LEADING SOCIAL ENTREPRENEURS

ASHOKA INNOVATORS FOR THE PUBLIC

A Tribute to R. Sargent Shriver

R. Sargent Shriver, who died on Tuesday, January 18, 2011, was one of the founding members of Ashoka's Councils and helped Ashoka in many ways over the decades.

The Ashoka community will miss him deeply.

He will always be a part of our history. As will his personal example of vision, values, humor, and commitment. And the professional example he set in creating and leading America's War on Poverty and the Peace Corps. The Special Olympics, one of the great examples of social entrepreneurship, which was created by and is now still led by members of the Shriver family, is another statement of his and his family's values.

Friends are working to create an Ashoka endowment in memory of this most remarkable friend and leader.

With sympathy to the Shriver family on behalf of the entire Ashoka community,

—*Bill Drayton, Chairman & CEO*

MANAGING EDITOR: Kelly Hicks

EDITORS: Rebecca Altman, Hanae Baruchel, Norma Dancis, Claire Fallender, Catherine Jaffe, Sarah Jefferson, Kulsoom Khan, David Nahmias, Farah Qureshi, Simon Stumph, Raquel Thompson, Michael Zakaras

ART DIRECTOR: Rachel Land

PRODUCTION ARTIST: Jennifer Geanakos

CONTRIBUTORS: Leila Akahloun, Claire Bangser, Siddharth Barthakur, Flavio Bassi, Iman Bibars, Chimene Chetty, Tina Choi, Abby Chroman, Amy Clark, Kenny Clewett, Elena Correas, Celia Cruz, Chris Cusano, Marie Isabel Espinoza, Anne Evans, Andres Falconer, Nicolina Farella, Maria Fonseca, Erin Fornoff, Leah Fotis, Ahmed Fouad, Konstanze Frischen, Silvia Giovannoni, Oda Heister, Ndeye Binta Houma, Doris Huang, Sarvam Kailasapathy, Nassir Katuramu, Ewa Konczal, Wil Kristin, Mira Kusumarini, Armando Laborde, Guillermina Lazzaro, Tiana Lins, Catriona Maclay, Sarah Mariotte, Valeria Merino, Arnaud Mourot, Abubaker Musuuza, Anna Obem, Paul O'Hara, Roshan Paul, Eitan Perry, Maria Clara Pinhiero, Neela Rajendra, Paula Recart, Maria Lucia Roa, Monica de Roure, Ranya Saadawi, Shreen Saroor, Dawn Scales, Pritha Sen, Sadhana Shrestha, Supriya Sankaran, Jessica Soley, David Strelneck, Beverly Schwartz, Seyda Taluk, Fazlyn Toeffie, Natalia Toledo, Coumba Toure, Nir Tsuk, Filip Vagac, Jan Visick, Michael Vollmann, Maria Zapata

Ashoka Fellow Sasin Chalermlarp of Thailand, meets with Karen health volunteers to discuss communal health services within the Western Forest, the largest remaining continuous forest in Southeast Asia, where forest inhabitants are no longer evicted but instead work with park officials as equal partners in conservation.

In addition, over 100 forest communities have agreed to common land use regulations and together guard against forest encroachment. Sasin is replicating this collaborative conservation approach in well over 100 other communities along the forest borders, to ensure lasting protection of forest, wildlife, and the right of indigenous communities to coexist with nature.

To read more about Sasin's work, go to page 79.

LEADING SOCIAL ENTREPRENEURS

ISBN-13: 978-0-9815279-5-6; ISBN-10: 0-9815279-5-7 Leading Social Entrepreneurs, 2011 Edition.

LEADING SOCIAL ENTREPRENEURS

ASHOKA INNOVATORS FOR THE PUBLIC

1700 North Moore Street | Suite 2000 | Arlington, VA 22209 USA
Tel: (703) 527-8300 | Fax: (703) 527-8383 | www.ashoka.org

PREFACE
Are You Ready?

Bill Drayton

Dear Friend,

For millennia the world has been organized around repetition. Individuals learned a skill and applied it for the rest of their lives. Institutions were designed for repetition—serving stable clients who wanted the same thing over and over. This explains their architecture. A few, who might think, directed everyone else through organizations of rules and enforcement and of walls.

This model is dying. It simply cannot survive in the world into which we are now going, a world defined not by repetition but by change.

There is a simple fact that explains why the world of repetition is dying. It is a fact. We cannot stop it. It is driving history hard.

This fact is that the rate of change is still escalating exponentially. This is mathematically true. It has been accelerating for roughly three centuries. We have now reached the juncture where we are about to go over the tipping point. To a world where the institutions simply cannot work.

Of course, there is still going to be repetition. We are still going to have to wash the dishes, I suspect. However, people will very quickly be valued chiefly in terms of whether and to what degree they can contribute to change.

The key factor for success for any society, city, company, citizen group, or religious house is increasingly—and in five or ten years from now will absolutely be defined as—what proportion of the people are changemakers, at what level of skill, and how flexibly and well does the group enable them to work together. This is a fundamentally different paradigm. Imagine ahead five or fifteen years. How can the hierarchical institution of rules and walls, where at best only a few people think, survive in this new world? There is no way. Everything around this group is changing—and each change bumps a dozen other things, forcing them to change. Moreover, the rate of change is not the only thing growing exponentially. So is the number of people causing change and, probably more important, the combinations of people and the combinations of combinations of people causing change.

What will replace institutions? We are moving rapidly into a world of teams—a global team of teams that comes together very flexibly.

Why are fluid, quick-changing teams of teams the new architecture? Because now value is contributing to change processes.

The clients are no longer institutions repeating and repeating—and therefore wanting suppliers that repeat. To serve a change process requires ever-changing combinations of people and skills. Providing value requires changing with change. This is a truly deeply, profoundly different world.

When you think about change, there is big change, there is small change. However, once in a very rare while, the world goes through the sort of tectonic change now upon us. These are changes in how humans work together—which changes everything. This sort of change is far more profound than the various technological revolutions, for example: the chemical or even the digital revolution.

This tectonic shift is upon us. We are right at the transition point.

In the world of change and teams, everyone must be an initiator. One does not have a team unless everyone is a player. Moreover, to be a player in this world, people must be able to see and contribute to change. Consider what this means. Every human being has to have a truly significantly different set of skills. That means we must redefine what success in growing up is. It also means that all of us must learn to lead and organize in very different ways. This is indeed a tectonic shift.

Why do we think we are now in the final tipping zone? History provides one very strong clue. From the end of the Roman Empire to 1700, there was no growth in average per capita income in the West. It went up and down with weather cycles. Then something happened. In the 1700s, per capita income went up 20 percent; in the 1800s, 200 percent; in the last century, 740 percent. What happened was that business did something very radical. It said: If you (anyone!) have a better idea and implement it, we are going to make you very happy—and we are going to copy you. That was a giant step towards an "everyone a changemaker™" world. It was the beginning of the end of elites running everything. It has driven history over these three centuries. It has spread from the North Atlantic to the rest of the world.

Over the last three decades it has swept into the citizen sector, which is now as competitive and entrepreneurial as business. Once the citizen sector made this structural jump around 1980 (which is why we set up Ashoka then), it entered a three-decade period of rapid catch-up with business in productivity, scale, and now globalization. It is this rapid catch-up that explains why the citizen sector is growing employment at two and a half to three times the rate of the rest of the OECD advanced economies.

Another very compelling piece of evidence is that we have a growing number of islands of the new team of teams world of change already in existence. Moreover, as is typical early in the development of a new architecture, the islands, although not highly skilled to begin with, are learning rapidly—not least because they are increasingly finding, connecting, and collaborating with one another. That is precisely why the web has come up just now.

Bangalore and Silicon Valley are obvious islands.

However, if you look closely, you will see them developing all over, often in some of the most unlikely places. Consider Procter & Gamble. It used to be known as the "Kremlin on the Ohio" because it insisted on developing everything internally. However, several years ago, the company realized that they simply would not be able to compete if they continued not taking advantage of all the creativity and ideas around the world. There are simply many more people and ideas outside than there ever will be inside. That is why P&G is now out looking for ideas across the world.

In fact, they have just invested in a radically different business/social hybrid way of delivering health that Ashoka has developed over the last several years (see "A New Alliance for Global Change" in the *Harvard Business Review* of September 2010) that unites safe drinking water, a micropharmacy, and distance diagnosis. P&G has invested, which is helping us to spread the model rapidly, because they saw its value both socially and to P&G as a new product and service model.

As a result, Ashoka is now—as part of the new global team of teams—a part of Procter & Gamble's new product development system. Something of a surprise to us, but there it is.

The world defined by change and organized in a fluid team of teams is all around us. As is almost always true in history, the reality is way ahead of perception.

This fact explains why it is so important for all of us to help the world consciously recognize that this change is happening— and what it means for every person and every group. The tipping process has a critical antechamber—the awareness tipping zone. We have entered that zone. Many people are now ready to listen to this description of the world they are entering both because it describes reality and because, increasingly, they are not afraid of being laughed at if they think such thoughts. The next and critical step in the tipping process comes when people begin to see those

around them talking about and beginning to respond to the new realities. Then they begin to fear being laughed at if they do not know what is going on and are not responding.

We will return to the implications of this tectonic shift for all of us shortly. However, it is important first to recognize how central the world's leading social entrepreneurs are to this process.

All the fundamental systems of the world will be changing— and as each changes, it will be bumping and causing change in other systems. The people who deal with system change *are* entrepreneurs. That is what defines them.

Social entrepreneurs are utterly essential to the healthy continuous evolution of the world going forward.

They are not defined by the subject area where they are working. Who is not involved in education, for example? What defines a social entrepreneur, instead, is the fact that, from deep inside their personalities, they (and therefore their work) are committed to the good of all.

There are many entrepreneurs who pursue narrower goals— self-interest, that of the shareholders, a particular ideological or religious point of view, etc. They and all the other forces at work are likely, especially as change accelerates and the traditional safeguards that typically are tied to old structures that are dying become ineffective, without even thinking to drive the world in unhealthy directions. For example, the world is now in grave danger of losing privacy, which is critical to creativity and freedom. Why? Because the world needs preventive surveillance to deal with terrorism; because the cost of connecting the dots now has almost disappeared; and because many business entrepreneurs in the digital field have a business model of providing value, getting information, and selling that information at a profit (e.g., via targeted advertising).

Society must have a powerful community of social entrepreneurs who will always be, like highly beneficial and very smart white blood cells, spotting where society is about to go off the rails and providing the necessarily highly savvy and powerful antidote.

For example, 40 percent (and rapidly growing) of the U.S. labor force now consists of freelancers. The existing organizations for workers are unable to serve them because their needs are so different. Our Ashoka colleague, Sara Horowitz, is well on the way to solving this problem through her Freelancers Union (which already has in the still-early stage of its development 165,000 members). Freelancers need insurance. I watched Sara work for 15 years to figure out how to solve that problem. She now has an insurance company registered in 38 states that is providing the needed service and is profitable. Freelancers also have a chronic challenge of workload peaks and valleys. Sara has developed a computer-based system that allows freelancers to help one another flatten out this terrain.

Here is another example: 30 to 40 percent of the pharmaceuticals in Africa may be fakes. Ashoka Fellow Bright Simons of Ghana has figured out how customers can determine whether or not a bottle is what it says it is or a fake by using their cell phones.

This volume introduces some of the recently elected Fellows. Five years from now over half of them will have changed national policy and three-quarters the pattern in their fields at a national level. As new problems come up, they will spot them and develop the antidotes.

There is another reason social entrepreneurs are so important. Their goal is to change the world, not to capture a market and dig a moat. Social entrepreneurs *want* other people to copy their ideas. Because, as a result, they make their ideas as simple, safe, and understandable as possible, each is typically able to get thousands of local people in thousands of communities to stand up and say: "This is a good idea that we need here. We're going to get together and make this change come to our community." When they do that, they have become changemakers—who recruit and are role models for many others. Some of them, moreover, will later be pattern-change entrepreneurs in their own way. Given that the central historical task now is to build an "everyone a changemaker™" world, the fact that social entrepreneurs are mass recruiters and facilitators of local changemakers is profoundly important.

Over the last half-dozen years, we have learned that there is something more important and more powerful than the individual entrepreneur. That is us entrepreneuring together. Such *collaborative entrepreneurship* is a giant step beyond solo entrepreneuring. It is also unprecedented in the world.

For example, 700 out of a total 3,000 Ashoka Fellows are focused on children and young people. Each is powerful individually. However, by thinking/entrepreneuring together, we have been able to move to an entirely different plane of power.

Our methodology begins by identifying the most important patterns cutting across the successful innovations of each Fellow. Then we must (1) move beyond what works today to understand what the new paradigm for the field is and (2) find the entrepreneurial jujitsu that will allow us in fact to tip the world. Then we and hundreds of the Fellows, especially those in the ten key parts of the world we must tip to tip the world, organize to execute that plan.

For example, the old paradigm of success in growing up was defined as: Master knowledge and rules. That was okay for the world of repetition but is utterly inadequate in a world of change.

The faster things change, the less rules cover. Any child who does not master the skill of empathy, therefore, will hurt people and disrupt institutions—and be thrown out regardless of whatever knowledge s/he may have. Thus, a key part of the new paradigm of growing up is that "Every Child Must Master Empathy" (see www.ashoka.org/collaborativeentrepreneurship and click on http://www.ashoka.org/sites/ashoka/files/Innovations_Collab_Ent_with_Empathy_Overview.pdf.

What are the implications of this profound tectonic shift for you, and for all of us?

First, you can help the world understand the transition from repetition to change and what it means for everyone—starting with the individuals and groups important to you and including friends who are writers or otherwise influencers. You can give them an invaluable map. This is probably the most highly leveraged thing any of us can do right now.

Second, as the example of empathy suggests, every human being needs a set of social skills to be able to contribute in a world defined by change—empathy, teamwork, and leadership for change. All these have to be learned. They are complicated. We need to have parents, schools, businesses, every group consistently help people build these skills. You can help with the individuals—from children to colleagues and with all the groups with whom you are dealing. Here again, you can also influence public thought.

Finally, we all have to change and grow. How do we lead? We cannot lead the old way. It is hugely important—and challenging—for you to take any group about which you care—be it a foundation, a citizen group, a business, or a government agency—and turn it into a team of teams.

The transition will be easier than we think. Once society as a whole has understood and is moving, we will be going with society as well as with history. And who doesn't want to be a changemaker or, even better, an entrepreneur or, best, a social entrepreneur?

Most sincerely,

Bill Drayton, CEO

ASHOKA INNOVATORS FOR THE PUBLIC

ASHOKA: INNOVATORS FOR THE PUBLIC is the global association of the world's leading social entrepreneurs—men and women with system-changing solutions—that address the world's most urgent social challenges. Since its founding in 1980, Ashoka has helped launch and then provided key long-term support to roughly 3,000 leading social entrepreneurs in over 70 countries. It provides these "Ashoka Fellows" start-up stipends, professional services and a powerful global network of top social and business entrepreneurs. It also helps them spread their innovations globally.

Ashoka uses a rigorous, highly refined, five-step process to identify the most important emerging social-change ideas and the entrepreneurs behind them who, together, will redefine their field, be it human rights or the environment or any other area of human need. This process focuses sharply on five key criteria:

- A big, pattern-setting New Idea

- Creativity in both goal-setting and problem-solving

- Entrepreneurial Quality

- The Social Impact of the New Idea

- Ethical Fiber

Once Fellows are elected, Ashoka makes sure that they have the supports and full freedom—including the ability to work full-time—they need to launch their visions and succeed. This includes providing a launch stipend to the degree it is needed for an average of three years, organizing a wide range of high leverage supports, and—most important—engaging them in a local to global collaborating fellowship of their peers.

By structuring, supporting, and routinizing such collaborations, Ashoka is also helping the world's leading social entrepreneurs come together to cause truly major changes, changes whose impacts far exceed the sum of the impacts of even these individual entrepreneurs. In recent years we have learned how, starting with the Fellows' innovations, to map the most critical transformations the world needs—and then through collaborative entrepreneurship among hundreds of top social entrapreneurs, in fact, to tip the world time and again. There has never been anything like this before.

Ashoka is also helping the emerging profession of social entrepreneurship to find the institutions and patterns that will serve it wisely long into the future.

In this volume, you will find profiles introducing the ideas and leading social entrepreneurs recently elected by Ashoka. They are grouped according to six broad fields: civic engagement, economic development, environment, health, human rights, and learning/education. These sketches introduce entrepreneurs and their ideas very early in their careers, years before the scale of their impacts will be obvious. However, annual Ashoka evaluations show that five years after their election and start-up launch, 90 percent of the Ashoka Fellows have seen independent institutions copy their idea and over half have changed national policy. Moreover, they encourage many, many, others to stand up and become changemakers. Both as role models and because, to succeed, they must—and do—find champions in community after community that adopt and spread their models.

Letter from the Ashoka President

Diana Wells

Dear Colleagues,

Ashoka was founded over thirty years ago by Bill Drayton who recognized that the most powerful force for change in the world is a big idea in the hands of an entrepreneur. As an exceptional entrepreneur himself, he applied this principle to social change and built Ashoka and the field of social entrepreneurship.

Today the strength and diversity of Ashoka's network, fueled by the constant sourcing of new Ashoka Fellows, enables us to serve social entrepreneurs and catalyze a collective social impact that goes both deeper and broader We are able to recognize patterns across our network of some 3,000 social entrepreneurs from more than 70 countries to extract actionable insights to tackle social change. And now, we are in the position to leverage these insights to provide valuable opportunities that enable social entrepreneurs to collectively scale their impact.

In this volume, we share with you the inspiring stories of the social entrepreneurs most recently elected to the Ashoka Fellowship. Take, for example, Kara Andrade. Elected to the Ashoka Fellowship this year, Kara is a social entrepreneur who is only in the early stages of her innovation but is already having large-scale impact. Kara is pioneering a citizen-based information sharing platform throughout Central America called HablaCentro.com. This local, mobile-driven network enables contributors, especially young people, to share and discuss information in various languages, including indigenous languages. Her grassroots model which began in Guatemala has been replicated in Honduras, El Salvador, Costa Rica, and Venezuela. Kara is fueling civic participation and transforming democracy throughout Latin America.

The Ashoka network consists of thousands of social entrepreneurs like Kara—changemakers who are not content to serve just one constituency but rather aim to create an entirely new democratic system. And with our global network of entrepreneurs, the opportunities for idea spread are now more than ever.

In 2010, Ashoka held its first Globalizer, a program which identifies leading Ashoka Fellows and connects them with global business entrepreneurs who have lead global expansion in their businesses. Together Ashoka Fellows and global business entrepreneurs develop practical wisdom on creating greater impact explicitly for the social sector.

Dr. Steve Collins was one of the first Ashoka Fellows to participate in the Globalizer. Dr. Collins has revolutionized community-based therapeutic care of severe acute malnutrition through ready-to-use food (RUTF). His organization, Valid Nutrition, developed a new method involving individual portions of RUTF administered directly by community members. This approach cut death rates five-fold while dramatically increasing coverage. Recognizing the opportunity to scale, Steve employed the corporate expansion model prevalent in this industry. Eager to maintain tight control over quality, Steve and his team built a factory, hired a distribution team, and established an entire supply chain under direct Valid Nutrition management. Steve eventually faced one of the central challenges in scaling social impact: as a target population increases, the complexity of the work can increase faster than an organization's capacity to manage it.

Steve's story exemplifies an emerging consensus from Globalizer: social entrepreneurs who wish to scale-up effectively must learn to transition "from an enterprise to an ecosystem." By bringing together our network of entrepreneurs at Globalizer, Ashoka was able to extract insight about how scaling in the social sector is unique from the business sector. We learned again that in the social sector it is not about scaling the organization, but about scaling impact. For Steve Collins, this means focusing in on his core mission and actively collaborating with other actors to expand the scope of impact.

One of the patterns for reaching broad scale is using smart networks—empowering individuals to create new networks that allow for greater impact. For example, Ashoka Fellow Bright Simons is improving the safety of pharmaceutical consumers by providing a way for them to identify fake drugs with the first system in the world by which consumers and patients can instantly verify the source of a purchased pharmaceutical at no cost, right at the point of purchase, using standard mobile phones and SMS messaging. His system provides a live, dynamic link between the customer and the manufacturer—a smart network that empowers consumers to be changemakers.

Of course, this work would not be possible without the Ashoka Fellows featured here and their fellow changemakers around the world. It would also not be possible without the support of the global Ashoka community—our staff, volunteers, partners, and supporters, including you. We hope you find the enclosed stories from the 2010 cohort of Ashoka Fellows as inspiring as we have.

Diana Wells, President

RESOURCES

RIPPLING
How Social Entrepreneurs Spread Innovation Throughout the World

By Beverly Schwartz, Foreword by Bill Drayton
Published by Wiley/Jossey-Bass, March 2012

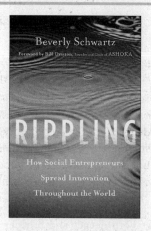

RIPPLING is the first book written solely about Ashoka and its approach to system change.

It presents a collection of innovative social solutions that have the capacity to "ripple" through and break down the walls of "not possible", "never been done", "can't change that", "it doesn't matter" and "not my problem" thinking. These solutions demonstrate how and when empathy, creativity, passion and persistence are combined; significant, world transformation is indeed possible.

The book describes how innovative, effective and scalable ideas can change communities, cities, regions and countries. It centers on the ability of Ashoka Fellows to change market dynamics, and institutional norms as they advance full citizenship and apply market forces to create social value – all the while utilizing empathy and a culture of changemaking as eco-system operating principles.

RIPPLING demonstrates how Ashoka Fellows apply an Everyone a Changemaker™ model to exponentially enable greater numbers of the world's population to be social problem solvers. It signifies a wave of innovation, inspiration and empowerment that marries possibility, people and hope with systemic and sustainable change the world over.

You can obtain a copy of the book after March 15, on Amazon.com or in a Barnes and Noble store.
Copies, signed by the author and Bill Drayton will be available with a donation to Ashoka. Visit Ashoka.org/Rippling to order.

Everyone a Changemaker:
Social Entrepreneurship's Ultimate Goal

By Bill Drayton
Published in Innovations magazine (MIT, Harvard, George Mason)

This article maps the future. It describes where the world and social entrepreneurship are going. It defines the ultimate goal for both—an "everyone a changemaker" world. This is a world where everyone, like smart white blood cells coursing through society, knows (s)he can cause change and can spot whatever is stuck and go and fix it. This world ends 12,000 years during which only a small elite had the initiative. It is also a world where the problems can no longer outrun the solutions. The article describes in practical terms several of the most important means of getting there, as well.

To obtain a copy of this publication, log on to our website, www.ashoka.org, and look under the "resources" section or send an email to info@ashoka.org.

How to Change the World
Social Entrepreneurs and the Power of New Ideas

By David Bornstein
Published by Oxford University Press; Penguin, and many others*

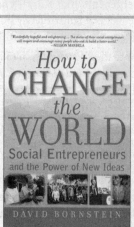

How to Change the World chronicles the historical transformation of the citizen sector and introduces you to the extraordinary social entrepreneurs leading the change. It starts with the stories of individuals with remarkable ideas that change the fabric of our society and identifies the characteristics and qualities that make social entrepreneurs the agents driving social change at a global level. It examines the systems and supports they need to accelerate and scale the growth of their ideas. It is, in effect, a roadmap to a different future—one which will change lives and draw the top level talent the field needs to progress faster. It will help leaders in government and in business, as well as within the citizen sector, understand the implications of their changed strategic environment, so that they can adapt far faster—to their and the social entrepreneur's benefit.

How to Change the World is available for purchase on Amazon.com, Barnes and Noble, or a book store near you.

* *How to Change the World* has also been published in Arabic, Bulgarian, Czech, Chinese (Simplified & Complex), Danish, Dutch, Estonian, Farsi, French, Finnish, German, Greek, Hebrew, Hindi, Hungarian, Indonesian, Italian, Japanese, Kannada, Korean, Pashto, Persian, Polish, Portuguese, Romanian, Russian, Serbian, Sinhalese, Slovenian, Spanish, Swedish, Tarmic, Tamil, Thai, Turkish, and Welsh.

Social Entrepreneurship
Theory and Practice

By Ryszard Praszkier and Andrzej Nowak
Published by Cambridge University Press

Social Entrepreneurship: Theory and Practice details how social entrepreneurship can creatively solve pressing and seemingly insurmountable social problems. Theories of social change are presented to help demystify the "magic" of making an immense, yet durable and irreversible social impact. In-depth case studies from multiple disciplines and from around the globe document how social entrepreneurs foster bottom-up change that empowers people and societies. The authors review the specific personality traits of social entrepreneurs and introduce the new leadership model required for 21st-century development. This book is valuable to undergraduate, graduate, and post-graduate students, while remaining accessible to non-academic readers due to its clear language, illustrative case studies, and guidelines on how to apply social entrepreneurship, or become a successful social entrepreneur.

Key Features

- Presents the concept of social entrepreneurship through the lenses of various theories such as dynamical systems theory, complexity and emergence theory, sociology and psychology, social networks analysis and theories of leadership

- Documents the hypothesis that social entrepreneurs pursue their social mission through launching a bottom-up process and through building social capital

- Links theory with diverse, colorful case studies from around the world, including photo documentation

- Identifies and analyzes the specific personality traits of social entrepreneurs as compared to social activists and the average of the society

To obtain a copy of this book and recieve a discount, please visit www.cambridge.org/us/9780521767316 or call 1.800.872.7423, enter Discount Code **SEPN11** at checkout. *This offer expires 01/31/2012.* Or visit Amazon or Barnes and Noble.

Dream of a Nation
Inspiring Ideas for a Better America

Edited by Tyson Miller; with chapters by Bill Drayton, Diana Wells, Roshan Paul and Ashoka Fellows
Published by SEE Innovation

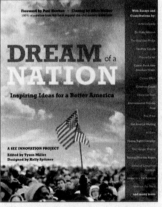

Dream of a Nation is a citizen handbook and national movement focused on big dreams, bold innovations, and the realization of our full potential as a nation. The project was created to elevate awareness, ignite passions, redefine priorities, inspire action on a range of critical social, economic, and environmental issues, and unite us all in dreaming the American dream.

More than 60 leading thinkers and civil society organizations are participating in the project including Alice Walker, NASA astronaut Jerry Linenger, Paul Hawken, Geoffrey Canada, Al Gore, Dr. Holly Atkinson, along with such organizations as the Union Of Concerned Scientists, Bipartisan Bridge, Citizen Effect, Common Cause, Free Press, Veterans For Peace and more than 50 others. The work brings complex issues to life and explores how we must put politics aside and share the task of rebuilding the economy, strengthening community, re-imagining business, removing money from politics, re-establishing more media integrity, revitalizing education, repowering America, ending poverty, waging peace and much more.

In reference to the project Alice Walker writes, "The most important thing humanity can do is believe in itself. That we can grow, we can change, we can rouse ourselves in time to make big changes happen. Dream of a Nation encourages movement in this direction. It offers hundreds of ideas and examples of how smart, committed, and daring we can be."

Dream of a Nation invites everyone to share in the work and the rewards of daring to dream once more.

To obtain a copy of this publication, log on to http://dreamofanation.org and look under "The Book" section. 100% of all royalties are returned to the 60+ organizations who shared their vision in the project.

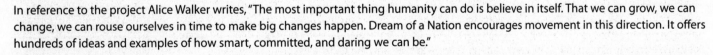

FOR ADDITIONAL ASHOKA RESOURCES VISIT US AT ASHOKA.ORG AND CHANGEMAKERS.COM

LEADING SOCIAL ENTREPRENEURS

2011 EDITION

The Social Entrepreneurs and Their Ideas

Organizing the Movement

ASHOKA FELLOWS
2011 EDITION

CIVIC ENGAGEMENT

MOHAMMED ABU AMERAH

JORDAN

Capacity Building

Cooperatives

Municipal Services

Mohammed Abu Amerah is reviving the traditional and cultural concept of the *harra* (neighborhood) and what it represents as a space for community participation, mutual respect, and protection for vulnerable groups. Mohammed is recreating the social and economic fabric of the harra by fostering community collaboration to solve the problems which have arisen due to modernization, namely, anonymity, neglect of public spaces, and a lack of safety nets.

THE NEW IDEA

Mohammed is promoting a sense of community ownership, which increases both the residents' sense of belonging and responsibility; his motto for the initiative, "Our Harra, Our City, Our Country." Through communal physical rehabilitation projects, the inhabitants of the neighborhood start developing a sense of belonging defined by common space, and through collaboration in those projects social networks are created and new bonds are cultivated superceding ethnic and tribal allegiances. To improve the livelihood of the Harra, Mohammed organizes capacity-building and educational programs where neighbors exchange skills and resources, and form consumer and trade cooperatives which leverage the collective purchasing power of the neighborhood.

The Harra Initiative is currently in its pilot stage in the Jabal al-Joffeh region of Amman, Jordan. Mohammed's Harra is a unique initiative in the Levant region, and has widespread relevance in the Arab World. He envisions Harra as a communal development model for developing countries, particularly when community erosion is the result of unplanned, rapid urban expansion, re-establishing a balance between urbanization, environmental health, communal well-being, and neighborly cooperation.

Mohammed is currently planting the seeds for more harras by identifying and training change agents; natural leaders who are dissatisfied with the status quo. Following this step, he will expand throughout Amman, then Jordan, and then into other Arab countries. While others are working in the field of community development, none involve the community in the development process to the same extent. In addition, unlike some other organizations, Harra started entirely as a grassroots effort, independent from the government and without the need of funding. It is the only initiative to work on building a social infrastructure by strengthening communal ties, and build more independent, self-reliant communities, committed to their own social development.

THE PROBLEM

Amman's explosive growth over the last five decades has caused the degeneration of harra and the support network that came with it. This growth is also largely due to unnatural causes. Jordan is one of the countries most affected by the Palestinian refugee problem: Over 60 percent of its population is of Palestinian origin. As a result, a class system has developed, encouraging discrimination and contributing to the degradation of community. As long as there is no reason for interaction, no communal goals, and no common social fabric, people become strangers; conflicts arise between strangers and escalate, as third parties have no interest in mediating. Mohammed was catalyzed into action by the shooting of his neighbor over a parking space.

Al-Jazeera reported on the initial stages of the Harra, and called the project a "model of community empowerment".

In contrast, there used to be a collective moral spirit within communities. Families would interact and help each other through difficult times. Traditionally, the Sheikh El Hara (in urban districts) would be the informal litigation authority in resolving local conflicts. Even though the position of "sheikh" was an informal one, their verdicts were widely respected in the community.

Today, neighbors in Arab cities barely interact. Seclusion and exclusion has become the norm for many families and individuals. Suspicion and intolerance has replaced inter-reliance, friendship, and understanding. The absence of communal ties means the absence of communal responsibilities. The result is a crumbling infrastructure and growing heaps of refuse. What the government fails to fix remains broken, as few take the initiative to care for land outside strict property lines.

People became strangers because of the weak social fabric, which borders on anonymity. For example, in these modern times, if a widow is evicted because she could not pay rent due to the cost of the funeral, her neighbors may not notice she left the building. In the days of stronger communities, neighbors would cook for her and share funeral costs, until she was able to recover from her grief and find a way to make ends meet.

There are a few other organizations in the Levant that specialize in community development. However, none are committed as strongly to *grassroots communal* development, development for the community, *by* the community.

THE STRATEGY

In 2005 Mohammed moved back to Amman, to the neighborhood where his family lived in East Amman, an area that didn't get enough attention from the government. He felt that residents were estranged from one another, and frequently witnessed violence in the streets, including a shooting over a parking space. Mohammed decided to restore the harra to how it was before. He sold his house and left his job at the Municipality of Amman to start change at a grassroots level.

Mohammed is reviving the concept of harra, a small community centered around a central pedestrian alley where community members congregate to discuss problems and launch community initiatives.

After five years in development, the Harra Initiative has laid the foundation for a strong, healthy community; the current Harra serves 85 families, about 500 people. It started with urban rehabilitation projects in the pilot. These involved defining and renewing the physical environment of the community, including removal of rubble and garbage, building and painting fences, repairing non-structural building problems, planting trees and gardens, using recycled graywater for watering plants, clearly sign-posting streets, and numbering houses. This has increased the residents' physical identity with the harra and sense of belonging; their social identity has become that of an interconnected group with common goals and shared responsibilities, instead of individual families or ethno-religious sects. Cologne University undertook a study to measure the effectiveness of the Harra's physical environmental rehabilitation project on society's well-being by interviewing community members. It concluded that the impact of the project was very effective, as individuals reported higher levels of trust, cooperation, and interaction with their neighbors. In addition, *Al-Jazeera* reported on the initial

stages of the Harra, calling the project a model of community empowerment.

In five years, Mohammed will expand the project to 20 harras in Amman, all composed of no more than 100 families; small enough to create strong bonds, sense of belonging, ownership, and participation. In the near term, Mohammed's goals are increased eco-awareness among 350 families, participation in specific communal development projects by 700 families, participation in the rehabilitation of the physical environment by 5,000 families, basic English education, Internet connections, and housing improvements, including upgraded electricity, and central heating.

The social benefit of these projects is the most important aspect. The cooperation required to make these projects successful brings the community together. These projects are especially important to fostering a tighter community for the next generation: Children watch their parents' participation and will emulate them. These cross-factional interactions spread to daily life. The neighbor next door who you first met while repainting the wall across the street becomes the woman who teaches your daughter to sew, not the Palestinian, for example. In this way, she becomes more than a neighbor; she becomes something closer to family. Multiply these relationships by the number of people who participate in Harra and the positive impact on the community as a whole is clear. The development of these relationships, simple as they may seem, increases community inter-reliance.

In the pilot community, Harra is also starting educational centers for the community's children within a designated house, offering language courses and IT training. It will also establish a women's committee to address issues of children, family, and health, as well as a committee for helping those in need (the poor, widows, and emergency health situations). Those in need will go before the committee, present their situation, after which the committee decides whether the community is able to help. Additionally, Harra organizes community events, such as sports activities and celebrations of children's academic achievements, to encourage healthy and rewarding lifestyles.

Finally, participation in the Harra Initiative includes economic benefits. Mohammed has developed a model for community and trade cooperatives, in which members pool resources to save costs on everything from groceries (i.e. tomatoes, potatoes, and chicken), to Internet service, to raw materials for businesses and tradesmen, at wholesale prices. This is yet another level on which community members will bond. These common funds will be accessible by majority approval in the case of a personal or family emergency, such as medical expenses, paying for a wedding or funeral, or emergency car repair.

Mohammed and the Harra Initative have encountered many obstacles along the way, including selecting the initial Harra, convincing people to participate, motivating people to continue working on their projects, and making the community leadership, usually affluent and influential people, understand the needs of the most destitute in the community and work toward addressing those needs. However, as the Harra pilot enters maturity, Mohammed is confident that the lessons he has learned from the project will serve him well in his replication and expansion efforts.

As he expands into other neighborhoods, Mohammed reaches out to natural leaders and has them, in turn, enlist the wider community's participation in the project, emphasizing full communal participation as a goal. Once participation has reached the crucial level, Mohammed and the community leaders form "community-based management teams," composed of 7 men, 5 women, and 10 children from each neighborhood. The teams then design development projects to address their needs and ameliorate problems, with some guidance from the leaders if needed.

After 10 harras have been established, they will join together as a district, with a districtwide democratically elected council. Once this network is firmly in place, Mohammed will establish an intra-communal conflict mediation program, with natural community leaders proposing even-handed solutions to community members' disputes, instead of expensive lawyers and unsympathetic judges. These leaders will be chosen by the community, in a democratic way.

"[Mohammed] has formed joint trading cooperatives, so villagers are able to pool their know-how and resources, share experiences and benefit from savings when making purchases. Cooperatives ... exist ... ranging from food retail to Internet shops and raw materials storage."

—*Hilti Foundation*

Each harra costs US$50,000, of which 20 percent is financed by in-kind contributions from the community, 40 percent through donor funds, and 40 percent through the business sector. In ten years, with enough funding, Mohammed envisions the completion of 3,000 harras throughout all of Jordan. There is also potential for export of the model to other areas that have experienced rapid community degeneration, such as slum areas in Cairo, where community relocation following the 1992 earthquake destroyed the existing social fabric, and in Moroccan immigrant communities in France and Spain.

THE PERSON

Mohammed's interest in community development stems initially from the example and influence of his parents, who were both active as community advisors, mediators, and philanthropists. Mohammed began his studies in Amman in a private school in a pleasant harra. He was one of the best students in his class, would defend weak students against the tyrants, and was particularly fond of public speaking. Then, in his fourth year his family moved to a more urban area in East Amman, and he transferred to a public school. The first day, he remembers being shocked by the disparities between the abilities of his former and current classmates and being slapped by his new English teacher, for no apparent reason. He became quite unhappy, his grades dropped, and his level of class participation and general interest in voicing his opinion fell off sharply.

After completing his B.Sc. in mathematical statistics from Yarmouk University, Mohammed trained as a trade advisor and enterprise management development consultant; he held a number of positions as an independent consultant and in consultancy firms early in his career.

Mohammed then served as an advisor to the Mayor of Amman for development projects, sitting on the Greater Amman Municipality board. His main duties were to initiate and plan development programs, draft policies, and supervise the execution of these programs. Over time, Mohammed found that most development initiatives targeting infrastructure projects were directed to subcontractors who sucked the money out of the project and diluted the original intent. He saw little qualitative impact and no increase in people's income, a result which only served to increase their sense of isolation and frustration with the government. In these communities, the physical environment suffers from the frustrations of the residents. When people have no sense of ownership of public property, they either willfully break things or allow things to deteriorate, as the only way they have to express their anger with the government.

Mohammed has been proactively involved in public and private community-related projects and activities for a long time. He is the founder of the "Be like Jordan & Belong to the Future, from Ramtha Bani to Davos" initiative. He is also CEO of Friends of Environment Society in Jordan. The development of these various initiatives has honed his entrepreneurial and capacity-building skills.

After his extensive efforts in the private sector and government, Mohammed decided to work independently, based on his belief in grassroots development as opposed to top-down solutions. So much so, that he sold his house in an affluent Ammani neighborhood to move back to the humble neighborhood where he grew up to finance the beginnings of Harra. Mohammed also left a comfortable and respected job to ensure that he could devote his full attention to his initiative. ◆

KARA ANDRADE

GUATEMALA

Citizen/Community Participation

Media/Communications

Technology/Information Technology

HablaCentro.com is a local mobile-driven network of regional citizen information websites in Latin America. Built on mobile phone networks and Internet "hub" sites, Kara's HablaCentro model has rapidly spread through the region, as grassroots demand for a reliable source of information has surged.

THE NEW IDEA

Coming precisely at the first time in nearly five decades that democracy has taken root in the region, HablaCentro is the first Central American news-sharing platform built on mobile phones: The most pervasive digital technological applications available in these countries. In a region where social media applications like Twitter and Facebook are still not widely used because of their reliance on the Internet and smart phones, HablaCentro is providing an easily accessible, user-friendly means for grassroots participation in news generation and consumption. HablaCentro's technology platform allows users to send and receive information via text messages that are also posted to local hub websites in each of the countries where HablaCentro currently operates (i.e. Guatemala, Honduras, El Salvador, Costa Rica, and Venezuela). The HablaCentro platform has already experienced such high demand that Kara's model has spread virally from Guatemala, where she began her operations in May 2009, to other countries through sheer local initiative.

Beyond being a mere communication platform, HablaCentro is designed to promote civic participation through citizen journalism and collective action calls. Through educational outreach— provided to schools and citizen groups—as well as basic online tutorials, HablaCentro encourages citizens to report news that is timely and relevant to their communities, thus creating a bottom-up flow of information to counterbalance the traditional top-down media. Kara is particularly interested in promoting citizen-based investigative journalism, a concept that is not well established in most of Central America. As a firm believer that news and information serve a larger purpose, Kara has also built the HablaCentro platform to facilitate community action calls by the users themselves, such as sending help to disaster zones or disseminating information about recent political events.

Kara also envisions the HablaCentro platforms to enable citizen organization (CO) partners to reach more people with their services and information. Characterized by rapid viral growth and extensive geographic coverage, the HablaCentro networks provide a way for COs working on health, poverty, education, and other issues to disseminate information, particularly to communities where they do not already have an operational presence. Besides providing HablaCentro with a potential revenue stream as COs pay to share information across the networks, partnering with COs also strengthens and enriches the network effect that is inherent to HablaCentro's success, attracting more users and creating more nodes of activity and communication.

THE PROBLEM

During the Cold War period, violent civil strife throughout Central America claimed hundreds of thousands of lives. In Guatemala alone, an estimated 150,000 to 200,000 people were killed and 40,000 to 50,000 disappeared within a few decades. While the killings themselves undoubtedly traumatized Central Americans, the lack of reliable news about the government's role in the atrocities only aggravated tensions further. A small group of elites, who valued their economic and political agendas more than democratic journalism, controlled the traditional media outlets, especially newspapers. Without an independent news sector to act as a watchdog, Central American societies already battered by armed conflict also grew disillusioned by a general sense of societal helplessness and passivity.

Even though most violent conflict in Central America ended in the 1990s, a largely disconnected, fractured citizenry and elite control of information have persisted. Relatively low literacy rates (e.g. 69 percent in Guatemala, 67.5 percent in Nicaragua, and 80 percent in Honduras and El Salvador) still prevent a significant number of Central Americans from reading periodicals, and the geographic isolation of many communities limits access to both newspapers and television. Whereas a growing number of citizens in industrialized economies rely on the Internet for news, Internet penetration in most Central American countries remains low. Community radio and mobile phones are the two communication channels that have a broader geographic reach in the region. Mobile phone penetration is already impressively high in parts of Central America (e.g. in 2007, mobile phone penetration was over 60 percent in Guatemala and El Salvador and close to 50 percent in Honduras) and is rapidly growing each year (e.g. mobile phone subscriptions grew by nearly 50 percent in Guatemala and El Salvador in 2007 and by 80 percent in Honduras).

The disjointed nature of Central American societies is reflected in the citizen sector as well, which is largely still in a process of consolidation after decades of political instability. Many COs remain increasingly isolated, particularly because of distrust, a lack of awareness, as well as an absence of infrastructure. For example, the Cultural Survival Community Radio Network helps public health COs distribute information to 500,000 Guatemalan listeners free of charge, but the distribution process involves saving data on compact discs and hand-delivering them to far-flung community radio stations, because broadband networks and rural mail delivery are non-existent. As a result, disseminating information in the citizen sector is cumbersome, expensive, and inefficient. COs have long struggled to find a more effective way to operate.

THE STRATEGY

At the heart of the HablaCentro strategy is the idea that access to timely, relevant information improves people's lives, especially if that information is used to fuel civic participation. Until recently, providing Central Americans with consistent, inexpensive access to such information was nearly impossible as violent civil strife gripped many countries and political elites stifled democratic decision-making. As democracy begins to take root in countries like Guatemala, Nicaragua, and El Salvador, the time is finally ripe for a mass communication platform built and used by citizens themselves.

Kara has created a mobile phone-based platform that allows people to send and receive SMS text messages to local telephone numbers, which are routed to a national hub website that aggregates submissions and disseminates them throughout the HablaCentro network (i.e. which is itself centered upon a regional hub called HablaCentro). The national hub websites enable users that do have Internet access, particularly users living outside of Central America, to learn about events on the ground in Central America and contribute their perspectives via web postings. For those Central Americans who still do not have access to mobile phones, Kara has created HablaRadio, which allows listeners to submit reports and comments by voice, using Spanish, English, or various indigenous languages. The HablaRadio audio files are also posted on the hub websites, where users can listen to the reports online or download them to their mobile phones. Kara and her team support the HablaCentro user experience through online technical assistance as well as tutorials for people who have Internet access and off-line community education. Her team places a special focus on teaching children and youth how to generate their own journalistic content and how to be responsible consumers of information.

To foment civic participation based on the HablaCentro information-sharing platform, Kara and her team are forging partnerships with a range of COs that can use the network to disseminate information about health, education, human rights, or any other social topics. For example, in the case of the Cultural Survival Community Radio Network (i.e. which distributes health information via radio stations), HablaCentro is piloting an Android-based application that allows 22 community radio stations to receive compressed audio files via mobile phone and upload them to an HablaCentro site. Users can then download files directly to their mobile phones—far more efficient than hand-delivering compact discs. Moreover, the incorporation of CO partners provides HablaCentro with a potential revenue stream as COs pay for distribution rights. Kara is not only forming journalistic partnerships with freelance investigative reporters who can find source contacts via HablaCentro's network, but she is also developing relationships with news organizations and bloggers to aggregate and disperse information for a wider audience. As with any network model, creating more partnerships helps extend HablaCentro's user base and enriches the diversity of sources and perspectives feeding into the information exchange.

Kara explains how to use HC's simple digital platform to receive information.

As a digital platform, the HablaCentro model is relatively simple to replicate in other countries, as has already been the case with the HablaCentro hubs that have sprung up in Honduras, El Salvador, Costa Rica, and Venezuela. While the growth of the HablaCentro network must remain viral and stay in citizens' hands, Kara realizes that certain centralized structural elements must also be put in place. The creation of national HablaCentro hubs in each country enables a degree of standardization and quality control, but also ensures that the information shared within that hub is both locally owned and consumed. Each national hub will become self-sustaining as it generates more partnerships with local COs and other actors, thereby extending its network of users. While Kara's current focus is on consolidating HablaCentro in the countries where it already exists, in the next five years she envisions supporting the implementation of HablaCentro hubs in other Latin American countries and setting the stage for a second iteration of HablaCentro; once smart phones become more widely available in Central America. Not every user will have to possess a smart phone for more sophisticated HablaCentro functionality to be developed and deployed, even the presence of a handful of smart phones in each community will create the possibility for faster and more complex information sharing.

THE PERSON

Kara was born in a town in Guatemala called Bananera, "Banana town," that provided a pool of cheap labor for the United Fruit Company from generations of families, such as her mother who put the stickers on bananas and her mother's mother who picked the best bananas to ship to the U.S. It was like something out of a Garcia Marquez story; they lived through summer bouts of cholera and malaria and then moved to the poor barrios in Guatemala City, where seven of them struggled to survive during the period of genocide, called *la violencia*. Eighty percent of the Maya indigenous population would be murdered by the time the Peace Accords were signed in 1996. Her mother headed North, through the Guatemalan border into Mexico and waded past the Rio Grande.

Kara was born at the beginning of this period of unrest, during Guatemala's Day of the Soldier, which meant, her mother told her, that she would be a fighter, and more importantly that she would pursue a cause for which she had great passion. Journalism is that passion for her because freedom of expression is not something she associated with Guatemala, a country where the police reported 5,338 murders in 2005, an average of more than 14 murders a day, and where 17 percent live on less than one dollar a day according to the 2005 USAID report. That citizen journalism could come out of this Guatemala, sprouting from the cracks, inspired her. She identified with Guatemalan's struggle to overcome their socioeconomic limitations as she struggled to overcome hers by gaining access to information that provided educational and financial opportunities to pursue a masters in Journalism. Kara created a quantum leap for herself simply by having access to the information she needed, the teachers and mentors to help her make informed decisions with that information, and then teaching those skills to others.

> "The site has become both a platform and a destination for what's happening in Honduras. HablaHonduras is about citizen journalism today and what it could become."
>
> —*Social Nerdia*

As a young professional, Kara accrued experience in public health, social work, as well as journalism, a combination that fulfilled her passion: The utilization of media as a tool to help low-income communities gain access to resources. After working for the *Oakland Tribune* as a young journalist and writing 40 front-page stories in three months, Kara enrolled in a master's program in journalism at the University of California at Berkeley. During this time, she began to research ways in which the Guatemalans who had stayed behind in her native country were expressing themselves and communicating with each other in the post-conflict period.

In the summer of 2008, Kara won a grant from the Pulitzer Center for Crisis Reporting to report from the remote Petén region of northern Guatemala where environmentalists were fighting environmentalists in a behind-the-scenes ideological conflict over how best to save the vast but rapidly shrinking Maya forest. She hiked through the jungle with a team of three fellow reporters and archaeologists to document the stories of citizens affected by transnational conflict in northern Guatemala. As Kara rested atop an excavated Mayan pyramid, she noticed that the three Guatemalan archaeologists accompanying her were all holding their mobile phones up to the sky, sending text messages in the middle of a remote jungle. Surprised, Kara began asking questions about mobile phone connectivity and penetration in Guatemala and quickly realized that mobile phones could be used to create a citizen-based information sharing platform in a country where Internet connectivity was still low. Technology in the shape of cellphones that are cheap, accessible and ubiquitous was transforming Latin America—home to 12 percent of the world's almost 4 billion mobile subscribers in 2009. Cellphones and the Internet create opportunities for governance, economic advantage, transmission of culture and skills.

Toward the end of 2008, Kara returned to the U.S. and submitted a proposal for the HablaCentro concept to the Fulbright Commission, which granted her a scholarship (2009 to 2010). With the Fulbright funding in hand, Kara moved to Guatemala to begin implementing her idea. Within its first year in operation, HablaCentro has grown rapidly in Guatemala and neighboring countries, largely thanks to grassroots demand for an information source that citizens can trust. Other hubs grew in Honduras, Venezuela, El Salvador, Costa Rica and many requests were made for other countries. HablaCentro now acts as both a "regional pulse meter" and a place for democratic, civic activities based on the sharing of information that is useful, relevant, has impact, geographic significance, timeliness and veracity.

Given Kara's life story of agile persistence and success against difficult odds, combined with her passion for empowering the disenfranchised through newly emerging digital journalism, she will not rest until she has democratized information access throughout Central and then Latin America through user-friendly and accessible technology. ♦

CHRIS BALME

UNITED STATES

Access to Learning/Education

Youth Development

Chris Balme is reducing school drop-out rates by turning workplaces into classrooms where disengaged middle school students receive personalized apprenticeships in their dream jobs and a reason to re-engage in their school experience.

THE NEW IDEA

By the time young people reach high school, many of those who have not thrived in the school environment quickly make the choice to leave it. Chris thus determined that middle school was a critical time to give young people the opportunity to dream about their futures, and he saw that opportunity in the office buildings surrounding city schools. Every working person's desk could become an engaging learning environment for a middle school student at risk of dropping out of school. Chris founded Spark to build this bridge between schools and their surrounding communities. Spark matches middle school students with apprentice teachers in the student's careers of choice and supports that experience with a curriculum that helps students make the connection between exciting apprenticeships and their classroom learning.

Spark finds the students most disengaged and thus most at risk of dropping out and asks them what they dream of doing in life. Spark then makes their dreams seem achievable by sending them into workplaces for one-on-one mentorship with accomplished professionals. Buttressed by an adaptable school curriculum, the experience helps make school learning relevant to the students. In the process, it engages adults in the education of their communities' young people and transforms workplaces into youth-friendly educational environments, increasing workplace morale in the process.

THE PROBLEM

Approximately a third of U.S. high school students do not graduate in four years, many dropping out of school for good. Drop-out rates are even higher among minority populations. Among the reasons cited by students for leaving school, disengagement ranks among the highest. Nearly half of those students who drop-out of school say they were not interested in their classes. Additionally, the majority of these students did not have positive parental involvement in their education.

Most efforts to address the high school drop-out crisis target high school students themselves. But by then, it may be too late. Students begin to make critical choices about their futures already in middle school. Many of the existing programs also focus solely on content and quality of education and afterschool programming, neglecting the issues of attitude and motivation at the heart of the problem. The problem suggests a need for individualized attention to students, but schools and educational programs are too resource-constrained to personalize their approach.

Work-based learning has developed as a way to connect students with real-world learning opportunities that take them outside of the classroom to experience career opportunities. However, these programs are almost exclusively provided to high school students and tend to have a vocational, job-training objective. These programs thus direct students toward a career but often fail to help students make the connection between the job experience and their school experience. Without a fundamental shift in attitude toward school, students remain at risk of dropping out.

By targeting middle school students, focusing on student motivation, and tapping the underutilized resource of workplaces to personalize the experience, Spark has created an effective and scalable model that pre-empts the problem of students dropping out at the high school level.

THE STRATEGY

The Spark model aims to provide middle school students at greatest risk of dropping out with a personalized apprenticeship that gives them a fun and different learning experience in a new environment, allows them to develop tangible skills in an area of interest, and helps them see the relevance of their classroom learning. At the same time, it builds community accountability for the education of young people and shifts adult perceptions of "lost cause" kids.

Through Spark, a middle school student is able to explore the day-to-day experiences of an executive chef.

The strategy has five component parts: Identifying students, identifying apprentice teachers, managing apprenticeships, administering the curriculum, and conducting follow-up and referral. This division allows Spark to strategically and flexibly adapt and delegate different aspects of the model for ease of spread and scale.

Intrinsic to Spark's approach is a redefining of student potential. Whereas many youth programs look for those students who have demonstrated potential in school, Spark instead finds the potential in those who have not. Therefore, Spark's intervention begins by having schools identify the "trouble" students, those most disengaged from the classroom experience. Then, unlike other organizations that channel students into a pre-determined program, Spark lets each student determine the specific content for him or herself. Spark staff assess whether the students can benefit from the program generally, but they let each one tell them what he or she would love to do someday.

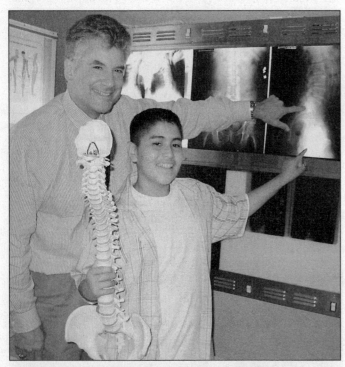

Spark connects students' apprenticeships with their school learning for tangible results.

Spark then invites accomplished professionals to play a unique volunteer role within the context of their work lives. Unlike mentoring programs that ask adults to play an amorphous role in the lives of disadvantaged youth, Spark approaches a potential volunteer with a discrete opportunity to use his or her specific skills to impact the life of a particular student who dreams of doing what that professional does. By approaching adults in their professional lives, Spark accesses an untapped volunteer market that other mentoring programs may not reach. Chris began by identifying individual apprentice teachers as the demand was created by student requests. To facilitate program growth, Spark is now building an online database of professionals willing to teach their professions to students. This database of profiles will allow students to browse and find careers they may not have otherwise

considered, and although screening of mentors will remain in Spark's hands for the time being, the database will also allow schools to take over the apprentice-teacher matching process.

While some programs bring professionals into the classroom to teach their skills, Spark takes the students out of the classroom environment that has failed to engage them, and sends them into the new and exciting work environments of the apprentice teachers. For 2 to 3 hours a week over the course of a semester or summer, the student works alongside the apprentice teacher in his or her workplace on a tangible project or skill. At the end of the apprenticeship, the student then presents that project or skill to parents, teachers, and peers. When the students "teach back" what they have learned to do, they show the adults in their lives that they are not hopeless. Furthermore, their peers learn about new potential careers and become excited about the Spark opportunity, building demand for the program.

The apprenticeship experience itself is often transformative for both student and apprentice teacher. Spark has an 85 percent retention rate among its students, most of the attrition being due to students moving or other family issues. Typically, 100 percent of the participating students report not only enjoying the experience but also experiencing growth in such areas as self-confidence, public speaking, teamwork, communication, and meeting new people. For the apprentice teachers, Spark's volunteer return rate is 92 percent, much higher than the national volunteer retention average of 65 percent. Apprentice teachers repeatedly report increased insight into their profession and increased self-confidence. Furthermore, the impact of the experience extends to their colleagues: Apprentice teachers report increased morale and team spirit in their offices. Spark's volunteer supply grows as colleagues of the apprentice teachers are inspired to take on their own apprentices.

While the apprenticeship gives students a fun and interesting experience, it only lasts for a few months, the objective being to create a spark that re-engages students in their school experience, keeping them from dropping out. As such, it is critical to Spark's success that students complete the program having clearly connected the apprenticeship experience to their school learning. Some of this connection happens organically as the students come across school concepts in their apprenticeships, such as a chef apprentice encountering fractions. But to reinforce this connection, during the semester or summer, the students participate in regular workshops through which Spark's leadership curriculum helps them understand the critical role that school plays in making their personal goals achievable. The curriculum pushes the students to develop three critical life skills: Self-awareness, community-awareness, and resourcefulness.

Although Spark's aim is to provide a short-term, targeted experience, Chris understands that the students need some continued support to make the most of that experience. Spark assists its students to make connections to other resources that will help them continue to internalize the learning. If they can benefit from another apprenticeship, Spark allows them to repeat the program. Spark also provides Alumni Leadership Coaching, which helps students refresh their Spark learning and connects them to other program resources in high school.

To spread the program, Spark is both replicating in other geographic areas and experimenting with models for scaling nationally. Spark currently operates in San Francisco and Redwood City, California, and is opening a new program in Los Angeles. By replicating in new cities, Chris hopes to demonstrate that the model is transferable. Spark will also gradually transfer more of the program, such as implementation of the curriculum and identification of apprentice teachers, to the schools themselves, allowing for more adaptability and faster spread. At the same time, Spark is developing a consulting capacity that will allow it to seed the idea in other locations around the country and ultimately serve as coordinator and trainer of a national network of middle school apprenticeship program implementers. Chris intends to leverage this position to push policy reform for the incorporation of apprenticeships into middle school curriculum nationwide.

"Chris Balme puts together
at-risk teens and business-world mentors
who show them a brighter future."

—*Christian Science Monitor*

THE PERSON

Chris adopted a love of teaching from his parents, who were freelance musicians and taught music to supplement their income. But growing up, Chris dreamt of becoming a successful business entrepreneur and was often creating little businesses. As a middle school student, he combined teaching with his entrepreneurial ambitions, starting a business teaching elderly people how to use computers.

Chris did not enjoy school but focused intensely on it, understanding the significance of doing well to achieving his career dreams. After years of working hard in school to maintain good grades, Chris studied abroad in Paris for a semester, where he suddenly found himself with very little work to do. He started wandering the streets of Paris, meeting people, and his perspective on life changed. Chris lost interest in his business dreams, and after graduating from college, he decided to pursue his intrest in teaching.

But after a year of part-time teaching in an urban middle school, where behavior was such a problem that students were required to cross their arms as they walked through the hallways, Chris felt he could do more for these students from outside the classroom. After spending a year researching school programs and finding very little for middle school students, he decided to take on the disengagement he had seen among the students in his classroom. He and his co-founder looked around at the office buildings surrounding city schools and thought that if they could pry open those doors and break disengaged students and often equally disengaged adults out of their school and work silos, they could revitalize the middle school experience and perhaps transform communities in the process. ◆

CONCHY BRETOS

UNITED STATES

Housing

Older People

Public Policy

Conchy Bretos has created an affordable assisted living model that allows low-income and disabled senior citizens living in public housing facilities to remain in their own homes instead of being forced into nursing homes against their will. Over the last 15 years, she has helped public housing authorities in 23 states renovate public housing buildings to comply with assisted living facility regulations and finance start-up operations through state and federal funding. Along with her team at MIA Consulting, Conchy is now poised to change public policy on elderly care through a pending national demonstration project with the Department of Housing and Urban Development and the Department of Health and Human Services.

THE NEW IDEA

In response to the deplorable public housing conditions that she witnessed as Florida's Secretary for Aging and Adult Services in the mid 1990s, Conchy created a new model for providing basic care services to the elderly while allowing them to stay in their own homes. Although private assisted living facilities (ALFs) have long existed for senior citizens who are able to pay hefty monthly fees, low-income and disabled senior citizens—many of whom live in public housing—are largely unattended by the market. Conchy's model makes ALFs affordable for these seniors by retrofitting existing public housing buildings to comply with ALF regulations and by leveraging state Medicaid waiver funding to finance the ALFs start-up operations. Not only do these affordable ALFs allow the elderly to continue living with relative independence and dignity in their own homes, but they also generate employment for single minority mothers in the daily care of the residents and the maintenance of the facilities, often leading to a gradual revitalization of the frequently derelict or decaying urban neighborhoods where these ALFs are located.

Preliminary studies of the results of Conchy's model have shown that residents' physical and cognitive health actually improves significantly in these affordable ALFs as compared to traditional nursing homes. As hospitalizations, emergency calls, and dependence on medications drop, so does the financial burden on the Medicaid program, which often ends up covering the medical expenses of low-income and disabled seniors. Consequently, Conchy's model not only helps the elderly stay in their own homes with basic services, but it also helps cut Medicaid costs at a time when both state and federal government budgets are becoming increasingly overwhelmed by public spending.

Conchy has already replicated her model in 40 ALF projects that serve approximately 5,000 seniors in 23 states through MIA Consulting, the for-profit group she founded in 1995 to help public housing authorities (PHAs) across the country adopt versions of her affordable ALF model. MIA Consulting works directly with interested PHAs to conduct feasibility studies, retrofit buildings to meet ALF standards, recruit residents and staff, manage day-to-day operations in the start-up phase, and conduct performance and impact evaluations. After an initial three- to five-year period of intensive involvement, MIA Consulting hands over the management of facilities to the local PHAs themselves. MIA Consulting is funded by contractor fees from PHAs and non-profit organizations that want to implement an affordable ALF model; all profits beyond the salaries of MIA Consulting's two principals (the CEO and COO) are reinvested in the organization to help subsidize low-cost and pro bono consulting services.

Conchy's work has received wide attention as a solutions-approach to what seemed a financially unsustainable situation.

THE PROBLEM

The many impending consequences of an aging population on American society—particularly on the health care system—have yet to be seen, but what is certain is that institutions in both the public and private sectors will have to change dramatically to accommodate these demographic changes. According to the American Association of Homes and Services of the Aging, in the next 20 years both America's elderly population and the country's Medicare costs are expected to double, whereas GDP is

projected to grow by only 75 percent in the same period. Senior citizens in low-income brackets or who are disabled are especially at risk of failing to receive the medical attention they need. Many of these elderly either live in public housing or are poor enough to be eligible for public housing, and studies have suggested that they tend to suffer from higher rates of chronic illness than their wealthier counterparts.

Unlike senior citizens in higher income brackets, these seniors cannot afford expensive private ALFs that often cost thousands of dollars a month, nor are they willing to enter nursing homes where many feel a loss of identity and where the quality of care is sometimes questionable. However, since laws require that public housing residents be able to live independently, once these low-income or disabled senior citizens are deemed unfit to support themselves, they are often ejected from public housing and are either sent to nursing homes or become homeless. Coupled with the effects of a society that values the contributions of the young over those of the old, this phenomenon results in many senior citizens being effectively abandoned with few choices as to how to live out the remainder of their lives.

In financial terms, the forcing of low-income and disabled senior citizens into nursing homes or homeless shelters against their will places an enormous strain on the Medicaid budget. Without an emphasis on monitoring and preventive health, many of these senior citizens only receive medical treatment when their health is in significant danger, which leads to higher public health care costs. Not only is Medicaid already operating at a deficit, but many states have also cut their Medicaid budgets as a result of the economic crisis (2008 to 2009). Without systemic reform, the current model of public spending on elderly care and medical treatment is unsustainable, as evidenced by the current national debate on health care.

Despite clear indications that low-income and disabled seniors are falling through holes in the social safety net and that public health care costs for the elderly are excessively high, changing public policy in this area is very difficult. As with any public policy problem, there is a great deal of inertia in the existing system, and a large number of stakeholders in the public, private, and social sectors must all be engaged in the debate. Nevertheless, given the heavy influence of the Federal Department of Housing and Urban Development (HUD) and Department of Health and Human Services (HHS) in elderly housing and care in America, working with government authorities is critical to reach national scale in this field.

THE STRATEGY

Conchy's mission is to make assisted living accessible to low-income and disabled seniors who either live or are eligible to live in public housing facilities. Interested PHAs contact MIA Consulting directly to initiate an inexpensive feasibility study where Conchy and her team determine local demand for assisted living services and explain the process of financing and operating an ALF to the PHA's staff and board of directors. If the PHA ultimately decides to move ahead with the project, then MIA Consulting guides the PHA through all the necessary steps to set up an effective and financially sound ALF, including retrofitting existing public housing buildings to meet government licensing standards for ALFs; hiring and training staff, many of whom are minority single mothers who also live in public housing; recruiting residents; buying supplies; monitoring regulatory compliance; and managing initial ALF operations. For the first two to three years, MIA Consulting staff are actively involved in the daily management of the ALF as well as data collection and impact assessment at 6- and 12-month intervals. Throughout this period of intensive accompaniment, Conchy draws upon more than 15 years of experience and contacts in the aging sector plus the political savvy gained from her public service as Florida's Secretary for Aging and Adult Services to assemble an affordable public-sector ALF in a highly expeditious manner.

> "Bretos became the driving force behind the nation's first public housing project to bring assisted living services to older adults who just need a little help to stay in their homes."
>
> —*Encore*

In recruiting residents, MIA Consulting looks first and foremost for vulnerable seniors, such as those who suffer from medical problems like blindness, diabetes, or heart problems or those who have no family. Residents can count on basic home care, round-the-clock monitoring, and transportation to medical appointments, but unlike many nursing homes, there are no doctors or full-time nurses on duty, thus dramatically reducing costs. Staff supervision gives both residents and their relatives the peace of mind that usually comes with a nursing home, but the fact that residents live in a home-like environment rather than an institutional one has been shown to boost both their mental and physical health. Conchy recalls that upon opening Helen Sawyer Plaza, her first pilot facility in downtown Miami, she explicitly decided not to lock up Alzheimer's patients in separate wards, as is common practice, because she believed that such a policy was inhumane. To the staff's surprise, under MIA Consulting's management not a single Alzheimer's patient got lost in the complex; the patient's sense of orientation was actually bolstered by all the support that they received from staff and fellow residents. The model also improves neighborhood security by providing a source of formal employment in urban areas that are often in need of regeneration, thus enabling many minority single mothers the opportunity to support their families through stable jobs.

Not only does Conchy's model improve low-income and disabled senior's quality of life, but it also creates enormous cost savings in the housing and care of some of the country's most disadvantaged seniors. Conchy finances the start-up costs of these assisted living facilities using federal housing and utilities subsidies from HUD and state Medicaid waivers that allocate money for seniors who do not enter nursing homes. On average, supporting these seniors in a public housing facility with assisted living services costs Medicaid $30 to $50 a day; putting them in nursing homes costs Medicaid $150 to $200 per day. Over the course of a year, this represents an average savings of $30,000 per resident in Florida alone. Moreover, Conchy is so effective at streamlining ALF operations that the facilities are often profitable by the time that MIA Consulting transfers management responsibilities to the local PHA. Helen Sawyer Plaza went from losing money when Conchy originally acquired the facility in 1995 to making a $1M profit in the year that MIA Consulting handed the facility back over to Miami-Dade County.

Although MIA Consulting has not been able to dedicate many resources to extensive documentation of its work, Conchy is conscious of the importance of independent impact evaluations and has collaborated with third-party evaluators. These evaluations are often prohibitively expensive, but Conchy's work has generated enough interest to attract Florida International University, which did an impact study of Helen Sawyer Plaza in the 1990s, and the news channel CBS, which researched and ran a report on one of MIA Consulting's projects and its associated cost savings for Medicare. Stephen Golant, an investigator from the University of Florida at Gainesville who specializes in gerontology, has been identified by HUD to rigorously evaluate the model's impact if a pending agreement between HUD and HHS to create a national pilot program based on Conchy's model is approved by both agencies.

Conchy is improving the dignity and quality of life of low-income and disabled seniors, with tremendous cost savings.

Given the influence of HUD's policies in PHA operations around the country, Conchy believes that the most effective approach to expanding her model nationally is via a shift in public policy. She has been heavily involved in drafting a memorandum of understanding (MOU) between HUD and HHS that would establish a pilot program for the public-sector assisted living facility model in eight different cities, funded by HUD and jointly overseen by both departments. The MOU has been endorsed by senior HHS officials, and Conchy expects that the agreement will be officially signed at the beginning of 2010. Under the terms of the MOU, MIA Consulting would retain its independence but would play a critical advisory role to the eight pilot projects. To achieve this, Conchy plans to expand MIA Consulting beyond its current capacity by hiring a chief financial officer, a program director, legal staff, and operations staff experienced in government reporting and compliance.

In the meantime, Conchy and her team are continuing to build relationships with individual PHAs in various locations around the U.S., which is how her model has spread to 23 states over the past 15 years. During this period Conchy has experimented with 11 different affordable ALF models, each with varying types and levels of services depending on local needs. This flexibility has allowed her to adapt to differing state and local regulations and preferences that greatly influence the design of each affordable ALF. Conchy believes that working with governments on a state-by-state basis will continue to be fundamental to her expansion strategy, given that housing policy and funding sources vary significantly by state. Securing the official support of HUD and HHS will facilitate and expedite her collaborations with individual PHAs as well as initiate a process of standardization across the country. Conchy has also received requests to export her affordable ALF model internationally to countries like Chile and Costa Rica, where she would be able to leverage both personal contacts and the Spanish language to lay the necessary groundwork for model facilities. She sees international expansion as the logical next step after consolidating the spread of her model throughout the U.S.

THE PERSON

Conchy was born and raised in Cuba by her grandmother, who she says greatly shaped her personality and character. The Cuban values with which Conchy grew up emphasized respect for elders and their critical role in society. When Conchy was 14-years-old, she joined 14,000 other unaccompanied minors who were flown to the U.S. under Operation Pedro Pan, a collaborative effort between the U.S. government and the Catholic church in Miami to shelter the children of Cubans who opposed Fidel Castro's new regime in the early 1960s. Conchy and her brother were sent to live in an orphanage in Lincoln, Nebraska, where she recalls feeling the first stirrings of a lifelong resistance to perceived injustice. Living in the orphanage also taught her resourcefulness and instilled in her the belief that individuals can take action to change their own reality.

At 30, Conchy enrolled in Oberlin College for her undergraduate degree while working full-time and raising three children. Her time at Oberlin, a liberal institution with a deep-seated social conscience,

represented a turning point in her life in terms of cementing her commitment to improving the lives of some of America's most vulnerable populations. After finishing her degree, she became very active in public sector agencies and citizen organizations like the World Health Organization, the United Negro College Fund, the Florida Commission on Hispanics, and the Miami-Dade Women's Fund, which she founded in 1991.

In the early 1990s Conchy made an unsuccessful but highly visible bid for public office in Miami, which prompted the governor to ask her to serve as Florida's Secretary for Aging and Adult Services in Tallahassee. It was during her time as Secretary that Conchy witnessed the squalid living conditions of many of Florida's low-income and disabled senior citizens. Upon leaving office in 1994, Conchy founded MIA Consulting with the dream of equipping public housing facilities with assisted living services for disadvantaged seniors. By leveraging her political connections and skills, she persuaded Miami-Dade County to allow her to use Helen Sawyer Plaza in Miami as a test case. She converted the failing public housing operation into a nationally acclaimed affordable assisted living facility using $1.27M in Medicaid waivers for residents who were able to stay in their homes rather than being moved to nursing homes. Conchy's early success led to similar contracts in states like Ohio, Tennessee, West Virginia, and Pennsylvania in ensuing years. In 2006 she was named one of the inaugural winners of the Purpose Prize, which recognizes leading social innovators in their encore careers, for her contributions to the fields of public housing and aging. The Purpose Prize brought increased visibility and funding to MIA Consulting, thus enabling Conchy and her team to expand their marketing and pro bono consulting efforts and to finance a new ALF in Tampa, Florida. ♦

DONNY B.U.

INDONESIA

Appropriate Technology

Conscious Consumerism

Media/Communications

Donny B.U. is building the foundation for the responsible use of online media in Indonesia through Internet Sehat, forging a nation of fully informed citizens and subtly preempting the possibility of new government limits to the freedom of expression.

THE NEW IDEA

Donny is creating a suite of strategies that put Indonesia's 38 million Internet users in charge of their own freedom of expression. His Internet Sehat (Healthy Internet) project encourages responsible Internet use by engaging many thousands of teachers, parents, and students to improve their online literacy and skills through various trainings and workshops in partnership with schools or held openly in public places. As part of this training, citizens encounter and agree to a "virtual code of conduct" that discourages the negative excesses of online activity. Together with Information and Communication Technology (ICT Watch), an organization he co-founded, Donny also catalyzes the development of Internet Sehat software applications—filtering software and a kid-safe browser, e.g. by local producers that reinforce the virtual code. His organization also supports the deployment of social media by citizen organizations (COs), engages bloggers and journalists and sponsors a blogging award to stimulate high-quality online content.

On the one hand, these services and others promote broad information citizenship, preparing millions of citizens to participate fully not just as responsible users of online information, but as active content creators and distributors who contribute to a rich and varied media universe. But indirectly, they also serve a crucial policy objective: The spread of responsible information citizenship on the Internet, achieved in partnership with government agencies, is meant to head off the looming threat of new regulations that would dramatically limit freedom of expression online. Donny is, essentially, solving a problem before political forces decide there is one.

THE PROBLEM

Access to Internet is no longer a problem for a majority of Indonesians. With Internet-ready cell phones that cost an average of US$100 widely available, people can now easily browse, post or connect to social networking sites. Indonesia now has 38 million

Internet users, including 25 million Facebook members (i.e. the third largest concentration in the world) and 4.6 million Twitter users (the most in Asia). But that proliferation has brought challenges: 60 percent of young Internet users, according to surveys, are susceptible to exposure to adult content, cyber addiction, or cyber-related crimes. The National Commission for Child Protection recently received 36 reports of Facebook-related crimes, including kidnappings.

This phenomenon has sparked outrage among conservative politicians—enough so that, 14 years after media deregulation firmly established freedom of expression for Indonesia media, a new round of proposed laws threatens to dramatically limit such freedom online. New laws on electronic information, defamation, and pornography specify stiff penalties for violations. A conviction for defamation online, for example, could lead to a maximum of six years in prison under the new electronic information law, compared to 14 months under the criminal code in the offline media. Meanwhile, a draft bill on Internet regulation proposes a government team to screen online content, sparking protests from news media, bloggers and other members of the online community.

Taken together, the recently enacted and proposed bills threaten to limit participation and innovation in online media. They promise to reverse the advancement of freedom of information that was the centerpiece of the nation's earlier media reform—which set off a dramatic expansion of news media. More important, these measures would have a chilling effect on free speech and access to information, both central features of effective democratic society.

THE STRATEGY

Donny is firmly committed to freedom of information and is keenly aware of the emerging threat to Indonesia's free speech laws. His strategy is carefully calibrated to counter this threat indirectly—by creating the conditions for responsible Internet use and the creation and distribution of high-quality online content, and by involving government as a partner in the program's proliferation.

> "Donny BU is known as a driving force and founder of the Internet Healthy ICT Watch, which conveys his experience in starting an Internet Healthy movement in Indonesia."
>
> —*Bloggerbekasi*

Through the Internet Sehat program Donny has endeavored to show the government that people can take responsibility for their online activities. For this, ICT Watch introduced a how-to module for parents and teachers, and a comic book for children/youngsters containing basic knowledge about the Internet, Internet hazards, and means of safety and privacy protection. These modules are patented under creative common license, and have been used by other organizations in various Internet skills training. ICT Watch also organizes various offline activities, such as workshops and trainings, public events, roadshows to thousands of schools and campuses, and provides online consultation and campaign on "good Internet ethics" using all media available (e.g. website, Twitter, Facebook, and so on). Tens of thousands of people have received the training, some organized directly and others in partnership with ICT Watch. Two to three short tips and tricks of "how to use the Internet safely and wisely" are posted daily and are responded to by more than 15,000 Facebook members and 950 Twitter followers.

Using refurbished donated computers, ICT Watch provides free community-based computer labs, helping local schools and community organizations to organize computer related trainings, from basic Internet to blogging and creative media. This lab also promotes the use and development of open source software among trainees and schools. Donny links the schools with prominent universities (e.g. Gunadharma and Bina Nusantara University) to provide volunteer tutors whenever necessary. From both online and offline community groups, this training model is independently replicated—combining technical skill with the Internet Sehat campaign. From a code name used by techie activists, Internet Sehat has now become a brand label for various local softwares, books, and Internet connection packages offered by local businesses. Various community nodes are even referring to the Internet Sehat model as a solution in opposition to the government censorship in the new draft bill.

ICT Watch also aims to build capacity among Indonesians for participation as creators and distributors of online content. It sponsors the Internet Sehat Blog Award to appreciate those who positively use the Internet for knowledge exchange. Two winners are chosen weekly from nine categories (i.e. education, family, student, travel and culinary, technology, citizen journalism, lifestyle, variety, and inspirational), and further included in monthly competition, best of the best quarterly winner, and annual super blog winner. A *pesantren* (religious school) in East Java replicated this award program among their *santri* (followers), and together with the ICT Watch team they eventually proved to the kyai, or religious leaders in the community, that the Internet can be used for positive purposes.

Currently ICT Watch is developing a curriculum for COs on how to optimally use the Internet and social media to achieve social change. Topics in the curriculum include social media, blogging, content strategy and privacy security where the journalism content has been integrated in the sessions. To accelerate replication, Donny is preparing Paguyuban Relawan Internet Sehat Indonesia (PRASASTI), a volunteer association to mobilize local scale activities independently, but with content support from ICT Watch. In addition, Donny ensures the research results are provided in Indonesian and posted for public use.

Donny and ICT Watch partnered with the Indonesia Internet Café Association that developed Domain Name System (DNS), which is essentially a voluntary filtering system. This allowed him to introduce Internet Sehat to leverage the social campaign of self-censorship at the individual, family, and education institution levels

among the Internet cafes. Even though not fully in agreement with the filtering system being applied, Donny found it a good way for the Internet providers to be held responsible. He believes this could be one of the alternative means to censorship. The Internet Sehat movement has inspired the Indonesia Internet Service Provider Association to partner with ICT Watch to market the Internet Sehat among the ISP members. Now, at least five of the largest ISPs, that reach out to millions of Internet users in Indonesia, have developed alternative Internet especially for families.

In Donny's opinion, the government should play an integral role in creating a supportive environment for healthy Internet usage. He is therefore lobbying with the Ministries of Education, Women's Empowerment and Communications and Information Technology to spread the Internet Sehat campaign. The draft bill has already been actively discussed by Internet users through social media. The success model of Internet Sehat has recently been shared among Asia ICT activists in a workshop held by OpenNet Initiative, and many have considered replicating the model in their countries.

Donny leads a workshop to increase online citizen understanding and literacy skills.

THE PERSON

Donny grew up in a family that believed in strict discipline and a simple way of living. He spent his childhood moving from one place to another, following his father who was an air force commander on duty. He learned about personal relationship building from his father, who took Donny with him on motorcycle rides, visiting and chatting with soldiers despite differences in military rank.

Always interested in technology and communications, Donny began his foray into this world after his parents bought him a typewriter. As a junior high and a high school student he was exposed to computers and Internet, and understood the enormity of this considerably new medium.

However, wishing to become a pilot like his father, Donny took the entrance test for military school but failed the psychology test due to his non-conformist beliefs. Instead, Donny enrolled in an undergraduate program majoring in informatics. He was more interested in the behavior of people in relation to technology rather than programming. Through his side job as reporter for detik.com, he tapped into a network of techies, ranging from Senior Fellow Onno Purbo's community to common users to underground hackers. His curiosity about social networking through the Internet made him choose communications for his postgraduate study. Donny learned how social networks developed in Indonesia, how Internet users communicate and interact with each other and how bloggers set up their own groups.

Donny experienced first hand Internet addiction following the online chatting boom of the late 1990s. Spending hours online with only a couple hours of sleep every night and becoming increasingly withdrawn from real social life made him realize how people should be prepared for the sometimes negative repercussions of Internet usage in order to benefit from it. Together with IT specialist colleagues, Donny was active in the Sekolah 2000 program, introducing the Internet to the public, particularly schools. Learning from the findings and envisioning a positive, healthy future of Internet users in Indonesia, in 2002 with colleagues from different professions including a teacher, lawyer, and reporter, Donny co-founded ICT Watch. ♦

BEN COKELET
MEXICO

Consumer Protection

Corruption

Democracy

Through the Project on Organizing, Development, Education, and Research (PODER), Ben Cokelet is training Latin American civil society organizations to become community guarantors of corporate transparency and accountability. The key to PODER is local capacity building, which can subsequently promote corporate accountability in a region where the concept is largely underdeveloped.

THE NEW IDEA

While working in corporate transparency, labor unions, and large civil society organizations (CSOs) for approximately 10 years in the United States and Mexico, Ben realized that very few actors possessed the strategies necessary to hold corporations accountable for their actions in Latin America. As a result, the concepts of corporate transparency and corporate accountability are much less developed in most Latin American countries, like Mexico, than they are in the U.S. Through his organization PODER, Ben's goal is to detonate a regional corporate accountability movement centered on local CSOs throughout Latin America, beginning with Mexico, where Ben has worked for years and currently lives.

The crux of PODER's model balances business intelligence gathering with multi-stakeholder approaches to guarantee corporate accountability. By conducting strategic corporate research through a combination of open sources (i.e. information that is publicly available but sometimes difficult to find) and human sources (i.e. a confidential network of contacts in companies, regulatory agencies, and the media), PODER uncovers information on undisclosed corporate practices and reputational risk factors that can be used as leverage with companies whose actions harm local communities or the environment. By involving various stakeholders like investors, creditors, shareholders, and community members, PODER works to change corporate behavior through strategic pressure from the inside rather than simply through whistle blowing from the outside. Rather than altering the individual attitudes of business executives, Ben's ultimate goals are to make corporate practices more transparent and empower CSOs in the process.

Ben is convinced that local CSOs are best placed to hold the companies in their communities accountable, particularly because the civil sector rarely has a voice in any business decisions across Latin America today. Using revenue from strategic corporate research for international clients, PODER builds the capacity of local CSOs to gather business intelligence and deploy it strategically in conjunction with other stakeholders to address corporate malfeasance. By embedding PODER staff in these local CSOs for several months, Ben ensures that the CSOs receive the long-term accompaniment necessary to become local corporate accountability partners. Local CSOs will thus gradually become a counterweight to entrenched business and political interests in making business decisions that affect all levels of Latin American society.

THE PROBLEM

Mexico is no exception to consolidated decision-making power, which only a small number of business and political elites hold throughout much of Latin America. For example, the 38 members of the Consejo Mexicano de Hombres de Negocios (Mexican Council of Businessmen) control major conglomerates that together account for an astonishing percentage of Mexican GDP. Through the collaboration and consent of politicians and regulators, crony capitalism undermines equitable economic growth and democracy in a country where democratic institutions are still being strengthened. Decisions of great economic importance, such as contracts for infrastructure projects or television broadcast rights, are routinely made by a small circle of the most powerful corporate executives in Mexico, most of whom are members of the above-mentioned Consejo Mexicano, which currently includes the chief executives of companies such as Bimbo, FEMSA, Televisa, and Banamex.

Ben's organization, PODER, increases the capacity of local CSOs to act as community guarantors of corporate transparency and accountability.

Corporate transparency and accountability are scarce in Mexico, particularly because company reporting standards required by the Mexican government are lax compared to those in more closely regulated markets like the U.S. For example, most publicly-traded holding companies only report consolidated financial statements for their entire groups rather than breaking them down by subsidiary. Corporate impunity is also a pervasive problem, ranging from white-collar crime to association with organized criminal groups.

> **"PODER accompanies civil society groups in Latin America to build power and, ultimately, a citizen-led corporate accountability movement."**
>
> —*Echoing Green*

The actors that traditionally hold corporations accountable in developed economies either have conflicts of interest or are ineffective in Mexico: government regulators are often impotent against corporate malfeasance or are in collusion with it; the major media outlets are controlled by the same powerful business families; and the judicial system is riddled with inefficiency and corruption. The few CSOs that do work on corporate accountability in Mexico tend to pursue what labor activists call "air campaigns," which refer to high-level public assaults on a company's image and reputation that are designed to produce consumer pressure and draw the company into changing its behavior. This strategy, however, rarely produces the desired effects. Many companies, particularly manufacturers, can simply pack up and move their operations elsewhere, leaving behind thousands of unemployed workers. Often these companies have undisclosed financial and legal liabilities that could be used as powerful negotiating tools for investors, creditors, and shareholders. But most human rights, labor, and environmental CSOs lack the expertise to systematically uncover such information, so the public never discovers that these liabilities even exist.

Local CSOs in Mexico do their best to represent community interests, but they have little influence over important business decisions. Even if they were allowed to participate in such negotiations, most local CSOs lack the specialized knowledge required to gain leverage. As a result, Mexican economic growth in the past few decades has not brought attendant income equality; according to the latest available Gini coefficient data, Mexico ranks as the 28th least equal country out of 134 countries worldwide. The benefits of capitalism in Mexico have been significantly distorted by asymmetric power structures.

THE STRATEGY

The cornerstone of PODER's work is strategic corporate research, or business intelligence gathering, in any of five areas—labor rights, human rights, environmental impact, corporate governance, and illicit activity. PODER's clients are all large international CSOs or labor organizations that commission specific studies on corporate practices. PODER will often uncover unforeseen information and advise clients on how to use it strategically while guarding the security of everyone involved. Unlike the private sector where firms like Kroll and McKinsey serve clients' business intelligence needs, few organizations until now have offered strategic corporate research services to the citizen sector. PODER's target market comprises trade unions, human rights, as well as environmental CSOs that have a presence in Latin America and generally possess annual budgets greater than $1 million, of which Ben estimates there are over one thousand in the U.S alone. Even in the first few years of PODER's operations, Ben has had to turn down paying clients in areas outside his core target. Ben and his team rely on a confidential network of contacts, whom Ben calls "human sources," within companies, regulatory agencies, and the media to complement information gleaned from open source information about corporate actions and their consequences. Since 2008, PODER has already conducted $200,000 worth of strategic corporate research and compliance services for ten different paying clients, uncovering previously unknown pieces of information that stakeholders have leveraged with the companies in question.

By training CSO staff, Ben is empowering CSOs to become a counterweight to business and political interests in Latin America.

Besides conducting strategic corporate research, PODER also partners with communities and other stakeholders to alter company behaviors that carry negative social and environmental consequences. Instead of immediately exposing any undisclosed liabilities to the media and antagonizing the companies involved, PODER determines the most effective course of action to take in each individual case. They select from a prioritized menu of tactics, which includes engaging the offending corporation in private; taking collective action against the company with employees and community members; pressuring the company financially by involving investors, creditors, and shareholders; sharing information with the media; and taking legal action, which is always the last resort. By focusing on industries that are not easily outsourced (i.e. such as mining, energy, and ports) or that are located in the most economically important cities, Ben concentrates PODER's resources on strategic cases where success will have a ripple effect across the national economy. For example,

in PODER's first project in 2008, a large labor organization asked PODER to investigate a Mexican mining accident for which a publicly traded mining and infrastructure conglomerate was ultimately responsible. Ben's team uncovered numerous strategic leverage points that were shared with shareholders, the media, and even U.S. regulators.

The revenue generated from these paying clients finances the pro bono heart of PODER's work: the long-term accompaniment and training of local CSOs to become corporate transparency and accountability guarantors. Using a train-the-trainer model, PODER embeds members of its own team in selected local CSOs—often worker or human rights groups—for several months to build these CSOs' capacities to conduct strategic corporate research on their own and implement multi-stakeholder approaches to pressure companies for change. In the long-term, Ben's goal is to create a region-wide corporate accountability movement led by the citizen sector in conjunction with investors, shareholders, local community members, and the government. Rather than spending time and money fighting isolated, short-lived campaigns against corporations in Latin America, PODER invests its resources to help local CSOs assume long-term responsibility for holding corporations accountable for their actions. In the 2008 mining and infrastructure conglomerate case, for example, Ben used the project revenue to train two Mexican CSOs dedicated to labor rights and transparency in the mining sector, so that they could continue to drive corporate accountability in this field. Three years later, both organizations are still working with PODER in a pro bono capacity.

While much of the information that PODER unearths must be carefully controlled, Ben sees an important opportunity to address the problem of asymmetrical information in markets suffering from lax financial disclosure standards. Part of the reason why corporate accountability is so challenging in Latin America is the limited access that investors and shareholders have to information that could affect their investment decisions. Ben has already begun working on a Web platform that will make some of PODER's information selectively available for more widespread use. He and his team are developing the "Who's Who Wiki" that will not only compile information about regional elites and their business interests, but will also allow users to add further information through a wiki feature. Ben's goal is to create a LexisNexis-like online resource for organizations and individuals working on corporate transparency throughout Latin America.

Ben projects that PODER will grow from serving ten paying clients today to 25 by 2014, with annual revenue of approximately $1.5M, 80 percent of which will come from project sales and 20 percent from philanthropic donations. He envisions two field offices in Mexico in addition to the current office in Mexico City and an additional office in South America, where there is also high CSO demand for strategic corporate research. Between 2010 and 2014, PODER plans to work with 30 different local CSOs on corporate accountability capacity building, thus creating a network of local PODER-like organizations with extensive geographic coverage. Through paid contracts and pro bono CSO accompaniment, Ben estimates that PODER will impact the lives of 2 million people in the next five years by improving corporate transparency and accountability in Latin America.

THE PERSON

Ben's passion for corporate transparency and building civil society capacity comes from over a decade of experience as a trade unionist and civil society advocate in the U.S. and Mexico. Even though PODER only came into being with a proof-of-concept project in 2008, Ben's expertise in corporate accountability springs from a much longer personal and professional history working in this field.

For many years Ben worked on traditional campaigns against multinational corporations, but in 2004 a particular experience in Mexico prompted him to reexamine the actions that most human and labor rights organizations take against the corporate sector. Over the course of a year, Ben managed a campaign against a textile factory in the state of Puebla that was notorious for employee abuse. One day, the factory owners suddenly decided to shut down the operation rather than continue dealing with the workers and their advocates, thus instantly eliminating thousands of jobs. It was a catastrophic result for the workers whose interests the campaign was promoting. Instead of gaining better pay and better working conditions, the workers lost both their jobs and voices necessary to negotiate with factory owners. Ben says that he learned two important lessons from that experience: "Never risk the livelihoods of the economically disadvantaged without knowing what you're up against, and never wage empty international campaigns without first developing local organizing capacity."

Two years later, the incarceration of a fellow activist from a partner advocacy organization once again forced Ben to question the effectiveness of traditional anti-corporate tactics. He felt that there was a lack of innovation and creativity in the strategies that were conventionally deployed in the human and labor rights sector and that oftentimes those strategies did not even achieve their stated purpose of protecting workers' and communities' rights, particularly when international organizations tried to wage local campaigns without first understanding local culture. Ben decided that the solution lay in empowering local civil sector groups to assume responsibility for corporate accountability in their communities.

In April of 2008, Ben began working as an independent researcher and consultant for large international CSOs, focusing on strategic corporate research paired with multi-stakeholder accountability approaches. That fall, he enrolled in an International Business and International Politics master's program at New York University to further develop the PODER concept; in the meantime, he hired a small team to continue implementing the idea in Mexico and the U.S. At NYU, Ben was a Catherine B. Reynolds Fellow in Social Entrepreneurship and, in 2009, PODER won NYU Stern School of Business's prestigious Social Venture Competition and $100,000 in seed funding. In 2010 Ben was named an Echoing Green fellow. Both the recognition and the money have been instrumental in helping Ben to rapidly scale PODER during this initial stage of growth. ◆

JEREMY DRUKER

CZECH REPUBLIC

Citizen/Community Participation

Democracy

Media/Communications

Jeremy Druker is developing the foundations for professional journalism in two critical markets: Central Asia, where independent journalism is constantly under threat, and Central Europe, where there is a strong need for industry standards. By placing emerging local journalists at the center of independent and professional journalism and connecting them through a pan-regional network, Jeremy seeds the field with "media multipliers" and institutionalizes benchmark standards for the media industry. His efforts are keeping the flame of independent journalism alive and strengthening civil society in some of the most repressive countries in the world.

THE NEW IDEA

Jeremy is creating the foundations of professional journalism in areas of the world where independent media remain fragile and journalists often work in an atmosphere of apprehension. Across Central Asia and Central Europe, Jeremy places young journalists at the center of changing these region's media industries. He believes that benchmark values for independent and professional journalism must be constantly reinforced in transitioning communities, and that the solution lies in emerging local journalists themselves. Jeremy's organization, Transitions (TOL), acts as an independent keeper of that vision by seeding the field with professional journalists who are trained to uphold only the highest core professional journalism standards in some of the most difficult contexts.

TOL offers journalists critical skills and on-the-job training to defend these standards and make their communication more effective, even as the industry undergoes drastic evolution toward citizen-produced media and new methods of content production that may undermine quality. TOL trains over 700 underserved and sometimes isolated journalists annually across 29 countries on topics such as writing sensitively about religion or ethnic minorities, new media techniques, election reporting, education, Roma issues, and many others. These journalists are encouraged to leverage new technologies, such as podcasting or blogging, in order to produce more "trendy" journalism while maintaining the highest standards and ethics. TOL also provides them with first-hand journalism experience by giving them the opportunity to be content producers for the *Transitions Online* news platform, where they are continually provided with feedback on their stories. Often for the first time, with access to professional support, local journalists are better equipped to dig deeper into social issues and act as watchdogs for their respective communities.

With the right training, tools, and networks, these journalists go on to create new ideas and further develop the industry in their home countries or elsewhere. By acquiring new skills and becoming part of a pan-regional peer network, young journalists play the role of "media multipliers," the most powerful force to change the industry. TOL acts as a catalyst for innovation led by local journalists by connecting them into theme-based communities and regional networks that represent the highest independent journalism standards in the region.

THE PROBLEM

In Central and Eastern Europe, the Balkans, and the former Soviet Union, democracy, pluralism, and freedom of information continue to suffer in great part because the media industry does not play a strong enough formative role in society. The governments of these countries all too often fail to provide legal, political, and economic protections to enable open and independent journalism. When media fall prey to government repression, commercial pressures, and their own self-censorship, industry core standards run astray and citizens in these regions no longer have access to a wide range of views and opinions.

Demanding the highest standards and ethics from his journalists, Jeremy's organization, TOL, trains local journalists in everything from writing on sensitive issues to leveraging new media technologies.

Young journalists, as the future keepers of these core standards, traditionally receive few, if any, training opportunities in the workplace, particularly the farther east they live. Specifically, they do not receive sufficient education in covering social and economic issues, investigative journalism, and other pressing issues of the day. Despite 20 years of international assistance and exposure, many journalism departments in former Soviet countries still stress theory over practical experience and end up employing professors who either have never worked in journalism or did so

many years ago. Unfortunately, quality journalism training centers (either non-profit or commercial) have not sprung up to fill the gap; while some countries are home to well-respected institutions, others have none. Many of these centers have also struggled to find sustainable business models, meaning they are often dependent on donors and therefore must adapt their training content to donors' whims. Without the right training, emerging journalists are disempowered to create the foundations necessary for professional and independent media to thrive.

Core standards are not only being undermined, but the amount of news content is also diminishing. With shrinking news budgets and the increased tabloidization of traditional media, the coverage of complicated social issues has also diminished. In this atmosphere, media outlets lack the funds or motivation to train their reporters in specialized journalism or "beat reporting," whereby journalists are able to build up a knowledge-base and gain familiarity with a particular sector, such as health, education, minorities, or the environment, European integration, economic reform, and so on. A major challenge facing emerging journalists is how to pursue serious journalism, while also incorporating new and trendy forms of media production and maintaining the highest professional standards.

In light of these obstacles, across Central Asia and Central Europe there is a strong need for an independent center to serve as the keeper of core professional journalism standards, and to carry out this function in a way that institutionalizes and continuously reinforces the foundations of a skilled, professional, ethical media industry.

THE STRATEGY

In 1999 Jeremy and three colleagues decided to transfer the print magazine they were working for into an online platform. Frustrated by the lack of other donors and more business income, the Soros Foundation cut part of the magazine's funding, leading to the exodus of senior staff. At that time in Central Europe, it was a radical move to shut down a print magazine and launch a startup on the Internet, but Jeremy and his colleagues were determined to prove that serious journalism covering the post-communist countries could survive on the Internet. With seed funding from the Open Society Foundation, *Transitions Online* thus became one of the first exclusively online magazines in Central Europe.

In the following years, with no fundraising, financial, or managerial experience, Jeremy, acting as executive director, and his small team learned on the fly how to run an online magazine startup. A major first learning experience for TOL was how often to publish content; monthly content updates turned into weekly updates, which eventually turned into daily updates. In response to the increasing need for content, Jeremy began to think creatively about engaging talented journalists from societies overlooked by mainstream media. TOL thus began to recruit local journalists to write about topics and issues that they could not often write about in their home countries due to political bias, censorship, or other reasons. As such, TOL became a space for local journalists to publish their stories internationally, while exemplifying professional standards to audiences back in their home countries. For example, a Kazakh journalist recently wrote an article on the large regional disparity in his country, which would have been next to impossible for him to publish in Kazakhstan due to censorship. Through TOL, the article reached 15,000 readers monthly, thousands more through syndication databases, and tens of thousands more through businessweek.com, which regularly reprints TOL articles. By involving local voices across Central Asia and Central Europe, Jeremy shifted TOL from a static print magazine to a dynamic platform of young, talented local journalists who learn skills that can drive independent and professional media in their local communities.

Jeremy soon realized that the exchange of numerous drafts and feedback with young journalists was essentially equivalent to on-the-job training, and it was all done virtually. Jeremy began to think more systematically about conducting trainings and in 2002, he launched TOL's first international training workshop on fundamental journalism skills. Over the next few years TOL began holding in-person journalism workshops, mainly in Prague and Sarajevo, training approximately 75 to 100 people annually. Numbers started to rise rapidly around 2006, as TOL began to train journalists from Central Asia, Russia, and Belarus, and added a distance-learning program. The number of trainees again rose once TOL expanded the training to cover new media and initiated programs in the southern Caucasus. For the last two years, TOL has hosted around 50 free-of-charge training events annually, reaching roughly 700 people across 29 countries.

TOL has multiple levels of impact. First, through creating a space for local reporters to uphold core industry standards while educating them in new media techniques, Jeremy and his team are keeping alive the flame of independent and professional journalism in some of the most repressive places. Second, TOL is acting as a "home" and enabling platform for talented journalists frustrated with state-dominated media or commercial media, empowering them to have much greater impact than they would without support. Finally, through its pan-regional networks, TOL is raising international awareness around topics that local journalists believe are important and deserve direct action, and which otherwise would not be picked up by mainstream media outlets.

More and more, the media industry is interested in the effective usage of new media and social communities. TOL was one of the first media development organizations in Central Europe to introduce training on new media, which represented a turning point in TOL's approach to journalism education in repressed countries. Jeremy realized that the use of new Internet-based media could offer an empowering and expanding toolbox for independent voices, particularly in countries with limited or no access to free media. In practice, such training workshops have directly led to innovative uses of new media to cover issues neglected by local media. After receiving TOL training, a participant in Azerbaijan organized video reporting on a YouTube channel on the attack on the Azerbaijan Oil Academy; in Belarus, another group launched a new social network to promote podcasting on socially important issues.

The several hundred TOL-like-minded journalists, who share similar ethics and standards for independent journalism, are becoming influential "media multipliers" by building professional journalism and civil society in their home countries. Empowering individual journalists with new skills, knowledge, and the right network helps them become innovators within the industry, and encourages them to initiate their own startup blogs, launch low-cost Internet publications, or write as freelancers. For example, after receiving new media training participants sometimes have the opportunity to apply for micro-grants from TOL to put into practice what they have learned. Examples of successful grantees moving on to create their own media outlets include a woman from Georgia who started up a lifestyle blog for young people that is now one of the most popular blogs in the country. Another woman, a freelancer from Azerbaijan, launched a site about women in the Caucasus, focusing on Georgian minorities in Azerbaijan.

TOL's regional network also ensures the transfer of ideas among local journalists. For example, through the training and alumni network, journalists from a country such as Azerbaijan can learn more about countries, such as the Czech Republic, that are farther along in their transition, and vice versa. Jeremy's strategic plan calls for developing this network further to enable and empower the communities of journalists who work on specific topics often neglected by mainstream media. For instance, Jeremy has created an online site focusing on education-related journalism (chalkboard.tol.org) and may soon launch a site dedicated to environmental journalism in the region.

> "TOL publishes a high-quality Internet magazine covering 29 former communist countries. It also provides extensive media training for journalists from those post-communist countries."
>
> —Cesky Rozlas

Finally, TOL provides an important outlet for the international publication of the work of underserved and often isolated journalists. Today, there are around 500 paid subscribers to TOL, and readership can be multiplied by several hundred more. Visits to the website total to approximately 15,000 per month from both subscribers and non-subscribers and hundreds of thousands more have access to content via syndication agencies and partnerships with online news sites such as businessweek. com. Over the years, TOL articles have also appeared on CNN. com and in *The Guardian*. With one of the largest online archives of articles on Central and Eastern Europe, TOL has become a global reference point for many audiences. In order to increase readership and public discussion, within four to five years TOL is considering relaunching its Russian version and publishing more in Serbo-Croatian, further enabling journalism to truly be local and accessible to all.

Over the years, Jeremy has been spending a great deal of his time crafting a sustainable financing model for Internet journalism. He decided to strengthen the paid-training component of TOL, hoping it will become a model for the sustainable production of high-quality independent journalism. While TOL's commercial activities constitute 24 percent of the organizational budget, since 2005 the paid training component has been growing. In 2010 it constituted approximately 70 percent of the organization's total commercial income. Other commercial income streams have been developed, including magazine subscriptions, syndication, and advertising. Jeremy calls this a hybrid citizen organization/commercial model (grants still constitute approximately 75 to 80 percent of TOL income, but TOL aspires to be less and less dependent on grants). Increasing the paid training income, TOL has created tailored journalism courses for Hong Kong Baptist University recently and has provided lecturers for a course run by New York University in Prague.

Thinking strategically about the future, Jeremy hopes that other media outlets will replicate the TOL model for publishing serious journalism, especially in regards to a focus on underreported topics and on having multiple income streams. To raise awareness around the TOL model, Jeremy is interested in offering TOL in more languages and will also be putting into place systems to improve tracking of readership figures and public discussions about TOL's content. Over the next year, TOL will also begin to better track its network. Specifically, Jeremy plans to monitor the activities of alumni and the impact of their respective media outlets throughout the region. Jeremy likens his vision to a map of the countries where TOL-trained journalists work and where each journalist is represented by a light. As more and more journalists join the network, the number of lights spread exponentially over the years until the light overtakes the dark.

THE PERSON

Jeremy grew up in Brooklyn, NY. His parents, both descendents of immigrants from Eastern Europe, believed in getting Jeremy and his brother out of their Brooklyn neighborhood and exposing them to other parts of the city. Jeremy remembers seeing diversity among his peers every day on his baseball team and in his elementary school. In high school, Jeremy was captain of his baseball team and an editor of his school monthly literary journal.

As a young Harvard student, Jeremy continued to be involved in the school newspaper and recalls it being as central to his life as sports and studying. When he became assistant editor, he knew he was hooked on journalism. Toward the end of his time at Harvard, Jeremy attended a fascinating talk about how journalism was changing in Eastern Europe, and a conference in Prague on the topic. He followed up with the conference participants to learn how he could get involved in the field and soon started studying Czech on his own. In 1992 Jeremy traveled to Central Europe (Prague) for the first time, where he taught English and independently interviewed local journalists on their changing careers. It was at this point that his professional journalism career took off.

Working for various NGOs and an alternative weekly in Prague, Jeremy wrote interesting pieces on media transformation in Central and Eastern Europe. He was most proud when he was labeled as an "enemy of the state" by a member of former Prime Minister Vladimir Meciar's government for his report on the Slovak government's repression of the media. Jeremy also had a chance to travel to Belarus, Macedonia, and Albania and had eye-opening experiences regarding the quality of media and journalism education in these countries. Everywhere he traveled, Jeremy heard complaints about media bias, the overemphasis on theoretical training instead of practice, the lack of quality teachers, and so on. At this point, the dire need for reinforcing professional journalism in the region was becoming abundantly clear for Jeremy. These experiences laid the foundations for him to set up an organization that would build the skills and confidence of young journalists.

The transformative moment that shaped Jeremy as a person and influenced the development of TOL was the collapse of its print predecessor, *Transitions*. Although the magazine was successful, it relied on expensive printing and distribution costs. Jeremy believed the biggest problem was that it was over-dependent on one donor. When the magazine lost a major part of its funding, the management team decided to leave. This was a real blow for a young journalist like Jeremy—to see that a quality publication wasn't immune to failure. Thus, under Jeremy's direction, a group of four people (Jeremy, a Serb webmaster, a British intern, and an American copy editor) decided to transform the publication into an online format. Jeremy co-founded a new organization, Transitions, and began to look for funding to explore whether quality, public-service-oriented journalism could survive on the Internet. Ten years later TOL has not only survived, but it has flourished to become the leading cross-regional platform for the growth of independent journalism in some of the most repressed countries in Central Europe and Central Asia. ♦

CHRISTA GANNON

UNITED STATES

Citizen/Community Participation

Criminal Justice

Youth Development

Christa Gannon is reducing juvenile incarceration and recidivism rates and changing the culture of the juvenile justice system by getting the system to listen to young people and turning it into a place of transformation for troubled youth.

THE NEW IDEA

Despite various efforts to make the system rehabilitative, the punitive environment of juvenile justice tends to plunge troubled young people further into hopelessness and crime. Christa decided to take a different approach: She listened to the young people caught in this vicious circle, found out what they needed, and provided it. Adapting evidence-based practices in youth development to a previously unconsidered population, juvenile justice youth, she equips this neglected population with a positive, supportive community and the tools they need to imagine and pursue productive futures for themselves. A combination of legal education, mentorship and leadership development helps make the criminal justice system intelligible to these young people and empowers them to shed the "delinquent" label attached to them and change their behavior.

At the same time, Christa gives the system what it needs. By presenting a cost-effective alternative to incarceration, and one that has demonstrated a transformative effect on young people, Christa is showing the juvenile justice system a better option. Leveraging the status that her organization, Fresh Lifelines for Youth (FLY), has attained among judges, district attorneys, public defenders, and probation officers, Christa supports young people in the system to serve as reform consultants to these various players. This approach both aids leadership development of the youth and shows the system actors how listening can help them do their jobs better. By serving both young people and the system that previously has failed them, FLY is helping to build a juvenile justice system that is not only rehabilitative, but transformative.

THE PROBLEM

The juvenile justice system aspires to be a rehabilitative system that focuses on the best interests of children, even while it protects public safety. But it has struggled to achieve either of these goals to great effect. While most young people who come into contact with the juvenile justice system are not chronic offenders, those that get far enough into the system tend to keep coming back. National statistics show that nearly 60 percent of persons referred to juvenile court return before they reach the age of 18. Of those under state custody, 55 percent are rearrested and 25 percent reincarcerated as juveniles or adults. Twenty percent return with more serious offenses. Approximately 15 percent of youth on probation are readjudicated for offenses committed while on probation. California has some of the most dismal statistics. According to government data, California arrests 237,000 youth annually and has a 70 percent recidivism rate for incarcerated youth, within three years of release.

Most juvenile dispositions include a period of supervised probation, along with other requirements such as counseling, drug treatment, or community service. Though probation rates have declined over recent years, in 2003 in California, nearly 179,000 juveniles received probation dispositions, at an estimated cost of $8,000 per probationer. Incarceration costs are even higher, and overcrowding is a problem. In a 2002 national study, 36 percent of responding facilities reported more residents than beds.

Christa's organization, Fresh Lifelines for Youth, has proven effective in developing youth leadership and in providing options to transform the juvenile justice system.

Though many "juvenile delinquents" want something better for their lives, many adults have given up on them. In response, juvenile justice youth have given up on themselves. Many of these young people assume they will be dead or in prison by age 21. These outcomes seem inevitable because they grow up in communities with revolving doors into prison. Family members, friends, and neighbors come and go, such that prison becomes a rite of passage. Studies show that 9 out of 10 incarcerated youth do not have positive adult role models in their lives; 8 out of 10 have experienced significant trauma, whether being subjected to serious physical or emotional abuse or witnessing violent crime; and 8 out of 10 do not have the developmental resources they need to make healthy choices.

Yet the general public perceives of them as predators and a threat to public safety. As a result, the system has often taken a "get tough" approach to get these youth off the streets. But research shows that detention can have the opposite effect of making it more likely that young people will re-offend.

Various juvenile justice reform efforts have emerged over the years with different objectives, including reducing racial inequality in the system, reforming detention policies and addressing substance abuse among juveniles. All are contributing to developing a better system, but the voice of juveniles themselves has largely been left out of the conversation. Where young people are being asked for input, the effect is limited because it is done outside a context of trusting relationships and support for the young people to develop the assets they need to productively participate in the conversation.

Leadership development programs that take a youth-led approach are plentiful for disadvantaged young people with potential, but in the juvenile justice system, the approach has been very clinical and service-delivery-oriented. Juvenile justice youth are generally considered damaged persons in need of treatment. When perceived in this way, they are not empowered to overcome the obstacles to behavioral change. By making leadership development work for juvenile justice youth, Christa is showing that "juvenile delinquents" have just as much potential as their peers.

THE STRATEGY

FLY focuses on three different groups of people that are critical to achieving its vision: Young people in the juvenile justice system or at risk of ending up there, FLY's own staff and volunteers, and the juvenile justice community. The result is transformed young people, a community that supports youth in the system, and a more effective system.

FLY's direct programming with young people consists of legal education, mentoring, and leadership development. The legal education program equips them with the information they need to make better choices about their behavior and activities. Most young people do not understand the nuances of the law and its consequences. FLY conducts law classes with teenagers throughout the juvenile justice system. They teach them about the law, their rights, and the differences between various crimes and their consequences, while also helping them build skills in empathy, anger management, and problem solving.

> "Christa Gannon founded Fresh Lifelines for Youth to provide teenage criminals with positive role models and enable them to turn their lives around."
>
> —*SandHill*

Through these classes, FLY identifies from among teenagers on probation those who can most benefit from more individualized attention and supports them with mentors and leadership training. For one to two years, they have the support of FLY staff and a community of their peers to help them set and achieve personal goals. They create and execute service-learning projects that allow them to develop the leadership skills they need to transform their own lives and make a difference in the lives of others. These teenagers also serve in an advisory capacity to FLY, providing their input on program design and improvement. The program has

provided a family environment for many young people who have lacked positive support from their own families, created a ceasefire zone among rival gang members, and put numerous teenagers on a path away from the criminal justice system and toward college, jobs, and community service.

FLY provides a supportive community and the tools young people need to imagine and pursue productive futures for themselves.

While transforming the lives of individuals caught in the juvenile justice system, FLY is also building a community of people committed to these youth and capable of making a difference for them. Christa carefully selects staff, board members, and volunteers who have both compassion for them and high standards for achievement. FLY uses law students to help teach its law classes and serve as mentors, instilling an ethic of public service in the next generation of lawyers. It also brings in community volunteers to work alongside the program youth in their service projects, thus changing perceptions of probation youth.

Finally, FLY takes a customer service approach toward the system it is trying to change. Christa has positioned FLY as a solutions-oriented ally to the various players in the juvenile justice system. At the most basic level, FLY relies on the probation office to fill its programs. It provides probation a service by giving it a place to send its charges. By providing a program that delivers results, FLY gives probation officers and judges a reason to avoid the costly alternative of incarceration. FLY has won the system's trust through its collaborative and effective approach.

As a result, FLY is repeatedly invited into discussions of system reform, and it has developed a youth-centric consulting model to assist this reform. Santa Clara County called in FLY to help it address a 40 percent recidivism rate at its juvenile detention facility. FLY designed a workshop for youth at the facility to research, analyze, and present solution proposals to the county. The county took the recommendations and reduced its recidivism rate to 7 percent. FLY has used a similar process to assist the Public Defender's Office in learning how it can better serve its clients. As a result, not only is the culture of the system changing, it is becoming more effective, and it is the young people themselves who are guiding the shift.

Decreases in government funding and increased criticism of failure rates have juvenile justice systems around the country looking for programs that provide a high return on investment, thus presenting an opportunity for FLY. FLY currently serves over 3,000 young people a year in Santa Clara and San Mateo Counties. The juvenile justice systems in other counties have already begun requesting FLY's services, and Christa is making plans to replicate in Oakland and Sacramento, two large cities with a critical mass of young people on probation. FLY will use the lessons from these replication efforts to determine how it can best catalyze the idea nationally.

THE PERSON

Christa was molded from an early age by the two very different personalities of her parents. Her father, an air force pilot in Vietnam and a corporate executive, instilled an ethic of discipline, focus, and dedication, characteristics honed by Christa as a collegiate athlete. Her mother, a special education teacher, taught her compassion and empathy. The combination of these characteristics has shaped her as a leader and defined the culture of her organization. But it was some early transformational experiences that shaped the vision that those characteristics would ultimately serve.

When she was 16-years-old, Christa's best friend was raped, and she became determined to be a district attorney. But when she got to law school, she signed up to teach the Fourth Amendment at juvenile hall, and her life path changed. She saw something powerful happen as the group of Chicago kids she taught developed into a community where even gang loyalties relaxed. She was personally transformed by the experience of hearing them long for something better than what they saw ahead of them. Christa transferred to Stanford Law School after her first year but took her juvenile hall experience with her. She started a Street Law program at Stanford, similar to the program in Chicago, to teach incarcerated and other at-risk youth about the law. But this time, Christa built her own curriculum and was soon being asked to speak about it at national conferences.

While working with juvenile justice youth in California, she listened to them in a way others had not: What did they need to get out of the system and pursue better futures, and what could she do to help them? They came up with the programs that became the core of FLY's work. With a Soros Foundation Fellowship, Christa traveled around the country to see what else was being done for young people in the system and found very little for youth on probation, a population that most organizations were avoiding. She started with a crew of volunteers and a conviction that "juvenile delinquent" teenagers could change their own lives and change the system, if adults would just give them a chance. ◆

FELIPE HEUSSER

CHILE

Democracy

Media Communications

Technology/Information Technology

Felipe Heusser is promoting a culture of transparency and accountability in Chile and Latin America by creating incentives for politicians to disclose more information about their actions and by facilitating citizens' access to it. Felipe is using social media technologies and partnering with Chile's leading communications media to disseminate the data in a manner that encourages informed decision-making and greater civic participation.

THE NEW IDEA

While working in the public sector in Chile, Felipe witnessed a number of alarming transparency issues and detected a strong correlation between this situation and citizens' apathy toward politics and democratic rule. Felipe left the government as a result and is now creating a culture of political accountability in Chile. He is doing so by establishing incentives for politicians to make information about their daily work public and by transforming this newly accessible data into easily digestible information that can guide citizens in their civic engagement.

Felipe is harnessing the power of Internet technologies to create much needed avenues for communication and engagement between citizens and their elected representatives. He is promoting political literacy in Chilean society and fomenting the demand for transparency and access to information. Access to information, however, is merely the first step in promoting citizenship and transparency. What matters most is how the information is then used to further the common good. The platform Felipe has developed showcases public information in a way that is easy to assimilate for citizens, and leads to informed decision-making, which makes for a more vigorous democratic process. The data is also becoming an important tool for citizen organizations (COs) that seek to influence public policy, as well as for journalists, who finally have access to a reliable and multi-layered source of information.

THE PROBLEM

As a result of the highly centralized power structures that characterize Latin America's political and economic systems, public information tends to reflect the interests of a privileged few. In addition, a long history of corruption and secrecy at the government level has enduring consequences to this day: Commitments to transparency and access to information are only nascent phenomena in many Latin American countries. Information is particularly lacking in public decision-making processes—be they legislative or political—which is most evident during and right after electoral campaigns. Not only does the available data generally not reflect the reality and interests of most citizens, it is also extremely scarce and poorly organized. Such data makes it difficult for people to interpret information once they actually manage to access it.

Felipe is increasing the amount and quality of Chile's public information by using social media tools.

This situation leads to high levels of apathy toward government on the part of citizens and can significantly weaken democratic rule. It is made worse by the fact that most people do not even perceive the lack of information and transparency as significant problems. It should come as no surprise, therefore, that a survey of 18 Latin American countries—conducted by a Corporación Latinobarómetro, a Transparency International partner—revealed that in 2009, more than 50 percent of the population did not care whether or not it lived in a democracy, as long as the government could address the economic issues they faced. The result is that politicians lack incentives to do their jobs righteously, thus creating a fertile environment for corruption and mismanagement, as politicians have few incentives.

Moreover, the political arena in the region remains quite inaccessible. Most citizens are simply not aware of the policies created and/or dismissed by political parties. They generally do not know which laws are being discussed and who is responsible for each initiative. It is even more unclear whose interests specific projects might represent, which politicians actually attend each parliamentary session, or what is decided within them. There is an obvious and pressing need to establish strong parliamentary monitoring systems across Latin America.

Although new social media technologies could be a key instrument to foment a sense of transparency and responsibility within

political systems in the region, the size of the digital divide in Latin America remains an important challenge. Any strategy that utilizes social media strategies to engage citizens politically will need to include complementary tools to ensure the participation of all of society. Very few have taken up this important challenge until now, apart from Fundación Ciudadano Inteligente.

THE STRATEGY

To address these transparency issues, Felipe created Fundación Ciudadano Inteligente (Intelligent Citizen Foundation). His team comprises professionals from a diverse range of disciplines such as political scientists, sociologists, communication specialists, web developers, and bloggers. Felipe established the organization in 2009, thus strategically coinciding with the presidential elections in Chile—a time where citizens' and journalists' demand for information is logically higher than normal.

Votainteligente.cl, the foundation's web platform, has since established itself as a trustworthy, professional, and innovative tool for political and civic participation. Felipe and his team dig up information relating to political processes, aggregate and organize it, and make it publicly accessible to Chilean society at-large. They have conscientiously developed visual ways to present the information to make it both compelling and easy to understand. Fundación Ciudadano Inteligente is thus increasing the amount and quality of public information that reaches Chile's population through social media tools.

The foundation has developed softwares to "synch" digitalized information from the Congress and communication media onto votainteligente.cl. It has also created web applications that allow citizens to participate as accountability partners in the information building process through crowd-sourcing technologies. For example, during the last presidential elections, citizens were able to monitor illegal advertising and campaign promises through the platform by sending their written or image contributions through computers and text messaging.

The foundation is becoming one of Chile's main players in the field of transparency. Votainteligente.cl is now the most visited politically focused website in the country. During the 2009 elections it hosted more than 4,000 unique visitors per day and many more through Facebook and Twitter. This notoriety and their proven track record has allowed Felipe's organization to establish partnerships with Chile's leading academic institutions to provide them with up to date information about transparency issues in the country.

Given that a large portion of Chile's population does not have access to the Internet, Felipe has prioritized having a high media presence as an intricate part of his strategy. Ciudadano Inteligente works with the country's biggest media corporations such as CNN, EL Mostrador, El Mercurio, La Tercera, and various radio stations to disseminate the foundation's aggregated information broadly, especially as it relates to themes debated in the Chilean Congress. In less than one year, Fundación Ciudadano Inteligente has appeared more than 50 times in the media. Most recently, Felipe established an official partnership with one of Chile's most important newspapers to publish regular in-depth articles generated by the foundation on a regular basis, both online and in its paper version. He has also signed an agreement with one of the biggest television channels to provide them with information on a weekly basis as an official source for their reports.

One of Fundación Ciudadano Inteligente's most important contributions is to foment a previously nonexistent demand for such information. The organization is thus effectively building incentives for political figures to become more transparent. In the context of the 2009 elections, Ciudadano Inteligente through www.votainteligente.cl developed a transparency index to evaluate each of the presidential candidates based on the campaign information they had made public. Because the initial scores were mediocre, Felipe and Ciudadano Inteligente worked with the media to publicize these results and put pressure on the candidates to increase the quality and quantity of data available about their campaign and policy goals, as well as their funding sources and expenditures. The foundation ran the evaluation a total of four times throughout the elections. As a result of the public pressure, three of four electoral candidates increased the amount and quality of information published on their websites by an average of 18 percent. While in the first ranking exercise only one of four candidates had managed to obtain a score above 50 percent, by the end of the campaign all but one had well exceeded the 60 percent mark.

> "Using the Internet, Vote Smart seeks to inform and educate citizens in all matters relating to public administration."
>
> —CHW

Felipe and his team are currently working to replicate this experience through local partners in Argentina and other Latin American countries, leading up to their presidential and parliamentary elections. This expansion, as well as the startup of the initiative, is being supported by Open Society Foundations. Felipe's ultimate goal is to create a pan-Latin American network of such organizations promoting transparency and civic participation through technology. In November 2010, Fundación Ciudadano Inteligente was the first non-European organization to host the Personal Democracy Forum, an important international event on transparency and technology. In addition, the foundation has been called upon by the World Bank to lead capacity-building workshops for COs working on the topic in Latin America. Felipe is also beginning to explore how a similar approach could be applied to monitor consumer rights and foment citizen participation around corporate responsibility. Recently, Ciudadano Inteligente won the PRIX-ARS Electronica 2011 Award for 'Digital Communities' one of the worlds most important awards regarding digital development. Fundación Ciudadano Inteligente was chosen among 407 web projects nominated for the same category.

THE PERSON

As a child, Felipe moved from Chile to the U.S. with his parents who were completing postdoctorate degrees in New Haven at Yale University. This three-year experience exposed him to new realities and allowed him to learn English at a young age.

In high-school, Felipe began demonstrating strong leadership skills, but only after initiating a degree in law did he get involved with various COs addressing poverty alleviation in Chile. At law school, he was elected President of the Student Union. During his time at Un Techo Para Chile (A Roof for Chile) he developed an interest in the implementation of socially oriented public policies. After his studies, Felipe went on to pursue a short-lived career in government where he worked for the Ministry of Labor and the Ministry of Foreign Affairs. At the Ministry of Labor, he had the opportunity to lead the international agenda of the sub-secretariat of labor—an experience that allowed Felipe to participate in the Chilean delegation at the ILO in Geneva for two consecutive years.

Discouraged by the bureaucracy and the lack of transparency that permeated some public sector agencies. Felipe left the public sector to study these issues. He pursued a master's degree in public administration and a Ph.D. at the London School of Economics & Political Science. Both of these experiences allowed him to deepen his theoretical and practical knowledge relating to transparency and accountability globally; establishing strong relationships with leading organizations working in the field of transparency and technology around the world. As a result, Felipe now acts as advisor to many of those organizations, including the United Nations. Felipe currently dedicates his time to completing his doctoral research on Freedom of Information and to the strengthening of Fundación Ciudadano Inteligente in Chile, while also planning its expansion to other countries in Latin America. Recently, Felipe was selected as a 2011 to 2012 Fellow for the Berkman Center for Internet and Society at Harvard University. ◆

© Franklyn Pepleg

EMMANUEL KASPERSKI

FRANCE

Employment/Labor

New Structures

Faced with increasingly complex social and environmental challenges and the insufficient number of social entrepreneurs to address them, Emmanuel Kasperski is creating a supportive environment for everyone to become changemakers. Starting in a French region with some of the lowest levels of social entrepreneurship, Emmanuel is using the templates of successful French entrepreneurs and demonstrating that through local coalition building and adequate support, it is possible to foster the creation and growth of a critical mass of social enterprises, catalyze changemaker communities, and accelerate innovation.

THE NEW IDEA

Emmanuel is convinced that there is an enormous untapped pool of local changemakers with the creativity and dedication to adapt and scale systems-changing ideas across France. He is opening another route to accelerate social changes by mobilizing all the stakeholders in a community around their own self-interest in resolving a social or environmental problem. As such, he is piecing together all the elements needed for a social solution to be constructed. Through a process of collective entrepreneurship, he supports local changemakers in replicating the most successful social and environmental enterprise models from all across France and invents new ones when solutions have yet to be found. Emmanuel has increased by fourfold the number of social enterprises created each year in his region, enabling the creation of jobs for the most excluded and paving the way for the necessary infrastructure to support these types of enterprises.

The co-construction of social enterprises is an incremental process, in which local governments, local businesses, citizen groups, and staff members all take part in supporting a designated changemaker in his/her entrepreneurial endeavor. The individual enterprises then form a collective of social enterprises. To keep this collective model together, Emmanuel has engineered a very clever, unique equity ownership model, in which the group of stakeholders owns 50+1 percent of each enterprise and each enterprise owns 40 percent of the collective. This team-of-teams model fosters a self-sustaining dynamic and prevents the individual opt-out of collective members.

Emmanuel's model is relevant in areas where the context is too complex for individual entrepreneurs to succeed or where an urgent social gap has stayed chronically unfilled. He also engages

social entrepreneurs who have encountered similar issues in their respective regions. Through his work, Emmanuel is creating a platform to share best practices and to competitively incentivize and accelerate innovation in a given region.

THE PROBLEM

Social change over the past decades has demonstrated that the successful, systemic resolution of social and environmental problems often depends on individual initiatives of social entrepreneurs who have the vision, determination, and qualities to overcome obstacles and build successful social enterprise models. However, faced with the multiplicity and magnitude of the challenges we face, society is confronted with an insufficient number of social entrepreneurs. While initiatives like Ashoka's Youth Venture and others prepare young people to become social entrepreneurs in the coming years, issues are pressing and societies cannot wait any longer for solutions.

MOBILECO is a cooperative associated with REPLICA and aims to promote the use of eco-mobility solutions to businesses, communities and individuals.

At the local level, governments, citizen organizations (COs), businesses, and citizens have been organizing to address social and environmental challenges. However, they tend to operate in silos and are poorly equipped to act proportionally to society's needs. Indeed, social policies are subject to power issues and often lack the necessary pragmatism to embrace all economic, social, environmental, and cultural specificities of local contexts. Social sector organizations struggle to innovate because of their reliance on old intervention frameworks and their lack of a global perspective on the systemic causes of issues they are addressing. Businesses are driven by short-term economic objectives and fail to integrate the social return on investment created by social projects, and hence do not invest enough in high social value-added, low financial return initiatives. And finally, while citizens are increasingly aware of problems, they do not know how to take part in the solutions. They may volunteer, but very few are ready to take the risk of social entrepreneurship (i.e. such as lack of a fixed salary and professional and personal isolation).

Even when successful local social enterprise models do surface, they often fail to spread throughout the country. Various factors contribute to this. First, social entrepreneurs are often very isolated and do not have the means to grow their organizations. Those who succeed need years to build a local network, legitimacy, and local financial partnerships to survive or spread into new regions. Second, very innovative models raise the resistance of local governments and local COs, who often block the launch of such initiatives. And finally, entrepreneurial people who try to set up a solution often struggle to find capital and support: Nine projects out of ten are never launched. Consequently, very few social enterprises reach a regional scale, and even fewer reach a national scale. There is a true missed opportunity to create large-scale solutions and catalyze competitive innovations.

THE STRATEGY

Until 2005, despite an ambitious garbage selection program, the city of Montpellier in the south of France was failing to reach its paper recycling goals. With a population and business sector growing exponentially, the city was well below its 45 percent waste selection objective. In the meantime, in Rennes, a similar-sized city in Brittany, the social enterprise Feuille d'Erable was collecting 2,000 tons of paper from local businesses every year and recycling them through an integrated chain of social businesses, while employing 25 people who had long been out of work. However, there was no social entrepreneur in Montpellier to replicate this particular model and all attempts to create a new social enterprise around waste sorting and recycling had failed. Puzzled by such paradoxical situations, Emmanuel created REPLIC for any social or environmental challenge on a given territory, he has created a system to organize all local stakeholders to identify existing solutions from other contexts, adjust them, and then implement them.

> "Replica, a cooperative group of social enterprises, works for the establishment of new structures capable of responding, in an area, [where] the social and environmental problems are greatest."
>
> —Emploi, LR

Emmanuel knew that he had to recruit strong, qualified changemakers to create and lead the social enterprises his region needed. But since these changemakers often lacked the qualities of leading social entrepreneurs, they would only succeed if given the right tools and support to lift administrative and financial obstacles. As a result, Emmanuel designed a unique coalition model that brings together all the stakeholders needed to identify pressing social issues, decide on the most relevant social enterprise model and create a supportive environment for success. His coalition groups consist of 1) local government representatives from the regional and municipal levels, to bring legitimacy, financial means, and lift administrative barriers 2) social sector organizations, to help identify the gaps in the existing landscape and avoid any unnecessary competition 3) private companies to bring their expertise and networks 4) selected changemakers, with the qualifications to head and staff the social enterprise when it is launched.

To build these coalitions, Emmanuel has chosen the legal form of Collective Interest Cooperatives, a unique French model that allows for collective ownership of socially relevant enterprises. He engineered a mutual ownership system guaranteeing that all stakeholders stay engaged and that social enterprises created on a given territory develop synergies and cooperate, yet can still strive independently from each other. This mutual ownership system also allows for the viral spread of any successful social enterprise in the cooperative to other communities and regions.

Emmanuel's organization also works with La Table de Cana, a restaurant that seeks to hire and train those that have been excluded from the labor market.

For example, through REPLIC, Emmanuel and his coalition have lifted all obstacles to create Feuille d'Erable in Montpellier, the first recycling social enterprise. Shareholders pooled the 200K EUR (US$282,500) initial infrastructure investment and recruited and salaried a qualified project leader. With the advice of private entrepreneurs they have grown the business to employ 30 people who had long been excluded from the job market. As a result, the municipality changed their garbage collection tax and over 20,000 citizens have been informed about how to select their garbage and collect over 50 tons of paper every month. Like all other changemakers heading a social enterprise in REPLIC, the head of Feuille d'Erable would never have founded such a company had he been alone. But now, with the support of his peer changemakers, he is successfully managing a booming social business.

With the creation of five social businesses in Montpellier within five years, which in turn are replicated in adjacent territories, REPLIC has initiated a virtuous cycle of positive social and environmental change in the previously depressed region. Local governments, COs, and citizens now have the REPLIC reflex and ask for REPLIC's intervention when they see an unfilled social need. Emmanuel is looking to replicate REPLIC in other territories with the support of local stakeholders promoting the model. Many regions have already expressed a strong interest: Champagne-Ardennes has already raised the money to launch REPLIC, and Nord-Pas-de-Calais and Rhône-Alpes are building coalitions that will lay the groundwork to create REPLIC. By scaling up his mutual ownership model to a national scale, Emmanuel wants to create a platform of changemakers and social enterprises that will accelerate social innovation and share best practices.

THE PERSON

Emmanuel grew up in some of the most industrially and economically depressed areas in the North of France. He was nourished by stories from his two grandfathers, one a miner who died of silicosis, and the other, a local union leader. From a very young age, Emmanuel visited factories occupied by strikers and listened to stories of workers hardship—even building very strong ties with some of them. During those years, he attended summer camps and became a camp leader at age 17. Emmanuel developed a passion for working with at-risk and disadvantaged youth and loved how the right support could transform their self-esteem within three weeks.

When Emmanuel found out at 18 that his health would keep him from becoming a pilot as he had always dreamed, he decided to follow his heart and work with disempowered groups. Right out of business school he joined ADIE, the newly launched national microcredit federation and launched their delegation in the North of France. For the following three years Emmanuel supported excluded people in creating their businesses through microcredit. A natural-born problem-solver, Emmanuel immediately came up with new ideas and models: He replaced the caution model with a solidarity guarantee, created a catalogue and toolkits for standard models of enterprises, and launched the first material marketplace to help entrepreneurs limit their initial investments. But the federation, which only mainstreamed his ideas many years later, repeatedly inhibited his efforts.

Emmanuel went on to take over AIRDIE, a newly established microcredit and social investment platform in Montpellier. For the next 12 years he tested and implemented his ideas. In particular, he managed to convince local banks to delegate credit decisions to AIRDIE up to 23K EUR (US$32,490), thereby dramatically increasing investment possibilities. AIRDIE became France's regional microcredit institution with the best reach into low-income groups and the highest sustainability levels for created enterprises.

But these successes only underscored the fact that the region needed accelerated creativity and sustainability in developing social enterprises in order to integrate marginalized people and establish sustainable environmental businesses. Emmanuel recognized that most people are ill equipped to become entrepreneurs and lead their own enterprises. Year after year, he saw the large number of failed enterprises. In 2004, Emmanuel decided to organize a conference on the topic of "Replicating social innovations in the Languedoc Roussillon Region" where he brought together all the important local and national stakeholders and engaged them in the creation of REPLIC. Five years later, with a strong track record, Emmanuel now wants to step away from operations and focus on national expansion. ◆

MICHAEL KELLY

IRELAND

Agriculture

Community

Family

Health

Michael Kelly is catalyzing a nationwide movement to substantially increase the number of people growing their own food. Through Michael's viral organization, Grow It Yourself, he is creating simple structures to tap into and cross-pollinate existing knowledge, excite new participants, and spread food growing on a massive scale.

THE NEW IDEA

Michael is resurrecting the traditional Irish notion of *meitheal*, a practice that builds a spirit of community by working collectively on individual projects—much like a barn-raising—to exponentially increase the number of people with the skills to grow their own food. Michael is creating a national network of local Grow It Yourself (GIY) groups designed to provide a grassroots, tangible structure to the local food movement and spark new growers by capitalizing on the knowledge of mavens in the area. Through GIY, Michael is expanding meitheal to encompass group learning around food growing, by creating off-line and online knowledge networks of engaged citizens. Michael compares his structure to that of Alcoholics Anonymous, envisioning GIY meetings available everywhere and offering a well-established open community in every town and city. Rather than relying on expensive courses or politically-driven agendas, GIY groups provide a place where neophytes can mingle with master gardeners to learn the tips and tricks of growing food from one another, offering a mechanism to integrate structure into fragmented local food initiatives.

Michael has created an organizational model that facilitates viral spread—his program, offering free monthly meetings consisting of group skill-sharing around gardening, focuses specifically around building community between participants, and works equally well in cities, villages, rural areas, or corporate settings. Committed to wide-scale spread, Michael has structured GIY to be action-oriented and dynamic, eschewing the cost-prohibitive membership model that ossifies many community groups with minutes and motions, and allowing interested parties to set up groups within the structures of existing food organizations or create their own free-standing programs. Tapping into social networking, Michael offers local groups opportunities to connect with others around the country, and has built a structure that allows painless adoption, offering mavens a platform and guiding local champions to launch branches in their own communities. Currently fielding over 60 groups with roughly 5,000 members around Ireland within a year of the program's inception, he also has interested citizens furthering expansion of the program in three foreign countries.

THE PROBLEM

The current generation in Ireland is one of the first generations raised without the ability to grow food. The skills for strong self-sufficiency have been lost in today's world with increasing pressures on the global food chain. Eating has become an unthinking act of consumption or refueling, rather than the culmination of a long process of growing or rearing. With no sense of the actual process and connection to food, there is little consciousness about the longer-term repercussions of choices. Children believe that milk comes from a carton, peas come in cans and chicken breasts grow as if by magic in a plastic tray wrapped in cellophane. Five billion EUR worth of food is imported into Ireland that could be successfully grown in the country.

A search of the field reveals an arena cluttered with traditional garden clubs, farming associations, and a large number of for-profit courses on organic methods at demonstration farms and centers.

Frequently expensive or narrow in focus, these programs tend to pair experts with experts. Older people, many equipped with a lifetime of knowledge on food growing techniques, remain untapped.

Food, as a subset of the Green Movement, is a growing area of focus. However, the arena is fragmented and frequently ideological to the point of evangelism. Consumers are faced with the choice between local food or organic food, food miles or fair trade; chemical-free apples flown in from New Zealand or the regional ones grown with pesticides. Most of these specialized options are economically unfeasible for many ordinary citizens. The Green Movement has no central framework among its disparate pieces—from local food to organic, community carbon efforts to slow food, to the growing number of exhibit farms, community gardens, and allotments. The problem is detailed exhaustively while concerned citizens are left to navigate a seemingly endless number of proposed solutions.

THE STRATEGY

Michael estimates that more than 70 percent of GIY attendees are beginners at growing food and gardening, with the other 30 percent experienced growers there to share skills and pick up new techniques. GIY consists of free monthly meetings to teach people interested in learning how to grow their own food or expand their skill set together, share success stories and heart breaks, and collaborate on projects. The local group meetings are designed to be high impact, action-focused and interesting; these are not traditional club meetings with agenda items. Typically, each session consists of a speaker for half the time (e.g. speakers vary from a professional gardener or farmer to a local person with a story, demonstration, or tip to share), and then the group is broken into pods of six or seven, organized around particular

topics related to what to grow to how to grow, and any helpful tips. Members receive a "grower's calendar" to inform them about the steps for the next month. Michael is seeking to recreate the traditional knowledge exchange of "two guys talking over their back fence," by structuring the meetings to maximize conversation and relationship-building.

Michael's GIY is structured to grow organically—GIY groups have sprouted up in major cities, small towns, and isolated rural areas, as well as in company offices like Microsoft, Intel, and Anglo-Irish Bank. In roughly a year, Michael's program has grown to over 70 groups and more than 5,000 members. The program applies as much to city dwellers creating balcony gardens as people living in small towns and villages, and can be easily integrated into existing initiatives such as Transition Towns groups or community center offerings. Many local organic farms and growing centers across Ireland now host GIY meetings at their facilities. There is also an extensive social networking presence online, connecting groups around the country and places to share tips and tricks.

By providing a communal experience, GIY has created a space for neophytes to talk with master gardeners and given structure to fragmented local food initiatives.

Michael estimates that an average launch meeting, regardless of location, attracts roughly 70 people, which tends to distill down to a core group of roughly 25. Michael is adamant that GIY not adopt the structure of a traditional membership organization, and therefore offers the program for free to attract the maximum number of participants. GIY has grown at an astonishing clip—Michael had set a goal of 30 groups across Ireland by September 2010, and counted over 60 active groups by March 2010, with over 5,000 members. He has created a system of "local champions" across Ireland who help to launch new groups in their region and guide existing groups. The program has already begun international expansion into Scotland and Western Australia and Michael has been approached by groups in the U.S.

> "Grow It Yourself was started in Ireland by Mike Kelly. It is about creating local groups of people who share a passion in creating their own productive backyard gardens."
>
> —*Ward off Climate Change*

Frequently noted by participants and observers is the age range and diversity of the groups—teenagers to elderly, immigrants to locals. "They talk about growing the way lads talk about football in a pub." By removing the political underpinnings to environmentalism and food growing, Michael makes it more accessible to everyone. His work utilizes the practical skills of growing food as an entry point to larger consciousness about food chain and other environmental issues. The program "makes gardening sexy," and empowers participants with their own role in addressing the issue—a political act without being political.

Michael builds "communities of practice" around growing food through his GIY groups. He is working to resurrect the traditional Gaelic notion of a meitheal, or group effort, similar to an Amish barn-raising. Initial meitheal projects implemented by GIY include activities such as seed-sprouting, with each participant starting roughly 25 seeds of a particular plant, then exchanging the sprouts. Others include members of GIY helping one participant dig raised beds or other such activities accomplished more quickly with extra hands. The individual meitheal effort is still taking off, but many GIY groups have found that their energies turn more easily toward community meitheals—community or school gardens, town beautification, and tree planting. Michael is expanding his efforts to include school GIY programs, microfarms, allotment programs, and farmers' markets devoted solely to GIY member produce.

THE PERSON

As in many Irish families, Michael grew up with sacrosanct meal times. His parents cultivated an extensive and productive garden. As a result, he was raised with a deep understanding of how food was connected to the land. He and his wife began gardening out of financial need—"vegetables were expensive." When searching for an outlet to help guide him through his own gardening efforts, he found only a few flower clubs or pricey organic courses. Michael himself is the design customer for GIY. He left the corporate world, moved to the country and began hosting seminars on how to keep hens, and wrote a book on his journey. At his courses, Michael realized that their shared lunches, which were full of stories, advice, and tips was often the most useful for the participants. Michael wondered if he could recreate that experience in particular; the camaraderie and skill sharing spirit evolved into his initial GIY meeting. He placed a notice on a community bulletin board, and when he arrived on the evening he was shocked to find a packed room with over 100 interested people.

Over the course of a varied career, Michael has excelled in every field he has pursued. He began his career in an IT company which offered a great deal of freedom to be creative within the bounds of the work. There, he honed the skill of coming up with his own solutions to challenges. A Waterford native, he set up offices for the company there and in Cork. One day he had an epiphany—"I heard myself talking and realized I didn't care about a word I said." He decided to leave the IT field to pursue a dream of writing and journalism. He took a part-time course and within two months was writing for the *Irish Times*. Focusing on a broad range of topics, but especially passionate about social change, food, and issues of the natural world, Michael pitched a column called "Giving Up," where each week he would practice living without something—from shaving to meat to driving—and discuss the implications on his life and impact on the world.

As a journalist for *The Irish Times*, he was sent on an assignment to interview Ireland's first Ashoka Fellow Caroline Casey. He was deeply inspired by her work and courage. He recognized himself as she described the characteristics of a social entrepreneur. He cites the conversation with Caroline as a huge turning point for him; the spark that led him to launch GIY.

Currently gaining increasing national recognition, Michael has received support from Social Entrepreneurs Ireland and the Arthur Guinness Fund, and is working to manage the explosive viral growth of his organization. ♦

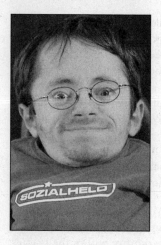

RAUL KRAUTHAUSEN

GERMANY

Aging

Disabilities

Raul Krauthausen is promoting the inclusion and awareness of urban wheelchair users through the first crowdsourced online map of wheelchair-friendly places around the world.

THE NEW IDEA

Raul built a crowdsourced online map of wheelchair-accessible and inaccessible places, to provide a simple and efficient way toward better inclusion for wheelchair users in Germany. The online map (www.wheelmap.org), serves the mobility of impaired communities in several distinct ways: First, it provides the first guide to wheelchair accessible places in Germany, and second, it provides a new and effective platform for creating greater public awareness and social mobilization around issues related to increasing the integration of disabled persons into everyday life in Germany. Raul believes that inaccessibility is not only a problem for people with impaired mobility, but it is an issue that affects all people and their right to an inclusive society. He challenges a discriminatory system that creates separate spaces for people with disabilities throughout their lives. Raul builds his approach on a simple insight: If wheelchair users know which public places are accessible, they are more likely to go there, engage in public life, and realize their full potential.

Raul puts the solution into the hands of everyone: His open data, OpenStreetMap mapping platform, with 40,000 active contributors worldwide, allows every user to tag public places as accessible, inaccessible, or partly accessible to wheelchairs. Thus, Raul radically simplifies the information about wheelchair accessibility. While existing certification schemes too often provide irrelevant and overly detailed data in user-unfriendly ways, wheelmap.org limits complexity and focuses on the relevant accessibility information. This information is easily searchable; it can be sorted and adopted to individual needs and shared with other users. Due to the fact that the user enters the information, in a similar fashion to Wikipedia, everyone helps to grow this powerful tool from the bottom up. By creating open and standardized interfaces to the data, Raul enables third parties to create lists, applications, and other services on top of his service. For example, identifying all educational facilities in Germany without wheelchair access by simply plugging in data from other

sources, or lobbying a cinema chain for better accessibility by making their inaccessibility public.

Wheelmap is in the start-up phase, having launched in March 2010 as a beta platform after 12 months of intensive preparation. The functionality will support open source competitions, call-in services, tagging parties, and partnerships. Raul expects wheelmap to be a market leader and cover its own costs through income streams from wheelchair manufacturers or large public events within a year. Thanks to the worldwide reach of OpenStreetMap, Raul intends to spread not only throughout Germany, but to other countries as well.

THE PROBLEM

There are 1.6 million wheelchair users in Germany, and many more individuals use them occasionally or rely on mobility aids such as rolling walkers. These numbers are expected to triple by 2050 as more elderly people will use mobility devices as a result of demographic change. Individuals relying on mobility aids all face a simple yet powerful problem: Not knowing whether a public place is accessible to wheelchairs. As a result, few wheelchair users take part in public life and a vicious cycle of exclusion emerges.

This challenge reflects a broader social problem: In Germany, as in many societies, the welfare system has created separate spaces for people with disabilities. These fall into separate schools from early on in their lives (i.e. with poor average educational achievement) to special workplaces later in their lives (i.e. typically subsidized and lie outside of the regular labor market). As a result, people with disabilities only associate with other disabled people and have far fewer chances to realize their full potential as active members of society.

> "Krauthausen attributes Wheelmap's success to its availability as an iPhone application and the 'Wiki principle' - the idea that anyone, anywhere can contribute."
>
> —*The Spinal Post*

So far, most efforts to improve the accessibility of public places for people with disabilities are regulated by the government and often require 20+ pages of detailed information that takes into account the span of mobility impairments such as blindness, deafness, short stature, or many others. Consequently, there is little stringent enforcement and very few institutions make the effort to comply and face prohibitive refitting costs.

Raul knew that in almost all cases, this depth of information is either superfluous or too difficult to navigate and use. A simple "(not or partly) accessible for wheelchairs" is sufficient for most people with disabilities. Also, this information does not have to be mandated or regulated by authorities, but can more efficiently be obtained from users themselves. This change in approach emphasizes a much-needed paradigm shift from integrating people with disabilities into "normal" life to including people with and without disabilities in truly shared spaces.

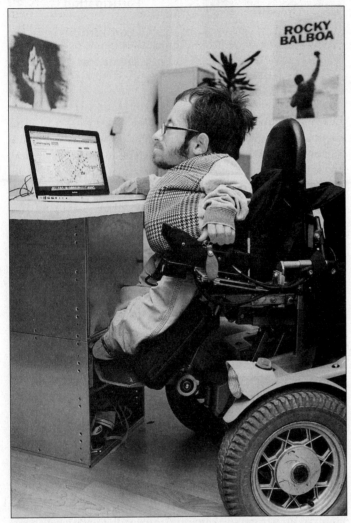

Raul's OpenStreetMap platform enables users to tag public places for wheelchair accessibility—making it simple to find accessible places and creating greater public awareness around issues related to the inclusion of disabled persons in everyday life.

THE STRATEGY

Raul recognized the power of open networks to bring about paradigm shifts in the area of disability rights. Set up as a free and open data platform, wheelmap.org provides a low barrier entry point and a powerful self-help tool to anyone interested in the issue. Built on top of OpenStreetMap systems, the technology comes free, already has a large mobilized user base, and will continue to develop to user needs over time. Every user can easily tag places as accessible, partly accessible, or not accessible to wheelchairs, and a blog and other features allow for additional information sharing and community organizing. The platform works with various input devices including mobile phones, and provides open programming interfaces for third-party applications and websites.

This type of open data online technology is bridging the mobility challenges of wheelchair users utilizing their huge online affinity as they are among the highest users of online technologies. Raul is galvanizing the first online open data application for this population and is growing a thriving community on his online-platform. Already, Raul's existing blogs and forums are very well known by impaired people in the German-speaking web. Through its additional functionalities wheelmap is not only a self-help tool but also an important interest group bringing people together who are interested in a more integrated society. For example, when a mainstream cinema sold Raul a ticket without telling him that the cinema hall was wheelchair inaccessible, 200 people immediately commented on the incident on wheelmap's twitter post. Consequently, the cinema called to apologize and soon after signalized the wheelchair accessible halls at the entrances and on their homepages.

Because wheelmap allows for easy identification of wheelchair accessible places within a category in a given geography, the community and its data place pressure on owners to improve the inclusiveness of their facilities. In contrast to existing projects, Raul does not limit wheelchair specific locations, such as therapy centers or toilets. Instead, he wants to include wheelchair users in daily life, focusing on public places of daily life including cafes, clubs, theaters, and basic public services, including public transportation, administrations and banks. Wheelmap.org also works to bridge the information gap between public policy and employer knowledge. The German government provides generous funds for improving accessibility to shop owners, barkeepers, and so on; however, the benefits are rarely utilized by employers because they do not know about them. Wheelmap publicizes this information, making it accessible to all parties and promoting the benefits of accessible locations. Raul therefore uses transparency not only as a tool to improve individual lives, but also to affect a shift in the dominant mindset and to challenge a system that segregates disabled people.

An expert in social marketing, Raul pulls all levers of stakeholder mobilization, including social media, events, and campaigning. He taps into market forces such as the tourism sector and its need to improve accessibility in the face of demographic change. Raul works with related projects and data sources to quickly generate 10,000 plus data points, which he estimates will mark a tipping point at which many chains of stores and restaurants will start contributing their own data.

Raul's funding strategy is built on leveraging engagement from users and volunteers and generating income from alliances with partners such as wheelchair manufacturers, city authorities and event managers, who can also use a "white label" version of the platform to create their own branded maps.

Wheelmap is the third major project of Raul's social innovation group, SOZIALHELDEN (German for social heroes). As wheelmap expands, Raul plans to launch new projects, in essence building an ecosystem of ideas to improve the inclusion of people with disabilities (i.e. carry-along folding ramps for wheelchair users).

THE PERSON

Raul is a marketing specialist dedicated to solving social problems, and making solving social problems fun. As a child, he lived in both Germany and Colombia, where he witnessed many stark economic divides. With his own genetic bone disorder confining him to a wheelchair, he experienced the social divides facing people with disabilities.

Returning to Berlin, Raul early on dedicated his life to creating social change. He enrolled at the Berlin University of Arts where he studied "strategic communication and planning" and created an award campaign for the Alternative Nobel Prize (Right Livelihood Award) and at the School of Design Thinking at the Hasso-Plattner-Institute where he studied "Design Thinking." Trained as a radio host, Raul later launched a call-in radio show for people in emotional distress, where he was confronted with poverty, abuse, and loneliness in the dark niches of the welfare state.

Reacting to these social issues with a spirit of inclusiveness, participation and entrepreneurship, Raul co-founded the SOZIALHELDEN platform, a multi-award-winning group of extraordinary changemakers, of which he is the creative mastermind. The group has a track record of creating successful, sustainable and well marketed social innovations, including "Pfandtastisch helfen!", Germany's most prominent recycling for social change project. Raul always felt the need to empower people with impaired mobility and to get them better integrated into a very segregated German society. Having many experiences with the German welfare system himself he always wanted to give wheelchair drivers a tool at-hand that makes them more independent and brings them closer together to support each other. While continuing to contribute to SOZIALHELDEN, Raul now fully concentrates on growing the wheelmap community. ◆

DOMINIK KSIĘSKI

POLAND

Citizen/Community Participation

Corruption

Democracy

Drawing on his considerable experience as a publisher of local newspapers, Dominik Księski is creating a new operating model to ensure that all Polish citizens have access to independent local press. His bottom-up approach has created a movement among first generation local publishers, strengthened their watchdog capabilities, and uncovered new sources of financial sustainability. Dominik's Association of Local Newspapers is increasingly seen as a reference point for neighboring countries.

THE NEW IDEA

Dominik is creating the future of independent local press, aiming at all citizens in Poland to have access to a neutral, accurate, and reliable press that takes on the government and vested interest groups and exposes corruption. Through his Association of Local Newspapers (ALN), he is mobilizing the first generation of private local publishers in Poland, and is enabling them to collaborate around issues that expand their footprint throughout Poland. Dominik's new operating model for local independent press—one that is networked, but decentralized, competitive, and sustainable—ensures that the movement toward accessible local independent press continues to grow rather than backtrack in the face of industry threats.

In Poland, three quarters of the population live outside big cities; however, 40 percent of these rural areas still do not have access to privately-run independent newspapers. Dominik is expanding geographically by targeting and helping local publishers set up independent newspapers in some of the most isolated communities in Poland, including post-collective farming areas where access to information is limited by municipality controlled press and low levels of citizenship awareness. These high-risk communities present a major political and strategic opportunity for the industry's long-term survival.

Having already built a movement that covers 60 percent of Polish localities, representing 107 independent newspapers, Dominik is creating systems to keep these independent newspapers sustainable. Recognizing that the survival of the sector depends on its financial independence, and its ability to remain competitive vis-à-vis media conglomerates, Dominik is diversifying the revenue sources of local newspapers. By establishing a shared advertisement service for the whole association, he has opened up the central advertising market to local publishers that would otherwise be unable to access it. Furthermore, to improve the attractiveness of local newspapers to advertising agencies, Dominik introduced the first readership survey of local weeklies, conducted by the same company that surveys regional and national newspapers.

Dominik is also working to ensure the long-term sustainable future of local independent press by placing curbs on newspapers subsidized by local governments. Members of his independent press movement publish watchdog articles daily and, without taking a point of view, they reveal local cases of corruption that would otherwise be left unturned. Dominik's press association is therefore contributing to transparency and healthy public life, while reducing the involvement of local governments in the press industry.

> Having already built a movement that covers 60 percent of Polish localities, representing 107 independent newspapers, Dominik is creating systems to keep these independent newspapers sustainable.

Finally, with an eye toward sustainability, Dominik is assisting this first generation of publishers in creating succession plans for their newspapers to ensure that ownership will remain local and dedicated to the same ideals—that the local independent press movement is ultimately about recognizing an opportunity to create effective citizenship at the local level and strengthening the social and ethical fiber of communities.

THE PROBLEM

Since 1990, when the new democratic era began, local publishers who provide readers with politically neutral, accurate and reliable sources of information have been facing a range of obstacles in running their businesses with a social mission.

After 20 years of democracy in Poland, during which hundreds of independent news outlets were established, government at all community levels continues to influence public opinion through the media. Local government-owned media presents only the official perspective and does not allow for the exchange of views or free-flow of information. Furthermore, central and regional newspapers do not provide readers with access to politically neutral, in-depth information about their own communities and daily realities. Citizens in Poland, particularly those from little communities, have only just begun to realize that the widespread corruption characteristic of the communist era does not have to be the norm today, and that local independent press is in fact a guarantor of reducing and eradicating corruption. For example, when the local government donated land to the church and a

priest built a house for himself instead of the promised church building, community members did not challenge the priest's decision for fear of being publically condemned during church service. Only the local journalist found the courage to disclose the story to the community.

In addition to fighting to promote their brand of unbiased and reliable news, independent local weeklies are struggling to compete against the dominance of international and national media corporations. For example, independent local weeklies are denied access to Poland's national readership survey, making them unattractive to the central advertising market, which serves as an important source of revenue for newspapers, especially since taking government subsidies is not an option. Without this official industry-wide recognition, local weeklies remain "substandard" to national and regional newspapers.

Furthermore, most of the publishers of local weeklies today are middle-aged and, though a majority of them will work past retirement age, they will soon face the challenge of succession in their businesses. However, only with training, advice, and a menu of succession options, will these publishers be able to plan for the future of their businesses and produce young successors who identify with the social mission of independent media and will serve as ambassadors of an independent local press.

Although local independent media can be a high-cost and risky industry, at the same time it is highly efficient as a business model that occupies a unique industry niche, as it is the only vehicle through which to provide citizens with the most accurate, locally-sourced information, and empower them to act and react as citizens. However, it will require a new model of operation in order for it to survive.

THE STRATEGY

In 2004 Dominik assumed leadership of the ALN, an organization of which he was a founding member in 1999. ALN was created as a platform of exchange between publishers from various places in order to improve their chances of success in a difficult market. However, when ALN encountered financial challenges, Dominik decided to realign and broaden the vision to ensure all localities across Poland have access to independent local press. He presented a new program for the association, which included three strategic goals for the long-term survival of locally produced independent news: Successfully reach the areas in Poland uncovered by the range of independent local weeklies; reduce the scope of government influence over local press; and finally, ensure its future financial and generational sustainability.

Dominik finds it particularly important to advise novice publishers on how to organize their newspaper to reach the maximum number of readers; for instance, it should be politically neutral, include content about issues important to local readers, and have the courage to write about unspoken issues. He also demonstrates to publishers the importance of training team members. Finally, Dominik provides advice on financial survival, including strategies to reach local advertisers. Together with a lawyer specializing in local press issues, he is also providing support to legal cases against local publishers.

Through the network of local publishers based throughout the country, Dominik is placing pressure on local governments to be transparent, follow the rules of democracy, and to step out from the domain of the local press outlets. These local news outlets publish watchdog articles on a daily basis that reveal local corruption scandals that would otherwise remain hidden. For example, one weekly wrote about a local politician who was accused of corruption and did not appear in court, claiming he was sick; however, during the same time, he attended city council meetings and collected allowances for it. Another example is the publication of lists of people who benefit from tax abatement. If the list is posted in the town hall, few people will read it; however, when it is published in the local newspaper, it is read by 50 percent of the citizens in that community who now understand the scope of local corruption transpiring in their communities.

In addition to assuring constant vigilance and pressure on local governments by publishers at the micro level, Dominik is also working at the public policy level to reduce government influence over local media. He has managed to unite members of the association, accustomed to working independently, to speak with one voice on issues related to fair competition in the press market. Dominik speaks on their behalf in the senate and advocates for legislation to limit the circulation of newspapers subsidized by local governments and their ability to sell adverts. He does not want to ban governments from speaking at all, but he believes they should do it in the form of official bulletins distributed for free, to make clear to readers which perspective they present.

Upon taking leadership, Dominik presented the feasible plan of entering the central advertising market as a way to diversify the revenue sources for local newspapers and therefore create a means to increase their independence and sustainability. Although others have played with the idea, no one has developed a strategy to successfully implement it. Dominik created a mechanism allowing an advertiser to reach readers of the entire network of local newspapers with a single simple order. In this win-win scenario, local publishers gain access to new sources of income and advertisers easily reach new customers in local communities across Poland. Just four months after taking over and revamping the association Dominik had created an ad network of 20 to 30 weeklies with 250,000 copies a week in circulation (i.e. representing all newspapers in the association's network). In 2010, the ad network covered a circulation of over 800,000 a week.

However, from the beginning, some media agencies remained unconvinced by the appeal of this offer. Thus, in 2004 Dominik initiated the first local press readership survey, which is carried out by the company that leads the national survey and employs the same survey methodology used for central and regional dailies in Poland. The survey showed that in some cases up to 51 percent of local community members read independent weeklies and that every copy is read on average by five readers. This was the first time that statistics on readership of local independent titles were calculated and published. The readership survey brought increased income from adverts in 2006 and during the following three years, revenue has continually increased, allowing the association to cover its operating costs and add new initiatives to its program, e.g. professional trainings for publishers and journalists. Still, some media houses doubted the survey's legitimacy. Thus, Dominik is now making efforts to formally include local press outlets in the Polish Readership Survey that embraces all daily and regional newspapers. To achieve this, he and 20 other ALN members signed up to the Press Distribution Controlling Union which runs the survey. Dominik is trying to change the rules of the readership survey, so that it will include the agenda of local publishers.

Recently Dominik began developing a solution to a new challenge: The intergenerational survival of independent local weeklies. On average, publishers of these weeklies are in their fifties and need to begin thinking of successors to continue their mission. To prepare for this sustainability challenge, Dominik is analyzing various models to create a database of succession options with pros and cons. Publishers will be able to choose from these and develop a sound succession strategy, along with providing advice and guidance for successful implementation. There is a huge opportunity for young people to not only continue the publishing work of their parents, but also to become ambassadors of the Polish model of independent local press as a tool to foster a healthy democracy at the grassroots level outside Poland.

THE PERSON

Dominik grew up in Southeastern Poland. His mother was the director of the culture promotion department in the Lublin Regional Center of Culture and his father worked in the literature department of a local Polish radio. Growing up, Dominik recalls summers he spent trekking in mountains with his grandmother and the rest of the family. When he was 17, he moved to Żnin, where he lives today and cares for his grandmother.

During his schooling, Dominik was an active organizer. In high school, he was the president of the student government. As a student of Polish literature and language—following the family tradition—he organized a library of underground books for students in his department. Later he distributed an illegal anti-communist bulletin. As a teacher in a primary school in Żnin, Dominik founded a hiking group that organized treks in the mountains. During the 1980s he managed the secret printing house in Wenecja close to Żnin, where press, posters and leaflets were printed for the underground movement. In 1989, he set up the political newspaper, *Volcano*, against communist rule. The newspaper was closed in 1990, only nine months later, just after first local elections that marked final end of the communist rule. However, citizens of Żnin continued to ask Dominik about the newspaper and in 1991 he founded a new politically neutral newspaper, *Paluki*, to provide readers with current, in-depth local news.

Dominik is characterized by his love for culture, poetry, literature and music. He believes the local media have a mission to protect freedom. In 1994 Dominik was nationally recognized along with five other local publishers in a competition for the Polish press. For the first time, he had the opportunity to meet with other publishers of local press, based elsewhere in the country, and discuss issues related to everyday publishing work and the real mission of local independent news outlets. Over the next five years, Dominik continued to meet with his colleagues to exchange professional experiences and views, while brainstorming on how to improve conditions of local publishing enterprises so that they could better perform in their social roles for society.

In 1999 Dominik and his colleagues set up ALN with the aim of gathering those publishers who share the mission of local newspapers: One that sets the boundaries of distribution as boundaries of information; is politically neutral; is financially independent and published where it will be distributed; and finally, holds the principle that local press is a foundation for local democracy through its watchdog and informational roles.

In the following years, the lack of strong leadership, individualism of members and lack of specific strategy for development led to financial crisis in the organization. The board resigned and Dominik was elected the new president of the association. He restructured it. Dominik has built the community of local publishers based on one-on-one relationships and values of trust and loyalty. He has a deep understanding of the local context and challenges in the work of a local press publisher who wants to pursue a social mission of nurturing democracy and building a sense of identity among community members. ◆

PAU LLOP FRANCH

SPAIN

Citizen/Community Participation

Media/Communications

News and media organizations have always played an essential role in free and democratic societies by connecting individuals to vital information about events and decisions that shape their worlds. These organizations are quickly losing relevance in an increasingly interconnected society where almost anyone can access and create free news. Through news-based social networking, Pau Llop Franch is providing an alternative media model that empowers citizens to become full participants in creating and sharing news. By engaging professional journalists as editors and coaches for the site's users, Pau's model also provides the quality control characteristic of traditional news institutions that open source initiatives often lack.

THE NEW IDEA

Pau has created a new media model, fully adapted to today's highly connected, informed and socially-minded individuals. His news-based social network, Bottup, connects citizens while enabling them to create and share reliable news. By involving ordinary individuals in the news creation process, Pau reduces production costs and extends the coverage of news to encompass local and international events that traditional media institutions are not able to cover. Moreover, the way the network is built ensures that as the number of participants increases, Bottup also grows in content, quality and relevance.

Pau's model is empowering citizens to exercise their right to inform and be informed accurately about the world around them. With the belief that citizen participation should extend beyond opinions and commentaries in reaction to professionally produced news, Pau is giving people the tools to be fully involved in the news creation process. Bottup users are taught how to collect information from different sources, contrast the facts, and publish news that follows journalistic principles such as accuracy, fairness and quality writing. As citizens share about specific affairs that concern them, they begin to establish the public news agenda, not through opinions but through direct participation. Through the process of writing and publishing, citizens are also equipped to understand and relate news at a deeper, more accurate level.

Maintaining high quality information is also a key aspect in Pau's model. In order to ensure Bottup's standards, Pau involves professional journalists as editors and coaches for citizen journalists. Instead of serving corporate controlled media interests as news-creators, Bottup's professional journalists serve citizens as news brokers, forming an editorial team that works with the users to assure information is verified and contrasted as well as assuring a good final presentation. The result is a quality news piece that follows strict journalistic principles.

THE PROBLEM

The business model of traditional media and news publication is failing. Readership is quickly decreasing as people turn to free newspapers and digital editions for their daily news. Advertising companies are also abandoning printed news publications as attention and money are being increasingly drawn toward Internet commerce and social networks. As these factors reduce traditional media's financial power, newspapers are forced to reduce journalist staff and travel which generally implies a serious reduction in the depth and breadth of news coverage and the ability to contrast sources. This endangers the quality and accuracy of news information, putting citizens' ability to receive accurate, vital information about events and decisions that shape their world at risk.

Pau's model is empowering citizens to exercise their right to inform and be informed accurately about the world around them.

Another contributing factor in the reduction of readership is the increasing lack of trust people feel toward traditional news institutions due to the political and corporate interests that often lie behind the main news companies. The news industry is composed of large corporations that are directly implicated in providing income to hire journalists and print publications. From the citizens' perspective, this often results in biased news coverage, influenced by political and corporate groups sponsoring the newspaper. In a recent Carnegie Corporation survey on citizen preferred news sources, traditional newspapers were considered the least trustworthy, up-to-date and useful source of news compared to local TV news and Internet-based news, among others *(Carnegie Corporation, 2003).*

Although digital news sources are abundant, they rarely provide in-depth and unbiased information. Most Internet-based news sources are divided into two categories: Digital editions of traditional newspapers and blogs or individual, and generally quite partisan, information websites. The first suffer from far worse under-sourcing problems than their counterpart paper-based editions and a patent inability to build a faithful reader base, partly due to their rigid top-down structures as well as to an understandable resistance to yield power to digitalized citizens. Blogs, on the other hand, lack significant quality control methods that ensure the veracity and fairness of their content. Even when these citizen writers attempt to apply journalistic principles to their research, they often do not have direct access to key

information that a press pass might offer and other tools, like editors and proof readers, which professional journalists depend upon.

With each passing day, the way people connect with media is shifting. The mass that once consumed mass media is fragmenting into ever more narrow audiences as individuals increasingly seek out only the information that interests them. This is proving to be an extra challenge for current media models that focus on information geared toward large audiences, and also signifies a reduction in citizens' tendency to seek out views very different from their own. Effective and independent journalism as a pillar of information for democratic participation could disappear if an alternative and reliable news source is not made available to citizens.

THE STRATEGY

Pau is using social networks as a model and an opportunity to reach people where they are and provide the skills they need to create, consume and share high quality news. By using technology that has already proven successful through companies like MySpace and Facebook, Pau is building a network with the capacity to grow quickly and exponentially, reaching citizens across Spain and Spanish speaking countries at a very fast pace.

The network revolves around an initial web-based platform which in appearance is much like a digital news portal. Interested readers become members by filling out a "citizen journalist card." This card is an adaptation of a typical social network profile, which includes topic interests and geographical location. As members participate, their card lists the news articles they have written or collaborated on, ratings they have been given by others and comments posted by the user. Although individuals begin participating on a specific issue or subject, the tendency is for them to meet other citizens and connect with them on new issues which they have not previously given much thought to.

Pau Llop Franch is providing an alternative media model that empowers citizens to become full participants in creating and sharing news.

Citizens are placed at the center of this network as contributors, researchers and consumers. Believing in the power of many to verify and develop facts on a given news issue, Pau has developed simple tools for citizens to pre-publish, aggregate information and rate other user's articles. Also, articles are not published and forgotten by the next day, but rather, are reviewed by an editing team and the original author can modify an article instantly. Issues that are important to citizens are kept alive for longer periods of time than in traditional newspapers. This way, citizens set the editorial line according to what is important to them.

Another key aspect to Pau's initiative is how the participating community is organized. As the network grows, Pau groups citizens around topics and geographical areas. In order to identify key participants or experts on a topic or geographical area, and place them as news-leaders for a particular group, he is developing logarithms that consider factors such as fellow user ratings, number of articles published and quality of articles. These leaders become an important asset as they assist the editorial board to train citizens on how to verify the facts and organize information more clearly and effectively to the rest of the community. These expert groups will also serve to carry out group research to verify facts over an issue that interests the community as a whole.

To control the quality of the news published on Bottup, Pau is engaging professional journalists to become editors and contributors, as well as training citizen participants to improve their research and writing through different partnerships with groups of university professors and professional journalists. Instead of simply accepting or declining user's articles depending on quality, these professionals work with citizen journalists to assure principles such as source verification, contrasting information, accuracy, and fairness have all been applied. This process not only improves the quality of the final product, but also helps citizens to gain literacy both in consuming as well as producing news.

Although still in an early pilot phase, Bottup already hosts over 1,000 registered citizen journalist members and receives between 40,000 to 60,000 unique visits a month. Pau aims to increase these numbers significantly in the next two years through a three-prong strategy concerning technology, staff sourcing and revenue models. His goal is to reach a significant readership that will allow the model to become fully sustainable, leveraging citizens and professional journalists to create high quality news with farther reach than current media companies.

Although Pau still has to take important steps in the way of fully establishing his model, Bottup has already given birth to a number of local news-networks in Spain and Latin America that have used it as a working model.

THE PERSON

For as long as he can remember, Pau has wanted to be a journalist. As a teenager, he was fascinated by how information is transmitted, and the power it had over the people around him. From newscasting playground soccer games from the classroom window to launching a newspaper during high school and working as head editor, he found countless ways to involve others in capturing current news and relaying it to a larger audience in a meaningful way. As he grew up, Pau began to understand journalism as a social service and felt an obligation as a journalist to help people understand what is happening around them.

In pursuing his dream to become a news professional at university, he was disappointed at the slow decay of the traditional media model. As citizens around the world were able to be informed through new technologies, he was surprised that many journalists and media opinion leaders received these ground-breaking innovations as a threat.

During the next few years, Pau's jobs included working for local newspapers as well as managing web content and communication for a very successful job-search website. As he developed innovations for his employers, Pau discovered the amazing tools technology offered to produce more comprehensive and engaging news products more quickly.

When he was 25, Pau left his job to build a team of fellow professional journalists and launch Bottup. ♦

KAMAL MOUZAWAK

LEBANON

Agriculture

Citizen/Community Participation

Intercultural Relations/ Race Relations

Because of Kamal Mouzawak's success in creating communities around organic, locally grown food, he has become the father of a movement in Lebanon that supports local farmers, educates urban communities, and gathers around the dinner table citizens of a country ravaged by decades of war.

THE NEW IDEA

Souk el-Tayeb in Arabic means the "Market of Good," and for founder Kamal, even more than affordable organic produce, or locally grown poultry, "good" is at the heart of his initiative. In the midst of divisive political tensions still prevalent after the Lebanese civil war (1975 to 1990) and continuing conflict between Lebanon and Israel, Kamal began Souk el-Tayeb. Souk el-Tayeb is the first inexpensive organic food market in Beirut, but more importantly, it serves as a platform for the people of Lebanon to forge a unified Lebanese heritage and identity based on their shared cuisine. A place where regardless of the religion or ethnic heritage—Druze, Shiite, Sunni, Maronite, Greek Orthodox, or Jew—the diverse peoples of Lebanon are united around a food experience.

Lebanon's tumultuous history of diversity and conflict has resulted in low agricultural production, massive internal migration, inadequate agriculture policies, and ethnic divisions. For each of these problems, Kamal's approach is part of a solution. Branching from Souk el-Tayeb, Kamal has begun a farmer visit and exchange program, a cultural tourism program, a producer restaurant, educational programming for youth, and inclusive national festivals to promote reconciliation in Lebanon. While Souk el-Tayeb is based in Beirut, due to Lebanon's compact size, farmers from the Niha Mountains to costal Saida can join together at weekly farmer's markets. Additional programs branching from the market, such as the farmer's exchange program, also connect farmers from across Lebanon in their own homes, and transnationally with investor networks in London, Galway, Amsterdam, New York, and Latakia. Based on the marked success of Souk el-Tayeb in Beirut, and the impact of its related initiatives in other parts of Lebanon, Kamal is working to introduce producers' restaurants in Dubai and farmers' platforms in Saudi Arabia. Using cuisine traditions and customs as a unifying social and cultural catalyst while also empowering and generating income to small-scale farmers and local communities—through food, Kamal is scaling peace in the Middle East.

Kamal's restaurant, Tawlet el-Tayeb, invites producers to prepare traditional dishes made from their produce, while educating visitors about the heritage of Lebanese cuisine.

THE PROBLEM

Lebanon boasts the highest percentage of cultivable arable land in the Arab World. Because of its geographic diversity and fertile valleys, it has natural water resources that are the envy of neighboring countries. However due to decades of war, conflict, and violence this land is underutilized, with agricultural production at only 5.4 percent of the GDP and with nearly 80 percent of food products imported into Lebanon. The Lebanese civil war dissolved relative regional stability, and Lebanon's system of Confessionalism (the balance of political power sharing between Lebanon's religious populations) led to a battle between political interests and religious groups. Between the presence of Syrian militia, Israeli troops, insurgent forces, and a massive influx of refugees, Lebanese soil became fertile with land mines, rockets, and gun fire instead of locally grown produce or grazing livestock. Massive population movement ensued, with farmers leaving their lands, hoping to maintain their landholdings once the violence ceased. However different religious and political groups repossessed the land and permanently displaced internal migrants. In contrast to pre-1975 when villages were diverse

microcosms of Lebanon with people of different religious groups living side by side, following the war, internal displacement now reflects Lebanon's internal divide with different settlements based around religion and ethnicity.

With prevalent social tensions and political instability, the Lebanese government has neglected creating supportive policies for farmers to help them re-establish their farms and redirect land use toward agriculture. According to Agriculture Minister Hussein Hajj Hassan, farmers in Lebanon are particularly under-represented as they do not join unions or cooperatives and therefore do not have a bargaining platform. Antoine Hwayek, President of the Lebanese Farmers Syndicate contends that agriculture is currently generating US$2B less than if the government created better policies regarding agriculture. Unable to compete with subsidized foreign exports, and faced with non-existent agriculture reform, moving to an urban environment is more attractive than attempting to resume farming activities. As a result of discouraged and disconnected farmers, fresh local produce is expensive and inaccessible to most of the population. Due to the high expenses associated with organic food and a lack of more accessible options, fast food meals are increasingly replacing their nutritious home-cooked counterparts. As a result, obesity, malnutrition, and an alienation of Lebanon's gastronomic heritage are growing threats.

THE STRATEGY

While many groups and individuals are working on easing socio-political tensions in Lebanon, Kamal's strategy is innovative because he addresses the symptoms of this problem—farmer under-representation, eroded market for local produce, migration, social disunity, and loss of cultural heritage—all at once. Kamal begins with the hub of Souk el-Tayeb and uses different programmatic branches to address a variety of issues. Although diverse in scope, each program shares the same underlying theme: They work closely with local people to connect them with one another and the land to facilitate a shared platform for celebrating and preserving Lebanon's cultural heritage and history of diversity.

Souk el-Tayeb begins by repairing farmer's fragmentation through gathering local farmers together under one umbrella organization so they are in a position to transform government policy and provide for their own livelihoods. In order to create market demand for farmers' products to sustainably provide revenue beyond the market, Kamal has established Tawlet el-Tayeb, a restaurant where producers from Souk el-Tayeb rotate through preparing traditional dishes made from their produce, and educating visitors about the heritage of Lebanese cuisine. Kamal also makes Souk el-Tayeb an inclusive community by providing uncertified "organic" produce alongside certified organic produce so as to appeal to different socioeconomic classes. As a result of these activities, participating farmers have created a cohesive group for their representation, and revenue to support their livelihoods. In 2004, the weekly market was the only source of revenue for most participating producers. By 2010, the farmers of Souk el-Tayeb observed about a 50 percent income increase due to new employment through the market growth, higher production, and stronger consumer demand. Farmers that started with a small plot of land and a single crop are now able to produce more crop varieties and acquire more land or communally cultivate crops.

In an effort to educate, inform, and promote nutrition and local heritage, as part of Souk el-Tayeb, Kamal has also begun the Food and Feast Festivals Program, the Farmers Exchange Program, Souk@Schools, and in partnership with the International Labor Organization the Beit Lubnon communal cultural home program. The Souk@Schools program rallies together teachers and students to choose a theme involving food, such as organic agriculture, and then Kamal helps them build a curriculum including site visits, or hands on collaborations, such as preparing a meal from "garden to table." In an effort to curb migration and provide local revenue generation for villages as a whole, Kamal's communal homes program coordinates with traditional village homes that represent regional culture, crafts, music, and cooking, and opens them to host visitors from urban areas. This model is increasing villages' income-generation potential and their ability to attract sustainable local tourism, both adding a steady revenue stream and reducing internal migration.

> **"Mouzawak's idea is to create links between communities fractured by sectarian divisions, by bringing them together around the table."**
>
> —*New York Times*

Additional initiatives range from shifting behavior patterns, such as Bala Nylon, a campaign launched by the farmers of Souk el-Tayeb to ban plastic bags in their communities. Or increasing sociocultural acceptance by rallying together restaurants in Beirut to join Kamal's Semsomiyat, a network of restaurants where each chef commits to featuring a traditional dish from each region, thus celebrating Lebanon's cultural diversity. Each of these programs uses a different approach to address Kamal's specific focus: Forming strong cultural, economic, and educational ties through food. From using food to engage with youth, to opening up personal homes, to uniting diverse communities in national celebrations, Kamal is transforming food into a social glue that will hold Lebanon together in future civil strife.

Kamal has engineered "a food not war" model that is replicable throughout the region. Kamal's approach to transform the market place into a safe space rising above sectarian politics and violence can be scaled and adopted in Egypt and Jordan where regional conflict is also the cause of local tensions. Kamal illustrated his technique on the anniversary of Lebanon's 30-year civil war, when he hosted Souk el-Tayeb at Martyr's Square in Beirut, and displayed a large map of Lebanon featuring the dish that each region is famous for instead of the names of its cities or villages. The UNDP commended this activity as part of its peace-building initiative and the *New York Times* called Souk el-Tayeb a "gastro-political awakening."

THE PERSON

Kamal fondly recalls how as a child, his grandmother's legendary cooking brought together his large family, making them forget any differences they may have had. Kamal saw how a mutual love of food could bring a family together, and he is applying this same basic principal to his communities in Lebanon.

As a student, Kamal studied graphic design and applied his artistic skills to his first startup business at age 16, selling handmade lamps to art galleries around Beirut. He later worked with Leonel Ghara, a man who opened a house called Art et Culture in order to support and share about arts and culture. With Art et Culture, Kamal gained experience leading trips in Lebanon and in Allepo, Syria, following the civil war, when travel was once again permitted. From this work, he was commissioned to write a guidebook about Lebanon, allowing him to tour the country between 1993 and 1994 in a gigantic Oldsmobile coupe.

During his travels, families from small villages invited him into their homes where he discovered the heart of Lebanon, and he fell in love with it. Kamal became a full-time travel and food writer. In 2003 he began weekly appearances on the cooking show Sohtak bil Sahenn (Your Health in Your Plate), a program hosted by Mariam Nour, a Lebanese macrobiotics and spirituality guru known throughout the Arab World. Kamal frequently traveled to Arab cities to host cooking workshops and promote his message of peace through food. In his presentation, he introduced people to the history behind each dish and talked about the importance of sharing food among the community.

In 2004 Kamal founded Souk el-Tayeb as a platform where he could use food, a non-threatening tool, to help the Lebanese people overcome their religious divides. He describes, "for the five million Lebanese in Lebanon, and the 15 million Lebanese around the world, it's not their language, history, costume, or architecture that they get nostalgic about; it's the kibbeh, tabbouleh and those huge red tomatoes that grandpa used to talk about."

Having witnessed his grandfather's hard work producing ripe tomatoes, and his grandmother's love transforming fruits into marmalade, Kamal learned from an early age that food is more than a commodity, it is the product of farmers' hard work and the glue of the Lebanese. Using this love of food and family, Kamal has found a way to reunite a Lebanese society torn apart by religious divides. ◆

Kamal has founded festivals and programs for farmers and schools, and partners with the International Labor Organization on the communal cultural home program.

DAMIÁN ELÍAS OSTA MATTOS

URUGUAY

Media/Communications

Damián Osta is creating a media platform that gives a voice to Uruguay's youth and incorporates new perspectives in the public discourse. Damián is leveraging the power of communication media to incite civic participation, connecting the news with social causes and informing the future of Uruguayan society.

THE NEW IDEA

Recognizing the transformational power of communications media, and the inadequacy of most efforts to harness that potential for social ends, Damián gathered a group of people to create La Diaria (The Daily): A new media space that awakens the muted voices of Uruguay's youth. In order to attract younger generations—40 percent of its readers are between the ages of 20 and 34—La Diaria writers and editors infuse their articles with catchy text and compelling photojournalism, while never compromising the quality of the content. The newspaper is published online and in print.

> "La Diaria is an independent news organization that connects young people to public discourse."
>
> —*Transnational Institute*

On one level, La Diaria is breaking the news monopoly currently occupied by a few antiquated media sources. Through it, La Diaria is redefining both the format and content of the news in order to promote a culture of civic engagement among Uruguayans, and most importantly, among its younger generations. It is the first newspaper in the country to have instituted the presence of a reader's ombudsman to ensure accountability. In addition, Damián has created the La Diaria Café: A space where Uruguayans can engage in meaningful debates and dialogue around important public policy issues, and take part in diverse cultural events. Both the newspaper and the café are providing an environment where youth—previously excluded from the public discourse— can participate along with politicians, journalists, and citizen organizations (COs) in discussions on such topics as education reform or communication legislation.

On another level, Damián is tackling the significant, but largely invisible problem posed by the way newspaper distributors control the market. By developing a new newspaper delivery system, and skipping the middlemen, La Diaria is driving the price of papers down while creating new jobs.

As La Diaria was being established, Damián was adamant about not making it simply another "alternative" news source. His goal, and he is well on his way to getting there, is to turn La Diaria into a "mainstream" newspaper, and transform the way the industry operates. Damián is determined to outpace the biggest Uruguayan daily within five years. Thanks to its innovative approach to news reporting, La Diaria's content is already beginning to permeate other mainstream media sources on the radio, on TV and in the press. Damián has established relationships with COs in the south of Brazil to replicate the model there.

THE PROBLEM

Although nearly 25 percent of Uruguay's population is between the ages of 15 and 30, few communication spaces have been designed or opened up to them historically. Youth are therefore left unrepresented and voiceless in the majority of Uruguay's news portals. This situation is disempowering and makes it hard to break the "myth" of youth apathy, thus contributing to the perpetuation of an "I can't" mentality. Uruguayan youth are rarely asked what they think about important social and political events, which nips in the bud their potential as changemakers and their creativity. In addition, few media sources have made the transition to online technologies, making the participation of younger generations all the more difficult.

This is due in significant part to the fact that Uruguay's news media is highly concentrated in the hands of a few conglomerates that cater to an older, elitist generation. As a result of both this level of concentration and the target population, news coverage is quite homogeneous and traditional. Mainstream media sources are mainly driven by their bottom line and serious reporting on social and cultural issues is hard to come by.

In addition, although legislation around communications exists, it has been applied only haphazardly in the last 30 years. The level of nepotism in the distribution of radio and TV frequencies for example, is alarming. Similarly, newspaper distributors control a large part of the market, thus driving the prices quite high and making newspapers inaccessible to a large portion of the population. While this has important implications for freedom of expression in the country, it unfortunately remains a hidden issue to most citizens.

THE STRATEGY

La Diaria is a daily newspaper published from Monday to Friday and delivered right to each subscriber's footstep. In March 2006, when it was launched, La Diaria printed 1,200 copies per day; four years later it has become the third most read daily in Uruguay, with 7,000 subscribers. (The country's biggest newspaper distributes 10,000 copies per day.) Damián and a group of people created this daily in order to counteract the homogeneity of today's news reporting in Uruguay. They are carving a space where youth can feel empowered to enter the public discourse and where new perspectives can be introduced. Its slogan is "La Diaria, the daily that depends only on you."

Damián and the other daily creators began by establishing a governance structure that would both ensure the paper's sustainability and its mission. He first reached out to a pool of 40 shareholders to provide the start-up capital. He chose them from a diversity of backgrounds: Citizen organizations, young professionals, thought leaders, and writers. Mario Benedetti and Eduardo Galeano, two of Uruguay's most accomplished writers and journalists were some of the first people to believe and invest in the idea. Those shareholders also acted as a sort of advisory committee in the beginning, helping him determine the functioning of the organization and the types of content that would be published in La Diaria. Its readers and workers now run La Diaria as a cooperative that operates as a not-for-profit and all of the revenue is re-invested into the organization. The board of directors is composed of five members, four of whom are elected by employees and one by the shareholders.

Although many of its articles can be read online through a web 2.0 platform that incites citizen-led journalism, some items are published exclusively in the print version, which is intentionally not sold in stores. Individuals must subscribe to it if they wish to read La Diaria. Because the newspaper is delivered directly to its reader's homes through an in-house distribution system, La Diaria does not have to deal with newspaper distributors, who control the market and bring newspaper prices up. Additionally, most newspapers in Uruguay cost between US$1 and US$2.50—a price that is inaccessible for many Uruguayans—La Diaria is sold for about fifty cents.

La Diaria is connecting the news with social causes to engage young people in Uruguayan society.

La Diaria is giving visibility to young people's perspectives on a variety of social, political, economic, and cultural issues. It is the most read newspaper by youth, with 40 percent of its readers between the ages of 20 and 34. The topics featured in La Diaria are often taken up by other media sources, as a result of a deliberate strategy to distribute 250 free copies daily of the publication to the country's most influential TV, radio, and written press organizations. Similarly, the La Diaria Café is providing younger generations with a much-needed physical space where they can gather and debate such topics as education reform on par with politicians, journalists, and citizen sector leaders.

Leading up to Uruguay's presidential elections, La Diaria—the newspaper and the café—launched a series on the future of education entitled: "El Uruguay que viene," (The Uruguay of tomorrow). It was the first time that youth from all of Uruguay's political parties participated in such a dialogue, and its success led various other youth fora outside of La Diaria later to take up the initiative. The voices of these youth were heard and every political party subsequently included the decentralization of public tertiary education to their platforms. They also each committed to strengthen the links between university education and the labor market. This is but one example of the way La Diaria is promoting civic participation and demonstrating to youth that they can indeed affect change.

Damián is also creating a space where communication legislation is discussed. He recently launched a TV show, recorded in the La Diaria Café and broadcast online on ladiaria.com, to expose issues relating to this topic. He has led a series of fora that involve business leaders, as well as audiovisual specialists and public authorities. Damián's goal is to create a strong network and strategic partnerships between cultural, business, and political leaders to affect new communication legislation guaranteeing the participation of small media organizations in the digital TV space that is currently being developed. One of his main focuses is to influence policy relating to the distribution of digital TV frequencies.

Like the majority of newspapers, La Diaria's sustainability relies on advertizing and subscriptions, which account for 30 percent and 70 percent of the budget respectively. Although he has been able to drive his newspaper prices down, thus increasing the potential for membership, Damián is developing other strategies to ensure the paper's sustainability in an increasingly challenged industry. One such strategy is the development of a classified ads space, much like Craigslist.org, which would be much more affordable and accessible than other newspapers over-priced classified ads. He is also incorporating text-messaging functionalities to ladiaria.com to ensure that those who do not have access to the Internet can still follow the news free of charge or at a small premium.

THE PERSON

Damián comes from a small town from the interior of Uruguay. At the age of 17, he decided to move to Montevideo to pursue university studies. Before moving there, however, as president of his high school's student council, he established a network of students from the interior of the country. This association's goal was to collaboratively resolve some of the common issues that affected students outside of Montevideo. One of their accomplishments was to create an affordable university student residence for themselves in Montevideo. This student residence still exists to this day.

Damián also participated in the creation of his university's student union through which he established a library, cafeteria, and the country's first student-run community radio station.

From 1995 to 2001 Damián worked as a consultant for the Center of Socioeconomic Studies of the Uruguayan Workers' Union. He created and administered the union's Communication Institute. In 1996 Damián also participated in crafting the *Annual Report on Human Rights of the Peace and Justice Service*, while coordinating their communication and press strategies.

Between 1999 and 2006 Damián worked in the environmental organization Redes Amigos de la Tierra, where he was in charge of the communications department and developed the communication strategy of the World Social Forum. After working relentlessly with various COs to help them harness the transformative power of communication for social change, he gathered a group of people to create La Diaria in 2006. ♦

ANIL PATEL

CANADA

Citizen/Community Participation

Income Generation

Volunteerism

Anil Patel is shifting citizens' approaches to volunteerism from a traditionally periodic commitment to an integrated and long-term engagement plan that enables volunteers to increase their "civic footprint." As a result, Anil is empowering the citizen sector to be a more efficient, interconnected and powerful system, while changing the mindsets of volunteers.

THE NEW IDEA

Anil is prompting volunteers to think and engage more strategically as citizens. By developing a model of "volunteer planning" he acts as a curator for civic participation. The same way individuals work with financial planners and physical trainers to create plans for managing their wealth and fitness, Anil offers support to citizens to create a long-term, sustained plan for their voluntary engagements and to learn how to maximize the impact of their volunteer hours. He is raising awareness about the benefits of long-term engagement and sees civic participation as a distinctive and powerful path for every citizen.

"Anil Patel is the Executive Director of the Framework Foundation, which empowers Canadians to 'get in the picture' to participate in volunteering and philanthropy."

—*Small Change Fund*

Anil catalyzes citizens' engagement through a series of events called TimeRaiser, which brings together potential volunteers, citizen organizations (COs), and artists to strengthen everyone's actions and reach. Volunteers bid on art with volunteer hours that are then invested into the CO of their choice. To contribute to the financial viability of the artists' professional careers, Anil also raises corporate funds to pay artists for their art donations. He is thus creating powerful new synergies; COs gain strategic outreach and can solicit high-quality and long-term volunteer commitments; volunteers have the unique opportunity to meet with an array of organizations and select where they may best contribute; and artists carve out a space where they can showcase and sell their art. Once citizens are "hooked," Anil ensures that they follow through and refine their approaches to volunteerism.

Although Anil developed these initiatives out of a deep commitment for civic engagement, he also wanted to address the citizen sector's chronic struggles with internal management and capacity issues, which in turn,

limits their social impact. He is addressing these issues more deeply through two nascent initiatives. Anil leverages these combined strategies to create value for the citizen sector and increase its potential impact.

THE PROBLEM

Canada's nonprofit and charitable sector mobilizes over US\$34B in revenue, employs 1.2 million people and engages 5 million volunteers each year. In spite of the sector's importance to community and societal well-being, it continues to be hobbled by antiquated operating models, chronic funding shortages, and inefficient deployment of human and financial resources.

Because many COs are significantly understaffed, they often have to rely on building robust teams of volunteers. However, very few of the volunteers on the market have ever truly asked themselves where their time could be best invested to make the greatest potential impact, and most organizations also lack the managerial resources to guide citizens as they explore these questions. As a result, COs often do not involve volunteers most effectively and experience difficulties recruiting and supporting new volunteers. As a result, volunteers engage only periodically, thus leading to greater inefficiencies in COs, which find themselves constantly training new short-term volunteers.

Although various provinces throughout Canada have focused on initiatives intended to increase volunteering, such as mandatory community service by high school students, it has been found that this involvement decreases drastically after high school. The wealth of opportunities available to volunteers also makes the task of deciding where to focus one's energies quite daunting. Before Anil introduced his idea to the Canadian landscape, citizens had little to no opportunities to interact with a variety of COs in an inviting environment. Neither did they have the chance to develop long-term visions for their involvement.

In addition, while the business sector developed many tools to be efficient, productive, sustainable, and profitable, the social sector has historically devoted more time and energy to their mission and fundraising, and not internal efficiency. Technology and management in small organizations is often not an expertise. Fundraising consumes much time and energy—sometimes more than what is dedicated to the organization's core mission. Volunteers are often under-employed in organizations, wasting valuable human resources and opportunities to add value and efficiency.

Existing norms suggest that nonprofit organizations should spend no more than 20 percent of operating costs on non-program activities. This creates little-to-no opportunity for learning and growing as an organization, yet it is often highly valued by funders. The information highway between funders and grantees needs to be rebuilt in order to build stronger organizations, share learning, and improve the outcomes and impact of COs.

THE STRATEGY

Anil is building a system with constant feedback loops to ensure that volunteers develop sustained and sustainable engagement strategies as critical participants in the citizen sector. He identified a powerful departure point in public events that not only raises awareness about volunteerism but also provides public reporting about yearly volunteering achievements and fosters a "competitive" atmosphere to see the quality and quantity of civic engagement rise year after year.

In 2004, Anil designed TimeRaiser events, large happenings in cities across Canada, bringing together each time up to up to 700 potential volunteers, 30 artists and 50 COs. Each year, Anil holds Timeraisers in seven Canadian cities. The events are organized as auctions, where people can bid up to 125 volunteer hours on pieces of art. To ensure that artists are paid market value for their works Anil fundraises from corporations and pays up to $1,000 per piece of art. (In Canada, although many artists struggle to make a living, most donate an average of eight works of art each year to charity). Five years later, a total of $410,000 has been funneled to artists, and 6,500 people have 74,000 volunteer hours in 300 COs throughout the country. In the next five years, Anil plans to organize TimeRaisers in 15 Canadian cities, thus directing $1 million in funding to artists, bringing 75,000 people to invest 50,000 volunteer hours each year. This is equivalent to creating 25 full time jobs each year for the citizen sector in Canada, and will significantly strengthen the citizen sector by investing in the creative class.

At a TimeRaiser event, you can bid on beautiful artwork, but with volunteer hours, not money!

TimesRaiser events are a strategic entry point to get people to continue volunteering. The continuity is being reinforced by the platform of Civic Footprint, which tracks and helps to augment the impact of volunteerism. Created in 2005, Civic Footprint responds to the desire of TimeRaiser participants to follow-up their bid hours with a long-term civic engagement plan. The online platform enables citizens to share opportunities for civic engagement as well as track their own contribution to the citizen sector, acting as a curator for civic participation. Anil is learning from financial planning and physical training models to infiltrate the same type of strategic long-term planning into volunteerism. Through the platform, citizens are asked to think about their "civic footprint" in the same way one might think about their carbon footprint—considering their full impact on society. Using Anil's tools, people can structure their volunteer work in a way that allows them to deliver value, and for organizations to gain value. As more and more citizens engage with Civic Footprint, Anil will develop a greater capacity to track the evolution of the volunteer sector and map topical trends that are of increasing importance to Canadians. He has begun doing so with such issues as food security and access to water.

With the aim of increasing the efficiency and impact of COs even further, Anil developed Organizational Pilates in 2008 to help COs "build their core strengths." Anil captures knowledge and disseminates expertise through specialized tools and short instructional videos. These tools include integrated and customized applications for computer and online software and online sharing of best practices to improve internal management of data, resources, documents, and communications. Participating COs pay US$10,000 per year for access to the platform, making it more affordable than any other management consulting. Organizational Pilates is a resource developed specifically for COs based on their specific needs and challenges. It is a social enterprise which reinvests its earned income into TimeRaiser.

Most recently, Anil launched Platformation, a platform for COs and foundations to have greater interaction and share data more fluently—a type of Facebook for funders and COs. He is thus beginning to rebuild the information highway between funders and grantees with the ultimate goal of improving the efficiency of the sector by making information readily available and transparent. Anil envisions that COs will share 95 percent of all non-confidential documentation on this platform, including information such as up-to-date annual plans, budgets, job descriptions, program reports, and social returns on investment methodologies, thus facilitating greater trust and collaboration within the sector. Anil is currently working with the largest foundation in Canada to make this vision a reality and give funders an opportunity to lead from the middle—changing the way they, as leaders, strategize about philanthropy to inspire and influence others.

THE PERSON

Anil grew up in a small city in Ontario where he and his siblings were strongly influenced and encouraged by their mother. A full-time professional, she was also an avid athlete and an active volunteer. In high school and university, Anil was a competitive swimmer, influenced by his mother's athleticism. He learned then about the importance of training and strengthening to improve performance results.

After university, Anil moved to Toronto looking for volunteer opportunities and work. It became abundantly clear to him that it was easier to find a job than a good volunteer opportunity. Turning to the for-profit sector for work, Anil worked as a business analyst. He saw how much time and money could go into developing ineffectual systems with low user adoption rates. Seeing this, he became interested in designing an efficient database to improve the flow of information. In his spare time, he started to study the issues and social problems affecting Toronto, visiting public libraries and city records offices. Anil read city reports to see what was going on in water and housing issues, debates between citizens and politicians, and any other city disputes he could access. As a visual thinker, Anil started to map issues together, connecting water issues to social issues and generating questions about their interconnections. During these two years of research, the goal was to understand the system.

When Anil's mother developed cancer, the family took the time to talk and reflect. His mother told him the easy way to channel his energy would be to "conquer cancer" but she explained the world is more complex than one disease or one issue. She made him promise not to take any short cuts when addressing systemic issues. Approximately six months later, in response to some of the trends and linkages he had mapped, Anil started thinking about a way to bring together COs, volunteers, and artists. The idea of TimeRaiser came to him in what he calls a "bhag" (big hairy audacious goal) moment. Anil immediately put himself to work to turn TimeRaiser into a reality, just as he'd promised his mother he would do. ◆

FRANCESCO PIAZZESI TOMMASI

MEXICO

Citizen/Community Participation

Housing

Social Enterprise

Drawing upon years of experience in the housing industry, Francesco Piazzesi Tommasi is addressing the lack of decent housing for Mexicans at the bottom of the pyramid through Échale a tu casa! This auto-construction model is focused on community-based financing and construction of safe, ecologically friendly, and adequate homes, in order to offer both dignity and (resale) value to low-income homeowners.

THE NEW IDEA

Through his program, Échale a tu casa! (Give your house a go!), Francesco has created a community-based model to help Mexican families at the bottom of the pyramid build their own homes. Échale is designed to bring community organization to the commonplace practice of self-construction in rural areas, in which families generally fend for themselves rather than work together. The centerpiece of the model is a local housing committee appointed by each community that assumes responsibility for the project along with the professional support of the Échale team. All construction work is done collectively, with teams of neighbors pooling their labor to help each other build their homes. Échale's social franchise replication model—which Francesco is now beginning to pilot—is also community-based, with local leaders assuming supervisory roles over multiple community construction projects in exchange for a commission.

Another key element of Échale's approach is the financing model via a legal structure known as a sociedad financiera comunitaria (community financial society) or SOFINCO in Spanish. Families who put their savings into a SOFINCO fund are essentially buying owner's shares in that fund, allowing their savings to be leveraged as a financial guarantee to obtain loans from the government or private banks. This overcomes the biggest financial barrier that families at the bottom of the pyramid face in Mexico: The inability to furnish a financial guarantee for credit. The SOFINCO funds, which are managed by the local community housing committee, can be combined with federal housing subsidies to finance an Échale self-construction project in that particular community.

The final innovative component of Francesco's model is the use of adobe blocks as the primary building material. Using special equipment known as an Adopress machine, participating families can create adobe blocks quickly and easily using locally sourced dirt. In addition to being much more aesthetically pleasing than the cheap, low-quality materials that are traditionally used in self-construction, the resulting adobe blocks (known as Adoblock) are also light, resistant, and environmentally friendly. Since the Adopress machines are simple to operate with minimal supervision, community members can assume responsibility for nearly the entire building process from raw materials to finished homes.

By working with communities at the grassroots level to build their own homes, Échale provides a deep sense of ownership and responsibility to each family in the process.

THE PROBLEM

Shoddily constructed or half-built abandoned houses are a common sight throughout rural and suburban Mexico. According to government estimates, 4.5 million families in lower socioeconomic brackets (i.e. 20 percent of the Mexican population) lack the knowledge, time, and financing to build safe and decent homes. Most of these families at the bottom of the pyramid do not have access to mortgage financing from Mexican banks because they cannot provide the financial guarantee needed to secure a loan. Instead, they fall into a long stop-and-start cycle of self-construction: Families build one part of a house at a time as their time and savings permit, an approach that is so inefficient that many families take 10 to 15 years to complete construction, if they ever finish at all. Since these families cannot afford to hire professional contractors, the construction process ends up being extremely disordered, with little or no advance planning. Combined with the use of cheap, poor-quality building materials, this lack of expertise often results in houses that at best have no patrimonial value and at worst can be unsafe for the families who live there.

This auto-construction process represents a significant economic loss to many Mexican families who invest years of savings into building something that has virtually no resale value. Another important opportunity cost of self-construction is lost wages from family members who must take time away from their jobs in order to work on their house. Even once they are completed, these poorly constructed houses can have a negative impact on both the physical and the psychological health of the families who inhabit them.

A number of social factors also play a role in the lack of decent housing in rural Mexico. First and foremost, distrust is pervasive in many rural communities where government agencies or Mexican and international citizen organizations (COs) have promoted housing projects in the past. Often these entities have made grand promises but either failed to deliver on them or imposed construction projects that ignored local community needs and preferences. As a result, many poor communities are now suspicious of, and even resistant to outside efforts offering affordable housing solutions. In addition, many of these rural communities have become fragmented by decades of chronic poverty and high migration rates. Much of the social cohesion that once knit communities together has deteriorated, leaving behind families who are focused on their own concerns rather than communal problems and solutions.

THE STRATEGY

The core of the Échale model is the organization of the traditional auto-construction process into a community-based effort. Once Échale identifies the communities that would most benefit from the program with the help of state and local governments, and occasionally COs and philanthropic organizations, Francesco and his team approach the community leaders with an explanation of how the project is structured. The Échale architects always offer to build a model home to gain the community's trust. In the end, the community must decide on its own whether to implement the project. If the residents decide to proceed, they elect a representative housing committee that becomes responsible for designing the homes, overseeing the project finances, and managing the project overall. Échale provides technical advice and support throughout the entire process as well as the machinery necessary for producing the building materials and payment for the labor that the families contribute to constructing their own homes. Neighbors band together into work groups that jointly produce the building materials and lay the foundations for every new home in the community, thus achieving economies of scale while strengthening social relationships between families. The efficiency of this collaborative auto-construction reduces the average time for completing a home in these communities from several years to just two months.

To solve the financing problem, Francesco recently launched a partnership with Ashoka Fellow Isabel Cruz to create a new type of community fund known as a community financial society (SOFINCO). By law, the SOFINCO fund structure allows families' savings to be used as a financial guarantee to obtain government or commercial bank loans. Each family that deposits savings into the SOFINCO is effectively buying shares in the fund, which incentivizes the families themselves as well as the elected

housing committee to manage the fund prudently. In general, approximately 10 percent of the cost of a house is covered by family savings, with another 40 percent covered by a government housing subsidy and the remainder financed by loans, although the exact proportions of funding coming from subsidies versus loans may vary depending on the availability of government subsidies.

From the families' perspective, one of the most valuable aspects of the Échale model is the use of adobe rather than cardboard, metal sheets, or concrete as the primary building material. Using machinery manufactured by Francesco's family's 50-year-old business, ITAL Mexicana, Francesco and his team teach the families how to produce adobe blocks (which Francesco calls Adoblock) that are strong, light, thermal, and ecologically friendly. Both men and women of all ages, including youth and even children, get involved in this stage of the construction process, gathering dirt, mixing it with water and small amounts of additives like lime or cement, and using the Adopress machines to create the Adoblock and dry it in the sun. Not only is the Adoblock inexpensive and aesthetically pleasing, but the Adopress machines make the production of the adobe blocks very simple and highly efficient so that non-experts can take charge of the process.

> "Francesco … helps low-income families
> build environmentally-friendly homes.
> Échale has built nearly 26,000 homes,
> all with adobe blocks from local soil."
>
> —New Ventures

Since 2006, when Échale took on its current form as a community-based auto-construction model, Francesco and his team have helped 2,000 families build their homes in nine Mexican states in addition to consulting on housing projects in other countries like Venezuela, El Salvador, and Haiti. This year Échale is supervising 2,200 more homes that are currently under construction throughout Mexico. While Francesco's goal is to eventually help communities build 10,000 homes a year, he understands that to truly scale his model, he will have to implement a social franchise model where community leaders with whom Échale has worked in the past will take on a supervisory role for auto-construction projects within a certain geographic region. Échale will continue to manage the back-office operations, including financing, but the day-to-day project management will be in the hands of the community leaders, who will be paid a commission for their work. Other former participants in the Échale program may also choose to employ the construction skills that they have learned to work as contractors in the social franchises new construction projects. Francesco has begun piloting this social franchise model in the states of Aguascalientes and San Luis Potosí, and he expects to implement many more franchises in the next two to three years.

THE PERSON

Francesco comes from a family of Italian immigrants who moved to Mexico to escape the effects of the world wars in Europe. In 1957 his father founded a family business called ITAL Mexicana that specialized in the manufacture and sale of construction machinery. Francesco began working for ITAL Mexicana when he was 17-years-old and today he is still involved in guiding the business along with his two brothers. When he first formally joined the company, ITAL Mexicana sold an average of 20 machines per year; now the company sells an average of 300 machines a year via distributors in virtually all the capital cities of Central and South America. The decades of experience that Francesco has accumulated in the construction industry have made him one of Mexico's foremost experts on housing issues.

Since he was young, Francesco has been motivated to find housing solutions for the poorest families who lack decent homes. In the 1980s, he took the initiative to collaborate with the CRATerre Institute at the architecture school in Grenoble, France to design a machine that could use dirt as the raw material for the auto-construction of homes. In 1985 Francesco tested the first Adopress machine—the same type of machine that Échale uses today to produce Adoblock—in a Chalcan community in the state of Estado de Mexico, and in 1987 Francesco founded the non-profit organization Adobe Home Aid to promote what he called social housing using the Adopress machine. A decade later, Francesco founded Ecoblock International, a for-profit structure that served as the necessary financial intermediary so that communities doing auto-construction and producing Adoblock commercially could be legally paid for their work.

Over the course of many years, Francesco regularly spent up to 30 percent of his work week and a significant part of his personal time on Adobe Home Aid, but by 2003 he could see that truly scaling his idea would be impossible using philanthropic means alone. He decided to enroll in a doctoral program at the Universidad Anahuac to focus on designing a more agile program structure. Francesco received his Ph.D. in 2006 after publishing an award-winning thesis on sustainable housing microfinance. Around the same time, Échale was established as the model that exists today under the umbrella of the pre-existing Ecoblock International. Francesco has achieved widespread recognition for his work, including the federal government's National Prize for Housing in 2007. ♦

MARTA PORTO

BRAZIL

Equality/Rights

Media/Communications

Marta Porto is driving lasting behavior change around key social issues that are poorly understood in Brazil. She has developed a new paradigm for communication whereby she tailors social messages through dozens of media tools in order to communicate with thousands of micro-audiences. By effectively targeting these communities, speaking to them in a language they understand and leading them through their behavioral changes, Marta is impacting the lives of thousands of people throughout Brazil.

THE NEW IDEA

Marta understands that hearing a message is not the same as understanding it. This is why she has developed an alternative to the common approach of targeting mass audiences solely through mass media; recognizing that such strategies often fail to reach those who most need information about pressing social issues such as tuberculosis or human right's abuses.

In 2004 Marta founded XBrasil: The country's first cause-oriented communication company operating as a social business. She has turned the idea of a communications/PR firm on its head and has shown that people's attitudes and behaviors can change if you begin to understand the needs of many different micro-audiences in a grassroots way, then use an array of media tools to reach them via hundreds of partners and organizations. Marta doesn't take clients; instead, she chooses causes. To prepare for a campaign, XBrasil undertakes a three-step process to acquire a deep understanding of a key social issue such as AIDS, TB or human rights through in depth conversations and research with thousands of micro-audiences from youth in Rio slums to isolated and poor farmers.

XBrasil works with a large network of producers, graphic designers, distributors, and artists, some of whom cooperate without charging XBrasil, and they develop a variety of media tools to reach this wide range of audiences with different levels of understanding about the social issue. Films, spots on community radio, text information to be sent by cell phone, podcasts, complete mini packages with DVDs, talking points, frequently asked questions and answers and telephone hotlines are all prepared. These partnerships and Marta's dissemination strategy have allowed her to create campaigns that cost 90 percent less than commercial, while still ensuring a return on investment for her organization. Marta has carried out 30 campaigns since 2004.

In a typical campaign, XBrasil develops partnerships with 35 TV stations, 1,000 community radio stations, 125 movie theater chains, 42 partner citizen organizations (COs) and 200 schools. In addition, the information is sent individually to thousands of small town mayors, clinics, schools, public health officials, and others so that they can become, in spite of having no local budgets, the reference points for high-quality information free of charge. They can get the materials to the people who will benefit the most, answer many of their questions and direct other questions and concerns to a national hotline, which also tells them where to go for testing, treatment, and how to change simple behaviors that have a major social impact.

The social impact of her approach was validated by a major study undertaken by the Global Fund in 2007, after her TB and AIDS prevention campaign.

Marta is now disseminating this approach to COs and other institutions by training their staff to help them develop their own campaigns without depending on XBrasil. She has trained 10 replicators using her toolkit and is in the process of systematizing the training modules to scale her model and reach an increasing amount of diverse audiences. Marta is also constantly creating new projects: Her newest venture is Lenses, a program that aims to give universal access to audiovisual cause-marketing content through social media. She is thus headed to spread XBrasil's methodological paradigm shift throughout Brazil and Latin America.

THE PROBLEM

Although Brazil has enjoyed significant economic growth in recent years, as of 2006 it was still the 10th least distributed wealth in the world according to the United Nations Development Program (UNDP). The UN Development Index does not simply measure income disparity but it also ranks countries according to citizen's access to different wealth enhancing assets such as education, information, private property, credit, and infrastructure, among others. The fact that Brazil is ranked so low on the UN Development Index makes it clear that inequality will only be addressed once it democratizes the access to knowledge and information. Unfortunately, it is much easier to build infrastructure and new services than it is to change behavioral patterns related to education, and public health, among others.

Such behavioral change could be greatly aided by increased information flows. The right messaging about the right topics to the right people could play a key role in stimulating individuals to become active citizens. However, the communication industry in Brazil often broadcasts information, in a top-down manner. This translates into significant challenges for the public, private and citizen sectors alike.

Governments often invest in traditional media campaigns that can cost up to R$9M (US$4.95M) and are highly ineffective: The communication industry's top down approach does not allow for a differentiated understanding of the issues from the point of view of the average citizen. Thus most publicly funded campaigns fail to reach the sectors of society that most need the information being relayed.

COs may have a deep understanding of social issues and have excellent solutions, but they have not been effective in explaining and communicating to diverse audiences with different levels of understanding. Until this powerful field of communication and knowledge production is perceived as strategic and highly relevant to social change, it will continue to be dominated by very few advertising and media companies with no commitment to social causes or public interest. For example, improving information about health issues could result in the prevention of certain diseases. The overall health indicators in Brazil remain terrible partly due to the fact that information and knowledge about preventative care simply does not get to the people who need it the most.

THE STRATEGY

Marta created XBrasil in 2005 to introduce a new communication paradigm capable of mobilizing different social networks, media outlets, government agencies, and communities to promote social and behavioral changes.

> In a typical campaign, XBrasil develops partnerships with 35 TV stations, 1,000 community radio stations, 125 movie theater chains, 42 partner citizen organizations and 200 schools.

She begins her work not by having a client but instead by choosing a key, poorly understood social issue in Brazil. Her team identifies a community's main challenges in order to define the social cause to focus on, either on behalf of another organization, a governmental agency or by XBrasil itself with the participation of a council of COs. Once that is accomplished, Marta's organization undertakes a macro-analytic exercise, carefully examining data, statistics and qualitative information about the targeted social issue. This process brings up questions about the main decision-makers and leaders engaged with this issue; the risks and opportunities; and the public and private resources available. XBrasil develops answers to these questions by engaging in a deep dialogue with the communities targeted through the campaigns. The organization turns existing public institutions (e.g. schools, libraries, and community centers) into spaces for civic engagement, thus introducing a bottom-up approach to the development of cause-related communication campaigns. After developing a differentiated understanding of a particular social issue and the way it affects citizens, XBrasil develops customized communication strategies to generate behavioral change.

By the end of this initial campaign building process, XBrasil will generally have developed three sets of products for implementation: An orientation guide (i.e. including an action plan, profiles of initiatives, guidelines for the creative process, and social branding), a stakeholder engagement plan, and a cause communication plan. It is only then that XBrasil begins the creative process. It attracts strategic partners, and pulls in various citizen groups, including social networks, COs, unions, community organizations, schools, and international organizations (i.e. the United Nations) to encourage increasing support for, and a diversity of insights into, cause-related communication campaigns, publications, ads, and special projects. XBrasil also puts a great deal of emphasis monitoring, supervising, and evaluating the quality of the end product and outcomes.

As a result, Marta's organization is able to develop innovative social messages with deep and proven social impact. For example, XBrasil established a partnership with the Ministry of Health to raise awareness about the treatment and prevention of TB. The goal was to inform the general public about the disease through simple and effective messaging, and to encourage them to take preventative measures, or to get diagnosed and treated. XBrasil launched a campaign broadcasted on major television channels throughout the country, including TV Globo, but also used a variety of other media, distributed through hundreds of other channels, including connecting directly with health clinics in order to prepare them with appropriate information and messaging for an influx of new patients.

The Global Fund to Fight AIDS, Tuberculosis and Malaria, supported this initiative and undertook an independent evaluation of XBrasil's campaign that demonstrated its significant impact. As a result of its tailored campaign, the Global Fund found a significant increase in the number of citizens that sought and received treatment at community health clinics: Achieving one of the main objectives of the campaign. In addition, by providing health clinics and call centers with new communication tools using XBrasil's tailored products and techniques, public organizations also learned how to interact differently and more effectively with their target audiences. Thus, it can be said that XBrasil very effectively caused behavioral change among previously disengaged portions of the population; something that no other traditional campaign (no matter how expensive) had been able to achieve.

Apart from the methodology used to develop the message, XBrasil also differentiates itself from typical marketing firms in the way it disseminates information to all those who need it. All campaigns produced by XBrasil are broadcasted for free: It is a company policy that public interest communication campaigns should not have to pay for media space. In order to turn this vision into a reality Marta has partnered with 35 TV stations, more than 1,000 radio stations in 125 municipalities and a few strategic players, such as: Educational Television Association of Iberoamerica (ATEI), TV Brasil, Integration Channel, SESC TV, community-based TVs, university channels, COs, YouTube, and many more. She targets, both, large media companies and smaller audiences through health clinics, schools, poor communities, international organizations, and digital media spaces. Not only has this strategy allowed XBrasil to directly reach and affect a wide audience it has also done so at about 10 percent of the cost of traditional media campaigns.

In order to strengthen the quality of the dialogue with smaller audiences, Marta also develops and manages special projects around social issues identified with the participation of a council of COs, social leaders, and experts. For example, XBrasil launched Universal Milestone in 2007 to generate public discussions and mobilization around chosen topics, every two years. Such civic engagement occurs through the dissemination of audiovisual materials, public debates and the active participation of individuals, collectives, and movements.

For example, in 2007 XBrasil and its coalition of citizen sector actors decided to examine the theme of "Human Rights: The Exception and the Rule." XBrasil disseminated documentaries through cultural and educational networks in more than 200 schools, universities, and public spaces. All participating institutions received a toolkit to guide them in organizing practical activities and presented various films on the topic to generate discussions. The project has enjoyed great success and recognition. The Special Secretariat for Human Rights selected it as the best project in human rights education in Brazil in 2008. It was also identified as a model to replicate by the UNs Office in Brazil. The launch and dissemination of this special project has brought together a network of artists, cultural producers, media, businesses, public agencies, and 42 COs. In addition, eight television stations showed XBrasil's documentaries in December 2008 to celebrate the 60th anniversary of the Universal Declaration of Human Rights.

Marta's vision for change is much more ambitious than affecting Brazil alone. She aims to spread her paradigm shift throughout Latin America by universalizing the access to social media content through the Internet. Marta is also training replicators by systematizing XBrasil's methodology, and training individuals and communities to help them develop their own campaigns and products independently from XBrasil throughout Latin America.

THE PERSON

Marta is in an early stage of her entrepreneurial life cycle but she has been through an extensive apprenticeship in which each step provided another building block which led to XBrasil.

Marta was born in the U.S. while her parents were exiled by the dictatorship in Brazil. She returned to Brazil and studied law and journalism in university but had to stop prematurely at the age of 19 when her father passed away. Her parent's experiences throughout the dictatorship made it clear to her that the field of communications had the unexplored potential of contributing to the resolution of social issues. Marta was sure that the strength of culture and communication could be unleashed to alter power dynamics and activate the citizenship of silenced or marginalized populations.

Marta began working in Porto Alegre for the State Culture Secretary and her job was to travel around the state to remote and isolated communities; she encountered a whole new world of Jewish, Polish, German, and Afro Brasilian communities, and she learned how to relate to and communicate with each. She married and moved to Belo Horizonte and worked with a state-owned bank, which was trying to reach out to small communities within the region. This helped her further understand how to reach out and communicate with diverse communities and audiences. After having a baby, Marta decided not to return to the bank but she and a couple of friends started a social project, the Association of Ideas, in which they sought government and private sector support for various social ideas.

This led Marta to launch her first innovative project in the city of Belo Horizonte: The Urban Object, an initiative that used a participatory process to revitalize an area of the city called Pampulha, according to the needs and desires identified by the communities living there. Largely as a result of this process, Pampulha was declared a World Heritage Site in 1994. Marta's success led Belo Horizonte's Secretary of Culture to invite her to lead the planning bureau, thus becoming the youngest member of City Hall with such high responsibilities. It is in this role that she launched an integrated information and planning platform that is still being used to this day. This tool also helped her develop the Urban Quality of Life Index, now widely utilized throughout Brazil.

Realizing the limitations of the public sector Marta went on to launching and directing UNESCO's operations in Rio for three years. She started a UNESCO Culture of Peace program in the slums of Rio, the first *favela* project ever to receive support from 12 different organizations. Marta's work paved the way for the organization's future work in Brazil. She left UNESCO when she realized that she had been as creative and innovative as the institution could possibly allow her, and therefore resolved to create her own initiative.

In 2004 Marta created XBrasil: An entirely new model of social communication, dramatically different from the conventional wisdom of mass marketing of social causes through mass media at incredibly high costs. Marta has all of the elements needed to replicate broadly, not just through her core group of replicators but by spreading her methodology as broadly as possible as a whole new concept of how to achieve social change. ◆

CHIRANUCH PREMCHAIPORN

THAILAND

Citizen/Community Participation

Democracy

Media/Communications

Chiranuch Premchaiporn has introduced a news and knowledge strategy that, by combining new media technologies with a flexible organization, ensures the free flow of information and exchange of diverse perspectives. Her online newspaper, Prachatai, is forging a more inclusive media environment, engaging tens of thousands of marginalized citizens and interest groups, at a moment when most of the Thailand's media is moving in the opposite direction. Because of Prachatai, informed and balanced discussion of issues is surviving in Thailand.

THE NEW IDEA

Chiranuch is using the Internet to preserve and advance core news and knowledge values in the face of continuing political efforts to systemically control and disrupt information. She is demonstrating that, while Internet technologies themselves are not solutions to freedom of expression, access to information, and quality knowledge, a strategy that shrewdly combines those technologies with powerful content and a flexible, decentralized organization can engage people with information as never before.

Chiranuch's Prachatai.com platform has blurred traditional roles of expert and news subject, giving voice to people historically marginalized by politics, economics, or race. Beyond delivering information in new ways, Chiranuch has also created a public space for open public discourse in Thai society. Even more popular than the Prachatai news website, the non-partisan Prachatai web board of opinions is used by hundreds of thousands of Thais per week to conduct interactive discussion and debate.

With a growing community of citizen reporters and ever-increasing reader interaction, Prachatai newspaper is a testament to the fertility of "cyberliberty"—free access to information and freedom of expression on the Internet—despite increasing censorship of new media in Thailand.

THE PROBLEM

Although information technology has been called a new era, today's generation of readers face the same journalistic limitations as they turn from print media to the Internet. As before, business and government influences still determine the news agenda. People without powerful backing are often spoken for by others, and many times fail to even make the headlines. Rural communities, laborers, ethnic minorities, and other marginalized groups are presented as victims or news subjects—rather than as actors with distinctive voices.

Across the world, newspaper, radio, and television editorial boards and journalists historically have determined the subjects for discussion, while readers have had little to no room for expression or debate. In Thailand, media recipients have been further limited by the amount of information they can access. In times of political instability, all forms of mass media in Thailand are pressured to self-censor or provide limited perspectives. Even on the Internet, arguably the most liberal form of mass media with cheap and instant ability to acquire and distribute information, the open exchange of information and opinions is stifled by state orders to close down web sites and, in some cases, press criminal charges.

For the past three years, new media users in Thailand have lived in the shadow of the Computer Crimes Act of 2007. Ratified by a military-appointed legislative assembly following the 2006 coup, this law has been used to monitor and prosecute online political activity. Five people have been accused of disseminating comments or images that defame the royal institution and threaten national security. One of whom has been sentenced to ten years in prison. Of some 100,000 web pages closed by government order over the past three years, many have coincided with political events. In May 2010, 1,150 websites were shut down in the days following a military dispersal of protesters in Bangkok, which resulted in a contested number of deaths and missing people.

Contrary to the intentions of law enforcement authorities, however, the effort to control online expression has only catalyzed Internet users' hunger for the exchange of alternative information and views. For instance, Thai membership of the Facebook interactive online community grew tenfold between January 2009 and January 2010—from 200,000 to 2 million users—and increased to 3 million users by mid 2010, coinciding with political unrest and state control of web sites. The increasing demand for free online expression has been made possible by the recent availability of affordable Internet connections, Internet applications on mobile phones, and Internet cafes in every peripheral town across Thailand.

Chiranuch continually reinforces among reporters that readers determine the editorial agenda.

THE STRATEGY

Chiranuch has created a news website called Prachatai.com, meaning "sovereign citizens," home to an interactive online newspaper that gives voice to otherwise marginalized people, views, and issues.

Established in 2004, the 10-person organization emphasizes a horizontal work structure that is focused on enabling citizen networks to determine the news agenda. The Prachatai team has trained approximately 100 volunteer citizen writers in basic journalism and multimedia reporting; collectively, these journalists contribute more than half of the website's content. One Prachatai editor is assigned solely to "community and network development," to link with a broad range of grassroots organizations and distant rural communities. This active outreach work has allowed the editorial team to report on many overlooked stories—at least 10 per day—including national coverage of labor, environmental and other public interest issues. Community networks of citizen reporters' link with one another through Prachatai, catalyzing collective awareness that marginalized issues are in fact concerns of the majority, and becoming themselves active agents in the production and distribution of news.

> "The International Women's Media Foundation says Chiranuch has shown dedication covering violence, corruption and social unrest. [She] exemplifies the crucial role of the press in society."
>
> —*Political Prisoners in Thailand*

Widely accepted as an independent and trustworthy source of information, Prachatai's readership has grown exponentially over the years, to a current estimate of 20,000 unique visitors daily. Chiranuch recognizes the unique quality of the Internet, which allows for immediate interaction and open debate. To encourage active reader participation, she created a space for comments at the end of news stories, at the time an unconventional practice in Thai journalism. Chiranuch soon discovered that many readers visited Prachatai to read and respond to other readers' comments, perhaps even more so than to read the news reports.

In 2008 this realization led to the creation of an independent website, the Prachatai webboard, for unedited exchanges of views and information. As website administrator, Chiranuch refrains from deleting unpopular comments or discussion topics. She has had to participate only in the occasional discussion to remind fellow users to respect minority viewpoints. As a result, the Prachatai webboard has become a public space that welcomes everyone, unlike other public forums available in Thai language which are heavily edited according to the political climate. Communities of people have emerged from this public space, evident in many users adopting Prachatai as their online surnames. In 2010, there were at least 30,000 registered users, 300 to 400 new topics daily and thousands of daily responses at the Prachatai webboard. This portion of Prachatai received two to three times more visitors than the news section, at 150,000 to 300,000 users per week. Chiranuch encourages Prachatai's reporters to follow discussions, constantly reinforcing the central conceit that readers determine the editorial agenda. In fact, many reader comments have been formally published as opinion pieces on the news website, and others have been the basis of further research for news articles.

Today, Prachatai has become a reference for some mainstream media. During the 2010 demonstrations, Thai mass media—including a major newspaper and a national public television station—referenced alternative information and commentaries from Prachatai.com. The issues raised by Prachatai are presented to create balance and diversity, as most mass media in Thailand is still owned by the military, or by businesses that conduct self-censorship to avoid political and financial consequences.

Chiranuch at a global village workshop in Toronto.

Prachatai has been called a threat to national security, because of its firm public commitment to providing space for diverse information and open debate. During the 2010 demonstrations and the ongoing declaration of State of Emergency, Prachatai online newspaper and Prachatai webboard were listed among the 36 websites to be shut down for national security purposes. Mobile phone operators voluntarily revoked Prachatai's text messaging news service. But readers seemed to seek information from Prachatai more than ever. Chiranuch has altered Prachatai's web address eight times, leading government censors on a cat-and-mouse chase, as a public statement that freedom of expression will not be easily contained on the Internet. She has also publicized tools for users to circumvent blocks, in addition to creating alternative ways to access and contribute to Prachatai news through online social networks like Facebook and Twitter, which are more difficult to censor in Thailand.

Chiranuch has been charged with violating the Computer Crimes Act, as administrator of a website that contains reader comments that defame the royal institution and thus are seen as a threat to national security. She denies the allegations, having fully cooperated with government censors in removing those comments when they came to her attention. In March 2009, Chiranuch was arrested at her office on 10 counts of computer crime violations, facing a maximum of 75 years imprisonment. Released on bail, she continues to develop Prachatai into a model of free flowing information and exchange. Chiranuch's case is being watched closely by cyberliberty advocates in Southeast Asia, Europe and North America, including the Southeast Asian Press Alliance, Reporters sans Frontieres, Freedom House, Opennet Initiative, Amnesty International, and Human Rights Watch. Her case is believed to set the precedent for freedom of online expression in Thailand.

THE PERSON

Chiranuch has always believed in the power of media to alter real-life behavior. Prior to Prachatai, she worked for 13 years as an AIDS awareness campaign officer. Back in the 1990s, public health campaigns in Thailand publicized fear instead of information, labeling certain populations as high-risk and tacitly blamed them for the cause of the AIDS. Chiranuch's organization was ahead of its time, promoting facts as the first step toward prevention. With her educational background in journalism and mass communications, she designed educational media and campaigns—mediums ranging from print media, radio, photography, and short film contests—to alter deep-rooted individual and collective behavior and perceptions.

Experienced in engaging a broad range of information recipients, Chiranuch has worked with diverse populations ranging from children with HIV, rural communities, to media practitioners themselves. Despite having left the field of AIDS work, she is still active in an independent partnership of AIDS workers that she co-founded, called We Understand, to ensure media sensitivity in portraying children with HIV. In addition, she co-founded a Women's Working Group on AIDS, in an effort to establish an alternative awareness of sexual health among Thai women.

Chiranuch has brought much of her experience to bear on Prachatai, a more controversial effort to alter public consciousness. Her ability to empower marginalized groups through information, by converting fear into open dialogue, has contributed to the effectiveness of Prachatai as a forum for transforming readers into active participants.

In May 2011, Chiranuch received the Courage in Journalism Award from the International Women's Media Foundation, for her commitment to free press despite personal threats and political pressure. ◆

PAUL RIECKHOFF

UNITED STATES

Citizen/Community Participation

Paul Rieckhoff is building a new type of veterans organization to meet the needs of a new generation of returning soldiers, nurture their leadership potential, and transform the national conversation around veterans issues and combat.

THE NEW IDEA

Veteran services organizations have played an important role historically in protecting the interests of veterans, but the old politicized models are failing and have become irrelevant to new veterans. Furthermore, the Department of Veterans Affairs (VA), stymied by bureaucracy, has failed to efficiently respond to the needs of this population. Paul is building a twenty-first century, non-partisan veteran's organization, using social media tools to organize and mobilize veterans of the wars in Iraq and Afghanistan and bridge the disconnect between veterans and the general population. In a time when less than 1 percent of the population serves in a volunteer military, most Americans have no personal connection to servicemembers or veterans. As a result, veterans often suffer the personal effects of combat in silence, and the country does not reap the benefit of their expertise on military and other issues. Through Iraq and Afghanistan Veterans of America (IAVA), Paul is changing this dynamic by equipping veterans in real time with information about resources they need to manage the transition back to civilian life and become leaders in their communities. He is also providing a non-partisan space for them to organize around veterans issues and building support among the general population for the community of veterans. The result is not just better care for veterans, but a population that is more thoughtful about future military conflicts because it better understands the causes and consequences of war.

THE PROBLEM

The veterans community suffers disproportionately from health and social problems. Approximately 20 percent of veterans from the wars in Iraq and Afghanistan have post traumatic stress disorder (PTSD) or serious depression. The same percentage are living with a traumatic brain injury. Additionally, suicide rates are increasing at an alarming rate. Among the remaining veterans of all U.S. wars, the VA estimates that 18 commit suicide each day. Among Iraq and Afghanistan veterans, at least 254 had committed suicide by 2006, on top of 230 suicides committed while still in Iraq or Afghanistan. Furthermore, unemployment among new veterans exceeded 11 percent in 2009, and more than 3,700 Iraq and Afghanistan veterans have already sought help from the VA homeless outreach program.

Soldiers and veterans are not the only ones who suffer the effects of combat. Nearly 2 million children have been affected by Iraq or Afghanistan deployments, and over half of military spouses report increased fear, anxiety, and behavioral problems among their children. Additionally, divorce rates among female veterans are significantly above the national average.

Few veterans are receiving the help they need in the face of these problems. Only 25 percent of veterans with PTSD or depression have received adequate treatment. Only half of veterans with PTSD or depression even sought care due to a strong mental health stigma in the military. In addition, many veterans and reservists are not promptly receiving the benefits to which they are entitled. The VA is notoriously slow in processing benefits claims, forcing many veterans to go into debt while they await their payments.

Historically, veteran services organizations (VSOs) like the American Legion and Veterans of Foreign Wars (VFW) have assisted veterans in the transition back to civilian life and sought to promote veteran interests. But the models are failing, and new veterans are not finding what they need at these institutions. First, these VSOs are funded in large measure by membership dues, and as World War II veterans die, revenue is falling rapidly. These organizations have operated through physical chapter buildings around the country, which they can no longer afford. Second, over time, these organizations developed a political bias, largely becoming conservative interest groups. This positioning does not resonate with all new veterans, and most veterans, especially those still enlisted, are reluctant to get involved in partisan politics. Third, VFW and American Legion halls are largely populated by aging white veterans from World War II, creating an environment where many of today's young veterans, particularly women and minorities, do not feel comfortable. Furthermore, today's veterans often find these organizations irrelevant to them, as the wars in Iraq and Afghanistan are different than past wars, and the existing VSOs are not responding to the unique issues faced by the new veterans.

Paul and his team march for Iraq and Afghanistan Veterans of America.

Among other differences, the new veterans are a much smaller percentage of the population and have served in an exclusively volunteer military. As a result, most Americans have no direct relationship with a servicemember or veteran, and thus do not have experience with the personal aftermath of combat, but rely on the media for all of their information about the war. Additionally, today's veterans have been subject to a different structure of multiple short deployments, as opposed to one long tour of duty, which creates different psychological issues. Finally, these new veterans are part of the social media generation, which communicates in very different ways than previous generations, using the Internet as their main source of information, networking, and communication.

Returning from Iraq himself, Paul was shocked by the lack of relevant and effective support for him and his fellow soldiers, as well as the disconnect between what he had experienced and what the general population knew about the war. He set out to modernize veterans services, creating a new model for a new generation that would change not only the experience of this group of veterans but would change how the U.S. supported its veterans and approached war for generations to come.

THE STRATEGY

IAVA uses social media tools toward three objectives: Community-building among Iraq and Afghanistan veterans to share information and facilitate access to resources, education of the American public about veterans issues, and targeted, non-partisan advocacy for policies that will significantly impact the lives of veterans.

> "IAVA advocates on behalf of their members on a range of issues from PTSD to homelessness and from the recent Don't Ask, Don't Tell bill to the New GI Bill."
>
> —*Fast Company*

IAVA is redefining veterans services through an interactive online community of veterans that replaces the old bricks and mortar VSO model. At less than 1 percent of the population, veterans of Iraq and Afghanistan often do not live in close proximity to a critical mass of other veterans. Because these veterans are isolated from their peers, the local VFW or American Legion hall is an unworkable model. Instead, IAVA has created an online version of these gathering places, responding both to the isolation problem and this generation's affinity for online social networking. In this exclusive online community, Iraq and Afghanistan veterans have a safe space in which to wrestle with the issues they face and seek the advice and support of their peers who are experiencing the same problems. Through forums on the various health and social issues that veterans face, the community serves to break down the stigma attached to many of these issues and encourages people to seek help.

Furthermore, by creating a free exchange of information among veterans, the community allows veterans to answer questions and access resources in a significantly more efficient way than if they had to contact the VA and wait for a response. Beyond the exchange within the online community, IAVA can rapidly disseminate information to its members. With a two-minute video that explains how to access a particular benefit, IAVA immediately equips veterans with clear information that it might otherwise have taken them a lot of time and effort to acquire and understand. In effect, IAVA is doing the VA's job much more cost-effectively, and in so doing, is forcing the VA to improve its outreach. And in contrast to old VSO models, which largely consisted of direct services, such as handing out blankets to homeless vets, IAVA has made veterans services about equipping and empowering veterans with the information and resources they need to realize their full civilian potential.

Paul is bringing attention to the issues of IAVA through social media, using community building, access to resources, education and targeted non-partisan advocacy.

IAVA is also rebranding veterans in the public eye by using the media and popular culture to educate large audiences about veterans. In the wake of Vietnam, veterans returned home to an unwelcoming environment, as the public directed their anger about the war toward those who had fought it. As a result, Vietnam veterans suffered tremendously, and the image of the homeless Vietnam veteran, invoking simultaneously sympathy and disdain, remains strong in the collective memory of the current American population. By facilitating veterans to become leaders in government, business, and the citizen sector, and by marketing that image to the general public, IAVA is pre-empting the victim perception and mobilizing public support for this community to reach its potential. Paul has strategically built a constant media and popular culture presence, which positions IAVA as a source of non-partisan information about the wars in Iraq and Afghanistan and a voice of the people who are fighting them. By educating the public about veterans issues, Paul aims to both build support for veterans and seed a more accurate and thoughtful national conversation around issues of military conflict.

Finally, IAVA leverages its community and media presence to push major policy initiatives through Washington. Among other legislative victories, IAVA has helped push through a new GI bill, which will allow thousands of veterans to go to college, retroactive stop-loss payments, which will ensure payment for the involuntary extension of servicemembers' terms of service, and mandatory, confidential mental health screenings for every servicemember returning from combat.

IAVA currently has 46,000 Iraq and Afghanistan veteran members—and twice as many other supporters—and continues to grow. Through a multi-year partnership with the Ad Council, IAVA has launched a public service advertising campaign directing returning servicemembers to the IAVA website and online community for support. In five years, Paul expects to have 175,000 veteran members and an additional 400,000 supporters. The online social network, new this year, has already drawn in 3,000 members. In 2010, IAVA piloted a local organizing structure to support and organize veterans locally in different geographic areas, merging the face-to-face element of the old VSO models with IAVA's modern social media approach.

THE PERSON

When Paul graduated from college, he was looking for a challenge, something tough that would teach him to be a leader. After considering both the Peace Corps and the military, Paul decided to join the Army Reserves. Needing to make money to help pay for health care for his mother, he then took a job on Wall Street. He had just left his Wall Street job on September 7, 2001, to pursue further military education, when the terrorist attacks of September 11th happened. That morning, he joined the volunteers assisting the rescue effort at the World Trade Towers. Eight months later, after additional military training, he volunteered for active duty, and in early 2003, he was deployed to Iraq, where he served in combat operations for a year and learned to "leave no man behind."

Although the 38 members of Paul's platoon returned alive, almost all of them struggled to transition back to civilian life. Many suffered from PTSD, six of them got divorced, and one lived at Walter Reed Medical Facility because he had lost both legs. Paul was shocked that there was so little support for those who had risked their lives and that there seemed to be a great disconnect between the national conversation about the war and what he and his fellow soldiers had experienced. He created an initiative called Operation Truth to try to change the conversation, but soon realized that what mattered more than whether the war was right or wrong was the lives of the individuals who were fighting it. Operation Truth became IAVA and took a fiercely non-partisan stance to improve the lives of veterans. ♦

© Todos Los Derechos reservados

RAÚL ROBERT

SPAIN

Housing

Raúl Robert is addressing Spain's chronic challenges for housing solutions by offering a new affordable housing model. Through a form of limited equity cooperative-based on relinquished usage rights that stop price speculation, he creates a larger permanent pool of affordable housing.

THE NEW IDEA

Raúl is introducing a new, non-speculative, housing cooperative model in Spain that combines characteristics from both ownership and renting regimes, allowing cheaper access to housing without reducing a sense of home ownership and responsibility. Raúl's model differs from others, such as traditional building cooperatives, in that it stops speculation over prices in the long-term, preventing unreasonable price increases that put houses out of reach for most people. Although traditional construction cooperatives coincide with Raúl's model, by making building costs affordable for cooperative members, they do not create a permanent pool of affordable housing, since, after construction the property goes on to become part of the speculative housing market.

The main characteristic of a relinquished usage cooperative, the model Raúl proposes, is that the cooperative itself perpetually holds the actual rights of property. Each cooperative member pays an entrance fee for his home (i.e. 9 times less than they would normally pay when buying a property) and then pays a monthly fee throughout the time the individual lives in the property. The fee tends to be less than a monthly rental fee at market price (i.e. 90 percent of a regular rent and 70 percent of a mortgage fee). Once the construction fees have been covered (by members of the cooperative), this monthly payment becomes a fund to cover improvements and loans to spread and disseminate the idea. The members of the cooperative have the right to use the property and are involved from the beginning in the design and management of the building. However, when an individual wishes to move, he returns the usage rights to the cooperative (i.e. recovering their entrance fee plus the improvement investments made as well as the increased appreciation). The cooperative, according to its statutes, will resell those rights to a new cooperative member.

Raúl's model prevents many of the speculative practices that rule traditional markets and place home ownership out of reach for most people, and instead builds a permanent and larger pool of fairly priced housing. Raúl's aim is to bring more flexibility to the housing market by offering an alternative model that adapts better to the population's needs, such as lower entry costs, long-term rights, and work-related mobility.

Raúl also intends to influence the housing policy at-large, including access to land. By launching pilot projects with this new affordable housing model, making already available legislative and financial tools applicable to the model, he is changing key aspects of legislation and spreading awareness of the model's benefits. Spain in particular is at a historic moment for a change in mentality concerning home ownership, which has been made explicit through the construction crisis. In a country where the average age of first-time homebuyers is 30 and work-related mobility is one of the lowest in Europe, there is a vast pool of young adults in need of affordable housing.

SostreCivic believes in an *ecological and holistic* transformation of the environment across neighborhood community plans that promote human relationships.

Additionally, due to the explosion of the construction bubble that had been growing since the mid 1970s, there is a large pool of half constructed buildings that cannot be sold in the regular market but could easily be converted into housing under Raúl's model. Local governments and companies have shown immense interest in Raúl's work as a solution to a housing crisis that Spain has been suffering from for years.

THE PROBLEM

Historically, Spain's housing policy has led to ownership. Only 15 percent of housing stock is available under the rental scheme (i.e. of which only 2 percent is public or subsidized). The tax system has favored home purchases and policies aimed to protect tenants and has discouraged owners to rent their empty property, intimidated by threats of deterioration of the building, non-payments, and longer lease contracts. Although measures have been introduced to encourage renting, they have proved insufficient to reverse the trend in Spain toward home ownership.

Consequently, housing in Spain is perceived narrowly as a speculative good rather than an asset with broad value beyond its speculative price. This narrow view results in a progressive increase in home value. In Spain, an average of 42 percent of a family's available income is dedicated to the acquisition or rental of housing. The impoverishment of families, caused by accumulated debts and heightened rent, reduces their ability to spend their income on other basic needs like health care, education and so forth. This reality is especially important for young people at the age of independence (between 25 to 34), whose low poverty rates hide under economic

dependence on their parents. For example, 60 percent of young people in Spain aged 25 to 29 still live with their parents compared to 20 to 22 percent in France, the U.K., or the Netherlands.

On the other hand, the supply of public housing is inadequate. In Spain, the social rental housing stock comprises 2 percent of total available housing (versus the 18 percent European average, which is as high as 35 percent in the Netherlands). Additionally, the current measures for public housing subsidized by the government do not create a permanent number of available housing because the subsidized properties re-enter the regular speculative housing market after a certain period of time. This leads to a misallocation of public funds to private flows (i.e. since the initial purchase of housing was already subsidized in different ways: Access to credits and subsidies). On top of this, the costs of governance for public housing are very high and the administration tends to outsource this managerial task to private service agencies without any social ambition.

Different ways to make housing more accessible have developed in the private sector, such as construction cooperatives that provide access to housing at cost price. However, these models do not break the speculative dynamics in the sale, which can take place once the construction phase is over. Economically, an unbalanced housing policy has negative long-term consequences. For example, the inflexibility of the housing market reduces the mobility of the labor seeking population and reduces their ability to better avail of offers of employment. This brings about greater labor market rigidities in the current context of alarming levels of unemployment.

> "SostreCivic promotes a model of urban planning and access to housing [where] property remains in the hands of the cooperative. Members enjoy their home by a right of use."
>
> —*Tas-Tas irrati librea*

THE STRATEGY

Raúl's goal is to change the governmental housing policy to include more flexible housing solutions based on a home's broader measure of utility rather than its narrower speculative market value. To achieve this he is working at different levels to influence public policy, making different legislative and financial tools available for its implementation, developing pilot projects to prove the models effectiveness, and carrying out communication efforts to spread the model.

From a policy perspective, Raúl is working at local, regional, and national levels to create an enabling environment for this model to be developed. On the one hand, he works with local municipalities to include the model in local housing plans, while influencing regional regulations that make subsidies and other financial tools available for this model to compete in equal conditions with other models, such as renting. One of his achievements, for instance, has been to have his model included in the Master Plan for Housing of the Catalonian government, thereby making it eligible for all subsidies and support mechanisms already available for rental homes. In other cases, such as one of his projects under negotiation, the city council has made land available for construction under this model. The government lends the land for a long period of time without losing its ownership, and therefore without losing assets in the long run. One of Raúl's objectives is to promote legislative change at a national level as well, so that more municipalities implement this form of access to land.

Raúl is also working on creating financial tools and products to finance the cooperatives projects. At the moment, Raúl is aiming toward the next two-year housing fund agreement, which will be signed by banks and the government ministry. His goal is for this agreement to include ethical banking institutions such as FIARE, which are willing to finance projects in the form of relinquished usage rights. Beyond the support mechanisms, Raúl is working through other platforms and regional governments to promote improvement in tax schemes for this model in order to make it more competitive with sale or rental regimes.

Raúl is launching a series of pilot projects with the goal of proving the models feasibility and offering successful showcase units. He has already launched a project with 9 families and 2 others that will accommodate 33 families and are in the final negotiation stages. These experiences are causing a viral effect in other municipalities that have shown interest and are looking for new models that suit the housing needs while reducing public expenditure in administrating social housing.

In addition to influencing public policy and creating financial tools, to ensure that the model of relinquished usage rights will have a widespread impact—and therefore contribute to balancing the structure of rent and property in Spain in the long-term—an awareness spreading effort is needed to explain the concept and show successful experiences that are underway. To achieve this, Raúl is launching an intense dissemination strategy through forums and platforms specialized in housing. Unlike other more activist movements, Raúl is using concrete proposals and pilot projects to talk with municipal councils so that they can test the model and share the results. Once these types of projects are approved, existing cooperative and cooperative managing entities can be used as channels as they adopt this model as another product in their range of promotions. In fact, larger players like traditional cooperatives, who were at first not very supportive, are showing interest in his model, as a new product to incorporate into their portfolio.

In order to achieve this broad impact, Raúl is integrating experts from many different fields—lawyers, urban planners, psychologists, and sociologists—to work in specialized and multidisciplinary teams. Working from a multidisciplinary perspective has been crucial in order to adapt the model to the complexity of Spanish context, with a very rigid housing policy history, and where local, regional, and national administrations have legislative and implementation competencies.

THE PERSON

Besides his passion for building things as an engineer, Raúl has been interested from childhood in building a society where more people have the opportunity to live in better conditions. This has led him to undertake a series of projects. For example, at university, along with some friends, Raúl launched a series of initiatives including a consumer cooperative (i.e. later replicated in another city) and an association supporting innovative cooperation initiatives in other countries.

After leaving university with a specialization in housing and construction, Raúl collided with a problem that—he soon discovered—many young people face: The impossibility of obtaining affordable housing in the city where he worked. To temporarily solve the problem he resolved to live in a farmhouse in a community with professionals from other sectors just outside Barcelona, where they commuted. During this time of constant interaction with people from other specialties, Raúl discovered the power of synergy of multidisciplinary work. Still, the experiment did not leave Raúl satisfied as he met more and more people looking for a solution to live near their place of work without having to deal with the insecurity of renting a home or the discomfort of living with parents.

During this time, Raúl began to travel with his work to Northern European countries (e.g. Germany, Denmark, England, and so on) where he found alternatives that did not fall into the category of rent or speculative buying and selling. With this in mind, he began to design an alternative housing model absorbing foreign experiences and adapting them to Spain's reality. Once Raúl had an idea, he began to talk with others from different fields with similar concerns; this later became the core team of SostreCivic (CivicRoof)—an organization that designs and carries out the implementation of relinquished usage cooperatives. ♦

SostreCivic promotes a new approach to housing access based on Use Cooperative Models, according to which the property of the dwellings always resides in the hands of the cooperative.

JAKE SHAPIRO

UNITED STATES

Media/Communications

Jake Shapiro is democratizing public media by creating an open architecture and marketplace that allows new producer entrants, delivers greater choice in programming, and guides the field from traditional broadcasting to a flexible and interactive multimedia approach.

THE NEW IDEA

In principle, public radio and television addresses the collapse of traditional commercial strategies for bringing quality, diverse content to Americans: Free to its 30 million listeners, it is supported by public and private grants. In reality, however, public media has ghettoized itself, providing relatively narrow content to a relatively narrow audience. Jake is democratizing both content production and distribution, leveraging new technologies to create powerful sharing networks for producers, distributors, and consumers that catalyze new levels of engagement. His Public Radio Exchange (PRX), formed in 2003, has 110,000 registered users and is public media's largest archive of on-demand programs for broadcast and digital use, housing tens of thousands of pieces. Grounded by a native knowledge of new media technologies and production, PRX is shaping public media's transition and using the moment to create new platforms, habits, expectations, and offerings in the early 21st century.

THE PROBLEM

Public broadcasting emerged about 30 years ago in the U.S. and has three main "legacy" operators. National Public Radio (NPR) was created in 1970 through congressional passage of the Public Broadcasting Act in 1967, which at the same time created the Corporation for Public Broadcasting (CPB), the government entity that funds both public radio and television (PBS). NPR is a privately and publicly funded membership organization and the country's leading provider of public radio content and distribution, now serving about 600 radio stations around the country. Its main content rival providers are American Public Media and Public Radio International (PRI).

While much of the content of public radio is produced at a high level of quality, it most typically resonates with a relatively limited and elite listenership, failing to appeal to younger, lower-income, and non-white audiences. In part, critics say, this disconnect stems from a lack of diversity in programming: The industry tends toward formulaic delivery geared to the sort of educated audiences it understands. While the NPR "voice" is distinctive, and while its journalism justifiably wins many awards, its "formula" has grown safe and not especially adaptive, just at the time when the industry needs—for reasons of its business model and its public mission—to cultivate, engage, and inform new listeners.

This conservatism stems from several sources. First, public broadcasting has been somewhat insulated from the economic forces wreaking havoc on commercial media: CPB revenue has stayed steady in the face of an advertizing downturn, as have private donations. So producers and stations haven't felt an urgent need for dramatic change. What's more, the structure of the public media "industry" has encouraged parochial strategies geared to protecting perceived strategic "turf" and market share.

The result: As the Internet and digital media introduce new possibilities for content creation and distribution, existing public broadcasting models have been slow to experiment, much less fully embrace the opportunity. Providers use the Internet as a distribution channel for established programming, but are not exploiting its full potential to move the industry to a place of greater democracy and engagement. Instead, content providers and member stations alike rely on vouched-for nationalist journalist packages, augmented with locally produced features, to deliver news to passive media consumers.

THE STRATEGY

Jake's strategy to democratize and reshape public media operates on several levels. His first and still core service, Public Radio Exchange, is an online marketplace that allows independent producers, listeners, and station programmers to find each other and share content. On this web-based platform, producers anywhere can upload their programs—and stations anywhere can download. PRX takes care of the technology and the licensing, creating a fair market for creative radio work that otherwise wouldn't be heard amid the public radio mainstream. Stations can easily assemble diverse and exceptional programming that fits their listenership and its (local) preferences and needs.

The Exchange reflects Jake's approach to content supply, forging a diverse portfolio that creates pathways for new content providers and attracts a broader range of listeners—all while building the PRX brand. He describes it as a pyramid approach: The base is completely open, meaning that anyone can register on the PRX site and share content according to technical specs. The second tier is partially curated, through machine and human review. Algorithms help to establish a basic rating for type of content, and the PRX reviewing community has options to rate for quality. At the pyramid's top, PRX showcases select offerings that it itself has produced, including The Moth Radio Hour and State of the Re-Union with Al Letson—two promising new programs of 2010.

Al Letson is the fruit of another content strategy—a discovery of the Public Radio Talent Quest, hosted in 2007 by PRX and the Corporation for Public Broadcasting. The five-round contest surfaced 1,400 contestants, most of them first-time producers. Supported by Jake and his team, Al Letson, one of three contest winners, shows the trajectory envisioned: Raw talent advancing fresh content is spotted, then helped along to production and national distribution at scale by PRX. Letson's program explores how American cities and towns create community and offers vital cultural narratives that show the uniqueness of locale. He explores area news, cultural happenings, and grassroots movements. The radio show is one-hour, released in blocks of five episodes and available to PRX and NPR member stations. (Prior to becoming a radio producer, Letson was a community organizer and poet in Florida. He is African-American, explicitly reflecting Jake's push for diverse programming.)

> "Jake Shapiro is connecting stations, producers and the public. PRX has been a leading innovator in public media, pioneering new digital distribution models and social media applications."
>
> —*National Conference for Media Reform*

But PRX is as much about diverse distribution as about diverse content. Jake sees that as demand for media moves online, PRX can broaden listenership by shaping new distribution channels for use by public stations and producers. Jake's team built and launched a series of streaming applications that brought programming from PRI and a host of stations to the Internet. This work led to the Public Radio Player, an iPhone application for public radio content—which in turn led to elegant iPhone apps for This American Life—which has been downloaded 80,000 times since February 2010—WBUR, and NPR News. The enthusiastic reception of these applications, developed by PRX's internal technical team, has brought other shows knocking to PRX's door. (PRX turned down one request from a program whose values and content were commercial and didn't sync with PRX's mission.) Jake sees a revenue stream emerging as PRX develops an expertise in the creation of smart phone applications that also advance the mission: Extend distribution for select content. The selection of application "clients" is another example of PRX's curatorial role in shaping the industry by subtly controlling, or guiding distribution.

While PRX tests out and advances new platforms and tools, Jake sees value in advancing the shared discussion with industry leaders. PRX is a wedge and anchor in discussions with the other three industry leaders. The latest iteration of this discussion is Public Media Platform, a consortium including PBS, NPR, PRI, and APM funded by the Corporation for Public Broadcasting and the Knight Foundation and currently in a six-month pilot phase. The goal: To create a unified online platform where all public media producers, distributors, stations, and listeners can upload and share their programming—a true interactive media experience that reaches a broad national (if not global) audience. The politics are daunting—a similar effort failed three years ago—but Jake is hopeful and is committing time to this. He sees the promise that the web affords in making public media truly public, and he believes that, as an outsider with deep new-media expertise, he and PRX are uniquely equipped to steward that pioneering shared strategy.

THE PERSON

Jake's early values were shaped by his parents, who pursued their passions: His father, a medical director of a non-profit psychiatric hospital, gained exposure to Russia through his musical interests—he was part of a university chorus that toured there in the early 1960s. Jake's mother, a musicologist and pianist, encouraged Jake's music interests as he learned cello and guitar.

Jake developed an early love for Russian language and culture and lived in Moscow in the early 1990s. He was hired to run a language and political studies program from 1992 to 1995, and built out its immersion components so that participants would have full exposure to the society, not just the safe or sanctioned elements. In Moscow, he witnessed the turbulent forming of a new democracy as the society restructured itself around new ideals and institutions.

Jake's interest in the Internet as a disruptive technological tool emerged from his experiences in music. He returned to Boston in 1995 to start a rock band—Two Ton Shoe—and an independent label, for which he developed a website, including some of the earliest open audio and MP3 distribution. Open file sharing bore surprising fruit in the form of a viral hit song in South Korea, a record deal, and sold-out tours in Seoul.

Jake was recruited as a producer for The Connection, a formative experience that ended in a high-profile firing of the host by the producer over ownership rights, causing Jake and the other producers to walk out and form an independent production company to carry the show for another year—experiencing the financial and other challenges of being a producer. Joining the Berkman Center for Internet and Society in 2001, he arrived just as new forms of media were emerging, and new behaviors were forming around them. There, he saw the power of shaping habits by guiding the emergence of new digital tools, such as the podcast.

Jake formed PRX in 2003 with producer Jay Allison and a consortium of station owners, which incubated PRX until 2008. PRX's early growth was enabled by the collapse of the dot.com industry around that time, and much of the early code was built at very low cost to the fledgling organization. PRX now has 10 full-time staff, and a strong volunteer base. ◆

CLEODON SILVA

BRAZIL

Technology/Information Technology

With respect and admiration, we remember the life and work of Ashoka Fellow Cleodon Silva. He changed the lives of all those he met.

Cleodon Silva created a model for civic participation through open source geo-refencing technology, in order to adequately help communities, citizen organizations, businesses and government entities identify local social needs and design appropriate solutions.

THE NEW IDEA

Cleodon created the Lidas Institute in order to provide citizens with information that can inform their civic engagement. Through participatory geopositioning exercises, he helps identify social needs, holds local government more accountable and reconnects people with their neighborhoods while promoting citizen participation. He does so by mapping existing information about cities through the agregation of existing data and scientific indicators, and by analysing them against knowledge produced by local communities.

Cleodon understood early on that the first step to producing relevant information was to rethink the way urban areas are divided-up and administered. In order to get citizens to connect to their surroundings, he has reorganized all the districts of Sao Paulo into subunits called Units of Participative Planning (UPP). The area covered by these UPP is determined according to the way the majority of citizens in any given part of the city interact with their environment.

With these urban subunits as its starting point, the Lidas Institute developed a virtual platform, Base Comum de Conhecmiento Cidadão (BCCC—Common Grounds of Citizen Knowledge). Using geopositioning techniques and open source software, this online space agregates various data points about each UPP, while making it visually easy to understand and absorb the information displayed. In order to further incite civic participation and deepen citizens' understanding of their neighborhoods, anyone can also add, edit and share information that might be relevant for their communities or for the city as a whole.

By thus merging scientific and popular knowledge, Cleodon facilitated the diagnostic of important socioeconomic and cultural issues. However, the BCCC is merely a tool he then uses to promote and design appropriate responses from the bottom up. Particularly concerned with the well-being and civic education of younger generations, and recognizing their propensity to readily assimilate the technological tools he has developed, Cleodon has therefore been training youth between the ages of 16 and 29 to master this tool. As a result, he helped create COOPLURB—the Cooperative of Urban Logistics—with these youth. They began by using the UPPs and the BCCC to design low-cost market research for small and medium enterprises looking to establish their businesses in low-income neighborhoods. They have since amplified the scope of their work in order to affect public policy on such issues as the rights of children and adolescents, and to facilitate the work of citizen organizations (COs). Cleodon established partnerships within COs in order to bring the methodology to other urban centers throughout Brazil.

THE PROBLEM

Although the digital divide in Brazil remains vast, it has decreased significantly in recent years. A growing number of Brazilians now have access to the Internet thus enabling the use and gradual democratization of various new social media tools that encourage online collaboration and information sharing. However, this increasing supply of data is rarely transformed into digestable knowledge, which has a series of important consequences.

> "Cleodon uses GIS techniques and new tools of information technology to facilitate the strengthening of civil society and a better ownership of the city by citizens."
>
> —*Lidas*

For example, the way governments handle official data poses a fundamental challenge. While the Brazilian state is obliged to make a large amount of information publicly accessible, some of it simply remains unavailable, and most is not well organized or properly disseminated. When the data does exist most people are unaware of it or don't know how to access it, and when they do, they often do not know how to use it. Moreover, because the data generally depicts a statistical average, it rarely represents the reality of each neighborhood, thus reinforcing the perception of many citizens that their local knowledge is inaccurate or, worst yet, irrelevant. Disagragated information makes it difficult for people to identify specific social needs or design appropriate responses. This is true as much for government entities when making important public policy decisions, as for COs and small businesses, which must understand the markets or communities they work in, in order to propose locally relevant solutions.

For individuals, this wealth of disagragated information tends to be overwhelming. As cities and the volume of virtual interactions continue to grow exponentially, citizens often become disconnected from their local communities. In most mega-cities, especially those that have undergone rapid urbanization such as

Sao Paulo, it is extremely common for people not to know what is happening in their very own neighborhoods, thus making it more difficult for them to get involved and participate in the resolution of important social issues.

This phenomenon is of course agravated by the way urban areas have been conceived and managed, at least within the Brazilian context. Historically, municipal governments have opted for the creation of large districts within cities. These districts tend to be administered in a centralized way, with little regard for the diversity of "realities" that co-exist in these vast areas. This not only leads to poor public policies and, often times, bad reporting—as a result of insufficient or inaccurate information— but it also encourages citizens to develop a generic and inaccurate understanding of their cities.

Although the many social media platforms that currently exist could serve the purpose of making neighborhoods and communities better, they rarely are used for more than the sharing of trivial information and do little to instill a strong sense of citizenship. Youth tend not to get the type of support they need to see that potential through and thus lose the opportunity to become knowledge producers. In public schools, for example, teachers are ill equipped to serve that role because they generally are not particularly adept users of such information technologies. While these virtual platforms could be used to transform citizens from mere consumers of information to producers and intepreters of knowledge, very few of them actually do. Even fewer have been able to employ such tools to the benefit of marginalized populations.

THE STRATEGY

The methodology Cleodon has developed has four distinct characteristics: 1) it divides urban areas into subunits to reflect the way citizens interact with their environments 2) it agregates existing official information in order to make it accessible and understandable for individuals through user-friendly, open source technology 3) it teaches individuals, COs and small businesses how to use this tool to develop appropriate community-based solutions and 4) it transforms individuals, and especially youth, into knowledge producers and disseminators.

By establishing UPP, Cleodon aims to help citizens reconnect with their communities. Whereas Sao Paulo's municipal census information has traditionally been classified by district, these UPP help to reorganize the city into smaller areas that accurately reflect the way space is used by all Paulistanos. The Lidas Institute then rearranges and aggrates the official data that relates to these areas and makes it publicly accessible, in order to provide citizens with information that reflects their UPP or community's reality.

It is through the BCCC—an online mapping tool—that the information can be accessed by citizens. All anyone needs to do is enter a specific address and postal code in order to find out which of the 270 UPP they belong to and have access to an expansive

amount of corresponding information. Realizing that official data alone cannot tell the whole story, Cleodon and the Lidas Institute went one step further by making the platform open source and interactive. Thus, Cleodon is turning tacit knowledge into hard data and citizens are now becoming one of the database's main sources of information. In addition, the BCCC is making it increasingly difficult for government entities to manipulate public data while democratizing the access to information. Although the platform is user-friendly, Cleodon's organization offers workshops and field work experience to teach individuals to use it.

Cleodon trained young people to do field research, use mapping and geo-referencing because he knew they could appropriate the technology quickly and that these skills would prove valuable in the future.

The Lidas Institute piloted the methodology in 2001, through a partnership with the CO Casa dos Meninos. It worked with 30 youth living in the borough of M'Boi Mirim—one of the most empoverished and violent parts of the city of Sao Paulo—in order to create a digital map of the area they lived in. Using official data, they developed local indicators relating to such things as the number of children between the ages of 0 and 6, the number of unemployed heads of the family, or the state of small businesses based in those 270 UPPs. They also mapped the location of schools, daycares, community centers, hospitals, health centers, and COs, among others.

The objective is obviously not to gather data for its own sake, rather it is to foster better decision-making and to encourage the design of appropriate solutions to social needs through broader information sharing. Believing in the technology's potential, Sao Paulo's Municipal Counsel on the Rights of Children and Adolescents (CMDCA-SP) partnered with the Lidas Institute in 2007 to lead a diagnosis of the rights of children and adolescents for the entire city of Sao Paulo. By accurately depicting the annual birth rate in a specific UPP, for instance, and comparing it to the number of existing public daycare centers, the Institute was not only able to inform citizens and COs about the level of social needs in that particular area, it also legitimized through scientific data a citizen-led demand for better access to childcare. This information, which can be constantly accessed and updated online, has been instrumental for the work of several COs, i.e. as Creche para Todos (the Daycare for All Movement)—but also for government entitites that did not previously have access to this level of accurate and detailed data.

In addition, this geo-referencing methodology is being used to develop low-cost market research services for small and medium size enterprises looking to set up shop in different areas of the city. Thus far, Cleodon has been able to develop these services through the creation of COOPLURB. Cleodon taught groups of youth how to conduct field research, use mapping, geo-referencing, mockup tecniques, and aggregate census information in order to create regional maps of local needs or demands, through the BCCC. Cleodon chose to work with young people because he recognized the propensity with which they could appropriate themselves to the technology because of the high-impact such skills could have on their lives. These youth now head-up the cooperative and have jobs with a high market value. Cleodon's goal was to train 30 youth per UPP in order to conduct similar initiatives throughout the city.

In 2003, the youth that lead COOPLURB established a "map-newspaper" that allowed them not only to report on important events that took place within their community, but also to locate them on the map, thus helping residents relate to the information. Cleodon opened a newsroom to teach youth between the ages of 18 and 29 about video-journalism techniques. The news reports they produce address social needs identified through the BCCC methodology and are inserted directly onto the maps, thus creating another level of interaction and information on the virtual platform. Cleodon facilitated a first experiment with the youth as part of their work with the CMDCA-SP. Through mapping exercises the youth identified areas with the highest need for childcare services. They then identified a number of abandoned facilities, such as community centers and schools, in those same areas and created a news report backed up with their hard data pleading for the government to transform the abandoned buildings into daycares. The report was embedded onto the interactive maps and the story was quickly picked up by a local TV station that disseminated the news even further.

Beyond partnerships with the citizen and private sectors, Cleodon worked with the government. His partnership with the Federal Ministry of Culture will be instrumental to spread his work. The two entities have partnered to use the BCCC methodology to map all information relating to the country's more than 4,000 "Cultural Hotspots" in 1,122 cities. (The Ministry of Culture developed Cultural Hotspots under Gilberto Gil's leadership to incentivize culture in the country's most remote areas.) By bringing this online platform to every region of Brazil, the Lidas Institute will not only be contributing to building better community-led information it will also pilot its use for government entities.

Cleodon built a stronger team with the youth trained through his program in order to develop the Lidas Institute's financial and organizational sustainability through fee-for-service activities and further capacity-building for his staff. Such institutional strengthening will allow the Lidas Institute to disseminate the intiative to other urban centers throughout Brazil.

THE PERSON

Cleodon was born in Garanhuns, a city located in the interior of the State of Pernambuco, in the Northeast of Brazil. He was strongly influenced by his father, who taught him about the importance of being autonomous in life. Although he came from a poor family, Cleodon was able to study in a private school thanks to a scholarship. This is an experience he does not look back fondly upon, and one through which he suffered a lot as a result of class discrimination.

As Cleodon was creating his high school's first student council in 1964, a military coup occured in Brazil. Despite the violence perpetrated by the state, he created a news bulletin to report on government abuses, but, out of fear, his parents quickly put a stop to it. The values he had so dispised in his private school were gaining a whole other dimension with the military regime.

At the same time Cleodon decided to give up a degree in the "hard sciences" to study philosophy, political science, and sociology in order to better understand Brazil's historical moment. This is how he first got involved with political movements in Brazil. He eventually began working with the unions in factories and became one of the leaders of Sao Paulo's large workers' strikes in the 1970s and 1980s, just as Lula Ignacio da Silva was heading similar battles in the Northeast of Brazil.

Cleodon learned about the precarious situation of workers and the lack of hard data about the inner-workings of the factory. He began aggregating and mapping data to understand the correlation between occupational health complications and working conditions within the factory. He did so by hand with the ultimate aim of using the hard data to push for workers' rights and reforms. He soon realized, however, that he would need to familiarize himself with computer programming to reach this goal. He taught himself codes and began developing his own mapping softwares. This is when he realized that by uniting his social work with geo-referencing he could achieve high potential impact.

In 1988 Cleodon created the Lidas Institute, an organization from which he led various projects to map risks associated with work conditions. In the 1990s, however, with substantial changes in the labor movement and the persecution of its leaders, the Lidas Institute changed its focus to work more broadly on urban policies with a strong emphasis on children and adolescents. In 1992 Cleodon initiated his first geo-referencing social project in the city of Sao Paulo. It is more recently with the advent of open source technology that the initiative began reaching its full potential. Despite these changes, he was always moved by the conviction that information and knowledge are the basis of all democracies. ◆

CLAUDIA VIDIGAL

BRAZIL

Criminal Justice

Early Childhood Development

Claudia Vidigal is transforming the way childcare workers and the justice system interact with children and adolescents housed in child shelter homes. Claudia is introducing a simple methodology whereby: Children learn to create, share and value their personal life stories; childcare workers find new, simple ways to engage with them at an individual level; and judges can consider the children's perceived needs and desires in their court cases.

THE NEW IDEA

After volunteering as a psychologist in Brazil's child shelter system—temporary housing establishments for kids whose families cannot take care of them—Claudia was alarmed by the lack of attention paid to individualized care and its affects on children. She decided to introduce a simple methodology into shelters throughout Brazil to recover these children's life stories through regular, in depth interactions with the shelters' childcare workers and volunteers.

Claudia founded the Instituto Fazendo História (IFH—Making History Institute) in 2005, to demonstrate to children housed in shelters that their personal stories are valuable and that they are allowed to, and encourage to dream. She is thus helping them create new life paths, as autonomous and self-confident citizens.

Through the introduction of this simple approach to individualized childcare, Claudia is transforming the way shelter staff and volunteers interact with children and adolescents. In addition, she is organizing shelters into a network of learning practitioners who now understand the need to consider the personal and family histories of the kids they work with, as a way to improve their daily interactions with them, but most importantly, to help them develop as active citizens.

In 2009 alone, the IFH worked with 65 shelters, attending to the needs of more than 1,400 children (directly and indirectly), training approximately 785 childcare professionals and engaging more than 400 long-term volunteers. Claudia began her work in the state of Sao Paulo and has begun to spread to Maranhão, Paraná, Pará, and Ceará. She has already systematized her methodology in order to replicate it in other regions of Brazil.

Claudia has also begun to work with the justice system to introduce the children's stories in their court cases, as a sensible way to give them a voice.

THE PROBLEM

The Child and Adolescent Statute (ECA—Estatuto da Criança e do Adolescente)—passed into law in 1990 by the National Congress of Brazil—radically reformed the legal status of children and redefined the responsibilities of the state and civil society. For years prior to that, legislation relating to orphans and children whose families were not able to take care of them was weak and poorly implemented. The ECA however strove to ensure that shelters would remain temporary housing situations for kids, only to be used as a last resort. Children and adolescents are typically sent to these shelters when they are neglected by their parents (often for economic reasons), if they suffer from abuse in their families, or if they are orphans and do not have a legal tutor. The main mandate of these shelters is to strenghten and maintain affective bonds of children with their families, as well as facilitate their timely return home as soon as the situation gets better.

Despite the advances made through this statute, the situation of the more than 50,000 children and adolescents housed in shelters in Brazil remains precarious, thus jeopardizing the credibility of these institutions. Because the shelters' staff are often poorly trained and do not have the systems in place to take care of such a large amount of children, those housed in the shelters are usually treated as a uniform population, with little regard for their individual personalities, needs and desires. The relationships between educators, volunteers, and the children are generally quite weak and it is not uncommon for staff not to know even the children's names. In the case of volunteers, although they are driven by good intentions, they tend to get involved for short periods of time, and have little direction during their interactions with kids.

> "The work is not a learning, where employees teach a method, but a continuous exchange of experience that enables a rich gathering of stories, respecting the uniqueness of each child."
>
> —*itodas*

These establishments therefore become a place where children and adolescents feel abandoned or marginalized by society and their families, and where many lose their identities and stop dreaming. By ignoring their life stories—to avoid pain—they are done a great disservice. A study undertaken by the Institute of Applied Economic Research in 2005 found that the lack of individualized care in shelters results in affective deficiencies, difficulties establishing bonds with others, low self-esteem, delayed psychomotor development, and a lack of familiarity with family routines. Such institutional childcare, if experienced during a long period of time, not only violates children's rights, but also causes permanent trauma in children who do not feel they belong anywhere, and face serious difficulties adapting to other situations, and reintegrating into their families and communities.

This reintegration is made further complicated by the inability of the justice system to take children's opinions and desires into account. Although by law, the ECA requires that children's voices be heard in their own court cases, few respectful avenues exist for them to do so. This serves as a confirmation for many children and adolescents that their personal stories are not valued. Judges are ill equipped to deal delicately with such issues and often make decisions, such as separating siblings, that are not only illegal but also inconsiderate of the children's actual needs.

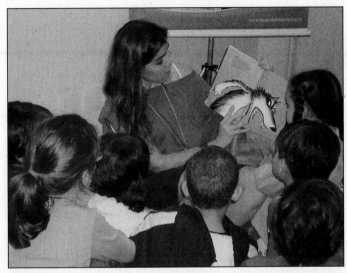

Claudia reads a story to children at a child shelter home.

THE STRATEGY

Claudia recognized these deep-seated issues as a result of her own experiences volunteering as a psychologist for a child shelter home. After piloting several approaches to respond to children's developmental needs outside these institutions, she realized that in order to resolve some of these important challenges she would have to gently transform the shelters from the inside out. She understood that her initiative would need to involve working side by side with its childcare workers, educators, and volunteers in order to change the nature of their relationships and behaviors with children and adolescents.

Claudia therefore developed a methodology to help the children acknowledge and share their stories, acknowledging the past but focusing on the future. The approach became a tool not only to help children develop a sense of belonging and self-awareness, but also to identify and resolve some of the problems, emotional and otherwise, that occur during their stays in shelters. Her flagship program is called Fazendo Minha História (Building My Own Story).

Whenever she enters an institution with this program, Claudia first establishes a partnership with them and trains their staff and volunteers on three core aspects of the program: 1) stimulating reading by using strategically chosen books as a way to begin the conversation 2) working with children on developing their life stories, recognizing the challenges the exercise may incur and 3) acknowledging the importance of establishing strong bonds with the children in order to accomplish their mission as individuals and institutions. The volunteers are always supervised by the shelter's staff members who in turn receive advice and support from IFH. Claudia's staff organizes regular meetings with their partners in order to discuss particular challenges that arise throughout the process and to monitor whether the program's guiding principles become an intricate part of daily life in the shelters.

Once the childcare workers and volunteers are trained, IFH works with them to build a library in their shelters. Each library contains approximately 150 children and youth books appropriate for every age group and every type of reading ability. Most importantly, the books are chosen specifically due to their focus on life stories and because they reflect the diversity of realities lived by children and adolescents housed in shelters. The goal is to create an environment where the childrens' imaginations are stimulated on a daily basis, and to set the tone for conversations about their own lives and desires.

Each child and adolescent is then paired up with the same pscyhologist, childcare worker or volunteer educator on a weekly basis for a period of approximately one year (unless the child leaves the institution earlier). The adults are prepared to read with them and listen to them in order to record the children's personal life stories together. During those encounters, they also participate in playful activities, using drawings, pictures, and collages that are then incorporated in the child's album. By the end of the program, the children and youth come away with their own personal story books. In the medium term, Claudia plans to digitalize the collection of books. The exercise and the end product demonstrate to the children that their versions of the story are valuable, and are in fact a priority. The children thus become the protagonists of their own narratives. In 2009 alone, the Fazendo Minha História program worked with more than 700 children and youth, involving and training approximately 400 shelter staff and 230 volunteers.

Claudia has also adapted the methodology for babies, to guarantee that their personal stories are also recorded and to ensure the creation of strong bonds between them and their caregivers. The program began in 2009 and has already engaged 37 babies, 14 teenage mothers and more than 50 childcare workers.

Recognizing that many children need much more than recording their stories, the institute also began a program called Com Tato (With Tact), offering psychological support to those who need it. The volunteer psychotherapists are themselves supported by people that have navigated the child shelter home world for many years. In 2009, 34 psychologists saw 88 patients from 18 different partner shelters.

From the very beginning, it was obvious to Claudia that the problem faced by children in shelter homes was not simply a result of their life stories, but also intricately related with the way the shelters themselves were managed. She created the Perspectives Program to work directly with institutional childcare technicians, managers, coordinators and educators. She aims to transform the institutional culture of these establishments and their workers by stimulating greater reflection around their missions and daily practices. Thus far, this program has engaged workers from 12 different partner institutions, including more than 200 participants on a regular basis. It has also delivered three workshops to more than 100 professionals on these topics. Most interestingly, the program has catalyzed the creation of a learning network of practitioners by establishing partnerships that did not previously exist between childcare institutions.

The IFH has already worked with 25 shelters in the State of Sao Paulo, five each in Maranhão, Paraíba, and Ceará and one in Foz de Iguacú. Its activities are financed through individual, corporate and government donations. Claudia has for example received funding from the Municipal Fund for Children and Adolescent Rights, the Municipal Council of Children and Adolescents, as well as from the Ministry of Culture, which financed the establishments of many shelter libraries. She aims to strengthen and formalize these relationships in order to spread her approach nationally. Claudia's organization is also sustained through charging fees for services delivered to shelters that are usually financed through patnerships with corporations and citizen organizations (COs). To supplement these two sources of funding, the institute also organizes regular fundraising events and counts on the help of numerous pro bono partners.

Claudia has worked alongside a number of other COs dedicated to the well-being of children and adolescents to craft a law that would improve certain sections of the Child and Adolescent Statute relating to the topic of adoption. The law passed in 2009 and specifies, among other things, that children cannot stay for more than two years in shelters before being adopted or reintegrated in their families. It also reiterates the need to give children and adolescents a voice in their own court cases. Claudia understands that this law may facilitate the spread of her approach to a number of jurisdictions throughout Brazil. She has already demonstrated in a few court cases that the children's story books are a great tool for judges to assess their versions of the facts in a sensible manner. A number of her programs have already been financed by the Court of Justice and the Child and Youth Court in the North East of Brazil. Claudia has her eyes set on establishing a partnership with Brazil's National Association of Judges, recognizing that if they buy-in to the approach, she will be able to spread it much more easily throughout the country.

THE PERSON

Claudia studied psychology out of a desire to understand people's personal stories and help them make sense of them. Five years after graduating as a psychologist, Claudia was working in one of Sao Paulo's most respected clinics, attending to more than 20 patients. However, she did not find the experience fulfilling and began looking for other initiatives to get involved with.

Claudia began participating in the Semear Project by volunteering in shelter homes and immediately developed a strong interest in the challenges faced by the children, the workers and the institutions as a whole. At first, she brought the children to her clinic but quickly realized that a real and impactful tranformation could only happen from within. However, it is only after working as the corporate social responsibility coordinator for a small business that she began truly tackling this issue. Claudia developed a volunteer project with pregnant teenagers living in shelters to help them record their life stories. The project was not successful, but she did not give up. Quite to the contrary, Claudia realized that she had to immerse herself in the idea if she were to make it a success.

Claudia left her job and created the IFH. One year later, she created the methodology using literature to help children engage with, recognize and record their own stories. The first project was implemented in 2002 in eight shelters, engaging more than 100 volunteers. The methodology proved successful, but Claudia knew it still needed fine-tuning.

Claudia is tirelessly working to protect children and adolescent rights in the context of shelter homes for children, using their personal stories to ensure strong family and affective bonds. She recognizes that she has a lot of work ahead that will positively impact children, childcare workers and educators, as well as the justice system. ♦

ENVIRONMENT

© Todos Los Derechos reservados

MARTIN ASCACÍBAR

SPAIN

Capacity Building

Rural Development

Martin Ascacíbar is creating vibrant, profitable new businesses in rural Spain by restructuring value chains and processes related to biomass. These structures engage local small producers and businesses who then reap significant economic benefits that previously only went to larger non-resident investors and industries. The new vertically linked enterprises are accelerating rural development, providing livelihoods for dwindling rural populations, and helping steward and preserve Spain's remaining forest lands.

THE NEW IDEA

Martin is developing a new biomass model that is socially empowering, economically feasible, and environmentally sustainable. Through a vertically integrated business model based on cross capital participation (i.e. with each element of the value chain holding an interest, either through individually held or corporately held equity, in other segments of the value chain), Martin is demonstrating how a new type of enterprise, which incorporates an integrated value chain that includes small local producers as well as larger players, can succeed in biomass production where others have failed. The capital structure that Martin has pioneered allows full and transparent access to financial information, benefit sharing and most decision-making. In the process, it offers key incentives to all participants, from producers to consumers, to maximize the benefits of the whole system, and to ensure sustainable local development.

Starting at the local level, Martin establishes a biomass production plant. The forest owners—both public and private entities—that provide material for the plant (forest waste and other types of wood)—have a dual relationship with this plant as both owners and suppliers of raw materials. Producers hold capital shares of the plant and also commercial agreements that guarantee fair prices for their material. This structure allows for the growth and profits of the plant to translate into double benefits for the producer: As a shareholder, and through higher raw material prices. Martin's different plants are geographically distributed and share a central body, Enerpellet, which is in charge of logistics and distribution as well as marketing and commercialization of every plant's production. To round up the capital structure of the model, Enerpellet participates in all the producing plants with shares and vice-versa.

This model allows the biomass industry to act as an engine of local economic development and environmental preservation. Martin's model distributes returns of capitals and passes them down to the primary producers, addressing the inefficiency of existing business structures markets where the producers of primary (commodities) rarely reap the full benefit from the profits generated in their channels. Thus, he is promoting local development, ensuring sustainability, and responding efficiently to future energy needs of the population.

THE PROBLEM

Spain's recent long period of vigorous growth before recession did not sufficiently reach rural areas, as evidenced by the resulting pattern of population concentration in larger cities and the backwardness of rural areas with regards to many economic and social indicators. However, there is movement to try to shift these trends in Spain. For example, the new Law on Sustainable Development of Rural Areas includes employment and economic development as a main priority, along with addressing environmental concerns promoting sustainable development for rural areas. In fact, in today's crisis, rural areas are starting to be regarded as a new source of employment and wealth creation, while contributing solutions to environmental challenges.

Enerpellet aims to build clean and renewable raw materials such as wood products; renewable energy sources capable of replacing the fossil fuels we consume today.

There are no virgin forests in Spain, and survival of existing forests depends on resource intensive management. Forests require constant stewardship and frequent thinning and clearing of underbrush to avoid natural fires and other threats. Traditionally, forests were naturally maintained, thanks to the economic value of its resources (dry wood and resin); however, as rural life is increasingly independent from its closest natural resources, maintaining forests is not only unprofitable, but a costly activity for municipalities. Additionally, today the producers in the primary sector, especially in forestry, very seldom benefit from the returns generated by their own resources. As small producers at the earliest stages of the biomass production chain, with multiple competitors, rural producers have little pricing power and are often pressured to sell below production costs.

During his years as Director of Innovation for the Basque Government, Martin worked with many primary sector producers and small companies. He understood the barriers they encounter when attempting to compete efficiently with larger businesses, especially when there is no cooperation among the smaller businesses. In traditional value chains each independent player, from producer to consumer, is only interested in maximizing his own individual profits; there are no incentives to cooperate and the chains generally create negative effects for other participants. On the other hand, Martin found that existing models such as cooperatives were bound to fail due to the lack of incentives for workers to maximize future returns. Traditional cooperatives distribute the benefits in the hands of all owners, who usually have an employee mentality rather than that of a shareholder motivated to invest in long-term growth. On top of that, traditional cooperatives have proven inefficient to integrate multiple players of different sizes and sectors, or to build a sustainable model of relationship between cooperatives vertically integrated.

Martin saw an opportunity for changing this pattern in the biomass sector, where traditional production was being handled at a very large-scale, with very high environmental impact from heavy and intensive transportation and few, if any, economic returns to the primary producers or the regions in which the primary commodities were grown. If no alternative solutions are successfully implemented, there is a risk of forests being degraded for poorly and costly management. Also, if larger energy companies step in with the establishment of large capacity biomass plants, producers will not hold a strong enough position to protect environment values and will remain part of a disintegrated value chain, unable to fully enjoy generated returns.

The wood pellets are 100 percent pure sawdust. They do not contain residues or additives that could harm emissions during combustion.

> The Enerpellet network is structured so that 80 percent of benefits delivered by the marketing/distribution activities are returned to the biomass production plants.

THE STRATEGY

Martin's model is based on maximizing profits (or sharing losses) for all participants in the biomass production value chain. He does this by locating production facilities close to the raw material source and by aggregating production from small production facilities to create a national, reliable brand of cost efficient energy suitable for home and select business uses. The glue that holds the diverse stakeholders together in this value chain is the unique capital structure of Enerpellet, with segments of the value chain holding equity in other segments of the chain, ensuring that forest owners, biomass producers, and commercializing bodies' interests are all balanced.

Unlike other top-down larger infrastructure solutions driven by corporate business principles, Martin works bottom-up to gain the trust and buy-in from municipalities and other forest owners in order to build a new biomass production plant. These partners benefit from the economies of scale emerging from having a centralized body, Enerpellet, which will assume the marketing and distribution function. All plants will benefit from a well-known brand, name, and ensured quality. This positions them at the same level of quality and service of other fossil fuel providers.

In keeping with its sustainability objectives, the business model requires locally-based plants adapted to, but not exceeding, the local forest production capacity, which in turn ensures the geographical distribution of benefits and economic regeneration in Spain's rural areas, minimizing long-distance environmental impact and costs. The value to rural communities is further enhanced by the creation of undervalued jobs, which contributes to rural development and to keeping populations in rural areas.

Given the challenge of growing the biomass market, which can entail significant conversion costs for energy users, Martin has also included other strategic partners in the Enerpellet structure, such as larger companies involved in the sector, leveraging the added value they bring from their specific expertise (e.g. boiler companies, gas companies, and financing firms) These firms help to build a strong competitive brand to position Enerpellet as a true competitor to other providers.

A significant component of the growth strategy is working with communities to develop "local communities of energy management." Martin and Enerpellet work with the municipalities that build the plants to buy the pellets from Enerpellet. This offers steady pricing due to negotiations between Enerpellet and the production plants which link price adjustments to inflation and helps to avoid wide swings in the speculative energy markets.

The Enerpellet network is structured so that 80 percent of benefits delivered by the marketing/distribution activities are returned to the biomass production plants. Because Enerpellet holds equity in the plants, it is in its best interest to perform well commercially. As the benefits cascade down to the plants, the producers (shareholders of the plants) will benefit from them, and will have all the information needed to renegotiate prices. The 20 percent of benefits that remain in Enerpellet will help to replicate the model in other regions in Spain and elsewhere. Today there are three plants in Spain, one in negotiation to join Enerpellet, and Martin plans expansion into France, Italy, and Chile. Municipalities, as well as individual neighbors, are becoming the lead investors in the construction of a new plant. Given the importance of scale and attracting expertise to the success of the venture, the model also includes other strategic partners, such as a large industrial firm. Martin is building a solid company with the expertise of many players; giving Enerpellet a strong competitive advantage.

Martin's model is redefining the way all members of a value chain collaborate and maximize benefits for all, meeting rural, environmental, and local development criteria.

THE PERSON

Martin is an entrepreneur moved by his obsession to find solutions to primary producers' problems, and a deep conviction that he can drive important changes. Strongly involved with his local community since childhood, Martin has led different initiatives to mobilize youth in driving change. For example, when he was a teenager he organized summer camps with other children to visit elders in a community residency.

Martin is a systems thinker with extensive entrepreneurial experience. As Director of Innovation within the Basque Government, he piloted initiatives with fishermen cooperatives and agriculture e-commerce to remove intermediaries from the markets and translate more benefits down the value chain.

When he was the director of a dairy group, he worked to change an obsolete model and faced strong opposition internally and from the union of transporters. Martin's aim was to transform the traditional culture of the company, to instill more participation and trust while creating short distribution channels to surrounding neighborhoods and villages to employ local people at-risk of exclusion. To prove this was possible, he set up a small business with the at-risk youth in the area. This initiative began a deep transformation in these young people, as they learned new skills that moved them out of marginalization.

Based on all Martin's previous learnings, in 2006 he established Enerpellet, where he acts as CEO (holding no equity). Although he is convinced this model applies for all primary sectors, he is focused on strengthening and positioning Enerpellet before expanding to other sectors. ◆

VICTOR BERRUETA

MEXICO

Capacity Building

Rural Development

With a focus on user appropriation of rural technology, Victor Berrueta has overcome a significant barrier to the lasting adoption of energy-efficient cookstoves to replace traditional cooking fires in the Mexican countryside. By innovatively linking long-term user accompaniment with financing through carbon emissions offset trading, Victor has created a sustainable and scalable model to ensure that rural families reap the health and environmental benefits that are promised to them.

THE NEW IDEA

The Patsari Project tackles the failures characteristic of energy-efficient stove projects by incorporating an improved, user-tested stove design with long-term user accompaniment financed by proceeds from international carbon credit sales. For decades, governments and citizen organizations (COs) in Latin America have promoted the installation of energy-efficient cooking stoves in rural areas. However, in general such initiatives have failed to produce lasting results. The users, mostly rural women, tend to abandon the stoves either because they are too accustomed to cooking over an open fire or because the stoves—often designed cheaply with little durability—fall apart. Project funders are so focused on installation numbers that they often neglect to finance user accompaniment over the medium to long term, contributing to the high rates of stove abandonment throughout the region.

Having identified a number of systemic gaps among typical energy-efficient stove initiatives, Victor has designed a strategy that integrates elements of user-tested design, close contact and follow-up with rural user households, sustainable financing through carbon credit sales, and a long-term plan for replication that embraces other types of appropriate rural technology in addition to stoves. At the core of Victor's work is the appropriation of rural technology by end users, usually indigenous Mexican women. Realizing that many other attempts at installing these stoves in Mexico and elsewhere in Latin America have failed because the stove designs and programs do not take into account users' preferences and needs, Victor has set out to ensure that the end user actually adopts the new technology in the long term, thus securing the attendant health and environmental benefits.

One of Victor's key insights is that user-friendly stove design is simply the first step on the road to technology appropriation; a human-centered approach to user accompaniment over time is also critical, as is a sustainable financing mechanism to pay for the entire cycle of technology appropriation. Understanding that the medium- to long-term monitoring and accompaniment process can actually be more costly than the building and installation of the stoves themselves, Victor seized upon the idea of aggregating the carbon emissions offset by thousands of rural families using Patsari stoves, selling those savings as credits in the voluntary carbon market, and using that unrestricted revenue to fund the user appropriation component of his Patsari Project. In one stroke, this financing mechanism helps eliminate the single most important bottleneck in the long-term success of rural technology appropriation. Victor is clear that the money generated from carbon credit sales "belongs" to the end users, since they are the ones generating the carbon savings; Grupo Interdisciplinario de Tecnología Rural Apropiada (GIRA—Interdisciplinary Group for Appropriate Rural Technology), the umbrella CO to which the Patsari Project belongs, uses those funds to pay for the follow-up visits and maintenance and repair of the users' stoves.

Victor's plan for expansion does not only involve installing increasing numbers of Patsari stoves, but also lifting the entire rural technology sector in Mexico—and beyond—out of its current dependency on traditional funding sources and beyond its focus on installation instead of long-term user appropriation. He is already applying his experience with carbon credit sales to give other social-sector projects that reduce carbon emissions access to the voluntary carbon market. These COs, whose technologies include not only wood-burning stoves but also biodigesters, solar panels, and other energy-efficient devices, are too small to attract carbon credit buyers on their own. Victor is leveraging his understanding of the voluntary carbon market to help link these COs to a sustainable funding source. Within the next five years, Victor envisions this portfolio of COs evolving into what he calls a Social Carbon Fund that will aggregate the environmental and social impact of the COs and give them a proportional share of revenues from carbon credit sales to pay for follow-up services, ultimately transforming how the rural technology sector operates in Latin America.

THE PROBLEM

While in theory energy-efficient wood-burning stoves are an ideal replacement for traditional open cooking fires, in reality the general failure of initiatives to install them has led to widespread skepticism about their effectiveness. Still, the negative effects of using open cooking fires are well documented. The fires consume heavy amounts of wood, thus contributing to deforestation and prompting rural families to spend time and money gathering or buying firewood. Wood smoke also releases significant amounts of greenhouse gases, exacerbating air quality and carbon emissions problems. Finally, women and children who spend many hours every day cooking or playing by indoor fires are susceptible to various respiratory illnesses that could otherwise be easily preventable.

Nevertheless, despite the clear advantages of replacing cooking fires with energy-efficient stoves, thousands of installed stoves are abandoned every year in Mexico for two main reasons. First, many of the stoves installed by government agencies, COs, foundations, or private businesses are of inadequate design for sustained rural use. Many are shoddily built of sheet metal, which

normally gives the stoves a lifespan of only two to three years if they are not well maintained. The metal also allows the stoves to become dangerously hot during cooking—temperatures of up to 300 degrees Centigrade have been recorded—which poses a safety problem to children in particular. In the case of government installation programs, the stoves are usually manufactured by a third-party contractor that is disconnected from the reality of life in rural Mexico. This results in designs that are ill-adapted to the actual customs and needs of the families themselves, who are reluctant to modify their traditional cooking habits.

Second, donors tend to have an overwhelming interest in seeing as many stoves installed as possible but little or no interest in paying for accompaniment and follow-up with the end users, which can be equally expensive as the installation itself. These funders generally measure their success by the number of stoves installed rather than the number of stoves still in use or the amount of carbon emissions saved in the long term. Many donors underestimate the challenge of changing rural women's cooking habits from open fires to energy-efficient stoves, so at best a brief orientation is given before or when a stove is installed, but usually no funding is available for any monitoring afterwards. Consequently, Victor estimates that actual adoption rates of stoves in rural Mexico are no higher than 30 percent in the case of poor stove design and 50 to 60 percent in the case of a good stove design that still lacks user accompaniment. Not only do abandoned stoves represent a waste of time and money, but they also do not ensure rural families the longer-term health and environmental benefits that they are supposed to bring.

THE STRATEGY

Having identified user appropriation as the key ingredient for these projects' success, Victor set out to achieve two goals: First, designing a much-improved stove and user orientation and follow-up methodology to ensure the long-term adoption of energy-efficient rural technology; and second, finding a reliable financing mechanism for this critical, though undervalued, stage of any rural technology program. His overall strategy relies on the human element of the relationship with the users, empowering them to adopt the stoves into their lives while returning the profits of his carbon credit sales to the communities to support their use of appropriate, energy-saving technology.

The Patsari Project revolves entirely around the user experience. Built from construction-grade brick, the durable Patsari stove has a far greater lifespan and requires less maintenance than other similar stoves, which Victor and his team of rural engineers have found is a major factor in determining whether an end user adopts the technology or not in the long term. The design has been refined over several years of user feedback and input. In terms of outreach, Victor and his team visit rural communities and give workshops to explain to families the problems associated with traditional cooking fires and the health and environmental benefits of switching to a Patsari stove. If the families consent to trying the stove, the GIRA team installs the stoves directly in their homes or yards.

Whereas in most stove projects the end user is left on her own after the stove has been installed, with the Patsari Project the installation is merely the beginning of an extended relationship between GIRA and the end user. Three months and six months after installation, the GIRA team schedules individual follow-up visits to help each user and her family adopt the Patsari stove into their daily cooking routine. GIRA maintains a relationship with each family for up to three years post-installation, not only to ensure that the users truly appropriate the stoves but also to repair any stove damage and to measure long-term carbon offsets at the family level, a requirement to receive the Gold Standard certification needed to sell carbon credits on the voluntary market. Victor estimates that most stove projects without follow-up attain stove adoption rates of 50 to 60 percent six months following installation; the Patsari Project attains adoption of 85 to 95 percent with its follow-up scheme. Abandonment of the stoves in the medium term (four to five years after installation) is another common problem with many stove projects. The Patsari team will begin to evaluate this metric as well once the program reaches its fourth and fifth years of operation; it is currently in its second year.

> ## At the core of Victor's work is the appropriation of rural technology by end users, usually indigenous Mexican women.

Financing the essential user accompaniment process has traditionally been a barrier for most stove projects, but Victor has resolved the problem through an innovative strategy of aggregating the stoves' carbon offsets into carbon credits and commercializing them on the international voluntary carbon market. A meticulous impact measurement process designed in concert with Mexico's leading public university, the Universidad Nacional Autónoma de México (UNAM—National Autonomous University of Mexico), distinguishes the Patsari Project from similar initiatives. Victor equips his field engineers and technicians with smart phones to capture the carbon emissions data necessary for external audits as well as GIRA's own records. With a single smart phone, an engineer can capture a photo of the end user with her stove, the geographic coordinates of the end user's home, firewood use and carbon emissions data, a timestamp, and the end user's digital signature. All the data can then be uploaded to GIRA's central server for rapid access and data analysis. Eventually, Victor plans to hire local community members to gather this data using smart phones, rather than relying on GIRA or partner CO staff.

Once armed with the data, Victor aggregates the carbon offsets into carbon credits and packages them for sale through South Pole Carbon Asset Management, a carbon credit broker. In 2009, Victor secured a seven-year contract to sell carbon offsets to Carbon Neutral Group, a consortium of European businesses obligated by their national governments to offset their emissions. By the end of 2016, the Patsari Project will have offset some 400,000 cumulative tons of carbon through the installation and continued use of over 30,000 stoves. The Patsari Project is currently undergoing a rigorous annual seller certification process with Gold Standard, an internationally recognized carbon credit certification agency. Victor's contract with South Pole is conditional upon the Patsari Project's compliance with yearly stove installation targets as well as annual certification by

Gold Standard. The profits generated by the carbon credit sales are reinvested in the communities that have adopted the stoves, as the emissions offsets—and the resultant profits—are earned through the dedication and commitment of the families to using their energy-efficient stoves. End users have the right to ask for ongoing training and maintenance visit whenever necessary, all of which are paid for by carbon credit sales. Each stove generates approximately 150 to 200 Mexican pesos (US$12 to US$17) of economic value per year, of which half covers the operational and administrative costs of the Patsari Project and partner COs and half directly toward community training, stove maintenance, and parts replacement for the end users. This scheme reinforces the Patsari Project's model of empowering rural households to improve their own quality of life.

Victor's longer-term goal is to create what he calls a Social Carbon Fund with a portfolio of multiple COs that aggregate carbon offsets through promoting various types of energy-efficient rural technology. With this fund, Victor will share with other COs his knowledge of how the voluntary carbon market works as well as his established relationships with brokers and buyers, thus shifting the Mexican rural technology sector away from its current reliance on philanthropic funding and its focus on installation statistics rather than long-term appropriation. As of 2010, he has already signed agreements with three other COs that install energy-efficient stoves, and he is working closely with them to meet the reporting and certification standards required to participate in the carbon credits trading. He also plans to leverage his rural distribution network to help partner COs bring other types of appropriate technology to isolated communities, such as water filtration systems, composters, and solar heating systems. He envisions rural technology promoters advising families throughout the Mexican countryside on affordable rural technology, much like the model of health and social welfare promoters that the Mexican government and some COs have already implemented in those fields. The Social Carbon Fund will therefore be a mechanism that can finance user accompaniment in the entire energy-efficient rural technology sector, rather than being limited to GIRA and stoves alone. While he believes that much work lies ahead of him in Mexico, Victor is purposely designing the Patsari Project using an open architecture so that interested COs elsewhere in Latin America can draw from GIRA's experience to replicate the model in their own countries.

THE PERSON

The three passions in life that have led Victor to his work with the Patsari stoves and the international carbon market are his experiences living with rural indigenous communities, his engineering talent and background, and his love of applying research to improve quality of life. As a young man, Victor was actively involved in numerous school and church service trips, and one particular missionary trip to northeast Mexico left him with a lifelong drive to improve rural standards of living. During an extended stay in the impoverished Tarahumara region, Victor was asked to accompany a local indigenous man as he bore his three-year-old son's body to church for mourning. The child had died of pneumonia, which Victor knew could have been easily prevented had the family enjoyed decent living conditions, but like so many other people in the region, they lacked even the most basic food and shelter. From that point on, Victor became determined to apply his talents in engineering design and research to help rural families improve their health and quality of life.

Victor immersed himself in his engineer training through both academic preparation and practical field experience. He continued to harbor an interest in working with applied rural technology, putting his engineering skills to the test in designing and implementing tools like a solar-powered coffee bean dryer in the coffee-growing highlands of the Mexican state of Chiapas. Victor has always insisted that rural technology design must take into account the end user's culture, habits, and preferences; otherwise, no matter how brilliant the design is from an engineering point of view, the technology will inevitably fail to change users' lives in the long term. As a result, his engineering projects have always involved working very closely with rural and indigenous communities. His work in rural technology helped garner him the renowned Ashden Award in 2006, which opened the opportunity to pilot a small-scale carbon bond contract with the United Kingdom-based broker Climate Care in 2006 to 2007. This experience inspired Victor to design and implement his carbon credit financing strategy.

After getting married and having three children, Victor joined the CO GIRA to pursue his passion for developing applied rural technology, which has always been GIRA's primary focus. At GIRA, Victor has been able to dedicate himself full-time to the combination of research, design, and implementation of rural technologies that has always been his driving force. Victor originally joined GIRA's stove project team while he was studying for his doctorate degree in energy engineering at the National Autonomous University of Mexico. Upon finishing his doctorate, Victor was invited to join GIRA as a full-time staff member, and as the director of the Rural Energy Program, an autonomous programmatic area, he is considered one of GIRA's six principal partners.

Although he works under the umbrella of GIRA, Victor enjoys full autonomy to personally direct the Patsari Project within the Rural Energy Program. Victor independently administers his own budget and staff and reports directly to GIRA's Board of Directors. Victor's Patsari Project also has the personal backing of Omar Macera, a founding partner of GIRA and Victor's academic and professional mentor. Omar is a member of the Nobel Prize-winning International Panel on Climate Change and thus is personally invested in Victor's work with the voluntary carbon market. His affiliation with GIRA grants Victor all the benefits of a respected, established Mexican CO with a long track record in rural technology without circumscribing his freedom to guide the Patsari Project. His plan is to continue operating under this non-profit scheme until the time when the Social Carbon Fund grows large enough to be spun out independently from GIRA, at which point he will seek an independent non-profit legal structure or trust to administer the fund. Today, as the director of the Rural Energy Program, Victor runs his Patsari Project full-time, for which he has garnered both national and international recognition. For Victor, the Patsari Project represents an enormous opportunity to improve thousands of rural families' quality of life while also reducing greenhouse gas emissions in hard-to-reach rural areas. ◆

JORGE ALBERTO CAPPATO

ARGENTINA

Appropriate Technology

Cooperatives

Natural Resource Management

Jorge Cappato is expanding riverine communities' economic opportunities in northeastern Argentina by redefining the role they can play within the fishing industry's value chain. Jorge is thus preserving their culture and identity, increasing their well-being and mitigating their economic need to migrate to urban centers.

THE NEW IDEA

Riverine communities in Argentina are among the poorest in the country and have for years been forgotten by the government and marginalized by large agricultural corporations. Jorge seeks to redress the economic viability of these communities by helping them devise productive strategies that redefine the role of local inhabitants in the fisheries' value chain.

> "Jorge Cappato is one of the pioneers of the environmental movement in South America."
>
> —*Global 500 Forum*

Jorge recognizes that cultural preservation does not have to come at the expense of economic independence, and argues that for this independence to be sustainable culture can play a vital role. He works with northeastern riverine communities to increase their quality of life by unleashing their productive capacity, using culture and identity as one of their main assets. Local knowledge and motivation are central to the approach. Because some of the people most affected by the region's poverty and environmental degradation are young people and women, Jorge focuses a good deal of his interventions on these two segments of the population. As a result of his work, hundreds of jobs have been created, and the income of participating fisher-families has more than doubled. In addition, by creating viable, local economic opportunities, Jorge is mitigating the need of riverine communities to migrate urban areas.

A central aspect of Jorge's work deals with creating strong networks among the inhabitants of riverine communities, including government officials and industry leaders. He has, for instance, led the creation of two associations, Redepesca and Recopades, communities of practice, whose main goal is to build knowledge and best practices around capacity-building and collaboration, and the sustainable use of natural resources in riverine and wetland areas. Such knowledge exchange in turn helps to improve the productive capacity of these communities, while also being instrumental in the proposition of new public policies.

THE PROBLEM

Although the northeastern region of Argentina is one of the nations richest in natural resources, its population remains the poorest in the country. Of Argentina's five most underprivileged provinces, four of them—Santa Fe, Corrientes, Chaco, and Entre Ríos—are located in the northeast. Fifty percent of the region's population is said to live below the poverty line. Such factors as the monopolization of the agricultural sector by large producers, the migration of rural inhabitants to medium-sized and big cities, and ever-increasing unemployment rates, contribute greatly to this economic situation.

Jorge and his team have created over 200 jobs and helped fisher-families double their income.

Among the Northeast's most forgotten population are riverine communities. Their existence is constantly threatened as a result of their loss of access to natural resources, especially within the fishing industry. Insufficient measures have been taken to promote environmental preservation and the management of the fishing sector in the region. The large companies that have moved in to the area have not only taken jobs away from local fishermen, they are also causing grave environmental damage. The economic and social consequences for the small fishermen are obvious, but this situation also affects the entire region and its inhabitant's ability to sustain themselves, be it through trade or tourism.

In addition, government services simply do not get to these riverine areas. This means that small fishermen and their families, for the most part, do not have access to social security, education, health or financial support. They are often "informal laborers", and therefore do not benefit from recognized worker's rights. These poor conditions increase the vulnerability of riverine inhabitants and lead many of them to leave their culture and communities behind to migrate to bigger cities in the hope of achieving a better quality of life.

The region also lacks networks that bring together fishermen, government and the industry. The fishing industry today does not

rely on sustainable practices in terms of fish extraction, pricing strategies, and worker's rights. There is a real need to develop initiatives in the region that promote environmental sustainability and increased productivity for the benefit of riverine communities. Unfortunately, riverine communities in Chile, Brazil and Uruguay, as well as in part of Africa and Asia, are equally invisible and marginalized. The need to intervene is real and it is urgent.

THE STRATEGY

Jorge co-founded the Proteger Foundation, a citizen organization dedicated to the local economic development and environmental preservation of riverine communities, with a focus on influencing public policy and developing communities of knowledge and practice.

The Proteger Foundation works directly with fishermen communities. It has promoted the creation of four fishing cooperatives in various parts of the region. The foundation helps them develop and commercialize value-added fish products and derivatives. The cooperatives benefit from a range of supports including legal, marketing, product design, and microcredit services. The ultimate goal is to counteract the monopolization of the fishing industry by large corporations, and ensure better revenue distribution toward small producers at various points in the value chain.

As a result of this work, Jorge and his team have created 200 jobs and helped fisher-families double their income. Most importantly, the Proteger Foundation is creating viable alternatives to urban migration—albeit, an impact that is difficult to measure. Whereas fishermen used to sell their fish at modicum prices to large corporations, because they had little bargaining power, by organizing themselves through cooperatives the power balance is beginning to shift. Moreover, the riverine communities now sell gourmet fish products that have been processed—by youth and women, for the most part—into smoked fish, fish pâté and high-quality artifacts made of fish leather, among others. Their newly acquired abilities allow them to increase the value of their products by 300 percent, without necessarily going through large intermediaries. In addition, by organizing themselves into cooperatives, fisher-communities have gained new rights, as they can now be officially recognized as workers, toward whom the government has responsibilities.

The Proteger Foundation has created a microcredit fund that allows fisher cooperatives and associations in Sante Fe, Chaco, and Entre Ríos to develop other productive projects. Jorge's organization has for example supported 25 families to purchase small boats for an ecotourism enterprise. Although such initiatives have important economic repercussions on these communities, they are also instrumental in restoring their self-esteem and catalyzing greater aspirations.

After working diligently with fisher-communities, Jorge realized there were certain needs that could be addressed through the development or adaptation of technologies. The Proteger Foundation therefore began designing and promoting the implementation of socially appropriate technologies, incorporating the use of renewable energy, in order to increase the quality of life of riverine communities while protecting the environment. The foundation has partnered with the Universidad del Litoral to deliver and develop various capacity-building courses on the use of such technologies in various regions of Argentina. Together they have for example created environmentally friendly and affordable refrigeration units. They are thus giving fisher-communities the opportunity to sell the fish on the market themselves instead of having to sell it quickly to intermediaries at a very low price.

The Proteger Foundation created a microcredit fund that has assisted 25 families to purchase small boats for ecotourism and other initiatives.

The Proteger Foundation is notorious for its work on developing and pushing for adequate legislations that promote the economic development of Argentina's northeastern communities. The foundation has also played a fundamental role in the establishment and implementation of Santa Fe's Provincial Fishing Law. One of its most important contributions has been to create regulatory norms on catching, breeding and farming fish. This law also regulates research and capacity-building; commercialization and industrialization; monitoring of the fishing industry and the registration of any boat, or fishing product and its derivatives. In order to agree on the contents of this new law, Jorge led a series of participatory debates that brought together riverine communities, industry leaders and government officials. The law, and the process through which it was developed, have since become models on the matter in Argentina. In addition, it has led to the creation of the Regional Treaty of the Northeast for the Sustainable Management of Fishing Resources; a treaty which is now ratified by the executive branch of three provinces in the region.

Jorge and the foundation are locally and internationally recognized as leaders in environmental protection, especially as it relates to riverine and wetland communities. He has developed strong communication strategies that have played an important role in positioning his organization as a leader in Argentina. For example, Jorge's organization's website is the second most

visited environmentally focused website after Greenpeace. The Proteger Foundation is a member of the International Union for Conservation of Nature (IUCN), the Alliance of the Paraguay-Paraná System, the Community Network of Artisan Fishermen for Sustainable Development (RECOPADES) and of the Waterkeeper Alliance, among other international networks.

Jorge has also played an instrumental role in the creation of Redepesca in Argentina, a network of 20 fishermen groups and communities operating in five different provinces. The network serves a total of 3,400 families and fishermen. Redespeca focuses on the development of public policies, knowledge sharing and capacity-building directed at fisher-communities, government officials, and other actors that affect the fishing industry.

Jorge has begun spreading his work to fisher-communities in Bolivia and Paraguay, and is sharing knowledge and best practices with organizations in Brazil, including that of Ashoka Fellow René Schärer.

THE PERSON

Jorge was born and raised in the province of Sante Fe, in direct contact with rivers and riverine communities. His grandfather was a fisherman and taught him to love and appreciate nature's gifts. These early connections with the environment have shaped Jorge's life and aspirations.

From an early age, he demonstrated a strong interest in the intersection of environmental preservation and social change. At the age of 12, some of Jorge's favorite things to do were to teach his young neighbors about the structure of atoms, hunt lizards to study them, and row throughout the Paraná streams. In 1978 Jorge was invited to join a group of ecologists for which he dedicated many volunteer years to further environmental conservation. He also worked for many years to establish and strengthen provincial and national environmental movements by organizing numerous events. Jorge's leadership was instrumental to the establishment of the First National Meeting of Non-Government Environmentalist Organizations that took place in Santa Fe in 1983.

During the 2000s Jorge worked diligently to address the effects of Argentina's economic crisis on artisanal fishing communities. He began focusing on network building to strengthen existing organizations—i.e. through the creation of Redepesca—and developed capacity-building workshops to improve the education of riverine women and youth.

As of 2010, Jorge is the President of the Regional Committee of South American Members of the IUCN, as well as its national coordinator for Argentina. In addition, he has led the development and implementation of the Communication, Education and Public Awareness Program of the Ramsar Convention on Wetlands in Latin America.

Jorge considers himself a social facilitator in northeastern Argentina, the Plata Basin, and South America. He is an innovator and a communications specialist, who has developed new methodologies to address socioeconomic issues affecting riverine communities. ◆

SASIN CHALERMLARP

THAILAND

Conservation/Preservation

Cultural Preservation

Natural Resource Management

Sasin Chalermlarp is developing a conflict management mechanism to protect the largest remaining forest complex in Southeast Asia. By restoring the credibility of indigenous ways of life, he has enabled forest inhabitants not only to remain in the forest, but also to collaborate in conservation efforts alongside government officials as equals.

THE NEW IDEA

Sasin is changing the consciousness of forestry officials and turning indigenous people into potential partners, rather than enemies. He has employed a series of conversation starters to create mutual understanding with inhabitants of the forest and the forestry department. Top-level bureaucrats and field officers alike now recognize indigenous mechanisms of forest and wildlife preservation and, despite legal limitations, have revised conservation practices on the ground to include the local forest community.

Sasin is also reuniting forest communities who had previously been under threat by conservation officials. He is reviving old community networks—such as watershed neighborhoods, community doctors, and barter and trade channels with low environmental impact—thus developing alternative models of low-impact communal infrastructure and services. More importantly, these networks are creating and strengthening mechanisms for the community to voice its concerns.

As a result, whereas arrests of forest inhabitants were a common practice in the Western Forest Complex, these have practically ceased to exist. In addition, over 100 forest communities have agreed to common land use regulations and together guard against forest encroachment. Sasin is replicating this collaborative conservation approach in well over 100 other communities along the forest borders, to ensure lasting protection of forest, wildlife, and the right of indigenous communities to coexist with nature.

THE PROBLEM

Environmental conservation efforts in Thailand have long been characterized by conflict between the state and the people. Ethnic minorities inhabiting some of the most valuable forests of Thailand and Southeast Asia have been particularly affected by these conflicts.

The Western Forest Complex, encompassing a Natural World Heritage Site and nearly 18,000 km² on Thailand's western border

with Myanmar, is the largest remaining continuous forest in Southeast Asia. Located at the juncture of four biogeographical zones, the Western Forest contains unparalleled biological diversity—at least ten different types of forest ecosystems, one-third of all terrestrial vertebrates in mainland Southeast Asia, and many endemic and globally-endangered species. Some 10,000 inhabitants who practice *swidden* (rotational) agriculture also populate this forest, a tradition that has endured for at least 200 years.

Contrary to common perception by Thai government officials and the general public, this traditional form of agriculture preserves both forest areas and biological diversity. Swidden agriculture, or shifting cultivation, involves clearing a patch of forest for cultivation and, after the growing season, leaving the land to lie fallow for six to ten years, until a secondary forest grows back and nutrients return to the soil, at which time the farmer returns to cultivate the same field. However, government authorities view all types of human activity and settlement as a threat to forest protection. Accordingly, swidden farming has been denounced by various government departments, mass media and popular discourse as "slash and burn agriculture," practiced by backward "hill tribes."

> "The foundation was established to carry on the dedication shown by late forestry official Seub Nakhasathien, who devoted his life to the conservation of forests, wildlife and natural resources."
>
> —*Bangkok Post*

In an attempt to protect the Western Forest, the Thai government has established 17 legally-protected wildlife sanctuaries and national parks. By law, any form of agriculture qualifies as forest invasion, thus leading to crop destruction and daily arrests of forest inhabitants. In return, indigenous communities view forestry officials as enemies. Swidden farmers are compelled to clear more land than they might otherwise need, in case of government confiscation. Some farmers burn and cultivate watershed forests in vengeance. In short, it has become an open battle between conservation officials and indigenous communities, with the Western Forest Complex held hostage.

The construction of road networks within the Western Forest for convenient government access has, ironically, introduced an even more powerful threat to forest protection. Roads have become important trade corridors, encouraging swidden farmers to switch to marketable crops and chemical-dependent monoculture. Nearby communities also have convenient access to the fertile soil of the Western Forest. In short, there are now growing threats of true slash-and-burn farms, owned by some forest inhabitants and many outsiders. The common perception, however, is that indigenous communities are the enemies of forest conservation.

THE STRATEGY

Sasin is enabling mutual acceptance between forestry officials and forest inhabitants, at an unprecedented scale in Thailand. He has translated indigenous practices and beliefs into formal land use regulations, establishing credibility and accountability to forest communities' way of life. Moreover, he has revived and improved existing community infrastructure, demonstrating to both conservationists and indigenous communities that human and forest coexistence has a future.

Sasin has changed the practice of conservation, encouraging conservationists to identify common ground between environmental and human rights protection. It is the first time his conservation organization—the Seub Nakhasathien Foundation, established by the death of a park ranger 20 years ago—is working with communities.

Since 2004 Sasin has initiated conversations within the forest. The first few years of his work was focused on earning the trust of community leaders in 14 Karen villages, located in the heart of the Western Forest Complex. Simultaneously, he opened dialogue among local forestry officials and park rangers, who wanted to find a more effective way of protecting the Western Forest than daily arrests of villagers. The forest communities, who once refused to speak to any conservationist or official, now allow Sasin's team and forestry officials to participate in monthly village meetings.

To establish credibility for indigenous practices of coexistence with the forest, Sasin has introduced joint forest mapping to facilitate mutual understanding. Forestry officials, who once refused to share information with forest inhabitants for fear of further destruction, now realize that villagers know more about the forest. On joint forest surveys, villagers have the rare opportunity to explain to park officials about traditional conservation practices, such as the rotation cycle for swidden agriculture, the precise criteria for extractive gathering of forest products, and the strict spiritual belief to preserve watersheds and primary forests. After many walks and extensive conversation, villagers translate their traditional practices into formal land use regulations. Using global positioning system (GPS) data, villagers map the distinct boundaries between their swidden fields, forest areas for extractive use, and protected forests. An elected village committee and an advisory group of village elders are ready to administer financial and social penalties, ensuring that forest inhabitants respect these boundaries.

This zoning map and land use regulations has become the contract between forest communities and park officials. Villagers commit to using the forest within the existing boundaries, which allow for swidden fields and forest extraction. Park officials commit to ceasing arrests and crop destruction. Instead, Sasin has convinced both the Department of Forestry and Department of National Parks to an alternative interpretation of the law. In the Wildlife Reservation and Protection Act and the National Parks Act, field officers are permitted to exercise their best judgment in the interest of conservation. To date, 106 communities who live in and use the Western Forest are benefitting from this agreement,

as well as three wildlife sanctuaries, eight national parks, and one future forest reserve within the Western Forest Complex.

Even as the open conflict subsides, Sasin recognizes the encroaching threat of cash crops and chemical agriculture. He has worked with villages inside and along the borders of the Western Forest to establish communal services, promote low-impact income-generation activities and most importantly, revive a sense of community.

Sasin is adapting various livelihood improvement and community empowerment programs to the Western Forest Complex, an area of unique ecology, ethnic diversity, and history. For instance, he has revived the network of "revolutionary doctors," who received advanced medical training from the Communist Army, during the open conflict between the Community Party of Thailand and the Royal Thai government in early 1970s. Sasin has brought some 20 doctors in 14 Karen villages back together for the first time in almost 40 years. Since 2006, this network of Community Health Volunteers receives regular supplies of medicine and equipment, replenished twice a year and financed by donations from one temple, several private businesses, and many veterans of the attempted Communist Revolution. Community Health Volunteers provide herbal as well as Western medical care—ranging from prescription drugs to emergency surgical procedures—to forest inhabitants who live one to two days drive away from the nearest health facility.

Sasin works with villages in regard to health supplies, land use agreements and forest gathering practices.

Other community services include the chili-salt barter program. Building on historic traditions of exchanging the famous Karen chili grown in swidden fields with salt from traveling traders, Sasin has set up a modern-day barter program to engage both forest communities and forestry officials. Once a year, Sasin's field officers trade salt for Karen chili, to encourage swidden agriculture, and gives the chili to park rangers to sell, in order to raise funds for purchasing more salt for the next year. Other services include eight learning centers for agroforestry, providing forest communities and surrounding villages with training, and tree seedlings. In 2009 Sasin initiated a trade agreement with Thailand's most prominent herbal medicine company, for communities practicing agroforestry on the borders of the Western Forest to provide the company with sustainably-grown herbs.

In addition to livelihood improvement, these services focus on creating a sense of community in the Western Forest Complex. There is now a network called the Mae Chan Watershed Community, comprised of villages along the Mae Chan river in the heart of the Western Forest, who agree to conserve the forest together with park officials. Another community network in the nearby wildlife sanctuary issued a collective statement "against corn-growing." Peer pressure, coupled with support for alternative practices, has effectively convinced most forest inhabitants to maintain their low-impact way of life.

Recognizing that the biggest threats to forest survival come from outside, not within, Sasin is conducting intensive outreach work with "gateway" villages along roads that lead to the Western Forest. Since 2006 he has facilitated local land use agreements in some 30 villages whose agricultural and forest gathering practices may threaten the Western Forest. At the regional level, he has set up active community forest networks in five provinces to promote community coexistence with the forest, with support from hundreds of volunteer forest patrols, local forestry officials, as well as governors and other high-level bureaucrats. At the Department of Forestry and Department of National Parks headquarters in Bangkok, Sasin is integrating more and more of his activities into the annual budget and regular conservation duties.

Today, Sasin is part of the Working Group to register another Natural World Heritage Site in Thailand. His contributions on community conflict management will be crucial, as this site along Thailand's southern coast is abound with opposing interests among local communities, government departments and the tourism industry.

As a testament to the unique and critical impact of Sasin's work, the Danish International Development Agency (DANIDA) extended its initial funding from one to five years, totaling approximately US$10M, before necessarily closing its operations in Thailand in 2009 due to Danish national policy. DANIDA, however, continues to work in neighboring countries Burma and Cambodia, and showcases the results of Sasin's initiative worldwide as a prominent model of effective participation in natural resource management.

Sasin has embarked on active public communications campaigns, to share his approach and change common perceptions around conservation and community rights. In addition to hiring a media professional to his staff, Sasin is working closely with a broad range of journalists and contributing regular articles to a major national newspaper. Furthermore, he is using the Internet to engage new partners through almost-daily updates and photographs from field offices. He plans to translate the website content into foreign languages in the future.

Sasin has been able to open dialogue between community leaders, forestry officials and park rangers to find more effective ways of protecting the Western Forest.

THE PERSON

Sasin's education in natural science coincided with the beginning of Thailand's messy struggle with environmental conservation. As a third year university student in geology in 1989, the Department of Forestry banned a century's worth of timber concessions and declared its commitment to protecting the remaining forest areas. In the years to follow, Sasin witnessed human rights violations across Thailand—thousands of households being forcefully evicted from the forest, time and again. Contrary to expectations, this approach only resulted in more deforestation, not to mention violent resistance. Indigenous communities could not adjust to their new settlements and returned to their familiar ways of life in the forest.

Sasin's graduate study in geology led him to a career in academia, but always with a people-centered orientation. Throughout his 13 years as university professor, Sasin conducted research on community and environmental impacts of mining projects, as well as founded and advised the student club for social and environmental services. He has also served on the National Human Rights Commission Subcommittee on Water, Coastal, Mineral and Environmental Resources, where he conducted investigations of community rights violations.

Sasin believes that being born into a family of government employees has helped him work effectively with government officials. As Secretary General of the Seub Nakhasathien Foundation, a nationally-respected conservation organization with close ties to the Department of Forestry, Sasin has been able to earn the trust of policymakers and park rangers more easily than other citizen sector workers. His unique background has enabled him to achieve unusual success in harmonizing the often-conflicting concerns for environmental conservation and human rights protection. ♦

STUART COHEN

UNITED STATES

Urban Development

Stuart Cohen is creating new tools to reverse the paradigm of growth away from sprawling big box development, and to instead revitalize our existing towns and cities by planning for people, not cars—a reversal that has tremendous potential to reduce global warming pollution and improve social outcomes as the country grows by 100 million by 2050.

THE NEW IDEA

Stuart sees that creating vibrant, healthy and affordable communities requires bringing together diverse stakeholders to achieve systematic change at many scales. His first victories were at a regional scale, leading efforts for a smart growth visioning and winning billions for public transportation. The smart growth vision pointed to a better way and was quickly replicated in other major regions of California. Stuart then built diverse campaigns and partnered with agencies to raise over $6 billion toward new public transit, bicycle and pedestrian infrastructure, and affordable homes near transit.

Stuart and his team are now creating new tools and incentives to align the needs of citizens and neighbors, city planners and developers. The first major effort is to make community voices a constructive heart of planning a neighborhood's future, and help avoid the oppositional dynamics that blunt progress. Through the Great Communities Collaborative, tools, training, and technical assistance help neighbors identify not just what they want to preserve, but what they may want to make more complete communities, whether safer streets, parks, or more services like health or childcare facilities.

A more recent innovation is a third-party certification for buildings, called GreenTRIP, which supports cities and developers that plan for low-traffic, low-carbon developments. GreenTRIP certification is given to projects that are designed to cut traffic, with incentives like free transit passes or CarSharing on-site, instead of excessive parking. This certification helps foster community support to get the best developments approved while giving property owners a marketing edge. Having emerged from pilot projects in the Bay Area, Stuart's team is now spreading the approach to other regions in California, where the policy environment is supportive, and then to other parts of the country.

THE PROBLEM

Over the last 50 years, poorly planned growth that assumed people would drive for every single trip has dominated in the United States; with devastating environmental, social and economic consequences. Supported with billions in highway subsidies we've been paving over farms, forests, and open space at an astonishing rate. Cars now cause 80 percent of the air pollution in many urban areas, and transportation is by far the country's largest source of greenhouse gas emissions.

The long distances between home and destinations have left many people with grinding commutes, few transit options, and less time with friends or to engage in civic activities. But the impacts are most intense for low-income families. With so many jobs moved out to corporate parks, commuters that rely on transit can now access just 1/9th as many jobs as those that are able to drive. While owning one or more cars can improve access, average transportation costs for low-income families now amounts to 30 percent of income.

Fortunately, there is tremendous demand for a new way of growing. Walkable towns and villages with a mix of housing, shops, parks and community facilities have huge market demand. And growing this way could have a tremendous impact; with enough people easily able to get to transit stations we can make public transportation more frequent and affordable. In the Bay Area, people who live and work close to transit are ten times more likely to use it. And local foot traffic keeps local businesses bustling and neighborhoods thriving and vibrant.

Compact, infill development is being supported by improved policy environments throughout the country, especially in the San Francisco Bay Area, Portland (Oregon), and Denver. In California, pioneering legislation to reduce greenhouse gas emissions—SB 375—requires that the state's 18 major regions develop plans for more transit-oriented communities that can reduce how much people drive.

But locally, complicated zoning and incentives challenge even the most enlightened planner or city councilmember. Builders are often required to build two or more parking spaces per home or apartment unit, even though in transit-oriented areas or walkable communities, fewer are needed. With the cost of each parking space at $45,000 for land and construction, there is less space for homes and each one becomes more expensive. It also means less or no profit for the developer, and certainly no funding left for community amenities and benefits. While this means there is a focus on high-end units, there are few policies in place locally to prevent displacement of existing, lower-income residents or businesses.

Compounding the problem is distrust among the various stakeholders. Neighbors often are left out of planning, do not trust city staff, and despise developers. They almost instinctively oppose change that seems thrust upon them from outside—gaining the moniker NIMBY—Not In My Back Yard. Unfortunately, this just leads cities and developers to craft ways to minimize their involvement. This oppositional paradigm leaves almost no room for uncovering ways to design projects or whole communities that can benefit everyone. These unhealthy dynamics block the enabling environment needed for cities to work swiftly to move policy into practice.

THE STRATEGY

To achieve a real shift in how we plan for urban growth, Stuart sees that it will not be possible to change without a supportive policy environment, where regional and state policies reinvest in existing communities and in transportation alternatives. With early policy wins, including building coalitions that helped gain more than $6B for expanding public transportation and bike lanes in the Bay Area, Stuart and his team began to see that actual neighborhood level change would not just happen by itself or from some big regional mandate. He realized the Bay Area and other regions could only make positive change at the local level by changing incentives, deeply engaging residents in planning their communities. But more than engagement, they needed tools and resources that could bring residents, planners, and developers to explore and discover their common interests.

While there were certainly some great examples of smart planning with great outcomes, Stuart realized making just a few great communities may have some local benefits but would not garner the tremendous regional benefits of a whole region moving in that direction; benefits like greater job access, open space preservation and reducing air pollution. In 2005 he co-founded the Great Communities Collaborative, a unique partnership of three Bay Area community foundations working in tandem with transportation, environmental, housing, and social equity groups.

> "By combining high-quality policy analysis with coalition building and strategic media efforts, TransForm has become a powerful voice for world class transit and walkable communities."
> —Robert & Patricia Switzer Foundation

By coordinating the work of experts and organizers at a regional scale they were able to work in 25 communities over three years, providing tools that help residents identify crucial needs early on, and then providing technical assistance and trainings so residents have a strong voice in shaping the future of their communities. But engagement itself is not enough. The Collaborative created a host of tools that demystified issues, for example using complex transportation models to show how growing in the right places, and doing it in a way that houses more people than cars (with reduced parking requirements) can actually reduce overall traffic, save families thousands of dollars in transportation costs, and reduce spending for cities, all while developers would be able to meet growing market demand for walkable communities.

Stuart and his colleagues have built the Collaborative to be a powerful anchor to shift policies into practice, and a participatory spirit through cross-sector resolve, aggregated resources, and an expansive shared vision. The Collaborative is now sharing this model with other regions in California and across the nation.

With the broader citizen-base mobilized and engaged on planning, Stuart and his team are taking on a critical roadblock: How to make specific developments (i.e. not just broader community plans) reinforce this more collaborative planning and support great projects. This is especially critical to break a vicious cycle where planners require vastly too much parking for new homes in walkable communities near transit. This reduces the space available for homes or community amentias. And with all that parking there is no incentive (or funding left) to promote the use of alternatives with free transit passes and so on. It also comes with an overprediction of car trips and traffic, which gets the community up in arms.

But nobody trusts developers who want to do the right thing; asking for a variance from these codes opens them up to even more delay and litigation. And updating codes is not only cumbersome but can quickly get out of date.

So Stuart is helping spearhead an independent certification approach that specifically looks at new development through the a holistic lens of transportation and community impacts, addressing such questions as: Does this development maximally equip new residents with the tools, information, and opportunities they need to use public transit as an alternative to owning and using cars? Does this development make homes affordable?

This certification, called GreenTRIP, solves several problems at once, and aligns public and private interests that have been assumed to be oppositional. Essentially, the appeal of GreenTRIP to builders: Let us, a trusted third party be engaged from the design phase forward, and help you get quickly through the entitlement process by making sure the building works optimally for the community, for the environment, and for your bottom line. (To builders, every month of delay is costly, so the incentive is high to participate.) TransForm staff advise developers early in the process on what it takes to meet these standards, and help quantify the costs and benefits of various solutions. The appeal to residents is not just a much better development, but that the claims of benefits are coming from an outside community-based organization that is motivated by environmental and social outcomes, not profits.

At a micro level, what does success look like from these combined efforts? Let's look at San Leandro, south of Oakland. Through the Great Communities Collaborative, TransForm garnered broad citizen engagement and the zoning for their downtown was changed to allow 3,500 instead of 500 homes. The final plan included community requests for an affordable childcare center, and safer streets—identified early in the process. Bolstered by tremendous citizen support for this plan, though much more "density" was now allowed a local landowner, designed ground on a 300-home development that is certified transit-friendly. By cutting its parking in half, the development offers 100 affordable units instead of the required 60, more profit for the developer, and free space on the ground floor (i.e. initially sketched as a parking lot) for the childcare center the community wanted. To get a GreenTRIP certification they have separated the cost of the parking from the rent and offer tremendous discounts on transit passes, allowing families to save more money while creating an incentive to own fewer vehicles and drive less. And the local government helps meet climate change targets. The proposal garnered huge community support, and by finding efficiencies and reducing cost, it is one of the only developments of its kind ready to break ground in the Bay Area during the financial downturn.

Begun in 2009, GreenTRIP is moving out of its pilot, having certified five buildings in San Jose and several other Bay Area locations. The developments to date are varied in size and all are residential, ranging from 100 to 800 housing units. Stuart and his team are moving to the second round, incorporating feedback from all sides. They expect to certify 10 to 12 developments in the Bay Area, then create a business plan for expanding to enthusiastic partners in Sacramento and San Diego. Stuart is already finding that a certification program may be able to nurture whole markets to innovate trip reduction measures. For example, areas whose transit agencies do not offer bulk passes, or that do not have carsharing, are trying to bring them in so that developments there can get GreenTRIP certified. And as new ideas like bikesharing take hold these can be quickly incorporated into the standards.

After, Stuart and his team will move the idea out nationally, so that GreenTRIP becomes an established norm (similar to LEED). In the first pilot, TransForm did not charge developers; but a fee-based system to cover most or all costs is being formulated. Stuart feels it is imperative for TransForm not to profit from GreenTRIP financially, or it can damage the independence and trust from the community.

TransForm is now setting up another program, TravelChoice, to provide "travel concierge" services to existing transit-oriented buildings; working with management to introduce commuter incentives and educating residents about ways to cut their car and commute costs. This has the potential to spin-off as a consulting service and supply a revenue stream to TransForm, and other transportation advocacy groups that may do it in their regions.

THE PERSON

Stuart grew up in the suburbs of Long Island, where sprawling development made driving to every activity the norm, but hiking and skiing with his family, he gained an appreciation for the natural world. At age 17, with almost no prior exposure to social change, he saw the film *Gandhi* and was overcome by the powerful story of one person orchestrating an entire civil movement and redirecting the course of a nation through peaceful protest—this was his introduction to the idea that people can shape and lead positive, transformative change at a large-scale.

During college, Stuart began to apply Gandhian sensibilities about change to his passion for environmental preservation. He started a Greenpeace chapter, and engaged students in civil disobedience at proposed nuclear plants and toxic incinerators. A student of social anthropology, he also wanted to explore the world and learn from others. In 1990 Stuart traveled to Indonesia to organize the only Earth Day in that country during the event's 20th anniversary. He also learned Nepalese and as a volunteer with the Annapurna Conservation Area Project set up a self-sustaining cultural and environmental information center in Pokhara, Nepal.

Stuart's interest in land use began in earnest at age 24, when he moved from a cycling-friendly college town to New York City, and witnessed how cyclists had to risk their lives in a place that could be tailor made for short bike trips. He began to notice how the design of cities directs everyday choices for transportation, for housing, for social interactions, and the quality and cost of living. While pursuing a master's in public policy at UC Berkeley, with a focus on planning, he saw that no Bay Area group was trying to impact transportation and land use at a regional level. While working with others to start a regional advocacy effort, he secured $25,000 to be able to work full-time upon graduating in 1997. Another small grant helped sustain him for 20 months working from his home, at which point multiple foundations started giving and he hired his first colleague, Jeff Hobson (who continues as TransForm's Deputy Director). Stuart's staff has grown to foster these collaborative and innovative programs, and now stands at 32 in three offices. ♦

© Darnel Lindor

GRÉGORY GENDRE

FRANCE

Energy

Waste Management/ Sanitation

Grégory Gendre is building a new environmental paradigm by setting up a national network of professional and local recycling communities. Grégory has proven the economic and environmental efficiency of local waste management, from collection to treatment and production of added-value recycling products and services. Using his methodology of selecting creative and entrepreneurial communities, Grégory will spread his model on a national scale and foster an unprecedented double bottom-line set of recycling actors.

THE NEW IDEA

To encourage environmentally and economically rational waste management, Grégory empowers local stakeholders and creates recycling communities. Starting in Oléron, on the French West Coast, he has successfully gathered various actors along a local cooking oil recycling chain, including public institutions, restaurants, camping institutions, oil suppliers, and the general public. Grégory demonstrates to each of them the benefits and common interests in participating in the local recycling system, such as avoided expenses connected to the treatment of waste output, corporate social responsibility, and communication benefits toward tourists (i.e. for instance, fun and punchy messages about using the cooking oil for one's French fries as a biofuel for the local scenic railway). Beyond the significant reduction in the environmental print of recycling, Grégory uses his system as a leverage to raise awareness on environmental issues and to deeply influence behaviors around recycling.

The success of Grégory's model is primarily based on the community principle. Indeed, the involvement of a large range of actors around cooking oil has a domino effect on the entire recycling system. Beyond the 25,000 liters of cooking oil collected and recycled every year (i.e. more than half of the total oil deposit of the region), the stakeholders have put into place new practices, i.e. camping institutions have created Mister Waste seasonal jobs to optimize waste sorting. The community-based system also generates a bottom-up sourcing of local waste issues and opens up new opportunities to build recycling chains. For instance, fishermen and oyster-farmers were able to raise the issue of having no solutions in regards to the rotten shells that were polluting their tanks. Thanks to a partnership with a research and development laboratory, Grégory is currently setting up a new recycling chain to collect these shells and create recycled bags for the mussel and oyster industry.

Grégory is spreading his model to other communities, with the goal of setting up systems to recycle everything, everywhere. With this objective in mind, he carefully selects local actors, such as environmental citizen organizations (COs), public institutions, or professional groups, and trains them to become committed and creative recyclers. All affiliated organizations become part of the national community and can share best practices and solutions. By scaling up, Grégory builds a new set of market-based actors who can recycle waste innovatively and efficiently.

THE PROBLEM

Over the last few years, governments and citizen initiatives have made great efforts to raise awareness on environmental issues such as global warming and carbon footprints. The French Agency on Environment and Energy has led national awareness campaigns and people are more sensitized and feel the responsibility to do something. A basic level of environmental consciousness seems to have been reached; in 2009, 68 percent of French people declared being well informed about recycling and waste sorting.

Beyond the significant reduction in the environmental print of recycling, Grégory raises awareness on environmental issues and deeply influences behaviors around recycling.

Nevertheless, playing an active role on an individual level can be difficult and the national recycling rate of domestic waste fluctuates in reality between 15 and 20 percent. Some initiatives show that community-based projects are more willing to engage organizations and individuals in social and environmental issues. A telling example is the creation of a new agricultural production and distribution system to encourage local consumption. For instance, the Cocagne Gardens, a social initiative led by a French Senior Ashoka Fellow allows thousands of citizens to collaborate together on local green agriculture projects.

Conditions are thus present to engage new actors collectively, and now is a historical moment to build community-based models to recycle better. Current models are not working. There is a missing piece in the recycling scheme between individual volunteers who sporadically clean up waste and large private companies disinterested in local scale. Industrial recyclers like Veolia are unable to deal with door-to-door collection and individualized support to professionals who produce waste. Instead, they rely on a simple commercial relationship where one pays to get rid of waste. As a result, recycling rates remain low.

There is a profound lack of economic and environmental rationality in the current system, and recycling processes (i.e. collection plus treatment) can in the end generate more pollution than intended. For instance, before Grégory's initiative, the cooking oil in Oléron was collected at the local waste reception center; however, without regulations producers preferred to deposit the oil at uncontrolled dumpsites. The oil that was successfully collected at the waste reception center was sent by truck to a recycling center in the south of France and then to Germany for chemical treatment. On a national-scale, better collection and recycling of half of the total oil deposited into nature today would save 50M EUR. There is a huge opportunity to create a more efficient, cost effective, and environmentally-friendly waste management system for cooking oil and other waste.

> "Roule my fries" recycles used frying oils in order to transform it into diesel fuel."
>
> —Erla Technologies

THE STRATEGY

Since 2007 Grégory has been developing a dynamic system in Oléron, the region where he collects cooking oil, filters it, transforms it into a biofuel, and promotes its local use for the scenic railway or fishing machines. All community stakeholders are involved, share the same values, and are collectively building a virtuous circle where they all gain various economic and communication advantages. Professional members (i.e. restaurants, camping businesses, and oil suppliers) benefit from the free collection of their oil (versus paying 0,23 EUR per litre at the local waste center), access to a cheap biofuel, and advice to globally improve their environmental practices (i.e. reducing cooking temperatures, not using palm oil, and better sorting methods). They are also able to promote their social responsibility to their clients and partners. Furthermore, local authorities work with the association as a partner to develop new solutions for environmental protection, raise awareness, and handle the huge growth in the island's population during the tourist season (where the population grows from 30,000 to 300,000 people). Local authorities have a direct interest in recycling oil since 20,000 EUR (US$28,256) are paid each year to clean the sewer pipes, clogged by oil. They also benefit from promoting environmental innovation to locals, tourists, and students. For example, they promote the association's social awareness programs on environmental issues; workshops in school, shows and plays in tourist sites, and on local TV. By building communities around recycling, further positive actions are set up and continue to drive a cycle of local awareness, change, and improvement.

Oléron and the surrounding region are now recognized as environmentally innovative and exemplary sites. This recognition facilitates the spread of Grégory's innovative model. Since the beginning, while building the first recycling community, he created the conditions to spread his idea nationally. Grégory partnered with a research and development laboratory, Valagro, to jointly lead experimentations and validate them scientifically. This professional partnership has yielded great results: Monitoring the amount of collected oil has demonstrated the system's impressive capability and for the first time in France, the use of naturally filtrated oil-fuel in vehicles is permitted. This unprecedented decision will facilitate the implementation of oil recycling projects in other regions, and open doors to experimenting with recycling innovations based on waste issues sourced by the affiliated communities.

Grégory has gathered various actors along a local cooking oil recycling chain, including public institutions, restaurants, camping institutions, oil suppliers, and the general public.

To build his network of affiliated recycling communities, Grégory has established selection criteria and designed a turn-key replication methodology, the Kit Huileo. Grégory relies on three types of existing organizations to spread his model: Environmental COs, professional groups, and local authorities. The package they buy as affiliated members offers them a 15-day training, all the materials to quickly collect and filtrate oil, and ideas for community management. Starting with cooking oil is an easy way to launch a local recycling system and allows the network to have at least one common project to share nationally. However, Grégory also pays attention to developing the creativity of the local communities and encourages them to think of new products and services to recycle particular local waste or to use the recycled products. Members then make the new initiative possible by working with the R&D lab and sharing best practices. Currently, the association is half financed by local government and half by revenue from membership fees, the sale of oil, and TV programs, among other income-generating schemes. Already, Grégory is launching five new local recycling communities in France, demonstrating that community members themselves can control and reduce their environmental footprint.

THE PERSON

Grégory grew up on the island of Oléron and had the chance to experience a great feeling of freedom. When he was young, he would play outside—biking, surfing, and playing with children from the village. Grégory's secondary school and high school periods as a boarder in a big city might have been harder if he had not found an escape in books. Spending most of his time in the school library, Grégory read a great deal about various topics. These activities have helped him develop into a creative, curious, and passionate adult.

Grégory's unquenchable thirst for knowledge led him to study journalism. He worked as a free-lance journalist for several years and participated in the creation of two new media communication start-up companies. Grégory seized all opportunities to travel to cover news and his social engagement grew stronger over the years as he observed social and environmental issues all over the planet. In 2005 he decided to launch the company's first social project in Africa, to reinforce local media by bringing computers and other material resources to local organizations. At the same time, an oil spill was ruining the South West coast of France. Grégory quickly returned to France and engaged in the local clean-up of the beaches and coastland. He then pursued environmental work with a job at Greenpeace in the communications department. His work provided him with accelerated training on environmental causes, waste management and recycling, especially during his last mission, covering the asbestos issue on the French aircraft carrier Clemenceau disassembly process.

At that time, Grégory realized that denouncing these problems was not enough. He returned to Oléron and decided to develop his own solution. Grégory started investigating and discovered an oil biofuel project in the South of France. He realized how cooking oil could be a punchy starting point for his recycling community model given that Oléron is a tourist island where everyone eats French fries. His previous experiences and communications work helped the project grow rapidly and benefit from powerful media coverage, even at the Copenhagen Summit. Wearing several hats, Grégory not only has great communication skills but is also a coordinator in the field, a great spokesman with scientific expertise on recycling, and a strategic entrepreneur. Grégory is part of the network Entrepreneurs of the Future and helps develop social entrepreneurship in his region, while paying attention to his role as a husband, father, and stepfather to three children. ♦

BRENT KOPPERSON

CANADA

Energy

Brent Kopperson is transforming Canada's electricity generation and distribution systems from highly centralized ones, dominated by non-renewable resources, to more decentralized, green and locally-owned systems. He is bridging social sector engagement and provincial level policy change to remove the structural barriers that have until now impeded the large-scale emergence of community-led and owned green energy sector. Brent is giving citizens the tools and incentives to become energy entrepreneurs, empowering communities across Canada to become self-reliant in energy-use and conservation.

THE NEW IDEA

Brent uses a combination of community engagement and policy change to enable citizens and communities to become conservers and generators of electrical generation installations, moving toward renewable energy investment. By transforming the electricity system into one where everyone can be a producer, Brent is helping to put electricity systems back into the hands of individual consumers, communities, and small-scale entrepreneurs at the lowest possible cost. He is implementing a model of Community Power by reducing dependence on fossil fuels and nuclear energy, preventing climate change, creating local jobs, encouraging entrepreneurial spirit, and economic opportunities.

Brent is working on multiple fronts to lay the groundwork for a transformed electricity system in Ontario. He is creating outreach programs and educational tools while removing structural barriers to policy change. In addition, Brent's initiative catalyzes broad-reaching coalitions. He is working directly with Aboriginal communities, rural and urban cooperatives, farmers, and individual homeowners to implement small-scale electrical generation projects and instil a sense of collective grassroots power. Brent piloted his project in Aboriginal communities where he saw the greatest need, but also openness to this approach. He used the experience as a proof of concept and has replicated the approach to other rural and urban settings in Ontario.

Brent and the communities and organizations he works with are building community-managed windfarms and solar energy systems. He is creating a new movement where "green energy consumers-producers" are leading the sustainable development movement by investing in renewable energy systems in Canada. To ensure these groups continue to have incentives—economic, social, and environmental—Brent is also changing the infrastructure within which the energy sector operates. He has played an instrumental role in introducing the first Green Energy Act in Ontario, which is now setting the tone for other green energy legislation in provinces across Canada. He is democratizing energy production and making green energy accessible and widely distributed.

THE PROBLEM

The concentration of electricity production and distribution with highly centralized generation facilities has created systems that are resistant to change. In Ontario, the energy matrix is dominated by large nuclear, fossil fuel, and hydro facilities, and electricity monopolies are obviously not thrilled about the idea of relinquishing autonomous control over the energy industry to community-based organizations. The efforts made in recent years to advance the cause of renewable power, energy efficiency, and the decentralization of energy grids have therefore not found fertile grounds to grow. Energy production was not always dominated by large producers, in fact, until the industrial revolution individual families and communities were the main energy producers. The rapid expansion of industrial electricity in the twentieth century led to the production and distribution of electricity falling into the hands of monopolies and oligopolies. Until recently, few examples of community-owned electricity production existed in Canada.

> "Brent Kopperson was an advisor to the Canadian government for three years at the United Nations climate change treaty negotiations (Kyoto Protocol)."
>
> —*Green Solutions*

It is not just the grid technologies and tariff structures that are based on a centralized system, but also the legal, policy, and financial frameworks. It is this structure combined with Canada's politically conservative attitude that has prevented progress being made toward a green energy strategy. Europe has been the leader in green energy with clear incentives to encourage development. It was after seeing the progress made in Europe that Brent started working to overcome the barriers in Ontario by changing policy and bringing back more community focused green energy production.

Across Canada, there are a number of barriers to a transition to renewable energy. Electrical systems in Ontario are designed for a limited number of large central generation sources with a one-way distribution grid to bring electricity from these large sources to homes and industries across the province. The grid technologies, tariff structures, legal, policy, and financial frameworks are all compatible with this centralized structure.

THE STRATEGY

Driven by a desire to empower local communities and have more efficient and sustainable mechanisms to produce and use energy at the local level, Brent developed a way for them to regain control of and benefit from energy production. His model involves bringing green energy to communities, and creating dialogue between multiple stakeholders, including governments, communities, investors, and advocacy groups.

From the initial creation of the Windfall Ecology Centre in 1998, Brent has been pursuing small-scale energy production as a means of community development. He developed a cooperative model called Community Power, where a community creates and owns a fund to buy shares in a social enterprise, which produces energy. The model ensures that each project provides the community with democratic control, community ownership, and shared economic value distribution. The first attempt was on Georgina Islands where Brent had an existing relationship with the First Nations community. The ability to conduct this pilot in a relatively isolated environment allowed Brent to refine the methodology to eventually replicate it in other rural and urban settings throughout Ontario.

Compared to other commercial energy projects, the Community Power model can create two to three times the number of local jobs and 5 times the amount of local spending whilst retaining almost all the earnings within the community. For example, in 2003, the Pukwis Energy Co-Op was founded with a US$6M pilot project that managed to achieve a 10 percent reduction in energy costs. An additional six pilot projects consisting of 10 windmills with a 20 megawatt capacity will generate enough electricity to serve 7,000 homes and replace 15,000 tonnes of greenhouse gases every year. Once the renewable energy infrastructure is complete, the community will become entirely self-sufficient in its energy production.

Melinda Zytaruk and Debra Doncaster from the Ontario Sustainable Energy Association, Dr. David Suzuki, and Brent Kopperson, OSEA Chair and Windfall Ecology Centre Executive Director.

The green energy sector is relatively new in Ontario and as Brent develops Community Power projects, various policy or regulatory issues inevitably arise. By founding several nonprofits, Brent has been able to overcome some entrenched policy and regulatory barriers. The Ontario Sustainable Energy Association and the Canadian Renewable Energy Alliance are two examples of organizations he has created that have assisted in developing the green energy sector. Brent and his colleagues were largely responsible for conceptualizing, advocating, and consolidating The Green Energy Act, a pioneering law passed by the provincial Government of Ontario. He also introduced a policy on Feed In Tariffs, which ensures that electricity from renewable energy projects is purchased at a rate profitable for small producers. These

new regulations are the first of their kind in Canada and have since inspired other provinces to follow suit.

Although the Green Energy Act will help guarantee income, renewable energy projects typically involve large capital expenditures for the infrastructure. To alleviate this problem, Brent has worked with the financial community and founded the Community Power Fund to promote local power generation and in an effort to find long-term financing solutions. Brent's organization, Windfall Ecology Centre, also provides expertise in project development, financing, construction, and operations to help local community actors manage and control this process. In addition, Brent's leadership has motivated Ontario Hydro (Ontario's largest energy provider) to develop technologies that incorporate some small-scale decentralized electricity into the grid.

To date, Brent's organization has developed community-based renewable energy projects in six communities, and he has played a central role in a wide range of other initiatives to catalyze and expand this sector. Together, these initiatives will unlock a latent demand for green energy projects, increase community empowerment, and shift energy production from million dollar mega-projects to small community-driven projects. In 2009 there were around 100 community energy projects, which Brent is determined to increase to 200,000 installations over a period of ten years. These initiatives and new policies have turned Ontario into a leader in green energy practice in North America. Recent changes have already attracted a lot of attention from large investors, such as Samsung, who recently committed to invest CA$6.6B in the province of Ontario's green energy sector.

THE PERSON

It was in the 1980s as a young pilot that Brent realized the effects of air pollution. As he flew over urban centers across Canada, it was clear to him that air quality was deteriorating due to inefficient and unhealthy energy production. However, it was not until a few years later, when his life hit a low point that he faced a turning point.

Brent comes from a strong business sector background. He co-founded a telecommunication company that became the foundation of an entertainment merchandising company. Backstage Pass Inc. provided communications and marketing services to over 200 performance artists, including Madonna, U2, and Bruce Springsteen. Brent succeeded in achieving both wealth and fame, yet this career came to an abrupt end when he was the victim of fraud. Left with nothing, and in need of a change and some time to think things over, Brent took a job as a cemetery gardener.

Upon returning from work one day, Brent noticed a farm with a windmill and solar panel. Intrigued, he stopped to talk with the owner. With growing interest, he listened as the owner explained ways to reduce peoples' ecological footprints through green energy. Since that day, Brent has focused his attention on climate change and the role of the Ontario energy sector. Soon after that conversation, Brent started working with individuals, communities, and the government to find solutions to environmental problems. The Windfall Ecology Centre was the first of a series of organizations he founded, aimed to promote green energy, empower the community, and change policy. ◆

TOBIAS LEENAERT

BELGIUM

Conscious Consumerism

Tobias Leenaert has developed high-impact and socially acceptable solutions to the health and environmental issues related to meat consumption that can be achieved with modest changes in our consumer lifestyles. Tobias has developed a partnership with one of the leading enterprises in Europe, and his public campaign has spread from Belgium to Germany, France, Brazil, the U.S., and South Africa.

THE NEW IDEA

There is clear evidence that the current level of meat consumption is not sustainable to ecological and social equilibriums, and to human health. Recognizing the lack of awareness surrounding the problem and the challenges to shift deeply culturally and socially rooted eating habits, Tobias has embarked on a quest to subtly shift market forces and incentivize a higher demand for vegetarian food and a stronger implication for businesses.

To increase the consumption of vegetarian meals and influence consumer behavior, Tobias has changed the discourse around vegetarianism in Belgium and has been promoting it in a new way. The usual vegetarian stance, often linked with animal rights and protection, is highly normative and has led to a situation where meat consumption is a polarizing and taboo subject. Tobias, on the contrary, is mobilizing customers to change their behavior toward more healthy and sustainable food, while proving that this shift can be at the same time easy, fun and tasty. Furthermore, he is also educating the public about the multi-dimensional consequences of one's eating habits.

Tobias is making vegetarian meals attractive and accessible through a large number of creative initiatives based on positive and attractive messages. His "veggie city" plans, his vegetarian cooking courses, his seven-course gourmet dinners, his Veggielympics and his multimedia campaigns show that vegetarian food is tasty and readily available. Tobias is taking a progressive approach to promote the integration of vegetarian meals into everybody's diet, rather than promoting the more difficult shift to full vegetarianism. As such, he developed an approach that is completely socially acceptable—and that offers the possibility for each citizen to contribute in a positive way to a more sustainable society.

In parallel, Tobias has developed a business-friendly approach that is opening ways for businesses to be socially responsible

and profitable at the same time. For example, partnerships with the restaurant industry are enabling him to incentivize and train chefs so that they can offer high-quality and tasty dishes without meat. He is also partnering with agro-industrial groups who develop meatless products or meat alternatives to go mainstream. As the market shifts, Tobias is working up the value chain and influencing a steadily deeper change in the meat supply landscape.

To catalyze the change triggered on both ends and to increase his leverage, Tobias creates an atmosphere where "meat" becomes a politically safe subject. This is a far cry from the polarizing subject it had become. He is engineering an enabling institutional environment through cooperation with public authorities and business. To effectively engage these stakeholders, Tobias developed the inspiring and powerful concept of "Veggie Day." He launched the "Thursday Veggie Day" campaign in the city of Ghent, Flanders, where on this day the city services and many local businesses promote a vegetarian option. More than 40 kindergartens and 35 primary schools now offer a vegetarian lunch as their default option every Thursday. This idea is spreading like wildfire across Europe and the rest of the world, such as Brazil, and is creating a global movement of sensible vegetarians and sensible meat eaters who are preparing for a more sustainable future.

EVA association was awarded the Culture Prize for Social-Cultural Adult Work for their work on the promotion of vegetarian food.

THE PROBLEM

Tobias is tackling some specific food related problems. While the consequences of transport or energy consumption are well known, the consequences of the Western staple diet with an emphasis on animal products are still underestimated. Not only that: The issue of meat consumption is for many still a taboo and is overall a polarizing issue with little middle ground.

In fact, our current and increasing levels of meat consumption are contributing dramatically to some of the most daunting challenges that we face locally and globally—climate change, food insecurity, health problems, and the inhumane treatment of animals.

Our meat consumption, and consequently meat production, has been exponentially increasing since the 1950s. Between 1950 and 2000, the world's population doubled from 2.7 to 6.7 billion people while meat production increased fivefold from 45 to 233 million tons per year. The Food and Agriculture Organization predicts now that the production of meat will double within the next 50 years, to reach 465 million tons in 2050.

Consumption is particularly high in Western countries, with developing countries following example. For instance, people in Belgium eat on average 160 grams of (mostly animal) protein a day, which is 60 percent more than the recommended maximum.

These levels of meat production and consumption have dramatic impacts:

- The meat industry is contributing vastly to climate change. Many people are surprised to learn that the contribution of the livestock sector to global warming amounts to 18 percent of greenhouse gas emissions, through the production of carbon dioxide, methane, and nitrous oxides.

- At the individual level, excessive meat consumption has a direct effect on human health; the excessive intake of animal fat leads to obesity, and to an increase in several health risks (i.e. heart diseases and cholesterol).

- On a more macro level, the methods of the meat industry have a very negative impact on the food security of millions of people. Feeding millions of animals uses up to 25 percent of arable land, and 45 percent of all wheat is produced for animal feed. This inflates subsistence food prices and accelerates the global food crisis.

- The market dynamics of an increase in production tied to cost containment forces billions of animals to spend their short life in inhumane conditions.

These insights should have already led to important changes in meat consumption—yet this has not been the case. Exacerbating these negative externalities are the following four issues, all of which Tobias is directly tackling:

First, the debate on meat has up to now mostly been dominated by animal rights "ideologists" who are primarily motivated by and focus on the animal rights issue—and present the issue as black and white—you eat meat, or you do not. In their world, there is no middle ground.

Second, animal rights "ideologists" have almost no interest in the other meat related problems; however, the animal rights argument is for most people not as strong as the other ones (i.e. climate, health, and food security), which remain largely unknown by the general public and decision-makers.

Third, the market does not provide enough diverse, qualitative and well-marketed alternative options for meatless meals that could counterbalance prevailing consumption patterns.

And fourth, due to the prevailing messages, "meat" is considered a provocative and polarizing issue—something policymakers

better keep their hands off. What one eats is then very much considered as a private matter, and institutional actors tend to play a very limited role in the market. Existing regulations focus on guaranteeing some quality in processes and ingredients, and not by moderating the behaviors of consumers, producers, and food suppliers (i.e. restaurants, schools, and companies).

THE STRATEGY

Tobias is simultaneously tackling all angles of the problem, by motivating rather than moralizing all stakeholders and incentivizing them to change their behavior.

Seeing the need to foster a very broad base of support to trigger sufficient change and impact, Tobias targets consumers and decision-makers with the best-adapted strategies. To reach the general public, he informs and offers inspiration. On the information side, he focuses on the health and environmental impact of meat. To inspire consumers to take different choices, Tobias imagines and develops a range of public events and attracts the media to reach an even broader audience. For example, the Golden Carrot Award is an annual prize recognizing a person who made a special contribution to vegetarian food. Another example is the organization of seven-course gourmet dinners that bring vegetarian haute cuisine to the table of all interested. A cook trained at the world's number one restaurant, El Bulli, prepares the menu.

> "It is, indeed, the first time that the authorities of a major city, and a modest association specializing in the promotion of vegetarianism, decided to proclaim a day of the week day without meat."
>
> —*Steunpuntjeugd*

Tobias created the Ethical Vegetarian Association (EVA) to frame his actions and to facilitate his impact. The history of EVA is a history full of events to convince the general population that to eat more vegetarian food is not only necessary, but is tasty and fun. This is crucial in a culture where people consider eating good food as an essential element of life and where sharing good food is an essential part of social interaction.

Tobias indeed produces and leverages accessible information that focuses on the multi-dimensional consequences of our meat consumption. Well aware of the sensitivity of the issue and to prevent counter-publicity, he is working closely with scientists to back all pieces of information with scientific data. To reach decision-makers, he organizes high-level meetings and seminars and even developed a Vegetarian Info Centre with information for decision-makers to build more sensible policies.

But Tobias is going much further than just advocacy: He is stimulating behavior change among a large number of citizens. To empower people to considerably reduce their meat consumption, he sees the necessity to increase the visibility and accessibility of vegetarian food. He is educating consumers on how to cook without meat, through real life and online lessons and is showing them where to purchase meatless products, through the production and distribution of Veggie maps. These veggie maps are powerful marketing tools as 200,000 of them have already been distributed, incentivizing the restaurant industry to offer vegetarian options. Tobias is also supporting restaurants through training courses for traditional chefs and a veggie chef cookbook.

The history of EVA is a history full of events to convince the general population that to eat more vegetarian food is not only necessary, but is tasty and fun.

Tobias is building strong partnerships with businesses by developing formulas that will be sustainable and profitable. To stimulate the supply side, he is building partnerships with agro-industrial firms who are offering sustainable solutions. An example of such a company is Alpro, a large distributor of soy products in Europe that is involved in developing sustainable alternatives for the traditional meat-producers.

To catalyze and accelerate the shift in demand and supply, Tobias is engaging institutions in fostering a more enabling environment. He demonstrates to local governments and companies their personal interest in reducing the meat consumption of their constituents, for example, to reduce their carbon footprint or to improve the health of their citizens. He then offers them easy, low-cost and high value-added tools to join the movement. Tobias created Thursday Veggie Day, a nationwide campaign where all institutional actors join in a campaign to offer vegetarian meals on Thursdays. Veggie Day has received worldwide attention, and its growth is viral—citizens and decision-makers everywhere are approaching Tobias for advice and support.

THE PERSON

Tobias is 36-years-old and was born in Ghent, Belgium. His mother was a teacher of mathematics to high school students and his father was a businessman, buying antiques (i.e. rugs, jewelry,

and artwork) in central Asia and selling them in Belgium. Both his parents raised their children with the belief that it is important to do good, and that it is essential to be excellent in what one does. Both elements are very much present in the personality of Tobias.

Tobias studied Germanic philology, the study of Dutch and English languages and literature for a master's degree, followed by a master's degree in Comparative Cultural Sciences, which is similar to the field of anthropology. He obtained a teacher's degree and also obtained a degree as an analyst-programmer.

Tobias first taught IT in a high school, and later worked at the university language center combining language, teaching and IT skills. All this time he was already heading EVA (founded in 2000) as a volunteer, after hours from his apartment.

When EVA became possibly the first vegetarian organization in the world to receive structural government subsidies (after having submitted a well received strategic plan) there was the possibility to pay for its first two full-time staff members. Tobias chose not to be one of them, as he felt he could already do a lot as a volunteer, and instead used the funds to recruit other people for a bigger workforce. However, after two external directors and a three-month period of introspection in South America, Tobias decided the best thing to do would be to become director himself, a position he still holds.

Tobias' evolution has been quite remarkable—from a rather shy boy, he developed into a person full of creative ideas, with the confidence to launch these ideas, and to make them real. He also evolved from a die-hard vegetarian into someone who focuses on change, and goes for the middle ground where impact is maximal. As an example, Tobias has no problems entering into negotiations with McDonald's.

For Tobias, this is the work of a lifetime. He intends to remain director for a long time to come, but wants to dedicate more time on the vision, the strategy, and the development of the organization so that it may grow to its fullest potential. This is why EVA recently hired a HR manager—to take management work out of his hands. ♦

GÜLCAN NITSCH

GERMANY

**Intercultural Relations/
Race Relations**

Gülcan Nitsch develops new approaches to recruit Germany's largest minority group, Turkish immigrants, in environmental protection efforts. Gülcan is diversifying and broadening the base of the country's environmental movement, she is creating a healthier environment and helping to foster better integrated communities.

THE NEW IDEA

Using a highly personalized and high touch communications approach, Gülcan works directly with Turkish media and the Turkish community to mobilize Turks around environmental issues. From the preparation of information materials to the community empowerment strategies she adapts, Gülcan focuses on the day-to-day world and the everyday language of her target group. Tailoring the messages and strategies to her audience often means leaving behind complicated modern environmental protection mechanisms, and instead, focusing on basic concepts that appeal directly to the needs of her target group, i.e. being more economical with household resources and energy.

To roll out her ideas and programs, Gülcan founded Yesil Cember (Turkish for Green Circle) in 2006. While her first priority was to develop adequate Turkish information materials about simple and hands-on ways to protect the environment (i.e. the usage of energy saving light bulbs, recycling, and how to avoid toxic chemicals), the initiative has developed into a knowledge hub for effective approaches to raise awareness about environmental protection among migrant groups. Yesil Cember began with public relations (e.g. every year Gülcan organizes the national Turkish environmental day), and moved toward more hands-on projects, including training migrant women to become environmental consultants for their communities. After a 30-hour training they begin to consult friends and relatives, then, step by step, reach out to their community, gaining more self-confidence and feeling a strong sense of responsibility for their environment.

Ultimately, Gülcan's approach to sensitizing the Turkish community to environmental causes could be spread not only to more immigrant communities but also to other public issues such as participation in democracy or violence prevention.

THE PROBLEM

Many immigrant communities in Germany, in particular, the large population of Turkish immigrants, remain disconnected from environmental protection efforts. Environmental groups have failed to integrate the Turkish community as well as other immigrant populations into their efforts. This results in key segments of German society not yet embracing environmental concerns as one key shared challenge facing the country.

A lack of understanding of environmental issues and knowledge about environmental protection measures among the Turkish community in Germany results partially from the fact that there are no materials available in Turkish nor educational activities reflecting Turkish cultural and educational background or living realities. Another reason for the lack of mobilization around environmental issues is that issues such as employment, integration, education, and low income are often placed higher on the agendas of Turkish communities.

Yesil Cember focuses on resources for its target group, migrants, with awareness raising, training and hands-on projects.

Before Gülcan began her work, German environmental organizations had not seen migrants as a relevant target group and therefore had no mechanisms by which to engage them. Migrant organizations, similarly, did not perceive environmental protection as a relevant subject of their work. Until now, they have worked largely without connections on both the institutional and individual levels and did not realize the potential synergies of their specific competences and experiences.

THE STRATEGY

Gülcan recognized that simply translating existing German materials into Turkish was not a sufficient measure to solve the problems facing Germany's environmental community. Instead, she started to develop her own hands-on Turkish information material which includes pictures, metaphors, and references to Turkish daily life that could be easily understood by everyone, including the semi-illiterate. Parallel to the development of these materials, which nowadays can be found at almost all information stands in Turkish community centers around Germany, Gülcan convinced influential Turkish community associations (i.e. which exist in almost every Turkish community throughout Germany) to partner with her in organizing the first Turkish Environmental Day in Berlin. In spite of great skepticism, the event was a huge success. It has become an annual event, attracting hundreds of people and triggering many more environmental activities for the migrant communities.

Having intensified her collaboration with Turkish migrant associations, Gülcan and her team started giving two-hour lessons on environmental protection at countless Turkish community centers throughout Berlin and other cities in Germany. They quickly realized that women were especially eager to learn how to save energy and therefore money, how to avoid toxic cleaning agents and plastics, as well and other environmentally unfriendly actions. Behavioral changes as a result of the trainings do not only result in positive effects for the environment, but also in the better integration of the training's beneficiaries in their neighborhoods and ultimately, in society.

Looking for ways to scale her impact and the number of people being reached by Yesil Cember, Gülcan developed a 30-hour training course that educates women to be multipliers in their communities. Through its trainings Yesil Cember is catalyzing new local changemakers, thus spreading the model and its impact in ways that would have been impossible without encouraging community-members to take initiative. These local changemakers go to the homes of their peers for environmental counseling free of charge. Although the women are paid for their initial counseling, Gülcan found that women often continue their work even after funding ceases, mainly because they enjoy the responsibility they have been given, often for the first time in their lives.

The whole initiative is backed through the support of Turkish Community Associations, which provide space and financial support. This is extremely important as it gives Yesil Cember tremendous visibility and builds trust within the Turkish community. Backed financially by the German Environment Foundation and scientifically evaluated by the University of Cottbus, Gülcan is now replicating the model in at least seven other German cities by training members of local Turkish community organizations to become representatives of Yesil Cember. These local representatives train new multipliers and oversee their face-to-face counseling.

> "Nitsch is reaching out to the Turkish community in Germany, talking about environmental issues and distributing reusable shopping bags along with Turkish-language pamphlets on the environment."
>
> —*Treehugger*

Besides developing new information materials, organizing community activities and training multipliers, Gülcan is extensively promoting collaboration between German environmental organizations, Turkish migrant associations, state agencies, Turkish and German media corporations, and other relevant stakeholders. An expert in the field of environmental education for migrants, Gülcan is invited to share her experiences at conferences and seminars, and is training other environmental organizations in how to adapt her experiences in their work. Eager to find new ways to maximize her impact Gülcan is currently developing trainings for Turkish businesses, helping them to save energy and become carbon-conscious companies.

THE PERSON

Gülcan has dedicated her life to environmental education and the full integration of immigrants and other marginalized communities. She was born in Berlin as the second daughter of four to Turkish parents who belong to the first generation Turkish immigrants. Since her childhood, Gülcan seized opportunities where others saw only problems. For example, at the age of 18, she formed the first German-Turkish self-help group for stutterers.

By training women, Yesil Cember is catalyzing new local changemakers, thus spreading the model and its impact in ways that would have been impossible without encouraging community-members to take the initiative.

Realizing at an early age that humans have to live in balance with nature, Gülcan pursued her studies in biology at the Free University of Berlin—after attending elementary school in Turkey and finishing high school in Germany. Gülcan has worked with many leading environmental and human rights organizations, including Greenpeace, Amnesty International, the WWF, and the German Green Party—investing the majority of her free time to societal causes and the improvement of society. In her late twenties, Gülcan joined Friends of the Earth (BUND), Germany's biggest environmental association, which she used as the platform to introduce many of her successful programs. Gülcan launched Yesil Cember at BUND (i.e. the first time a BUND volunteer had ever created and launched a nationwide program) and to this day, uses BUND as a fiscal umbrella, while managing all aspects of the program and fundraising.

Often referred to as the "Green-Turk" by the German press, Gülcan is a calm listener filled with a deep-rooted passion for change. She has been a powerful voice advocating for new and innovative ways to advance environmental protection measures. While public speaking, Gülcan delivers her messages with both affection and great insistence, always tailoring her message to connect with the specific needs and traditions of her audiences, whether that be a group of semi-illiterate Turkish women in a Berlin neighborhood or a delegation of 25 mayors from Turkey willing to learn about how to adapt her approaches to their country context. ♦

MATTHIEU OUÉDRAOGO

BURKINA FASO

Agriculture

Income Generation

Natural Resource Management

Throughout the southern frontier of the Sahel desert, southern Mauritania, north and western Senegal, parts of northern and western Mali, the northern region of Burkina Faso and then eastward, desertification has advanced steadily since the mid twentieth century, taking away arable land, and threatening the agricultural livelihoods of small producers in Burkina Faso. However, along the edge of this southern "semi-desert," small family farms passed down from generation to generation still grow cereals such as millet and sorghum. Matthieu Ouédraogo believes family farms are at the heart of regional innovation. By assisting the growth and regeneration of local plants, to helping to build communities of small producers that replicate local innovations, Matthieu hopes to foster a spirit of entrepreneurship among farmers across the region.

THE NEW IDEA

Local farmers have developed various techniques for assisting plant regeneration in this semi-desert belt, particularly in growing new forests and water systems that can trap humidity and increase crop yield. One example of an innovative farming practice is the construction of a contoured barrier of small stones which guides and evenly disperses infrequent rainfall around crops. However, unlike a regular water canal, the stone barriers also act as depositories where seeds carried by the rainfall can take root and eventually offer shade to crops. Another example of naturally assisted regrowth is when local farmers feed tree seeds to their livestock and then plant the manure (including the tree seeds) and cereal seeds in *zains*—small carefully dug holes. Eventually, the fertilizer assists the seeds to grow, resulting in fertile cereal plants and trees that can shade them.

Matthieu's understanding of naturally assisted regeneration extends to innovations in distribution. For example, an innovative small producer in Matthieu's network has engineered a method for storing potatoes in large underground cellars which is an entirely new approach in the Sahel. This allows the farmer to protect their crop yield and that of surrounding farmers until well after the harvest, when the price of potatoes increases substantially. This particular idea was inspired by a trip to Europe sponsored by Swiss volunteers, where the farmer saw a wine cave and realized

that he could keep potatoes cool without refrigeration in a 50 foot deep cellar with adequate air circulation, even if summer surface temperature exceeded 120 degrees.

Matthieu plans to connect small farmers to each others new ideas, and to introduce farmers to more effective uses of locally available natural resources. He will achieve this by a) creating improved supply chains through working together with business entrepreneurs b) working with local governments, particularly with respect to gaining formal recognition for traditional land rights so that small farmers can use their land as collateral in taking out small loans and c) urging other citizen organizations (COs) to identify and encourage innovative small farmers to foster a community of small farmer-innovators.

By assisting the growth and regeneration of local plants, to helping to build communities of small producers that replicate local innovations, Matthieu hopes to foster a spirit of entrepreneurship among farmers across the region.

THE PROBLEM

The government and the citizen sector responded to increasing desertification in the Sahel in the 1970s with widely publicized reforestation. While the campaigns initially were a strong and much needed movement, ultimately these campaigns failed for a variety of reasons. Due to a limited follow-up movement and the government's focus on agriculture which emphasized less on empowering small farmers and more on providing subsidies, small farmers become passive and did not mobilize around this movement. When gradual desertification forced a shift in commercial cultivation, the government diverted resources to new commercial cultivation rather than combating the problem. This left small farmers in the most affected areas to fend for themselves.

Small farmers in arid territories also struggle to create sustainable livelihoods from farming as a result of increased pressure on the land from government land purchases. The Burkina Faso government has formal legal rights to all land except those specifically ceded by the government through concession. In an effort to privatize agriculture, the government has now created a system for transferring traditional farming rights to formally owned land, however this process is currently too expensive for small farmers. As a result, this system instead favors investors who are willing to buy up small traditional landholdings and convert them into commercial farming ventures. This has not yet impacted small farmers in extremely arid regions, as agro-industry investors have found better opportunities in other parts of the country which offer the prospect of better economic returns. However, this shift inflicts increasing pressure on desert land which now must yield more resources to support the needs of communities. While small producers in the semi-desert belt are demonstrating that farmer-led innovation makes environmentally sustainable productivity possible on small farms, the government's unwillingness to allow small farmers formal access to their land rights and to financial services hampers the ability of small farmers to fully explore these innovations.

THE STRATEGY

Matthieu's strategy is divided into three steps. His first step is to select and create an association of innovative small farmers. The selection criteria for these farmers are whether they use original and innovative applications and approaches to new ideas. Matthieu tests these ideas by how much interest they attract. Thus far, he has found that generally these innovations have attracted the interest of anywhere from 15 to 50 small farmers. Using this criterion, Matthieu has selected 64 innovative small farmer association members in Sanmatenge, 47 in Passore, 55 in Yatenga, and 43 in Zondoma. These regions are in the four driest northern provinces of Burkina Faso.

> "Matthieu Ouédraogo assembled the farmers in his area, and they were experimenting with techniques to restore the soil, some of them traditions that Ouédraogo had heard about in school."
>
> —*National Geographic Magazine*

Matthieu's second step is to mobilize farmers who have adopted an innovation of the association members and to encourage them to create new innovations of their own. This could be a refinement of what they have already learned, a combination of innovations from other members of the association, or a brand new approach that they want to introduce. Matthieu's short-term goal is to increase the number of farming families affected by his members to grow by 50-fold in the next several years through word of mouth communication between his association and

networks of farmers in neighboring countries such as Mali, Ivory Coast, and Ghana.

The third step in Matthieu's strategy is to draw attention to this initiative in Burkina Faso as well as in neighboring countries where small farmers are struggling with similar challenges. In Burkina Faso, Matthieu needs the government to formally agree to lower the cost for small farmers to own land, and the government's active cooperation thus permitting the process of land ownership to run fairly and effectively. He also wants to spread his approach out to the most arid provinces in central Burkina Faso, and to other regions of the country where naturally assisted regeneration can curb and mitigate recently created pockets of deforestation. Decades of field work and research have taught Matthieu that conditions in the region degrade rapidly when significant areas are deforested. Without forest growth, the desert areas lose their critical source of humidity thus stunting other vegetation and accelerating the likelihood of further desertification.

THE PERSON

Matthieu was born to a poor family in Bourcy, the northern and driest region of Burkina Faso. He worked from a very young age to support his family, briefly attending a Koranic school when he was nine-years-old, but otherwise spending most of his time working for his livelihood. Matthieu was baptized in the Catholic Church when he was 18, and he learned to read and write while living in a Catholic monastery for three years in his early twenties. During this time, he worked as a gardener. He continued to work in agriculture after he returned to Bourcy and worked with Peace Corps volunteers on a series of gardening and reforestation projects. Matthieu also taught himself to cook, and was hired as a chef by a succession of foreign families, while he continued his work with Peace Corps Volunteers.

From 1985 until 2002 Matthieu operated a series of agro-forestry projects, first with Oxfam, and then with ORFA, an organization focused on conducting grassroots-level research. In 2002 he decided to leave ORFA to determine whether a more "assisted" approach to working with small producers rather than a "technical" one would yield improved results. Matthieu experimented for six years with this concept until he felt certain that selecting and working with innovative small farmers held the greatest promise for harnessing the ideas of innovators and creating a realistic basis for guiding future agro-development. In 2008 he began to attract attention to his work through radio programs, public speaking engagements, and the "Theatre Forum" framework created by Ashoka Fellow Prosper Kompaoré.

Matthieu believes that naturally assisted regeneration carried forward by small farmers' innovations will create sufficient forest cover to trap humidity, to increase crop yield (i.e. especially for cereals and smaller vegetable plots), and to provide sufficient forage for livestock. Matthieu believes encouraging farmers to innovate is an answer to creating a vibrant farm economy that can combat desertification in the Sahel. ♦

KARIN RESSEL

GERMANY

Capacity Building

Youth Development

Karin Ressel empowers students to realize their potential in vocational careers by reinventing their relationship between each other, their schools, and future employers. Through hands-on learning modules based on practical experiences and skills, students' assess their interests and aptitudes, while prospective employers increase their recruitment and retention rates.

THE NEW IDEA

Karin has invented a set of hands-on learning modules that simulate real-life work experiences in order to support young people to identify their strengths and to prepare them for the practical aspects of a future career. Berufsparcours® (which roughly translates as Profession Circuit) targets young people from grades 8 to 10 who, during one day, pass through individual learning stations where they can test different technical professions, from a mechanic to a policeman or a secretary, in a very practical manner. To create a long-term and effective intervention for youth, Karin works with schools to implement her modules and toolkits into curricula to provide outlets for youth to test their interests.

Karin has also brought her learning modules to companies. She works with employers (i.e. many of Germany's largest industrial enterprises) to integrate them into local job fairs and recruitment processes, thereby allowing for direct, hands-on interaction between recruiters and applicants. Berufsparcours® is transforming the recruitment practices of companies, from a reactive application process to a process that involves proactive, personal outreach and the qualifications of broader target groups.

Each year Berufsparcours® conducts 110 Profession Tours in schools and 90 company fairs in eight German counties, reaching approximately 50,000 pupils yearly. The success of Berufsparcours® has led Karin to license her modules to student-run companies and schools directly, who then spread the product further.

THE PROBLEM

In Germany, despite high levels of youth unemployment, many companies are unable to fill their training vacancies (i.e. particularly in apprenticeship programs) due to a lack of suited applicants. Firms requiring technical skills forecast huge problems for their industries in coming years due to shortages of skilled labor. In March 2010, more than 240,000 young people were registered as looking for employment, though companies had more

than 200,000 vacancies. This trend has companies increasingly worrying about a shortage of skilled workers.

This shortage is especially problematic in the field of technical professions, with experts predicting a lack of more than 175,000 suited trainees in five years. They complain about badly trained applicants lacking practical knowledge and necessary personal skills. What is more, they incur high costs due to the handling of thousands of applications reaching them each year with little indication if the person has the necessary talent and skills for the job. Nevertheless, they stick to their recruiting strategy based on glossy brochures at conventional job fairs. Karin has calculated that 1,000 young people applying to 100 companies cost the companies around 22M EUR (US$2.783M) in initial screenings.

Young people, on the other hand, lack the practical education to prepare them for these placements, and they have little support in identifying what industries and positions would be suited to their talents and interests. For example, half of Germany's graduates from Hauptschule (i.e. a secondary school geared toward students who will enter technical trades) fail to find an apprenticeship within one year of graduation. The result is unemployment and its many negative psychological effects and high social costs.

Schools typically do not have the means to solve this problem on their own. With too few resources and rigid, state mandated curricula, they are too focused on theory and not enough on practical experience. Schools rarely actively assist their students to discover their individual talents and translate these into the best-suited jobs.

Students, on the other hand, know little about the richness of more than 150 potential apprenticeships available in Germany, and most end up applying to the 15 to 20 most common with little knowledge about what they can expect from them. This narrow focus is especially true for girls in technical professions, since company recruitment, technical courses in school, family, and public opinion is still dominated by a male perspective. Left alone at this difficult transitional period between school and professional life, most applicants lack the endurance and motivation needed for successful applications. This contributes to a high youth unemployment rate, which stood at 10 percent among 19 to 25-year-olds in 2009.

> "Adolescents often have little knowledge about occupations. As an antidote, a large number of young people in a matter of hours meet and evaluate 14 professions."
>
> —*Der Paritatische*

THE STRATEGY

Karin knows that hands-on practical experience is the best way to excite and engage young people. It is also the only way for them to find out what their talents are and what they enjoy doing. She created Berufsparcours® in 1994 to provide young people with these experiences and is implementing them through her organization Technikzentrum Minden-Lübbecke e.V., with a staff of 12 full and part-time professionals and 18 volunteers.

At the core of Karin's strategy is to offer young people simple practical exercises, each developed to synthesize a core aspect of a profession. The exercises require mental and physical manipulation which allows students to test out, discover, and understand what working in a particular technical profession may actually entail. Karin is implementing this hands-on experience at different levels: She offers professional tours to schools, where 300 pupils for one day can experience 20 professions in a practical manner (i.e. based upon the 440 modules she has created so far). Teachers are each responsible for one module, thus learning the methodology, but also realizing the talents and potential of their pupils. Schools pay 2,400 EUR (US$3,337) per "school course" and as most do not have the funding to cover all costs, Karin and her organization assist them to apply for suitable funds. Each year, Karin offers around 110 school courses.

Each year Berufsparcours® conducts 110 Profession Tours in schools and 90 company fairs in eight German counties, reaching approximately 50,000 pupils yearly.

Companies can take part in "company tours" where approximately 50 local companies and 400 to 500 young people from surrounding schools participate. For a fee, Karin helps companies design the practical exercises, which are supervised by company recruiters. Young people interested in the profession can directly get in contact with the firms and get a better understanding of the skills required. The companies benefit from directly testing the talent and motivation of the potential applicant.

Additionally, Karin expands her concept through the development, production, and distribution of her modules. She also organizes competitions, in which student-run companies develop modules as well as distribution strategies, thus generating income and learning entrepreneurial and practical skills on the job. What is more, Technikzentrum has developed a licensing model, through which it is training other organizations on how to facilitate her courses and use her modules for both school and company settings. So far around 50 licenses have been sold.

An important part of the success of the Berufsparcours® lies in Karin's attention to detail. It is also important that pupils get a thorough introduction before they start the course. They need to understand that their success in life partially depends on their ability to find a job which they actually like doing. Another important aspect is her ability to bring together all necessary stakeholders and implement Berufsparcours® among existing systems, working with and licensing her model to schools, educational institutions, companies, governmental agencies, and conventional job fairs.

Third, Karin has a special focus on making technical professions interesting for girls, using simple techniques, i.e. providing tools and gloves suited for smaller female hands, and changing exercise goals from producing cars into producing picture frames or flowers.

Since founding Berufsparcours®, Karin has trained 500,000 young people, 10,000 teachers, and 2,700 companies in eight German counties. Approximately 200 schools use her system regularly as well as 45 institutions (i.e. the Ministry of Economy in Baden-Wurttemberg). Additionally, Karin has placed approximately 325 adults, who supported the organization and supervision of courses, in jobs. Although the impact of this has not yet been measured scientifically, anecdotal evidence shows that all involved stakeholders change their attitudes: Girls begin to consider a career in technical professions, pupils report having found something they really like, and teachers see their pupils with more respect for their abilities. Additionally, companies realize how much money and energy they save through this method of recruiting—with much better results.

Karin's vision is to train even more schools and companies to implement her hands-on learning modules in their yearly recruiting/job training routine and engage more young people in manufacturing and inventing modules. What is more, she is working on establishing profession centers, where kids can go to experience professions and discover their talents.

THE PERSON

Karin has always been drawn to technical work, inventing her own alarm or sound system while still at school. As women were not encouraged to take on technical professions she studied administrative studies and worked as a career counselor at the Federal Defense Administration. After eight years, she gave up her status as a civil servant and its lifetime security, when she realized she could not change the system while working within it.

Karin studied educational science and additionally taught courses on career counseling for pupils at 27 different education centers. Her focus on students gradually expanded to adults, especially women. Karin invented courses to bring day-to-day technical know-how to women, teaching them how to work with tools, materials, and objects. Together with 25 other women she founded an association for women interested in technical professions and craftsmanship.

Karin started to cooperate closely with the equal opportunities officer of Bochum, developing several training programs for technically interested girls, counseling offers for women reentering the workforce, and women setting up their own businesses. After several other initiatives and jobs, from founding an environmental women's village to inventing a new pedagogical focused waste separation program, Karin founded the association, SEFRA with 60 women in 1994, changing its name into Technikzentrum in 2000. Her early focus was to encourage girls and women to take on technical professions, then, step by step she expanded the target group to boys as well as to other professions. When Karin had to move out of their training center in 2001 because the city had to demolish the building, she invented the idea of mobile support—instead of having pupils come to her center, Karin reached out to them, creating Berufsparcours®. ◆

PENCHOM SAETANG

THAILAND

Capacity Building

Conservation Preservation

By initiating citizen-led industrial pollution monitoring, Penchom Saetang is amplifying the Thai public demand for corporate and government accountability to community health and the environment, at the neighborhood level, as well as national policy.

THE NEW IDEA

Penchom established the first citizen network to monitor industrial pollution in Thailand. In the face of pro-industry economic policies and ineffective environmental guidelines, she is equipping communities impacted by industrial pollution with the tools needed to independently demand socially and environmentally responsible industry practices.

Penchom's work targets "fence-line" communities living in the shadow of Thailand's rapid development. Her efforts cover a wide spectrum of areas: Enhancement of neighborhood capacity to collect pollutant data; support of environmental litigation; and advocacy for a national policy to guarantee the public "right to know" of released pollutants. Penchom has also created an unusual opportunity for Thai scientists, otherwise silenced by organizational policy, to support the citizen sector in demanding corporate and government accountability.

> "The main components of Pollution Watch are research, monitoring industrial policy and pollution problems, empowerment and support for environmental justice."
>
> —*Kairos*

To ensure that citizen concerns are represented in the latest negotiations by industries and the government on climate change, Penchom has pioneered a national campaign for "climate justice." She works with a broad range of citizen networks across Thailand to demand that measureable changes be made to create a socially and environmentally responsible industry in developing countries.

THE PROBLEM

Industrial development's adverse health and environmental effects have largely been unchecked and unnoticed for more than three decades in Thailand. Each year, industries produce approximately 1 million tons of hazardous waste, of which an indeterminately large portion is improperly disposed and presumed to be illegally dumped in open landfills, vacant land, nearby waterways and the sea. Factories do not receive penalties or other measures of accountability for improperly disposing of hazardous waste. While transporters can be subjected to a fine, it is nominal—the highest fee of 2,000 baht (US$60) for open dumping—and rarely enforced.

Due in great part to community resistance, at least 10 heavily-polluting industries have been delayed in the last decade, including coal mining operations and coal-fired power plants.

The public largely lacks information about hazardous industrial chemicals, which often pose the greatest threat to low-income populations. In 1991, the illegal disposal of chemicals was suspected to have caused a chemical explosion and three-day fire in central Bangkok—the largest chemical accident to date. The fire destroyed the homes of more than 5,000 slum residents and hospitalized 1,700 patients from chemical exposure. While estimates revealed that the fire burned more than 3,000 chemicals, the government only released a list of 23 substances. Doctors protested that they were unable to provide accurate treatment. Yet two decades later, similar chemical accidents, along with complaints of open dumping and toxic effects from industrial pollution, still occur regularly across Thailand.

Corruption within government agencies has produced an institutional unwillingness to acknowledge or address the negative impacts that industrial waste has on community health and environmental conditions. While multiple government agencies maintain independent records of the import, transfer, treatment, and disposal of hazardous material, they possess no collective inventory. Even scientists working in laboratories backed by government or industrial funds, have had little opportunity to contribute data on this controversial issue.

Approximately 20 years ago, the Ministry of Public Health founded the National Institute for Occupational and Environmental Medicine to investigate possible causes of deaths at an electronics factory. The institute published a report suggesting that workers died from lead poisoning in the factory. Within weeks, government officials removed the institute from the investigation and appointed a new commission composed entirely of industrial hygienists, rather than physicians. After conducting tests on working conditions—and not workers' health—the newly appointed agency published a report vindicating the factory. No government agency with active budget allocation is directly responsible for investigating and treating the health and environmental effects of industrial waste.

THE STRATEGY

Despite political and financial pressures preventing the public disclosure of industrial pollution's hazardous effects, Penchom has established the first independent agency to empower disadvantaged fence-line communities with scientific information and the know-how to detect industrial pollution to negotiate for increased government and corporate accountability.

An important component of Penchom's work has always been to create public pressure for the government disclosure of information—a key component to solving the country's hazardous waste problems. In response to the 1991 explosion of chemical warehouses in Bangkok, Penchom co-founded a campaign demanding the release of information regarding the 3,000 involved chemicals. Collaborating with workers' rights advocates and Ashoka Fellows Somboon Srikhamdokkae and Saree Aongsomwang, they established a committee consisting of affected slum residents and relevant professionals, to demand investigations into the health damage caused by the accident. In 1993 Penchom joined a local campaign exposing the government's burial of the fire's chemical wastes across a pristine forest located in Western Thailand. The campaign sparked national controversy and ultimately compelled the government to excavate the hazardous remains and rebury them, using the proper safety measures.

Bypassing institutional obstacles, Penchom has established direct partnerships between citizen networks and relevant professionals to initiate pollution-detection trainings for fence-line communities. Community members also learn how to present scientifically sound evidence at negotiation tables with factory owners, public authorities, policymakers and, on occasion, judges. In late 1997 Penchom founded the Campaign for Alternative Industry Network (CAIN), a national group to link disadvantaged communities most heavily-affected by Thailand's industrial development projects, such as coal-fired power plants, petrochemical factories, oil refineries, steel mills, lead mines, and landfills.

In 2004, in collaboration with the international environmental monitoring groups Greenpeace and Global Community Monitor, CAIN released the first analysis of toxic air contaminants in Map Ta Phut Industrial Estate, the world's eighth largest petrochemicals hub located on Thailand's eastern shore. Her group collected the air pollution data and continuously monitored the air pollution. They used a simple bucket device to collect the air samples for analysis. Penchom and her group joined the Bucket Brigade of Global Community Monitor in California and the Community Environmental Monitor group in India. The results and accompanying community campaigns led to further disclosure of other pollutant information. For instance, earlier findings from the National Cancer Institute revealed that Map Ta Phut residents were three-times more likely to develop cancer. More scientists and students came to conduct research in Map Ta Phut, leading

to an unusual abundance of scientific data on industrial pollution and health impacts. The findings played a crucial role in winning two famous lawsuits: In March and December 2009, two court rulings declared a national government agency "negligent" in declaring pollution control measures and ordered the halt of all 76 new industrial projects in the area.

Penchom's organization has created a rare opportunity for Thai scientists to provide controversial data. She has created partnerships between residents affected by industrial pollution and researchers in human biology, plant biology, environmental engineering, and oncology. Moreover, sympathetic government employees often leak useful information to Penchom's organization. Penchom shares research findings and pollutant information not only among neighborhood residents, but also with communities across Thailand that face similar risks.

Penchom's work has created an information exchange gathering for the past 12 years, which is now enabling communities to start negotiating for better safety standards. She has garnered national support from academics as well as scientists and doctors for health impact assessments (HIA) of new industrial projects. The HIA concept is gaining interest from top policymakers as well as national institutions. Introducing the concept of the Community Right-to-Know Act, Penchom is also conducting the policy study for a Pollutant Release and Transfer Register, to publish information on industrial chemicals and their whereabouts, thus making it widely available on the Internet in future and increasing pressure for the government and private industries to be accountable for pollutants.

Penchom works with a broad range of citizen networks across Thailand to demand that measurable changes be made to create socially and environmentally responsible industries in developing countries.

Until safety measures against industrial waste represent the norm in Thai society, Penchom and the allied civil society continues to enable communities to resist unsafe industries and industrial policies. Due to strong community resistance, at least 10 heavily-polluting industries have been delayed in the last decade, including coal mining operations and coal-fired power plants. It has, however, been at the expense of at least 10 assassinations of environmentalists in the past decade. Penchom herself has been harassed, and some of her funding agencies have been called in by government authorities for questioning.

Nonetheless, Penchom continues to link local community struggles with national campaigns for social and environmental justice in Thailand's industrial development policies. For instance, in 2007, Penchom led an international campaign to publicize the contents of a bilateral trade agreement, in which Thailand was to import Japan's hazardous waste in exchange for tariff reductions. Penchom collaborated with a coalition of Japanese citizen organizations (COs) to petition both Thai and Japanese governments for the removal of the clause on hazardous waste import. Her campaign again stirred national and international controversy, but fell on deaf ears with the military junta.

Most recently, Penchom has expanded her coalition of partners within the citizen sector. In 2008, she co-founded the Thailand Working Group for Climate Justice—a national effort of civil society and community organizations that specialize in environmental, health, and community education as well as human rights issues—to pressure corporations and the Thai government to address social and environmental justice as they define and invest in climate change programs. At the Climate Conference in Copenhagen last year, Penchom voiced demands on behalf of Thailand's citizen sector and pressured industrialized countries to cut emissions. In Thailand, she is part of a working group that is proposing alternatives to the 10-year Global Warming Master Plan currently tendered by the national government.

In 2009 Penchom registered her organization as a foundation to highlight its neutral stance as an independent monitoring group. The Ecological Alert and Recovery-Thailand (EARTH) Foundation plans to bridge formal partnerships between affected communities, universities, and government laboratories.

THE PERSON

Born into a working class household of eight siblings, Penchom was the first-generation college graduate. In addition to conducting volunteer work with Bangkok's slum communities, she spent her later years as an undergraduate traveling to rural areas with an alternative theater group. Instead of performing for the audience, she joined to teach children theatrical skills.

Working in Bangkok during the chemical explosion in 1991, Penchom joined citizen advocates to pressure the military junta to release chemical information. Since then, she has developed numerous reports on the health and environmental impact of various hazardous waste instances. Penchom and the local community have also exposed the underlying corruption behind industrial pollution management, publishing reports that link corporate negligence with political interests. She has been appointed as the CO representative to many working groups, including the Senate subcommittee to study national health problems, and the subcommittee to investigate corruption and promote good governance.

In 2006 Penchom received the prestigious Asian Public Intellectual Fellowship, funded by the Nippon Foundation. She chose to study the Japanese citizen movement following severe methylmercury poisoning from industrial wastewater, now widely recognized as the incurable Minamata disease which has affected over 200,000 local residents and more than 10,000 patients. ◆

FULL ECONOMIC
CITIZENSHIP

RODRIGO AGUIRRE DE CÁRCER

SPAIN

Conscious Consumerism

Financial Services/Markets

Rodrigo Aguirre de Cárcer has created a channel through which citizen organizations can monetize the value of in-kind donations from businesses and individuals. By leveraging Internet auction platforms such as eBay, he is reaching large numbers of citizens in a continuous and scalable way, offering them public opportunities to contribute to the citizen sector while also getting great deals on products, services, and experiences.

THE NEW IDEA

Rodrigo has created a new channel through which citizen organizations (COs) can extract liquid value out of in-kind donations from businesses and individuals. SocialBid, his organization, uses online auction platforms—such as eBay—to monetize in-kind donations by selling them to e-consumers. SocialBid accepts and markets a wide variety of products and services (from iPods to holiday trips) that are sold using existing platforms to millions of users with varying interests. Through his online bidding tool, Rodrigo is engaging new contributors that traditional charity auctions and fundraising campaigns generally cannot reach. He is also tapping into a new pool of resources by opening the door for more types of businesses to participate in funding the citizen sector, whose donations of products and services were previously difficult to accept on behalf of most COs.

For example, in 2009 a travel agency wanted to donate what they do best: Organized holiday travel packages. Previously, this donation would have been practically useless and most likely would have been rejected by most COs. SocialBid, AeA (Help in Action), a well-known CO that conducts development programs across the world, and a travel agency worked together to organize an auction that offered 24 holiday trips starting from 1€! The successful campaign raised over 10,000€ for AeA and also raised awareness among thousands of online bidders about AeA's work.

Rodrigo offers a varied marketplace in which businesses contribute, citizens purchase, and COs benefit. In contrast to other approaches, SocialBid provides a continuous flow of monetary exchanges that result in financing for COs. The model, however, goes beyond simply providing liquidity: Rodrigo aims to build a culture where businesses and individuals play a legitimate and recognized role in building a strong citizen sector. On one hand, Rodrigo brings value to in-kind donations from businesses in order for them not only to become useful to COs but also, by

monetizing their value, to help businesses achieve legitimate tax reductions for donations that previously did not apply to in-kind donations. Citizens are drawn to contribute mainly because they find the available products and services cheap and attractive. However, they are also attracted to the fact that their purchases are opportunities to contribute to socially minded initiatives. By bringing these three groups together—businesses, COs, and citizens—Rodrigo is creating synergies that increase funding and awareness through new and large communities of Internet users.

THE PROBLEM

It has always been a challenge for COs to leverage financial resources, particularly liquid funding. In Spain, organizations depend heavily on public funding, comprising an average of 40 percent of CO's budgets. As organizations increase in size and number, and governments decrease their financial support, COs are forced to find new funding sources in order to survive. Moreover, depending on high levels of existing government funding is unhealthy for the sector, as it often limits an organization's freedom in setting goals independent of political interests. Organizations are discovering that diversifying funding sources and including new participants (such as private businesses) is vital not only for their long-term survival, but also for building a strong and competitive citizen sector.

> "SocialBid work ... both benefits donors and NGOs. With zero cost, the non-profit institutions have at their disposal a new sustainable source of income over time and political independence."
>
> —*El Pais*

As COs turn to private businesses for funding, they have discovered that a gap often exists between what they are requesting and what businesses are interested in giving. Increasingly, successful companies are offering in-kind services and products instead of simply handing over cash. Although this trend, often referred to as corporate social responsibility, is theoretically bringing the private sector closer to the citizen sector, it can also present a serious barrier for collaboration. Many times the services and products that businesses offer simply are not useful to the CO in question. For example, a private olive oil manufacturer in Spain, impressed with the work of a CO in an African country, decides to donate what it does best: Prime quality olive oil. However, the sheer logistical costs and complications of bringing that oil to Africa makes it impossible to accept on behalf of the receiving organization, obliging them to decline the offer and lose an opportunity to form an important relationship with a corporate entity.

On paper, the monetary value of in-kind donations that businesses and individuals offer is often much higher than they would be able to give in monetary funding. However, so far there have been very few successful attempts at capturing that value in order for COs to profit fully from quality donations. One such attempt has been the traditional charity auctions in which an intermediate organization gathers high valued objects—generally from celebrities or wealthy individuals (i.e. Babe Ruth baseball bats)—and puts them on sale, donating the benefits to COs of choice. Although these auctions have indeed resulted in needed liquidity for the receiving entities, they are limited to intermittent periods (there are only so many Babe Ruth bats) and to a narrow interest group. Without a channel through which to make in-kind donations profitable to COs, a great opportunity is lost to involve new players in the citizen sector.

THE STRATEGY

SocialBid has quickly become one of the largest eBay shops in Spain, with a community of over 15,000 buyers. In this time, Rodrigo has generated over 400,000€ for COs through the sale of over 7,000 products and services.

Rodrigo is leveraging online auction platforms such as eBay, which alone reaches over 4 million Internet consumers in Spain, to enable a constant flow of exchanges that create liquidity for COs. With this large market of consumers at hand, Rodrigo can commercialize a wide variety of products and services. While on paper the in-kind donations from businesses are made directly to the desired CO, SocialBid handles the logistics, placement, and sales process. This way Rodrigo is able to offer potential buyers thousands of products, services, and experiences (e.g. from mp3 players, to swimsuits, to dinners with celebrities) in a professional and efficient way. Through key partnerships with eBay, Rodrigo has gained privileged placement on the top of search lists as well as in key advertising space.

Rodrigo recognizes that he must make SocialBid's channel cheap, simple, and fast to attract and maintain his users. This requires a highly professional structure able to compete with other online stores. To achieve this, Rodrigo has built his organization as a social business (it receives no profit) that charges small commissions for monetizing in-kind donations. Instead of having a fixed fee for every auction, he charges the donating businesses small-scale commissions on the final price of the items and only if they are sold. Once the items are sold, COs receive the amount raised and are able to give their donors a receipt for the precise amount that was raised through their donation. Businesses can then apply for important tax deductions on their contributions. The simplicity of the process and variety of sellable products has enabled many companies to recycle immobilized stock while contributing toward the social sector without losing brand value. On the other hand, COs are not only receiving much needed liquid donations, but are also developing new links with private companies that opens doors for further engagement opportunities. Rodrigo believes that these relationships are essential to model the synergies produced by different kinds of organizations working together to strengthen the citizen sector. Already a number of non-profit organizations are partnering with for-profit firms on other programs, after having connected through SocialBid.

Rodrigo is also very aware of the important role individual citizen's play in giving real value to in-kind donations made by businesses to COs. As much of Rodrigo's strategy involves identifying incentives for businesses, COs, and individuals to extract value out of this system, he spends a great deal of time analyzing how people initially engage with SocialBid. He found that people learn about SocialBid through different motivations: Some are interested in contributing to a given COs activity, others find the idea interesting, and others simply want a well-priced item that SocialBid offers. However, Rodrigo's aim is for all to know where their money is going and to begin to understand their ability to use their consumer power for social good. He achieves this end with two strategies: First, he includes a small summary of the beneficiary CO's work in the product description that users read while verifying the product's characteristics. Second, Rodrigo is building an online social network of buyers and others interested in using their purchasing power to contribute to the citizen sector. From this network, with already over 3,000 users, he plans to launch other initiatives focused on providing opportunities for further involvement.

Rodrigo is tapping into a new pool of resources by opening the door for more types of businesses to participate in funding the citizen sector, whose donations of products and services were previously difficult to accept on behalf of most COs.

Having engaged over 40 COs and 180 donating businesses and individuals in SocialBid, Rodrigo is focusing on improving the user experience to gain speed and efficiency as well as incorporating new and creative ideas to increase the organization's reach. One of the key aspects Rodrigo is developing is marketing. He has discovered that SocialBid is an excellent platform for both COs to share their work as well as for businesses to show their social commitment to clients. To leverage this capacity, SocialBid has put a series of indicators in place in order to measure the impact that each auction campaign has achieved. This is instrumental in helping Rodrigo stress to COs the importance of communicating their message well and to show businesses that their contributions are important. Rodrigo is now developing a series of studies with strong media impact and strengthening ties with offline media to reach new people, increase traffic to their site, and raise awareness on opportunities for individuals to support the citizen sector.

Rodrigo's goal is that shopping for products that contribute toward social good becomes a central consideration in citizen's consumer routines. He believes that consumer habits can be channeled to support social good and that as people realize this, businesses will find themselves under pressure to prove they are contributing to the citizen sector. To reach this, Rodrigo is focusing on building a critical mass of organizations and individuals involved in SocialBid Spain. As this network is consolidated, Rodrigo has plans to use his multinational partners (eBay as well as participating COs and businesses with international reach) to replicate the model in different countries where e-commerce markets are more stable than in Spain. He is also developing SocialBid's own selling platform to increase traffic as well as test and develop new initiatives.

THE PERSON

As a son of a diplomat, Rodrigo spent his childhood and youth in 4 different continents, giving him the chance to see firsthand important social inequalities between countries and people. For example, when Rodrigo was 10 he moved from the U.S.—where he had spent 5 years—to Pretoria, South Africa. He recalls having great difficulties in understanding why black people were treated so differently from whites and why he couldn't befriend them as he did in the U.S. He was particularly confused when he was asked to vote whether black children could attend his school or not, shortly after Apartheid ended. When he was older, he began carrying out volunteer work to better understand and learn how to solve some of these injustices. It was during this time that Rodrigo also became convinced of the importance of bringing economic resources to COs so that they could become motors of change to bring about social change.

At university, Rodrigo studied economics as a means to help solve social injustices from a financial perspective. He then spent time learning the trade in top firms such as Goldman Sachs and Bain & Co., where he worked on projects in corporate strategy and private equity, among others. At Bain he developed a pioneer pro bono initiative to source COs with high level consulting to improve their practices. Rodrigo also began planning a series of initiatives that connected COs and businesses in significant ways.

While talking with a senior partner at Bain about the possibility of using eBay to sell an in-kind donation of many tons of olive oil to support an organization in Africa, Rodrigo became aware of the vast pool of resources that businesses could generate through non-financial donations. In a relatively short time and with the support of a few key partners, Rodrigo developed the basics of an initiative that would place citizens as the central element in tapping into these resources and, in the process, bring businesses and COs together to improve the citizen sector. He engaged eBay Spain as a key partner and began to develop his Internet auction interface to test his idea with a variety of donated products. The next step included knocking on doors of hundreds of COs and businesses to engage them in the initiative. During this period Rodrigo developed key aspects of his idea, enriched by conversations with experienced people in both the for-profit and non-profit sectors.

When SocialBid became a reality, Rodrigo knew his commitment needed to be complete in order for it to prove successful. Therefore, he left his high paying job at Bain—who had offered to sponsor him for an MBA at INSEAD in Paris—so that he would be able to dedicate himself full-time to take SocialBid to a level where all citizens can have access to contributing to COs in a lasting manner. ◆

SOFIA APPELGREN

SWEDEN

Employment/Labor

**Intercultural Relations/
Race Relations**

In the close-knit culture of Sweden, corporate hiring operates on networking, personal relationships, and references. To a large degree, immigrant communities do not have access to these resources. Sofia Appelgren has launched a program that matches the most dynamic and entrepreneurial young women with Swedish entrepreneurs and corporate leaders. Beginning in Goteborg on Sweden's West Coast, the program is poised to spread to Stockholm and Malmo.

THE NEW IDEA

Sofia is tapping the most driven of immigrant girls in Sweden to launch them into the labor market. She connects with schools and principals to gain the legitimacy that many immigrants place on the education system. She seeks out those immigrant girls with "true will" and ambition and enrolls them in a for-profit program called Mitt Liv (My Life). Mitt Liv partners with traditional companies to build mentor relationships between these girls and company employees, as well as to expand educational opportunities into the extracurricular space through short courses on Swedish society, life-planning, and labor market competitiveness.

Overturning the structure of traditional mentorship models, Sofia has created a professional solution, creating a win-win, symbiotic interactive program for participating partner companies. She charges companies for participation and services, drawing mentors from company employees and in turn, positions her young participants as experts for the companies. The girls offer their knowledge of immigrant life and markets through paid lectures, participation in consumer research focus groups and testers, forums, and field trips, offering an inside look at globalization.

Furthermore, Sofia's Mitt Liv program creates a win-win interactive program for these girls by building networks, personal relationships, and life-plans—giving the girls solid contacts for future opportunities and success to incubate their own ideas and develop their entrepreneurial skills.

THE PROBLEM

In Sweden, the prevalence of segregated communities limits career opportunities for immigrants. A generous refugee policy has resulted in 1.3 million foreign born residents living in Sweden, with young immigrant girls facing the highest levels of joblessness of any demographic in the nation. Immigrants have gravitated—whether driven by price considerations, government housing initiatives, or existing expat communities—toward the suburbs, reinforcing a segregated society. Specifically, the government's low-cost high-rise housing projects have further exacerbated issue of highly concentrated and segregated immigrant populations; in fact, in the suburbs of the Sweden's most segregated cities, Goteborg and Malmo, over 80 percent of its residents were born outside of Sweden.

Sofia's program creates a win-win program for girls by building networks, personal relationships, and life-plans—providing solid contacts for opportunities and developing their entrepreneurial skills.

The labor market is less accessible to immigrants; employers take fewer risks in hiring "unknowns." Often described as the "invisible wall," this division makes employment and integration into the business world difficult for immigrants. The problem will only increase as 27 percent of Swedish residents are predicted to be born outside of Sweden by 2015. Contacts are the currency of gaining employment in Sweden; employers tend to favor familiar names and source their hiring efforts from within their community. Some estimate that 90 percent of jobs are secured through contacts. Heavily segregated immigrant communities with few contacts and limited CVs lack access to this close-knit Swedish cultural landscape. In particular, women immigrants face an uphill climb to employment—young immigrant women have the highest unemployment of any demographic in Sweden. The Minister of Immigration estimates that female immigrants fight two and half times harder for every opportunity.

Sweden does not have a strong focus or great love for entrepreneurship, an area where immigrants particularly excel. Companies lack access to immigrant communities. Swedish companies are faced with a dramatically globalizing world and are struggling to keep up with the new cultural arena.

THE STRATEGY

Sofia's approach allows the immigrant community to see and the greater community to believe that immigrant women can follow their dreams. The program focuses on sourcing the most driven women and equipping them with the tools to function in Swedish society. The work is currently operating in Goteborg, in the western region of Sweden, with imminent plans for expansion. Sofia searches for immigrant girls with "true will" in her selection process. Each participating girl is matched with a mentor with similar interests and career path. Drawn from local schools (i.e. to acquire the legitimacy of the educational system, which is highly valued among immigrant communities), the girls move through individual courses that cover topics from work environment to social norms in Swedish working life. These courses are designed to ease the transition into the labor market and provide the skills to be competitive, while raising participant self-esteem. The courses, which are spaced over the course of a year, award diplomas, and can also enhance a participant's CV. Sofia has built an agreement with local school principals to recruit

participants, and requires that girls be fluent in Swedish and demonstrate strong will and interest in their applications. Their goal is to support the women to "see their own dreams as an option," offer them the tools to be competitive, and build a culture of entrepreneurship in a demographic inclined toward it.

Sofia's Mitt Liv is structured as a mutually beneficial mentorship model where women are not "victims" to be helped, but rather contributing partners on an equal footing, providing insight and education to company employees as experts. Sofia feels that "a relationship well-built has profound impact." The girls provide their services in return as guest lecturers, participants in discussion groups, members of focus groups, and testers for products such as veils. The girls have helped critique and craft ad campaigns for their demographic and regional areas.

> "[Sofia] had a dream of eliminating barriers for immigrants to enter the labor market and to focus on our differences as assets. The dream became a reality when she created Mitt Liv AB."
>
> —Partnership for Change

Companies pay for the privilege of working with the girls and employing their services—the joint partnership is celebrated and its high visibility attracts new people to the idea. Sofia has created a for-profit, self-sustaining model for Mitt Liv by partnering with companies who purchase the service and participate in the program. Mitt Liv generates income by selling the partner package deal to a broad range of companies—from cosmetics to finance—containing access to guest lectures, discussion groups, mentoring, a forum to exchange experiences between partners within both internal and external diversity efforts. Mentors, drawn from partner companies, work with the girls to craft life-plans and establish incremental goals for the future. Currently, Mitt Liv works with 21 partner companies—many international—in a broad range of fields from cosmetics to insurance, each paying 150,000 Swedish Kroner for the package. Partners include Mary Kay, JKL Group, Volvo and Vinge, one of the largest law firms in Sweden, whose broad reach and many locations will be a boon to Mitt Liv's expansion efforts. The work, while still in the early stages, is poised to expand quickly. The program currently (year 2011) has 60 girls paired with 60 mentors, with participants from 28 countries who speak 40 languages. The program is now in Stockholm and Gothenburg and during next year, the program is about to expand to Malmö. They are now looking at how to scale their impact wider.

Mitt Liv's mentorship approach is in a state of continuous evolution and growth. In an approved agreement (2010), Sofia has begun work with the Swedish state to receive government funding for women's place in the program.

THE PERSON

A serial entrepreneur, Sofia founded two companies before she was 20-years-old. Sofia had to earn her own money and be independent from an early age. At 16, she began a party and event planning business, organizing schools and local businesses (i.e. restaurants, bars, and nightclubs) around themed events at affordable rates. She made enough money from this business to buy a car, help support herself during college, and seed a second business designing clothes for a local boutique.

While at university studying communications, Sofia became a young parent. She points to the experience as a turning point, and one which opened her to "profound empathy" and taught her resilience through adversity. Her husband, a Turkish Swedish born immigrant, second generation and he put immigration and integration issues into stark focus: "When I go to Turkey, people are curious. When my husband comes to Sweden, he meets whole other challenges."

Mitt Liv's mentorship program benefits the girls as much as the professionals participating in the program.

Unable to support herself both as a college student and young mother, Sofia opened a small salad bar, Wild n' Fresh, at 23. She employed one part-time staff member. Approached by the powerful local union in Goteborg to sign a collective agreement, Sofia asked her employee to look over the terms. Her worker found that Sofia provided better pay and benefits than the union contract, and asked to remain external. Through a series of increasingly aggressive letters and visits, the union demanded she join. Sofia refused. Eventually, the union set up a 20 person blockade outside her business, passing out flyers and shouting into bullhorns outside her store for four months. Sofia received numerous death threats and had to have a police escort. Refusing the union, which had made a habit of using tactics of intimidation, placed Sofia in the national spotlight. Sofia's story became the most widely read news piece in Sweden 2006. Rather than acquiesce, she sold her business and wrote a book about the experience.

Offered lucrative fees to speak about the issue, Sofia had no interest in the ideological debates that ensued, and decided to focus on breaking down the walls of discrimination that keep immigrants out of the labor market. Armed with ample contacts from the union experience, she applied them to bring the idea of Mitt Liv to life.

Sofia was awarded 2011, by The Swedish Chamber of Commerce, as this years west Swedish and was picked as one of ten from one of the biggest morning papers in Sweden, to be the one in the future to put Gothenburg on the Swedish map for her work with immigrants. ♦

ARNAUD CASTAGNÈDE

FRANCE

Employment/Labor

Poverty Alleviation

Arnaud Castagnède is opening up a new track to efficiently rehabilitate disqualified and long-term unemployed persons. Arnaud is tipping the job rehabilitation sector by designing an integrated market-based process whose success lies in the combination of professional qualification and social support with real work experience and the engagement of private companies.

THE NEW IDEA

To facilitate the professional reintegration of the most excluded unemployed populations, Arnaud has designed an integrated process of rehabilitation based on the renovation of historical patrimony. By helping participants through social support, vocational guidance, and professional experience in construction and renovation work, Arnaud offers an adapted, high-value and certified job qualification program, the first of its kind in France. Participants of his program, who are also paid employees, learn how to master cutting-edge techniques in the eco-construction field, such as eco-friendly lime and hemp thermal insulation. Equipped with specialized skills, these formerly unemployed individuals now make up a workforce in high demand by private construction companies who lack qualified employees for emerging markets.

> "Acta Vista addresses both unemployment and building restoration by employing people, including those excluded from society [and] immigrants on sites that restore and maintain heritage sites."
>
> —Schwab Foundation

Arnaud has built a social business that has gained recognition as a market leader in the job rehabilitation field. His organization, Acta Vista, has six regional branches and turns over 8M EUR; it is considered the leader among professional rehabilitation companies in the south of France (the Bouches-du-Rhône region). Through systematized sub and co-contracting with large private construction firms, Arnaud reinforces synergies with the private sector. He demonstrates the value of skilled employees, facilitates their hiring processes, and deeply changes recruitment practices. As a result, 65 percent of Acta Vista's employees are hired or continue their training after their six-month or one-year contracts with Acta Vista, a success rate four times the national average for professional rehabilitation programs.

Fully aware that his approach to job integration can inform diverse situations of exclusion and is easily replicable, the impact he aims to deliver is approved and recognized at the European level. Arnaud plans to spread Acta Vista to the global market by multiplying his program around renovation sites of historical patrimony. He thus builds the infrastructure to train other rehabilitation companies and raises awareness of private companies on his rehabilitation approach. Furthermore, Arnaud's training center delivers certification degrees in eco-construction and social entrepreneurship.

Each year, more than 350 people are supported and trained by Acta Vista.

THE PROBLEM

Over the past 40 years, fast economic, political and demographic changes in Europe have resulted in the exclusion of more and more people from the labor market, leading them to precarious situations. Non-qualified workers, immigrants, and people from underserved areas are the first victims of inequality in a two-tiered Europe. In France, for example, 7 million people live below the poverty line and over 1 million are unemployed for more than a year.

Since the 1970s social entrepreneurs have decided to tackle the problem of unemployment by creating subsidized rehabilitation companies to facilitate the reintegration of the most excluded populations into social and professional life. However, despite the growth of these public companies across France, they have never succeeded in coping with the large and complex issue of exclusion: On average, only 17 percent of people who go through the first step of the reintegration process successfully obtain a job or training. This is partly due to the fragmentation of the rehabilitation sector. An unemployed individual will typically go from one rehabilitation company to another, with no coordination between the companies, and will spend most of his time on occupational activities, rather than professional trainings and specialized qualification. Without professional or specialized skills, participants of rehabilitation programs have trouble getting hired, as they already suffer from a bad reputation among employers by being considered "at-risk workers."

In terms of demand, growing markets are looking for low-qualified workers, but are having difficulty recruiting them. For example, in the construction sector 500,000 jobs remain vacant each year. This gap could be filled through appropriate professional trainings and qualifications. The chance of being unemployed decreases as an individual's qualifications grow: The unemployment rate for people with no qualifications is 38 percent, while it is only 16 percent for people with a vocational qualification and 6 percent with a university degree.

Systematizing vocational trainings would double the chances of marginalized people finding a job. It would also create new opportunities for the private sector by connecting corporations with the appropriate qualified workers. Finally, with public subsidies for rehabilitation programs on the decline, partnering with private firms opens up entirely new sources of funding. Built on a new economic model independent from public funding, rehabilitation companies could have a successful future in European and global markets.

THE STRATEGY

Arnaud is seizing these opportunities to open a groundbreaking path for the next generation of professional rehabilitation players. In 2001 he founded Acta Vista, recognizing the huge potential of a historical patrimony market that demands the revival of eco-construction competencies. His innovative and personalized rehabilitation process offers a three-fold package:

1. Certified qualification, obtained by on-site and classroom courses on eco-construction techniques

2. Support that determines each individual's situation of exclusion and connects them to vocational guidance and solutions tailored to their specific needs (e.g. alphabetization, driving license, and so on)

3. Support at the end of their rehabilitation contract that facilitates hiring by monitoring the job market and introducing workers to private companies

Each year, more than 350 people are supported and trained by Acta Vista. During their training period they work on enhancive jobs among the six branches operating on 20 historical and natural patrimony renovation sites. During their six-month to one-year trainings, participants benefit from 540 hours of professional training. For the first time ever in the rehabilitation field, Arnaud makes it possible for participants to obtain a certified professional qualification at the end of their training period. Now recognized as official qualifications, French institutions in charge of collecting continuing education tax from employers pay for Acta Vista trainings.

Combining professionalism and efficiency, Acta Vista's unprecedented success shifts the bad reputation of professional reintegration organizations, from inefficient publicly subsidized programs to high-value recruitment partners for construction companies. Arnaud seizes this opportunity by co-contracting or sub-contracting with companies by operating common renovation sites and sharing human resources management. He has also strategically associated Acta Vista with France's national association of traditional construction techniques and with the National Forest Agency. These strategies reinforce his economic model and guarantee Acta Vista's sustainability if public subsidies were to disappear in the years to come.

To build and sustain relationships with construction companies, Arnaud has built a non-profit group with six branches that can anchor their activities in a given territory and integrate the local business networks. Structured as a network of regional branches, Acta Vista can also lower his costs by mutualizing some departments (i.e. supplier, accountability, or communications) Acta Vista currently has a team of 43, with 40 percent dedicated to social support and 60 percent to the vocational training on-site and in the classroom.

To optimize the professional placement of participants once their training comes to an end, Arnaud has created a dedicated department in charge of monitoring regional labor markets, identifying job offers, and matching them with the appropriate workers from Acta Vista, thanks to a centralized tracking database. He has also launched a temporary job agency which targets low-qualified people, and is managed by former Acta Vista employees.

For each development, protection, and rehabilitation, Acta Vista recruits and employs those socially excluded and engages in professional integration.

As the last ten years have highlighted developing a quality model, Arnaud now wants to spread his idea into other regions and countries with historical patrimony and restoration needs, such as Morocco. He will also systematize his innovative methodology based on personalized support and high-value trainings. To structure his development strategy at a European level, Arnaud has instigated a working group supported by the European Union and is gathering construction firms and citizen organizations (COs) from Mediterranean basin countries, such as Italy, Cyprus, and Malta. This has led to the launch of the construction of the first European training center on historical patrimony techniques and social entrepreneurship. In September 2010 it offered common trainings to the workers of reintegration companies, business construction firms, and European COs that would like to build a professional integration department. The center offers a European diploma and is the first certified training center managed by a rehabilitation company.

THE PERSON

Graduating as a surveyor topographer, Arnaud began his career in French Guyana as an engineer for the National Forest Agency. He moved up quickly and became fond of working on community-based projects to develop housing and tourist infrastructure. These projects involved the local Amerindian population in community development and gave Arnaud the idea to base the construction work in his rehabilitation company on local know-how, ancestral techniques, and natural materials. A few years later, Arnaud also applied his community-based development experiences to an eco-friendly mining project, where he combined employment rehabilitation of the excluded Hmong population with eco-friendly techniques to preserve the environment surrounding the mine.

Enriched by these experiences, Arnaud returned to France where he ended his surveyor career to continue on job integration projects. As lack of mobility is one of the main obstacles for employment, Arnaud first launched an associative driving school for job seekers. He began to see the disconnection between the labor market and job seekers, and observed the inefficiency of the integration sector. Arnaud decided to create his own system, Acta Vista, and led by his previous experiences, he chose the renovation of historical patrimony to serve his rehabilitation work. From the beginning, Acta Vista distinguished itself from the other integration players by its eco-construction position, professionalism, and the efficiency of its economic model.

Arnaud has created a social business at the frontier of the private and citizen sector. In line with his goal to provide access to state-of-the-art eco-construction trainings to the most excluded people, he has joined several networks to maintain an edge of new innovations. The PRIDES label allows him to regularly collect information on new techniques and meet key players. This is how he has developed strong competitive advantages and now mastered lime and hemp thermal insulation.

Arnaud is also deeply committed and recognized in social entrepreneurship networks in France. Convinced that his job integration process could be easily replicated, he wishes to spread his methodologies in the field. For instance, the database and knowledge management software applications he specifically developed to better track his beneficiaries, is now available to other integration companies. ◆

RAGHDA EL EBRASHI

EGYPT

Employment/Labor

Financial Services/Markets

Raghda El Ebrashi is creating employment for marginalized youth through a market-based sustainable model catering to business sector needs and market needs, thus, bridging the gap between the social sector and the business sector and professionalizing the citizen sector. Raghda's model has as its workforce volunteer university students from the student clubs affiliated with her citizen organization (CO), Alashanek Ya Balady (AYB—Association for Sustainable Development).

THE NEW IDEA

Raghda's organization began as a student club involving youth in development activities and is now a CO with affiliated student clubs in leading universities in Cairo based on a franchise system. The franchise system allows for swift replication of the model and spread of the impact. While each franchise is responsible for following the founding principles and operating procedures as AYB, the student leadership of each franchise has control over which social challenges to address according to its constituency. AYB, as Raghda imagined, is now a change engine for people on both sides of the equation, the volunteers and the people who find jobs.

Acting as an employment office, AYB offers a service to the corporate sector by selecting, training, and mentoring employees from marginalized communities who would otherwise not have access to the labor market. AYB also creates income-generation opportunities in the informal sector by offering youth training and microcredit to start their own projects.

THE PROBLEM

In Egypt, 16 to 25-year-olds, as a sector in society, are today the largest, most dynamic group with the potential to change the direction of the nation and elevate its development to a new level. However, studies that specifically monitor youth unemployment—in a nation where the median age is 20—estimate that 25 percent of men and 59 percent of women are without work. To put it another way, young people represent nearly half of the unemployed workers in Arab countries. Unemployment among youth can be superficially attributed to apathy, but it finds its true roots in a basic lack of the appropriate soft and technical skills, including English proficiency, and IT skills. When youth are excluded from the labor force, a country's society and economy stagnates. Arab states cannot hope to ever build stable, educated middle classes with approximately a quarter of their young people out of work.

Another reason for the employment problem is that there is a lack of consistency between the outcomes of the educational system and the needs and requirements of the labor market in terms of various specializations and skills. Youth generally have a very poor understanding of which skills they will need to master to improve their chances of finding employment.

In addition, youth, and in particular marginalized youth, have an "unemployable" stigma, because employers' experience in hiring them has been negative in terms of caliber, commitment, and discipline. There exists a virtual absence of effective systems of public and private employment agencies and a lack of programs aimed specifically at the employment of youth. The imbalances between a shrinking demand and growing supply of labor expose the realities of the labor markets with the outcome of escalating rates of unemployment and underemployment.

New entrants to the labor force, particularly the youth that do not find appropriate jobs, are more of a social threat than the long-term unemployed that would have joined the informal sector and adjusted their lifestyles accordingly. Some serious consequences of youth unemployment and insecurity are linked to the exclusion of young people from a productive role in the adult world of work that could demoralize them, undermine social cohesion, and lead to social problems such as crime, drug abuse, vandalism, religious fanaticism, and general alienation in the vicious circle of poverty. Such patterns will persist in the future if no holistic approach is initiated to alter the employment situation.

Education and training is a major instrument, if not the instrument for enhancing the employability, productivity, and income-earning capacity of youth. Young people need broad, general, employable skills combined with training in specific skills and exposure to the world of work that will ease the transition from school to work. Women also need education and training to give them access to more and better jobs in the labor market and to overcome the syndrome of poverty and social exclusion. Skills possessed by young people are a significant factor in determining employment of youth. Studies show that employment outcomes are increasingly determined by the level and quality of education and training relevance to labor markets' needs and opportunities. The mechanisms deployed to facilitate young peoples' transition from school to work, such as apprenticeships and alternate training, also play a vital role in their future employability.

COs and government initiatives in Egypt and the Arab World generally provide training for youth without consulting future employers, thus leaving youth even more frustrated with their inability to find jobs as a result of their raised expectations after the training they received. On the other hand, employment offices only cater to privileged youth, matching them with existing jobs and not exerting any efforts to correct market imbalances.

THE STRATEGY

Raghda started AYB in 2002 at the American University in Cairo (AUC), by inviting her fellow students to join her in creating real, long-lasting, and sustainable development in their country. Instead of giving charity to the poor, they would dedicate their time to becoming change agents for entire communities. Despite initial skepticism from the student population, AYB quickly grew in numbers, attracting those students who also yearned for meaningful life education, outside of the classroom. The success of AYB led Raghda to register it as a CO in 2005, following her graduation, and in franchising the student club to other universities around Egypt. AYB is now operating in eight governorates in addition to Cairo, namely Dakahlya, Munofia, Sharkya, Gharbia, Fayum, Qena, Beny Suif, and El Menya.

The model started as a volunteer development activity to improve the skills of marginalized youth so they could find jobs. Though a number of youth found jobs, Raghda soon realized that she needed to develop a more proactive strategy: "I wanted to create economic opportunities, not leave youth's employment to chance." She knew that companies would not hire youth out of goodwill, nor would they devote significant resources to training them, even if they had multiple vacancies in entry-level positions. There was also no possible way the two parties would naturally interact, particularly as youth from marginalized communities remained stigmatized as incompetent and dishonest.

> "These programs empower the community to take charge of their development by providing vocational training, microloans, and handicraft production to provide income for women."
>
> —*Synergos*

Raghda decided that AYB would fill the missing link, so she began identifying companies' needs and proceeded to tailor training for marginalized youth to enable them to fit the job requirements. In 2008, AYB signed its first contract to select, train, and mentor youth for sales and customer service positions at a company. AYB now offers a quality service to the corporate sector in exchange for a fee, providing the training and job placement for free to marginalized youth. After this, AYB continues to provide occupational stability to both sides, coaching the new hires on the job, and monitoring their progress for the first three months. AYB also ensures that the graduates of its program always receive a fair income. Frequently, graduates are so satisfied with their experience at AYB that they return as trainers later on.

Since the development of this service, 2,000 people have been trained in Old Cairo and several companies have used AYB as an employment office, including Aramex and Vodafone. Vodafone paid AYB 2M EGP (US$335,460) to provide employment candidates in eight governorates. Aramex signed a one-year contract for 60,000 LE and hired 40 employees.

AYB charges for its employment service respective of the client organization's ability to pay. Raghda designed a three-tier fee system, where formal sector companies pay full price, followed in amount by informal businesses, then COs, while factories do not

yet have to pay, because training is basic and she is still introducing the concept to the industry.

For those unable to find employment in the formal sector due to health problems, family obligations, or social norms, AYB creates income-generation opportunities in the informal sector, training youth on producing handicrafts, so they could work with small workshops or start their own projects. For those who do decide to start their own projects, AYB offers microcredit and marketing training; to date, 500 people have received microloans to start or expand their small businesses. Also, AYB is selling products to generate more income, Zaytoona (Arabic for olive) is the brand name given to the products of the community's vocational center in Old Cairo. The vocational center was established in Old Cairo in 2006 and turned into a social venture in 2007. It produces high-quality, handmade products targeting upper- and upper-middle-class women and girls in Egypt and the Middle East. Zaytoona is paired with the Vocational Training program, which trains poor communities in Egypt on sewing skills, leather making, and handicraft production. The best trainees from the vocational center are hired by Zaytoona to produce the branded products. These products are sold in various locations in Cairo, including fancy shopping malls. Zaytoona not only provides employment for the poor, but is transforming widely held stereotypes that the poor cannot produce high-quality products, and that COs are not able to sell their products at competitive market rates.

AYB's volunteers provide the human resources needed to make both programs work, starting from identifying companies' needs, scanning the marginalized community to find those who have the potential to fill these needs, and training promising youth to be hired by the company. Also, it is AYB volunteers who train youth and women on handicrafts, follow up on disbursed loans, and help market the products. For this reason—free labor—Raghda is able to charge businesses a lower fee for AYB's employment service than the market rate, ensuring AYB's competitive edge.

Raghda developed and expanded AYB according to the franchise system. The franchise system in business is a method a company uses to distribute its products or services through retail outlets owned by independent, third-party operators. The independent operator (the franchisee) does business using the marketing methods, trademarked goods and services, and the "goodwill" and name recognition developed by the company (franchisor). In exchange, the independent operator (franchisee) pays an initial fee and royalties to the owner of the franchise.

AYB is the first CO to apply the franchise system to social development. The franchise system of AYB operates as the franchise system in business; however, instead of the franchisee (student groups) paying a royalty fee to AYB (the franchisor), the franchisee contributes to the overall goals of AYB by creating organization growth in terms of volunteers and general resources. So far, from its founding location at American University of Cairo, AYB has franchised to Ain Shams University, Cairo University, the German University of Cairo, and Université Française d'Egypte. Raghda plans to expand throughout Egypt.

By using volunteer university students, Raghda is able to keep costs low for her clients, and ensure AYB's competitive edge.

To cover the costs of her formal and informal sector employment program, Raghda uses the income from her social ventures, Revive and Tafanin. Social ventures are among of AYB's most innovative strategies and are new to the Arab World. Revive offers specialized and soft skills trainings for youth in universities, institutional development courses for COs, capacity-building for students in schools, and professional courses for multinationals and SMEs. This social venture is paired with the Training and Career Guidance Program (TCGP). All curricula produced by Revive are translated into Arabic so as to be used for training low-income youth and women to find employment opportunities. In addition, Revive training consultants use the curricula to train community members on a volunteer basis. Tafanin, (Arabic for creative art), promotes social responsibility through art and culture. Tafanin produces corporate social responsibility campaigns that solve community problems, while creating marketing opportunities for companies. In addition, Tafanin innovates social businesses that create social impact among low-income populations.

Today, AYB for sustainable development is one of the most successful and innovative youth COs in Egypt. It has the potential to generate 15,000+ jobs in the next five years. AYB, as Raghda first imagined it, is a change engine for people on both ends of the social spectrum.

THE PERSON

As a naïve 12-year-old from a privileged family, Raghda's first school trip outside Cairo was to Bel-bayes, Sharkeya, to visit a home for the elderly. There she found Om Fathy, an old and seemingly very poor woman, the home's cleaning lady. Raghda, caught up in her comfortable, even luxurious life in Cairo, had

never before seen the face of true poverty. She remembers standing very still and watching Om Fathy, her young mind unable to fully understand this frail woman, in worn-out clothes. Om Fathy approached her with a warm smile and gentle words, saying that she—Raghda—was the same age as her own children. Om Fathy invited Raghda to her home to meet her children.

Taken in by the kind invitation and curious to know more about this woman, Raghda went along with Om Fathy, and saw the reality of a destitute life whose existence she had never even imagined. She frequently returned to visit Om Fathy and her children, who welcomed her as one of them. Raghda visited her the day before she died. Her only dying wish was that Raghda would continue to work with the people of her community.

Om Fathy taught Raghda that there is nothing called charity, it's always a mutual exchange, and that what matters is being with people not just giving charity and leaving. It is on this foundation that Raghda built AYB, to be the first developmental student club at a time when everyone else focused on charity.

Throughout her high school years, Raghda volunteered with many COs, three with Ashoka Fellows, Hisham El Rouby, Ehaab Abdou and Maher Bushra. Inspired by them, Raghda entered university with high expectations of finding enthusiastic students like her. Unfortunately, her hopes soon vanished as she discovered how most students considered and treated people of lower-income levels with disdain. Even those who had tried reaching out to people in need did so only in the traditional forms of charity.

After much reflection, Raghda developed a strategy to link educated students to Egypt's less privileged. Her belief was, and still is, if every able citizen believed in his/her ability to help and started helping those in need, then there would be no poverty in this country. She knew she had to begin by educating her peers in the concepts of civic engagement and social development, to turn them away from seasonal, pity-driven charity and toward a sustainable effort to improve the lives of the disadvantaged in the long-term.

After graduation, Raghda realized the business sector was not for her. She pursued studies and work in the social sector. Now, in addition to her work with AYB Raghda is teaching strategic management at the German University in Cairo and is finishing her Ph.D. thesis on social entrepreneurship. She aims to introduce social entrepreneurship as a major course of study at the German University in Cairo. With Raghda's scholarship, she is developing a social entrepreneurship curriculum for several universities in Egypt.

Over the years, Raghda and AYB have received many awards and media recognition, including the AUC Award for Community Service. She is a Synergos Social Entrepreneur, a recipient of the King Abdullah II Award for Youth Innovation and Achievement, a recipient of the 35 Under 35 Award, given by *World Business Magazine* and the Shell Corporation for the top female social entrepreneurs in the world, and was recognized by the United Nations Development Program as one of the 100 leading social entrepreneurs under 30. Raghda has not let the recognition go to her head and is continually working to improve her model and her own capabilities. ◆

© Darnel Lindor

MAJID EL JARROUDI

FRANCE

Employment/Labor

Equality/Rights

Urban Development

Every year, big companies spend billions of euros in procurement, but discriminate against local entrepreneurs who lack the right networks or the right reputation. Majid El Jarroudi is bridging this gap by setting all entrepreneurs on an equal footing through a unique platform that connects procurement officers' needs with the potential of entrepreneurs in disadvantaged areas.

THE NEW IDEA

Majid is radically transforming the purchase practices of companies by revealing the untapped potential of doing business with underserved entrepreneurs in marginalized neighborhoods. By targeting France's young generation of procurement officers and connecting them to potential suppliers in these localities, he manages to break down stereotypes, create more competitive and fair business practices, and foster a community of like-minded, diversity-conscious decision-makers. To accelerate this shift, Majid has designed his organization, Agency for Diversity in Entrepreneurship—Adive, as a marketplace where large companies can submit their calls for tenders to entrepreneurs in marginalized neighborhoods and entrepreneurs can promote their services.

Through local networks, Majid identifies and vets a large number of entrepreneurs working in underserved areas who have the potential to meet the needs of big companies. In addition to opening up new markets to them, he helps the entrepreneurs build capacity and trains them to the specificities of the tendering processes. Among the 200 entrepreneurs on Adive's platform, one-third has successfully won bids. Furthermore, in a "satisfaction evaluation" 83 percent of entrepreneurs reported being "very satisfied" with Adive's service and commented that their businesses would no longer exist without Adive. By acting as a bridge between big business networks and an emerging generation of talented, but marginalized, entrepreneurs, Majid's marketplace strengthens vulnerable communities by building sustainable local companies, creating employment, opening up economic opportunities, and developing positive role models for youth.

Within a year and a half, Adive has had a tremendous impact on the business practices of 35 leading companies, who have purchased over 500,000 Euros worth of goods and services from companies they would have previously overlooked and undervalued. More recently, European Aeronautic Defence and

Space Company N.V. (EADS) decided to dedicate 50M EUR (US$70.644M) in purchase from the entrepreneurs supported by Adive. Starting with the 40 largest firms in France, Majid is fostering a world where all companies have the intuition and reflex to choose their suppliers among entrepreneurs from marginalized and underprivileged backgrounds, while still maintaining competitiveness.

THE PROBLEM

The 2005 riots in France shed dramatic light on social, cultural, and economic discrimination toward low-income, high diversity neighborhoods and their inhabitants. Since then, and thanks to the work of leading social entrepreneurs, companies have made some progress in recruiting from these neighborhoods and cultural perceptions of underserved individuals have somewhat evolved. However, companies still fail to see the economic potential of local businesses and discrimination still prevails in procurement processes. The cultural stereotypes of procurement officers are reinforced by the fact that most of them have never stepped foot in an underprivileged neighborhood or have met entrepreneurs from diverse backgrounds. Instead, the attitude remains that "you do business with people you know."

© Darnel Lindor

Majid and his team at Adive vet entrepreneurs working in underserved areas who have the potential to meet the needs of big companies.

Besides, the priority of procurement officers is to kill costs and the easiest way for them to do this is to give priority to their traditional networks of suppliers. As a result, only 5 percent of suppliers to big French companies are located in underprivileged areas, even though the business creation ratio in at-risk neighborhoods is 20 percent above the French average. It is often economically nonsensical: A company in Paris can have a paper supplier in Marseille and a printer in Lille, while they could access more price-competitive, high-quality services in a disadvantaged neighborhood only 5 kilometers away. There is a truly missed opportunity to tap into the goods and services of an emerging sector of innovative, low-cost and effective companies.

Entrepreneurs from marginalized neighborhoods have many obstacles blocking their entry into mainstream markets. For one, they tend to have lower levels of studies or degrees from public universities rather than elite colleges. They also tend to remain isolated from traditional business networks and do not know how to navigate the system to access procurement opportunities. Moreover, they remain invisible due to the lack of precise economic data from underprivileged areas. Confronted by these obstacles, these entrepreneurs struggle to keep their businesses afloat. This is evident in the fact that, when isolated and ignored, entrepreneurial endeavors in underprivileged areas create a third fewer jobs and have a third fewer chances of survival after three years than the national average.

> "Adive connects procurement officers' needs and the potential of entrepreneurs in disadvantaged territories, which reveals a new generation of first-class entrepreneurs."
>
> —*Echoing Green*

Adding to these obstacles is a policy framework that limits and even hinders the success of underserved entrepreneurs. European Union legislation prevents companies from targeting their calls for tenders to specific categories of suppliers. Policies cannot change without available information on underserved entrepreneurs and their economic and social value to communities. In France, however, since large companies are not authorized to request ethnic criteria and other personal background criteria from their suppliers, it is impossible to quantify the economic benefits arising from underserved entrepreneurs. Furthermore, because diversity is only valued in terms of corporate social responsibility and not in terms of economic competitiveness, there is no measurement of these entrepreneurs double or triple bottom-line impact on communities.

THE STRATEGY

Majid has developed a threefold approach to change the behaviors and mentalities of decision-makers in big companies toward underserved business entrepreneurs. First, through in-person meetings, informational breakfasts, workshops, and field-visits, Majid assists companies assess their current procurement processes and helps them to become aware of opportunities to find suppliers in discriminated areas. He thus breaks the first barrier of prejudice by connecting procurement officers interested in diversity opportunities into a community of peers, which fosters emulation and shares best practice.

Next, Majid encourages companies to create a position of interface between human resources, diversity and procurement departments, which is solely dedicated to the issue of supplier diversity. For example, the pharmaceutical laboratory of Bristol-Myers Squibbs has designated a manager to ensure all the company's calls for tenders target underserved entrepreneurs and that the company pays special attention to the bids they receive from disadvantaged neighborhoods. In the long-term, Majid is fostering the creation of this diversity-oriented position in each company of the CAC 40 (i.e. the benchmark French Stock Market Index which includes the country's 40 largest corporations) so that a focus on diversity is part of the daily business of these firms.

Finally, Majid works upstream to shift the culture of future decision-makers by giving specific trainings in leading business schools, like INSEAD. His goal is to integrate the question of "diversity" into all existing responsible procurement training programs.

Convinced that his integration efforts will only work if they make sense economically as well as socially, Majid has designed Adive as a marketplace to facilitate commercial relations between large companies and underserved entrepreneurs. Relying on local partners to identify entrepreneurs, his platform uses a set of precise criteria to methodically qualify an entrepreneur's activities, assess his/her capacity to supply to big companies and match the entrepreneur with the most appropriate calls for tenders. Adive also provides entrepreneurs with training, thanks to a partnership with HEC Business School, and ongoing feedback throughout the tendering process. These capacity-building efforts ensure the entrepreneurs are recognized for their quality and competitiveness, so that they may enter and remain in big business networks.

Majid's marketplace works both ways. It helps large companies connect with a diverse range of entrepreneurs, but also allows emerging entrepreneurs with highly innovative goods and services to enter Adive's database and use its platform to promote their offers to businesses. This allows them to kick-start their business and to be at the cutting edge of technology and innovation. It also demonstrates the great innovation potential of companies in emerging neighborhoods.

Adive provides entrepreneurs with training and ongoing feedback throughout the tendering process.

A year and a half into the creation of Adive, Majid has demonstrated on a small-scale the potential of his marketplace model and is virally engaging increasing numbers of large companies and potential suppliers in the Paris area. In line with his strategy to include all discriminated groups into good procurement practices, he is expanding his networks to Marseilles, Lyon, and the North of France by connecting with the local branches of his current partners.

Majid's unique template has the potential to bring many other discriminated groups into the mainstream economy. He is preparing for the inclusion of entrepreneurs in other regions in France as well as entrepreneurs who suffer from other forms of discrimination, such as women and the handicapped. Additionally, Majid is working on much needed studies to evaluate precisely the economic weight and impact of discriminated entrepreneurs. Since national data on the diverse background of suppliers does not exist, Majid is developing criteria to measure the impact of these entrepreneurs. He is therefore creating the necessary conditions to make up for the lack of information on and visibility around these entrepreneurs. Moreover, Majid also identifies high potential entrepreneurs, whose products or services are so innovative that they do not enter into traditional supply chains. By connecting them with large companies, he accelerates their entry into the market and provides a cutting edge to companies who play by the rules of diversity.

THE PERSON

Majid was raised with the understanding that you have to fight for your dreams to come true. His Moroccan father succeeded as a boxer in Algeria and was the first professional boxer in France. But he had different ambitions for his son and did not allow 14-year-old Majid to become a professional soccer player when a famous Parisian team approached him. Instead, Majid pursued high-level business and journalism studies. As a student, an aspiring entrepreneur, and always eager to discover new initiatives, Majid traveled alone across Canada and the U.S. and was struck by the entrepreneurial spirit and success stories of underserved entrepreneurs in America. He became intrigued with the American Small Business Act and wondered how to foster such an entrepreneurial energy in France.

Returning to France, Majid started his first company at the age of 22 and continued to launch new initiatives and businesses to support entrepreneurs in their success, including a strategy consultancy firm, a real estate agency (both dedicated to entrepreneurs) and a cultural café. Working alongside many entrepreneurs struggling due to their social and cultural origins, Majid took an active part in many initiatives to promote diversity and entrepreneurship, such as working with Ashoka Fellow Abdellah Aboulharjan in starting Jeunes Entrepreneurs de France (JEF), to help young entrepreneurs successfully launch their companies. As honorary roles, he still takes part in Jeunes Entrepreneurs de l'Union Européenne, a European network based on the same model as JEF, and is Vice-President of Humanity in Action, an international non-profit working on the protection of the rights of minorities.

Seeing the limits of all other approaches and with the Small Business Act in mind, Majid set up Adive at the end of 2008 and has since then gained increasing recognition for his work. He is now considered an expert in the fields of diversity and entrepreneurship; spreading his vision and expertise through lectures in some of France's leading business schools (HEC, and INSEAD), at national media interventions, and conferences. In May 2010 Majid represented France at Barack Obama's 2010 Entrepreneurship Summit in Washington, D.C. ♦

MARCOS FLÁVIO CORREA AZZI

BRAZIL

Capacity Building

Financial Services/Markets

Marcos Flávio Azzi is creating a philanthropic culture in Brazil by introducing new management and educational mechanisms that encourage sound social investments. Marcos Flávio is bringing wealthy individuals to define their social causes, invest in them strategically and sustainably, and strengthen the citizen sector as a result.

THE NEW IDEA

Deeply concerned about income disparities in Brazil, Marcos Flávio is pioneering the field of strategic philanthropy while building bridges between wealthy people and citizen organizations (COs). Skillfully using his banking expertise, Marcos Flávio is combining financial market and management tools, with social impact measurements to build a strategic social investment model with the direct involvement of investors.

The Azzi Institute is creating a culture of accountability, preventing potential investors from supporting corrupt organizations and mitigating risk and uncertainty by helping investors identify and monitor successful projects that tackle social causes of interest to them. Although there are similar models in the world—i.e. the Institute for Philanthropy in England or WISE in Switzerland—the Azzi Institute differentiates itself by moving beyond philanthropy education and investor network building. Marcos Flávio's approach is transforming traditional family legacy investments into strategic, impactful philanthropy. The Azzi Institute's greatest contribution has been to bring principles of social investment to family-owned business managements (family councils), thus helping them build long-term investment commitments. Investors are now using a percentage of their patrimony to determine the size of their initial investments and gradually increase that percentage over time to build a legacy for their families. As a result COs are gaining access to previously untapped resources and are constantly challenged by the Azzi Institute to strengthen their organizational capacity and become increasingly financially sound and transparent.

As a result, these new types of investors are contributing to the development of Brazil's citizen sector while fostering new social values for future generations. Barely two years after its launch, the institute has already built a portfolio of more than 600 social investors and 100 registered organizations. In 2009, 25 organizations received more than R$1M (US$556,000). Within the next five years Marcos Flávio plans to have grown this investment pool to R$10M (US$5.56M) and by 2012 he plans to spread the institute to Rio de Janeiro and other major Brazilian capitals.

THE PROBLEM

Despite significant economic growth in recent years, Brazil remains one of the world's most socioeconomically disparate countries. Approximately 10 percent of the population owns 45.8 percent of the gross domestic product. Brazil is the 10th largest economy in the world, yet it ranks 69th on the human development index. Such disparities are all the more apparent in capital cities. The city of Sao Paulo, for example, is home to some of the world's wealthiest people. It is the only city on the planet to have three Tiffany stores, and the number of Ferrari sport car sales are higher there than anywhere else.

Unlike the U.S., Brazil does not have an established culture of philanthropy, be it organized, strategic or charitable. Less than 14 percent of citizen sector funding comes from individuals, and the average Brazilian donates approximately R$158 (US$88). Although this may seem like a large sum to many Brazilians, it pales in comparison to individual donations in the U.S., where 70 percent of the adult population donates approximately US$1,017 yearly *(Brito, Márcia & Melo, Maria Emília. Hábitos de doar e captar recursos no Brasil, São Paulo, Peirópolis, 2007)*. It is true that nearly half of Brazil's adult population with a family income greater than 20 minimum salaries donates to COs, however 65 percent of those donations are fragmented and average less than R$100 (US$56). In addition, families whose wages are equal to or lower than a minimum wage income donate about 3.6 percent of their salaries to social causes, while those that make the equivalent of 20 minimum salaries barely donate 0.8 percent of their income.

The small portion of Brazil's population that decides to engage in philanthropy is usually confronted with the challenge of not knowing how to choose one social cause over another or how to link it to their family legacies.

Brazil has one of the fastest growing populations of millionaires. By increasing their interest in responsible private social investments they could have a deep impact on the redistribution of wealth as well as on the creation of a value-based culture of philanthropy for generations to come. Nevertheless, family philanthropy in Brazil is still not valued. Family Councils are common in big cities, yet they tend to focus on discussing procedural norms as opposed to ways in which they can give back a portion of their profits to society.

THE STRATEGY

In 2007 Marcos Flávio realized that it was possible to help address problems of income distribution and support social change by significantly increasing and strategically directing the amount of money going into philanthropy. Marcos Flávio is applying the management tools and techniques he used when he helped create Brazil's first private wealth management firm. He founded the Azzi Institute to stimulate and channel investments from wealthy individuals to strong COs, thus simultaneously ensuring transparency, enabling the emergence of a strategic philanthropic culture in Brazil, and strengthening the citizen sector.

The institute works with two target populations: The first consists of wealthy investors, and the second is made up of COs with a proven social impact. In order to reach out to the wealthy individuals, the institute's staff set annual and biannual goals to increase the number of contacts, meetings, proposals and new investments or renewals. Marcos Flávio's organization also disseminates the concept of strategic philanthropy and best practices through conferences and written publications.

> "Since its founding, Azzi and his four colleagues have directed over $1.14 million from 20 individual donors to 40 worthy organizations in São Paulo and the surrounding region."
>
> —*Americas Quarterly*

At the beginning of a relationship with a potential investor, the institute first offers advice and evaluates investments previously made by the donor, should they exist. If the person is thinking of investing for the first time, Marcos Flávio's team seeks to understand the potential donor's interests and begins to jointly define the cause to be invested in as well as the amount. Throughout the process, the institute strives to involve more than one member of the same family. Once the cause has been defined and agreed to, the team of advisers introduces the potential investors to COs with proven track records. The institute monitors the investments and provides donors with regular reports about the projects while also providing support to the organizations in question.

Marcos Flávio has developed an online platform to allow donors to follow their investments at the click of a button (i.e. a model he replicated from his experience working in the private wealth management firm). Thus, the Azzi Institute centralizes wealthy individual's social investments in a practical, efficient and transparent manner. In instances where investors would like to dedicate their time and expertise to the cause chosen, the institute identifies organizations within which their volunteering would have the highest potential impact.

The secret to Marcos Flávio's success has been his ability to help investors define their causes and direct them to credible projects that could truly benefit from such investments. He strives to transform the way wealthy individuals think about donating and to create a lasting philanthropic culture in Brazil. The Azzi Institute therefore spends a considerable amount of time educating the potential donors about the causes they express an interest in, providing them with as much background information as possible about the issues chosen and the organizations that tackle them. Involving various family members in this process has the dual role of helping them create family legacies while also ensuring the entrenchment of this philanthropic culture.

Marcos Flávio is also working hard to dismantle the widely accepted stereotype that COs in Brazil are corrupt and/or poorly managed. In his work with COs, therefore, he focuses extensively on due diligence making sure that they have a solid organizational structure and are financially transparent. This also has the added benefit of reducing the risk of investing, thus building up the Azzi Institute's credibility with its investors. The institute evaluates four core aspects of COs before including them in their portfolio: Stability, good management, potential impact and transparency. These are the parameters used to define an Organization Quality Index (OQI). The OQI is calculated by a software in order to ensure an impartial process. The institute follows up these initial evaluations with periodic investment monitoring and site visits.

Currently, the Azzi Institute is a not-for-profit organization entirely supported by a percentage of Marcos Flávio's personal patrimony and that of two other investors. To guarantee its full sustainability, in two years Marcos Flávio plans additionally to charge investors 10 percent overhead to be reinvested in the institute's scaling up efforts. In 2009, in order to secure 18 new investments, the institute had to establish contact with approximately 600 potential investors and organized more than 90 meetings. Barely two years after its inception, the Azzi Institute has already directed more than R$1M (US$556,000) in investments to 25 COs. The goal is to reach the R$10M (US$5.56M) mark within the next five years in the city of Sao Paulo. Marco Flávio plans to open four new offices in Brazil by 2020. His vision is to aggressively scale this model in order to create the equivalent of five huge foundations in Brazil that will operate under the highest standards of professionalism and will invest in organized, transparent and honest philanthropic projects. Marcos Flávio is thus building and spreading a strategic and impactful philanthropic culture in Brazil.

THE PERSON

Marcos Flávio was born in a lower-middle-class family in a town of 20,000 inhabitants of the interior of Minas Gerais. His mother has always been involved with social work in the region and instilled a desire in her children to treat people with care and respect.

After completing high school in the public educational system, Marcos Flávio joined the army with the goal of one day serving as a United Nations peacekeeper. After two years of training, he grew frustrated of the strong corporate hierarchy embedded in the military and felt that he could make a greater contribution to society by continuing his studies. He studied administration at a private university in Sao Paulo and in 1994 he began working at Citibank. The following year, he left Citibank to find a smaller company within which he could grow and explore his potential. He began working with Hedging-Griffo, a company founded at the time as an Absolute Return Fund and became Brazil's first private wealth management firm. Driven by the motivation to develop close relationships with clients, Marcos Flávio created the firm's commercial area from scratch. He thus developed a valuable expertise and became responsible for an important portfolio of clients and relationships. His innovative approach—introducing care and personal interactions to the financial market, addressing customers not as mere investors, but also as people looking for support and guidance—was highly successful.

Four years later, Marcos Flávio became a shareholder of Hedging-Griffo and, with his increased income, he was finally able to unleash his vocation for social transformation. In 2003, in addition to creating the company's Social Responsibility Institute, he started saving part of his patrimony to invest in his own social investment in housing, a field which he has always seen as a priority. In the first year, 60 popular houses were built in the suburbs of Sao Paulo and 200 more followed a year later. He quickly realized however, that much like his bank clients, his social investment was too fragmented to make a significant impact. He needed to develop a more strategic approach to social investing, and began seeking his social cause.

This is how Marcos Flávio understood that he could foster a strategic culture of family social investment in Brazil by creating a mechanism that would bring potential investors together with COs. Weaving his expertise and resources from the successful sale of Hedging-Griffo to Credit Suisse in 2007, Marcos Flávio created the Azzi Institute. He is helping investors discover their social causes and build family legacies for future generations. ◆

RIKIN GANDHI

INDIA

Agriculture

Appropriate Technology

Capacity Building

Through interventions based on modern technology in Jharkhand, Karnataka, Madhya Pradesh, and Orissa, India, Rikin Gandhi is focusing on the efficiency of information dissemination and application and creating new knowledge networks for agriculture extension services. Rikin's method entails replacing the old architecture of agriculture extension services with a new one; and the community is involved in the creation, dissemination, facilitation, and evaluation of locally relevant content.

THE NEW IDEA

Rikin launched Digital Green after carefully studying agriculture extension services. The success of the system is based on the extension officer and his mobility; often the information only reaches big landowners and farmers. The Digital Green method recreates the relationship between the agriculture extension worker and the community and creates a new ecosystem of community learning where the community creates, disseminates, and evaluates the information.

> "[The] simple videos starring local farmers themselves, for every dollar spent, persuaded seven times as many farmers to adopt new ideas as an existing program of training and visits."
>
> —*Technology Review*

The intervention uses video as a basis for disseminating agriculture practices. The medium in many ways is optimally designed for interacting with smallholders, as it overcomes problems of illiteracy and is an intuitively accessible technology, especially when the advice and information in the video is conveyed by local and progressive farmers. Cropping patterns, weather patterns and agricultural practices of a particular area are studied and content is created with the help of community members. The videos feature a progressive farmer explaining effective practices that he/she is using to increase yield. Seeing a fellow farmer use a particular method in a context and a language that is relevant creates incentive among other farmers to adopt the practice.

While technology is the tool that is employed in the Digital Green intervention, an integral feature is the feedback mechanism

which ascertains the effectiveness of the method. Through this mechanism the community members become creators and facilitators of the content, thereby becoming part of a new knowledge infrastructure.

The Digital Green team is developing a management dashboard to see how many screenings a farmer attended, the videos a farmer watched, the kinds of questions asked, practices adopted by them, and videos in which they can be featured in the future. Community members involved in mediating video screenings in their communities capture this data on customized paper formats and provide follow-up support to farmers in the field as and when requested to do so. The data from these paper formats is relayed to district-level hubs where they are reviewed and uploaded into a central database by the partner staff members and Community Resource Persons involved in video production, to inform the next iteration of videos that are produced and to better schedule the videos shown during screenings. While in the traditional method the cost to convince one person to adopt a farming practice is US$30, in the Digital Green method it is merely US$3. The multiple feedback loops created in the process is what makes Digital Green score over traditional extension services.

To keep costs low, Digital Green works in partnership with other citizen organizations (COs) that have a relationship with farming communities and have an existing system of extension work. Digital Green embeds its tools and training into the work that these partner organizations are doing with the communities. Eventually, Digital Green transfers ownership of the process to the partner organization and moves onto newer geographical areas.

THE PROBLEM

The Indian agricultural situation shows that though farmers spend long hours at their field, productivity and economic benefits continue to evade many of the small landholders. A major reason for this is that access to available technology and inputs in farming is uneven. Food security requires a stronger production response. Agricultural extension services and research can help reduce the differential between actual and potential yield and also promote other goals, such as linking farmers to markets. India has more than 100,000 people employed in the agriculture extension system: The second largest labor force committed to extension services after China. Though enough money has been invested in extension services by the government, the interventions have not had the desired outcomes. This is due to the fact that India is a large, diverse, and complex country. The number of extension workers per farmer is low and there are serious constraints on the mobility of staff to implement and monitor programs due to limited operational budgets. Due to numerous households being assigned to one officer, it also becomes difficult to establish rapport with all the farmers. The cost of the transfer of knowledge per farmer thus becomes high.

Another problem is that the content that is discussed with the farmers is often not sourced from the community. Given India's varying climate zones there are disparities between urban and rural, irrigated and rain-fed areas. The "one-size-fits all" assumption creates information that is not locally relevant. In the absence of localized content extension programs fail to optimally encourage local development or adaptation of technologies. Needs of specific categories of clients cannot be addressed and farmer to farmer extension is not supported. Thus, collective as well as individual behavior of farmers cannot be influenced. Often the small landholder and the woman farmer end up being neglected. There is a need to source locally relevant content and create smallholder community networks that will help in sharing information, experience and ideas, and pass them to other farming groups. Local facilitators from within the community need to be identified and trained to achieve a "multiplier effect."

By taking videos of farmers, many more were curious to adopt new ideas and technology, and thus, increased their income.

In the absence of an effective feedback system there is little reinforcement of the information that is conveyed to the farmers. Implementation of a large number of schemes (i.e. state schemes, central sector schemes, centrally sponsored schemes, and externally assisted schemes) with specific targets on demonstrations, distribution of subsidised inputs, and subsidies and training, leaves only a little time for extension workers to assist farmers with advice to solve specific field problems. Often farmers can meet the extension worker only once in a fortnight during his fixed village visit. The nearest office of the Department of Agriculture is at the block level, which is far away from most of the villages. As a result, farmers find it difficult to resolve their queries, making their absorption of the shared content low.

THE STRATEGY

In a one-year trial (2007 to 2008) involving 20 villages (1,470 households), Digital Green increased the adoption of certain agriculture practices sevenfold over a classic Training & Visit-based approach. Digital Green builds on the support of the existing extension system, but works to address its weakness and makes it effective by using relevant content and a local presence to connect with farmers on a sustained basis. On a cost per adoption basis, Digital Green was shown to be at least ten-times more effective, per dollar spent, than a classical approach to agricultural

extension. Digital Green is scaling its model to 1,200 villages over the next three years through the work of partner COs. Ultimately, they expect 15,000 farmers will adopt the new agricultural practices over 18 months and begin to improve their livelihoods. Rikin eventually plans to scale his model to Uganda.

The final goal of Digital Green is to help famers adopt new practices and technologies and increase their income. This will happen more effectively if the community owns the process as theirs. In order to help them have ownership of the entire process of video creation, Digital Green makes the community participate in both content creation and information dissemination. At the heart of the system are Community Resource Persons (CRPs) and Community Service Providers (CSPs). CRPs help in the creation of the videos: They create a survey of the needs and interests of the farmers and are trained to create a story board, to capture information using a camera, editing the information and finally creating the video. A CRP is chosen based on their background, interest, education (i.e. a high school graduate), knowledge of handling electronics, and some knowledge regarding agricultural practices. The videos are usually 8 to 10 minutes in duration and cover varied topics like seed collection, treating the seed, land development and land preparation, crop pattern systems, vermicompost, and improving land assets. Many videos also cover information which aid agriculture, for example, self-help group formation, credit facilities in agriculture, and access to government schemes. Farmers are divided into groups of 15 to 20 people and the videos are screened one to three times per week. The videos are contextualized to the local conditions of the region. Local and familiar farmers are featured in the videos as opposed to outside experts. Members of the community (i.e. CSPs), facilitate the screening of the videos to ensure that farmers use the content regularly. The video-based content and use of low-cost technologies like TV, DVD player and pico projectors improve the diffusion of better farming practices and reduces the expert support required for each farmer.

Currently Digital Green is working with partners like Pradan, BAIF, Samaj Pragati Sahayog, Green Foundation in Karnataka, Madhya Pradesh, Jharkhand, and Orissa. Partners are chosen through a rigorous process in which their domain expertise, scale, and community is checked and verified. Some new partners are also engaging the government's Agriculture Technology Management Agency (ATMA) program which intends to reform the public extension system through interventions like farmer field schools and crop demonstrations. By working with partners involved with ATMA, Digital Green is trying to develop a better understanding of how best to integrate with the government's agricultural extension system to achieve scale and sustainability over the long-term. Digital Green is also diversifying its partnerships with organizations of larger and smaller sizes; varying investments that trade intensity and breadth; maintaining their focus on increasing the cost-effectiveness of each partner; and, assuring quality throughout the system.

In the Digital Green model, costs are shared between Digital Green, CO partners and the farming communities. Hardware equipment is split 50-50 in the cost-share structure, as is the cost of a village mediator. The cost approximately amounts to Rs 2 to 4 per community member. The partner organization bears the cost of the CRP.

To measure its success, qualitative in-depth interviews with project participants, including extension staff and farmers, are sampled before and after the project. Convenience sampling is used for collecting the data. All the required information is collected using various types of structured questionnaires. For the purpose of evaluation, populations are matched in terms of geography, agroecology, demographics, irrigation availability, and the prior intervention of a partner.

In order to scale, Digital Green is working on a franchisee model. They will provide franchisees with documentation on their gender strategy, monitoring and evaluation framework, and administrative operations. As franchisees extend the Digital Green model, Digital Green will provide guidance on a case-by-case basis. In particular, they will help franchisees select cost-appropriate technologies, such as video cameras and pico projectors, to ensure acceptable quality content. Franchisees will also be provided with the software tools and processes to maintain adequate systems for capturing data from the field and accessing the Digital Green video repository. Digital Green's software platform will also allow franchisees and core partners to share content and experiences. The ownership of the system will be transitioned with the current set of partners.

THE PERSON

Rikin was born and raised in the U.S. and studied computer science and physics at Carnegie Mellon University. He went on to study Aeronautical and Astronautical Engineering from Massachusetts Institute of Technology. Growing up, Rikin aspired to join the U.S. Air Force, but lacking perfect eyesight, was told to undergo a very painful eye surgery to be considered. Not one to let go of his passion he decided to go ahead with the eye surgery despite the pain. His aspirations to join the Air Force sparked a journey that led him to work at a private space tourism company, earn a private pilot license, and venture halfway across the globe to make his contribution to the social sector.

Due to bureaucratic procedures, Rikin took a year hiatus from work after the surgery, and then joined the Air Force. This period provided him with a lot of time for introspection and he often found himself thinking about the earth and its sustainable development. During this time, he joined Oracle as a member of the technical staff on Oracle's Secure Enterprise Search team from February 2005 to September 2006. Oracle was just beginning its foray into developing a search product and he was given the role of a researcher. Rikin investigated the development of algorithms that could be used to search for proper nouns, like a person's name, based on the way it sounds. He co-invented two pending patents while at Oracle.

After working at Oracle and on the verge of joining the U.S. Air Force, he changed course to see how he could contribute toward eliminating poverty. Rikin "reverse-migrated" to India to help start a biodiesel venture on the wastelands of Maharashtra. During this journey he spent a lot of time in rural India and became conversant with the Indian agricultural system. As the biodiesel venture did not pan out the way he had hoped, he joined the Microsoft Research India team in Bangalore in the Technology for Emerging Markets program where his idea for Digital Green was formed. ♦

GUILLA GIFTY

BURKINA FASO

Agriculture

Guilla Gifty is facilitating small farming families to become more self-aware by guiding them to create a "Balance Sheet of Personal Competencies," an exercise for farmers to reflect on their families and businesses and become more effective. In addition to developing this exercise, Guilla gathers farmers to share ideas and support, thus helping them create more efficient enterprises. Guilia's support groups build individualized action plans for improved family and cultivation practices, ultimately empowering small farming families to change the economic landscape for local farming communities. Through these farmer networks, farmers are also emboldened to apply pressure on their governments to introduce policy reform that includes local farmer's needs.

THE NEW IDEA

Guilla believes that the key to unlocking productivity gains among small farmers is creating trust-based groups that allow small farmers the space for self reflection. She challenges small farmers in a safe collective space to ask: "Who am I?" and listen to their answers. This process helps to set in motion a transformation among farmers, from self-discovery, to self-assessment, to a mode of mobilization solidified by the creation of a family action plan.

By providing an avenue for dialogue and reflection, Guillia opens the doors for small farmer families to move forward together in creating group innovation, and collaborative family enterprises. In each case, the process is designed for a small group of farmers and their families (i.e. typically 7 to 10 families) and by making this process a group effort, participants gain support internally from their families and externally from other members moving through the same steps.

These sessions become the space for new ideas, with farmers guiding each other and aspiring to improve many facets of their enterprises. Together, farmers evolve their farming operations (i.e. more efficient planning of planting and follow up), they enhance their knowledge (i.e. deciding to enroll in agricultural courses about water management and crop cultivation), and they adopt new technologies (i.e. better seed varieties and the use of manure for organic compost). Farmers are encouraged to reflect upon and change their personal family dynamics, such as working on their family relations (i.e. opening communication between husband and wife and in polygamous families, the husband and several wives), and their self-discipline and self-confidence (i.e. learning how to ride a bicycle, or deciding to enroll their children in the local school).

THE PROBLEM

The small family farm in Burkina Faso has historically failed as a unit of sustainable family livelihood. Small family farms make up more than 90 percent of agricultural production, but more than half of all farm families live in a state of absolute poverty. The UNDP global ranking of comparative farmer livelihood classifies adult rural poverty as earning less than US$200 per year, placing Burkina Faso as the 176th highest country for adult rural poverty out of 177 countries.

In spite of recent reforms, most small farmers cannot collateralize their land holdings to make investments that would lead to an introduction of new technologies and higher product yields. This is due largely to government ownership of all land not formally given by concession, and because the government has not yet implemented an approved process allowing small farmers to gain formal titles to their land.

Guilla conducts a workshop with family's learning about group innovation and collaborative family enterprises.

Instead, the recent trend in government policy has been to create incentives for large-scale commercial agriculture by granting land concessions, but not by offering a contextually useful set of incentives to small farmers. As a result of the highly publicized recent successes of Ashoka Fellows Rosalie Ouoba, Ini Damien, and Claude Ariste, the government is now rethinking how to engage with small farmers more broadly to encourage small farmer sustainability.

Guilla believes that an important key to this transformation is farmer self-awareness as a family unit, and better communication of this externally. After undergoing this process of self-realization and self-awareness, farmers become clearer about their goals and demands. With this improved understanding of their own situations, Guilla then encourages farmers to organize and present their demands to the government, thus applying targeted pressure for more appropriate policy changes. In this manner, Guilla empowers the farmers to become community activists and influential participants of societal reform. With this increased public pressure for government officials to translate the entrepreneurial visions of small farmers into more favorable public policy, farmers will also evoke a more empathic response from professionals working in the sector as they learn to have more respect for the farmers.

THE STRATEGY

After promoting the cotton textiles of women artisans for a decade, Guilla noticed that repeatedly the most common problem was that women could not create a sufficient amount of free time to do this work. When she investigated why women struggled to become established, she realized that there was little communication between men and women about how to manage farming and non-farming work. She concluded that the family unit needed to better determine how to draw on all of the family's resources to create a shared vision of happiness tied to productive livelihoods.

Guilla gathers farmers to share ideas and support, thus helping them create more efficient enterprises.

Launched as a pilot in 2007 to 2008, Guilla is now completing a quantitative evaluation of the pilot's impact in five areas of the country, with farmers from diverse cultures who are engaged in unique cultivation practices. Guilla is looking to extend this approach beyond small farmers to government officials working in agricultural extension. To increase her capacity and further tailor her approach to other groups who impact the lives of small farmers, she is collaborating with the University of Ouagadougou and a regional association of professionals specializing in water management.

Guilla began with pilot projects in six provinces (Gourma, Houet, Bulkiemde, Kourweogo, Sissili, and Yatenga) involving 250 people. The objective was to gauge reactions from people with varying ethnic backgrounds engaged in different crop cultivation practices. In two of the pilots, the farmer families chose to undertake new joint projects involving the cultivation of crops such as peanuts and sorghum. A third group launched a joint organic composting project, and two other groups decided to organize sessions with other farmers to encourage them to engage in creating family action plans that improve crop planting and maintenance. Additionally 17 people agreed to be trained as future facilitators of this process with new farmer groups.

This success has led to a number of growing projects. The fruit juice company DAFANI is financing a joint venture with the Ministry of Youth and Employment of Burkina Faso to give Guilla the resources to help identify, train, and launch the founders of 225 new youth led agricultural enterprises. Another successful project involves extending one of the provincial level pilots to an additional 1,000 small farmer families. The National Association of Water Project Professionals has provided ten facilitators now trained in the intervention process, and have agreed to supply as many as 500 more facilitators for training over the next three years. A partnership between the University of Ouagadougou and FAO to produce agricultural professionals has also identified 20 students to be trained by Guilla's organization as facilitators.

In Guilla's work, she also focuses on properly scaling her method of engaging small farmer communities so it can effectively function as it grows into a nationwide network. One project she is leading is a mobile-based counseling and assistance program, where engaged farm families can reach out to other members for advice, from the technical to the more personal issues related to small farmers. She foresees a ready demand within a short period for this service from as many as 10,000 farmer families. Guilla expects to extend her work in the next few years to Benin and Mali, leveraging close contacts between farmers' associations in Burkina Faso, and similar farmers' associations in these neighboring countries.

THE PERSON

Guilla was born and raised in Ghana to a Burkina mother, although she spent her childhood with her maternal grandmother. While living with her grandmother, Guilla developed autonomy, self-sufficiency, and a strong work ethic. She was then sent to her mother on the Ivory Coast where she faced rejection within her new family, as they struggled under poverty and could not support another child. In this environment, Guilla realized that being an excellent student was her best hope for advancement. Although her family did not provide her with economic or educational assistance, Guilla managed to be one of just a few women chosen to enroll in the Institute of Mathematics and Physics in Ouagadougou in 1990. She completed her postgraduate work in Agricultural Engineering, but realized she was more interested in social rather than technical issues, and that she wanted to work on what she calls "a much broader canvas." For this reason, Guilla decided to take classes in sociology while working.

Guilla realized that improving communication between men and women is key in determining the family's shared vision of happiness.

Guilla's first job after graduating was researching and testing a range of new technologies related to dried fruits and vegetables. In 2002 she shifted from working on technical issues when she assumed the position of Director of the Burkina Artisans' Promotion Program. As Director, Guilla launched a successful program to promote cotton textiles produced by women's cooperatives. While working with the co-ops, she realized that in creating sustainable livelihoods for farmer families the one crucial element previously unaddressed is the functioning of the small farmer family unit.

Seeking to improve farmer family dynamics, Guilla attended a SwissAid course aimed to help development professionals assess their strengths and weaknesses. The course, "Creating a Balance Sheet of Your Competencies," became a source of inspiration as she began to think about how best to approach small farmer families from a personal, rather than a specific results-oriented development perspective. ♦

HAZER GUL

PAKISTAN

Cooperatives

Hazer Gul is eliminating the system of bonded labor in the cottage industry sector of Pakistan. Starting with the weaver community in Swat, Hazer is establishing rights awareness, collective power, education, and is integrating informal workers as key players in the economy. Rather than demonize the powerful middlemen in the value chain, he has developed peaceful, mutually beneficial solutions to break through a traditionally exploitive system.

THE NEW IDEA

Having freed himself from life as a bonded laborer, Hazer has an informed and thorough understanding of the problems that plague people working in cottage industries throughout Pakistan, and has developed a plan to empower laborers involved in the sector. Through the Islampur Cottage Industries Association Hazer educates laborers about their rights, helps them come together to assert those rights, links them to banks and goods suppliers, and guides them through the process of producing and marketing their products while keeping the middlemen involved.

"Islampur is bent on keeping its cottage hand loom industry up and running. Local artisans and industry owners are determined to revive their industry."

—*The Express Tribune*

Hazer implements his plan at various levels: He identifies a problem within a community and organizes the workers within the community to come together to overcome the issue, such as poor working conditions, or lack of monetary compensation. A worker's association is formed to provide training and networking services to gain access to a wider market, price their products at a competitive level, and negotiate with middlemen. At the household level, Hazer works with other citizen organizations (COs) and the government to introduce family planning and access to formal education. At the industry level, Hazer engages designers and professionals from the industry to help improve weaving tools and provide product design services. At the government level, Hazer campaigns for the recognition of the rights of the cottage industry workers and lobbies to change and implement worker protection laws.

THE PROBLEM

Pakistan has a thriving cottage industry, renowned in South Asia for its expertise in textiles, weaving, woodwork, and pottery. According to various surveys, there are nearly 10 million home-based workers in Pakistan's cottage industry. Despite the large number of people involved in this industry, it is still considered an informal sector and a majority of these workers are exploited daily by middlemen and other power players in the economy.

Swat, located in northern Pakistan, has the largest weaving community in the country. An independent state until 1967, Swat still lacks labor legislation and worker protection laws, thus, home-based workers are not recognized by law. This has led to the establishment of a labor-based caste system, whereby weavers are considered of a lower caste, and bonded labor has become an entrenched reality in society. Workers live and work in unhealthy and unsanitary conditions and are paid with food; never able to save enough money to break out of this cycle of exploitation. As a result, illiteracy is high, and the lack of government services, such as public schooling, only exacerbate the problem. In the past, weavers have come up with ideas to improve their situation. For example, families have resorted to having more children in the hopes of increased productivity (i.e. with children and adults weaving together) to increase their financial standing. But this strategy led only to more mouths to feed and no way to move into a cash economy. Instead, it only increased the debt and financial hardships of the community.

Many organizations have tried to ameliorate this problem by removing the middleman and encouraging the weavers and laborers to directly apply for loans, open their own shops and sell their own products in the market place. This approach has backfired time and again as the middlemen undercut their prices and even managed to coerce the national bank to increase interest rates, making it impossible for weavers to pay the principal amount or the interest. The middlemen never pay in cash because they do not want the weavers to compete with them by starting their own businesses. The overall working and living conditions are poor, a significant cause of the workers declining health.

THE STRATEGY

Hazer worked as a weaver for a middleman for more than 8 years and encountered a number of the problems cottage industry workers face each day. He identified the root causes of these problems as the lack of collective bargaining power, laws, education, and awareness. Hazer's organization, Islampur Cottage Industry Association, works toward addressing and changing each of these issues.

Hazer begins by studying a community and identifying a problem they collectively face. Since most families with the same occupation tend to live together as a community, Hazer educates them on their rights and benefits from the existing policies of their professions. Once they are united under the Islampur Cottage Industry Association, they campaign the local government for recognition and protection under the law. The Islampur Cottage Industry Association currently has 463 members, of which 53 are women.

Hazer's organization then acts as an intermediary for market information for the workers, who use this information for collective bargaining power with the middlemen. His program now includes training in marketing to the weavers to help them improve their bargaining skills and continued market surveys to identify where the value addition is done and the market for the value-added products. The middlemen are not cut out from the process—they are an essential part of it. A number of middlemen serve on the advisory board and also help with the technical feasibility studies. By doing this, Hazer has ensured a peaceful working relationship between the workers and middlemen; both he believes are integral players in the industry.

Hazer educates workers about their rights, links them to banks and goods suppliers, and guides them through the process of producing and marketing their products.

Hazer also realized early on that once he provided information on the supply-side of the market to workers, they were more motivated to improve their tools, and so he brought outside professionals to help the weaving community develop their new products. The modified version of the traditional weaving tools are easily adjustable, even in small rooms, and do not require the weavers to work outdoors in harsh weather conditions common in the northern regions of Pakistan.

Another aspect of Hazer's work revolves around providing education and health awareness to the families of the workers. His organization carries out family planning education and tries to change the perception that "more kids means more workers." His organization also educates communities on investing and capacity-building, and placing cash and assets directly in the hands of the workers. As a result, there are now 5,000 looms in Islampur owned by the community, as opposed to 1,200 in 1998.

Integral to Hazer's work has been convincing local banks to give interest-free and low markup loans to workers. Earlier, the national bank had been pressured by the powerful middlemen to increase interest rates, making it impossible for laborers to borrow money. The province of Khyber Pakhtunkhwa has recently attained much more autonomy, leading to more banks being opened in the region. Hazer has taken advantage of this opportunity to work with local banks and has worked out programs for laborers to borrow money at very low interest rates.

By ensuring that the workers are able to articulate their problems and lobby for governmental support, while also produce and sell their goods at competitive prices, Hazer is building an educated society which works in tandem with the middlemen, and contributes to uplifting the national economy.

In 2009, as a result of one of his campaigns, the Ministry of Industries in the Khyber declared Khyber Pakhtunkhwa Province Islampur a model village and granted 100 canals of land and a substantial amount of money (Pakistani Rupees 68M or US$805,690) for its development. The government, in collaboration with Hazer's organization, is constructing a facility to address the problems of underserved and marginalized workers. This facility includes a state-of-the-art weaving college and training center, a school for the worker's children, 100 units of weaving looms for the neediest, a branch of the Industrial Development Bank to provide interest free/low markup loans, a park for the women and children, and small residential units for poor workers. With the help of the government, Hazer has the financial flexibility to replicate this project in other areas of Pakistan.

THE PERSON

Born in Islampur, Swat in 1976 to a low-income family, Hazer began working as a firewood collector at the age of eight to support his family and then as a weaver at 16. Although working over 9 hours a day, he could never accumulate enough cash to feed his family. Witnessing the exploitation of the weaving community at the hands of the middlemen, Hazer realized that the solution had to come from within the affected community. He worked as a weaver until the age of 24, and studied the community's problems to escape the cycle of debt and exploitation. Managing to break free from the hold of the middleman, Hazer attended school. In college he began working as a pump operator at the Public Health Engineering Department. Looking into improving the water supply to his village, Hazer organized the households to form the Islampur Alfalah Tanzeem, a community-based organization established to create awareness around problems in the community, and developed a better understanding of how issues at the household and community levels, such as large family size, increasing pollution, and illiteracy were all linked to their working issues as weavers.

Hazer believes that if this problem of bonded labor among home-based workers is not solved, it will lead to huge numbers of jobless men and women and/or conflict between workers and middlemen. The military and militants pay well and will be seen as an attractive alternative to home-based poorly paid work. The economy will not develop. If the problems of the poor are solved, Hazer envisions educated cottage industry communities gradually integrated into a cash economy that contributes to the national economy. He believes there will be less conflict and increased opportunities; peace will then be ensured.

Motivated by his personal circumstances and his deep understanding of the problems faced by the cottage industry workers, Hazer collaborated with Ashoka Fellows Mohammad Ali and Shaukat Sharar in Swat to carry out preliminary research on cottage industry communities in the north. The results prompted him to establish the Islampur Cottage Industries Association in 2004 for all craft workers in Swat and Khyber Pakhtunkhwa province. ◆

WAMUYU MAHINDA

KENYA

Agriculture

Wamuyu Mahinda is catalyzing entrepreneurship among Kenya's rural and urban youth by focusing on re-designing the entire infrastructure that these youth-led businesses need to grow to scale, while inspiring youth from disadvantaged groups to engage in entrepreneurship.

THE NEW IDEA

Over 20 years, Wamuyu has had a hand in creating a movement of young Kenyan entrepreneurs and is building on this success to support more young people in rural and urban Kenya to succeed in their entrepreneurial ventures. She founded Youth Banner to work with youth serving organizations all over Kenya in applying the success principles she has learnt over the years to better empower their target groups. Through partner organizations, Wamuyu is setting up Youth Enterprise Clubs at the district level all over Kenya as a forum to facilitate peer learning and support among young and aspiring entrepreneurs. She is establishing a network of business mentors and setting up an information directory that will become a reference point for any young entrepreneur seeking guidance and or support to start or grow their business. Wamuyu is further expanding the scope of the Business Enterprise Clubs to address the unique challenges facing young and rural business women among other socioeconomic issues.

Wamuyu's goal is to create a generation of enterprising young people, most of whom are women and the majority of whom are rural. Though many people have commented on the demographic transition occurring in Africa, few seem as optimistic and proactive as Wamuyu when thinking about how to transform countries where a majority of the citizens are young. In Kenya, for example, more than 70 percent of the population is under the age of 35 and yet there is no clear strategy on how this critical mass of young people can be leveraged to cause development. Where others are foreboding and pessimistic, Wamuyu is energized by the success she has had in sparking youth entrepreneurship and is taking steps through Youth Banner to establish a framework that others can tap into to emulate her success.

As her work continues to grow and spread across the country, Wamuyu is beginning to use this platform to raise health, gender, and other social issues. As such, she is ensuring that the young people she is serving are empowered not only to be confident and independent business people but also socially responsible citizens.

THE PROBLEM

Like many African countries, Kenya's population is comprised mostly of young people below the age of 35. This group accounts for over 77 percent of Kenya's population. Still among the world's poorest countries, Kenya's poverty level stands at over 50 percent with 80 percent of its population living in rural areas. Unemployment, a major perpetuator of this status quo, stands at over 40 percent on a national level with rural based youth accounting for 64 percent of this number. Amidst this grim picture, the situation of young women is even worse. Women account for over 60 percent of Kenya's poor and over 70 percent of the unemployed youth. The unique situation of women is perpetuated by sociocultural and religious beliefs that generally put women in a more disadvantaged position compared to their male counterparts. They have less opportunity and support to grow and succeed in a highly competitive and capitalist environment.

The above statistics beckon quick and focused action that puts young people and women at the center stage of development strategies. Subsequently, the Government of Kenya with other citizen organizations (COs) has made youth empowerment and enterprise development a core strategic area of focus. Investing over 5 billion Kenyan Shillings (US$59.5M) per year in youth enterprise initiatives through the government run Youth Enterprise Program, the Government of Kenya is doing a lot to spark off a wave of entrepreneurship within Kenya's young demographic. In addition to the education curriculum, business startup grants and business planning competitions are among the interventions implemented to spur enterprise development among Kenya's youth. But all these well intentioned efforts have not enabled the majority of youth businesses to succeed.

> "With a membership of 150,000,
> the Girl Guides of Kenya
> is the largest single organization of
> girls and young women in Kenya."
>
> —*African Woman and Child Service*

Part of Wamuyu's assessment is that with the rise in entrepreneurial activity comes the need for mentorship and business growth support which is currently grossly under-looked. This, in addition to high levels of corruption and a lack of access to alternative startup capital options, has contributed to the high failure rate of entrepreneurial startups. Over 80 percent of all startups fail in the first year and over 80 percent of those that survive the first year fail in the second year. On top of that, anecdotal evidence suggests that the minority of these startups are launched by rural-based entrepreneurs, and far fewer by women. It is this critical insight that forms the basis of Wamuyu's work. Having worked in the youth development sector for over 20 years, she sees that the next logical step is to build the infrastructure that will boost not only the launch of more youth enterprises, but also the growth and longevity of these important organizations and businesses.

THE STRATEGY

The first phase of Wamuyu's profession started almost 20 years ago with her involvement in the Kenya Girl Guides Association. Over the years, she rose to the top of this organization, eventually becoming its Chief Commissioner before she was elected to the World Board of Girl Guides and Girl Scouts Associations. This, among other occupations all concerned with youth empowerment, has given Wamuyu a unique and intimate understanding of the challenges facing youth today—particularly rural based young women. She sees the gaps in current interventions designed to help young people climb out of poverty, and knows that merely waving the banner of entrepreneurship at young people is not enough to get them to jump into the deep end; rather, what will make them succeed is the presence of an appropriate support structure. It is this insight that paves the way for the second phase of Wamuyu's work.

Wamuyu begins by consolidating the experience and successes she has had working with young people to create a template that can be applied by other youth serving organizations. Cognizant of the many government and civil society led programs targeting youth all around Kenya, Youth Banner's mandate is to facilitate knowledge sharing among these organizations and programs. By working with this wide network of organizations and programs, Youth Banner is better leveraged and positioned to serve the millions of young people they represent in a sustainable and systematic way.

Having access to young people all over the country, Wamuyu's next challenge is to establish a system that complements the work of her partners by delivering the resources and support young people in business need to grow and succeed. To do this, she works closely with her partners to establish Youth Enterprise Clubs that serve their respective constituencies. The Youth Enterprise Clubs are youth-led spaces that facilitate peer learning and support between young and aspiring entrepreneurs. Successful young entrepreneurs have the opportunity to inspire their peers though a platform that enables them to learn from and inspire each other. The clubs are also an avenue for Wamuyu to provide mentorship support to budding young entrepreneurs through an extensive network of successful and seasoned business people. In so doing, Wamuyu has created the first and only recognized and accessible network of business mentors in Kenya. The scope of the clubs stretches further to facilitate discussions about sociocultural issues including HIV/AIDS, gender equality, and global warming, among others to foster social responsibility among the youth.

With a keen concern for women who form the majority of the poor as well as the unemployed youth in Kenya's urban and rural settlements, Wamuyu has designed a separate but complementary program, Amka Tujiinue (meaning "Stand up and let's lift ourselves" in Swahili) to empower rural young women in entrepreneurship. The program combines business and financial education with creation of access to markets and credit. Amka Tujiinue is a hands-on project with lessons and insights that feed directly into Youth Banner to benefit other youth-serving organizations that pay special attention to the empowerment of young women.

THE PERSON

Wamuyu grew up in rural central Kenya in a middle-class family that was able to give her a good education and fairly comfortable upbringing. While at home, she spent time working on her family's farm. At school, she was active in the Girl Guides Association, a group she continued to participate in throughout her education.

Wamuyu got married early, just before she entered university. The responsibility of starting a family did not detract her from her commitment to pursue and complete her education. After graduation, Wamuyu was employed as a lecturer at the Kenya Polytechnic, a job she held for five years. As a lecturer, she continued to serve as a volunteer with the Kenya Girl Guides Association as a mentor to the girls. To supplement her income as a lecturer, she started a bridal gown business in her house. Soon, the business grew and demanded her full attention which forced her to leave her job as a lecturer. Five years later, Wamuyu needed a change from the thriving bridal gown business. She closed the shop and enrolled in an MBA course, after which she worked for several years at the helm of organizations focused on youth enterprise development, including the Kenya Youth Business Trust, Technoserve, and Allavida. In 2007, while at Technoserve, Wamuyu led the largest business plan competition in Kenya's history in partnership with the Ministry of Youth and launched 100 youth led enterprises. At Allavida she raised US$1M to support a youth development program before stepping down to found Youth Banner. ◆

EDUARDO MALLMAN

BRAZIL

Appropriate Technology

Capacity Building

Energy

Eduardo Mallman is creating the capacity to produce social bio-ethanol through micro-biorefineries managed by groups of smallholders. Eduardo is thus increasing the energy independence of family farmers, combating the tendency toward mono-cropping associated with most efforts to produce biofuel and generating new sources of income for smallholders and cooperatives.

THE NEW IDEA

Eduardo is facilitating the entry of smallholder families in Brazil's booming green energy market by way of micro-biorefineries. He has developed a compact technology that produces social bio-ethanol through the use of sweet sorghum, sweet potatoes, and cassava, among other crops. Before introducing this technology and methodology to the market, there existed nearly no opportunities for small farmers to reap the benefits of this emerging economy since biorefineries are extremely expensive and have typically been designed to respond to the needs of a few large-scale producers.

Eduardo's Usinas Sociais Inteligentes (USI—Intelligent Social Factories) occupy very little space (100 m²) and are much more affordable than other technologies. They have been designed to foment the economic development and energy independence of rural communities in an environmentally sustainable manner. The alcohol is not only produced with several ingredients that are generally thrown out, but its by-products are also transformed into food, animal feed or fertilizer in order to further reduce waste and increase economic outputs. In addition, Eduardo is combating the tendency toward monocultures by deliberately using crops that necessitate agronomic rotation.

Through the use of USIs, smallholders are now able to produce between 400 and 2,000 liters of renewable bio-fuel per day, at a cost of R$ 0.30/L (US$0.17/L)—where the average market cost for bioethanol in Brazil amounts to R$1.70/L (US$0.96/L). This quantity is sufficient to respond to the energy needs of a small farm and generate a small surplus. Eduardo's vision is to facilitate the creation of groups of about 30 smallholders to increase their capacity to produce bio-ethanol at a marketable scale. Several micro-biofuel projects are already under way in the south of Brazil. The government of Rio Grande do Sul has purchased 120 micro-biorefineries to be used by 3,000 families, thus generating 12,000 new jobs. Eduardo is now looking to expand the model to Sergipe and other northeastern Brazilian states where there is a much larger number of low-income rural families and where the need is greater. Cognizant of the fact that USIs also have important and promising application for Africa and South Asia, Eduardo is establishing strong links with international organizations such as the World Bank and the European Commission.

THE PROBLEM

Recognizing the global need for clean, affordable and alternative fuel sources, as well as the economic opportunity they represent, Brazil has become the world's second largest ethanol producer and the world's first exporter. Although the country is praised internationally for its advances in the production of bio-fuels, most of these efforts also have a series of accompanying negative consequences.

Eduardo is making bio-fuel available to smallholders by reducing the price of production, diversifying the agricultural output of farmers and increasing their energy independence.

For instance, small farmers have largely been left out of the bio-fuel industry thus far. Although the main objective of the National Program for Production and Use of Biodiesel (PNPB) was to transform smallholders into Brazil's leading energy producers, a recent study revealed that of the 200,000 families targeted initially, only 36,700 families were included in the program. As a result, the enormous job creation and economic growth potential of this promising industry is not trickling down to those who most need it. This is due in part to the fact that most of the bio-fuel technology on the market has been developed for large producers and is therefore unaffordable and inappropriate for smallholders. Parenthetically, much of these families' income is eaten up by their farm's high-energy needs. This problem could be significantly addressed were a larger number of small farmers able to produce

their own fuel. Not only would it help them diversify their agricultural outputs, it would also create new sources of income for their families.

Brazil's largest energy producers thus continue to be the ones reaping the fruits of this booming industry. The production of energy is concentrated in the hands of very few large industries and the only entity allowed to commercialize fuel in Brazil remains Petrobras. With little regard for the ecosystems and populations that surround their immense properties, many of these corporations are deforesting large natural areas to make way for monocultures—of sugarcane or soy, for example—which cause alarming rates of soil erosion losses. The best plots of land are now reserved for crops used for bio-fuel at the expense of food crops, thus influencing both the availability and cost of foodstuff. In addition, although the big energy producers are often praised for introducing bio-fuels to the market, little attention is paid to the significant amount of energy wasted and trash produced as a result of this process. This situation is mirrored several times over in parts of Latin America, Asia and sub-Saharan Africa.

THE STRATEGY

Eduardo created Usinas Sociais Inteligentes Biorefinarias—a name referring both to the organization and the technology—in order to include smallholders in the emerging bio-fuel market. The micro-biorefinery model emerged as a result of elaborate research projects and viability studies, which sought to bring the price of bio-fuel production down while diversifying the agricultural outputs of family farmers and increasing their energy independence. It uses renewable crops such as sweet sorghum, sweet potatoes, sugar cane and cassava to produce high-quality bio-ethanol. It is the only bio-fuel produced through micro-refineries to have been officially certified by the National Agency of Petroleum.

Recognizing the need to adapt bio-fuel technologies to the needs and circumstances of small farmers, Eduardo developed a machine that is small, compact and easy to maintain and can produce up to 2,000 liters of bio-ethanol per day at a cost nearly six times lower than the market cost. In order to decrease the consumption of heat and energy typically required to produce bio-ethanol and to accelerate the process overall, the USIs use an enzyme that facilitates both the hydrolysis and saccharification processes. The bio-ethanol can be used as fuel for energy generators, kitchen appliances and motor vehicles, among others.

The capital investment required to purchase a USI ranges between R$140,000 and R$200,000 (US$80,000 and US$114,000). In order to make the technology accessible to his target audience—smallholders—Eduardo has established a partnership with Brazil's National Social and Economic Development Bank (BNDES). Through its family agriculture program (Pronaf-Eco) smallholders who want to purchase the USI as individuals, cooperatives or citizen organizations (COs) have guaranteed access to 12-year loans at a 1 percent interest rate. Eduardo and his team work closely with each family or cooperative to inform them about the financing plan and to teach them about the benefits of the technology and how to use it.

"Social bioethanol," as termed by Eduardo, serves the dual function of increasing smallholders' socioeconomic well-being while limiting environmental damage.

At the socioeconomic level, smallholders now have the opportunity to increase their energy independence and to diversify their agricultural outputs. Not only do the USIs allow them to reduce their monthly fuel expenditures by a factor of six and thus raise their quality of life, they are also contributing to the local economy through job creation. In addition, every crop used in the production of bio-ethanol serves multiple purposes. In the case of sweet sorghum, for example, the seeds are used to produce sorghum milk and flour for human consumption; ethanol is produced with sorghum syrup; and the waste serves as animal feed. Eduardo has thus found a way to reconcile what are often competing interests between producing food, feed or fuel while diversifying smallholders' production.

> "In Brazil, the USI was sought by the government of Rio Grande do Sul, which is negotiating the purchase of 120 mini-mills for household use by 3,000, generating a total of 12,000 jobs."
>
> —Rede de Technologia Social

This last example also highlights one obvious environmental benefit related to the production of social bio-ethanol: The reduction of waste. Eduardo is replicating this experience with cassava flour producers in Sergipe, northeastern Brazil. Each cassava flour factory produces 1,000 liters per day of manipuera—a poisonous liquid that is generally discarded into the earth thus causing alarming rates of groundwater pollution. Yet, this same liquid is rich in starch and can be used as a raw ingredient in the fermentation process. Consequently, Eduardo and his team have transformed poisonous waste into an alternative source of energy that has a higher profit margin than cassava flour.

One of social bio-ethanol's most important environmental contributions is that it can be produced from a diversity of crops. Unlike sugarcane, which requires a year to grow and large amounts of irrigation water, sweet sorghum has a 125-day production cycle, and needs about one-third the amount of water used by sugarcane crops. Sweet sorghum has been called a "camel among crops," owing to its wide adaptability, its marked resistance to drought and saline-alkaline soils, and tolerance to high temperatures.

In Rio Grande do Sul and Santa Catarina, Eduardo has worked closely with small farmer's cooperatives associated with important social movements, such as the Movement of People Threatened by Dams and the Movement of Small Farmers (MPA), which were the first to purchase and use the USIs. He has found that working with cooperatives of 28 to 30 small farms facilitates both the financing and viability of social bio-ethanol production, since many smallholders own 15 to 20 hectares of land. The income generated by these families increased significantly as a result of this initiative. Most recently, the government of Rio Grande do Sul bought 120 micro-refineries that will be used by 3,000 families thus creating 12,000 new jobs.

This is a model Eduardo is beginning to replicate in northeastern Brazil, where rural communities are more impoverished and where he believes the impact can be greater. In addition, Eduardo is establishing partnerships with the World Bank and the European Commission to bring the social bio-ethanol model to Kenya, Nigeria, and Ethiopia. In 2010, he installed the first USI in Uruguay as a result of collaboration with a local fuel agency.

THE PERSON

Eduardo grew up in a family that pushed him, from a young age, to think ahead of the curve. His grandfather was one of the first Brazilian medical doctors to get a doctorate degree in France in 1927. At the age of 47 he decided to dedicate himself to preventative medicine, a specialization that was unheard of at the time. He was also a rural entrepreneur who introduced irrigated rice farming to the state of Rio Grande do Sul and opened the first private school to be accessible to the children of domestic workers. Eduardo lost his father, a civil engineer and humanist, when he was 10-years-old. Both his parents instilled in him a sense of social responsibility and entrepreneurship. As a child, Eduardo began participating in his family's business activities.

Following in his father's footstep, Eduardo graduated in 1982 as a civil engineer from the Federal University of Rio Grande do Sul, committed to finding new solutions for the rural communities he had grown up with. In 2003, he developed a pioneering rural development project in small communities in Venezuela. A few years later, he created a school associated with Comitê de Democractização da Internet, Ashoka Fellow Rodrigo Baggio's organization, to promote digital inclusion.

Eduardo's inflection point, however, came in 2007 when he met Harry Stokes, Director of the Gaia Project. After learning about the way the quality of life of Ethiopian refugees had dramatically increased as a result of the conscientious introduction of renewable energy technologies, Eduardo was convinced that this was the path he had to follow. He created the concept of social bio-ethanol and the micro-biorefinery model. ♦

GUADALUPE ORTIZ MONTASTERIO CANDA

MEXICO

Agriculture

Conservation/Preservation

Natural Resource Management

Guadalupe Ortiz's Canasta de Semillas (Basket of Seeds) model combines the preservation and organic production of native Mexican seeds with a hub-and-spoke distribution network that ensures that rural families can access those seeds for subsistence farming. By linking the food security of rural Mexicans to the preservation of native seeds, Canasta de Semillas simultaneously tackles both the social consequences of subsistence farmer's nutritional and economic vulnerability and the environmental consequences of declining biodiversity.

THE NEW IDEA

When an organic farming project that Guadalupe was leading with a group of indigenous women in 2003 stalled because no native organic seeds were readily available, Guadalupe was spurred into researching the native seed market in Mexico. To her dismay, she learned that for years native varieties of many fruit and vegetable seeds—such as tomato, eggplant, squash, and lettuce— had begun to fade into extinction as rural families abandoned subsistence agriculture and as Mexico's industrial farming sector imported ever larger amounts of seeds from abroad. Seeing an opportunity to link the recovery of native seed varieties to the improvement of rural families' food security, Guadalupe founded Canasta de Semillas in 2004 with the goal of tackling both problems at once. Her strategy is to revive subsistence farming as a food "safety net" for millions of rural Mexicans by involving the families in the production and distribution of organic native seed varieties that are best suited to the diverse climatic and soil conditions throughout Mexico.

While many other citizen organizations (COs) already promote backyard gardens as a small-scale solution to the problem of food security, Guadalupe's innovative idea is to link those backyard gardens to a new network of community seed banks and regional seed reserves that collect seed samples from individual gardens, reproduce and preserve them, and make them available to even more rural families for use in subsistence farming. The result is a growing domestic supply of organic native seeds that, while ill-suited to large-scale industrial agriculture, perform better under local growing conditions without the use of irrigation, pesticides, or fertilizers. Not only does Guadalupe's network strategy improve food security for a greater number of families, it also begins to restore Mexico's endangered plant biodiversity.

Guadalupe is currently completing three demonstration "nodes"— each of which consists of a regional seed reserve linked to a set of community seed banks and individual backyard gardens—in different parts of Mexico that will serve as models for replication by potential allies like rural development COs or government agencies. Canasta de Semillas has received government financing to have four fully operational nodes by the end of 2010, and within the next five years Guadalupe's goal is to have one complete node up and running in each of the 31 Mexican states by partnering with local organizations and government entities. Once Canasta de Semillas has accumulated a critical mass of organic seeds from its network of backyard gardens, Guadalupe plans to commercialize the seeds to provide a new revenue stream for rural families. Her ultimate goal is to help establish similar hub-and-spoke networks in other countries, thus creating a Seeds Without Borders that can help bolster rural food security through the international exchange of seeds that have adapted to different regions and climates.

By supplying rural Mexicans with native seeds, Canasta de Semillas links food security with the preservation of native seeds.

THE PROBLEM

Many of the 25 million rural Mexicans who have traditionally relied on subsistence farming have increasingly abandoned the cultivation of their land, thereby putting their families' and their communities' food security at greater risk. In the wake of Mexico's debt crisis in 1982, the government began a series of attempts to liberalize various sectors of the Mexican economy, including the agricultural sector. The gradual removal of subsidies and the push toward more open markets signaled the beginning of a structural shift in Mexican agriculture, fueling the growth of large industrial farms while smaller farmers lost the income they once earned from selling excess crops at government-supported prices. The advent of the North American Free Trade Agreement (NAFTA) in 1994, with its incentives to export Mexican agricultural output to the U.S., further favored the large-scale agricultural sector, which in turn began importing genetically modified seeds and chemical inputs to dramatically increase crop yields. Today more than 90 percent of the seeds that are used in Mexico are imported, with the vast majority being varieties that do not reproduce and that require chemical pesticides and fertilizers to thrive.

These developments in the last 30 years have had profound consequences for subsistence farmers in rural Mexico, many of whom were already dealing with low productivity in communal farming arrangements known as *ejidos*, a holdover from populist land reforms of the 1930s. With shrinking land plots and few incentives for capital investment, subsistence farmers began losing the tradition of producing and exchanging regionally adapted native seeds, which became increasingly replaced by imported seeds. More and more rural families began abandoning their land altogether, creating a large population of Mexican women, children, and elderly adults who have become dependent upon remittances sent from migrants to feed their families. Not only is this reliance on remittances precarious, but it also furthers the vicious cycle of seed loss and deterioration of rural communities.

"The Seed Bank aims to retrieve, produce and store the seeds of life in our region, those who have the ability to reproduce the same characteristics of their parents, who are already acclimatized or adapted to our climate."

—*Valle Naturale*

A critical factor that has contributed to the decline of subsistence farming in Mexico is the absence of seed producers focused on supplying this market segment. Private companies are uninterested in the lack of profitability in the subsistence farming sector and therefore focus instead on importing highly productive hybrid seeds designed for industrial farms. Despite public concerns about adverse consequences for Mexican food security, the one government entity that did play an important social role in supplying seeds to small farmers—the Productora Nacional de Semillas (PRONASE)—was dismantled in 2007, largely because of doubts as to whether the government should be involved in mass seed production. Since PRONASE was shut down, no other supplier has stepped in to fill this gap. The few academic seed banks in Mexico are run primarily for research purposes and are disconnected from rural families who do not have access to seeds, and even COs that promote rural development through backyard garden projects must buy their seeds year after year, usually from foreign suppliers. Most of these seeds are not well suited to the challenging and highly diverse growing conditions that subsistence farmers face in different areas of Mexico, including varied climates, soil types, terrain, and precipitation levels.

On a national level, the decline of subsistence farming—particularly in the farther-flung southern regions of Mexico—increases the country's vulnerability in terms of food security. Not only does Mexico's overwhelming reliance on seed imports represent a tenuous position, but the deluge of foreign seeds is also threatening the country's plant biodiversity. Along with Central America,

southern Mexico is considered one of eight regions of the world where plant domestication originated, specifically for species such as maize, beans, sweet potato, pepper, papaya, guava, cherry tomatoes, and cacao. Native varieties of these species are increasingly at risk of extinction as imported seeds spread throughout Mexico. As Mexico's plant biodiversity shrinks, so do the chances that varieties that are particularly well suited to different regions and conditions survive and remain available to farmers.

THE STRATEGY

Canasta de Semillas is a network solution that both produces native organic seeds and distributes them to rural families through a loan-and-deposit seed bank system. The basic unit of the network is what Guadalupe calls a regional node, which consists of a set of individual family backyard gardens linked to local seed banks, which are in turn linked to a single seed reserve for that region. To launch a node, Canasta de Semillas procures native organic seeds from a variety of sources within a given region, including academic seed banks and individual families who have managed to preserve some seeds themselves. These become the starter seeds for each community seed bank, which is simply a collection of seed varieties managed by a "seed guardian" in that town or village, usually a local family or indigenous elder with longstanding experience with seeds.

The community seed bank can then loan seed samples to ordinary local families with at least a small plot of land. With the assistance either of Canasta de Semillas itself or rural development CO partners, these families learn organic techniques for growing an entire range of native fruits and vegetables—from spinach and celery to carrots and tomatoes—in their backyards. Two or three harvest cycles may be required before the families become adept at backyard cultivation, but as early as the first year the small plots of land—which are often located in semi-urban as well as rural areas—begin producing a supply not only of nutritious food for household consumption but also of seeds for future rounds of planting, thus ensuring the families self-reliance in food security. Once the families have returned the original seed "loan" that was made to them by their community seed bank after a couple of harvest cycles, they also have the opportunity to sell excess seeds produced in their gardens to the seed bank for additional income. The seeds that are reproduced in the backyard gardens vary from region to region according to local growing conditions, thus capturing the rich diversity of Mexico's native fruit and vegetable varieties.

In turn, the community seed banks within a given region send seed samples to the regional seed reserve, a facility that is run by a technician and includes a greenhouse, a solar-powered freezer for seed storage, and terraced gardens for experiments and research. Each reserve is responsible for cataloging and preserving native seeds from its region; reproducing those seeds to achieve sufficient volume to be distributed throughout the Canasta de Semillas network, including back to community seed banks for further loans to rural families; and serving as a resource center for rural families in the area who can come to the reserve for guidance and technical advice. Guadalupe also wants to equip each reserve to be an educational center for local schoolchildren, college students and academic researchers, and scout troops who can come to learn about the importance of seed preservation and small-scale organic agriculture.

In Guadalupe's network, family backyard gardens link to local seed banks, which are in turn linked to a single seed reserve in the region, make up a regional node.

Seeds Without Borders that promotes the exchange of seeds and best practices on an international scale.

THE PERSON

Despite growing up far away from Mexico's rural communities in Mexico City, Guadalupe has been fascinated by indigenous cultures ever since she was a girl and has dedicated much of her work to preserving their traditions and values. In one of her earliest jobs working in the public relations office of the president of the Institutional Revolutionary Party, a major Mexican political party, Guadalupe had the opportunity to interact frequently with the leaders of rural communities. Even though she has long since distanced herself from politics, the experience gave her a window not only into how the Mexican government works but also into the particular challenges facing the Mexican countryside, particularly indigenous groups.

In 1993 Guadalupe combined her entrepreneurial abilities and her knowledge of indigenous cultures by launching a business that helped indigenous communities commercialize artisanal products for export to New Zealand, Argentina, and Spain. When declining market demand forced her to close the business after four years of operations, Guadalupe realized that in order to have a greater impact on these communities and their needs, she would have to work much more directly with them. In 1997 she founded México Tierra Mágica, a CO dedicated to the sustainable economic development of indigenous communities. She traveled to the southern Mexican state of Oaxaca to work with the Triqui people—notorious for being a closed society that is hostile toward outsiders. For years Guadalupe patiently but persistently dialogued with local leaders—all men in the beginning—to jointly identify the most pressing needs and implement effective solutions by leveraging funds that Guadalupe raised elsewhere in Mexico. She gradually won the community's trust as she demonstrated her collegiality and her ability to deliver on her agreements with the community, such as an ambulance to be shared between various Triqui villages and a long-range radio communication system.

Each of these nodes is connected to other regional nodes through the Red de Semillas (Seed Network), thus enabling the exchange of seeds between different regions and the sharing of best practices. Even though Canasta de Semillas is in the early stages of growth, Guadalupe has specifically designed the node model to facilitate replication by third parties—most likely rural development COs and government agencies—following protocol and standards set by Canasta de Semillas. With financing and institutional support from two key government entities, the National Institute for Social Development (INDESOL) and the Secretary of Agriculture (SAGARPA), Canasta de Semillas completed four demonstration nodes in 2010 which served as models for interested third parties who want to join the Red de Semillas. SAGARPA in particular, will be a critical ally in helping Guadalupe to convince local and state politicians to adopt her model. Within five years, her goal is to have a fully operational node in all 31 Mexican states, largely through collaboration with locally-based COs and government agencies.

Once Canasta de Semillas has accumulated a critical mass of seeds from its network, Guadalupe plans to commercialize the organic seeds under a single registered Canasta de Semillas brand. She has already shared her plans with organic certification agencies who have verified that her entire network can be certified, allowing profits from seed sales to be shared among all members of the Red de Semillas. The opportunity to participate in this collaborative business venture will give rural families added incentive to continue cultivating their backyard gardens year after year. Guadalupe's other medium to long-term goal is to export the Canasta de Semillas model to other countries with large rural populations; with the ultimate intention of linking seed networks in different countries to each other in a

By 2003, local male Triqui leaders trusted Guadalupe enough to allow her to begin working with Triqui women, something that was virtually unheard of for an outsider. Concerned about the unbalanced gender roles that she had observed in these communities over the years, Guadalupe formed the Red de Mujeres Indígenas Triqui (Network of Indigenous Triqui Women), comprised of two female representatives from each community, and organized a workshop on small-scale organic agriculture for the women using greenhouse and drip irrigation techniques. It was during this workshop that Guadalupe realized to her great surprise that despite the availability of land and basic agricultural technology, the most basic component of organic agriculture—the seeds—was missing. When her independent research into the matter revealed that rural communities were losing their tradition of preserving seeds and that no one was any longer producing native seeds on a commercial scale, Guadalupe was convinced that immediate action had to be taken to address Mexico's vulnerable food security situation. Her work through Canasta de Semillas from 2004 to the present is coupling the preservation of native seeds with sustainable, small-scale rural development to achieve not only social but economic and environmental impact that can be rapidly scaled through strategic partnerships. ◆

SYLVESTRE OUEDRAOGO

BURKINA FASO

Access to Learning/Education

Agriculture

Social Enterprise

Sylvestre Ouedraogo is leading a Burkina-based regional movement to use information technology to spur the development of decentralized knowledge networks used by small farmers. These initiatives also ensure more energy efficient and dependably networked computers in rural areas, and SMS linked database information systems for small farmers.

THE NEW IDEA

Sylvestre believes that the first key to success, especially in the area of small family farming, is to build transparent and accessible knowledge networks from the ground up that shift the focus of information aggregation to farmer groups. This allows small farmers to easily and instantly articulate what they are farming, the size of their farms, and the challenges that they face. Using these platforms, farmers link directly to resources and markets, as well as effectively plan their work. A recent strategic element of Sylvestre's work has been to build computer skills confidence among ten of the most transparent, effective, and widespread farmer-related organizations in Burkina Faso. In several of these organizations, he has taken the next step to creating decentralized networks that integrate computer-based and mobile platforms, allowing member farmers to acquire regular updates and solicit information from each other and from their associations. Sylvestre is also integrating capacity-building into his work. He has a Wiki with technical experts as contributors, writing on seed selection, crop cultivation, animal husbandry, and other farm-related disciplines that have increased in size in the last 12 months to 400+ active members, including people from Mali and Senegal.

Burkina Faso is ranked among the poorest countries in the world, and as a result, decisions about investing in digital architecture cannot overlook the important role of the government. To direct the government toward the most effective route of action, Sylvestre has submitted a set of recommendations to overhaul the way information about agriculture is gathered and disseminated. Considered controversial by some, Sylvestre believes that it is only a matter of time before accelerating social and economic forces lead the government to implement more efficient, up-to-date, and transparent ways of working with small farmers.

THE PROBLEM

The government's approach to agriculture in Burkina Faso was originally designed as a centralized system providing inputs to small farmers and the government as a purchaser of staple crops. This approach required detailed knowledge of what and when

farmers planted, farmer fidelity in selling to the government, (i.e. regardless of the market price), and confidence in the government's prescriptions about what constituted best practice.

Recently this strategy has faced severe challenges. Burkina Faso's agriculture is largely based around small-scale farming, and the government does not have an extensive grasp of what farmers are planting and when. As a result, when there are seed shortages, there are widespread stories of seed sent to the wrong farmers. Rather than risk losing seeds, farmers and their families often simply prepare them for raw consumption than for proper cultivation.

Sylvestre is building the capacity of farmer-related organizations to use the resources, access to markets and knowledge base of integrated computer-based and mobile platforms to inform their work.

Other challenges require more drastic measures than shifting government seed distribution strategies. Burkina Faso is bordered by seven countries, and has a limited ability to monitor the flow of agriculture traffic across its borders. Though there have recently been food shortages in Nigeria, a relatively wealthy country, as a result buyers simply cross one of the adjoining countries to purchase the food they want at prices much higher than would be demanded in the local market; thus, accelerating local food shortages.

Another challenge is related to the shifting weather patterns across the region. Under French colonization, legislatures created this system based on the assumptions that the region of cotton in the center of the country would remain stable. With desertification, cotton has disappeared from the central region and farmers in the north and central regions are facing constant fluctuations in weather. The existing support system to farmers does not accommodate the creativity and flexibility necessary for farmers to survive these conditions. The result has been an erosion of the government's ability to respond effectively to the needs of small farmers.

THE STRATEGY

Sylvestre's initiatives are grounded in creating a decentralized computer server located in rural areas in Burkina Faso. This server is designed to ensure that, in case of a range of possible interruptions or problems, all up-to-date agricultural information and data will continue to be independently accessible by small farmers and their associations.

Sylvestre also encourages the emergence of new knowledge networks, and broadened grassroots access to resources and opportunities across the sub-region. For example, until now, a mango producer in Gaoua, a southern city in Burkina, has not had online access to a wide range of offers from buyers from any number of its neighboring countries. Without up to date information including photos or other video information, buyers and sellers have not had pertinent information, on what, when, and how many products are available. With the knowledge system tools Sylvestre is introducing, it will be possible to create efficient, user-rated online systems for the purchase and sale of these products across the West African sub-region.

Sylvestre's next big challenge is to create customized farmer knowledge of solutions. This knowledge will reflect his and his team's experience with farmer groups which would evaluate farmer knowledge and needs by the size and by the location of a farmer's landholding. At the moment, Sylvestre envisions creating a series of 1, 5 and 10 hectare acre modules around which farmers might usefully organize learning communities.

THE PERSON

When Sylvestre was very young he was involved in a Christian youth volunteer club which was the early years of the Boy and Girl Scouts. He enjoyed planting trees, and he made a small business out of selling hand made toys such as cars to other children. He also helped his mother make hand-sewn clothes. At the age of 13, with no support provided other than school enrolment fees, his father sent him to Ouagadougou to attend middle school. At the time, he struggled to find his way, but convinced the school administration to give him room/board and small jobs to pay his fees. Sylvestre joined a very active science club and through this found a group of curious people who enjoyed using the scientific method of experimentation.

> "The association has been a pioneer in the field of training young people in New Technologies and the International Institute for Communication and Development in knowledge exchange."
>
> —*Africa Burkina*

At the University of Ouagadougou where he studied math, Sylvestre worked to pay his school fees and room/board. In his spare time he set up a black and white processing lab on the campus and began experimenting with the first computers available at the university lab. After graduation, Sylvestre initiated a computer club modeled on the science club he had participated in during secondary school. The first members of his computer club were recently graduated university students. The club spent their time inventing new and engaging ways to teach people how to use computers.

In 2003 Sylvestre and his team were approached for help to increase computer literacy by several of the leading citizen organizations dealing with women's issues and farming in Burkina Faso. What followed was what Sylvestre described as a three year "initiation" into farming, in which the team designed new ways to approach digital literacy. At the same time, Internet use and mobile telephone technology were becoming increasingly available. With experience and vision, Sylvestre and his team realized they had a historic opportunity to improve the lives of small farmers, and they decided to focus on creating a technological platform mobilizing on-the-ground solutions for rural farmers. ◆

BIPLAB PAUL

INDIA

Agriculture

Income Generation

Rural Development

Biplab Paul has come up with a cost-effective and affordable solution to water scarcity that provides a reliable system of irrigation. In the rural areas of arid Gujarat, high saline soil creates an impermeable layer that prevents rain water from percolating; marginal farmers are unable to farm their crops and are eventually forced to abandon the land to join the growing workforce of migratory labor. Biplab's approach improves the lives of the rural poor through this unique participatory irrigation system based on rainwater harvesting. Through his organization, Naireeta Services Private Limited, Biplab empowers rural women to contribute to agriculture and to restore the biodiversity of the region.

THE NEW IDEA

Beginning with over a 100 existing farmer clusters in the rain-scarce and salinity-prone West Indian state of Gujarat, Biplab has created a system of irrigation that is run by women. The community-led initiative does not require any initial investment by the potential beneficiaries, while it assures guaranteed returns from the very next crop.

Biplab has introduced a five-stage process for solving the irrigation problem with the re-introduction of Bhungroo (meaning straw in Gujarati). This concept does not warrant farmers to pay anything upfront, instead, they agree to a five-year contract to repay the services of water logging-freeing and irrigation water through their cash crop. Naireeta Services Private Limited and SHGs take loans from financial institutions to install the infrastructure (i.e. bore-wells, pumps, piping systems, and other overhead costs) as well as the cost for supplying irrigation water to farmers for the next five years. Irrigation cost for food crop (monsoon crop) is waived, so poor and marginal farmers are able to access food security. Eventually, farmers are allowed to pay 30 percent of their standing winter crop (cash crops). Instead of fixed cash payment, farmers are allowed to pay their preferred crop and crop type, which facilitates a farmer-centric flexible payment system. This process stems from a farmer-defined unique agro system based on an innovative technology and implementation process. This also attracts more small and marginal farmers to access the services of Bhungroo. After the stipulated time, whole hardware technology/ systems along with need-based training are handed over to the group of participating farmers.

At a basic level, Biplab's idea addresses the threefold problem of the absence of year-round irrigation, lack of women's empowerment, and low crop productivity. He has developed a network of citizen organizations (COs) to spread his work in different regions of India. Biplab also works closely with universities and governments for a faster transfer of the technology to a wider audience.

THE PROBLEM

Older irrigation systems divert water from rivers to be used in the cities which leads to a decrease in farming and an increase in migration to the cities. The scarcity of water causes both domestic and social violence. Women are most adversely affected by the water crisis, and as a result, they rarely break free from the patriarchal system.

Biplab's idea addresses the problem of the absence of year-round irrigation, lack of women's empowerment, and low crop productivity.

High salinity adds to the problem. Salt deposits on the surface and the aquifer salinity adversely affect the local ecology; agriculture dwindles while human health deteriorates. Scanty monsoon rainfall of 416 mm pours over a short span of 10 to 15 days which causes water logging for three to four months during the peak cropping season. The salt does not allow the water to percolate while the standing water increases topsoil salinity due to capillary action. As per 2001 reports of the Ministry of Agriculture, 12 states in India account for 300 million farmers and over 15 million hectares of agricultural land, affected by salinity.

Due to overexploitation of groundwater, the water table has receded in the last few decades and depleting green cover has reduced moisture formation which eventually has led to desertification of fresh areas. An innumerable amount of deep tube wells has lead to the over-exploitation of ground water and the formation of a "water mafia" which controls the water. The poor villagers who purchase water from the mafia (well owners) eventually slip into a vicious debt trap. Water scarcity results in a class divide, and a powerful "water-owner class" controlling the water sources, ultimately gives rise to violence.

With the state's emphasis on industrialization there has been a battle raging between the poor farmers and the industrial lobby. The state acquires these "farmlands with high salinity" at cheaper prices which are then transferred to industrial houses at higher prices under concepts like the special economic zone (SEZ). The marginal farmer loses the price of the land as well as the only source of livelihood that has provided food and cash for many generations. The same farmers are employed at less than minimum wage in the manufacturing sector.

Fragmented landholding lowers the bargaining power of the marginal farmers. High input costs push prices upwards and farmers lose collective bargaining power; the economies of scale are lost. As a result, rural inhabitants are pushed further toward extreme poverty, while the forced migration for livelihood puts immense pressure on urban resources.

THE STRATEGY

In 2007 Biplab conceptualized the social enterprise Naireeta Services Private Limited, a community-based organization, managed by women. As an entry strategy, Biplab's team of 11 experts and 131 volunteers mobilize women to come together in groups. Biplab has borrowed the concept of peer accountability as social collateral from the Grameen Bank. The five women who form a Bhungroo group cannot default on any of the deliverables.

A big underground water reservoir enables the farmers to store the rainwater and avail of dual cropping during the monsoon and winter. This massive underground reservoir can hold as much as 40 million liters of rain water. It harvests water for just about 10 days per year and can supply water for as long as seven months. Artificially recharging aquifers by adding rainwater to underground water reservoirs through induced infiltration enables the communities to continue farming over seven to eight months in a year. The non-saline rainwater when mixed with the underground saline water brings down the salinity of the groundwater making it fit for agricultural use.

> Biplab's approach improves the lives of the rural poor through this unique participatory irrigation system based on rainwater harvesting.

Central to Biplab's solution is the simplification of the idea for technology-averse illiterate farmers. The five-step process that Biplab has introduced involves technical and social evaluations of feasibility of Bhungroo in a given village. In the first stage of this process, women SHG members identify the below poverty line women members of a village with the help of Biplab's team. They ascertain the land ownership, poverty status, creditworthiness, and measure the gradient of the land. All information is crosschecked by SHG members through a three-tier selection process at the village level, cluster level, and organization level. When the poorest woman of the group is identified, her land is selected for construction of Bhungroo. In the second step the women members check simple geohydrological feasibilities, for example, the gradient of the land, without any high-tech scientific equipment. Their lands do not necessarily have to be contiguous, only the gradient is ascertained. In the third stage of the process documents such as land revenue records, bank details or internal borrowing records, ration cards, and migratory status are collected from each member by Biplab's team, which are then authenticated by the local panchayat. All five participants brought together by Biplab's team sit together and agree to the rules of engagement, i.e. specific roles within the group and sharing the costs of maintenance. In the fourth stage the documents go to the "cluster": A cluster is representatives of SHGs from different villages. The application and the relevant documents are then evaluated by the SHGs. Finally, in the last stage, Biplab's team constructs the Bhungroo free of charge for those five farmers and the water lifting and filtration systems are put in place.

People are hired to construct the drainage systems and the five participating families drill. A pipe five inches in diameter is hand-drilled into the surface from the lowest point of the catchments area where the rainwater rushes and accumulates to a maximum depth of 110 feet to touch the subsoil aquifer. The pipe then guides the captured water to the saline aquifer. It frees the surface of the land from water logging while it dilutes the salinity of the aquifer water. The atmospheric moisture helps to grow crops for the duration of the next month while the water is stored there for the rest of the year. Evaporation barely happens due to the thick earth surface and farmers can use non-saline water for the next eight months.

One of the five women gives a part of her land for construction of the Bhungroo while the other members contribute their labor, bringing an added sense of teamwork. A one-time investment of Rs 2,500 was initially given to them as a grant by Biplab, but now his organization takes loans from the bank and pays them back in nine months, when the Bhungroo is operational. Biplab targets the small and marginal farmers and enables them to get their land free from water logging through the existing unused tube wells.

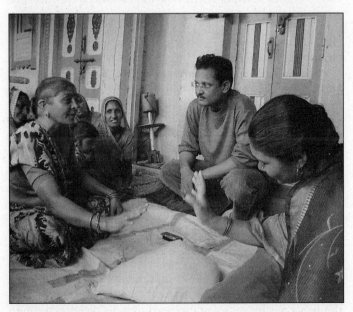

Biplab borrowed the idea of peer accountability as social collateral from the Grameen Bank.

Traditionally land ownership rights rest with a male member of the family, but with this new process a power-of-attorney is obtained in the name of the woman member from the male member (i.e. the husband or brother) to make the land a part of the Bhungroo initiative. The male member of the family usually agrees to the conditions because he clearly sees how the increased productivity would generate a higher income for the family. There is a lot of potential for women's empowerment throughout this process; women members pay back with one-third of the crop produced by each of the participants to the SHG and the SHG then sells the crop in the market and reimburses the bank; the break-even period varies from 9 to 11 months.

The farmer's work in collectives and they exercise better bargaining power with the input selling agencies now. It has become a fully women-driven process from repairing the water pumps to transporting them from one place to another and has drastically reduced rural-to-urban migration and land ownership transfers to the manufacturing lobby.

Biplab also talks to opinion leaders and policymakers and creates connections for expansion. Gujarat Ecology Commission has replicated this model in other parts of the state while the state education board has incorporated the idea into students' school curriculum. Biplab has collaborated with an international CO for a national level replication of the idea through 178 partner organizations. He has also collaborated with a couple of COs that are replicating the concept in the saline coastal regions of West Bengal and Orissa. Change Agent, a Boston-based organization has helped Biplab spread his idea to parts of Africa, venture capital companies such as Angel India Investment Network and Wisecraft, while Boston-based is in conversations with him about financially assisting the replication of his work in areas where banks are not coming forward. In 1999 Biplab participated in the Global Water Summit in Foz de Iguassu in Brazil where he shared the idea of Bhungroo.

THE PERSON

Born in 1970 in the small town of Chinsurah in West Bengal, Biplab went to a local school where he engaged in Indian Scouts and Guides. He fondly remembers his scouts training as teaching him to be empathetic to the needs of others. Here, Biplab started becoming recognized as a star in Indian Scouts and Guides activities. Later he studied humanities, which increased his passion for peoples' welfare. At the age of 10, Biplab witnessed a devastating flood and realized the destructive power of uncontrolled water, and at 14, the water scarcity among the tribal people of Purulia in West Bengal, where he had gone as part of a mountaineering expedition.

Biplab completed his master's degree in economics from Jadavpur University of Kolkata (1994) before taking a course on environmental education at the Center for Environment Education, Ahmedabad. He also joined a philanthropy organization working under the Aga Khan Development Network. Biplab's time of over a year exposed him to the problems of the rural poor in an arid region of Gujarat. This changed his perspective and he began to understand the importance of using technology to improve the lives of those in underserved communities. Biplab observed the dramatic decline of child health due to fluorisis (i.e. early aging children), malnutrition, anemia, the forced migration of farmers, and their subsequent conversion into the status of bonded labor, the resulting deterioration of their socioeconomic position, and the emergence of a class that controlled the water sources and the lives of the poor farmers. This painful experience convinced him that water is a basic need for people to lead better lives. Biplab then started working toward an innovative solution that could eventually reduce gender violence, maternity mortality, child mortality, and social conflict, besides known problems such as crop failure and poverty.

In 1997, after seeing his work in western Gujarat, a local CO, Lok Vikas, invited Biplab to provide technical know-how to solve critical drinking water issues. In 2001 Biplab conducted a biodiversity analysis of 59 villages which revealed that traditional varieties of crops were lost due to too much emphasis on commercial cropping; the nexus among agro input sellers, the deep tube well owners, and the industrial lobby who buy the agricultural produce from the farmers further aggravated the situation. After the 2001 Gujarat earthquake, Biplab provided relief services and organized illiterate women to develop remediation plans for their water issues, realizing that if mobilized, women can make high-impact social change at a faster rate.

Biplab was a part of the panel that drafted the alternative water vision for the state of Gujarat in 2002. This brought him a number of awards such as the Ambassador for Peace Award from Universal Peace Foundation of New York, recognition as Young Leader on Water Resource Management from the U.S. Department of State, the World Bank's India Development Market Place Award (2007) and the Aga Khan Innovation Award.

The World Bank also supported a documentary of Biplab's work. He was selected the conceiver of one of the best social entrepreneurship ideas by Maruti-Suzuki Motor Company, as part of a national business ideas competition. In the meantime, Biplab built a competent second line to run Lok Vikas while he prepared himself to become a full-time water expert. By the end of 2009 he quit Lok Vikas to start his own organization.

Biplab lives in Ahmedabad with his wife Trupti, a LEAD's Fellow and a Rockefeller Foundation Fellow, in addition to being a Commonwealth scholar. The couple has a nine-year-old daughter, Naireeta, whose name coincidentally means "the best cloud for cropping" according to the *Vedas*. ◆

© Andy Bodycombe/SolarAid

NICK SIREAU

UNITED KINGDOM

Appropriate Technology

Conscious Consumerism

Energy

Nick Sireau is applying the insights of modern consumer marketing to solve the basic energy needs of the rural poor in Africa. Nick's idea is to trail blaze new consumer norms for customers who are off the electricity grid: A trusted sales force, low price and high-quality products, and good customer service. In opposition to the aid- and technology-driven approaches which see end users merely as beneficiaries, Nick is changing this paradigm by developing a novel citizen-driven supply and distribution chain for clean energy products, viewing people as consumers rather than passive recipients of help.

THE NEW IDEA

To really address the energy needs of the poor, the supply and distribution of products needs to be fundamentally reoriented to the end user. Nick is developing a citizen-driven consumer approach which is based on the ability to find the right salespeople to deliver the right products, using the right processes. By focusing on the consumer power of impoverished rural Africans, rather than on the technology that they lack, Nick is creating an effective and constantly evolving distribution mechanism for products that are in demand by paying customers.

Nick has created SunnyMoney, the first micro-franchise brand of clean energy products for the rural poor in Africa. Nick realized that most distribution mechanisms in Africa do not reach people because they fail to understand how to sell to their customers in the local environment. SunnyMoney's model focuses on identifying the best salespeople for the consumer group in question: Those who inspire the confidence of customers in both the products and the service. Franchisees come from local communities and are selected by their neighbors and peers following an election campaign, which secures the loyalty of the customer base and ensures that the franchisee is ethical, entrepreneurial, and will be committed to the work. By circumventing the need for conventional sales and distribution channels and tapping into the best sales force possible, SunnyMoney avoids being limited by the constraints of third-party distributors or bureaucratic aid agencies. This local distribution model also provides franchisees with the opportunity to improve their independence and standard of living through a reliable source of increased income, thereby creating a sustainable economic approach to address development needs.

To reorient the demand side of the value chain, Nick is creating a strong brand identity focused on the benefits to the end customer rather than on the advantages of any particular product or technology. Recognizing that a successful brand will provide incentives that "pull" customers in rather than "push" them to any particular product, Nick and his team have developed a strict set of governance rules for franchisees in order to establish and protect the reputation of high-quality and affordable energy solutions.

Central to the consumer-facing model is the commitment to develop and source the most appropriate products to meet customer need, rather than finding great products and then introducing them to communities. For example, SunnyMoney found that a significant unmet need for rural villagers was to be able to light the area immediately above the door and outside their homes, as if the village home had access to electricity from the grid, so SunnyMoney is developing a product to meet this demand. All products are constantly re-evaluated to be maximally suited to the target populations they are designed for—they must be inexpensive, simple, robust, useful, and easy to maintain.

Clients enjoying their new SunnyMoney products!

Nick's approach to the supply of energy converts a need into a demand: While solar solutions may seem to be the perfect solution to energy needs in Africa, many communities remain unaware of the possibilities and unable to access affordable products. By activating a trusted local sales force a market is created, with customers for the products and a feedback mechanism (through the franchisee) about what products are the most appropriate. This approach exemplifies an ethical distribution system which is geared toward end user needs. This model has the potential to change the way markets reach the bottom of the pyramid for a vast range of products beyond solar, which empowers the end user over any other part of the supply chain.

THE PROBLEM

There are many organizations producing and distributing clean energy technologies in Africa, often wedded to a particular technology or energy source. Rather than delivering on the promise of the technology, they have created an unsustainable system reliant on handouts, which has failed to provide mechanisms for product maintenance or consumer feedback. Especially in the context of scarcity of resources, the system is vulnerable to market distortions,

corruption, and power politics. The technological solutions have therefore failed to achieve significant reach as a variety of distribution and supply mechanisms have failed to get the appropriate technology to the right people. Nick developed his approach by understanding the failures of this market and responding to genuine customer needs.

Many citizen organizations (COs) distribute solar equipment for free, which both undermines the development of scalable market-based solutions (as people have no reason to buy solar products), and prevents the natural feedback loop of finding the most appropriate products for the communities concerned. Some COs have taken the route of acting as third-party distributors for energy products (especially solar), buying products in bulk and selling them on through their own networks. This approach is restricted by the limitations of these organizations themselves—it relies on their own growth strategies to reach any scale. For-profit outfits working through third-party distributors are unable to control the price, meaning the retail price is beyond the means of most potential customers.

Few other options for distributing products remain. With a complete lack of infrastructure and stable distribution networks across many African countries, most goods remain produced and sold within local communities. Very few goods are distributed on a national scale, let alone further across the continent, which has so far prevented solar and other renewable energy generation mechanisms reaching those who could use them. Part of the result is that the market fails to support the evolution of the right kinds of products. Much of solar power production has focussed on large-scale power generation to power a community. The cost of such equipment remains out of reach of many poor, rural communities. In addition, many of the products available are not suited to the needs of those on the ground—large and highly technical equipment is not easily transported, and there is a lack of local knowledge to maintain it. Without an appropriate supply and distribution chain, the market fails to develop the right products.

Underlying these problems is one key issue: None of these mechanisms are helping to develop a mainstream economy which is viable and scalable and gives individuals the opportunity to earn a reliable income, while supporting the wider economic development of their communities. Solutions so far have isolated the issue of energy needs from other key development issues. People not only need clean and affordable energy, but they need a mechanism to distribute it which can both scale up and support wider development.

THE STRATEGY

Nick's strategy to redesign the supply and distribution channels for clean energy products focuses on three aspects: Finding the right sales force to distribute products, developing the appropriate processes, and then codifying the model to make it appropriate for further spread to other areas and industries. Nick is continually evolving his model of how he delivers in each of these three areas, determined to constantly re-evaluate every step of the process by testing ideas and trying something else if they don't work.

The original strategy involved training a number of micro entrepreneurs who would go on to sell SolarAid's goods. This proved problematic—from a large initial pool of interested trainees, few completed the training course, even fewer went on to actually sell SolarAid goods, and very few were able to sell them successfully. For such a large investment there were minimal positive results. It was this initial challenge which brought Nick to realize that the key to the success of SolarAid would lie in developing a distribution channel that worked on the ground. The micro-franchising idea grew out of this analysis.

The central idea behind Nick's franchise model is identifying the right people from within local communities. SunnyMoney believes that franchisees need to be both ethical and entrepreneurial, and have the respect of their potential customers. The best way to find this out is to let the potential customers decide, while also ensuring a significant level of commitment from potential franchisees before they can access any training. Following a demonstration of SolarAid products to a rural community, interested potential franchisees are required to run a week long election campaign in the community. The entire community votes on who they trust to be the local SunnyMoney franchisee, so by winning an election the franchisee demonstrates that they already have a customer base. To encourage gender balance and female involvement in the process men must vote on behalf of women and vice versa. Election winners are then interviewed in detail to select the most appropriate candidates from the community-selected pool. The winner of the election must also be approved by the local chief of police and tribal leaders before they are allowed to begin the week-long training course. There are currently 179 franchisees in Malawi and 20 in Kenya.

> "SolarAid launched and runs SunnyMoney, a programme that identifies, recruits, trains and manages a growing network of solar entrepreneurs in East and southern Africa."
>
> —Oxford Jam

Once loyal and committed franchisees are found, the business model is designed to ensure them a comfortable and sustainable source of income. As long as they sell 50 products a month the franchisee will be able to live comfortably off the franchise sales without the need for additional income. Once the local market has been saturated with starter goods (i.e. it is estimated that there will be a 10 percent reduction in sales of the core solar products each year), ongoing income is provided through the sale of the rechargeable batteries which are needed for the solar systems and need to be replaced approximately every year. In addition, gaps are left between communities when assigning franchises to a geographical location in order to allow individual franchisees to take on more territory if they are successful. In addition, SunnyMoney franchisees are entitled to be part of a social security scheme, whereby a proportion of their profits are paid into a fund that will support them in times of ill health or political instability. SolarAid is now partnering with MFIs to offer credit to franchisees and customers, and is also thinking about working with others to offer formal micro-insurance. To keep people within the franchise network incentivized there are opportunities available for increased responsibility within the network. SunnyMoney is currently experimenting with the idea of having the best franchisees grow their own sales force in order to expand faster. Nick is also exploring the option of helping franchisees

create fixed shops for their products, following feedback from franchisees that this would help them increase sales. By providing opportunities for franchisees to earn a reliable income the SolarAid model is helping to build an approach to development that is economically and socially sustainable.

Besides a solid community-led franchise model, Nick recognized that a further aspect of the success of the SunnyMoney brand is quality control: The name SunnyMoney stands for high-quality and affordable energy solutions, and therefore a range of mechanisms are in place to establish and protect this reputation. The brand name was chosen after research with consumers that suggested the name SolarAid had negative connotations due to the term "aid," and instead SunnyMoney focuses on a positive economic situation (i.e. it is not a reference to finance arrangements). There are a strict set of rules governing the standards franchisees must adhere to: All goods come with a one-year warranty which must be honored; franchisees may not sell other goods along with SunnyMoney goods so as not to damage the brand by being associated with inferior products; franchisees must adhere to the official retail price; and they may only sell in their allocated area. SolarAid has also been working with Transparency International to develop a strong anti-corruption policy to ensure that bribes are not taken so the integrity of the SunnyMoney brand is not compromised. As soon as a sale is made it is transferred via MPESA (a mobile phone-based money transfer system), so a franchisee's income can be tracked and the amount of cash they carry at any time is limited. Nick is also developing an in depth staff recruitment process to help him identify the very best candidates for every position. Following problematic experiences with bad hires in the past, Nick is adamant that SolarAid only employs the most committed and talented individuals. He is currently introducing a recruitment process called Top Grading to investigate each candidate in great depth, rather than the traditional process of competency-based interviews. The process involves a series of longer interviews based on life history and personal characteristics as much as work experience, giving Nick a greater insight into the people who will run SolarAid operations. By taking the best practises of sophisticated consumer companies Nick ensures brand integrity and the consistency of service to customers.

Nick describes SolarAid as "product agnostic": Their role is not to develop products and then persuade people that they need them, but to focus on the need and find the best technology available. In practise, many of SolarAid's own designs are innovative, but they will happily buy and distribute other goods if this makes social and economic sense. Paramount is customer benefit and not any particular product or energy source. Learning from franchisees about what kind of products are in demand and remaining competitive in terms of the range and quality of goods offered is seen as central to the success of the franchise network. Once a successful and reliable distribution channel is established, it can and should be used for a range of goods which improve the quality of life of the rural poor in Africa.

The most important aspect of the entire model is not the details as they stand at any particular point, but the commitment to continually experiment with the best ways to recruit, train, and incentivize salespeople; how they will sell; what they will sell; how transparency will be maintained; and what the customer follow up will be. In each of these areas SolarAid stands for innovative ideas and ways of working which will develop differently in different geographies and as customers' demands develop.

SolarAid has undergone the extensive Gold Standard accreditation process for carbon credits, meaning that SolarAid receives one carbon credit for every 10 products used each year. During the accreditation process SolarAid had the opportunity to thoroughly scrutinize all its activities to prove the social and environmental effects of its work. As product sales rise, the income from carbon credits will enable further investment into expansion. In January 2010, SolarAid was awarded its first carbon credits by the Gold Standard—the first time the Gold Standard had ever issued carbon credits for sub-Saharan Africa. SolarAid also has a branch of operations which installs conventional macro-solar panels in schools and other community business. This is a significant but declining part of overall operations which cross-subsidises the residential micro-solar distribution.

Families can save up to 70 percent of their income by using these products, and the health benefits of living free from the toxic gasses, emitted by burning kerosene, are even greater.

Nick's approach to scale is to focus on expanding market share in existing locations and perfecting the model over the next few years, before moving to other areas. The model that is currently working best in Kenya (in both rural and urban areas) first needs to be fully rolled out to the other three countries where SolarAid is operational (Malawi, Tanzania, and Zambia). A pilot in Latin America at invitation of Avina is not core to SolarAid's own activity, but will demonstrate the viability of the concept in different contexts. Nick is currently raising £1.2M (US$2M) in loan finance (half of which has already been secured from a range of social investors) to be able to invest in increased production of goods, as demand from franchisees for more products far outstrips supply. Once the model is optimized and market share is increased in East Africa, Nick will develop the expansion strategy for the rest of Africa, Asia, and possibly Latin America. Nick's overall objective is to work with others to codify and popularise micro-franchise approaches like that developed at SolarAid, as a means to fostering the significant scaling of product distribution to alleviate poverty. Nick is also working with a leading South African expert on microfranchising on collating and codifying the learning on—micro-franchising—in a book for practitioners in other geographies and sectors. In addition, he is seeking out the right networks within social entrepreneurship to popularize

this approach to doing business: His aim is that in 10 years micro-franchising is as common a practise as microfinance is today. Nick's work is gaining momentum through his openness to incorporating the ideas of others and his increasing range of partnerships.

THE PERSON

Nick was influenced by growing up in an entrepreneurial family in France and the U.K., spending weekends doing door-to-door advertizing for his parent's business, and doing name generation activities over the kitchen table. Early in his career Nick began working for faith-based development organizations, following a strong personal faith and a desire to be involved in socially conscious work. He gained experience working in developing countries in Africa and became increasingly disillusioned with what he saw as the failures of traditional development approaches. He worked as the Director of Communications of a large organization for five years, where he set up, led a new team, and led a re-brand of the organisation. While working, he completed a Ph.D. on the "Making Poverty History" campaign which helped him form his own ideas about the direction development work should take.

Apart from the intrapreneurial work Nick was leading inside development organizations, he also set up an organization tackling another problem. When he found out that his sons were suffering from Alkaptonuria (AKU), an extremely rare genetic disease causing serious health problems, Nick observed that such very rare "orphan" diseases, which have a prevalence of less than 1 in 10,000 of the population, lack the patient-base to generate either the economic incentives to find cures, or the professional incentives for doctors to become experts in them. Nick founded the AKU Society in 2003 with an AKU sufferer. It has created a community of interest around the illness, identifying and connecting all those with AKU in the U.K., facilitating new diagnoses, creating a body of evidence for research, and funding medical researchers for a cure. Leading innovation in this field, Nick is now replicating the AKU Society in France, and has built a model which can be applied to a large number of other orphan diseases. Driven by the personal relationship with the issue, he created a platform which has widely benefitted many other people. The AKU Society now has full-time staff that handle the day to day running of all activities.

Having honed his entrepreneurial skills with the AKU Society, Nick began looking for an opportunity to develop his own ideas in the area of development. He developed a relationship with Solar Century (i.e. a respected U.K.-based solar energy company) who wanted someone to develop an organization to bring solar power to developing countries. Nick began working on this project but soon realized that SolarAid needed to take an entirely different approach from one technology-focused if it was going to have any social impact. His approach to developing his ideas is to be a "one man market research machine" and his work is an ongoing project in understanding the problems he is tackling. Rather than focusing on solar energy, he realized that the issue was the nature of the distribution system rather than the technology, which led him to develop SolarAid as it exists today. It was this process of trial and error which led to the micro-franchise network, which changes the nature of the work and opens up a range of possibilities beyond solar. His focus on best practise and his ever-evolving model has seen Nick emerge as a thought leader in the field of micro-franchising and development. ◆

ANTOINE SOMBIÉ

BURKINA FASO

Agriculture

Population

Antoine Sombié has created Association Wouol, the first regional-scale, commercial hybrid value chain that joins European businesses with small local women's vegetable and fruit producers from across West Africa. Antoine's program focuses on expanding and legitimizing organically certified food by creating health incentives for local farmers, and developing economic partnerships with food distributors such as AKCO, a major European food company. In particular, Antoine is challenging current operating standards by building a network of producers that are locally supported with benefits such as mutual health insurance and education programs, as well as professional growth opportunities.

THE NEW IDEA

An integral requirement for Antoine's Association Wouol is that each member is entrepreneurial. Antoine believes that his venture must not only connect the distribution skills of his joint venture partners, but also facilitate the abilities of individual producers seeking new ways to produce, process, and sell the food they grow. He began experimenting with this approach by establishing the first women's producer company in Burkina Faso in 1994, and then in 1999 pioneering another network of small producers, primarily women. The successes of this producer program enabled women's associations to be active producers of organically certified produce in Burkina Faso for the first time.

In these programs, Antoine gained experience exporting products and acquired a deep understanding of necessary product quality standards. As a result, he has implemented a system that requires association members to meet certain performance standards by designating them with specialized jobs and responsibilities. This process both provides members with the opportunity for professional development as well as ensures the highest possible quality of the final product. Beginning in 2001, Antoine transformed this association into the equivalent of a cooperative production company owned by the farmers. Integral to this approach is that every member of the producer group understands each step in the value chain, why it is important, and who is responsible for its successful operation.

Association Wouol successfully operates because Antoine uses consumer trends, and current knowledge on the functioning of worldwide organic supply chains to direct the association's operations. He assures his buyers that the association's products are approved directly by European organic certification institutions such as Ecocert, as opposed to locally conceived organic

certification programs. Because he guarantees certification by legitimate European programs, he gives his producer members a marketable competitive advantage compared to producers using illegal methods. Through this network of European certified small producers, Antoine has shifted production from solely domestic markets to international buyers who offer higher prices and viable opportunities for producer members.

THE PROBLEM

Recently, partnerships between European and local African food producers have been beset by problems. In the past decade, the EU began offering financial incentives for European companies to partner with African producers in hopes to fuel economic development. However, after European companies had maximized their profits from these incentives, African producer groups were effectively cast aside. Resulting court cases are currently making their way through national and international courts, however, this has strained partnerships between local and international producers. Additionally, local producers have complained that EU partners operate in name only, leaving the food producer to pursue practices that focus simply on aggregating raw material at the lowest possible price, without local producers accruing further benefits.

> "Association WOUOL promotes good agricultural practice amongst its members and actively trains in organic farming. Members are also encouraged to diversify into new activities."
>
> *—Tropical Whole Foods*

An alternative approach to these failed partnerships is for European or foreign entrepreneurs to create small-scale organic farming experiments that target the international market in a social enterprise model. These businesses frequently contain clauses that allow small farmers to earn equity in operations over a period of time at a below market purchase price. Unfortunately, even this solution has not been error-free as international investors report that a low product quality has resulted from workers' lack of commitment and interest. Antoine believes that the core problem of these approaches is that they do not systematically encourage creativity and innovation in the families of small producers. Without proper support or encouragement, local producer groups find themselves the target of complaints from international buyers regarding food produce quality, which strains vital investment relations.

THE STRATEGY

Antoine's strategy taps into an overlooked partner to help transform producer relationships: Local women farmers. Among the more than 3,000 people of Association Wouol, 90 percent are women. By positioning women as effective producers and production process managers, Antoine has found that women are more reliable, and with the right training opportunities, the benefits of their involvement reach a greater portion of society, elevating education and health.

Antoine works with women as much on their health and their social and cultural activities as on the production process itself, from farming to packaging and marketing produce. He believes that, to fully impact the lives of women and their families in education, health, and economic livelihood, a woman producer has to be able to secure health care in addition to professional development that provides the space for creativity. For this reason, Antoine's program supports its women producers by organizing music and art festivals, educational competitions, local health clinics, and instructional classes in basic subjects.

Antoine believes he has now reached a point where the "network effect" of his various efforts can begin to take root. Rather than working with isolated health initiatives, he is creating a regionwide mutual health insurance scheme for his producers. The next step will be to create village level entrepreneur programs, starting with association member's children and extending out to other members in each community. Due to his program's successes, government officials in Burkina Faso and Mali are actively supporting the creation of regionwide health programs and adopting his model for youth entrepreneurship schemes.

THE PERSON

Antoine was born into a matrilineal society in Beragoudougou where his mother's family owned little land and his household included 18 siblings. He went to a Catholic elementary school, and was one of four among 56 children who continued to middle school. A key turning point for him was the opportunity to pursue a high school diploma in Tropical Agronomy at Bingervilles in Cote d'Ivoire. At Bingervilles, Antoine was exposed to the functioning of large-scale banana and cocoa plantations. Antoine continued his studies of agricultural technology by pursuing a graduate degree in Paris and then working in marketing with a multinational company in Abidjan. His studies and this first job prepared him to work with farmers and private companies in West Africa.

From 1972 to 1980 Antoine worked in Banfora as the local representative of SOSUCO, a large sugarcane producer. Through this experience, he became disenchanted with the impact of the plantation on neighboring farms and eventually left SOSUCO to work on several research projects with an Ouagadougou-based organization, SERAGRI. After SERAGRI, in 1991, he returned to the area where he grew up and began working at the local level organizing women's production groups. Through his different work experiences, he became convinced that there are better ways to collaborate with small producers and he felt ready to make a difference in his region. By 1999 Antoine had assembled a critical mass of several hundred producers and founded Association Wouol to respond to different problems that small producers faced. Wouol has since become a highly professional, women-focused collective that is the precedent for joint venture hybrid value chains in the sub-region.

At each stage in the evolution of his work, Antoine collaborated with government officials to ensure that his association best supports women producers, first as small producer groups, then as collectives, and now as private partners in the international joint venture. Government officials in Burkina Faso and Mali are pointing to his joint venture agreement as the "best practice" model for small farmer groups seeking to enter international markets. With the legal framework in place allowing him to work interregionally and internationally, Antoine has demonstrated that small women agricultural producers can become key partners in the global market for organic food. ◆

HARON WACHIRA

KENYA

Agriculture

Microenterprise

Poverty Alleviation

Through a model that relies jointly on aggregating production, co-ownership of agricultural businesses, and retooled value chains, Haron Wachira has created a surprising win-win scenario for subsistence farmers and agro-processing businesses in Kenya. This is impressive not only because of the unlikely partnerships formed, but because the agricultural sector in East Africa is chronically mismanaged and poorly coordinated.

THE NEW IDEA

Seeing the ineffectiveness of current approaches in improving the livelihood of farmers, Haron uses his business experience and entrepreneurial acumen to develop a full system approach that connects farmers to the private sector through specialized value chains. In his innovative win-win model, this approach has both parties invested in each other's success in a mutually beneficial partnership that has the farmers earning more while boosting the capacity and revenue of their private sector partners.

Haron is organizing smallholder farmers in an effective production unit much the way an efficient and results-oriented business would. Organized into groups of 10 households, each group is armed with a vision, committed and hardworking members, skills, financial literacy, a product, accountability structures, performance standards, and a processing and marketing partner. Haron is also rejuvenating the underperforming industrial sector, increasing the incomes of farmers in the short-term and also setting them on the path of long-term wealth creation. By negotiating a partnership with processing companies that has the farmers owning a majority stake in the processing company, he is turning small-scale subsistence farmers into visionary agro business owners.

The value chains around which Haron is organizing smallholder farmers are built on locally available farm produce. Through an existing local company, this produce is processed and sold to a local and existing market. Haron's approach can be tailored around virtually any kind of farm produce which, when processed, has an existing local market. This, of course, means that the model is inherently replicable and scalable and that the potential benefit for small-scale and subsistence farmers is huge.

THE PROBLEM

After its independence in 1963, Kenya experienced rapid economic growth that went on until the mid 1970s. This growth was characterized mainly by extensive industrial development in the food processing sector which in turn created a market for local smallholder farmers who produced most of the sectors raw material. However, mired in corruption and unfavorable policies for local industries and farm producers, the economy of Kenya started to plummet through the 1980s and to date has yet to turn around.

This economic downturn has affected different stakeholders, particularly smallholder farmers whose primary source of livelihood is agriculture. Without a thriving industrial sector to buy their produce and without the economies of scale to compete on the international scene, smallholder farmers have resigned to subsistence farming, wallowing in poverty and hardship. The poor circumstance of farmers in Kenya has lingered on for decades and has been blamed on a dysfunctional extension services system, bad policies, lack of access to credit, poor infrastructure, tribal conflict, land wrangles, and corruption, among other barriers.

> "[Haron's] built successful businesses and he appears to bring that same disciplined systems approach that one gets at the big consulting firms to his new passion: development and poverty reduction."
>
> —Speaking of Faith, Carl Blogs, Kenya

Despite these challenges and obstacles, agriculture, even at its current small-scale and given its mostly subsistence nature, contributes 30 percent to Kenya's GDP and is the primary source of livelihood for 80 percent of Kenya's population. Important not only to Kenya's economy but also to the survival of its mostly rural based population, agriculture has taken center stage in development efforts—both local and international. Development of agriculture has become synonymous with poverty eradication and attracts millions of donor funds every year. Value chain development, market access, information technology, farm inputs, and access to credit, among other issues, are being addressed to uplift farmers. With high levels of corruption, uncoordinated efforts, low capacity to perform in the public sector, and an unsupportive policy environment, little success is being registered. Kenya's industrial sector is still operating at only 10 percent of its capacity and over 50 percent of Kenya's population is still poor after over a decade of such interventions.

THE STRATEGY

Although Haron's model is built fundamentally around highly efficient units of production, before he sets these units up, he first establishes a market for what it will produce. He therefore starts by identifying an underperforming processing company whose raw material is locally available. When he finds one, he convinces them to sell part of their stake to a group of farmers who would guarantee them a stable and consistent supply of raw material

at a subsidized cost. When negotiations are concluded, Haron then finds and organizes farmers already producing the needed raw material into a basic group of 10 households called "Nyumba Kumi," or not surprisingly, "Ten Houses" in Kiswahili. The number of groups he sets up depends on the production capacity of each group versus the company's demand. To join a group, each household has to be vetted and recommended by the rest of the members of the group. Each group runs by high accountability and performance standards. Members are trained on financial literacy, specialization, production management, and team work, among other skills.

This training of farmers, paired with the restructured and tightly managed businesses that Haron has launched, are professionalizing and transforming the agricultural sector in Kenya where, in the past, layers of inefficiencies and mismanagement had led to dismal underperformance. Now, once a Nyumba Kumi group has been set up, it follows a strict delivery schedule in order not to upset the rest of the value chain. Delivery of raw material is done at dedicated bulking centers for collection by processing companies. Haron has convinced local district councils to allocate part of their budget to the construction of bulking centers. Through this strategy, he has already raised nearly US$700,000 to construct bulking centers in over 20 districts around Kenya. When a group delivers produce to the bulking center according to agreed upon timelines and quantities, 90 percent of what the group is owed is paid to them in cash and the remaining 10 percent in equity. This payment model is maintained until the farmers acquire 80 percent of the processing company.

Haron has developed a full system approach that connects farmers to the private sector through specialized value chains.

"Akili," which means cleverness or knowledge, is the name attached to each of the products and is now becoming a well-known brand in Kenya. There are currently seven value chains and partnerships running under Haron's model, producing, processing, and marketing coffee products, leather products, food supplements, fresh fruit beverages, herbal products, products of apiculture, and dairy products. Since each product is branded Akili, consumers of Akili Honey, Akili Nutrimix, and Akili

Aloe Vera, for example, know that they are supporting groups of farmers and producer-owned companies. Though only launched in 2008, Haron's work with Akili Holdings was recently recognized by the United Nations Development Programme, with whose support he plans to replicate his model of wealth creation for farmers in 15 constituencies around Kenya in an important step toward the realization of his vision to see a proliferation of value chains and industries co-owned by farmers all over East Africa.

THE PERSON

Haron was born, raised, and educated in a village in Kirinyaga District in Eastern Kenya. He attributes his character to the lessons he learnt from his grandfather and teachers in school. From a young age, Haron demonstrated a keen interest in learning about and solving problems. An interesting case is when he met an engineer in a neighboring village and convinced him to teach he and his brothers how to construct a well. Haron and his brothers then went on to construct over 200 wells all around his village.

As a young professional, Haron demonstrated a similar knack for innovation and leadership, first in starting up the first and only major computer assembly plant in Kenya, commanding 30 percent of the computer supply market in Kenya. Next, as an auditor in the coveted PricewaterhouseCoopers, he quickly rose to become a partner. At PwC Haron was responsible for cutting down the firm's desk space by 50 percent, ultimately saving them millions in rent by introducing and implementing an innovative resource sharing technology across the firm. Haron went on to chair the board of Tana Water Service, an experience that got him to once again engage with rural communities all across Kenya.

It was during this time that his previous experience as a high level executive started to shape his view of how poor rural communities could be helped more sustainably. Interacting more with rural communities, he started to see and understand their challenges more clearly. He was now able to see the gaps in the interventions on the ground and was able to use his business mind and experience to craft alternative solutions. Ousted from the board of Tana Water Services a few years later for taking a stand against corrupt officials, Haron saw and seized the opportunity to make a difference where his passion always was—in rural communities. This was the beginning of his work with farmers on value chains. ◆

K.D.N. WEERASINGHE

SRI LANKA

Appropriate Technology

Microenterprise

Professor K.D.N. Weerasinghe or "Weera" has invented several innovative applications to rejuvenate Sri Lanka's declining cinnamon industry. Weera's inventions include a cinnamon peeling device, a processing bench, scrapers, and a poly cam, are collectively creating a technological revolution across Sri Lanka. Some of the social benefits include increasing worker efficiency; improving work and sanitary conditions; eliminating caste prejudice; and, increasing local investment.

THE NEW IDEA

Weera is revitalizing the stagnant cinnamon industry in Sri Lanka by actively spearheading a global campaign to reposition the country as the premium producer of the finest cinnamon. Weera has worked tirelessly since 1986 to improve the status of the cinnamon industry and its workers. Recently, he developed technology that has proven to increase production of better quality cinnamon. Weera's interventions comprehensively and holistically address the problems of small stakeholders by improving the image, productivity, and profitability of the industry.

Weera founded a unique incubator company, located within Ruhuna University, and helps graduates use the technology and technical expertise free of charge so that they may pursue their own socially responsible business ventures.

Weera's technology has mechanized the cinnamon peeling process and increased the productivity, safety, and efficiency of workers. However, his innovations are much more than technical; they also address socioeconomic issues such as caste prejudices, unemployment, as well as gender and disability rights.

THE PROBLEM

With a market share of about 70 percent, Sri Lanka is the largest producer of Ceylon cinnamon in the world, with Mexico, Columbia, and the United States being its main buyers. Ceylon cinnamon is one of the earliest known spices and is a derivative of the Sri Lankan aromatic perennial tree, Cinnamomum zeylanicum.

The cinnamon industry supports the livelihood of more than 85,000 cinnamon growers. Currently, more than 150,000 peelers are engaged in the southern province, where approximately 75,000 acres of land are used to cultivate the perennial crop (i.e. a single tree can grow for over 50 years with minimum maintenance, which helps to minimize its water usage and carbon footprint). However, the industry has been stagnant for centuries and, in the last decade, began declining rapidly.

The cinnamon industry uses both indigenous and traditional tools that yield limited to medium quality cinnamon. The low supply and quality of Ceylon cinnamon has led to a decrease in the demand for Ceylon cinnamon and an increase in the demand for Chinese cinnamon. Chinese cinnamon is considered to be less healthy than Ceylon cinnamon, as it contains a higher concentration of coumarin, a moderately toxic compound.

In addition to the low supply and quality of the cinnamon, the industry is witnessing a quick withdrawal because the Salagama caste people, who are directly associated with cinnamon peeling, and have been abandoning the occupation; plagued with health issues, caste prejudice and low returns, they are looking for jobs in the more lucrative tourism industry. The caste prejudice against Salagama or any other "low" caste is analogous to racism: It confines a person to the lowest status in society purely by virtue of birth. Sri Lankan society often identifies cinnamon peelers by their odor. Thus, cinnamon peeler's interactions have been tightly restricted for decades.

In addition to caste prejudice, the cinnamon industry also excludes women and disabled people—unable to work because of unhealthy conditions and physical limitations. The lack of employment for women and disabled people in areas that are dominated by the cinnamon industry leaves them and their dependents struggling to survive.

Finally, the traditional method of making Ceylon cinnamon does not meet the sanitary conditions of many countries. The processing of cinnamon is traditionally carried out on the ground, which leads to contamination as well as health issues for workers, such as postural stress, fatigue, and pain.

THE STRATEGY

After years of observing and studying Sri Lanka's cinnamon industry, Weera created a cinnamon peeling machine and accompanying technology. During years of study, he recognized the importance of the cinnamon industry to the Sri Lankan economy. Inspired by his findings, he set out on a mission to not only increase workers' efficiency, but to also improve the economy of Sri Lanka, increase profits of small stakeholders, and improve labor conditions.

Weera began his campaign to improve the cinnamon industry in 1986 when he carried out a research project with Ruhuna University to address the issues plaguing cinnamon workers. His research allowed him to gain insights into mechanizing the process. He spent many years designing and testing the machinery.

In 1998 Weera and Ruhuna University's faculty members organized a workshop with all stakeholder institutions on the revitalization of the cinnamon industry in Sri Lanka. Following the workshop, Weera spearheaded a campaign to introduce machinery mechanizing the processing of cinnamon.

Weera's diligent efforts yielded inventions such as a cinnamon peeling device (International Patent Certification, B27J-3/00.A23N-7/10, 11/00), a poly cam mechanism to improve the cinnamon mechanization process (International Patent Classification A23N 7/10, 11/00 B27J 3/00 Go5G 17/00, 2005), cinnamon processing bench, (Registration of Industrial Design No; 7628, 24th Nov. 2005), a cinnamon sticks making table, cinnamon scrapers, and a cinnamon bark remover. These inventions have successfully increased the efficiency of workers by 40 percent and have improved the quality of the quills produced.

Weera's innovations for the cinnamon industry are also addressing socio-economic issues, such as caste prejudices, unemployment, as well as gender and disability rights.

The mechanization of cinnamon processing has also solved health and sanitation issues plaguing the industry. Mechanization has discontinued the need for processing to take place on the ground. With Weera's technology, workers can now process while sitting in chairs and benches. The mechanization has also limited direct contact between workers and cinnamon, hence decreasing contamination and removing the odor of cinnamon from workers' skin and attire. As a result, the Salagama caste is now much less likely to suffer caste-based prejudice.

Mechanization has also opened doors for women and disabled people. The technology allows both women and those with disabilities to join the processing line, which has been simplified from Weera's technology. Their reintegration alleviates the financial and social conditions that they experience, thus allowing them to support themselves and their dependents.

The increase in cinnamon workers efficiency and the quality of quills has attracted new investments in the cinnamon industry. The mechanization of the process, coupled with the increase in investment, has attracted youth to the industry. As a professor at Ruhuna University and through his involvement in the cinnamon industry, Weera inspires youth to improve the industry through innovation and investment.

Weera's inventions targeting the cinnamon industry led him to create an incubator company within the university called Ruhuna Business Incubator (RBI), established in partnership with UNIDO and Ruhuna University. The first model business incubator in Sri Lanka, RBI was used to test his inventions and mentor young students who then furthered his innovations and promoted the new technology. Leading by example, Weera mentors undergraduate and graduate students to think beyond making money and instead, begin embarking on positively impacting communities, he is creating a new generation of social entrepreneurs.

Through the RBI, Weera also opened a new chapter in the Sri Lankan university system. RBI creates a space for intellectuals, students, development agencies, banks, and business people to introduce new development activities by diverting promising graduates to the businesses. The RBI model provides business services and creates a supportive environment for startup and early-stage enterprises in innovation-based products and services. Its linkage to a local knowledge base, business community and government agencies ensures the sustainability and social entrepreneurship culture while contributing significantly to the economy of Matara District and the Southern Province. RBI has played an instrumental role in increasing investment and attracting social entrepreneurs to the industry.

In 2009 Weera carried out two major projects that had a large impact on the cinnamon industry. The first was a workshop aimed at increasing investment by bringing all stakeholders of the cinnamon industry together, along with the Export Development Board, Central Bank, as well as local and international actors. Following the workshop, Weera and his colleagues formed the consortium U-10, which ensures that cinnamon produced in Sri Lanka meets the health and processing standards of EU markets. Through this consortium, Weera and his colleagues gave small stakeholders access to European markets.

> Weera's interventions comprehensively and holistically address the problems of small stakeholders by improving the image, productivity, and profitability of the industry.

As the global cinnamon market expands, the product's quality is expected to improve. Sri Lanka is only able to compete with other countries due to the technological revolution created by Weera. He has been a key player in bringing new investors into the industry through his workshops, training programs, and technology. Weera has also encouraged tea plantation owners to diversify their plantations by inserting cinnamon into the marginal lands where tea cultivation cannot be practiced. Thus, tea plantation owners have become investors in the cinnamon industry.

In the years to come, Weera plans to increase investments by devising a scheme that allows migrant workers to invest part of their earned income back into the cinnamon industry. Such an initiative would guarantee the financial and long-term sustainability for both migrant workers and the cinnamon industry.

Weera has chosen to lend his technology to the indigenous medicine industry and other industries in Sri Lanka so that they too may increase efficiency and decrease contamination. Such a sharing arrangement is highly unusual in Sri Lanka, as university resources are limited and often segregated from local communities. Refusing to conform, Weera broke this trend and used the technology along with the incubator company to develop small export crops as well as the ayurvedic sector—a move that allows farming communities to improve their income and social status. Thus, his technology currently has an impact beyond the cinnamon industry.

Through the introduction of his technology, Weera has already made an immense impact on the cinnamon industry. His involvement has been further cemented by the University Grants Commission, which assigned him the task of improving the cinnamon industry. By carrying out more research, trainings and workshops, he hopes to improve worker's lives, create more social entrepreneurs, and make cinnamon one of the largest export crops in Sri Lanka.

THE PERSON

Professor Weera was born in Agalawatha (Central Province). His father and mother were school teachers. Weera grew up around the cinnamon industry. His childhood home was surrounded by cinnamon plantations which he frequently visited and explored. As a child, Weera noted the hardships and prejudice that cinnamon workers faced. In keeping with his agricultural interests, Weera pursued physics, chemistry, botany, and zoology for his advanced level studies at Isipthana Maha Vidyalaya in Colombo.

Weera studied how agronomy can be used to improve the lives of people in the agricultural industry. His mentor, Pekinio Hesus Pieris guided him during his formative years to combine his passion for inventing and helping people in the agricultural industry.

During a six-month break from university, Weera worked at a prestigious bank in Sri Lanka as the first agricultural officer. His work at the bank reintroduced him to the agricultural industry. He successfully helped to improve the lives of farmers through a lending system. After his successful stint, despite being offered a more lucrative job, Weera chose to pursue his passion for servicing the community through technological inventions.

Weera received his Ph.D. in 1980 and joined Ruhuna University as a lecturer. Initially, he struggled to implement the entrepreneurial ideas he had learned from the agricultural industry in Sri Lanka. He faced many road blocks and critics during his career. However, his passion to invent and improve the lives of people drove him to overcome hurdles. With this drive, Weera pioneered the trend of using academia to address humanitarian issues and created a technological revolution in the cinnamon industry. Weera continues to be a maverick and is challenging the present ideologies held by the Sri Lankan people to help them improve their lives. ◆

FALK ZIENTZ

GERMANY

Financial Services/ Markets

Falk Zientz is building a self-sustaining microfinance distribution system which links traditional banks and non-banking organizations in Germany. Through this new system of micro lending, Falk is empowering tens of thousands of entrepreneurs to access new forms of capital and create lasting change for themselves and their communities.

THE NEW IDEA

Microloans have proven a key tool for the empowerment of business entrepreneurs not only in developing but also developed economies. However, more than 100,000 small entrepreneurs in Germany have no access to capital, which constitutes a powerful barrier to lifting people out of unemployment and poverty. Moreover, without adequate microfinance, developments in a great number of market innovations are severely restricted. After ten years of pioneering microfinance in Germany, Falk is unleashing new forms of capital for microenterprises through a superior model for the distribution and handling of microloans.

> "In 2000, Falk Zientz developed an integrated cooperation of Ministries, Banks, start-up centers, consulting companies and local authorities to provide finance to microentrepreneurs."
>
> —*Reseau Europeen*

Falk trains local "non-banks," mostly small business associations, to become microfinance institutes. He has found that small business associations are ideally best suited to provide the social and skills context for high repayment rates and low transaction costs. These institutes, upon being certified, handle applications and business plan reviews locally. Falk puts systems in place to process the credits for the institutes and provides financial incentives. This new model breaks the cost barrier, penetrates the niches, and creates a financially sustainable platform.

Falk has embedded this strategy with key stakeholders, thereby institutionalizing it in financial markets. At the GLS Bank, Germany's largest alternative bank, he has created a backend platform for the efficient administration of the micro loans. A

Microfinance Fund serves as guarantor with €100M in backup funding from the European Union and the German government. The German Microcredit Institute, a platform co-founded by Falk in the mid 2000s, serves as a training provider and certifier for the individual local microfinance institutes. Falk has already trained 40+ microfinance institutes (MFIs) and plans to issue 4,000 microloans annually once the platform has reached its target size. With this structure, Falk is building the first self-sustaining, distributed micro credit platform to reach critical size in Germany.

Ultimately, Falk will take the concept to other areas of finance at the intersection of public interest and private banking, empowering the financial sector to serve the needs of micro entrepreneurs in areas such as education, the environment, and many others.

THE PROBLEM

In Germany, there are more than 150,000 startups founded every year which bring people out of unemployment. This number is impressive and has been rising due to the launch of various government programs in the 2000s targeting small enterprises. Although the majority of startups persist (only 10 percent of business entrepreneurs become unemployed after five years of founding their startups), the majority of employees never reach a sufficient income. A major reason for this is a lack of access to capital. For at least 150,000 entrepreneurs, microloans are the only alternative, as they lack the necessary securities and expected income streams to be considered clients by banks.

Because microloans have been shown to create or save 1.5 jobs on average, a large number of microfinance initiatives have been deployed in Germany with public funding. Despite this, the microfinance industry in Germany is still very small, with little capitalization, and few institutions either offering loans or working with potential borrowers to ensure their success. Furthermore, loan underwriters have few incentives as they do not have a stake in the loan. Instead, they are merely channeling borrowers to other institutions, thus hindering the growth of the whole industry. Most of the existing microfinance initiatives failed to become financially self-sustainable due to high distribution and processing costs per loan. In addition, many commercial banks shy away from offering microloans at higher interest rates due to fears of adverse public relations. Most importantly, however, the lack of supportive and enabling communities around borrowers and a lack of expertise among industry financiers concerning the requirements of the potential borrowers (i.e. unlike in many developing communities) results in a high default rate. Thus, no microcredit platform in Germany has succeeded in achieving sustainability outside of limited niches, i.e. long-term unemployed youth.

THE STRATEGY

Falk recognized that for microcredit to be successful in Germany it required scaling up. The industry needed to secure more access to capital by building and enhancing the number and capacity of loan providers and their affiliated institutions which both identify and assist borrowers in launching successful businesses. He recognized that the only way to do this was to rely on non-traditional banks as distributors. To work, these distributors, which must have deep ties and developed trust in local communities, will rely on larger intermediaries in the banking sector, which could provide both training and access to capital. With longstanding experience as a central player in many microfinance initiatives in Germany, Falk created Mikrofinanzinitiative (German for Microfinance Initiative), as a platform to bring together the necessary stakeholders.

Fauk's approach is an innovative delivery system, which first secures the largest pool of capital heretofore available to the MFI sector. He then implements a structured series of incentives to the MFIs themselves, in which they are evaluated on the numbers of loans they provide in addition to how each loan performs over time. MFIs thus have "skin in the deal" and are both encouraged to do more underwriting without diminishing their due diligence and the services provided to borrowers.

Through a new system of micro lending, Falk is empowering tens of thousands of entrepreneurs to access new forms of capital and create lasting change for themselves and their communities.

A further critical element in helping the sector scale up is how the Mikrofinanzinitiative works with local business associations, and the many existing startup and SME support and infrastructure organizations, many working in less developed regions and cities, or for less economically integrated constituencies, i.e. migrants or young people. These entities are becoming the key distribution points for microloans. Though most have not been engaged in lending activities in their work, providing microloans is a great opportunity for the associations to better serve their target groups. To become certified Microfinance Institutes, each prospective

MFI receives an initial one-day workshop with Falk. Next they are trained by the German Microfinance Institute (DMI), in loan processing, business plan evaluation, and other relevant processes. The certified MIFs work with micro entrepreneurs seeking microloans ranging from 1,000 EUR to 20,000 EUR. Examples of MFIs include a cooperative of small to medium enterprises in Dortmund, an association of Turkish business people in Bielefeld, and a self-help group of migrants in Berlin. With this bottom-up approach it becomes possible to reach into the niches of the market, break the cost barrier, and generate a high level of self-organization among all market participants.

Falk has also created a program with GLS Bank for online backend credit processing. All payments are being made to and from GLS Bank, which pays a gratification for each approved loan to the MFI as an incentive. The fund which Falk established through the GLS Bank is backed by 100M EUR (i.e. operates with the capital interest from this sum) from the European Social Fund and the German federal government, both of which also support the marketing and communication around the fund.

THE PERSON

Falk grew up in a small village in the Black Forest among the Green movement and other active citizen organizations. From a young age, he actively campaigned for environmental causes. While studying in Berlin, Falk initiated and coordinated a 500,000 EUR tour of 350 students, entrepreneurs, and artists to the former Soviet Union and Mongolia, leveraging his talents as a master organizer and convener of disparate partners. After his studies, Falk got exited about the concept of "new labor" and the power of micro entrepreneurship; deciding to work in this field.

Falk joined the GLS Bank in its pioneering stage as an "ethical bank", where he gained key on-the-ground insights to credit processing. After five years, he quit the bank to support microfinance initiatives in other regions, such as Eastern Europe and Russia and to found a number of microfinance-related initiatives in Germany; which came to shape his life mission to radically change the state of microfinance in Germany. After having set up several smaller funds together with Deutsche Bank Foundation and some MFIs, Falk co-founded the German Microfinance Institute as a center for further education and capacity-building in the field of microfinance. He finally re-joined GLS Bank as an independent agent with the authority to develop and pioneer microfinance activities. Falk's affiliation with GLS has been central to his ability to secure the infusion of significant capital into the sector, and to continue to innovate at the interfaces of public interest and commercial banking. Today, the German government frequently asks Falk for consultation on innovative social finance mechanisms. ◆

HEALTH

MADELEINE CLARKE

IRELAND

Disabilities

Unity

Madeleine Clarke is crafting a strategy to nationally overhaul the disability field in Ireland. She has created a new set of standards and a unique selection process to determine the most community-focused, integrated, and cost-effective initiatives, and has set up structures to scale these initiatives at a policy level. Madeleine is creating a convergence for a fragmented sector, building cohesion and a more powerful voice for actors working throughout the physical, mental, and intellectual disability realm.

THE NEW IDEA

To transform the disability field, Madeleine has designed a replicable selection process to find the most innovative and successful solutions in the field, and then using a unique cross-sector methodology she helps to scale them so they become standards in the field. Her work shifts the disability field toward a collective effort, bringing representatives from mental, physical, and intellectual disabilities together with a focus on outcomes and improved quality of life for all disabled persons. Using a set of measures related to outcomes, easy to understand for policymakers and practitioners alike, Madeleine has determined the 23 most effective programs in the disability field in Ireland—such as community care for mentally disabled adults and select direct payment programs that allow programs to individualize their services—prioritizing those that place the disabled person at the center of decision-making and community life.

Madeleine's selection process sifted through over 650 programs to find the 23 to place at the center of the new disability paradigm, focusing on those most cost effective and integrated interventions. After finding the most effective programs based on criterion such as a person-centered approach, community integration, quality of life improvement, and cost-effectiveness, she gathered evidence on their efficacy and is capturing these grassroots examples to make them standards in the field. Recognizing the need to influence governmental standards, she is scaling the innovations at a policy level through a government fund which invests in the alternatives and shifts funding from traditional approaches. Madeleine has created a process to shift a field from one abiding focus to another—it includes a step by step method for system-wide policy and practice transformation that has large implications globally.

THE PROBLEM

There is little cohesion among the various sectors within the disability field. Physical disabilities, intellectual disabilities, and mental health disabilities are fragmented and poorly coordinated. There is ample opportunity to blend strengths and minimize weaknesses within the field: For example, the physical disability field has a history of poor advocacy, and the mental health field is primarily state run and vulnerable to political whim, while intellectual disability initiatives are driven by the citizen sector and suffer from unstable funding. This fragmentation is particularly unproductive as each subset has similar aspirations: Self-determination, community involvement, and better quality of life.

Despite considerable investment, the disability field has not changed considerably since the early 1980s. Though a search through the field yields a plethora of initiatives, programs, and strategies, these tend to be directed toward the disabled rather than guided by the disabled; there is a collective systems failure to provide the supports and opportunities that people with disabilities need to participate in society as equal citizens. Health and specialist interventions are given a disproportionate emphasis as if people with disabilities are primarily, and constantly, ill. Grouping people together to "fit" them into available services rather than customizing support on an individual basis leads to significant compromises. Furthermore, programs are either underfunded or wasting excess resources.

In the disability field, there is a growing shift toward people-centered and community-based approaches that treat the disabled as "whole" people with a unique skill set. A number of service providers have begun to customize their services on the basis of what the person with the disability identifies as being most important in helping them achieve a full and valued life. Programs that utilize family members and community are also growing. For example, Danish Ashoka Fellow Thorkil Sonne is offering job opportunities to autistics through a consulting company designed to capitalize on the strengths of disabled individuals, while Irish Fellow Tara Cunningham is teaching speech therapy techniques to parents of disabled children to ease the burden on low-paid professionals. The field is poised at an important moment to move fully into this realm. The development of policy to support people with disabilities to reach their full potential is welcome, but there is a particularly poor track record of policy implementation in this field, as in many other similar areas in Ireland. The most conservative estimate indicates that 8.1 percent of the Irish population has a disability. Over 56 percent of persons with intellectual disabilities are reported to be awaiting new or enhanced services or will need services before 2012. At least 55 percent of people with physical or sensory disabilities are either not getting the desired level of service or are waiting for assessments in order to be placed on waiting lists to access services. These statistics and the many obstacles confronting the disabilities field indicate the need for a new systems approach aimed at making the field more efficient, effective, and cohesive.

By creating a new set of national standards, Madeleine is determining the most community-focused, integrated, and cost-effective initiatives to overhaul the disability field in Ireland.

THE STRATEGY

In 2007 Madeleine established Genio to sit at the intersection between government, philanthropic, advocacy and service providing agencies in the area of disabilities. Her goal was to forge an alliance between government, private, and non-profit interests to enable people with disabilities to take control of their own lives with the aid of tailored, cost-effective supports and services through an agreed-upon, system-wide strategy.

There is a particular and growing emphasis in national policy on a more individualized, *"person-centered"* approach to meeting the needs of disabled people. The extent to which service users are satisfied that services fit their needs, rather than the reverse, is becoming the most important benchmark of quality. For example, it is growing policy to deinstitutionalize people with intellectual disabilities, to close psychiatric hospitals in favor of community-based care, offer specialist services for the mentally ill, involve disabled caretakers in developing services, educate special needs children in inclusive, non-segregated environments, and incorporate services into a disabled person's life, rather than dictating or dominating it. Programs that meet these needs are often more cost-effective in the long-run and provide greater quality of life.

Madeleine has launched an extensive research effort and selection process to determine the best and most cost effective of these options, building in a strong advocacy voice from the recipients of the services. Central to this evaluation is a set of weighted markers that determine which disability services and initiatives have the greatest impact on quality of life for the disabled; for example, to what extent a disabled person is able to drive their own life, such as whether a person is living in a location they choose, the number of paid versus

unpaid people in their life, and whether they have a valued role in a community. The research also determines the cost-effective and self-funding options and pinpoints places where funding may be excessive or too stingy, wasted or trapped, or scattered in unconnected service provision. Out of over 650 program applications, Madeleine has currently identified 23 that are cost effective and place the disabled person at the center of decision-making for their own care. Her organization offers grants of 300,000 Euros to these best practices, capacity-building, and mechanisms to expand the work dramatically. A condition of the grant is evaluative research and learning events to help spread the best practice. Prioritizing natural supports, such as family and existing community, over paid professionals for disability care is a two part win, in that it improves quality of life and is less expensive. An example of this would be programs that remove mentally disabled adults from state-run institutions and allow communities to "adopt" them. Madeleine has grouped these 23 as the core of her strategy, and is focused on building the structures to turn these 23 best practices in person-centered disability into standard practice nationwide.

Madeleine is using distribution strategies in the private sector as an unofficial template for her own spread and scale. While the private health industry broadcasts nationally and internationally within days a new cure for a disease, the dissemination of learning and solutions in the disability field is haphazard. Madeleine is engineering the tools for distribution—a "cost effective transfer," to move funding from ineffective and paternalistic interventions to these identified best practices. Realizing the impossibility of a sudden about-face in strategy, and the logistical impracticalities of redeploying resources suddenly, she is building a transfer fund to allow governments to transition from existing approaches to best practices, linking funding to outcomes. She has received 3M Euros from the Irish government for funding the implementing of the strategy over the first year. She is also building a marketplace where disabled people can choose how to individualize their services, with options approved by both users and providers. For example, a disabled person could choose to move from an institution to live at home, with an allotted 20 hours a week of paid support, which he could choose how to "spend"—i.e. direct it toward what help he determines most needed, such as support getting dressed.

> ## "The Genio Trust, with a budget of €3.4m, financially supports a range of services tailored to the needs of the person with a disability."
>
> —*Independent*

Madeleine has articulated a clear vision for where she is guiding each arm of disability—intellectual, physical, and mental. In terms of intellectual disability, in five years she envisions more public resources supporting community inclusion and integration, and any new public money used to support individual services and people in the community. With the help of Genio, the resources are beginning to move in that direction. Madeleine and Genio are providing the only innovation funding for disability in Ireland, working in cooperation with decision-makers to direct it. In terms of intellectual disability, her strategy also includes ending funding for institutions and substantial numbers of residents moving out into community support programs. Madeleine has directly contributed to a new national policy to this end, which is creating a system of small group homes to support independent living for the intellectually disabled—a move supported by 80 percent of service providers. The law was drawn directly from Genio's research and success stories.

Madeleine is guiding the physical disability field toward a broad direct payment approach that would allow users to be paid and choose their own supports. Using the UN Declaration of Disabled Rights as a focus, she envisions a much stronger voice in policy and in the public space, as the physical disability arena has the weakest voice of any in the field. She is building a cadre of strong advocates working in collaboration. Finally, within the physical disability space she is pushing for significantly increased employment, specifically among those with spinal injuries, through "supportive employment opportunities," assistive technologies, and training to give people the "tools and courage" to enter the job market.

Madeleine talks with Pat McLoughlin and Finbar Flood, Chair of her Board of Trustees and Chair of her Board.

Mental disability has a distinctly different set of challenges than either intellectual or physical, having far fewer citizen organizations (COs) providing services. Mental disability services are almost entirely provided in state-run hospitals, making policy more difficult to shift. As such, Madeleine has shifted her strategy to support any groups that close "acute wards" or institutional beds and replace them with community supports. She is creating a national organization of service users to strengthen programs, generate user feedback and satisfaction levels, and publish the results. In five years time Madeleine envisions a culture where users can hold service providers accountable and where the voice of users is gaining traction and less dominated by medical or psychiatric representatives. Her five-year plan calls for a reduction by half in the number of patients in institutions, paralleled with more robust community supports. Madeleine imagines a landscape similar to the U.S. state of Vermont, which has nearly 100 percent community care for the mentally disabled and no institutional culture.

Madeleine is blending sectors in a field renowned for their divide—business, government, COs, and physical, intellectual, and mental disabilities—together with the disabled voice in a "convergence opportunity around government, service providers, process and methods." Currently her roster includes people with disabilities, the Office for Disability and Mental Health in the Department of Health and Children, the HSE, National Advocacy Groups, and service provider coalitions both in Ireland and internationally.

Beyond a government efficiency campaign or association building, Madeleine is engineering structures and a step-by-step strategy to ensure genuine policy implication and systems change across the disability field. Her work is designed to combat the passivity of disabled groups by placing them at the center of advocacy and decision-making and by defining self-determination in a much larger context—from choosing between services to choosing which services are on offer, and where money goes on a policy level. There are large implications for her approach to fields beyond disability as well.

THE PERSON

A child with a strongly developed social conscience, Madeleine began fundraising for social causes early on in her youth, selling homemade items at her garden gate at age nine to benefit children in war-torn Biafra. Studying psychology, she became highly-credentialed in her field. As a practicing psychologist, Madeleine saw the impact that disability can have on families—part of her role saw her diagnosing young children with lifetime disabilities. The conversations where she informed their parents had a profound effect on her. Madeleine grew to be a pioneer in her field, one of the first in Ireland to focus on evaluative impact. She defied expectations to pursue traditional psychological assessments and turned her attention to service evaluation and communication tools for those who could not use language. Working with a group, she co-designed a new, simplified version of Irish Sign Language manageable for those with intellectual disabilities or limited manual dexterity. She began to design service improvement initiatives and disseminate them through national organizations—an early apprenticeship for her work with Genio.

Later, Madeleine rose to deputy CEO at Barnardos, Ireland's largest children's charity. There she learned the machinations of a large-scale CO and sharpened her skills, rebuilding the organization's funding structure to be more sustainable and creating a national chain of children's services. Turning down an offer of the CEO position, she left Barnardos to become co-founder of Children's Rights Alliance. Designed to build consensus between governments and various CO groups in the context of the Convention on the Rights of the Child, her work with Children's Rights Alliance was a crash course in getting disparate groups to work together.

A weary veteran of traditional CO approaches, Madeleine found she had "lost interest in pilots," and grown tired of the uncoordinated, piecemeal approaches prevalent in so much well-intentioned work. She began a short-term effort with a foundation to map the disability field in Ireland, and was dismayed to find that the field had not changed in the 20 years since she had last worked in it. Madeleine became compelled by the idea of a united strategy for the transformation of the field, and founded Genio. ◆

PHIL CONWAY

UNITED KINGDOM

Child Care

Disabilities

Phil Conway is redefining the industry around the care of disabled children by introducing a flexible, personalized model of care based on the real needs of the clients. Recognizing that, like all children, disabled children need "fun, friendship and fresh air," he is using modern recruitment techniques to bring entirely new types of carers into the system: Open-minded, energetic young people. By introducing a new type of "personal assistant" into the homecare industry, Phil is shifting society's expectations about the visibility and inclusion of the disabled.

THE NEW IDEA

The Cool2Care model is based on the concept of a "personal assistant"; a youthful and energetic role model who is a friend to a disabled child and part of the fabric of family life. Rather than employing an unskilled older woman who watches over the disabled child while the parents get a break, a young personal assistant aged 18 to 28-years gives the child access to fun experiences and youth culture. They bring enthusiasm and an open-minded approach to the care of the disabled. In contrast to the standardized and medicalized notion of care promoted by most agencies, the principle behind Cool2Care is that the process should be made more personal for families; they should be directly involved in choosing and shaping the support they want, based on their particular needs.

Founded in 2008, Cool2Care uses corporate recruitment strategies to attract young people through youth magazines and the Internet, a stark contrast to the gray box repeated weekly in job pages for low skilled workers. Personal assistants are carefully matched to the needs of families by Cool2Care staff members who know the families personally. The arrangement gives families an easy avenue to find the kind of carer they want, rather than navigate the impersonal agency system or find their own support. Meanwhile, the young personal assistant gains an opportunity to work in a career which was previously considered unattractive, while also playing a role in the wider inclusion of disabled children in society.

Having scaled to 30 locations in the U.K. in only three years, Phil has identified a model which is both highly attractive to families and financially sustainable. Rather than rely on the traditional centralized agency model, Cool2Care is an *introduction* service, focused on careful matching of client to carer. Once the match is made, the family builds a contract directly with the carer, rather than Cool2Care, and pays the carer directly. Local authorities can

also contract with Cool2Care to serve their particular area. The income provided from local authority contracts and introduction fees ensure an ongoing revenue stream which is then reinvested into Cool2Care.

Phil is now working to change the provision of care for disabled children internationally. He is setting up a Cool2Care charitable foundation that will aim to promote understanding and share best practices across the world. He began by sending a group of students to map the disability field globally, developing an overview of best practices and the needs of the sector. Now that the connections have been made, Phil intends to create a self-supporting global network of likeminded practitioners who are creating a better system of care for disabled children and their families.

THE PROBLEM

There are 770,000 disabled children living in the U.K., with the vast majority living in the care of their families. Having a disabled child is a life-changing experience for the whole family, especially with regards to the new care burdens. New challenges, such as integrating care services into daily life, often put enormous mental and physical stress on parents. Surveys show that over 80 percent of disabled families are "at a breaking point." The divorce rate among families of disabled children is 33 percent higher than families without disabled children. There is also a strong correlation between families with disabled children and higher levels of poverty, as parents find themselves unable to work due to the time consuming responsibility of caring for their child: 34 percent of disabled children live in households where both parents are unemployed and 60 percent of disabled children live in or at the margins of poverty. As these statistics show, the consequences of not finding suitable care or not being able to afford suitable childcare, can be devastating.

Finding an appropriate carer for a disabled child is extremely difficult. Parents have a choice between either finding a carer through networks and community pin boards or through using a care agency. One of the system's major weaknesses is its pattern of standardized service, which is supply-driven and does not allow for individualization: Parents cannot decide which care-assistant to employ and their preferences around a carer's skills, personality traits, or willingness for weekend/evening work are not considered. Most conventional agencies employ older, unskilled people who choose the work out of circumstance rather than choice. Agencies focus on supplying a responsible adult to deal with the basic physical requirements of the child; enjoyment is therefore not the objective, and activities like leaving the house are forbidden because they are not insured. Disabled children therefore remain out of sight, and cut off from youth culture.

Furthermore, high-quality care under the British care sector is often expensive. According to recent research reports, finding childcare for a disabled child is the challenge most often cited by parents wishing to take on paid work.

Consequently, there is a disconnect between the care services that families need and the services offered by the care industry. Cool2Care aims to close this gap by making care more demand-driven.

THE STRATEGY

Phil aims to transform the entire care industry by irrevocably changing families' expectations about the types and quality of care for disabled children, thereby forcing other agencies to follow suit and change their own practices. Phil believes that competition from other companies will be a sign of progress toward the landscape of care for disabled children.

Phil's strategy begins with scaling Cool2Care across the U.K. The Cool2Care business model rests on three core pillars: The recruitment of personal assistants, their training, and tailored placement of carers into families. Families are identified with the help of the local authority, although any family may refer themselves. Phil's vision of changing the care sector begins with his recruitment strategy for personal assistants. His recruitment target groups differ from conventional care recruitment profiles; Phil is looking for young people, including students, existing nannies, and young migrant workers, who can provide friendship and a connection with youth culture.

> Having scaled to 30 locations in the U.K. in only three years, Phil has identified a model which is both highly attractive to families and financially sustainable.

A major goal of Phil's marketing strategy is to communicate that working with disabled children is a fun way to earn a living. Phil uses his previous experience at IBM to develop a recruitment campaign that targets young people in particular over the Internet and in their universities. Cool2Care has developed a tailored training course to give recruitees the confidence and skills to be personal assistants. Candidates complete a basic social care training course organized in six half-day classes over the course of three weeks. Upon completion of this first level of training, Cool2Care places the personal assistants with families.

Cool2Care makes introductions to families rather than employ the personal assistants directly. Cool2Care staff work to carefully understand the needs of the family in terms of type of personal assistant required and hours needed. In contrast to other care agencies that contract their clients directly, Cool2Care families privately employ the personal assistant on mutually acceptable, flexible terms. Families who want their carers to have more significant training can work this out directly with the carer. This flexibility is key to Phil's model: If the family needs to change their arrangements one day, they can resolve this directly with the personal assistant rather than going through an agency. Cool2Care only receives an introduction fee, thereby directly transferring the hourly rate paid to the personal assistant. Cool2Care advises the families on how to simplify and manage the care worker employment process, and provides support if problems should arise. In addition, Cool2Care explains how to effectively access state funding sources to help families pay for the personal assistant. These processes reflect Phil's concern with empowering a whole new generation of care assistants and beneficiary families. They are designed to not only offer the highest possible degree of individualized care, but also to foster confidence between the personal assistants and the families.

All Cool2Care's employees work part-time, and many are working mothers. Phil's recruitment strategy for his own staff has rested on the principle that staff could best cater to the needs of the client if they mirrored them in some way. He identified the part-time arrangement as a way to ensure that Cool2Care staff share and understand the same concerns as their clients.

Phil is now working with international partners to identify the leading approaches to working with disabled children from around the world. The process began with sending students to Brazil, Thailand, Cambodia, Sri Lanka, India, China, and Indonesia to research the sectors and identify best practices among citizen organizations. Phil wants the Cool2Care foundation to act as an international connector and center of excellence, which provides a platform to the best innovators while allowing them to exchange resources and expertise, and together acting as a louder voice for the needs of disabled children. Meanwhile, Cool2Care's model is transferable to a range of other social care needs, such as care of the elderly.

THE PERSON

Phil spent 20 years at IBM, a time he describes as feeling like a frustrated "intrapreneur" who always felt the urge to create something innovative with a bigger impact. He was constantly making proposals to his superiors, including insisting on a transfer to Asia to work on a new market despite being told "no" several times. He initiated and implemented several new business strategies within IBM, for example running software marketing for Asia when its market was just opening up.

Phil's life changed when his first son, Shaun, was born with significant physical disabilities. Shaun's disability became apparent after his first year of life after missing key developmental milestones. Suddenly Phil was confronted with disability issues and care service delivery, and found that all family life was consumed by these new concerns. He was frustrated by how hard it was to find the right kind of carer for Shaun—the family tried several agencies and by going through their own networks, but none of the people seemed to fit. At the core of the problem was that Phil and his family did not just want a babysitter, but someone who would be a fun peer and role model for Shaun. He realized that many families wanted the same for their disabled children, and were struggling with a range of inappropriate choices.

Phil began to explore how he could address the problems families like his faced. He first joined the board of a large charity working with the families of disabled children, which he saw as a valuable traineeship. Yet, he remained frustrated with existing approaches. Phil then became increasingly fascinated by social enterprise as a means for tackling social problems. He also remained convinced that the prevailing system of caring failed to meet the actual needs of disabled families, and that a new business model could underpin a better approach. Phil rapidly built up Cool2Care on the principle that it would only affect the industry if it quickly operated nationally. Phil is now exploring how the Cool2Care model can adapt to different target groups and geographies. ♦

ERIKA FOUREAUX

BRAZIL

Appropriate Technology

Early Childhood Development

Erika Foureaux is driven by the conviction that all children, whether they are "differently-abled" or not, must be given the opportunity to reach their full potential as citizens and community members. She is developing products and services that respect the principles of universal design in order to promote the integration of "diffabled" children in Brazilian society.

THE NEW IDEA

After giving birth to a daughter with cerebral palsy, Erika quickly became aware of the pressing need to promote the integration of children with different abilities in Brazilian society. She founded the Noisinho da Silva Institute, whose target audiences are children between the ages of one and six as well as their families, to "normalize" interactions between children of all abilities in schools and in their homes. In order to do so, she is developing a series of products and methodologies that adhere to the concept of universal design. Universal design refers to a broad-spectrum solution that brings about products and environments usable and effective for everyone, not just people with disabilities.

> "Erika Foureaux founded [the] Institute to work [for] the social inclusion of children with disabilities through inclusive design. In 2009, Ciranda [was] awarded the International Excellence Award, as well as the trophy in medical science."
>
> —*Sonia Pessoa Communications*

One of Erika's flagship products is the Ciranda, a new type of chair that allows children with "diffabilities" to sit on the floor on their own. The Ciranda makes it possible for them to play with their siblings and peers in ways never before possible, and without constant supervision or support from adults. This innovative technology has the merit of responding to two different market needs. On the one hand, Erika has developed an upscale model of the Ciranda to respond to the demand of middle-class parents who seek inclusive solutions for their children. On the other hand, Erika also developed a Ciranda that can be built and assembled by low-income families at no cost to them through Ciranda-making workshops. The workshops are at once therapeutic and

educational, and are financed through corporate sponsorships, as well as government and citizen organization (CO) funding. Since 2007, a total of 2,400 people have benefitted from the Ciranda: 600 children and their families now have access to a technology that enables the greater inclusion of diffabled children in Brazilian society.

Through the institute, Erika is also developing other lines of products such as the Socially Inclusive Desk used in classrooms. This product has already benefitted more than 100 children in the states of Rio de Janeiro and Minas Gerais thanks to a partnership with the Ministry of Finance. Both the Ciranda and the Desk are beginning to be sold to the government and to high-income populations in order to contribute to the financial sustainability of the organization and to enable it to serve an increasing number of low-income families. As a result of her work, Erika is also diligently raising awareness about the rights of people with physical disabilities, tackling prejudice and exclusion, intervening in public policy debates, and establishing partnerships with various companies and government entities to expand the reach and range of her products and services in the Brazilian market. She also aims to replicate the Ciranda-making workshops throughout Brazil by developing a distance education course.

THE PROBLEM

Brazil is home to a large number of children with diffabilities. According to Banco do Brasil's Bank of Social Technology, 12 percent of Brazilian children between the ages of one and six suffer from motor-skill deficiencies. Of these 2.3 million children, it is estimated that nearly one-fifth cannot sit up on their own or experience difficulties in doing so. As a result, children with diffabilities and their families also experience a number of related challenges.

A child's inability to sit up on his or her own, coupled with the lack of access to appropriate and affordable technologies to assist him or her, generally lead to various physical and developmental issues. For instance, children often suffer from respiratory, gastro-intestinal and orthopedic problems as a result of being confined to their wheelchairs or remaining in a horizontal position all day. Most diffabled children who cannot sit on the floor with their peers or be marginally mobile have trouble playing and interacting with other children and their surroundings. This is particularly relevant during early childhood since these types of activities are crucial to the social, emotional and physical development of all children. It is through games and interactions with others and their physical environments that children learn how to interpret the world they live in. Moreover, various studies have shown that children who lack such experiences during their early childhood are more likely to face difficulties in the classroom.

The lack of autonomy that these problems entail also has significant consequences for parents. Many feel an extreme sense of guilt and helplessness when confronted with the situations of dependency and, often, suffering endured by their children. Regrettably, guilt and helplessness can easily be transformed into sentiments of shame and low self-esteem, which in turn leave children all the more isolated from the rest of society. Fearful of the way others might react to their presence many parents inadvertently make their children invisible.

In addition, the majority of Brazilian households, schools and hospitals cannot afford furniture and technologies that might facilitate diffabled children's integration. The few products that do exist tend to draw more attention to the differences between people with and without disabilities and are rarely pleasing to the eye, thus perpetuating discrimination and doing little to increase the self-esteem of diffabled people. The concept of universal design—design solutions that are available to everyone, whether they are differently-abled or not—is only now entering the Brazilian market thanks in significant part to Erika's work.

The Ciranda seat rests on the floor and is equipped with two straps that allow children with physical disabilities to sit up and play with their peers.

Although Brazil recognizes inclusion as a right for people with disabilities, all three levels of government as well as many health and education institutions remain unprepared to respond to the issues people with diffabilities have to face on a daily basis. Families are quite lost and often do not know where to go to get the support they and their children need.

THE STRATEGY

In an effort to increase the quality of life and inclusion of people with diffabilities, Erika founded the Noisinho da Silva Institute in Belo Horizonte in 2003. She is using the principles of universal design in developing a series of products and services that are equally suited for children with and without disabilities.

The institute's flagship program is the Ciranda-making workshop. The Ciranda is a seat that rests on the floor and is equipped with two straps that allow children with physical disabilities to sit up and play on the ground with their peers. Low-income families whose children have physical disabilities build these seats with low-cost, environmentally friendly materials in the span of a single weekend. The workshops involve the entire family: While the parents are learning how to build the Ciranda, the diffabled children, their friends and siblings are having fun playing "universal" games with trained educators.

Forty chairs can be produced by up to 400 people per workshop. Each family leaves the course with its own Ciranda, an official

certificate, and a manual with step-by-step instructions to guide them as they build the seat. Those more entrepreneurial parents also leave with a new income generation opportunity should they decide to start building the Ciranda for other community members. The institute has begun inviting wood-workers from the community to make the affordable technology available in a greater number of localities, even when workshops are not offered. Families are asked during the class and periodically thereafter to report any problems and benefits their children have experienced in using the Ciranda.

Thanks to corporate sponsorships and funding from various government entities and foundations, more than 2,400 people have participated in the Ciranda-making workshops since 2007 and 600 children in the states of Minas Gerias, Sao Paulo and Rio de Janeiro now benefit from using this technology in their homes. Many more children have also used the Ciranda in schools, kindergartens and other institutions that attend to the needs of children with different abilities. Beyond the obvious health benefits (respiratory, gastric, and orthopedic) that come as a result of the use of the Ciranda, children also gain the ability to interact with their environment and their peers in ways previously unimaginable. Their newly found autonomy permits new types of learning opportunities and aspirations, thus increasing diffabled children's self-esteem. As a result, their families and friends also begin developing new perspectives on the capabilities and potential of people with disabilities. This realization in turn radically transforms group dynamics and relationships between people of varying physical abilities.

It is important to note that the workshops also serve certain therapeutic and healing functions for parents. They become so proud of their craftsmanship and of the new possibilities they have created for their children that their own self-esteem rises and the sense of guilt they may have struggled with for years suddenly begins to dissipate. Their children, who were once invisible to the rest of society—either because they were ashamed to bring them out in public or because they simply did not have the right tools to facilitate their inclusion—suddenly become visible citizens.

To implement the workshops in different cities, the Noisinho da Silva Institute first searches for local partners who share their vision and mission. The institute then contacts city halls, health and education organizations, as well as other institutions that work with people with disabilities. These partners are in charge of reaching out to families with diffabled children between the ages of one and six. The institute then organizes meetings with the partners, parents and children to inform them about the initiative's goals. It also conducts interviews with the children and their families to determine whether or not the Ciranda would be appropriate for them.

Determined to develop a diverse line of universal design products that contribute to the integration and autonomy of diffabled children in their homes but also in their schools, Erika created Brazil's first Socially Inclusive Desk. This classroom desk, which is pleasing to the eye, is suited for children of all abilities. By introducing this type of furniture into schools, Erika aims to educate teachers about inclusion, and improve the confidence, self-esteem, autonomy, and level of participation of diffabled children in their classrooms. Thanks to a partnership with the Ministry of Development of Minas Gerais, 150 desks are being used in classrooms in Belo Horizonte and Vale de Jequitinhonha.

With the organization's growth and sustainability in mind, Erika has also developed an upscale model of the Ciranda, which she aims to sell to middle-class families in Brazil. Not only will the institute thus reach a larger number of children, it will also be able to offer the Ciranda-making workshops to an increasing number of people thanks to the generated revenue. Similarly, Erika plans to sell the Socially Inclusive Desk on the market within the next year or two. She is establishing partnerships with associations of physiotherapists and COs who play an important role in advising institutions working with people with disabilities in their furniture purchases—including schools and large hospitals. In the same vein, Erika is developing a partnership with the Secretary of Education of Minas Gerais to introduce her desks into public schools. Finally, in order to replicate the workshops in more localities, she is creating a distance education course that will be administered through local partners. The institute will make the Ciranda molds available to each partner to also facilitate local production.

THE PERSON

Due in significant part to being exiled in France with her parents at a very young age, Erika developed an early commitment to social justice. In the initial years of her degree in Industrial Design, she created a working group with her colleagues to think of ways they could use their newly acquired abilities to serve the social good. This is when she started promoting the concept of Universal Design.

Erika is the mother or three girls. When Sophie—her middle child—was born with cerebral palsy, Erika began developing home-made solutions to ensure that all three of her children could play and interact in an environment that would enhance Sophie's development and be friendly for the whole family without making her stand out.

Years earlier, Erika had been offered exclusive franchising rights to bring VIBEL's upscale children's furniture to Brazil. After Sophie's birth, she quickly realized that people with different abilities could not use these fixtures. Equipped with extensive training as an architect and the experience of designing and distributing VIBEL furniture in Brazil, Erika therefore began developing new types of products and services that adhere to the principles of Universal Design.

Since founding the Noisinho da Silva Institute, Erika has become the recipient of several national and international prizes. In 2005, she won the Top Social Prize and the following year her work was officially recognized for its importance and innovation at the Handitex Fair in Paris. She also received an award from Banco do Brasil in partnership with UNICEF for the impact reached through the institute's Ciranda workshops. Most recently, Erika became a finalist of the Social Entrepreneurship Prize presented by Folha de Sao Paulo and the Schwab Foundation. ♦

FRANK HOFFMANN

GERMANY

Disabilities

Employment/Labor

Health Care Delivery

Reproductive Health

Dr. Frank Hoffmann pioneers a diagnostically superior, personal, low-cost breast examination method by training blind people as skilled diagnosticians. Frank's approach integrates them into the primary health care infrastructure, while enhancing women's health care experience and opening an entirely new professional path to a differently-abled constituency.

THE NEW IDEA

In Germany, preventive breast cancer diagnosis is either offered through mammography—which is expensive and therefore only routinely available for women over 50—or a superficial (i.e. limited to a few minutes by most German insurance options) manual breast examination available to all women, performed by doctors who do not employ a standardized technique (i.e. there is no mandatory in-depth training for physicians in Germany). As a result of the impersonal and often stressful experience, many women choose not to undergo preventative diagnosis. Consequently, Germany has the lowest participation rate for breast-cancer diagnosis in Europe—an indicator of the broader challenge potentially facing many Western health systems where escalating costs create pressures on patient care.

As prevention is critical in the fight against breast cancer, Frank recognized that the existing system required new resources and more cost efficient processes. He found this new resource among blind people, who possess a far better sense of touch and are widely neglected in the German labor market. (A mere 30 percent of Germany's 1.2 million visually impaired people actually work for an income.) Frank developed the program, Discovering Hands®, which trains blind women to become Medical Tactile Examiners (MTEs). Their superior sensitive touch gives them a higher precision rate and enables them to detect breast cancer earlier than the average doctor. The first scientific study deducted within half a year has shown that in 450 cases, MTEs found more and smaller tumors than doctors. Moreover, the 30-minute breast examination, as compared to the usual 3-minute exam, gives women more time to ask questions and be reassured that they are healthy.

With this model, Frank is not only offering improved and more cost-effective early preventive breast cancer diagnosis, but is also creating a new profession, opening the medical field to the blind. Furthermore, Frank's program helps seeing patients become aware of blind people's unique capacities; turning blindness, often considered a disability, into an asset.

THE PROBLEM

Breast cancer is the most frequent cause of death for women between 40 and 44 and is the most common type of cancer for women between 25 and 74. There are 58,000 new cases and 18,000 deaths every year in Germany alone. One out of ten women will suffer from breast cancer within their lifetime.

> "Blind women can develop their special tactile gifts in a medical profession which, in return, supports the social integration of people with disability."
>
> —*Ralf Esser, MyHandicap*

The mortality rate from breast cancer depends largely on early detection. Halving the time between the emergence of cancer and its detection typically doubles the survival rate. Despite this fact, the conditions for early diagnosis in Germany have deteriorated in past years. After legislative changes in 2005, high tech and cost intensive annual mammography is only reimbursed to women over 50, while women under 50 receive only a brief manual breast exam, typically lasting a few minutes. There is no standardized curriculum for doctors on how to perform an exam, nor is it part of an in-depth on-the-job training. What is more, insurance companies only cover costs for "normal" short breast examinations, thus leaving doctors and patients with uncertainty about the results.

The tension between preventative imperatives and cost is indicative for the broader challenge of health systems and demographic change. While breast cancer represents a particularly common and well-understood disease, many more medical conditions face a similar need for creative yet medically sound approaches, new resources, and more human-oriented solutions.

For Frank, blind people are the natural answer to the problem of effective breast cancer diagnosis. There are about 1.2 million people with less than 30 percent of normal vision in Germany. Of the 160,000 completely blind people, approximately 36,000 are in the employable age between 15 to 60 years, yet only 30 percent of them actually work, compared to 75 percent of the seeing population. Few professions are open to blind people, and they still face major discrimination when trying to enter the workforce. The health sector is a key field of productive work for them. For example, in physiotherapy many blind people combine the use of highly sensitized touch with verbal skills to provide superior health services.

THE STRATEGY

Frank designed a standardized system of orientation for breast examiners based on braille strips. This mapping system is an innovative solution on its own and has already been adopted by other gynecologists. It consists of five adhesive strips placed around a woman's breast with both braille and color coordinates that allow any abnormality/lump to be pinpointed by two dimensional coordinates. This allows blind women to carry out breast examinations with complete autonomy. Trained as MTEs—a completely new profession that Frank created through his standardized training curriculum—they are also able to accomplish other daily tasks of a seeing medical assistant, including the maintenance of medical records.

Due to the personal nature of the procedure, Frank has only trained women. His method humanizes medicine by giving more attention to patients through individual contact and longer, more personal examinations. An MTE reports to the doctor as an assistant, not a replacement, and their examination feeds into the doctors ultimate diagnosis. When an abnormality is located, the doctor proceeds, most often with ultrasounds and mammography.

A study conducted by Essen University's women's clinic concluded that in 450 cases, MTEs found more and smaller tumors than doctors. The identification of smaller lumps allows earlier diagnosis and more effective treatment. Another advantage of employing MTEs is their ability to dedicate more time to patient examinations. Whereas a doctor is able to spend only a few minutes on each examination, MTEs can commit a half hour due to their lower labor costs. At 30 EUR (US$45) per breast exam (with a duration of 30 minutes) Frank's model costs four times less than a mammography examination.

Discovering Hands® trains blind women to become MTEs—a higher precision rate enables them to detect breast cancer earlier than the average doctor.

The training of MTEs takes place at the BFW occupational school in Düren, a center located in western Germany for individuals no longer able to continue their profession as a result of visual impairment or blindness. The testing phase of the project (2006 to 2008) is completed and Frank is spreading the Discovering Hands® method through a newly found non-profit organization to all other German occupational schools, which then will be licensed to instruct MTEs on the standardized training curricula. Until now, 10 blind women have qualified as MTEs and all have found permanent employment. Frank graduated another 10 MTEs at the end of 2010. The program has been acclaimed a success by both patients and practitioners in Germany. Health services in Europe including Ireland, France, Denmark, U.K., and Austria have shown interest in launcing an equivalent system in their countries.

The program is based on a process that can be paid through the existing cost covering system of insurance companies. Thus, it is profitable for every doctor able to return license fees to Discovering Hands®. In this way, it is one of the very few health innovations that is self-financing from the very beginning and thus, able to greatly expand. It also has enormous potential in countries without high-tech medicine.

THE PERSON

Frank always looked for opportunities to improve existing systems that solve social and health problems. After working in a gynecological clinic, Frank, as a young gynecologist, took over a medical practice from his predecessor, who died unexpectedly, shortly after his arrival. After expanding his medical practice, the father of two children quickly recognized that single practices in suburban regions were no longer competitive nor sustainable organizational models. He used his entrepreneurial talent to convince other doctors to open a joint practice with him, becoming one of the first gynecological joint practices in a suburban region.

Eventually, Frank and seven other gynecologists merged their practices into what is today the biggest joint practice in the Duisburg region, the Praxis für Frauen. A leader in the field of gynecology, in 2001 Frank founded Quality Circle of Gynecologists in Duisburg, a round table guaranteeing standardized quality control in the region of Duisburg, and led it until 2009. In 2009 he set up a service company to outsource the administrative and IT work of his joint medical practice. This for-profit venture is one of the first of its kind and a pioneering model of how medical practices could become more efficient and fit for future changes in the health care system. After the mammography law changed in 2005 Frank could no longer serve his patients with the quality of care he wanted. When he realized that his idea could offer employment for blind people, a group highly excluded from the labor market, he wanted to institutionalize his idea and make it known. Since 2004 Frank has developed Discovering Hands® mainly in his free time. In 2010 he founded a nonprofit organization to spread the Discovering Hands® method. ♦

MIRIAM ISRAEL

MEXICO

Health Care Delivery

Nutrition/Wellness

Inspired by successful palliative care experiences in the U.S., and determined to find new ingredients that would allow the approach to succeed where previous attempts have failed, Miriam Israel is creating a culture of end-of-life care in Mexico. She has developed a set of integrated services to help patients and their families cope with the emotional, psychological, physical, and legal or socioeconomic consequences of death. Miriam is beginning to spread her approach through the budding National Palliative Care Network, with members in 24 Mexican states.

THE NEW IDEA

As a Mexican native, Miriam was first exposed to the specialized palliative care of a hospice while visiting her stepfather, who was dying of cancer in the U.S. In that moment she realized the complete lack of similar end-of-life care for patients in Mexico, where death and suffering are simply accepted by the majority as an intricate part of life against which nothing can be done. Aside from Miriam's organization in Mexico City, the only other places where palliative care is offered are Guadalajara and Tijuana, where a handful of Mexican doctors underwent medical training in the U.S. However, these services are usually priced out of reach of many of the terminally ill patients in Mexico. Even pain clinics that have purportedly begun offering end-of-life care do not address the psychological and emotional toll both on the patient and his or her family. Miriam therefore became determined to create a culture of palliative care in Mexico's health care system, founding the Centro de Cuidados Paliativos de México, IAP (CECPAM—Center for Palliative Care in Mexico).

CECPAM's palliative care model centers upon the delivery of integrated services through an interdisciplinary team consisting of a doctor, a nurse, a thanatologist (i.e. a health worker who specializes in death and dying), and a social worker, who is sent to the patient's home to provide an initial assessment of the patient's and the family's needs, followed by regular home visits. CECPAM also offers psychological services to family members dealing with grief for up to one year after the death of the patient. The care model ensures that the patient enjoys the highest quality of life possible at the end of his or her life and that the family is trained, sensitive, and aware of their own needs as well as those of their loved one.

CECPAM has become a leading voice in Mexico's nascent palliative care sector, and it is establishing its presence in numerous clinics and hospitals. Since the vast majority of Mexicans are unaware of palliative care, Miriam is working to spread the word about CECPAM's services and to have her two current teams working at full capacity. In time, she plans to expand beyond Mexico City and the Estado de Mexico, where her services are currently offered, through the National Palliative Care Network that she launched in Mexico to integrate more medical professionals, academics, and the general public into her association. Her goal is to create a citizen-led national palliative care movement—where all Mexican states are represented—to spread this culture and establish national palliative care standards and certifications.

Miriam and her staff offer integrated services to patients and their families to cope with end-of-life care.

THE PROBLEM

According to Mexico's Health Secretariat, one-third of the country's yearly deaths are caused by terminal illnesses—with cancer as the leading cause, and HIV/AIDS, Chronic Obstructive Pulmonary Disease, diabetes and neurological sicknesses not far behind. This situation should logically elucidate an interest among Mexican health officials to offer specialized services that enhance the quality of life of patients at the end of their lives, instead of only pushing forward with curative treatment options, but this is unfortunately not the case.

For people diagnosed with cancer or other terminal illnesses, the psychological effects of the disease can be just as significant as its debilitating physical symptoms. It is quite common for terminally ill patients to become depressed and develop a negative self-image. Recurring thoughts and fears about death make it difficult for them to stop negative thoughts from taking over their daily lives. This is true also for their family members who feel powerless in front of so much suffering. Similarly, medical caregivers struggle with their patient's pain. They often treat patients as clinical cases, instead of individuals, to protect themselves emotionally. In addition, their technical medical training fails to provide them with the empathetic and emotional skills they need to cope with the difficult situations they are faced with.

Although the concept of palliative care has been widely adopted in the U.S., Canada, and much of Europe, it has not yet made its way into Mexico's public health institutions and medical schools. Health professionals are trained and equipped to administer curative treatments but, when those fail, palliative care is rarely considered to be a viable alternative. Even when full recovery is clearly out of the question, many doctors insist on continuing with a treatment that ultimately will not help their patients. This not only takes an emotional toll on patients and their families, but it also further weakens Mexico's health care infrastructure.

THE STRATEGY

Miriam first learned about palliative care and its benefits after visiting her stepfather who was dying of cancer in the U.S. She was both surprised and moved to see that there existed non-curative treatments that could help patients and their families cope with death as peacefully as possible. Upon her return home to Mexico City, she resolved to bring this culture of end-of-life care to her country. In the beginning, Miriam looked for like-minded people who understood the need for and benefits of palliative care in order to devise a strategy that would turn their vision into a reality. They began meeting up once a week for a few years to advance their thinking on this issue.

Frustrated with the group's lack of action—and with its focus on devising a business strategy that would end up bringing palliative care only to the select few who could afford it—Miriam decided to quit her job and used her personal savings to start what would eventually become CECPAM. From the contacts she had made through her research and the aforementioned working group, Miriam found a thanatologist, a reflexologist and a well-connected individual who shared her vision. Together they began reaching out to various hospitals, clinics and other health institutions to introduce them to the concept of palliative care and encourage them to refer their terminally ill patients to her budding organization. She now works in partnership with 10 pain clinics and three public hospitals, which refer their patients to CECPAM when appropriate. Beyond these referrals, Miriam uses communications media—with radio as the most powerful and effective tool—to educate the public about palliative care and CECPAM's work. Many of her clients come to her organization as a result of these strategic communication campaigns (i.e. using the web, radio, television, and the written press), as well as from public speaking engagements at various conferences.

CECPAM has formed two multi-disciplinary teams, each includes one thanatologist (i.e. a specialist in death and dying), one algologist (i.e. a specialist in the medical treatment of pain), one nurse and one social worker. The thanatologist helps patients and their families understand their emotions, promote dialogue among family members, and tries to strengthen their bonds. Her role is to help families navigate the first four emotional stages related to illness and death—denial, anger, regret and depression—in order to get to the final stage: Acceptance. The algologist, on the other hand, focuses on the physical needs of the patient, with a special emphasis on alleviating pain. The nurse, in turn, teaches the patient and his or her family members about nutrition, exercises that increase mobility, and the necessary hygienic procedures they will need to administer in order to prevent the body's deterioration. As a result, all family members learn how to share caregiving responsibilities, which has both financial and emotional advantages. Finally, the social worker is in charge of understanding the socioeconomic situation of the family to gauge whether or not they are able to take care of the patient and whether they can afford CECPAM's services. The social worker and sometimes a notary also assist family members as they prepare the legal documents required once the patient passes away.

The CECPAM team delivers its integrated services directly in patients' homes. During the first visit, the full team visits the patient and his or her family together to evaluate their physical and psychological health, as well as the emotional and financial situation of the family members. Special attention is also paid to the state of family-patient relations, which tend to get strained by the challenges of providing or improvising end-of-life care for their loved ones. Subsequently, patients are visited twice by the algologist, four times by the nurse and two to four times by the thanatologist each month. The nurse and thanatologist visit the patient's home together: While the thanatologist looks after the needs of the family members in one room, the nurse examines the patient. The nurse next reports back to the family about the patient's health while the thanatologist has a private session with the patient. When an emergency need arises outside of the planned visits, CECPAM also sends a doctor to the patient's home to resolve the problem and appease the patient and his or her family.

CECPAM has the capacity to care for 80 patients monthly throughout the city of Mexico and its surroundings. Since 2007, CECPAM has attended to 436 patients and 1,131 family members. On average patients need CECPAM's services for a period of 1 to 18 months. These services cost CECPAM 3,500 pesos (US$270) per patient per month, but it charges most of its clients between 100 and 500 pesos per month (US$8 to $40), depending on their ability to pay. Although many clients pay the full price, Miriam is committed to ensuring that all families can access CECPAM services: Hence, the tiered-pricing system.

Without CECPAM's support, these families would have to take on astronomical debts or would be forced to forego any type of professional support. Miriam intends to get this model of end-of-life care replicated by other organizations through the nascent National Palliative Care Network, with CECPAM playing an advisory role.

Miriam recognizes that there is a huge gap in Mexico's health system in terms of the number of medical professionals that are trained to administer end-of-life treatments. In order to address this systemic failure, she knew that new health policies that recognized and regulated such treatments were needed. Miriam therefore joined the efforts of others to help draft and push a national law on palliative care, which was approved by Mexico's Senate on January 5, 2009. Among other things, this law gives Mexicans the right to suspend curative treatment at the end of their lives in favor of palliative care.

"Miriam is a social entrepreneur, founder of Hospice of Mexico, and works hard to provide the opportunity for a decent life for terminal patients and their families from diagnosis to death."

—Enlacejudio

Although a few institutions offer certificates in algology and thanatology, medical students are not required to take classes related to these specializations throughout their studies. Miriam's medium-term goal is to change this situation and ensure that palliative care becomes a recognized specialization in Mexico's medical schools. In addition, she is establishing strategic partnerships with large national foundations such as Fundación Flin, which combats the prevalence of nosocomial infections in Mexico. For the first year of this partnership, Fundación Flin has agreed to subsidize the training of two doctors and two nurses in palliative care, with a strong focus on the psycho-emotional health of patients and their families. In the near future, Miriam aims to open up a hospice for short-term care—to allow the patient's family to go on vacation, for example, without leaving their loved-ones unattended.

Most importantly, Miriam understands the critical importance of growing the palliative care community in all regions of Mexico. For this reason, she has begun forming the National Palliative Care Network: A group of health professionals and like minded individuals who share Miriam's vision of creating a movement of palliative care nationally. To date, the network has 127 members from 24 Mexican states. It acts as a community of learning and as a connector to ensure that terminally ill patients who live outside of Mexico City and Guadalajara—the best served cities—also have access to doctors, nurses, and social workers that are knowledgeable about palliative care. Miriam's goal is for CECPAM to become the leading national organization dedicated to palliative care: An organization that will establish national palliative care standards and certifications, which could then spread and be replicated by members of the National Palliative Care Network.

THE PERSON

From an early age, Miriam was involved with social causes. She remembers joining her mother, when she was six-years-old, to assist children with disabilities in summer camps. She was also a dedicated Girl Scout for many years. These experiences shaped her values and gave her the opportunity to develop leadership skills at a young age.

Miriam began her career as a business entrepreneur, opening up the first Ralph Lauren franchises in Mexico with her husband. They established their store in the first condominium mall in the city. Miriam acted as the mall committee's vice president for two years, and then became president for 11 consecutive years. During that time, she defended the shop owner's rights, negotiated agreements with the chamber of commerce, and turned the mall into one of the neighborhood's key attractions.

Although Miriam never lost touch with her commitment to the social sector, she did not immerse herself completely in it until she had a life-changing experience when her stepfather passed away in the U.S. She was impressed by the effectiveness of the palliative care treatment he and her mother received at the end of his life. Returning to Mexico, she took it upon herself to introduce a culture of palliative care to Mexico. In order to understand what thanatologists and algologists go through when they treat patients, she took all the certificates and courses she could to familiarize herself with the field. Although Miriam knew that her vocation was not necessarily to be a health professional herself, she recognized that developing a deep knowledge of the profession would be crucial for her to introduce it and spread it throughout Mexican society.

Miriam is a firm believer that, as one of her professors told her: "One of the most important things in life is to know what your vocation is. Once you find it, you stop working and simply begin to enjoy yourself." ◆

PAULA JOHNS

BRAZIL

Substance Abuse

Paula Johns is systematically addressing the question of tobacco control in Brazil by framing it as a sustainable development and public health issue, as opposed to an issue of individual choice. Paula is buiding a citizen-led movement to make the government and the tobacco industry accountable for the systemic problems related to tobacco production and consumption, with a strong focus on defending the rights of Brazil's most vulnerable populations.

THE NEW IDEA

Paula created the first citizen organization (CO) to effectively take on the issue of tobacco control in Brazil, a field that has traditionally been dominated by short-term government-led initiatives. She established the Alliance for the Control of Tobacco Use (ACT) in 2003 in order to push the Brazilian government to sign on to, and implement the international Framework Convention on Tobacco Control (FCTC). Through Paula's work she has tranformed the field from one that is uniquely focused on individual health issues related to tobacco use to one that is intricately linked to broader sustainable development and public interest questions.

Paula focuses on four main strategies. To begin, she is influencing government policies regarding tobacco control. Additionally, she is broadening the focus of tobacco control activities to include considerations for human rights, gender, race, economic development, and environmental protection, among others. Paula is also building research and communication tools to counteract the power of the industry's lobby with scientific data and to change perceptions around tobacco use among the general population. Finally, she is creating alliances with small producers to ensure that with decreased tobacco consumption they will continue to have a secure source of income while ensuring greater well-being.

Some of Paula's most impactful work has been around mobilizing the citizen sector to influence public policies on the issue of tobacco control. For example, her ACT has led an effort to elaborate and implement the first state laws transforming enclosed public spaces into non-smoking spaces. ACT has also led policy debates that have resulted in the implementation of stricter advertizing regulations for the tobacco industry and has disseminated influential public opinion research about second-hand smoke. Her initiatives are already reaching a national level. However, she has her sights set on much bigger goals. That is why she is actively participating in regional tobacco networks throughout the Americas and has become a member of the Framework Convention Alliance through which she has helped create similar citizen sector alliances to her own in Mozambique, Ecuador, and Argentina.

THE PROBLEM

According to the Brazilian Institute of Geography and Statistics (IBGE), about 24.6 million Brazilians aged 15 and up are smokers. This accounts for more than 17 percent of this age group, more than half of whom say they want to quit. As a result of this addiction and second-hand smoke, approximately 200,000 Brazilians die from tobacco-related diseases every year. Agricultural workers who produce tobacco are also a forgotten segment of the population. The consequences of manipulating large amounts of chemicals on a daily basis and their poor working conditions are often debilitating for their health and general well-being. All in all, tobacco puts a heavy burden on public health systems but despite the size of the issue, the Brazilian government invests an average of US$8M per year on anti-smoking activities, in comparison, it spends US$400M yearly on combatting HIV/AIDS.

Paula participates at the Union for International Cancer Control conference.

A step forward in addressing the effects of second-hand smoke came when Brazil ratified the World Health Organization FCTC—the first international public health treaty of its kind. When Brazil signed on, it committed to adopting the recommended measures, including making smoking prohibited in enclosed public spaces and in the workplace. Although a few states have made advances, the federal legislation on second-hand smoke has yet to be implemented in the majority of the country. This is to say that there have been sporadic attempts by the Government of Brazil to control tobacco use. For years it was the only entity active on this issue. However, as the industry grew, the government quickly lost interest. As a result of the government's previous leadership on tobacco related issues, the citizen sector has been

far behind much of the world and slow to take up the cause. The power of the industry has made most citizen sector work in this field ineffective, until very recently.

Brazil is now the second largest exporter of tobacco in the world, after China. Looking out for its bottom line, large companies regularly oppose any regulation aiming to decrease tobacco consumption. The industry yields much of its power by financing political campaigns and lobbying the higher echelons of government thus pointing to a clear lack of transparency and accountability. This multi-billion dollar industry therefore has a considerable amount of influence on public policies and is currently challenging state laws regulating smoking in enclosed public spaces.

> "[Paula] is the founder and director of a Brazilian coalition of over 300 organizations, created to monitor and support ratification and implementation of the WHO-FCTC in Brazil."
>
> —World Conference on Tobacco or Health

In addition, Brazil does not yet have effective public controls on tobacco advertizing. The marketing departments of tobacco companies operate like well-oiled machines in order to increase tobacco consumption. For example, though youth cannot legally be targeted by tobacco ads, large cigarette producers often sponsor hip university events and very little is done to stop them. By keeping the price of cigarettes extremely low consumption increases; and when prices go up, illegal trade rises with it. Youth, low-income populations, women, and black populations are among the most affected by the effects of cigarette use.

It is important to change Brazilian perceptions of smoking as an individual choice, and disregard the effects it has on the rest of society. Tobacco consumption is a sustainable development issue. It affects the environment, the livelihood and well-being of small farmers, human rights, issues of race and gender, as well as the health of individuals.

THE STRATEGY

At the end of the 2003, Paula led an initiative—while she was still working at Redeh (Brazil's National Network of Human Development)—that brought together citizen sector and governmental organizations from seven Brazilian states to create the ACT. She used the development of the international FCTC as a mobilizing force to begin a citizen-led movement in Brazil. Paula started by establishing a multi-disciplinary team of doctors, sociologists, psychologists, lawyers, and marketing professionals to systemically address issues related to tobacco production and consumption. She initially partnered with Health Bridge and the Canadian International Development Agency to get her organization off the ground. ACT is now an independent organization. It is currently headquartered in Sao Paulo, and has an office in Rio de Janeiro and representatives in Salvador, Brasilia, and Porto Alegre.

Setting out for an anti-tobacco campaign in Rio.

By increasing access to information on issues related to the tobacco industry and facilitating the creation of citizen-led networks, ACT is building avenues for civic participation in activities relating to tobacco regulations and their implementation. One of ACT's primary functions is to monitor and advocate for the development and implementation of the FCTC; compare annual analyses on progress made with regards to anti-tobacco legislation; highlight the government's commitment, or lack thereof, to the ratified treaty; and even monitor the tobacco industry's interference with such processes. Members of ACT are able to strengthen their strategies, including lobbying, as a result of this new flow of information, but also thanks to the contacts and campaign materials developed by Paula's organization. They are thus making both the government and the tobacco industry increasingly accountable and transparent, with the ultimate goal of shifting public opinion nationwide about the need for tobacco control.

ACT is also giving a voice to citizens and raising awareness among society-at-large about the inner workings of the tobacco industry as well as the effects of second-hand smoke. Paula's organization is building popular support for stronger tobacco control regulations and creating the transparency and accountability mechanisms necessary to increase the political will to act on these issues. Many studies have been conducted in partnership with Instituto Datafolha, one of the most respected research institutes in the country. The information obtained guides ACT's strategies, both in terms of communication and legislation.

ACT dedicates a significant amount of its resources to educating the segments of the population that have been found to be most likely to take up smoking. In addition, ACT led a campaign with its pro bono partner Neogama—a communications business— entitled, "Any enclosed space is too small for smoke." The campaign included the dissemination of information through pamphlets, billboards, radio, and television ads. ACT also reached out to a number of COs throughout Brazil with this information.

In 2009, ACT and INCA received funding from the World Lung Foundation to create a similar national campaign.

As a result of this work, and using public opinion research as one of its main data points, ACT has successfully influenced the state of Sao Paulo to pass the country's first law stipulating that people are to be prohbited from smoking in bars and restaurants. It is also working on getting a bill approved in the Senate to turn any enclosed space into non-smoking spaces. Following the passing of Sao Paulo's anti-smoking law, ACT established a partnership with Johns Hopkins Bloomberg School of Public Health to quantify the amount of nicotine pollution in bars and restaurants in the city of Sao Paulo before and after the law passed. The study showed that nicotine levels detected in the air of bars and restaurants had dropped by 72 percent, on average; thus signalling general compliance with the law and an improved environment for clients and workers alike.

Chief among Paula's goals is to address sustainable development issues related to tobacco production and consumption. She is particularly cogniscent of the affects of the tobacco industry on marginalized populations, such as low-income communities, women, and tobacco producers. Paula pays close attention to the issue of race relations as well. ACT, for example, established a partnership with organizations that work on gender relations in 2009 to better understand the relationship between tobacco consumption and gender, and disseminate those findings. These efforts led to the publication of four scientific articles on the topic and guides her organization's strategies. With regard to tobacco producers, Paula has created strong alliances with their associations to understand their concerns with the new tobacco legislation, to document the effects of cultivating tobacco on their health, and to gradually develop alternatives to tobacco production.

Paula has established strategic alliances with some of the sector's most important actors, both nationally and internatoinally. ACT is a member of the Framework Convention Alliance, composed of 350 organizations in more than 100 countries, whose mission is to promote the implementation of the treaty. Paula's organization also participates in the State Committee for the Promotion of Smoke-Free Spaces, an organization that brings together 40 governmental institutions, COs and student-led groups. It has participated heavily in advocating for Sao Paulo's Anti-Smoking Law in 2009.

The impact of Paula's work is becoming apparent. Brazil's population is increasingly aware of the negative effects of smoking and second-hand smoke, and a number of laws are now going into effect to regulate smoking in public spaces throughout Brazil. In addition, ACT's member organizations are now better equipped to work along with legislators and government officials on influencing and implementing public policy.

ACT is getting ready to replicate the law passed in Sao Paulo in other states and municipalities, putting a strong emphasis on the health of restaurant and bar employees. In the medium term, Paula will continue to work on policy change to increase the price and taxes imposed on cigarettes, as well as enforce stronger restrictions on advertizing by the tobacco industry in order to reduce consumption levels. She realizes however, that with rising prices, illegal trade will likely go up as well. This is an issue she has already begun to address with partner organizations in Uruguay, Paraguay, and Argentina. Paula is also determined to develop a strong strategy with tobacco producers to ensure they also benefit from the new tobacco legislation she advocates.

THE PERSON

Paula was born in Sao Paulo and developed an interest early on in learning about different cultures. As a teenager, she travelled to Denmark and studied at a boarding school out of an interest to learn in an foreign environment. She was quite shy and her inability to speak Danish at first made her integration all the more difficult. As Paula felt the need to socialize with her peers, she took up the habit of smoking and remained a smoker for 18 years.

Upon her return to Brazil, she worked for five years in the Consulate of Denmark in Rio de Janeiro. A few years later she returned to Denmark to pursue undergraduate and master degrees in the social sciences and international development. Her studies allowed her to do field research in Guiné-Bissau where she realized that she needed to contribute in one way or another to social change. Paula came to the conclusion that she would be much more "useful" if she worked in Brazil where social needs were higher and where she identified more deeply with the culture. She was always struck by the levels of injustice and inequality in Brazil despite growing up in a privileged environment.

After giving birth to her first daughter and finishing her degree, Paula returned to Brazil a second time to work with Redeh: The Network of Human Development. Through her work at Redeh, she began to examine the question of tobacco control for the first time as a result of a project she coordinated between 2001 and 2003. The objective was to increase the amount of information on health issues related to tobacco consumption by organizing seminars for organizations throughout Brazil. By the end of the project, she realized that she had created a network of organizations who were now aware of and passionate about the issue of tobacco control. However, if she stopped leading this work, her efforts would have been in vain. Paula also understood that given the citizen sectors' dismall contribution to this issue in the past, there was a real need to keep them involved and engaged.

From the beginning, Paula has followed the negotiations of the FCTC, at a time when the National Cancer Institute was particularly active on this issue in Brazil. However, it had never managed to include citizen-led efforts in developing its policy strategies. It was also quite vulnerable to political changes. This is how Paula decided to create the ACT and three years later, in 2006, she began to gain recognition in the sector for her leadership. She was invited as the keynote speaker at an event where Bill Gates and Michael Bloomberg announced joint investments in combatting the global pandemic caused by tobacco. Since then, Paula has actively participated in political decisions regarding tobacco in Brazil. ◆

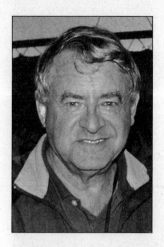

BASIL KRANSDORFF

SOUTH AFRICA

Nutrition/Wellness

Basil Kransdorff is addressing the critical problem of malnutrition in Africa and changing the realm of food production and consumption through the introduction of "bio-available" food supplements into mainstream African society.

THE NEW IDEA

Nutrient repleteness—or our body's ability to absorb micronutrients—is the basis of good health, well-being, and sustainable development. Making human beings nutrient replete and therefore physiologically functional is the new paradigm Basil wants to bring to the world. Moving away from activities that deliver partial solutions and an approach to food that is focused on quantity (or calories), his innovative approach helps change the "rules" and shifts the emphasis to food quality (or nutrient content). The result: a food system in which all decisions are designed to achieve nutrient repleteness. Nutrient repleteness encourages a holistic approach to solutions that include changing the way food is grown, processed and prepared. It encourages new scientific approaches to fortification that mimic nature to ensure better bioavailability of nutrients.

Basil has invented a unique nutritional supplement in the form of a modified version of a staple food in Southern Africa called "pap". He has taken pap, which is a porridge made from ground maize and soy, and invented 'e'Pap', which is an affordable package of ready to eat, fortified food. Basil, and his business partner and wife Rose, developed this technology approach to achieve "nutrient repleteness" to combat malnutrition and poverty. The objective of nutrient repleteness hinges on the hypothesis that the body performs optimally when it absorbs the necessary quantities of nutrients. The objective—a physiologically functional human being.

Basil wants to help decision-makers better understand the issues to fix our food chain so that all human beings can become nutrient replete. The e'Pap technology approach shows how it is possible to bring a human being back to nutrient repleteness. It is necessary to bring understanding as to why current approaches to address the "nutritional crisis" are part of our problem. The lessons learnt and the technologies and science that supports e'Pap Technologies can be applied to not only how we grow our food but also to how we process package and distribute our food chain.

Through the development and promotion of micronutrient rich foods, Basil is cost effectively improving the health and well being of malnourished people in over 15 countries across rural and urban Africa. Furthermore, Basil is changing agricultural norms around food production and the value placed on nutrient dense foods. The effect of the new idea, taken to its logical conclusion, will revolutionize the way a farmer is incentivized to approach food production. Rather than being paid according to weight, or in terms of a product's appearance, the measure of commercial value would be the nutrient content of the food. Basil is also transforming the way big agribusinesses, COs, and the international donor community manage food production and aid. With the locally produced e'Pap, countries can become less dependent on foreign food aid, pharmaceutical supplements, unhealthy processed foods, and expensive imported fortified foods.

THE PROBLEM

The idea of "nutrient repleteness" was pioneered decades ago in terms of how our bodies operate. There are many studies that highlight the fact that micronutrients in the "wrong form" are not taken up effectively by the body because they have been refined into what is called an "isolate form". It has been aptly described as trying to post an envelope without an address. Because refined nutrients are seen by the bodies' biological machinery as "foreign objects", they are then filtered out by "body processes" and tend to collect in the liver and other organs or liberated out through urine and faeces. Large accumulations in the body can sometimes become toxic. In Africa the urgency of the need for "nutrient dense" food has several dimensions, from healthcare implications to food security and sustainable development.

Nutrient repleteness encourages a holistic approach to solutions that include changing the way food is grown, processed and prepared. It encourages new scientific approaches to fortification that mimic nature to ensure better bioavailability of nutrients.

There is a well-known need for those suffering from chronic diseases to eat as nutritiously as possible so they can fight off opportunistic infections and absorb strong medications. An HIV/AIDS patient, for example, who is consuming a diet that is micronutrient deficient or otherwise malnourished, is less likely to adhere to treatment plans and take anti-retrovirals, because an undernourished person's constitution is not able to effectively handle harsh medications. In addition to non-compliance with HIV treatment in those who are malnourished, TB patients also have a significant need for nutrient replete foods. In South Africa, it is estimated that 70 percent of people carry TB in their lungs. TB is a poverty related disease and shifts from being present and dormant, to being active if a person is nutrient depleted. In South Africa, there are 6 million people living with HIV/AIDS and it is estimated that 80 percent of TB cases are co-infections with HIV. Currently, 20 percent of all TB cases in South Africa are reported as drug resistant. If nutrient replete foods are available to TB patients and their families, then the risk to TB infections will be reduced and most common forms of TB can rapidly respond to drugs.

In addition to health issues, in Africa, and especially in countries that rely heavily on food aid and food subsidies to meet basic nutritional needs, a key element to the problem of malnutrition is ignorance or disagreement with the emerging science around "nutrition repleteness." Like the naysayers who choose to underplay the importance of climate change, the science that supports the cheapest forms of food fortification revolves around protecting vested interests, and this often results in non-effective interventions. The placement of inactive micronutrients in foods is supported by the pharmaceutical industry and mainstream international guidelines. The result are low levels of biological uptake, higher levels of micronutrient recommended daily intakes and a consequence of a range of questionable side effects, some known, some still under investigation.

Countries that are receiving aid are at the whim of industrial giants who often place political and business objectives as well as profit considerations over the actual well-being of their aid recipients. Aid organisations have developed a "common practice" over the past 60 years that precludes real change in thought.

Current approaches to food security and nutrition such as the fortification of processed foods and the development of resistant strains of crops are often expensive and inappropriate solutions to problems of food scarcity and agricultural output. The traditional pharmaceutical approach to food fortification using isolated refined nutrients are not effective in addressing the deficiencies and often can create more problems because of the toxic effects of a build up of nutrients not biologically absorbed by the body. The public is often confused, "hoping" that organic foods are more nutrient rich than regular goods. Organic foods may be on the right track and might omit pesticides, but that does not necessarily make that food effectively "nutrient dense". Maximising nutrient density of food involves the health of the soil. What is needed in the farming industry is a closer examination of a range of agricultural practices to see which growing approaches deliver the high concentrations of bio-available nutrients. In the same vein, optimal growing practices might include a combination of non-organic applications, depending on the specific environment in which food is being cultivated.

Local farmers are undermined in the current model of food aid by big agri-business and international pharmaceuticals and foodstuff companies. Mass food fortification of cereals is often ineffective because of the addition of the wrong form of nutrients. At the moment, no one is incentivized to produce food that is nutrient dense. Nutrient dense food could be a great opportunity for farmers to increase the value of their crops, tap into new markets, and generate sustainable streams of income.

THE STRATEGY

Basil has embarked upon a multipronged strategy to change how producers and consumers view nutrient replete foods through targeted research, education and marketing efforts.

His current strategy rests on three key insights gained over the last ten years:

- National government contracts are often so riddled with "hidden agendas" that it is not possible to buy into them.

- Until there is a recognized set of standards around achieving an objective of nutrient repleteness as a diagnosis of human condition, the measurement of a food's value in terms of its ability to achieve nutrient repleteness is unlikely to change.

- Until the protocols change, the best way to proceed is to use existing academic institutions, NGO networks, and local supermarkets to spread word of the product's value.

Given these findings, Basil's strategy to date has been to work through the citizen and corporate sectors to increase awareness around an objective and the importance of achieving nutrient repleteness as the basis to market e'Pap, and to spread word of its effectiveness.

Basil and the e'Pap team have devised a specific strategy involving academic institutions and accredited scientific research to legitimize and popularize the concept of nutrient replete foods. They are currently conducting a clinical investigation into the use and benefit of e'Pap in conjunction with the School of Public Health at Witwatersrand Medical School, a leading academic institution. Part of this research will focus on developing a non-invasive measurement technique of nutrient repleteness to evaluate and determine the cost benefit ratio of their products. The establishment of a scientific accreditation around measuring the condition of nutrient repleteness will be groundbreaking in terms of showcasing the humanitarian and nutritional implications of effective supplements. It will be a critical tipping point to change traditional thinking around creating an objective to achieve nutrient replete human beings. It positions e'Pap as a leader in this emerging field. It could also shift the way food is valued: i.e. priced for nutritional value based on how effectively the nutrients are bio availably absorbed.

Well-recognized South African bodies have conducted studies on the efficacy of e'Pap. This has strengthened Basil and Rose's legitimacy and increased the spread of their idea. According to the South African Tuberculosis Association (SANTA), patients who are fed a regular diet of e'Pap have a 39 percent higher cure rate. They also have evidence that regular consumption of nutrients reduces the likelihood of TB recurrence by 75 percent. The reality is that 80 percent of TB patients in S.A. are now co-infections with HIV and nearly half of the infections are now re-infections. With an HIV infection pool of over 6 million people living with HIV in South Africa, this represents an enormous potential TB threat. There is clinical evidence that indicates the re-infections can be reduced by as much as 60 percent if the patient is kept nutrient replete. Basil believes that co-infections of HIV patients

with TB could be reduced dramatically if the patients are made nutrient replete. Fortunately, the South African TB Association has officially endorsed e'Pap, and is currently seeking to finance the feeding of e'Pap to the entire TB infected population of South Africa and their families, as a way of safeguarding them.

When people start ART therapy from very low CD counts, complications often result in morbidity. A recent investigation done by PEPFAR confirmed there is a 6-fold higher morbidity for malnourished people on ARVs than for those who were better nourished. In South Africa, where ARVs are now available to all, there is a 15 percent drop out. Medical practitioners partly explain this drop out being a result of the nausea and lack of drug compliance that results from using drugs on malnourished bodies. Getting a body back to nutrient repleteness prior to ART treatment with e'Pap addresses this challenge and also makes the benefits of ART more effective.

Basil is cost effectively improving the health and well-being of malnourished people in over 15 countries across rural and urban Africa.

This new approach results in healthy weight gain, and their studies show that when people eat a nutrient replete diet, weight gain is not just "fat" based (BMI), but rather attributed to muscle gain (lean body mass). There are documented cases of highly malnourished people eating e'Pap as a morning food supplement and putting on between 2-5 kilograms within 2-4 weeks. In addition to healthy weight gain, studies show that the consumption of e'Pap increases energy and concentration; suppressed medical conditions become visible and treatable; and it slows AIDS-related diseases and opportunistic infections. Particularly relevant in the African context, e'Pap has proven to improve digestion and lessen cases of diarrhoea, a serious condition for the malnourished and those suffering from HIV, TB and dysentery.

The e'Pap team has done contextually appropriate clinical research to support the safety and efficacy of their work as a way to ensure the uptake of e'Pap and the Kransdorffs are systematically spreading their idea by disseminating results from their research and expertise in nutrition workshops, conferences, under trees in rural communities, township meetings, and high-level briefings to interested parties across the continent. They share information about bioavailability through Internet forums as well.

Through these outreach efforts, Basil is shifting the way people perceive the importance of nutrition. Historically, there has been the prevailing notion that fortified foods are intended only for those inflicted with HIV/AIDS and other diseases. They are currently marketing e'Pap in the Alexandra Township, just outside Johannesburg effectively re-branding e'Pap as a food that is good for young children. Within South Africa and in numerous countries in Africa, the Kransdorffs are developing marketing opportunities to ensure that their products are recognised for their superior nutritional value. They have engaged the international donor community and corporate sectors as partners.

In terms of awareness and brand recognition, the strategy has been to develop familiar food products that local communities recognise and, in most cases, are already part of their daily diet. In South Africa, the production of fortified maize porridge, e'Pap, has been the product of choice as it forms part of the local staple diet. With the expansion into the rest of Africa and possibly to the Far East, products like bread, spreads, fortified drinks, soup, rice and cereal facilitate for assimilation of the products in other regions of the world. Basil's ability to repackage e'Pap products to suit the market and to produce foodstuffs with nutritional value, but with mass appeal, has created a noticeable impact in terms of their ability to scale. In the last two years, their products are beginning to emerge in mainstream supermarkets as healthy alternative foods.

There are 15 African countries that currently sell and distribute e'Pap as well as the extension products of e'Drink and e'Soup. Over 100 million food portions have been sold into malnourished communities. There are increasing numbers of farmers, corporate entities, international donor and aid organisations from within South Africa and the rest of Africa that are using the product. Basil has put in place a retail distribution scheme and is bringing large international COs, governments and everyday consumers to understand the importance of nutrient repleteness. This understanding is resulting in e'Pap being used as a priority foodstuff for health and social service programs as well as disaster relief efforts.

The e'Pap business is self-funding and growing exponentially. The profits from the business are reinvested into the company, and used to finance the development of the manufacturing processes, equipment, and the entire economic value chain to get the product to market. To date, Basil and e'Pap have donated over 2 million Rand of their profits to CO's working in communities in countries across Africa. The initial start-up capital was funded out of family resources. Today the highly mechanized factory has a current monthly production capacity of 200 tons and is expandable up to 500 tons. The unit cost of an e'Pap meal is affordable to the average South African. It is equivalent to about 16 U.S. cents and going to scale will bring that price down.

As part of building the e'Pap business internationally, they have started a HACCP certification process in food safety that results in international accreditation. e'Pap is registered with the following authorities: South African Department of Health, South African Medical Control Council, SAFSIS Food Safety Certification, Glycemic Institute and has received both Kosher and Halaal certification.

THE PERSON

Basil was born into an entrepreneurial family in Zimbabwe. As a child he worked with his mother to create an arts and crafts business that utilised the talents of local women in the country. Starting from a zero base, the business in ten years had a turnover of a quarter of a million rand/month and provided jobs and sustainable income to thousands of rural craft workers. Basil set up a business that innovated solutions on how to maintain workable deep level mining environments miles underground and how to deploy technological applications for what to do with mining slurry.

e'Pap Technologies resulted from a project his wife Rose was doing helping Jenny Marcus start a project to support people in HIV lines at Johannesburg Hospital. The HIV pandemic was just hitting South Africa in 2000. There were no drugs available and the only advice for patients was to go home and eat a healthy well balanced diet. It was advice that few poor South African's could afford. Rose was able to help facilitate a large donation from the Elton John Foundation to set up the support group, CARE (Community Aids Response). Part of this donor support was food parcels and their involvement was to bring some science to the package.

It was the "miracle stories" that resulted from those first unmarked pre-cooked fortified foods that Basil and Rose distributed in the food parcels and the requests from patients to purchase it that sparked the Kransdorffs to set up Econocom Foods. As social entrepreneurs, they decided to distribute the product via a "job creation" and community distribution network as a way to empower those living in the community and those with HIV. The business model they created allowed them to make large cash and product donations to those at the forefront of fighting the pandemic.

Basil's partner in business and life is his wife, Rose. To e'Pap she brings many experiences gained as a qualified social worker, advocate for social justice, management consultant, and community empowerment worker with work experience in South Africa, France, and Australia. Working extensively with communities, corporations, and vast networks, Rose recognised the need for nutritionally replete food as a basis for health, education and overcoming poverty. She joined Basil at Econocom Foods to design, manufacture and distribute e'Pap. ♦

© Sarah Gauthier

CLAUDINE LABELLE

CANADA

Nutrition/Wellness

Youth Development

Claudine Labelle is creating strong community networks to put sports back into the lives of teenage girls. She is increasing their self-esteem, and thereby improving their health, nutrition, and wellness as a whole through the use of sport and physical activity.

THE NEW IDEA

Claudine is creating community support networks to motivate young girls to become more active and to develop confidence and a positive self-image. She is working in multiple cities in Canada, bringing together professional athletes, career women, schools and amateur sport organizations. Olympians give conferences to inspire teenage girls and help them reflect on healthy lifestyles and self-development. Claudine invites teenagers to participate in FitClub and athletic challenges organized by teachers and accompanied by mentors—professional women and athletes. Her goal is to prevent unhealthy lifestyles by developing early habits for physical activities. Claudine offers teenage girls opportunities to interact with role models—athletes as well as women of all ages who have integrated sport into their lives in different ways, but who benefit from it in similar ways. They all enjoy it thoroughly, have used it as a self-development tool, and as a way to improve their health and develop support networks. Through big sport events, amateur sport organizations, schools, and mentors, teenage girls experiment with fun and interesting sports and games. With ongoing activities and network support, inactive girls make and sustain commitments to physical activity, trying new sports and developing new behaviors. The community clusters are constantly expanding to increase the motivation of young girls and their sense of belonging. As a result, Claudine is also preventing future eating and emotional disorders.

One of the most important players in the life of a teenager is the school system, and Claudine is strengthening its capacity to support girls in their physical, mental, and social development. She is developing train-the-trainer relationships with schools and teachers, getting them involved in supporting young girls to become more active. Claudine works closely with teachers to create FitClub's that enable young girls, who are often intimidated by sports, to get together to exercise. The training plan is

designed for all fitness levels so anyone can participate. The more active FitClub members are invited to motivate their less active teammates to get moving. Claudine also brings extra resources to schools, like kinesiologists and nutritionists, and thus changes mindsets within the school system by introducing a much needed focus on teenage girls' health. Furthermore, she offers a service to youth organizations that gives young women the opportunity to partake in sports. This gives girls the chance to experiment with a variety of physical activities, all in an unthreatening and casual environment. Claudine also partners with large citizen organizations (COs), like the YWCA and creates programs for their members.

THE PROBLEM

The adverse affects attributable to an absence of physical activity are striking in North American society, and young girls in Canada are particularly affected by this situation. The number of active youth drops significantly in teenage years, but this is more much noticeable for girls. At age 11, 68 percent of boys are active, while only 46 percent of girls active. Between 14 and 16 years old, only 27 percent of girls exercise compared to 46 percent of boys. At 16 and 17-years-old, the number drops dramatically down to only 11 percent. In addition to a decrease in physical activity, dieting is alarmingly prevalent among teenage girls: At 9-years-old 50 percent of girls are on some form of diet. By the time they reach the age of 10 or 11, 80 percent are dieting. Once teenage girls reach high school, 70 percent of healthy girls categorize themselves as being fat.

A team of girls from Quebec happily participated in FitSpirit's surfing workshops.

A startling fact about these statistics is that many studies show that young girls understand the importance of physical activity for their health. These same studies reveal that young girls want to increase their participation in some type of physical activity. The fact that the participation levels remain low suggests that social and cultural barriers are impeding their involvement. Among these barriers are limited opportunities for them to become active; the inaccurate assumption that boys and girls all enjoy the same activities; the limited choice of activities that are promoted to girls and young women; poor time management and a lack of financial resources.

Even with these statistics, schools tend to have dismal physical education programs, and their decline has been steady in the last few decades. Very few school resources are dedicated to sport and many high schools only offer one hour of physical education per week. Furthermore, when physical activities are offered, they are often in a competitive environment, which has been shown to be particularly intimidating for girls.

THE STRATEGY

In 2006, following a severe biking accident which took her out of professional sports, Claudine founded FitSpirit and began by mobilizing athletes to give speaking tours in high schools. When invited, these Olympic and professional athletes are asked to speak about their personal challenges and experiences as they relate not only to sports but to their lives in general as teenagers. Through their long-term involvement, the athletes become inspiring role models. Claudine also shows many different sides of sports to teenage girls by involving professional, career-oriented women who practice sport on a regular basis. The women work closely with the teenage girls, and share their experiences with sport and physical activity. Claudine invites them to become mentors to girls in specific activities she organizes.

> "Ms. Labelle founded FitSpirit, a training and nutrition program that uses sport as a conduit to build self-esteem and encourage active lifestyles among teen girls – no boys allowed."
>
> —*The Globe and Mail*

After the conferences, Claudine engages teachers, through train-the-trainer programs, to develop their own FitClub—a running program which lasts approximately 6 weeks and involves visits from nutritionists, kinesiologists, athletes, and mentors. The girls learn about the benefits of being active, become comfortable with trying new sports, and have the support of their group to start becoming active. The FitClubs take place during school hours, at lunch or afterschool, and become a tool for teachers to emphasize the importance of healthy living and to connect with their students at a non-academic level.

Beyond the FitClubs, Claudine also organizes a number of events with local COs and women's associations of amateur sports are invited as partners. For example, in 2009, Rugged Riders (snowboarders), Country Skiing clubs and Skirtboarders all got involved in the program, giving teenagers the opportunity to learn new and fun sports while doing so without pressure or competitiveness. The events are designed for girls to participate

in and experiment with new sports, while witnessing how other women are also benefiting from staying active. The events are much more than just a place to try out a different sport, they provide a space for athletes, mentors, teachers, families, and teenagers to strengthen their relationships and bring a strong group of people together with the goal of supporting teenage girls in their healthy life choices. Events are the catalyst for long-term network support. Partners of these events include a variety of ski centers, sport centers, instructors, families, schools, communities, and local sport organizations.

Claudine, an excellent role model, cross-country skiing in Quebec.

In the first three years of operation, Claudine worked with 50 athletes who engaged with 40,000 girls in more than 100 schools in Ontario and Quebec. The FitSpirit conferences are the first step in showing teenagers why physical activity can be so inspiring. In 2010, a total of 1,000 girls became involved in the larger FitSpirit events and FitClub. She is engaging school principals and teachers to include girl-only activities in the school, putting a strong emphasis on the necessity to approach sports differently with girls. This is representative of Claudine's work to change the behaviors and mindsets within the school system to allow for sport and healthy living to take a more important role. She is simultaneously strengthening the youth sector to engage teenage girls in sports. Claudine has partnered with the Quebec Federation of Physical Educators, to engage their members in FitSpirit, and to allow for long-term follow-up with the girls. She has also developed a network of teachers who currently perform health assessments, while also leading and participating in the FitClub.

In addition, Claudine is creating community networks that support the involvement of young girls in physical activities of all types. In 2009, in the Laurentian region (Quebec), the first pilot project was put in place and served as a model for replication in Richmond Hill and Peterborough (Ontario), and later in Montreal, Verdun, Estrie, and Quebec City (Quebec). The pilot model brings together five schools, five teachers, two professional athletes, and 25 professional women acting as mentors. In 2009

2,000 girls attended the Laurentian conference. As a result, three FitClubs were organized, 100 girls participated, and four large events were organized around running, wakeboarding, surfing, and various other sport activities. Because the FitClub and the activities involve different partners like ski centers, sport organizations, schools, and families, a large array of actors are involved in supporting girls to become more active. To increase FitSpirit's long-term impact, FitClub alumni are also invited to become mentors for younger girls.

THE PERSON

As a child, Claudine was a very reserved girl who found a way to express herself through sports. She began playing soccer at the age of five and cross-country skiing at seven. Claudine was a competitive athlete in both of these sports, training 20 hours per week, until she reached her teenage years. At 13, after having gained a spot on the national ski team, a teenage crisis got the best of her. Seeing her change in behavior, her physical education teacher approached her and inspired her to continue with sport. After beginning a running regiment with her teacher, Claudine got involved in triathlons at 17 and qualified for the World Championships in France at 20.

Years later, while working in an office, Claudine organized a running group to walk and run together at lunchtime, supporting each other to run for their respective causes. When Claudine decided to take a 90-day cycling trip, she was looking for a cause to dedicate the trip to, but could not find one appealing to her. This is when the idea of FitSpirit germinated.

At 21, Claudine was an elite athlete actively training to become a professional road cyclist. While in a training session, she was hit by a car and: in an instant, her ambitions of becoming an Olympian athlete were crushed. Claudine was devastated, but not defeated. In October 2006, two years after her accident, determined to share the joy and benefit of sport, Claudine created FitSpirit, a girl-only training and nutrition program dedicated to helping teenagers learn sports and give them the support needed to develop their best attitudes toward both sports and their health. ◆

EMILIE MEESSEN

BELGIUM

Health Care Delivery

With nearly 3 million homeless people living on the streets of European cities, street social workers struggle to find adequate answers to help the most excluded change their situation. Through a revolutionary process that bridges life on the streets with the traditional health care system, Emilie Meessen is supporting homeless people's dignity and self-esteem while facilitating their social and professional rehabilitation. Emilie has successfully created a network of "watchdogs" that act as an early warning system. Using hygiene as a stepping-stone, they are empowering the long-term homeless by helping them to take charge of their own bodies and lives.

THE NEW IDEA

Emilie has invented a dynamic, incremental process to empower the homeless to care for their own hygiene and progressively reclaim responsibility over their lives. Aware that careless hygiene is a starting point and catalyst for the exclusion of already marginalized people, Emilie has designed an approach that reconnects homeless people with their bodies. By using this method in street work and targeting the long-term homeless, she is building a holistic pathway to self-awareness and physical, mental, and environmental health. Infirmiers de Rue follows hundreds of homeless people every year with promising results: The intensive follow-up process led nearly 70 percent of the most excluded homeless people to proper hygiene and social reintegration. As an example of the potential of her method, over a three-month period Emilie succeeded in reintegrating a person that all other organizations failed to help over the past 15 years.

In order to catalyze the impact of her approach and allow for more targeted, effective street work, Emilie is training, organizing, and strengthening a network of watchdogs to support the homeless people's empowerment process. Citizens, shop holders, security staff, park rangers, and street social workers are all taught to use the same barometer to assess a homeless person's degree of risk, and as a result, are together able to track and monitor the progress of the most excluded people.

Emilie is also creating an enabling environment to make the system of street-workers more efficient, by reinforcing existing infrastructures and improving their accessibility. She is shedding light on what knowledge already exists for street-workers to use (i.e. street maps and lists of places where it is possible to take a shower, drink water, or use toilets). In doing so, Emilie constructively engages local authorities to fill infrastructure gaps. Already Emilie's approach is being adopted in three other cities in Belgium and is receiving attention from other European countries, particularly Finland and Switzerland.

THE PROBLEM

There are 17,000 homeless people in Belgium and 3 million in Europe, and these numbers continue to rise. In spite of the existence of numerous street work citizen organizations (COs) and intervention programs, their health remains a pressing issue. For example, in Flanders, 75 percent of homeless people report adverse health conditions and 58 percent suffer from mental disorders. The poor monitoring of the health of homeless populations is one of the first causes of street mortality.

The deterioration of hygiene is often the starting point of a vicious cycle of exclusion. A person living day after day on the streets will progressively neglect hygiene and appearance, which often leads to the loss of self-esteem. Dirt and body odors generate rejection and marginalization from society, which accelerates the degradation of a homeless person's physical and mental health. This gradual social exclusion further reduces their chance of finding a job, a place to live and an outlet from life on the streets.

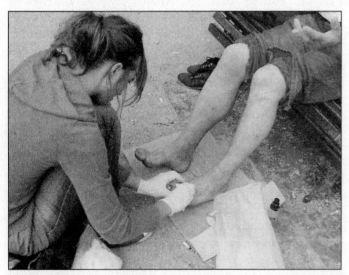

Emilie's work on the street consists of decentralizing health care and meeting homeless people where they are.

Advocates in the traditional street work system do not address the issue of hygiene for two reasons: Hygiene problems are taboo because they are considered intimate and personal and most professionals consider hygiene as outside their scope of intervention. Just as the role of physicians is to make a diagnosis and provide a medical response, social workers are meant to help the homeless find employment, housing, and fill administrative duties.

A further challenge in addressing hygiene issues among homeless people is the siloed nature of the field. Daytime shelters, night emergency shelters, and street workers, do not coordinate their efforts. Consequently, there is no real tracking of changes in a homeless person's situation, which prevents any comprehensive health management.

There are many untapped resources that could be leveraged to better manage the hygiene of homeless people. For instance, those in contact with the homeless on a daily basis, such as park wardens, shopkeepers, and security officers, are overlooked in the role of sentry they could play to help with the social integration of the homeless. Furthermore, public infrastructures (i.e. public toilets, water fountains, showers, and so on) and services offered by the city and other COs are unknown, sometimes misused, and often inadequate.

> "Nurses travel through the streets of Brussels, to meet the homeless. When necessary, they provide care on site. But most often they try to guide people to care under good conditions."
>
> —*Action Vivre Ensemble*

THE STRATEGY

When Emilie began working as a nurse with homeless people, she identified a clear gap: Most of the health-related social street work was conducted when a situation had reached a level of emergency, and most often occurred at night. The reason for this was that most homeless resisted stepping into existing health care centers which were open and accessible during the day. Emilie created Infirmiers de Rue (IDR) to build the missing link between reality on the streets and existing health care centers.

Emilie has developed a strategy that progressively builds trust and step-by-step brings the homeless closer to the mainstream health system. Pairs of nurses meet the homeless on the street with a non-intimidating approach (i.e. by foot, not in uniform, and only if the person accepts a conversation). Nurses are informed of a situation by neighbors, shopkeepers, COs, or by meeting the homeless on their regular patrols. The first encounter is a way to get to know each other and conduct a first diagnosis of the homeless person's state of hygiene and health. During the process, the nurses respect a homeless person's autonomy and openly discuss the situation with him/her.

The patient usually falls into one of two categories depending on their health situation. For the less serious cases, IDR is reorienting the homeless with the most relevant players. For the most critical cases, IDR develops "intensive monitoring," a file for the individual is opened and each week the nurses will assess progress, set goals, and organize cooperation with other institutions. IDR calls upon all stakeholders that are in contact with the patient (i.e. hospitals, social services, and street-workers) to exchange information and coordinate the various steps.

In Brussels, IDR has proven the importance of placing the person at the center of a collaborative network, to establish prevention mechanisms and improve the impact of each respective intervention. To strengthen, integrate and equip this network, Emilie has created tools and common assessment standards. The evaluation and selection of priority target populations are based on a "BCB score" (body, clothing, and behavior), measured by personal hygiene, cleanliness of clothing, and behavior on the margins of society (i.e. mental disorder, social misfit, and so on). Each criterion is rated between 0 and 3 and each person is graded from a maximum of 9 points. Anyone with a score below 6 is considered a patient at-risk and therefore, a priority. The BCB scoring tool was presented at the National Institute of Health Insurance Disability, which wants to use it as a national standard.

On the streets, IDR meets people who are often rejected by society, excluded and marginalized because of their different way of life. This inequality is unacceptable.

To deepen and strengthen the watchdog networks and improve their impact on each territory, IDR is leveraging its expertise to develop and implement training programs for professions that interact with the homeless, including medical and social professionals, security guards, maintenance staff, and shopkeepers. Based on the experience acquired in identifying symptoms related to levels of hygiene and adapting treatments for street patients, these trainings aim to:

- Teach the causes and consequences of poor hygiene, and explain respective possible roles to play

- Train participants on how to deal with questions of hygiene

- Raise awareness on the importance of a concerted management of health issues and using coordination tools

For example, IDR trains medical professionals (i.e. doctors and nurses from local hospitals, clinics, Samu Social, and Médecins du

Monde) to adapt their treatment requirements to living conditions on the streets. For security guards, IDR teaches how to maintain order and cleanliness in a station or a park with people who have little access to water, toilets, and showers, and how to manage possible confrontations between the homeless and passengers. As an illustration of the high satisfaction and enthusiasm generated by the trainings, the Belgian National Railway Company decided to increase more than tenfold the number of employees that will attend IDR trainings in 2011.

These training programs are a key accelerator for IDR's impact. Already conducted in three Belgian cities in addition to Brussels (Charleroi, Namur, and Liège), these trainings empower stakeholders to work together and equip a broad range of professionals to work toward the rehabilitation of homeless people.

THE PERSON

From a very young age, Emilie was attracted to street work and humanitarian work. During her studies as a nurse, she chose to volunteer in a homeless center in Brussels. She spent her free time and holidays in close contact with the homeless and soon after, decided to specialize in community health. Emilie wanted to break the cycle that trapped at-risk populations and she had the intuition that hygiene was a key part of the solution.

First pursuing her dream of doing humanitarian work in Africa, Emilie traveled extensively and wrote her dissertation in Burkina Faso on "Raising Awareness Around Hygiene and Wound Care". Seeing firsthand the challenges of humanitarian work, she returned to Brussels to focus on hygiene work in a place she was more familiar. While finishing her specialization in tropical medicine, Emilie pragmatically conducted a field study on the needs of homeless people in Brussels and identified the missing link between people on the streets and existing institutions. When none of the organizations she identified seemed able to fill that gap, Emilie founded the Association Infirmiers de Rue in 2006.

While developing IDR, Emilie continued working part-time as a community health nurse in homeless centers. This allowed her to deepen her knowledge of the field and get to know all the key actors in Belgium. In just two years, Emilie quickly grew the organization to the point where it was necessary for her to work full-time.

Determined to bring her idea from a national to the European level, Emilie is guided by the conviction that everyone can be an agent of change around the situation of the homeless. Emilie states, "What I am truly passionate about is connecting people with themselves and increasing their autonomy." This desire is what leads her to give every citizen a chance to act and participate in empowering the homeless they see everyday on the street. ♦

JEAN-LOUP MOUYSSET

FRANCE

Health Care Industry

Jean-Loup Mouysset, trained as an oncologist, is revolutionizing the handling of chronic diseases by involving citizens in the process of follow-up and long-term support. The results of his pilot with cancer patients demonstrates the efficiency of his mindful community-based approach by influencing compliance to treatment, improving physical and psychological well-being, and reducing relapse and mortality rates. Drawing from a wide range of sources, Jean-Loup has created the continent's first center of excellence focused on community support for chronic diseases.

THE NEW IDEA

Over the last few years the French medical system has made strides on research for chronic diseases such as cancer, but its patient treatment remains traditional, elitist, and closed-minded. Without focus on a holistic vision of disease, it denies a patient's singularity and thus targets pathologies with standardized methodologies. This system has traditionally defined treatment as purely medical and limited to delivery by doctors. Jean-Loup's systems-changing community model of handling chronic disease involves patients and citizens in the treatment process and creates a new ability for medical institutions to care for the patient as a unique person by providing a set of innovative and personalized treatments. Starting with cancer, Jean-Loup envisions a system of care where chemo- and radiotherapy are only two of many aspects of cancer treatment, and he is now providing patients with those missing elements.

Fully aware that improving compliance to and results of treatment entails dealing with every aspect of a patient's life, Jean-Loup sets up working groups that systematically deal with psychological support, social counseling, or aesthetical and physical well-being. These communities of practice involve medical and non-medical specialists, social workers, psychologists, and families, and surround patients throughout and after their illnesses. Mutual aid expression groups where 10 to 12 patients share accomplishments, fears, solutions, and psychological support play a crucial role in providing patients with a strong community and network throughout illness. No longer isolated by their suffering, they become central actors in their healing, rather than passive observers of their diseases.

These communities not only improve the treatment of patients, but they also play a major role in transforming the medical system and shifting perceptions around chronic diseases. Jean-Loup is anchoring a movement of informed patients, professionals, and families that gives strength to his model by spreading the word and promoting it through unprecedented large-scale informational meetings (i.e. each with an average of 4,000 participants). Thus, beyond his first center, more and more empowered patients are beginning to request Jean-Loup's innovative therapy. He is also spreading his model through trainings to volunteers and doctors and through implementing therapeutic centers in new regions. Jean-Loup envisions his community-based model as the new norm to tackle chronic disease.

THE PROBLEM

Chronic disease such as cancer afflicts societies in a unique way. Cancer has become the first cause of mortality in France, killing 12 people each day. To fight this "epidemic," many researchers have experimented with innovative treatments, but none of their advances have been formally integrated into medical treatments. In 1990 Dr. David Spiegel, a well-known psychiatrist at Stanford University, observed that patients lived twice as long when they were treated with his psychological support methodology. Furthermore, Dr. Barbara Andersen from Ohio State University set up a new methodology of therapeutic education to explain the healing process to breast-cancer patients, and she managed to decrease relapse rates by 50 percent. There is growing evidence that taking care of the psychological well-being of patients has a positive influence on their recovery; however, to date in France, these types of psychological therapeutic approaches toward chronic disease remain outside the traditional medical system. While several medical departments provide sporadic, temporary, and scattered aesthetical care, the only psychological support legally implemented in France is a one-hour interview with a social worker at the beginning of chemotherapy.

> "Association of Resource Aix-en-Provence by Dr. Jean-Loup Mouysset offers a different view of cancer, a more human-centered care and wellness for patients and their families."
>
> —*Blog Nutrition Sante*

In France cancer is still considered the "other" disease; many citizens believe cancer will never affect them in their lifetime, plus, it remains taboo and misunderstood as a disease. As a result, the traumatizing dimension for patients and their relatives is not being taken into account. Furthermore, the issue of life after cancer for recovered patients remains an untouched issue. There is no support for long-term physical and psychological trauma, heavy convalescence, and the high-risk of relapse. The lack of societal support leads to feelings of vulnerability and powerlessness at levels proportionate to the trauma undergone by war veterans or victims of natural disasters or rape. In the traditional one-to-one doctor-patient relationship, the suffering person is unable to understand the treatment and remains isolated in a passive recipient model. Instead, creating a community around the patient has been proven to help him/her fight isolation and loneliness.

The elitism and paternalism of the French medical system is anchored in traditional practices, and new therapies are hardly ever integrated. However, new therapies have long-term cost-saving benefits in terms of preventing relapse. With the cost of breast cancer relapse at 300M EUR per year, there is an urgent need to implement innovative treatment models that reduce the medical costs of handling chronic disease. Despite the fact that fighting cancer is now considered a national priority, after the French government launched the Plan Cancer 2009—2013, the government spent 150 times the amount of money for H1N1 treatment than it dedicated to cancer treatment. Overall, no significant efforts have been made by the government to improve treatments, in ways that are particularly innovative or cost-effective.

Jean-Loup's systems-changing community model of handling chronic disease involves patients and citizens in the treatment process and creates a new ability for medical institutions to care for the patient as a unique person.

For the sustainability of the medical system, it is crucial to open up medical elites and decision-makers to new therapies. Beyond the case of cancer, newly appearing or poorly treated pathologies or disorders could benefit from such a shift in the medical field. One example is autism, which conceals a wide-range of poorly treated behavioral troubles. Another is Multiple Chemical Sensitivity (MCS), which concerns 4 percent of the population, however, individuals must go to the U.S. or Germany for treatment since the disease is untreatable in France. The need to set up an alternative framework to treat a spectrum of chronic diseases through a mindful approach is thus critical in a society where traditional medical treatment has shown to be insufficient for the well-being of the sick and ill.

THE STRATEGY

To meet the needs of patients undergoing treatment or in convalescence from disease, Jean-Loup gathers a unique group of practitioners and specialists who provide a wide-range of care with a mixed psychological and physical therapy model. Jean-Loup's association, Ressource, trains beauticians, experts in sophrology or reflexology, psychologists, social workers, occupational physicians, and other specialists to adapt their skills to the specific treatment of cancer patients. This diverse community has the capacity to answer the specific demands of patients coming to Ressource. Every aspect of patient suffering is dealt with to improve their well-being and thus their ability to undergo treatments or get

through the rehabilitation process. The community is reinforced by the patients themselves: In addition to receiving treatment, every patient visiting Ressource gets involved in support and expression groups with ten other patients. These groups provide the space for patients, former patients, families, and relatives, to share accomplishments, fears, and solutions with one another.

Jean-Loup build upon experiments of support expression groups and therapeutic education developed by Drs. Spiegel and Andersen, who respectively demonstrated a 100 percent increase in patients' life expectancy and a 50 percent decrease of relapse rate for breast cancer patients. Jean-Loup upgraded and complemented these innovative methodologies through an *à la carte* community-based model that has benefited 1,500 persons since 2003. More than 10,000 treatments have drastically improved the living conditions and healing time of patients. Reaching a greater number of patients, he is now planning to implement a multidimensional impact evaluation that extends beyond previous research. It focuses on new aspects of enhancement for a patient's well-being, such as compliance to treatment, shifting to healthy lifestyles, and improvements in nutrition or stress management. Jean-Loup is thus driving a new integrative oncology in which chemo- and radiotherapy are only aspects of larger cancer treatment.

To give a concrete reality for the communities and reach the next step in implementing mindfulness in cancer treatment and the treatment of other chronic diseases, Jean-Loup has built a unique location to house the gathering of various actors and provide patients with diversified, innovative, and complementary care. In a non-medical center, which is easily accessible and therefore non-stigmatizing, a psychologist helps the patient work through a personalized one-year program. Each week for four months, then bimonthly over eight months, the patients come to the center to engage with experts in wellness treatments and social counseling. In the long-term, Jean-Loup plans to have in-patient treatments depending on the particular patient's situation. These specialists support the patient according to the needs he/she defined together with the community of caregivers and psychologists. To overcome institutional and medical corporate barriers, Jean-Loup follows his vision and empowers patients as central actors of his model. Thanks to a viral strategy using social networks and meetings, he is structuring a community of patients that spreads the word: Patients are now asking physicians to include Ressource in their treatment.

Jean-Loup is using Ressource as a tool to support the organization of unprecedented international meetings welcoming doctors, patients, and families. In 2008 and 2009, he gathered more than 8,000 individuals for a series of "Another Look at Cancer" conferences, where the most famous specialists of cancer or other diseases (including Drs. David Servan-Schreiber, Lucien Israel, and David Spiegel) called for a new way to handle heavy chronic diseases. Jean-Loup thus creates conditions for doctors and patients to change their perceptions toward treatment, and he is asked to organize these conferences on a regular basis. Networking with foreign specialists on the topic in Canada, the U.K., Switzerland, and Germany, Jean-Loup has already identified existing leverages to replicate and spread his model outside of France.

Generating sustainable funding and changing health policy are also strategic elements for spreading the Ressource model. Jean-Loup targets individual donations to advertise around Ressource and is now approaching for laboratories both financial support and to build partnerships around new hybrid treatment methodologies. On top of that, he is demonstrating potential savings implied by his model, to attain funding from regional health agencies willing to adopt cheaper solutions and to implement a Ressource center per Health Territory. Jean-Loup also raises awareness among local and regional physicians' unions to change practices and integrate new approaches in doctors' training. Eventually, he is also broadening his concept by opening up his pilot center to other types of chronic diseases, such as MCS. Jean-Loup is thus creating a network of hubs to allow specialists and patients dealing with a wide spectrum of disease to mutually work on the better handling of chronic diseases.

THE PERSON

Jean-Loup grew up in the South of France, exposed from a young age to the religious teachings of his parents. Engaged with the local parish, he participated in ecumenical summer camps led by a Jesuit organization throughout his youth years until becoming a camp supervisor when he was a teenager. Jean-Loup's time and engagement with the organization allowed him to develop a great sense of teamwork and community spirit, as well as altruism and care. For some time, he wanted to become a priest, but finally chose medicine as the most efficient way to help suffering people.

At the beginning of Jean-Loup's oncology career he understood his role as a doctor to pay more attention to the patient than the pathology. He began to read about Dr. David Spiegel's work during his studies at medical school in France and fought hard to get funding from his university to attend one of the psychiatrist's experiments on expression groups for cancer patients at Stanford University. At Damascus Road, this encounter helped him to build his own methodology to treat patients. Sensitive to other medical approaches, Jean-Loup sought training in various areas such as environmental bioscience, which helped him to understand the crucial role of the ecosystem around the patient and to implement a mindful vision of medical treatment. As a junior physician at the hospital La Timone in Marseille, his colleagues were impressed by his "medical rigor and commitment to the patients."

Step by step, Jean-Loup developed his model and created the first community with people enduring or having endured cancer as the key players. He believes they will really transform the system, placing them at the center of a large-range of citizens and professionals. Jean-Loup structured his patient model by recruiting part of his staff among former sick people. Suffering patients thus benefit from a highly profitable added-value: Understanding.

Jean-Loup has always thought that demonstrating the efficiency of a model is the best strategy to convince and accelerate change. In a closed minded and traditional medical world that is slow to innovate, he has built a new kind of private not-for-profit hospital, as a unique organization in the field of medical handling structures. Today, the community-based model Jean-Loup has initiated goes beyond the projects he is directly carrying out, and has the potential to transform medical practices. ◆

MICHEL NISCHAN
UNITED STATES

Agriculture

Michel Nischan is catalyzing demand among low-income urban consumers for locally grown, healthy foods through a financing approach that also fuels the growth and viability of small and mid-sized farms.

THE NEW IDEA

A chef and the grandson of farmers, Michel is re-creating local economies to nourish low-income families and support small and mid-size farmers. To bring about this market transformation, Michel enlists select local partners across the country, and with them, cultivates the largely untapped market among America's low-income families living in urban areas. To start off, he is introducing an incentive that doubles the buying power of low-income consumers at farmer's markets, a doubling that is made possible through blended financing of philanthropic and public investment. The incentive helps the market re-form around healthy food commerce and settle, longer-term, into a new and sustainable pattern with local food production and consumption for all at its core. Having begun in 2007, Michel and his team are working with 27 citizen organizations (COs) in 18 states, and showing significant results in 160 farmers' markets. Using this early success to attract the attention of policymakers, Michel and his co-founder aim to reach a scale that matters by redirecting a portion of appropriate federal and state funds (i.e. they are targeting the 2012 Farm Bill) and by cultivating philanthropic sources interested in creating a new system of local food commerce and healthier communities.

THE PROBLEM

There's a growing awareness of the link between poverty in America and diet-related health problems that debilitate millions and cause disease and, often, early death—these include sky-rocketing obesity rates in the last 20 years, and the advancement of diseases like Type II diabetes, which debilitate individuals and families, and contribute to a tremendous societal burden as measured in health care costs. Meanwhile, the U.S. government currently allocates $78 billion per annum for food assistance in the form of USDA's Supplemental Nutrition Assistance Program (SNAP), formerly known as food stamps; Women, Infants, and Children (WIC) for pregnant and nursing women and their young children; and various other benefits. Yet users of these benefits are among those groups showing the highest obesity and disease rates. At a macro level, money intended to help people and the society is supporting the purchase of unhealthy foods that cause disease, and contribute to escalating cost in human potential, happiness, productivity, and health care costs. The pattern also moves currency out of the community, rather than supporting healthy rebuilding of local food commerce.

While the main discussion around food reform is focused on food access, the reality is that fresh, healthy foods—locally grown or otherwise—are not affordable to poor families. Farmers' markets open in lower-income parts of town, and they fail— the same patterns are true of produce sections in grocery stores and many other efforts to increase food access without simultaneously addressing cost. These failures point some to the conclusion that low-income people don't want or like healthy, fresh foods, preferring instead fast food options—that what's lacking is demand.

Add to this picture the country's priorities in agricultural production, famously laid out in the Farm Bill, which subsidizes commercial-scale farms, while offering few supports to small and mid-sized farmers. These farmers struggle to find and grow a viable market, and many fold. The country's 5,000 farmers' markets offer a link to local economies; yet the markets serve a limited, affluent market. Even for farmers' markets that are equipped and certified to offer public benefit options, the SNAP redemption rates remain low—these markets are not attracting low-income customers, and the farmers who supply this network are not currently cultivating or connecting to this consumer.

THE STRATEGY

Michel and his team see untapped demand among low-income Americans for healthy, locally grown foods. To realize longer-term market transformation by reaching and converting these consumers, Michel is demonstrating that demand is there, affordability isn't (yet) and this is a key hurdle to changing purchasing and eating habits.

Starting with the existing network of famers' markets, Michel and his team are strongly signaling to low-income people that they are wanted as customers of fresh, nutritious foods—that the farmer's market is a place for them. To do this, they have structured an incentive that doubles the buying power of consumers who use public benefits. The set up is simple: Low-income customers swipe their SNAP card at the farmer's market, and receive tokens in double the amount to spend at the various market stands selling locally grown foods. The approach makes shopping for fresh foods affordable to low-income customers, and increases returns to the local farming community, thus stimulating the growth and viability of mid- and small-scale farms on the outskirts of urban centers. Most participating markets are showing increases of more than 300 percent in redemption rates of public benefits, a significant boost to total sales for participating farmers.

For greatest leverage and effectiveness, Michel partners with select local organizations—now 27 organizations in 18 states— that run markets and are trying to reach low-income customers. Partners receive a mini-grant from Michel and his team at his organization, Wholesome Wave, that allows them to start the incentive, begin messaging affordability to low-income clients, and proactively seek sustained local funding from investors interested in both health and local agriculture, and highly encouraged by the results. Michel's team also offers partners other supports to ensure success during their transition to attracting and retaining low-income consumers—help in setting up their market to accept SNAP benefits and applying incentives (i.e. markets need a laptop and typically wireless access in order to orchestrate the mechanics). They pay back with information, using easy-to-use templates for tracking and returning to Wholesome Wave the data they gather on changing consumer habits, so that nationally-aggregated data can be used to leverage policy change.

> "Nischan founded a nonprofit organization that brings fresh, local food to inner city communities. The organization accepts food stamps, and lets families get double their money's worth when they use them."
>
> —*Huffington Post*

Partner organizations are also welcomed into a network where the expectation is that everybody is helping everybody else by sharing best practices around reaching, exciting, and sustaining a consumer base of low-income people. This is important because the COs that operate farmers' markets do not typically have a chance to be part of a national movement, but instead operate in relative isolation. The Wholesome Wave team shapes the network to be self-supporting, and brings partners into a community that strengthens itself and advances the overall aim—some members are good at working with the media, some at reaching policymakers, some at outreach to the community, and so on. Michel and his team make the linkages and modestly fund collaboration so that, for example, a successful and long-term program partner in Chicago travels to Miami to help the partner there get a new market off the ground.

Michel and his team identify and select partners through their existing network and through nominations. They target organizations that are trying to reach low-income groups and have the right location, local clout and integrity with the communities to localize the approach so that it works for that place and the people who live there. Michel ensures that the partner shares the full vision of Wholesome Wave and can and will conduct effective outreach to low-income communities and share results—in other words, that the partner is well positioned to use the incentive to stimulate a longer-term market transformation. While partner selection has been primarily through networks to date, the team is formalizing selection criteria to ensure vision alignment.

Michel helps partners leverage his small investment for significant change in their city and state. He connects partners to local media and state officials to amplify their success, frame it in the context of a broader national reform approach, and show low-income people as a viable consumer base for local farmers. He and his team also help partners connect with and cultivate local philanthropic investors and secure government funding to sustain the incentives moving forward and attract individuals and foundations who want to support the emergence of local food commerce and do it in a way that also contributes to healthier low-income communities. Armed with data of redemption rates and aided by Michel and his team, partners have attracted government and foundation funds that are earmarked for the doubling incentive. For example, Wholesome Wave's program partner in San Diego, International Rescue Committee, just won a $500,000 HHS/CDC grant, over $200,000 of which is earmarked for double-value funds. In Minnesota, a program partner was able, with the leverage and frame Wholesome Wave allowed, to convince state agencies to mandate that farmers' markets across the state accept SNAP and WIC. These are early shifts that show the potential and viability of the effort to move money and public will to cultivate a new consumer group, and contribute to improved health of people and local economies.

In their first annual partner meeting, held earlier this year, Michel and his team of six brought to Washington its partners to share best practices and challenges with each other, and their success stories and experiences with legislators who may enable policy shifts in the allocation of federal funding. Michel and his co-founder have their sights set on demonstrating success (i.e. and showing it through nationwide data) in order to influence allocation in the next Farm Bill, to be passed in 2012, as well as to approach other sources of public financing so that public monies align with, rather than obstruct, the health of people and the rebuilding of local food commerce.

THE PERSON

Michel grew up in the suburbs of Chicago, where his parents had moved so that his father could find a job in industry. The family grew a garden that supplied them with food, and Michel's grandparents on both sides were farmers—one set in Missouri and the other in Kentucky. Michel spent a month each summer on the farms, helping his grandparents. While there was little money, his family was generous with what they had and one way of expressing this generosity was through food and having neighbors over for meals.

Michel decided early on to train to be a chef. He has become well-known, starting and running several restaurants in the Northeast, each focusing in some way on locally grown foods. From his perspective as a restaurant-owner and buyer, he has struggled to find locally grown foods, and has had to call around

to local farmers and cultivate one-on-one relationships to line up contracts—production is not well organized for smaller and mid-sized farms.

In the mid 1990s his second of five children, Chris, was diagnosed with Type I diabetes, and Michel began reading more about diabetes and its causes. He was alarmed to discover the link with nutrition (particularly with Type II diabetes), and the strong correlation with poverty and diet-related disease. This research helped him see food in a broader societal context, causing him to consider how best to channel his knowledge and experience to affect a broader system reform.

Knowing of their intersecting interests, a mutual friend introduced Michel to Gus Schumacher, a former Under Secretary at USDA, and former Massachusetts Commissioner of Food and Agriculture. During his 20 years working in agriculture, Gus had created policy work around food and agriculture, extending the WIC program to allow seniors and mothers to apply their benefits at farmers' markets. Michel and Gus co-founded Wholesome Wave in 2007.

Also in 2007, Michel created Dressing Room, an organic foods restaurant in Westport, CT, near his home. He opened it with Paul Newman's investment and partnership, and uses it to showcase healthy, locally grown foods. He recently transferred management of the restaurant to his wife so that he can focus full-time on Wholesome Wave. Michel continues to cook many weekend evenings because he loves it and because it's congruent with his work and allows him an entry point to change in communities—through high-end chefs. ◆

VERA PERINO

Conscious Consumerism

Nutrition/Wellness

Youth Development

Although Brazil struggled with issues of severe malnutrition in the past, since the 1990s obesity among children has become an increasingly alarming but unreported problem. Vera Perino is transforming the way Brazilian society perceives and addresses obesity by looking at both its causes and symptoms, while sparking deep behavior change and offering alternative lifestyle opportunities to low-income children and their families.

THE NEW IDEA

Brazilians have been slow to acknowledge the emergence of obesity as a serious problem to grapple with because of their country's traumatizing past with malnutrition. Various medical doctors have begun addressing the physical symptoms of the disease under the assumption that it can be quickly treated with drugs; but they usually fail to recognize the psychological, behavioral, and socioeconomic factors that lead to obesity. Vera is leading the way in addressing this issue among low-income overweight children and youth. She is dismantling the restrictive approach of diets and medical treatment, and replacing it with a methodology that positively incentivizes lasting behavior change. Vera is bringing psychologists, physiotherapists, nutritionists, physical education teachers, and endocrinologists together to address the various facets of the issue through fun and participative activities.

Vera began implementing her approach in 2004 when she founded the Movere Institute, which offers free treatment to low-income children and spreads awareness about this problem to health professionals, schools, governments, and Brazilian families. By working with both children and their families, Vera is having a lasting impact on their lives. The results could not be more tangible: Improved eating habits; reduction of body weight and fat; increased fitness levels; improved self-esteem; and disease prevention. Constant monitoring and evaluation have allowed Vera to improve her methodology and to become a leading expert in this field.

Vera operates by the motto: "Small changes. Great results." She has worked with more than 1,400 families, hundreds of schools and citizen organizations (COs), chefs throughout Brazil, and several recognized researchers in the field. Vera is on her way to

changing the manner in which Brazilian society perceives and addresses obesity. In order to ensure the institute's sustainability, Vera is diversifying Movere's organizational structure. She is getting ready to open a new facility to offer her services, free of charge, to low-income communities closer to their homes. This facility's operations will be "subsidized" by for-profit gyms that will focus on providing preventative health care services to the base of the pyramid. Movere is also developing a partnership with the Ministry of Health which will allow Vera to spread her approach throughout the country.

THE PROBLEM

Within the last 20 years, Brazil's rates of obesity among children have skyrocketed by 240 percent. Today, an alarming 10 percent of children and 17 percent of adolescents are overweight, regardless of socioeconomic status. This drastic increase can be traced back to a few critical social and economic factors, such as rapid urbanization and globalization, a historical culture of scarcity, and a reactive and restrictive medical culture.

Brazil's rapid economic growth and urbanization coupled with intense processes of globalization have caused several important changes, such as the emergence of a fast food culture; a dramatic increase in the number of women as heads of the family; and the largest poverty reduction effort in the past 14 years. As a result of these cultural and economic transformations, the Brazilian family's eating habits have changed drastically. However, unlike the U.S., Brazilian cities do not have structures and public spaces that promote physical education.

The Movere Institute provides an unprecedented alternative to children and families struggling with weight problems.

These problems are exacerbated by Brazil's recent history with prevalent malnutrition. The pervasive culture of scarcity this has engendered means that most Brazilians have a hard time worrying about eating too much. A significant number of adults, many of whom come from rural areas, have experienced hunger firsthand. Their traumatic personal experiences often make it difficult for them to impose seemingly unnecessary limitations on their children. Meanwhile, richer families tend to be embarrassed by the issue and therefore decide to ignore it. In addition, obese children and teenagers are discriminated against and often suffer from psychological and physical health problems. The psychological aspects of obesity often exacerbate its physical symptoms and degenerate into much graver health problem such as heart disease.

As a result of these historical and cultural factors, obesity has become an important public health problem in Brazil. It currently costs the state approximately R$1.5B a year (US$807M) to address this medical issue, representing 12 percent of the general health care budget. According to the Ministry of Health, the number of stomach reduction surgeries augmented by 542 percent between 2001 and 2009. This highlights Brazil's myopic emphasis on addressing the symptoms of obesity, as opposed to its causes. It is now common practice to treat overweight people by medicating them, thus ignoring the emotional and psychological causes of the disease as well as the need to change habits and behaviors through a cross-disciplinary approach.

In 2004, the World Health Organization published a study emphasizing the need to focus on the prevention of obesity among low-income populations in Brazil. Very few individuals, such as Vera, are acting on this recommendation. It is exactly because of the complexity of this problem that children and adolescents are particularly vulnerable: An obese child is 30 percent more likely than anyone else to remain obese into adulthood. This risk increases 50 percent for overweight adolescents. Dealing with this issue in Brazil entails coming to terms with many preconceived notions about hunger, poverty, and well-being.

THE STRATEGY

Throughout her professional life, Vera began to understand the complex correlations between obesity, poverty, education, and culture. She also noticed the disconnect between socioeconomic factors and the current treatment options offered to obese children in teaching hospitals. It became clear to her that their restrictive approach would never efficiently address the causes of this multi-pronged problem. She understood that she could attain sustainable impact by bringing together a multidisciplinary team of psychologists, physiotherapists, nutritionists, physical education teachers, and endocrinologists to simultaneously address the psychological and physical causes and symptoms of obesity. This eclectic group of professionals develops activities that serve as opportunities to change behaviors and bring families together.

Vera founded the Movere Institute in 2004 to provide an unprecedented alternative to children and families struggling with weight problems. She has developed a methodology where low-income, obese youth are given fun incentives to change their habits. They are taught to proactively enhance their own well-being through non-prescriptive measures: They write plays, share healthy recipes with their colleagues, suggest topics to discuss with the psychologist, and monitor their own achievements on a monthly basis. Thus, the children become subjects and leaders of change; they learn how to overcome challenges and begin to make conscious choices to become healthier and happier individuals.

They decide what and how much to eat, how long to spend in front of the television, what physical activities to engage in, whether to take the bus or walk. As a result, not only do they begin to develop better lifestyles, lose weight, and avoid developing other health problems, they also gain confidence in their abilities to surmount challenges, learn how to work in teams, and reduce their propensity to become self-conscious, depressed, and anxious.

At Movere, low-income children between the ages of six and seventeen come together three to five times a week to participate in experimental cooking classes and physical activities. Vera and her team choose participants by evaluating the children's clinical states and by engaging with their families from the very first day to determine whether there is an overall commitment to change. Ensuring that the whole family adheres to lessons learned at the Movere Institute has been crucial to the approach's effectiveness. This process of experiential education leads to significant behavior change and promotes conscious choices cross-generationally. Children learn about teamwork and discipline and become comfortable talking about their passions and preoccupations, while families get involved by participating in monthly meetings and field trips to the supermarket, clubs, museums, and sport tournaments. They also learn how to prepare affordable but healthy meals while minimizing waste.

> "The Moving Center for Sports - decided to create a non-governmental organization with a challenging mission: to prevent and combat obesity in children and teenagers."
>
> —*Vigor*

Although Movere began its work by focusing on re-educating youth and their families to adopt healthy behaviors, Vera has since expanded her organization's vision to share the Movere approach with cooks, school caretakers, and COs through delivering trainings. In addition, Movere implements in-depth courses targeting health professionals to disseminate the institute's methodology and transform the way they understand the complex factors that cause obesity. Finally, since Vera is concerned with transforming the way Brazilian's view this issue, she is also spreading awareness to key players and society as a whole.

This evolution in Vera's strategy began with the establishment of a partnership with PepsiCo that began in 2006 and lasted three years. She decided it was time to bring her approach to the public school system, thus benefitting approximately 1,000 children that year. Vera trained teachers to incorporate her methodology in their classrooms and physical education teachers received textbooks containing more than 100 lessons. All of the students benefitted from their interactions with her curriculum and Vera used this first experience to systematize her learnings through her Ph.D. thesis and the publication of a book entitled, *The Prevention of Obesity during Childhood and Teenage-hood:*

Exercise, Nutrition and Psychology. This book positioned her as a leader in this field and spread awareness nationwide about the issue of obesity.

By establishing partnerships with PepsiCo, Novartis, Brazil Foundation, and Eletropaulo, among others, Movere has worked with more than 1,400 families (approximately 7,000 individuals). Practically all participants have drastically changed their eating habits and improved their health. These results are monitored scientifically through physical and written exams, body language, and surveys. Most recently, Movere has partnered with Nestlé and Sao Paulo's Secretariat of Social Assistance, to train more than 300 schools and COs in seven states to become Movere cooks and educators. As a result of the program's success, Vera was invited by the secretariat of another principality to provide courses to local schools and government bodies.

Although these initiatives have been quite successful, Vera noticed early on that health professionals were still uncomfortable with the idea of cooperating across disciplines. She has therefore created an in-depth course to entrench her cross-disciplinary approach and disseminate it through lectures. Vera has been offering this course for four consecutive semesters and has provided training to 400 professionals at Brazil's most influential clinical laboratories: Fleury and Mars. The Santa Casa Medical School, where Vera did her Ph.D., is now planning to offer the institute's curriculum as a professional specialization course.

With a good initial track record, Vera is now thinking strategically about the institute's sustainability. She has all the elements in place to develop a revenue generating initiative. The strategy includes: Establishing the Movere Institute's Headquarters and Research Center on the east side of Sao Paulo (the poorest and most populated region) to offer free treatment to low-income communities; implementing fee-for-service, in-depth courses targeting professionals—Movere has already conducted a feasibility study to launch these courses; and operating gyms as social businesses that offer low-cost health activities to the bottom of the pyramid, thus subsidizing Movere's free activities.

By affecting three generations at the same time (i.e. children, parents, and their future families), this multi-pronged approach has the potential to reduce the health care cost related to obesity by at least 8 percent nationally. Thus, Vera is pursuing partnership opportunities with the Ministry of Health. Her ultimate goal is to re-establish a healthy link between human beings, the earth, and nourishment.

THE PERSON

Vera was strongly influenced as a child by her father's social commitment. He frequently took her and her siblings to different areas of the city to give them a true appreciation of different socioeconomic realities and to elicit a desire to become active citizens. He was an Attorney General and a community leader.

In high school, Vera became recognized as a leader as a result of proactively defending children who were being bullied, publishing newspaper articles in the 1970s (i.e. during the dictatorship) and by spearheading charitable activities. At the age of 17, Vera decided to become a mother, even though everyone encouraged her to remain an "independent woman." She confronted her parents, and society, and left with her boyfriend to raise her children. They became her priority and she decided that above all else, she would bring them up in a rich learning environment.

Nine years later, Vera realized that she needed a new challenge and she opened the region's first natural product store with her brother. She also decided to pursue postsecondary studies. Vera enrolled in university preparatory courses, and at the age of 33, she began her university degree. She originally thought of pursuing pharmaceutical studies, until she realized that physical education would provide her with exactly what she was looking for: A renewed connection between body and mind to promote better health. Driven by sheer determination (while she was still taking care of her children and the store) Vera became involved with community initiatives at the university. It was during her specialization that she first became aware of the issue of obesity and became passionate about it immediately.

Although Vera began her professional life relatively late, her experience as a mother was crucial to developing Movere's methodology. As a mother she could understand the complex factors that lead to obesity, pursuing her studies in a teaching hospital, Vera had the opportunity to attend to patients by creating an interdisciplinary connection with various professionals and specialists. She realized how important it was to adapt treatment to each patient, and encouraging lifestyle changes was equally important.

Initially, one of Vera's challenges was to find support for her approach among medical professionals. After 14 years of work and studies in the field of childhood obesity, she created the Movere Institute of Community Actions: An unprecedented initiative in Brazil that brings interdisciplinary care to overweight children from low-income backgrounds. Thanks to greater access to information about obesity and lifestyle changes, Vera hopes that one day obesity will cease to be such a prominent problem and attention will shift to prevention rather than treating its symptoms. ◆

HUMAN RIGHTS

ABBASS ABBASS

ISRAEL

Disabilities

The image of a lighthouse is a powerful one: It connotes safety, illumination, hope, and knowledge. For the blind and visually impaired Arab inhabitants of Israel—a marginalized community within a marginalized community—AlManarah (Lighthouse), a first-of-its-kind self-help organization in the Arab society in Israel, founded in 2005 by advocate Abbass Abbass, provides both hope and guidance, a sense of community and a path for personal and social transformation. Abbass seeks to change the way Arab society in Israel, and further afield, views and integrates those with visual and other disabilities, and seeks to turn exclusion into inclusion.

THE NEW IDEA

Justice and equality, dignity and empowerment—these are not new ideas. Unfortunately, in many places and for many people, they remain just that: Dreams that have yet to take root and be realized. For the blind and visually impaired Arab inhabitants of Israel, a very new idea would be to take the dream of universal rights and marry it to an actionable plan for social justice. Arabs in Israel are already at a cultural and political disadvantage, a minority (approximately 20 percent) in a country at war with some of its surrounding Arab nations—and the Arab blind must contend with the additional burdens of ancient stigmas and modern ignorance. Abbass seeks to challenge stereotypes and to build capacity through advocacy, education, and empowerment. Through a set of comprehensive programs, Abbass is creating the first self-help organization for people with disabilities in Israeli Arab society; providing a bridge between various elements within Arab society, Arab and Jewish communities in Israel, and creating a model for Israel and, indeed, for other Arab countries.

Abbass' concept for AlManarah is unique in its dialectic approach to the rights of the blind, in particular, and to disability rights in general. Although his focus is currently on the Arab blind of Israel, Abbass is committed to revolutionizing disability rights and social inclusion throughout the Arab World. He aims to transform both social perceptions and self-perceptions of the Arab blind; his organization fosters systemic social change through projects aimed at inclusion, integration and access, as well as self-change through therapy, community-building, and professional training. AlManarah utilizes two types of dialogue to achieve this goal. The first is intra-group dialogue—connection and collaboration

within the Arab blind community of Israel. Integral to Abbass' innovation is the idea of the blind helping each other. To do so, for instance, he has initiated the first Arabic Braille library in Israel, created an audio CD that informs the blind of their rights (i.e. now being adopted and distributed by the Israeli social security), and built a community center where blind Israeli Arabs can go for support, training, socializing, and employment advice.

The second kind of dialogue AlManarah facilitates is inter-group dialogue, integrating the blind into the larger Israeli Arab community through school and family outreach, leadership programs, parent and caregiver involvement, and supporting advocacy through the court system, and public education through the media. As part of this effort, Abbass is trying to encourage use of the term "persons with extra abilities" instead of "people with disabilities" or "disabled persons." "We called our association 'The Lighthouse' because we think that we should light the path. Not the path of the blind, but the path for society as a whole. Our society is blind. It fails to see the blind," Abbass told the Israeli newspaper *Ha'aretz*.

> Each year, more than 2,500 school children and adults from the Arab Israeli community are exposed to information about blindness through AlManarah's activities.

Abbass is the first person to have combined both self-help and societal change to assist the disabled Arabs in Israel. The innovation lies also in the approach and strategy: A rights-based approach for the empowerment of the individual, family and community, and action within society.

THE PROBLEM

In the Israeli Arab World, as in the wider Arab World, a rights-based approach for people in general, and for people with disabilities in particular, is less prevalent than in other parts of the world. Moreover, where special rights do exist, people tend not to be aware of them, and the authorities often do not make the effort to let people know what they are entitled to. At the most basic level, people who are brought up feeling disenfranchised, disempowered, and less than fully human, are not well placed to seek their full civil rights. This is therefore a problem on both the individual and the state side.

In addition, there is a traditional stigma attached to disability in many societies, including Israeli Arabs. At the family level, there is an attitude of guilt, shame, and inferiority (i.e. there is something wrong with the family). The tendency is to ignore the problem, to hide the people with disabilities away, and to feel a strong sense of shame. Lacking contact with people with disabilities, the disabled also lack vital role models. When disability issues are addressed, it is likely to be through a top-down sense of charity and compassion, rather than through empowerment and self-help.

The lack of support is felt at all levels of society, from the individual to the family unit to the community. Exclusion begins early in life; according to Abbass, the parents of visually disabled children do not have the resources, and in many cases the awareness, to deal with their children's special needs. The prevalent negative social attitude to disability also affects the personal realm, including finding a life partner.

The blind in the Israeli Arab community face steep challenges in many spheres. These include accessibility problems in Arab locales, ranging from neglected sidewalks to neglect by public institutions, and these extend to the blatant disregard of national disability rights in the Arab media and public sphere. The Arab community in Israel, more than ever before, is at the crossroads of three major dilemmas: The transition from tradition to modernity, the relationship between religious and secular life, and the tension between rural and urban communities. These tensions often leave aside the added concerns of those 100,000-plus Arabs with disabilities. In addition, in Israel, the Arab public's preoccupation with the Israeli-Palestinian conflict, and the campaign for a separate Palestinian state have contributed to the general ignorance about the exclusion of the thousands of Israeli Arab's with disabilities.

There are more than 6,000 blind and visually impaired Arab citizens of Israel. Not only are they socially excluded from their own community, but they also fail to receive resources and services from the Israeli state, which does not allocate sufficient resources for the Arab blind, and does not make an adequate effort to publicize the rights of the disabled. Communication between the blind and the government is usually conducted in Hebrew, which makes it difficult for the less educated to be independent. This disparity is compounded by ongoing budget shortfalls, and policies that, until recently, made it difficult for the blind to find work in either government ministries or the private sector without losing their disability allowance. "To employ people who have a certain disability, it is necessary to invest resources in adjustment, containment and understanding. This does not necessarily exist here, either in Arab society or in Jewish society," says Abbass.

THE STRATEGY

Abbass founded AlManarah in 2005, and staffed his organization primarily with Israeli Arab blind and visually impaired people. Through his organization, Abbass works to advance the status of the Arab blind and visually impaired on both the social and the individual level: By changing society's perceptions of the blind and by changing the self-perceptions of the blind—the dialectic approach mentioned. His is the first Arab organization of its kind in the region. By fostering social awareness through outreach and advocacy, Abbass seeks to change the traditional stereotypes and social stigmas common in Arab society toward the blind. AlManarah's activities include an extensive schedule of workshops and seminars, the distribution of relevant educational materials, leadership development, and self-help groups of Arab blind (and their parents, if relevant). In addition to outreach and support, Abbass and his colleagues advocate through the Israeli court system to ensure equal access and the protection of inalienable rights.

At the society level, Abbass works to remove the stigma of blindness by exposing the wider society to people with disabilities, and their condition, needs and views. He does this via work with schools, and through public events and publications. Each year, for example, more than 2,500 school children and adults from the Arab Israeli community are exposed to information about blindness through AlManarah's activities, and hundreds of Arab blind and visually impaired people within Israel receive the direct services of Lighthouse. Its center, located in Nazareth, opened in 2005, and is a multi-purpose facility with its core function to serve as a professional, educational, and social hub. Currently, the organization is focused on four main projects in pursuit of comprehensive social change: Awareness; empowerment and skills development; personal reading and guidance; and, the audio library project.

Abbass' organization seeks to educate the visually impaired about their rights, offers a mentoring program, raises awareness among families and caretakers, and works toward offering greater resources to the community.

To foster awareness, the center conducts workshops for parents and caretakers of the blind, and for the professionals serving them. Other workshops help to expose school children and university students to the world of the blind, including their needs and rights, which in turn serve to change attitudes and alter stereotypes. Abbass has created two models of school intervention to foster student awareness. The first model is simply a one-time workshop of an hour and a half, giving theoretical and practical background about being visually disabled, and provoking discussion and introspection about how to treat differently-abled people. The second model promotes the development of young leaders. Over 8 to 10 sessions, a group of students meets and designs a project to help the blind within their communities. One group, for instance, has published a book about blind people, while another embarked on an awareness campaign.

Abbass aims also to help individuals—first to know their rights, to know other people like themselves, and then to try to help themselves with the resources that his organization is building, such as the Braille library. The empowerment and skills development project works to overcome alienation through the establishment of self-help groups. These groups provide a framework for initiating mutual help, increasing self-confidence, and developing a cadre of Arab blind leaders to instigate social change. Several parallel initiatives are planned to augment the self-help groups. Abbass intends to broaden AlManarah's professional and communication platforms by building a website compatible with the needs of the Arab blind, and by conducting training programs in computer literacy, languages, and preparation for psychometric exams. The development of creative abilities, including music, art, and theater, will also be encouraged. He also helps the families of the visually disabled by taking people out, discussing their futures with them, and running a help-line to answer questions.

For AlManarah's third project, volunteers are recruited to serve as personal guides and reading assistants for blind Arab pupils and university students. Volunteers for this personal reading and guidance project undergo a uniquely designed training program that educates them on Abbass' self-directed approach. Finally, there is the audio library project. Due to a dearth of Arabic Braille and recorded material, this new initiative will establish the first Arab library for the blind in Israel. The library will provide learning, scientific and artistic materials—some recorded, others in Braille and large print.

Abbass is also in contact with a number of Jewish and Arab human rights organizations. The needs and the difficulties of Jewish and Arab disability populations do overlap to some extent, and a cultural gap can be bridged here. For example, Abbass runs a joint Arab-Israeli GMAT preparation course for the blind. A part of the association's budget comes from American-Jewish Joint Distribution Committee, within the Masira (Journey) Program for Advancing the Status of People with Disabilities in Arab Society in Israel. At the same time, Abbass' focus is specifically on the Arab public, and building bridges to similar programs in Jordan, Saudi Arabia, Egypt, and even the U.S. (i.e. as a guest of the U.S. State Department).

THE PERSON

Abbass, a Nazarene Arab and himself visually impaired, is dedicated to changing attitudes toward and treatment of Arab citizens with visual disabilities in Israel. As a role model, he aims to grow other role models to help the community. Despite losing his eyesight early due to genetic complications (his parents are cousins), Abbass has achieved a remarkable amount in his young life (born in 1978). His focus has always been on education and leadership. Abbass' father, a lawyer, provided a strong role model for him, while his large family of four brothers and two sisters was always there to act as a support system and sounding board. Combined with Abbass' own strong motivation and determination, it is of little surprise that he's achieved so much and is bubbling with new ideas and plans.

Abbass completed both his bachelor's degree and a master's degree in law at Hebrew University. After passing the Israeli bar exam and becoming a certified lawyer, he completed a master's degree

in business administration and the management of non-profit organizations at the University of Haifa. Commensurate with his interest in policy and advocacy, he is planning to obtain a doctorate in law, either at Hebrew University or abroad. His physical disability does not deter him. "It's as if there is a demon pursuing me," he says. "Instead of taking life easy, I have to be the best, to excel, to stand out. As if I owe someone something. That is what is instilled in us: For a blind person to stand out, he has to be the best." The fact that Abbass was appointed last month to be the first Arab member of the recently formed advisory council of the Commission for Equal Rights of Persons with Disabilities adds yet more proof to his success and the relevance of his work.

Abbass' passion for the rights of Israel's Arab blind, and their inclusion and empowerment, was fueled by moral outrage born from personal experience. After graduation, he applied for a job at an Israeli human rights organization, feeling confident that he was the ideal candidate for the job. However, reversing their over-the-phone demeanor, the staffers attempted to convince Abbass that he was "not right" for the job. Abbass suspected that their reversal was due to the fact that over the phone, he had not mentioned his blindness. Apparently, they felt it was an insurmountable barrier, despite his stellar qualifications.

Blindness, and the social and logistical obstacles it creates, has never stopped Abbass from pursuing his dreams. At school, when Braille textbooks were not available, he engaged students who volunteered to read aloud to him. He understands that the supposedly impossible can be accomplished through hard work and good organization, though he admits that being blind in a seeing society does require extra effort. It is his hope that his activity reduces the obstacles confronting blind people in the future; facilitating a full and normal engagement with life for those people who may have limited sight but no shortage of vision. ◆

AlManarah offers opportunities to the differently-abled to increase their independence, integration, and inclusion in Arab Israeli society.

CINDY BLACKSTOCK

CANADA

Child Care

Equality/Rights

Public Policy

Cindy Blackstock, a member of the Gitksan First Nation of British Columbia, is changing the discriminatory policies and actions toward First Nations children in Canada through a vibrant social movement. Cindy is building a new child welfare system by working directly with Aboriginal and non-Aboriginal communities and helping them translate their constructive and reconciliatory visions for child welfare into action.

THE NEW IDEA

Cindy is changing the mindsets of citizens—including politicians, businesspeople, and public servants—toward First Nations as well as their treatment by government. She works across disciplines and sectors to engage people within and beyond Canada to take action to bring equal funding, support, and resources to all Canadian children. Cindy works at all possible levels to make this vision a reality.

At the grassroots level, Cindy is creating a large reconciliation movement through the development of Touchstones of Hope, a process that brings together public child welfare practitioners and members of First Nations communities. Through patient network building, not only has Cindy succeeded in finding common ground among Canada's 233 divided First Nations groups, representing 30 different languages, she has also created unique spaces where Aboriginal and non-Aboriginal peoples can interact and plan their future collectively, putting their children's welfare in the forefront. Together, they identify processes to solutions and address the ongoing structural and systemic barriers that have made child welfare issues, inequalities, and conflict, seemingly intractable. Touchstones' design brings participants to the table without their titles or job functions. This creates an environment where participants are free to express their opinions and develop reconciliatory solutions while not being bound by mandate and policy or tribal protocol.

Equally important to Cindy's mission of addressing child welfare issues for all Canadians is the knowledge dissemination and research aspect of her work. Cindy is very clear about this strategy, saying she does research "out of necessity, to change things." She works with professional, high-caliber researchers to build a legitimate and scientifically-sound body of research on issues of child welfare. Cindy is systematically filling a critical knowledge gap and is using research as a tool to bridge the chasm between

Aboriginal and non-Aboriginal communities. In additiion, she disseminates First Nations knowledge (scientific and non-scientific) to spread awareness and build an action-focused movement through an online journal and nationwide awareness campaigns, such as "Seven Ways to Make a Difference" and "Be a Witness." Cindy is thus building the empathetic social fabric needed to pave the way toward equity. She is also creating compelling evidence that the Western and Aboriginal paths to knowledge and understanding mesh well together, and can in fact, complete each other.

After playing a leading role in passing a historical law, Jordan's Principle, a child-first principle to resolve jurisdictional disputes involving the care of First Nations children, Cindy is now leading the most publicly watched case in Canadian history. She is presenting a case in front of Canada's Human Rights Tribunal against the Canadian government. Cindy's goal, regardless of the final decision, is to engage a critical mass of Canadians in the cause of First Nations child welfare and highlight the current discrimination in health and education of First Nations families across Canada to further influence national policy.

Cindy won a decisive victory for children with Jordan's Principle, a law to ensure that no First Nations child could be denied proper medical and personal care due to arguments over jurisdictional funding for health services.

THE PROBLEM

Canada continues to grapple with its recent past of taking Aboriginal children away from their families to place them in Residential Schools. There, they were systematically stripped of their culture, and victims of physical and psychological abuse. In the wake of this long policy (i.e. the last Residential School closed its doors as recently as 1990), Aboriginal communities struggle to regain their cultures, languages, and sense of identity and community. Many First Nations communities now suffer from endemic social issues, including substance abuse and high drop out rates. These are symptoms of the continuing discriminatory policies enacted against First Nations throughout Canada. Federal and provincial governments allocate fewer financial and human resources to its most marginalized population: First Nations communities receive at least 22 percent less child welfare funding than other Canadians and $2,000 to $3,000 less elementary and secondary education funding per student. In addition, First Nations children are drastically over represented in child welfare care. Overall, there are more First Nations children in child welfare care in Canada than at the height of Residential Schools. As a result, First Nations children have poorer health, higher rates of youth suicide and incarceration, and many end up with substance abuse problems.

Although there are social service programs that aim to address some of these issues, they tend to address symptoms but not the systemic issues or its root causes. Child welfare services do not embrace local values and traditions but continue to use western methodologies. Within the government, many politicians and public servants are simply not aware of these issues. Among those who are, they generally do not have the power to change things. Others may have the power to change things but have other short-term priorities related to pending re-elections.

Among the Canadian and global public, there is lack of information about the conditions of First Nations. Moreover, the lack of knowledge and understanding of Canadian Aboriginal history creates a large gap in the identities and cultural heritage of all Canadians. In school, Aboriginal youth do not learn about their past, and grow up lacking self-confidence about their own culture. Non-Aboriginals show many misconceptions about First Nations communities, and those who are more aware often do not know how to take action.

THE STRATEGY

In the 1990s Cindy was working as a child protection worker in British Columbia and saw first-hand that there are insufficient services to help First Nations resolve very complex problems. She spent many years doing front-line service work in Aboriginal communities but realized that mindsets, relationships, and structures needed to change to break the cycle of poverty and neglect.

In 1999 Cindy became the first Executive Director of the Caring for First Nation Children Society. Prior to developing a strategy, she completed a 6-month field study to understand the expectations of First Nations communities regarding the health of their families. With this research, Cindy developed a curriculum for Aboriginal and non-Aboriginal social workers which is now part of the official program for any social worker dedicated to child protection in the province of British Columbia. It is a 13-week university program that includes an internship on a reserve. In 2010, more than 200 students attended this program, and a total of 600 social workers have been trained thus far. Cindy invited 15 Aboriginal people to contribute to the materials. Since many of them did not have the skills to write, they were paired with writers, and the Aboriginal authors were given copyright. This method ensured the curriculum reflect Aboriginal perspectives.

In 2002 Cindy co-founded the First Nations Child and Family Caring Society (FNCFCS) to promote equity for First Nations through research, advocacy, and curriculum development. Rather than creating direct programming, FNCFCS developed a national approach to child welfare program development, Touchstones of Hope. Touchstones is a set of policies and a comprehensive step by step approach to attain reconciliation by promoting truth-telling, acknowledging inequities, restoration, and long-term dialogue. Touchstones' uses a train-the-trainers model: In 2009, 30 trainers were trained across the country to facilitate workshops. In 2009 and 2010, 500 people participated in the program and

40 communities nationwide, in urban and remote areas, were offered the opportunity to implement this reconciliation approach. In British Columbia, the provincial government adopted this program in their practices to address First Nations issues. In total, more than 200 people, representing the government (i.e. Ministry of Aboriginal Affairs, Ministry of Education, and Ministry of Health) and citizen organizations (COs) use Touchstones. The implementation of Touchstones puts pressure on the government to tackle issues faced by First Nations.

> "[Cindy] has devoted her life to using reconciliation to address structural risks for First Nations children that are often exacerbated by conventional 'development' strategies."
>
> —Second International Conference on Gross National Happiness

Cindy found it equally important to fill the gaping knowledge gap that allows politicians and citizens alike to ignore the conditions of First Nations communities. She works with leading researchers to convince those that need to be convinced—usually the government—and speaks to them in their own language: That is to say quantitatively. This applied research program is used both as a public education tool as well as to support evidence to influence national public policy. The reports and documents are all freely accessible online. Cindy's quantitative and qualitative research defines a problem from legal, economic, political, cultural, and social perspectives, compares the cost of not dealing with the issues at-hand to the cost of taking action, and develops joint solutions with the government. These jointly-developed solutions are then implemented within a 12-month period. She is also channeling her impact through a very open and inclusive basic newsletter for children as well as sophisticated and academic reports using her Ph.D. Cindy is harmonizing the natural beliefs of her people with the highest possible levels of education. This is a true example of reconciliation. Education in Residential Schools was torturous, but Cindy is now harnessing the power of education for social good and for the advancement of the rights of First Nations.

Cindy recognizes that involving high-profile partners is key to change at a high level. She mobilizes other organizations to write independently about Aboriginal issues in Canada. To date, some examples include: UNICEF Canada's book on Aboriginal children's rights using Cindy's research; the Canadian Pediatric Society's annual report card and best practices, including Cindy's research as well; Amnesty International's Write for Rights (i.e. online support for policy solutions); and the Canadian Medical Association, which passed a motion to support Jordan's Principle. She also convinced the General Auditor of Canada, Sheila Fraser, to do her own research on the allocation of resources to Aboriginal communities and she came to the same conclusions as Cindy.

Cindy and the FNCFCS also work extensively on policy change. In 2007 Cindy won a historical national battle called Jordan's Principle to ensure that no First Nations child could be denied proper medical and personal care due to provincial/federal arguments over jurisdictional funding for health services. (Although health care is a provincial jurisdiction, First Nations health care is managed by the federal government.) Jordan's Principle now states that the child's well-being comes first and payment decisions can be reviewed post hoc. The same year, the Assembly of First Nations and Cindy's organization jointly filed a complaint with the Canadian Human Rights Commission alleging that Canada was racially discriminating against First Nations children. Cindy is using civil rights law to get legal recognition that there are financial and human resources inequities for First Nations families. It is the first time in history that Canada is being held to account before a judicial body with the power to order an enforceable remedy. The tribunal began in September of 2009 and she has engaged Paul Martin, former Prime Minister of Canada in this battle. Cindy is bringing significant national and international attention to human right's violations against Canada's Aboriginal people.

For her, the process is more important than the results. It is as much about public education and awareness raising, as it is about changing policy. She uses the tribunal as an engagement tool by inviting peoples of the world and organizations to join the "I am a witness" campaign. This web-based campaign provides a place for people to learn about the child welfare tribunal and invites them to register as a witness. Being a witness means that people/organizations agree to follow the case, listening carefully to both sides, and decide for themselves whether the government of Canada is treating First Nations children fairly. Registering is open to all ages in order to encourage the engagement of children and youth whom she is inviting to lead this social movement. In 2010, over 5,500 people from at least 10 countries signed on to be a witness making the First Nations child welfare tribunal the most formally watched court case in Canadian history. If Cindy wins the court case, the Government of Canada will have to address the funding inequities brought forward which ties in directly with the bigger vision, developed through the Touchstones process.

THE PERSON

Cindy was born in 1964 to a First Nations father and a non-Aboriginal mother and grew up in rural and remote communities in Northern British Columbia. Her childhood was colored by the oppressive racism against First Nations who were still being placed in Residential Schools with the aim of eradicating First Nations culture. These same schools only provided a grade three level of education as government officials believed First Nations children were only suited to household service and farming/labor. This reality coupled with the fact that federal laws had just been changed to allow First Nations people to attend high school and university meant that Cindy could not remember one First Nations person who graduated from high school, let alone went on to university. She was surrounded by stereotypes and judgments by non-Aboriginal Canadians who, not understanding the history, mistook the dramatic symptoms of government oppression as racial inadequacy.

Cindy was not comfortable with living an entire life trying to recover from the legacies of residential school and other forms of oppression—she was determined to go to university, overcoming the financial barriers. Cindy became a social worker in a bureaucracy where she learned how little the system was addressing the real problems of child welfare and poverty. She quickly realized that she did not fit there. In 1999 she became the executive director of the First Nations Caring Society where she established a successful professional development and policy institute for Aboriginal child welfare in British Columbia. She then co-created the Caring for First Nations Children Society to lead her movement for social reconciliation of First Nations and non First Nations communities.

In September of 2006 Cindy started her Ph.D. and finished in March 2009. She is an internationally recognized researcher and advocate for children's rights who can prick the conscience of the complacent bureaucrat, but moves beyond confrontation to engage the world as citizens who share certain values and seek collaborative solutions. Her blend of community development experience, policy development, and intellectual rigour have propelled her into a leadership role within the reconciliation movement—an effort to heal the wounds of Aboriginal children by fundamentally changing the Aboriginal child welfare system.

Cindy is deeply influenced by the voices of Elders. At many critical moments in her life and career, she has connected to a spirit around her, drawing on the voices of her ancestors to make decisions when at crossroads. This has also developed her sense of community—Cindy leads by community building and helping to advance the agenda of community priorities. She is learning how to fly, which she says gives her the free space she needs to consider and solve problems. ◆

PRAYONG DOKLAMYAI

THAILAND

Employment/Labor

Poverty Alleviation

Prayong Doklamyai has assembled the first nationwide coalition of farmers with land tenure insecurity. Formerly divided by ethnic or economic factors, these farmers are together proving to policymakers that land redistribution is not only necessary, but also viable, in the form of communal land ownership or "community land title."

THE NEW IDEA

Prayong has turned land reform into a tangible policy option and finally, a debate with a positive outcome. Working with landless farmer's networks nationwide, he has been able to offer Thailand's first working examples of communal land ownership, which he calls "community land title." Unlike government land handouts, the community land title protects arable land from private buy-outs through a system of financial disincentives, improvements on agricultural production, and other community-building mechanisms.

> After ten years, over 70 percent of redistributed land is being put to use, resulting in increased annual income ranging from 10,000 to 120,000 baht per household.

Prior to Prayong's efforts, the issue of land tenure insecurity has been portrayed as disparate circumstances and addressed, if at all, by disparate short-term government measures—such as land handouts, debt annulment, and temporary delays in arresting illegal tenants. The community land title, in contrast, offers long-term security for farmers' land and livelihood. In its pilot stage in nine locations, the community land title is already providing tenure security and income improvement for almost a thousand farming households. Farmer groups as well as the National Land Reform Committee are studying the pilot projects in order to develop Prayong's approach into a national-scale operation.

Ratified by the national presidential cabinet, and now in its last stage of legal endorsement, the community land title is a rare example of Thai policymaking, driven to the national sphere by tens of thousands of grassroots communities.

THE PROBLEM

In Thailand, as in many other emerging Third World economies, problems around land tenure are at a standstill due to a set of complex factors. An uneven structure for land ownership prevents small-scale farmers, the poor and the lower-middle class to access land for cultivation and housing. Some 4.8 million Thai farmers still lack sufficient land to earn above US$600 per year, while close to 900,000 farmers are landless. Meanwhile, the wealthiest 10 percent of the Thai population continues to acquire and own about 90 percent of all titled land.

Grassroots communities were able to bring the "community land title" into the national sphere to become policy.

This lack of farmland has also threatened the daily well-being of ethnic minority communities, who have lived in Thailand's forests for hundreds of years. Beginning in the mid 1990s, the Forestry Department has defined all land without title deeds as forests, turning 10 million indigenous people into illegal tenants overnight. Without land titles or proof of citizenship, these indigenous farmers have had no opportunity to negotiate with the government. They face daily harassment, arrests, heavy fines, forced eviction, and imprisonment. In short, they lack the security of a basic livelihood.

In the past, the Thai government has attempted to resolve land tenure problems by allocating new land titles for agricultural use. However, after 11 million acres of land allocation, there remains no mechanism to ensure that the land stays in farmers' possession. As much as 15 million acres, or 35 percent of all farmland in the country is mortgaged as debt security. Each year, more irrigated and arable land is sold for non-agricultural uses by banks or farmers.

As a wealthy minority of landowners continues to accumulate more land left unchecked by a negligible land tax, almost half of all privately owned land in the country is left fallow. Poor and landless farmers continue to be further disadvantaged by hostile market and legal mechanisms.

THE STRATEGY

Prayong is addressing the complex problem of land tenure insecurity through an alternative mechanism of market and legal measures for land redistribution. To ensure that land tenure problems are resolved in an integrated manner with long-term practicality, Prayong has united grassroots experiences and demands under the national farmers' movement, the Land Reform Network of Thailand.

For the past ten years, Prayong has conducted research, outreach, and mobilization work to engage hundreds of farming communities of different ethnicity and economic status, to increase their collective negotiating power. Farmers have studied the experiences of one another, and have concluded that without sufficient land and tenure security, they will always fall back to the vicious cycle of debt and landlessness. Starting with one group of some 200 landless farmers in Lamphun province who confiscated almost 200 acres of private land left fallow in 2000, Prayong has been working with farmers to develop a collective model of management mechanisms for communal land ownership.

Under the integrated approach, of community land title, farmers are entitled to land shares for agricultural production in which financial disincentives ensure that the land stays in farmers' possession. If a farmer decides to abandon the land, it must be sold back to a "community land bank" at a value reduced to only 30 percent of market price, to discourage farmers from selling land to repay debt. This community land bank, managed by a committee of elected representatives, also provides funds toward improving farmers' welfare, such as health benefits, savings groups, and microfinance. To discourage the wealthy from land accumulation, a progressive land tax is introduced, and a proportion of funds will be allocated to sustain the land bank.

In nine pilot locations in northern Thailand, Prayong is working closely with farmer groups and other community organizations to develop best practices for the community land title approach. They are experimenting with improvements on agricultural productivity and value-added products. After ten years, over 70 percent of redistributed land is being put to use, resulting in increased annual income ranging from 10,000 to 120,000 baht (US$300 to US$3,600) per household. Farmers are less compelled to abandon their hometowns to work as itinerant labor, increasing tenure security for the younger generation. These nine locations have inspired farmer groups elsewhere to independently establish their own community land titles, including one location of well over 300 acres in the arable outskirts of Bangkok. In 2005, farmer networks nationwide gathered at the first community land title site in Lamphun and founded the Land Reform Network of Thailand, with tens of thousands of members in 21 provinces.

Prayong's work has increased government accountability and responsiveness regarding land ownership and land redistribution. Some local offices of the Land Bureau have collaborated with the Land Reform Network to examine the land database for illegal titles. The Center for Poverty Eradication and Rural Development has officially included the community land title in its policy. Prayong sees government agencies as his first potential partners for formal implementation of the community land title, as government agencies own a considerable amount of land that is left idle, including several locations of Prayong's pilot projects.

Prayong has also worked closely with mass media to raise public pressure regarding land injustices. Within the past five years, the Land Reform Network has become a familiar name among Thai newspapers and television stations. Following a series of public events, a cross-country march and policy seminars, a four-day demonstration in front of Parliament in March 2009 led to the Cabinet Resolution later that year, agreeing to implement 30 community land titles as case studies for national policy. In addition, the Subcommittee to Study the Implementation of Land Redistribution Policy was established under the National Land Reform Committee, which was presided over by the prime minister.

Prayong has been able to keep the community land title legislation moving forward, despite political instability in Thailand. In fact, he has used the political situation to his advantage, convincing politicians that the community land title will benefit as many as 4.8 million voting farmers across Thailand. As of late July 2010, the Cabinet endorsed the policy and granted community land titles in 30 pilot locations. Meanwhile, the Land Reform Network continues to spread its influence in 21 provinces across Thailand, involving over 380 active communities in the northern region alone. As a recent member of the global farmers' movement La Via Campesina, based in the Philippines, the Land Reform Network has increased the leadership role of Thai farmer members. Through the Land Reform Network, Thai farmers have traveled abroad for study visits and workshops to share the community land title approach with farmer groups in neighboring countries and other developing countries where farmers face similar land tenure problems.

Using media visibility, policy seminars and outreach across the country, the Land Reform Network has continued to push legislation forward.

THE PERSON

As a teenager, Prayong witnessed his family losing two-thirds of their farmland just to pay for his older brother's tuition. Since then, he vowed to pursue whatever education and career that would keep the remaining four acres of his father's rice field.

This experience motivated Prayong to spend the past 20 years working in grassroots community development in northern Thailand on a range of issues faced by rural farmers. He has worked with ethnic minorities, threatened by the lack of citizenship and forced relocation and campaigned with rural communities impacted by adverse government projects, including dams, mines, and power plants. Prior to his work on the community land title, Prayong co-founded the Northern Farmers Association to represent the interests of small-scale farmers and ethnic minorities in land use conflicts.

As a highly regarded grassroots policy advocate, Prayong was elected as Secretary General of the Northern NGO Coordinating Committee for Development in 2004. ♦

ANA BELLA ESTÉVEZ JIMÉNEZ DE LOS GALANES

SPAIN

Gender Equity

Ana Bella Estévez is shifting the focus of support programs that address gender-related violence. She works to empower abused women by leveraging their strengths and capabilities in order to regain self-confidence to begin the separation process from their abuser. Ana Bella creates peer-to-peer support networks of surviving women, who by example of their own experience of recovery convey a positive message. Ana Bella's model is changing the current approach of available programs and resources to be better adapted to address women's specific needs, thereby lowering the barriers to recovery.

THE NEW IDEA

Ana Bella is challenging the traditional victim mindset and approach of resources intended for battered women. She has created a holistic approach that leverages their strengths and competencies over their victimization, and includes key stakeholders from multiple sectors.

Ana Bella is creating peer-to-peer networks that bring together women who have successfully overcome abuse with those who are undergoing abuse and want to break free. Through these networks, she has proven that close references and support from real women who have reconstructed their lives are more efficient in helping women to start their own process of separation and eventually legally report their abuser. To reach those 80 percent of battered women who do not legally report their abuser, Ana Bella focuses on the benefits of "breaking away" instead of the dangers of remaining in an abusive relationship. By building on the strengths of survivors (rather than only focus on treating the negative consequences of domestic violence), she is reducing the time it takes for women to begin the process of moving away from their abuse. Additionally, due to the simplicity of joining an informal peer-to-peer network, Ana Bella is creating shorter bridges for battered women to reach the point of reporting, which is generally the major access point to official resources and financial support. This network is also filling the gaps in existing resources, as volunteer networks provide key support more efficiently and are better adapted to women's real needs.

Ana Bella also works with the government to change the prevalent current approach of battered women as victims which is at the core of many of inefficiencies in the system. By focusing on the positive abilities women have developed through their tragic experience—strength, determination, and ability to work under extreme pressure—she is improving public resources for abused women. From how staff interacts with women when they first approach social services, to the type of financial support offered, including housing and work placement, Ana Bella is assisting these entities to become more efficient by learning from women survivors.

In order to transform the way society views women who have suffered abusive violence, Ana Bella also works with the media to change how domestic violence is portrayed. Instead of showcasing negative images of desperate, weak, violated and marginalized women, she provides positive examples of women living new lives. Ana Bella is proving that messages conveying hope and a plausible way out are more effective in encouraging women to initiate a separation process and report their abuser. This approach is also helping to change how corporations perceive and support abused women employees. By eliminating stigmatization at work and contributing to their speedier reintegration into the job market, women are able to achieve the necessary financial autonomy to safely rebuild their own lives.

THE PROBLEM

United Nations directed studies have found that one in three women around the world suffer gender-related violence at least once in their lifetime. These figures do not vary by age or social or economic status. According to the Spanish Institute for Women, 2 million women (about 10 percent of the female Spanish population) suffer gender-based violence and only 20 percent among them will report their perpetrator to the authorities. From 2001 to 2009, 554 women died in Spain as a result of gender-based violence.

Discourse condemning violence against women is a very much accepted and widespread in Spain. From the legislative point of view, regulations for the protection of victims and laws to promote equality between men and women have been well developed over the recent years. However, these legislative measures are insufficient to change negative attitudes and discriminatory behavior. Adding to this difficulty, the public system for abused women fails to provide support to women prior to reporting a perpetrator.

> To influence future generations of social workers and psychologists, Ana Bella is developing partnerships with universities to implement internship programs.

A root cause of the difficulty of coming out of an abusive situation is the psychological effects of abuse. Often, before actual physical violence, women suffer isolation from their support networks through psychological abuse that undermines their self-esteem; feeding a dangerous cycle of increasing isolation. This process worsens when the perpetrator also controls a woman's mobility and social contacts. This isolation combined with the stigmatizations from the media and other mainstream taboos toward abused women, make women hide their status and cloister themselves; complicating their ability to reach out for help. If they do so, in the end, they often feel rejection from society, which magnifies their fears, as well as their feeling of loneliness and sense of helplessness. Finally, if women do not feel empowered when they are breaking away from violent relationships, they may move from one abuser to another.

Solutions and concrete actions on behalf of the public administration focus on immediate help for a woman in danger or a woman who has criminally reported her abuser. This support takes the form of shelters, restraining orders, and official protection but overlooks the majority of women who have not yet taken this step, or have already used up their share of official aid programs. On the other hand, due to a lack of representation of this group in decision-making forums, abused women are not incorporated in the design of support measures. Therefore, these solutions are based mainly on a theoretical framework, designed by experts, but often lacking the pragmatism that would make them truly effective. Solutions emerging from civil society (including women's associations) in order to fill the gaps left by the public administration do not always deliver the necessary attention tailored to women's personal needs.

Additionally, media messages on the issue to often tend to focus on the immediate negative consequences of abuse, by showing images of defeated women. On the one hand, these messages discourage women from reporting their abuser, as they do not want to be identified with the negative pattern portrayed. On the other hand, society-at-large forms a negative image of women in these circumstances (instead of the abuse itself), perceiving them as marginalized, isolated, and weak. This makes their integration into the labor market more difficult and discourages other support from close networks and family contexts.

THE STRATEGY

Based upon the principle of portraying positive testimonies of survivors, Ana Bella is working at three different but complementary levels: Creating peer support networks, partnering with the public administration and other social agents to help them reach more women more efficiently, and influencing mass media.

Peer networks enabled by Ana Bella form around women volunteers who have successfully left abusive violence. Women suffering abuse have a difficult time admitting it to a stranger, but will often find it easier to talk to a volunteer from Ana Bella's foundation that has been through a similar experience. These relationships begin either through an e-mail or telephone call asking for information, or a casual meeting at one of the events hosted by the Ana Bella Foundation (workshops, stands at fairs, and fundraising occasions). The foundation connects the interested woman with the nearest volunteer or group, and step-by-step a peer relationship develops based on trust and empathy concerning a common traumatic experience. The volunteer not only shows her own example of breaking free from violence and reaching a successful current situation, she also guides and supports troubled women during their process. The support and professional network meets regularly to discuss each individual case and establish the most appropriate route to follow with each participant. This way Ana Bella provides a gradual trust building process that enables women who are not yet ready to report their partner (an estimated 80 percent of women suffering domestic violence) to gain confidence and support from the network to take the first steps in breaking away and access key support resources for gaining independence and protection.

Besides the peer-to-peer networks, Ana Bella uses other resources to help women build their self-esteem and start a new life based on their positive abilities. These resources include shelters, where women

can live temporarily until they find a more stable situation or flexible work at a small business. Ana Bella created, Comprehensive Support Services, to provide part-time jobs for women not yet fully available for the job market. These resources are not meant to duplicate existing official resources, but instead act as mediation points for women who for one reason or another cannot fully access what is available.

To expand this peer-to-peer network, Ana Bella is engaging many other women-related organizations that serve as geographical nodes to implement her approach and develop local networks. Through community-based support networks, Ana Bella empowers formally abused women to become true changemakers with leadership roles and autonomy to organize activities and events locally, with a decentralized model of resource mobilization. In the past year, Ana Bella's foundation has helped over 1,200 women. On average, 1 percent become actively involved in the support network and have directly helped about 300 other women. The impact over these 300 women is then indirectly multiplied as they serve of positive references reaching to a further 900 women. Starting in Seville, Ana Bella has expanded her network to five different regions and is also serving women in Latin America.

Ana Bella is welcomed to the Ashoka family.

In order to consolidate this work with other citizen organizations, Ana Bella is coordinating the creation of a federation that includes all women's associations that adopt the principle of portraying and tapping into the positive testimonies of survivors. Federated, these organizations will be better positioned to further influence the approach toward domestic violence at a national level, beginning by changing the current approach of campaigns to increase rates of reporting.

In regard to the public administration, Ana Bella works at different levels. Through an experience-based training methodology, she is helping social workers change the way they approach battered women, from a perspective of victimization to an empowerment approach that will help women start building a new life from day one, based on their needs and leveraging their capacities. This also avoids the possibility that a bad first experience with the public administration—often due to lack of empathy or excessive patronizing on behalf of the support service workers—may deter a woman from following through with the formal reporting process. To influence future generations of social workers and psychologists, Ana Bella is developing partnerships with universities to implement internship programs for social work students to learn through practice.

From the preventative side, Ana Bella works with students at schools and families to help prevent the development of aggressive behavior patterns and unhealthy relationships that may lead to domestic violence in the future. She works with both women and schools, where her volunteers teach workshops based on positive testimonies and strengthening women's capabilities.

With the media, Ana Bella works intensively to move the perspective away from victimization, and instead, to present women as empowered survivors. As Ana Bella herself has been portrayed positively in different documentaries, she has been sought by different media to find other ways to address this topic. Now she is also able to send volunteers who have successfully left their partners and rebuilt their lives, to represent survivors for media opportunities. Additionally, the foundation is producing radio programs and articles with its own positive content.

THE PERSON

After 11 years of being abused by her husband, Ana Bella managed to escape and raise a family of four children. In the process of separation and through interaction with other women in similar situations, she realized the potential within women who had overcome similar dreadful life situations. Ana Bella also saw how their inherent capacities as a result of their abusive relationships had not been recognized, even by themselves, and therefore, had not been leveraged by the existing support system.

During her breaking away process, Ana Bella also experienced the deficiencies of the public support system and began thinking of ways to help not dependent on the official support service's office hours, or the empathy of the civil servant in charge. She found that the empathy of people directly involved in the problem of gender violence (victims themselves, family, and friends) was key to help women who needed support. She began to meet informally with women to support each other and find ways to offer help to others. In particular, Ana Bella remembers the first woman she worked with: Leticia, from Cuba. Together with Leticia she consolidated the idea that women leaving abuse can become excellent multipliers of support. In Ana Bella's words, "I just helped Leticia, but Leticia then helped 30 other women on her own!"

To bring her work into a more systematized structure, Ana Bella launched a foundation with her limited funds in 2006. Since then, she has spent every hour possible providing resources and support to women on the path to breaking free from their abuser. Although she had opportunities to move away from this professional field and build another life—including a tempting offer to create a new life in the U.S. with her sister—she decided to continue working with battered women. Ana Bella is determined to transform how women leaving their abusers are supported by focusing on their abilities rather than only seeing the ailments that have produced the situation. ◆

FRANÇOIS GOUDENOVE

FRANCE

Disabilites

Contrary to many other parts of the world, such as the U.S., deaf people are highly excluded from French society and are often considered a burden. François Goudenove is changing this mindset. François is pioneering a society in which deaf people are full citizens, prejudices among the hearing towards the deaf have disappeared, and what was once considered a disability is an asset. François' innovative tools around sign language revolutionize deaf people's daily lives, restore their self-confidence, and empower them to play a fuller role in society.

THE NEW IDEA

François has developed a comprehensive set of tools that enable deaf people to broadly communicate using sign language. He empowers them to promote their identity. Examples of his innovations include new ways to make video phone calls, using live sign language interpreters, as well as a live news website in sign language. By facilitating communication and the accessibility of sign language, François has restored the autonomy and self-confidence of thousands of deaf people and has enabled them to act on an equal footing with hearing people. Moreover, he is promoting his organization, Websourd, as an integrative role model for deaf people into the mainstream workplace; currently employing 15 deaf people on a team of 20. By recruiting deaf people on their potential and skills, François offers them promising career paths.

In addition to directly serving the deaf community, François encourages hearing people to accept deaf people and feel comfortable with their differences. To break the taboo of deafness as a disability, he enables hearing people to have one-on-one communication with deaf people in sign language in the workplace and in public places. François also promotes sign language through highly visible tools, such as the first sign language avatar interpreter that will soon be accessible on large screens in 150 major French train stations. Furthermore, François creates job opportunities for hearing people to be sign language interpreters (from 280 interpreters today to 3,000 targeted in five years). He is also changing how academic institutions engage around the issue of deafness by developing trainings in sign language, soon to be available in several universities.

To fundamentally change French mentalities toward deaf people François knows he must demonstrate deaf people's value the whole of society. He is therefore developing training programs based on non-verbal communication skills, led by deaf people (i.e. 1,200 have been trained to date). To further revolutionize the role of deaf people in society, François is proving the value they bring to other sectors. He is working on a project with Airbus to design an airplane cockpit using deaf people's skills. In the mid-term, technologies developed initially for deaf people will be able to serve other populations (e.g. the elderly), thereby contributing to societal improvement. Beyond his national impact, François is currently working on two projects at a continental scale.

Websourd creates a stage for information access and develops software aimed at easing the deaf's access to society.

THE PROBLEM

There are an estimated 300,000 to 400,000 deaf people in France (i.e. one child out of 1,000 is born deaf). This population remains highly excluded from citizen and economic life; only 4 percent of deaf young people pursue their studies after they receive a high school diploma, while 50 percent are underemployed given their potential. This is partially due to the struggles they often encounter with reading and writing proficiency. Until 2005, the education provided to deaf people was based on oral learning and sign language was forbidden in schools. Communication with deaf people had to be oral, considerably limiting deaf people's interactions with hearing people outside their family. Daily exclusion from mainstream society strongly limited their autonomy. Exclusion was perceived as an unbearable moral violence by deaf people and led to deaf people progressively losing self-confidence (i.e. as shown by recent sociological studies in France). Exclusion is also one cause for the high rate of unemployment among deaf people (30 percent versus 10 percent of the whole population). However, the accessibility law passed in 2005 brought strong legislation improvements in France and after decades of oral learning, sign language became an official language in the French education system. Today, around 100,000 deaf people are fluent in sign language, as most have chosen this language to communicate within the deaf community.

The very recent acceptance of sign language has had three main consequences: The phenomenon of deaf people acting as an isolated community centered on itself; French hearing society feeling a powerful uneasiness regarding sign language; and, a fundamental lack of sign language interpreters in France. In total, 280 sign language interpreters currently exist in France (one for 200,000 inhabitants), when more than 3,000 would be required to implement the law on accessibility adopted in 2005. With 60 percent of interpreters concentrated in Toulouse and Paris, the lack of interpreters is even more apparent in the other regions. Given this gap, intermediaries are emerging with various profiles offering no guarantee of training or quality translation. New translation technologies represent a huge opportunity to bridge the gap between supply and demand of quality interpretation, particularly since the use of visual tools and the Internet is common within deaf populations.

Sign language is not a universal language as it is commonly believed. It reflects a country's culture, history, and geography, as any other language and thus differs from one country to another. Nevertheless, as deaf people have developed a sight-based mental structure (i.e. especially people who were born deaf or became deaf very early in life), the grammatical structure of sign languages is similar across countries. Vocabulary is the only thing that differs, and as it is a pictured language, some vocabularies even converge. Deaf people have therefore developed the capacity to rapidly communicate with other nationalities by inventing, in the moment, hybrid vocabulary. This easy convergence of sign languages and its overall grammatical similarity across countries lend tremendous potential to communication and accessibility solutions based on sign language, both on a continental and global scale.

> "The Toulouse-based company was selected by the European Union to work on the accessibility of emergency services for European people with disabilities, including the deaf."
>
> —*Objectif News*

THE STRATEGY

François' strategy focuses on working with both deaf and hearing communities and on creating the missing bridges between these two populations to reverse of isolation and stigmatization. To fulfil this mission, François has developed an organization mainly composed of deaf people and based on two goals: Develop tools adapted to deaf peoples' needs and empower deaf people in the workplace. Websourd is organized by the following divisions: To fight against the isolation of deaf people linked to a lack of daily information, François has created a web portal with 30,000 visitors per month. By providing daily news in sign language deaf people are equipped with up-to-date information about the services available to them. Websourd employs a team of journalists to maintain the web portal.

To make sign language more visible and to enable deaf people to access the same level of information as hearing people, Websourd has developed and is spreading the usage of the first sign language interpreter avatar. The technology is already effective in a major train station in Paris (i.e. and will soon be used in 150 French train stations). The tool's potential application is tremendous: There are hundreds of public places where citizens hear oral messages such as informative updates, advertisements, or urgency messages, whether in stations—train, tube, airport—or other public places such as commercial malls. A team of sign language experts oversee the design and implementation of the avatar tool and its training.

To enable deaf people to be autonomous in their public and professional lives—whether by making phone calls, accessing public services, or participating in meetings—a commercial team spreads the Visio technology (i.e. video phone calls facilitated by remote live sign language interpreters) in companies and public offices.

To recognize that the needs of the deaf community are continuously changing and evolving—a Research & Development team works on refining tools and developing new innovations.

Websourd is creating job opportunities for hearing people as sign language interpreters; with 280 interpreters today to an estimated 3,000 in five years.

Some activities, like the Visio, the avatar and the company trainings, are generating revenue which is 100 percent reinvested into Websourd, a social business. These activities make it possible for the organization to finance less profitable activities, such as the website or the R&D, and to guarantee that all the services developed by Websourd are accessible for free to deaf people.

François particularly targets his services and trainings toward companies and public services in order to change the perception of hearing people toward the deaf community within the mainstream workforce. He has been successful in demonstrating the interest of companies and public services in terms of their legal constraints, client relationships, employee satisfaction, human resource policies, and people development, such as company-wide complementary trainings. Companies have shown that they are willing to pay for the new tools, the interpreting hours, access to a sign language database, and the training, and thus participate in changing the perception of deaf people among employees and customers. One example of Websourd's impact within companies is its trainings led by deaf people, which allow hearing people to learn 10 different non-verbal communication skills, honed by deaf people. The trainings uniquely position deaf people with highly valued skills that hearing people do not naturally have.

Already 40 companies are using VisioPro and the system VisioGuichet is effective in 30 French towns (i.e. in town halls, tax bureaus, and public libraries). François' trainings have convinced 1,200 people that what used to be considered a disability can also enrich them with new and different skills. Spreading his model, François is negotiating national partnerships with some public institutions (e.g. with family allowances desks located in most French cities) and with large companies to ensure the broad implementation of Websourd tools and a change in sentiment throughout the country.

Reversing a pattern and shifting mindsets requires addressing not thousands, but millions of people. Aware of this challenging path, François has structured his organization to ensure the sustainability of his model while maintaining the quality of sign language interpreting. This requires greatly increasing the number of sign language interpreters in the world. François' strategy to reinforce interpreting includes two steps: First, provide quality live interpreting under the current constraint for immediate accessibility; second, develop the profession of interpreting while setting quality standards. For the second stage, François is creating partnerships with all stakeholders, such as universities to spread the teaching of sign language, with interpreter companies to provide complementary trainings, and with job agencies to source unemployed people as potential interpreters and offer them a high value job. He is also supporting interpreters in developing their own interpreting franchises that work with Websourd (i.e. with the ambition of reaching one interpreting cooperative structure of 20 interpreters per French sub-region in five to eight years). Not only is this expansion strategy of sign language interpreters critical in enabling François to spread his model, but most important, it contributes to making sign language a common academic study and interpreting a job opportunity for a growing number of hearing people.

The potential reach of François' solutions extends beyond national scale and he is currently working on projects at a European level. With four foreign partners in Belgium, Spain, Poland, and Austria, he participates in improving the training of deaf people, especially on new technologies. Working with 22 other partners across Europe, François continues to innovate for continued accessibility to communication by playing a key role in a European project on emergency phone numbers for deaf populations.

Websourd is centralized in Toulouse, which is considered to be the deaf peoples' capital in France, and even throughout Europe, as it gathers a huge deaf population. This central location has contributed to placing Websourd as a cornerstone of the "deaf people Silicon Valley." From Toulouse, François is well-positioned to set standards for high-quality accessibility and communication services for deaf people beyond French borders.

THE PERSON

Originating from a working class background in the North of France, François received an education strongly based on France's integration principles, beginning with speaking French. But he has also been instilled with teaching from his mother patois, Chti, the traditional language in the North of France. François' mother led a theater company in Chti and despite the fact that François and his brothers loved hearing and talking Chti, it was forbidden for them to do so outside their family home. As a child, he was included in numerous social activities with his father and naturally developed a sense of sharing. It contributed to his choice not to do his military service during one year, but to instead spend two years teaching math classes in Africa. François was thrilled by the experience of sharing his knowledge and fascinated by the way some words could have different meanings in different cultures.

Returning to France, François moved to Toulouse after hearing a song by the famous Claude Nougaro. Embracing the adventure of setting up in an unknown city, he quickly found a job at Airbus, where he spent 15 years with increasing responsibilities at a European level. François soon left his technical role, which he took due to his engineering background, to assume the role of a go-between, to facilitate the co-habitation of 44 nationalities with different backgrounds, culture and languages working at Airbus. He became passionate about the incapacity of many people to communicate and the levers to solve that issue.

When François' third son was born deaf, he spent two years hearing from a doctor that his son suffered from autism. Finally discovering that his son was deaf and not autistic, François rapidly began to understand the challenges of oral learning and sign language. Confronted with all the difficulties linked to integrating deaf people and the choices for deaf children's parents, François created an association to help and orient parents about their options. Meeting Jacques Sangla, a reference in the deaf community, he immediately shared his vision and decided to transform the concept of Websourd from an idea to a viable and large-scale activity. François' long experience at Airbus enabled him to benefit from high credibility and develop his leadership in a world mostly dominated by deaf people.

François' story is reminiscent to that of Graham Bell, the inventor of the telephone. Graham Bell had a deaf mother and worked all of his life to create sounds to help deaf people. Paradoxically, he created the phone. François' ambition is to fulfill Bell's initial goal to better reintegrate deaf people into society, bringing their unique value to the hearing world. ◆

SUYATNO HADIATMOJO

INDONESIA

Tolerance/Pluralism

To combat and reduce a rapid rise in religious conflicts across Indonesia, Father Suyatno Hadiatmojo—a Catholic priest—is building an interfaith movement. Working toward common humanitarian, social, and cultural goals, people from various religious backgrounds are developing respect and understanding for each other.

THE NEW IDEA

Using social and environmental causes as well as local traditions to bring people together, Suyatno has started an interfaith movement among people of different religious backgrounds. Through the forum he co-founded, People of Faith Fellowship Forum (Forum Persaudaraan Umat Beragama—FPUB), Suyatno offers citizens opportunities to demonstrate their religious values through non-divisive channels, particularly by serving their surrounding communities. Examples of service include interfaith village discussions, senior citizen visits, village gatherings, and community projects. Suyatno's efforts aim to bridge religious divides and reduce the conflict plaguing so many of Indonesia's communities.

Suyatno's movement is markedly different from past interfaith attempts, in that he has been careful not to market it as an effort to bridge religious divisions. Instead, FPUB organizes "social and cultural revitalization events." FPUB has inspired similar programs across the world and has facilitated the formation of interfaith forums in several areas in Central Java, Yogyakarta, Palembang, Medan, Lampung, and Aceh. Religious followers, journalists, and prominent religious leaders from more than 30 countries across Asia, Europe, America, and Australia have visited FPUB.

THE PROBLEM

Indonesia, which is home to six main religious faiths and a variety of other religious beliefs, is often beset by interfaith conflict. During the New Order era, the government used military repression to impose religious tolerance, which only resulted in a strict control over religious life. Despite the seemingly peaceful conditions, however, interfaith conflict remained latent.

Exacerbated by political interests and religious fanaticism, conflict soon erupted after the Reform era. In 2007, community groups experienced more than 32 religious clashes—many of which started from trivial disagreements among followers of different faiths, e.g. between Muslims and Christians in Ambon and Poso, located in Central Selawesi. In 2008, a freedom of religion demonstration in Monas, Jakarta experienced an attack, thus underscoring the gravity of the underlying conflicts.

While the government has attempted to formally initiate interfaith forums under the Department of Religion, unfortunately discourse only occurs among religious leaders, scholars, and citizen organizations (COs), rather than among ordinary citizens. Some religious fanatics even accuse people who try to broach interfaith discussions of being heretics. And, at the same time, religious institutions only make problems worse by fostering the cultivation of stereotypes and exclusivity.

THE STRATEGY

Having personally witnessed the disconnect between the interfaith discussions occurring among religious leaders and the daily conversations between most citizens, Father Suyatno—a strategic and effective long-term organizer—began mobilizing representatives from Indonesia's six major religious faiths to meet regularly. He convinced the representatives of the need to extend discourse to Indonesia's citizens. Together, through FPUB, the group held discussions about humanitarian issues with community members from various villages.

> "According to Suyatno Hadiatmojo, the people of Indonesia reaffirm the spirit of national unity.
> FPUB [encourages them] to feel concerned about spiritual issues, multiculturalism, and nationality."
>
> —*CyberNews*

Suyatno has strategically disguised the interfaith movement as a revitalization of cultural values. Furthermore, to obviate an endless discussion about religious beliefs, Suyatno distances the organization from religious goals, such as conversions or syncretism. Instead, he mobilizes members from various religious groups to collectivize and participate in social activities, such as dialogue, work, and celebration. Religious leaders and followers from all religious backgrounds participate together regularly in public events, thus providing powerful examples of interfaith practice for citizens.

Father Suyatno purposely emphasizes communal work, which has long been embedded in Indonesian culture, as a means of finding common ground among disparate groups of religious followers. Using social and environmental causes, he mobilizes and unites these various groups. The interfaith messages are delivered subtly and tactfully. When distributing relief aid and building clean water systems in the Turgo village, for example, Suyatno carefully tells members that "there's no such thing as Catholic rice, or Islamic rice, or Hindu water." As communal activities become more common and people begin working together to build religious facilities or even prepare festivities, interfaith collaboration begins to happen naturally. To further stress the importance of interfaith dialogue, FPUB focuses on sacred rituals such as village restoration projects, tree planting activities, and silent processions.

Father Suyatno, prompted by the need to extend discourse to Indonesia's citizens, regularly brings religious leaders together for interfaith discussions.

FPUB organizes regular Youth Camps to introduce the model to younger generations. As part of the Tsunami relief efforts, for instance, FPUB organized Life Skill Exchange sessions for Acehnese youth. Members attend various religious facilities to receive vocational training and to gain alternate perspectives about different faiths. By focusing on younger crowds, Suyatno hopes to foster the development of a generation of interfaith movement activists who can balance varying religious contexts around one unifying principle: The relationship to God and to each other.

FPUB organizes regular "peace campaigns" on national and religious grounds, which allows it to utilize traditional rituals as a means to promote understanding. For example, the ritual lampah ratri brings approximately 2,000 people together to march in silent procession, where they pray and reflect. Suyatno and his members also organize peace campaigns through other activities, such as flea markets, mobile medical services, savings groups, and reforestation programs.

FPUB has inspired the creation of hundreds of local interfaith forums, which were directly facilitated by staff members and even independently replicated in some cases. They effectively utilize the media to amplify their message and document lessons. *Jogja, the City of Tolerance* book and film series, cites FPUB as the best practice available to maintain peace among cities that were once plagued by riots. Through FPUB, Suyatno envisions a brotherhood that will ultimately dissolve all borders and respect all religious beliefs.

THE PERSON

Suyatno was born and raised in a poor family and had to pay his way through school by raising and selling chickens. He joined various student activities, including several sports and martial arts lessons. Suyatno's mother solely supported his choice to enter seminary and when she passed away, he almost dropped out from school. However, the rector helped him get support from Sister Martinet with the Soegiopranoto Foundation. Through the foundation, Suyatno and two of his colleagues began working with a charity to help the homeless and needy.

Spending every holiday with the charity helped Suyatno develop a strong sense of service. After working with beggars for long periods of time, he wanted to experience being in their shoes. Suyatno therefore began a month-long journey from Mertoyudan seminary to Bali, walking and hitchhiking as a beggar, even sleeping on church porches.

With his colleagues, Suyatno started a number of initiatives, such as selling used papers and "stealing" seminary food wasted during a month of Christian fasting to be distributed to the poor. He was later introduced to interfaith issues and grassroots community work through his mentor Romo Mangun (Fr. Y.B. Mangunwijaya), known for his advocacy and relief work in Kedungombo, a village drowned for the development of big dams, i.e. a victim of the government's development plan during the New Order era. ♦

LÁSZLÓ JAKUBINYI

HUNGARY

Disabilities

László Jakubinyi proves that individuals with intellectual disabilities, of all levels, can thrive as dedicated employees and live productive lives. László has created a replicable rural approach for people living with moderate to severe levels of intellectual disabilities. His approach is spreading to Poland, Romania, and Moldavia.

THE NEW IDEA

László has developed a new health care delivery system for moderately and severely disabled people. His approach facilitates the idea that people with significant autism and other mental disabilities can manage and excel in employment. To prepare intellectually disabled people for the workforce, László relies on a number of insights.

László believes a multi-stage rehabilitation model is the best way to prepare intellectually disabled people for independent lives. He begins with a physical space, where people with various intellectual disabilities are integrated, including non-disabled people. When participants are ready, they enter a "sheltered" employment program where they undergo paid work for four hours a day (i.e. contracted by László's organization), and experience on-the-job training according to their skills and capacities. Once comfortable in this environment they move on to a longer-term "transit" employment program with more stringent responsibilities (i.e. arriving to work on time and finding their own means of transportation to and from work), and undergo evaluations to prepare them for the open labor market. This staged process mimics the fundamental idea that humans first need basic shelter and food, then access to things like employment and a steady income, in order to achieve dignity and fulfillment in life.

László's second insight is that any approach to rehabilitation should mirror life's setbacks and successes. He therefore constructs his model so participants can retreat if needed, regain confidence, and then re-engage with the program. Emotional crises do occur, such as a death in a family or a break-up, which can jeopardize an individual's rehabilitation progression and set them back to the sheltered stage. Therefore, participants have access to a crisis center which offers therapy, including theater and puppetry therapies, to support them during emotional setbacks.

László also insists that rehabilitation services which integrate a broad range of disabilities are much more effective than a closed community limited to one or several disabilities. His open model differs from traditional services by providing services and activities that cut across numerous disabilities, physical to intellectual, and moderate to severe—and even incorporates non-disabled persons. For example, a blind person may work with a severely autistic person to train guide-dogs.

Szimbiózis works with mentally handicapped and autistic persons, with the aim to use examples of good practices in Miskolc to set up their happy farm, and alternative trainings and activities.

THE PROBLEM

In Hungary, 2.5 percent of the Hungarian population lives with autism and mental disabilities. Of this population, about one-half is enrolled in primary or secondary education, whereas only 7 percent is employed. Furthermore, 85 percent live at home, with parents who have dedicated their lives to their upbringing and rehabilitation, while 14 percent live in state-run institutions with over 300 people. They are quite isolated, which keeps them invisible from most of society. The final 1 percent live in independent apartment homes of approximately a dozen people; primarily managed by disability organizations. These numbers begin to uncover the significant opportunity to better integrate intellectually disabled people into society, particularly the employment sector and independent housing.

In Hungary during the 2000s, the disability field, particularly autism, was increasingly gaining attention. Questions such as, what services exist after school for children and adults when they are at the age to leave home? What happens when parents are no longer able to care for their disabled child? Parents and guardians wanted smaller, more intimate institutions to take care of their children so they set up associations to build more independent apartments. However, although these housing facilities offered leisure time and rehabilitation services, they were not sustainable solutions. Without opportunities for work and independence, their disabled inhabitants were bored and unfulfilled.

Another problem during this time was that existing rehabilitation programs in Europe often ignored the need to provide disabled people with the ability to cope with crisis situations. The occurrence of crisis situations decreases the possibility for people with intellectual disabilities to gain stable employment and live independently. This challenge is further strengthened by the prevailing notion that people with disabilities are rather problematic employees and do not add value to a company. In Hungary, 75 percent of adults with moderate disabilities and 97 percent of adults with profound intellectual disabilities are labeled as "unemployable" for the mainstream labor market.

The existing health care delivery system for disabled populations, which relies on institutions or personal caretakers, is unsustainable during an age where much consideration is given to human rights and human dignity, as well as to innovative solutions to pressing social problems. In the case of disabled populations, an entirely new European-wide approach is needed, along with a fundamental change in attitude toward the ability of moderately and severely disabled people to live independent and dignified lives.

THE STRATEGY

Over the years, as László worked closely with the intellectually disabled, he began to see that people with autism and severe mental disorders have the potential for almost entirely independent lives, including decent employment and an autonomous living situation. László is ending the notion of institutionalizing intellectually disabled people by demonstrating the success of open and independent living facilities where severely intellectually disabled people find paid work and those moderately disabled become prepared to enter the labor market.

> In Hungary, 75 percent of adults with moderate disabilities and 97 percent of adults with profound intellectual disabilities are labeled as "unemployable" for the mainstream labor market.

The core of László's approach is a farm, which acts as an open community; its disabled inhabitants engage in farming activities, animal husbandry, vegetable production, and crafts work. The farms provide a physical space for people with various intellectual disabilities to interact, but also includes non-disabled people, such as youth staying at the farm's hostel, buyers of the farm products, and participants of the open events organized by Szimbiózis. Szimbiózis farms have become the model for providing rehabilitation services to disabled people in Hungary's northeastern rural communities, and László is working to make his multi-stage approach the standard delivery service for disabled populations. With four farms established, László will spread to all 19 counties across Hungary and take his approach beyond Hungary, to nearby countries with similar service delivery problems.

A successful element to László's approach is the creative methods he uses to keep disabled persons engaged and working together across their spectrum of disabilities. In 2007 László began to interact and eventually employ people with physical disabilities, instead of only intellectual, on the Szimbiózis farm and its activities. He observed that the creative combination of disabled peoples' skills results in better work performance. László therefore has people with physical disabilities supervising and working with those with intellectual disabilities. For example, a woman with only one arm will work with a strong boy with a severe intellectual disability in the production of goat cheese. She oversees the process of cheese production and helps to instruct the boy, while he lifts heavy pots or other activities; or, a man with schizophrenia supervises the processing of vegetables in the kitchen with several other employees with autism able to efficiently peel the vegetables. In 2010 Szimbiózis' activities in Miskolc, a town in northeastern Hungary and the location of Szimbiózis' first site, employed over 160 people, of whom 100 are disabled.

Using pictogram flow charts that easily define and describe various work processes has also strengthened the results of the employee training program. Severely disabled persons receive simple pictured step-by-step instructions for their work, such as how to make handicrafts. These instructions leverage their skills, i.e. attention to detail, precision, and unerring focus that is common for people with autism, as well as other intellectual disabilities. The pictograms have also been used to define the work processes for employers. László advocates having pictograms as an accepted standard assistance tool for employees with severe disabilities. He is building a universal foundation for these tools by developing a European-wide database where pictograms are uploaded and employers can search for them depending on the work process they are implementing. The database will also spark new ideas among employees and rehabilitation organizations about the ways disabled people can be successfully employed.

László's work with guide dogs is a further example of the unique methodologies he employs to engage individuals across varying levels of disability. When he was approached by blind people to help them with employment opportunities, he decided to transform a building on the farm into a guide-dog training center. Besides benefitting the blind, this program created an additional job placement and therapeutic activity for people with severe autism to care for the dogs. This joint dog therapy approach has been so successful it has spread across Hungary and the municipality where Szimbiózis is located will fund an additional guide-dog center in town.

The majority of Szimbiózis' funding currently comes from the Hungarian government and the European Union. László is looking for ways to lessen the organization's reliance on government funding. He has viewed this as an opportunity to set up several related companies that have assumed some of the farm's activities, including a catering and a transportation company (i.e. to take disabled to and from the farm, and children with special needs to their schools). Szimbiózis coordinates with its disabled staff and the catering company to deliver lunches to various locations and organize the home delivery of milk. A hostel on the farm also welcomes school children who come to experience farm life as well as learn more about disabled life.

All the activities that fall under his model of social enterprise apply the idea of mixed working groups that complement each other with their specific skill-sets. Szimbiózis' business activities therefore generate a sustainable funding source (i.e. 10 percent of Szimbiózis' 2010 budget, and growing) which is reinvested back into organizational activities.

In 2003 László founded an agency that provides intermediary assistance to facilitate the matching process between companies interested in employing intellectually disabled and disabled people themselves. The agency helps to define their skills and provides proper on-the-job training. While the agency initially focused on people with mild disabilities and autism, after learning about the need of employers, he soon realized that people with severe disabilities could also be hired in settings outside of the farm. State employment offices soon began to send disabled individuals to László's intermediary employment agency. To date, two other organizations working with the physically disabled have replicated his employment matching model.

A successful element to László's approach is creatively pairing disabled persons across a spectrum of disabilities. In doing this, people work from their strengths and actively engage each other.

László has also begun to influence policy and gain attention in Hungary across a range of venues. He launched the Disability Work Group in the northern eastern region of Hungary to advocate for regulations enabling the employment of people with intellectual disabilities. Furthermore, László helped to finalize a court case this year which set a precedent for orphans with severe intellectual disabilities to be employed. He has also begun a media campaign to portray what it means to be employed for persons with disabilities. He produced a movie showing the meaningfulness of the first salary for disabled persons. With the slogan "I would like to pay taxes" in Hungary, the film has been received with great interest and significant attention. László is also partnering with local authorities to convince municipalities to transform public housing into flats for up two to three people with disabilities, who share its expenses. In 2007 the Szimbiózis Foundation inaugurated the first blocks of apartments for 12 people with severe intellectual disabilities and in January 2009 another block of flats opened.

László is now working on a strategy to find and help local community members to develop their own value chain of activities to serve disabled populations. For example, László and his team are working with parent groups from different towns and villages to help them to write a project proposal, obtain permission from the municipality, and attain government funding to replicate elements of the Szimbiózis model to their own contexts. He is also interested in creating a quality of life assurance system that measures the true quality of life of a disabled person, in addition to a knowledge base to facilitate the program's spread and to maintain its quality. The Disability Work Group is assisting to further replicate elements of the model, share methodologies, and develop standards for success (e.g. the home centers must be open and include various levels of disabilities both mental and physical). László's work with quality control, spreading networks, and creating industry standards is moving society closer to a world where institutions are phased out and a value chain that supports the independent living and employment of disabled persons has become the norm.

To date, Szimbiózis, has either established or assisted with the development of four farms across Hungary, with two others being developed in Romania. László is also advocating with state authorities to include people with intellectual disabilities in the mainstream labor market, and elements of his model are being picked up by other disability organizations. Ultimately, László envisions a world where disabled people are living independently, instead of excluded and isolated from mainstream society in institutions and homes.

THE PERSON

László was born in 1969 in the northern part of Romania in a commercial logging and mining town. His family background is a mixture of nationalities and cultures, i.e. it was normal to celebrate various religious holidays throughout the year. Although László's mother language is Hungarian, he was a minority in his town, speaking Hungarian at home and Romanian in school.

In the 1980s, when László was 14-years-old, he became involved in the underground Hungarian theater. The Securitate (Romanian communist security forces) picked him up, jailed him, and beat him for his involvement. However, László continued to reject social norms with which he disagreed. He soon became involved with a community group that collected food to bring to a local psychiatric hospital. The hospital's patients lived in atrocious conditions: Half-clothed men and women were kept in an attic of concrete, where there was only a hole for a toilet and metal beds to sleep in. After László brought food to them for the first time he was not able to eat that day; he was so disturbed by what he saw. Even the animals at his house did not live in such poor conditions. László began to return to the hospital once a week, then twice a week. He visited, bringing food and clothing for over three years. He believed that the patients waited for him and he had a duty to return. From this point, László devoted the rest of his life to bettering the lives of the intellectual disabled.

When László entered the Romanian army at 18 he immediately sought out a psychiatric hospital where he could volunteer. After the army he decided to organize summer camps for disabled people, and with 8 other young people he received free space from a church to develop a center. However, funding was always a challenge for his work and it was hard to get the center up and running. László decided to study special education in Budapest, but lacking adequate financing and struggling to be accepted by the school for his revolutionary ideas on how to best serve disabled populations, it took him 13 years to complete his studies.

In 1992 funding from the Knights of St. Columba enabled László to build the church space into a rehabilitation center for intellectually disabled individuals, but in 1997 he ran out of funding and was unable to convince the Romanian government to support him, refusing to recognize his Hungarian degree. Feeling tired, he accepted a job as a teacher in Hungary and also worked for a citizen organization to set up a home center for disabled adults. László experienced setting up home centers with a local church and the Budapest municipality. All along, he knew a home center is not a solution for the integration of disabled adults into society. The centers remained against the employment approach for which László strongly advocated. László therefore founded the Szimbiózis Foundation in 1999. For the first three years he worked as a volunteer and in 2003 he made the decision to become a full-time staff person and has been committed in this capacity ever since. László's approach is now to focus more energy and efforts on scaling to a national and regional level. ♦

MARK JOHNSON

UNITED KINGDOM

Citizen/Community Participation

Criminial Justice

Mark Johnson believes that only offenders can stop re-offending. Offenders are the key to their own rehabilitation, and the key to improving the system that is supposed to perform that function. Through his organization, User Voice, Mark is challenging the system's assumption that "punishment should mean silence" by giving offenders a voice in designing the system. Through his flagship program of Prison Councils, and through activities which give offenders representation at a policy level, Mark demonstrates that rehabilitation only works if people have an opportunity to take responsibility for themselves.

THE NEW IDEA

Mark is designing practical strategies for incorporating the voice of prisoners and imprisoned addicts in tackling the failures of the prison and rehabilitation systems. Two parallel and complementary processes are key to his innovation. First, he proposes that as in all other sectors, the views of service users be integral to developing the best solutions. The knowledge from service users about which services are most valuable and impactful need to be integrated into planning and commissioning. Applying this approach to criminal justice is controversial and challenging, however, with User Voice, Mark shows how ultimately service users know best about what will be successful.

The second process at play is a more significant and internal one. In order to be full citizens and members of society, all people need to be in a position to take responsibility for themselves and the world around them. In prison, prisoners are systematically denied these opportunities in a meaningful way. However, when offenders are released into society, they are expected to take on this role outside of the prison gates. Mark is overcoming this "democratic deficit" by empowering prisoners to give their opinions, and to take responsibility for co-designing systems while still in prison; thereby, putting in place the first building blocks for ex-offenders to become full citizens in the outside world.

The flagship program for giving prison users voice is Prison Councils. Mark works with prison authorities to develop a Prison Council where prisoners are asked to form and run particular parties, each representing common challenges faced by prisoners and the prison system. The success of a Prison Council is measured not by individual attendance or individual attitude change, but community indicators: At one prison site complaints from prisoners dropped by 37 percent, as problems were dealt with closer to the source; at another, the number of segregations days (e.g. prisoners are kept in isolation—often resulting from protest actions) dropped from 160 to 47. The rates of prisoner participation in the councils now surpass 50 percent. These examples of improved engagement with the community and with social processes indicate a personal level of responsibility-taking—the first step to real social rehabilitation.

Mark's aim is to change the industry of offender support services. He wants to see it shaped by the voices of those who are most affected by it, and driven by the positive influence of successful ex-offenders who become role models for others. Mark wants to see a system which enables ex-offenders to succeed and then go on to help other people do the same. This multiplier effect of ex-offenders helping other ex-offenders, and society-at-large in tackling the problems they know best, is key to individual rehabilitation and to finding society-wide solutions to crime. Mark is supporting his frontline work with widespread advocacy through a newspaper column, high profile events, and lobbying policymakers. In this way, he works at all levels toward a mindshift in society, which sees offenders as part of the solution.

THE PROBLEM

The U.K. prison system is widely recognized as a failing system, with prisons stretched beyond capacity and a re-offending rate of 55 percent for adults and 75 percent for juveniles. The U.K. has the highest incarceration rate in Western Europe. The cycle of reoffending is costly, and damaging to victims and perpetrators alike.

The industry of therapeutic and rehabilitative service providers built around the criminal justice system does not currently provide scalable and impactful solutions. Part of the problem is a perverse incentive structure which sees providers responding to short-term targets rather than effective solutions. Currently, a wide array of service providers competes to retain their slice of resources in developing programs for ex-offenders. Their own interests are best served by winning contracts, rather than developing the impact of those contracts and success is measured by how many people attend rather than by their impact on those that attend. The result is a crowded sector of people providing solutions that do not work. Those with the greatest stake in seeing solutions work—the users—are largely excluded from service design and provision, leaving service providers to speak and act on their behalf.

The issue of "user voice" in prisons is highly controversial and challenging. Prison is intended to remove one's liberties as punishment for their crime. Democratic voice is assumed by many to be one of those liberties which prisoners should be denied. Prison staff perceives their own role as one of control, and the general public clamour for harsh treatment of prisoners. This approach successfully fulfils the punishment function of a prison. However, it potentially reduces the opportunity for rehabilitation; in reducing people's ability to make responsible choices, they are prevented from becoming active agents of change. Most prisoner programs fail to give prisoners the experience of taking meaningful responsibility for their lives.

THE STRATEGY

Mark's strategy involves working at every level of society to reconfigure people's expectations about the importance of using the voices of offenders in designing services.

The centerpiece of Mark's approach is Prisoner Councils. Currently, User Voice operates four prison councils inside prisons, and five councils in the community with ex-offenders. More are planned to launch around the country. Loosely described, they are structured, deliberative, democratic forums, although within the regulations of a prison environment (or within the law, when taking place in the community). They are a tool to help to inform and improve the quality of prison management, while also underpinning the rehabilitation process. Prison councils are based on moral notions of both prisoner rights and responsibilities. Such an approach provides a firm basis upon which to further build work in helping prisoners to become law-abiding, contributing citizens. The principles behind the councils are that the format should be flexible, the council must work within regulations, and it must be solutions focused, representative, enjoyable, transparent, and accountable. Prisoners are asked to form and manage particular parties, each representing common challenges faced by prisoners and the prison system. For example one party will be concerned with preparation for return into the community and through-the-gate services. Another party focuses on strengthening and improving the relationships between prisoners and with staff. The prison councils have reduced complaints in the prison, "protest" actions among prisoners, conflict between staff and inmates, and have contributed to changes in prison policy, for example relating to adjustments in family visiting arrangements and to incentives schemes for prisoners. The councils demonstrate both the rehabilitative power of giving prisoners a voice, and the practical implications of improved feedback from service users.

> "Mark Johnson is on a mission to explain his new role advising policy makers how drug addicts and young offenders can be turned round."
>
> —The Guardian

Another important strand of User Voice's work lies in developing meaningful consultative processes to help government agencies listen to their "hard to reach" clients. Mark is working with a range of organizations to help them listen to their users, including the Probation Service, the Youth Justice Board, Drug Strategy Units, and the College for Social Work. For example, one project is seeing User Voice recruit and work with people who have engaged with social services in order to inform a center for excellence in social work. All projects rest on the principles that they are giving voice to excluded service users involved in the criminal justice system; they use other ex-offenders to access those service users; and they directly influence decision-makers. Mark is developing a pipeline of similar projects to ingrain the views of service users into the commissioning and design of services.

In addition to directly facilitating practical examples of user voice by improving systems and services, Mark is creating a national debate around the causes of offending, and the way to find solutions. Mark has a regular column in a national newspaper where he challenges public perceptions about the nature of people in prison, and what their role should be in stopping crime. He also carefully places and seeks media coverage of positive stories about ex-offenders taking responsibility; for example, at an event, excluded young people presented their recommendations to policymakers. Mark consciously uses his own story publicly as living evidence of his approach, and as an inspiration for other ex-offenders. He has published a best-selling book about his life, and is currently writing a second book about emotional development of excluded young people.

Perhaps the most important aspect of Mark's strategy is creating a pipeline of role models. User Voice is not only an organization undertaking a set of activities, but is by its very existence is a platform for ex-offenders who are articulate, socially responsible, and successful individuals. All of User Voice's frontline staff are successful ex-offenders who have turned their lives around, and are also engaged in helping other people to do the same. Mark recruits qualified and talented ex-offenders to lead the organization and to carry out its frontline work, for example, one ex-offender is leading the expansion into the north of England. This has a profound impact on employees' self-confidence and transforms their long-term employment prospects. More broadly, User Voice demonstrates the hugely positive role ex-offenders can play given the right circumstances. These individuals are key to Mark's strategy of changing perceptions both inside and outside the criminal justice system about what is possible and achievable. They are role models to other ex-offenders, and are key to the public perception that ex-offenders are part of the solution. They are also central to his scale strategy. Rather than directly scale User Voice from the center, Mark will recruit and train entrepreneurial ex-offenders to set up regional operations that are context-appropriate. The peripheral operations will then develop locally relevant services with ex-offenders, while the central operation will focus on the core advocacy work. Only through a larger number of ex-offenders who understand the system and are empowered to take responsibility for its improvement, can society successfully tackle the core problems in the criminal justice system.

THE PERSON

Mark arrived at the principles behind User Voice through first-hand experience of the failures of the prison system. He wrote an autobiography chronicling his childhood surrounded by abuse and addiction, and his own journey into—and out of—crime, homelessness, and heroin addiction. Mark spent 15 years in a downward cycle and ended up living on the streets of London before turning his life around. After successfully giving up drugs and gaining stability in his life, Mark set up a tree surgery business focused on employing other ex-offenders and recovering addicts. The business was very successful, but Mark wanted to take a role in improving the criminal justice system, and began advising others on projects working with ex-offenders. He spearheaded several innovative projects, including a peer mentoring project. Realizing that there were very few people like him, able to effectively speak with the experience of ex-offending, he determined that he needed to give voice to other successful ex-offenders, who could both act as viable role models, and more accurately access the important information that prisoners hold about what works. Mark has demonstrated through personal example that when given a voice and the chance to take responsibility, ex-offenders can not only be rehabilitated, but create the space for other people to act as influencers of change. ♦

EVA MARSZEWSKI

CANADA

Citizen/Community Participation

Conflict Resolution

Law and Legal Reform

Through Peacebuilding Circles and mediation, and conflict management training, Eva Marszewski is equipping high-risk communities to preventing violence and other anti-social behaviors from being first addressed through the judicial system. Eva is thus averting future juvenile delinquency as well as empowering communities to cope with problems as they appear. She is engaging with the court system, police, and schools to entrench this user-friendly and highly preventative tool and is building ordinary citizens' capacity to help youth in conflict grow into healthy, productive, civically-minded adults.

THE NEW IDEA

Eva is shifting the decision-making power in the youth justice system away from the courts and into the hands of schools, community centers, and communities. She is engaging ordinary individuals to help others heal and change their behavior through Peacebuilding Circles, collective decision-making, conflict resolution, and other peacebuilding tools. Eva has developed tools that handle multi-party conflict, providing youth in the criminal justice system, and in other difficult situations, options and opportunities to fulfill their personal needs and offers them support from friends, colleagues, and neighbors. Eva is partnering with elementary schools, high schools, universities, COs, police centers, and the Canadian court system to teach the value of peace and conflict resolution, giving community members and organizations greater decision-making power in determining the course of action needed for youth in conflict.

Eva is helping communities develop conflict resolution competencies to give them the ability to handle and take ownership of their conflicts without immediately resorting to police or court interventions for troubled youth. Conflict resolution competency in effect de-escalates conflict situations as Eva's methodology has the capacity to stabilize neighborhoods and communities to come up with creative and innovative local solutions to deal with diverse issues at the root of the conflict. Eva believes that sustainable personal change comes from within and is not brought about by coercion or shaming. Her approach reaches youth at a deeper level and motivates them to want to re-examine their values and principles, and align themselves to appropriate values by discarding behaviors that do not match up.

THE PROBLEM

There is a systemic struggle, both from the legal and civic communities, to build capacity for egalitarian, effective governance systems. This struggle and lack of community capacity in community conflict resolution competency forms a fertile ground for conflict escalation, leading to an increased involvement of children and youth in the criminal justice system.

Despite the increasing referral of youth to the justice system, about 45 percent of all youth charged with various criminal charges end up with the charges against them either withdrawn or stayed. Of the 55 percent that do proceed into the justice system, a smaller percentage of youth are sentenced to jail. The youth in conflict tend to be students who struggle under the weight of social, economic, health, and other challenges who are simply overwhelmed by their lack of personal resiliency and social skills. Poverty, lack of available/any parents, negative or oppressive peers, special needs, and health issues all challenge these youth. These issues are compounded by the systemic failure of governance systems institutions to operate with a coordinated and well thought out child and youth policy structure. Many youth are particularly challenged to make smart choices and fail to take advantage of educational opportunities.

About half of Ontario's jail sentences for youth are less than 30 days in length, indicating that a lot of the youth that are imprisoned for such a short time frame have committed minor offenses. The issues range from established types of misbehavior such as theft and assault to newer challenges such as bullying, cyber-bullying, Facebook and social media abuses, as well as group/gang induced issues. Society is squandering costly and scarce policing and justice resources on children and youth that do not need to be in the justice system. There is a scarcity of conflict resolution training among professionals, such as teachers and school administrators, who are required to deal with a multitude of conflicts on a daily basis. Furthermore, existing conflict resolution tools are not very good at dealing with group issues.

THE STRATEGY

Eva founded Peacebuilders International in 2002, after being inspired by Aboriginal communities' use of healing circles. Eva's adapted Peacebuilding Circles are a deliberative process which has been consciously constructed to combine the structure of traditional circles, which include the use of a talking piece (i.e. but without their ceremonial or governance aspects), with a contemporary understanding of consensus-building processes. Eva's approach has now been piloted, tested, and evaluated, and has received recognition, acceptance, and enthusiastic embrace by prosecution and defense officials, teachers, principals, police, and community members.

Peacebuilders International's mission is to create cross-cultural partnerships among youth and adults through capacity-building for peaceful and sustainable communities.

Eva's Peacebuilding Circles encourages communal dialogue, and address the emotional, psychological, and societal causes and repercussions of youth conflict behavior. The Peacebuilders Circle program establishes an effective detour from existing harsh disciplinary and court proceedings. It enables a diverse group of civil agents such as youth, community members, consultants, and teachers to address, as peers to the youth in conflict, sensitive areas and topics of conflict and youth rebellion. To date 100 percent of Peacebuilder reports back to principals, police, judges, prosecution, probation, and defense counsels have been approved. Due to the success of Eva's program, the court system has developed a strong partnership with Peacebuilders and has offered her a fixed office in Canada's busiest youth courthouse. This court system is partnering with Eva's vision to shift the cases from the court system to community resolution.

Peacebuilders' selects volunteers from among high school and university students, graduates, law students, teachers, police agents, and citizen sector leaders. All are primarily caring individuals who understand youth and are willing to help them identify their challenges and strategies to move forward. Peacebuilders' engages and trains their volunteers and seeks those who are representative of the communities in which they work. Currently, Eva has 12 trainers using the methodology, 100 trainees per year, and 50 circle facilitators.

Peacebuilder's Circle process enables a group of participants to address difficult issues in a safe, contained, and monitored environment. Events and conflicts are deconstructed, examined piece by piece, challenges and underlying causes are identified, and plans are developed to address them over time under the guidance and mentorship of the Circle Group. Subgroups may also assemble under the overall direction of the trained Lead Circle Keeper or trained Circle Keepers. The Circle Group also follows-up on monitoring implementation and addressing further

issues as they arise. On average, there are three Circle Keepers, two of whom are youth, with one professional consultant or mediator to provide guidance, direction, and support.

In order to scale the impact of the program, Eva envisions building neighborhood-based capacity to respond to and prevent conflict in a timely manner. Thus, youth and their families will be able to avail themselves of local resources to address their own pressing issues. They will be spared from having to attend youth court anywhere from 5 to 15 times prior to trial (i.e. the average in Toronto courts). Trainings for Circle facilitators will become local. Longer term, given trained community partners, Peacebuilders will develop a community triage system so that community representatives and youth will be able to establish a Circle to address local youth issues. Peacebuilders Youth Circles program intervenes at each of these three levels. The Circle teams seek to identify and address root causes, if at all possible, including involving members from the business communities, health sciences, and other needed disciplines so that the plan for each youth enables them to move toward a healthier life in which they can thrive. They also examine the youth's schooling situation and seek to place the youth into the most appropriate educational context available.

> "Youth Circles is an aboriginal-style peacemaking process intended to help inner-city Toronto youth stay out of trouble with the law, reduce violence and build safer schools and communities."
>
> —The Star

Eva has three distinct goals she is working toward through Peacebuilders. First, through her Circle programs, and partnership with the Canadian legal system, she aims to reduce the number of arrests by reducing the number of cases going into the court system. As a result, highly skilled judges and legal officials can apply their skills to more serious cases that need more time and specialized attention. By partnering with community officers and engaging them in her peace and conflict resolution methodology, Eva will be able to impact the relationship between youth in conflict and community officers by tutoring officers on how to engage with and determine the appropriate course of action for youth facing potential mischief charges. Therefore, Eva is working toward creating a system where the police officer, who is the first avenue of response, is not immediately charging the youth but rather cautioning, warning, or sending the youth to a conflict-resolution program, breaking away from the community-triage-system.

Second, Eva is teaming with elementary schools, high schools, and universities in Toronto. Her goal is to enter into the university curriculum for law schools to have conflict resolution as a mandatory program. Eva is currently also training student-teachers to have the capacity to manage difference and conflicts in their classrooms, in effect, giving a better capacity to handle conflict and discipline in a multicultural and ethnically diverse society. She is also working with a conflict resolution masters program by building relationships with their graduates; who provide opportunities and open new communities for Peacebuilders to train people, while introducing their methodology on conflict resolution and management.

THE PERSON

Eva has always been passionate about social justice issues, and comes from a family of social activists. Her parents fought for Poland's freedom; an experience that has shaped her family's view of the importance of freedom of opportunity. Eva was raised during her formative years in Venezuela, and was exposed to the disparity between the rich and poor, which transformed her perceptions of what is and what can be.

For three decades Eva worked within and around the justice system. First as a civil litigator on family law cases as well as on a Public Commission of inquiry into certain activities of the Royal Canadian Mounted Police; as a labor arbitrator for matters involving labor unions and management; and then as a mediator of civil disputes in court cases in Toronto. Through these roles and responsibilities, Eva was able to observe many dysfunctional aspects of the justice system.

Eva has an awareness of the importance of human connection and the perils of disconnection; a temperament predisposed to mediate and help others solve their problems or come to terms with their differences.

Fifteen years ago, a retired judge from the Territorial Court of the Yukon invited Eva to be a part of an Aboriginal peacemaking circle in Haines Junction in the Yukon, where she saw the power of a diverse group of social agents come together to address the conflicting nature of a young male who had committed arson to a community member's home. As they discussed the issue and learned about the young man, the community—through facilitated dialogue and traditional practice—were able to decide the appropriate means of action that would benefit both the youth and the man whose house was burnt, without resorting to a court sentence. This was a formative experience that led her to adapt the traditional practice, and later embed it in various social structures in Canada. ◆

WENDY PEKEUR

SOUTH AFRICA

Agriculture

Employment/Labor

Law and Legal Reform

Wendy Jasmine Pekeur has established the first women-focused trade union in South Africa to champion the employee rights of female farmers. Wendy works in the Western Cape Province of South Africa, the country's foremost wine producing region. In applying the trade union model to a farm setting, Wendy is empowering women (most seasonal laborers) to break the cycles of poverty, disenfranchisement, and alcoholism.

THE NEW IDEA

Though women make up a majority of the agricultural workforce in South Africa today, and a number of historical, societal, and economic factors; women on patriarchal, industrial-scale South African farms still have little power over their lives. In the past, formal labor contracts had been signed with men and only through their husbands were women guaranteed work on farms. Though the roles of men and women farm laborers have changed over the years and since the end of Apartheid, many female farmers have yet to exercise their full rights. In 2004, in this challenging setting, Wendy formed Sikhula Sonke (meaning "We grow Together" in isiXhosa). Through Sikhula Sonke, Wendy is ensuring the equality of people on farms, with a particular focus on women and seasonal workers who, to date, have had little (if any) representation. Today, Wendy and her team ensure that minimum employment standards are adhered to by farm owners; these include providing farm laborers and seasonal workers with livable minimum wages, health benefits, safe working conditions, and fair mediation of the termination contracts.

To eradicate the high levels of fetal alcohol syndrome (FAS), spousal abuse, and alcohol and drug addictions, Sikhula Sonke trade union is introducing a new code of behavior and professionalism to the farming environment in South Africa. In addition to demanding fair wages paid in legal tender and not in bottles of wine, Sikhula Sonke is changing the cultural norms surrounding seasonal farm work. The union and its members are promoting a new ethos that values empathy and respect for farm workers, particularly women, the disabled, and temporary employees. Men committed to this new system can join too, but those who wish to be represented by the union are required to first sign a resolution to desist from practicing any form of violence against women.

With its growing support base and bargaining power, Sikhula Sonke has been able to better negotiate with farm owners on behalf of farm workers. As a result, the union has been successful in expanding and revolutionizing the support being offered to people on farms. Some of Sikhula Sonke's hard-fought victories since its founding include setting a minimum wage standard for farm workers, securing childcare services on farms, providing access to savings plans to cover the costs of funerals (a vital social service), and ensuring better working hours and working conditions.

> "This passionate trade union leader has triumphed over personal hardship and devoted her life to the fight against injustice."
>
> —*Kristin Palitza*

THE PROBLEM

In South Africa the debate around land ownership and the rights of farm laborers has been a deeply contested historical issue. During Apartheid, land was owned mainly by white Afrikaner South Africans. The land in question had been forcibly taken from black landowners who were reduced to the status of farm laborers with no claim of ownership over the land. This created an exploitative (and legislatively sanctioned) situation where the power to employ and house the laborer—or not—rested wholly in hands of white farm owners. Generally, the farm owner provided employment, housing, and some land to the farm workers in return for their labor. However the farmer had total control while the laborer had little or no recourse when their rights were affected.

At the time, the practice was that permanent farm labor contracts were signed with the male farm worker. Since this contract typically included housing, employment, and a small parcel of land for subsistence farming, the family of the farm worker was dependant on this provision. However, should the farm owner be displeased with the individual farm laborer—the entire family would be reduced to destitution and lose not only their source of income, but their home and garden as well. Women were specifically affected by these conditions. In many cases, women worked in various roles on farms to contribute to the family income. However as tenure contracts were only undertaken with the male in the family, wives and daughters were subject to losing their employment if their husbands or fathers lost their positions on the farms.

Additionally, it has been the practice, particularly in the Western Cape, to pay salaries in the form of wine concessions know as the "tot system." This has resulted in extremely high rates of alcohol abuse and in particular, high percentages of infants born with FAS

in the area. It was also often found that physical and emotional abuse of women by male partners was rife. The dependence on the abuser for physical security further compromised women's abilities to leave abusive relationships and undermined the safety of women and their children. Tragically, the social and living conditions of farmwomen and their daughters today is still, for many of these same reasons, extremely harsh. A 2001 study found that the Western Cape has the highest incidence of FAS in the world, with 40 to 46 per 1,000 first graders showing symptoms of FAS. The legacy of alcoholism and FAS remains pervasive on the farmlands.

Much has changed since the fall of Apartheid, but even in the face of a many welcome improvements to labor and tenure laws aimed at protecting the rights of farm workers and dwellers, conditions remain much the same; farm life continues to be characterized by an extreme power imbalance between the industrial farmer and his work force, with women farm workers being some of the most disadvantaged and vulnerable in South Africa. Despite the minimum wage legislation now in place for agricultural workers, most farm laborers still do not make enough money to live comfortably in the face of rising food prices and precarious housing and living conditions. Women farm workers therefore need a representative organization to raise demands with employers and the government. Traditional agricultural trade unions are not proactive on farms, especially with regard to women workers.

Wendy realized that it is impossible to effectively tackle the issue of labor rights without an integrated approach that addresses the full range of threats to farmwomen's livelihoods. She also knew trade unions would have to be willing to become true social movements of the marginalized. By using the trade union as a unit to organize and empower the feminized workforce, Wendy saw the potential for the roles and rights of women farm workers to be recognized and expanded.

Wendy speaks at the launch of the *Sikhula Sonke* newspaper and cd.

THE STRATEGY

Wendy felt that organizing women laborers was necessary to address the interconnected issues of livelihood security, abuse, and the exploitation of women farm workers. But creating the trade union was just the first stage of her intervention; by addressing critical issues around labor in a growingly feminized labor force, further interventions could be attempted to ensure the place of all farm workers as full economic citizens.

Sikhula Sonke has taken the form of a trade union that addresses many diverse issues. Farm worker rights are just the entry point for improving general conditions and the lives of female farm workers. Sikhula Sonke's successes include providing secure housing with women as title holders, better health benefits, better safety standards, and increased wages. Sikhula Sonke addresses gender issues to create strong leadership structures that include women at all levels and reflect their needs.

Since the early 1990s, the organization, Women on Farms, has represented the interests of a number of South African farm workers but has concentrated on social issues rather than labor issues. Despite their good and charitable work, increasing cases of labor exploitation of women living and working on farms demanded a different approach. Wendy created Sikhule Sonke to respond to these needs. She believes that farm women should be able to access land ownership through agrarian reform and ensure food security for their own produce without being threatened by the farm owner. The organization also focuses on finding new and innovative ways of organizing, taking into account all the changes in the world of employment.

Sikhula Sonke expects to further expand their area of intervention and consolidate their work in the Western Cape, where an estimated 350,000 farm workers are employed. Though they will remain focused on women, Sikhula Sonke is developing a strategy to specifically defend the rights of pensioners, disabled people, young people, and the unemployed who also live on the farms. The union currently has more than 5,000 members and serves a total of some 20,000 people when all dependents and relatives of members are included. Sikhula Sonke hopes to expand membership to 8,000 members (on an estimated 300 farms) by 2011, but growing the ranks is only one part of the union's strategy. The union aims to diversify the membership, including men, but also ensuring that a minimum of 66 percent of the members remain women and hitting targets of 40 percent seasonal workers and 40 percent speakers of an African language, other than Afrikaans. On this last goal, language has been a particularly divisive issue, due to the fact that Afrikaans remains the local language and serves to divide farm workers who speak Afrikaans from those who do not. People who do not speak Afrikaans, as one might expect, are often disenfranchised. With the first step of organizing women farm workers achieved, Wendy has set her sights on improving the effectiveness of Farm Committees to provide better and more expanded services to members.

Still, there is a definite gap in the legislation in terms of addressing the needs of women farm workers. In the next year, Sikhula Sonke

intends to lobby the government to improve the enforcement and compliance mechanisms of all labor legislation so that women farm workers derive maximum benefit. Some of these benefits will include improved access to housing, a higher minimum wage, paid sick leave, paid annual leave, and unemployment insurance. The union will also help women worker's access housing on farms, paid maternity leave, and improved working conditions, from protective clothing to better latrines. By engaging the government and challenging labor laws and policies, Sikhula Sonke has the potential to affect nearly 1 million farm workers nationwide.

THE PERSON

Wendy grew up on a farm and, as in the stories of so many farm workers in South Africa, themes of alcohol abuse and child neglect were deeply woven into her life. Despite these challenges, even as a young girl, Wendy was driven by a deep desire to ensure the equal treatment of women farm workers. Soon enough, Wendy would experience the many challenges confronting women farm workers; her first job was as a seasonal farm worker in the Western Cape.

Although there was a worker representative structure in place, Wendy saw that it did not cater to the needs of seasonal workers. Instead, having an ineffective structure in place reduced the power and the ability of seasonal farm workers to best represent their interests. Given her experiences and her intrinsic drive for equality, she became more involved in helping to transform the lives of farm workers and move toward land tenure for these potential small farmers. Specifically, Wendy's personal struggle with farm owners practicing the tot system, led to her broader understanding of these systemic issues and the need to create a voice for women farm workers.

Today, Wendy, 31, is still motivated by the need to create more equity and equality in rural communities for those marginalized due to gender, language, culture, and perceived powerlessness. As the only female and youngest General Secretary in the organized labor movement in South Africa, Wendy is a trailblazer challenging male-dominated social institutions and reinventing the role for women on farms and in society. ◆

ANA LÚCIA VILLELA

BRAZIL

Child Protection

Conscious Consumerism

Law and Legal Reform

Ana Lúcia Villela is promoting healthy childhood development in Brazil by implementing the first citizen-led mechanisms to regulate the advertizing industry. Ana Lúcia is thus empowering society to honor children and to protect them from the harmful effects of an increasingly consumerist culture, such as childhood obesity and materialism.

THE NEW IDEA

Throughout her life, Ana Lúcia has been committed to the field of childhood development. She is concerned with creating an environment where children can thrive and she has identified consumerist culture as one of the first obstacles to surmount in order to make this vision a reality. Ads have been proven to lead to over-consumption amongst children: Girls are maturing sexually earlier than they would otherwise; kids are gaining weight, socializing less and overvaluing things over experiences. Ana Lúcia is therefore developing mechanisms to control the commercialization of childhood.

In 2005 Ana Lúcia created Projeto Criança e Consumo (Children and Consumerism Project), which is housed within the Alana Institute. This is the first project of its kind in Brazil to spark a debate about the effects of ads on childhood development and to challenge the legal frameworks that allow the advertizing industry to thrive by targeting young audiences. She is working tirelessly to ensure that kids can soon begin to enjoy commercial free childhoods. In order to do so, Ana Lúcia has created channels of communication to give the public access to news and information about this topic and equip them with tools they need to take action once marketing abuses are identified. She is also working with influential decision-makers (i.e. in government and big advertizing companies) to change their approaches and introduce new norms to regulate the publicity industry.

As a result of her work, Ana Lúcia has successfully entrenched this issue in Brazil's social and political agenda. She has not simply focused on changing the minds of media and communications professionals; she is creating crosscutting alliances by involving academics, students, public servants and large businesses in the debate. The Alana Institute has secured important legal victories that have increased regulatory norms for ads targeting children; the institute has championed hundreds of legal cases; and disseminated more than 500 news stories about the topic in 2009 alone, thus incentivizing the public to report thousands of abuses by the advertizing industry. With the support of the News Agency for Children's Rights–ANDI network, Ana Lúcia plans to spread this initiative beyond the five states where she currently operates to reach all of Latin America. She sees the entrenchment of a commercial free childhood as merely one step to guaranteeing healthy childhood development, and she intends to broaden her horizons once that goal has been achieved.

THE PROBLEM

According to a study entitled "Kids Power" *(TNS/InterScience)* 83 percent of Brazilian children are influenced by advertizing, 72 percent are particularly attracted to products associated to famous people, 42 percent are influenced by their friends' consumption habits, and colorful packaging affects 35 percent of children. In other words, children are extremely sensitive to marketing efforts. This sensitivity is exacerbated in Brazil, as children there watch more television than in any other country, including the U.S. The average Brazilian child between the ages of four and eleven spends about five hours per day in front of the television and approximately 85.5 percent of kids between six and twelve-years-old watch TV on a daily basis. They spend more time watching shows than interacting with their families or attending classes.

> "Ana Lúcia Villela sparked a growing and effective movement in Brazil to stop the commercial exploitation of children. [She] has just been awarded Brazil's top education award."
>
> *—Campaign for a Commercial Free Childhood*

What is more, the messaging in ads targeting children teaches them that there is a direct relationship between happiness and acquiring certain goods or services. Unlike adults, children interpret messages literally and are usually unable to discern persuasive metaphors from reality. They are also often incapable of discerning advertizing from other sorts of television programming. The influence of commercials has been proven to contribute to materialism, eating disorders, and precocious sexual behaviors, addictions to tobacco and alcohol, and household tensions, among others.

Obesity is one of the most telling consequences of the commercialization of childhood. Nowadays, 30 percent of Brazilian children are overweight. It is telling that 50 percent of advertizing targeted at young audiences sells food products, and more than 80 percent of those ads are for unhealthy goods, rich in sugar, sodium and fat. There is no doubt that advertizing is one of the factors contributing to the upward trend of childhood obesity.

To make this situation even worse, there are no laws in Brazil that regulate ads targeting children. It is neither the state nor an organized civil society that controls advertizing decisions, but rather the National Advertizing Council of Self-Regulation (CONAR). CONAR is made up of big advertizing companies, their owners and representatives from communication companies. Until now, the main justification for self-regulation has been that an external effort to regulate the sector would be an infringement on free speech and would be perceived as an act of censorship.

In a country like Brazil that is experiencing such drastic economic growth, it is important that this growth be accompanied by a renewed commitment to the social development of its future generations. However, Brazilian society tends to ignore the overall needs of children and has yet to make long-term investments in healthy childhood development. Ana Lúcia seeks to reverse this trend and put children back at the center of Brazilian society.

THE STRATEGY

After working for ten years to promote healthy childhood development through the Alana Institute, Ana Lúcia realized that any successful attempt to honor children's needs would have to directly address the hidden problem of consumerism and its harmful effects. Thus Projeto Criança e Consumo (PCC) was founded in 2005. Driven by the notion that limitless desires of consumption are detrimental to a child's healthy development, Ana Lúcia has developed a three-pillared approach (i.e. legal, educational and communications-based) to turn the vision of a commercial-free childhood into a reality. She has chosen to take a diversified approach to tackle the harmful effects of consumerism by creating a multidisciplinary team of psychologists, lawyers, teachers, journalists, and social workers, among others.

The Projeto's Legal-Institutional Program keeps track of activities of the executive, legislative, and judiciary branches of government; supports bills related to introducing advertizing regulations in Brazil and monitors businesses' marketing tactics. In addition, PCC receives complaints and reports from consumers when an advertizing company goes too far and it undertakes legal actions against them. In order to expand the number and diversity of actors involved with this issue, PCC also establishes alliances with competent organizations and decision-makers. Since 2005, the institute led 105 legal cases against companies that disseminate advertizing campaigns that are harmful to children's rights. Every month, Ana Lúcia and her team receive more than 90 complaints from citizens through the program's web platform and through a strategic partnership with the Public Ministry.

Projeto Criança e Consumo also has an area of research and education that is establishing itself as Brazil's first scientific and cultural reference center on the issue of consumerism. It produces and disseminates educational curricula for teachers. One of its most successful initiatives has been the InFormation Program developed in partnership with the ANDI network to increase the pool of knowledge about children and consumption by engaging senior undergraduate students. The program offers selected students interested in writing their final thesis about children, consumption and media, a R $350 (US$150) scholarship to help them develop their research. For the past two years, this national competition has resulted in the support and dissemination of 24 academic theses on this theme. At the end of 2008, the institute also promoted another contest in partnership with a leading educational magazine (Revista Nova Escola da Fundação Victor Civita) that selected and published the three best educational activities that dealt with questions of consumerism in school.

In order to further disseminate information about the topic of advertizing regulations, Ana Lúcia found that it was crucial to develop an area of communications and events, within Projeto Criança e Consumo. This department is responsible for tracking news relating to this issue on a daily basis; suggesting article topics to the media; developing communication campaigns; and organizing such events as the International Forum on Children and Consumption. This event is already in its third edition and is increasingly recognized

as a leading forum worldwide. It has generated an important debate in the media, most specifically about CONAR's regulatory mechanisms and children's advertizing.

Beyond contributing to daily behavioral transformations by educating the public about the commercialization of childhood, Ana Lúcia's approach has also found allies in organizations such as CONAR, government bodies, and companies who agree that is necessary to control ads targeting children and teenagers. Thanks to her efforts, new rules and restrictions have been introduced. For example, in 2008 the National Health Surveillance Agency (ANVISA) presented a new regulatory proposal to prohibit ads targeting children for products that are high in fats, trans-fats, sodium and sugar. In the legal sphere, Ana Lúcia also made considerable advances. A 2008 bill 5921/01 which deals with the prohibition of ads targeting children was voted on and approved by the Commission on Consumer Protection in the Chamber of Deputies. This bill influenced TV Cultura (a public television channel) to remove all commercials targeting children from its airwaves. The Commission of Economic Development, Industry, and Commerce passed this same bill in 2009. As a result, Brazil's 24 biggest food companies decided to sign a document recognizing the harmful effects of children's advertizing and made a commitment to discontinuing the dissemination of such ads. The Alana Institute has also been working with the Federal Ministries of Justice, Culture, and Education among others.

Ana Lúcia's Projeto Criança e Consumo is already operating in five Brazilian states. Within the next few years, she plans to expand throughout Latin America in partnership with the ANDI network. Ana Lúcia is increasingly participating (and sometimes leading the way) in national and international networks. She has chosen to focus on turning her vision of a commercial free childhood into a reality, but she sees this goal as merely one step among many others to create an environment where children can thrive and develop healthily.

THE PERSON

At the age of eight, after losing her parents in a plane accident, Ana Lúcia began to feel the effect that environments—not just material but also emotional—have on a child. She became "obsessed" with this insight and decided to write her thesis in teacher's college about how to create an optimal environment that stimulates a child's full and healthy development. Ana Lúcia, of course, focused on the impact of ads on children's health.

With the money she inherited from her parents, Ana Lúcia created the Alana Institute. Initially, it focused on increasing the quality of life of low-income families and their children, in a community of 25,000 people on the eastern outskirts of Sao Paulo. This project, now entitled Espaço Alana, allowed Ana Lúcia to understand the social realities of low-income children. This experience made it all the more obvious to her that a child's environment has deep consequences on his/her development. She saw innumerous examples of the harmful effects of childhood consumerism in that community, despite their low socioeconomic standing.

Ana Lúcia became increasingly convinced that this issue could only be addressed through a systemic and diversified approach involving the media, communication agencies, governments, the private sector, and all of society. Through Projeto Criança e Consumo (now the Alana Institute's focal program) Ana Lúcia is strengthening her life-long commitment to children's development. ◆

LEARNING & POWER

ADINA BAR-SHALOM

ISRAEL

Access to Learning/Education

Adult Education

Capacity Building

If information is power, knowledge is a pivotal personal and social asset, and education is an essential gateway for economic, political, and developmental progress. The integration of the several large ultra-Orthodox Jewish communities within wider Israeli society—henceforth "the ultra-Orthodox community"—in terms of education, employment, obligations and contributions, and general mutual acceptance, is one of the toughest faced by the state and the community. By creating the first structure in which ultra-Orthodox women (and recently, men) are able acquire academic qualifications and professional skills in harmony with their identities and traditions, Adina Bar-Shalom is not only contributing to their economic well-being, but also opening a door to inclusion and improved status within larger society.

THE NEW IDEA

Since the ultra-Orthodox community is growing at a disproportionately rapid pace in comparison with the rest of Israel, and now constitutes almost 15 percent of Israel's population, the challenge of integration, transformation and self-sustainability is growing more urgent and acute. Adina has set out to change the situation of the ultra-Orthodox community. Her innovation is to offer "academization" as she calls it, to ultra-Orthodox women (and now men) in Israel, while fully respecting their traditions, and the range of other demands on them. She observes that Israeli society as a whole is becoming increasingly academized, and those without academic degrees miss out on employment opportunities. The women who enter the college she founded in 2001, Haredi College in Jerusalem, are often the main or sole support for their families, which are often large, and live under the close supervision of rabbis or rabbinical bodies. The men are often restricted to a life of religious study that does not include paid employment. For both, the opportunity to learn academic subjects (education, economics, computer programming, or laboratory sciences are just a few examples) and to acquire professional skills (law is popular) provides personal dignity, much needed remuneration, and access to the wider society on the basis of mutual respect. Menachem Ben-Sasson, President of Hebrew University, says "Society must adjust itself to the changes taking place in traditional societies around the world, to encourage the acquisition of higher education and to take part in bearing the economic responsibility borne by the society as a whole."

Like other entrepreneurial and successful projects that deal with coexistence and the integration of marginalized communities, this

initiative deals with "the politics of interests" much more than with the trendier "politics of identity." Rather than talking about mutual understanding and the acceptance of the other's values and beliefs, Adina's Haredi College equips its graduates with concrete knowledge and tools that enable them to satisfy their personal, communal, material, and spiritual interests, yet also feel a bit closer to the rest of the society. Rather than discussing emotions and fears in what often turn out to be pleasant, yet fruitless, mixed group deliberations, Haredi College faces the issues of exclusion, inadequate skills and alienation head on by addressing the most crucial practical needs and the most concrete interests of the ultra-Orthodox community in Israel. Doing this in ways that are accepted and recognized by the rest of society brings the graduates and their families a step closer to the social mainstream.

Through influencing public policy, speaking engagements, and conference participation, her message is brought to traditional communities, as well as policymakers in many countries. A good example of her influence—beyond the activity of her college— is the new ambitious program of Mr. Benjamin Netanyahu, the Israeli Prime Minister, to specifically encourage employment of ultra-Orthodox women via tax breaks and other incentives, and by so doing improve Israel's general GDP and ranking in terms of productivity and economic performance.

THE PROBLEM

Judaism covers a wide range of cultures and practices, ranging from strict belief and observance, with cultural separatism, to cultural identification combined with a secular or humanistic outlook. "Orthodox Judaism" refers to the various streams of Judaism which adhere, to a large extent, to ancient beliefs and practices, based on a particular choice of ancient texts—the Old Testament, for example. Within this category, "Modern Orthodoxy" allows for some reinterpretation of religious law to accommodate social and historical changes, and for some measure of participation in and contribution to the secular world. In contrast, "ultra-Orthodoxy" (in Hebrew, the views of the Haredim or a Haredi outlook) tends not to accept the process of reinterpretation of religious law, but favors seclusion from the wider world, particularly from secular education and secular places of commerce. The Jewish law in question applies particularly to food, the Sabbath, sexuality, and synagogue practice.

In the ultra-Orthodox or Haredi world, certain cultural practices are followed to indicate belonging; among these are modest dress for women, especially the covering of the hair in some fashion, and formal dress, head coverings, and full beards for men. It is the custom in these communities to have very large families, for wives to support the families, and for men to engage in religious study for as long as possible in their lives. The sexes are traditionally strictly separated outside of the home. Because of their beliefs and practices, the community frequently lives in isolated "ghettos," which are afflicted by poverty and a variety of social problems—made worse by a general taboo to discuss these issues. Their attitudes to employment—i.e. to participation in national economic life—as well their traditional exemption from the otherwise universal army service, arouse the distrust and resentment of mainstream Israelis.

The Jewish ultra-Orthodox community in Israel is perceived by the rest of the Israeli society as one of the most unproductive, exploitative, and willfully alienated. More than 60 years after the establishment of the State of Israel, this community—concentrated in the cities of Jerusalem, Bnei Brak, Beit Shemesh, Beitar and Elad—continues to grow at a rapid rate (i.e. with an average of 5.6 children per family, compared with the national average of 2.3), to rely heavily on public funding, and to stick, by choice, with relatively low-skilled jobs. In general, it continues to serve as an irritant to the secular majority. At the same time, the community suffers widespread poverty and its related social problems, due to the employment structure and choices. Women are under particular pressure in being expected to manage large families and to earn the family's living.

Adina with the mayor of Jerusalem, Mr. Nir Barkat, and her college's executive director, Mr. Ariel Deri, at the college's 10th anniversary celebration.

THE STRATEGY

Adina understood that in order to improve the socioeconomic condition of the ultra-Orthodox population, as well as to raise its status and image in Israeli society in general, much better employment solutions had to be developed. This, in turn, required much better, more accessible and broader higher educational opportunities. Since non-religious higher education, or indeed, any sort of academic training, was considered impermissible in this community prior to her innovations, Adina used her pedigree and connections—as the daughter of an eminent Mizrahi (i.e. Jews who immigrated from Muslim lands) rabbi—in order to launch her quiet revolution, trying to remove these obstacles to higher education slowly and respectfully from within.

Adina's solution was to establish an academic college that meets the highest academic standards and which uses the knowledge, experience and personnel of the best Israeli universities—but at the same time, caters for the special needs of the ultra-Orthodox community. She has achieved this with the blessings (literally) of the most prominent and respected leaders of this, her own community, and the college provides its services in the most nonthreatening and accessible way, and at minimal cost to the students. Adina also widened the array of possible career choices; where once teaching was so popular a career choice for women that it could only absorb a

small fraction of the graduates qualified to teach, now a number of practical and professional subjects can be studied. This has greatly relieved the widespread unemployment of women in the community, and thus raised the general economic level.

Believing in social change rather than charity—that is, in finding practical solutions as opposed to waiting for help from heaven or other quarters—Adina decided to create an institution that would be accepted by the ultra-Orthodox community (i.e. ultra-Orthodox women, at the outset), but which, at the same time, could serve as a possible bridge to the rest of society, a gateway for inclusion, self-esteem, and better socioeconomic conditions. Social problems in the ultra-Orthodox community are now being addressed by graduates who are positioned to open up discussion on "taboo" topics. After the first five years, academic tracks were also opened to men at Haredi College. (In accord with tradition, men and women do not mix, and traditional dress and presentation is expected of the women, though not of lecturers.) This, too, constitutes a major change in the culture, as men have traditionally been expected to study and not to work for pay—or, if required to work, to work in low-skilled and low-paid jobs.

Haredi College in Jerusalem opened its gates in 2001 (i.e. with an initial intake of 23 women and approval from the Council of Higher Education) and is now offering a variety of degrees to both ultra-Orthodox women and men. Courses of study in social work, medical laboratory science, computer programming, speech therapy and other communications disorders, social work, and economics and logistics, are all taught 275by teachers from Bar Ilan University (i.e. Israel's second largest academic institution, in Ramat Gan) and elsewhere. Scholarships are given to students in need and a daycare center is operated on campus to help married students, many of them mothers of babies and young children.

> "[Adina's] valiant work is bringing higher education to both men and women in the rapidly expanding and increasingly impoverished Haredi population in Israel, so that they can better support their families."
>
> —*Jewish Daily Forward*

The results are unequivocal: Two such colleges, Haredi College in Jerusalem and another in Bnei Brak produce 540 of graduates every year who, in turn, achieve impressive placements rates of 94 percent in a wide variety of jobs. In Israel and other places, not only colleges are being established following Adina's pioneering work and ideas, but also other, less academic employment initiatives, which show both the religious communities and their surroundings the power of professional integration: Call centers have been opening in ultra-Orthodox towns in Israel and a dozen of local high tech companies realized that this community can provide reliable and skillful workers, if the companies are clever and sensitive enough to cater for their special needs.

In a statement summing up her approach and beliefs, Adina says, "I don't know if this is a revolution. But it is possible to talk about a significant change in the attitude of the ultra-Orthodox community toward education. The leaders of the ultra-Orthodox community realize that it's impossible to sit on the fence if they don't want this community to wallow in poverty all its life, I entered this field in order to open a door to masses of girls. This is my aim."

Adina speaks widely and participates in numerous conferences on a variety of topics, including social work, psychology, and mental health. Through these activities, her message is spread. It is a message that extends to ultra-Orthodox Jewish communities in Europe and the U.S. and elsewhere: As noted above, colleges inspired by hers have since opened in the U.S., the U.K., and France. Beyond that, as the president of Hebrew University was quoted as saying, her message extends to "traditional societies around the world," in which women (and men) can be helped, through education, to participate in the economic life of the nation, and to draw closer to the nation's mainstream.

THE PERSON

Born in Israel in 1945, Adina was the first child of Rabbi Ovadia Yosef, an Iraqi from Basra who has served as Sephardi Chief Rabbi of Israel, and who later become the unchallenged spiritual leader of the Sephardic/Mizrahi (i.e. Jews from Muslim lands, or originating from Spain) religious community in Israel. Rabbi Yosef has also worked to improve the status of non-Ashkenazi Jews in Israel. Adina believes that she inherited her sense of leadership and social justice from her father, who continues to be her source of inspiration and advice, and who has consistently backed her project. Indeed, to quote *HaAretz* (the Israeli *New York Times*), "Adina can allow herself to stand up to the Ashkenazi rabbinical establishment as Rabbi Ovidiah and the Shas Council of Sages are standing behind her…" Her father's support and her own determination and strategy show some powerful results—the outcomes speak for themselves.

Adina first developed her skills by taking responsibility for her ten brothers and sisters in her youth; assuming the burdens of housework and the care of her siblings when her mother became ill. One of her turning points occurred just before high school, when her parents decided that she should attend a professional school (i.e. in which she learned dressmaking) instead of the more prestigious general high school, to pursue a teaching career. Her mother dreamt that Adina would become a seamstress, and she did indeed become one as a married woman, making wedding dresses and wedding wear. Adina is not resentful, but regretted having been unable to pursue her education or to choose her own future, and she was unhappy with the limited options open to young women like herself.

At the age of 17, she was married to a Yeshiva (i.e. religious academy) graduate who was introduced to her by her father—after she discussed with the man the principles which have guided her throughout her life, and was sure they were compatible with his.

When he had difficulties in finding a suitable rabbinical job in Jerusalem, the couple moved to Tel Aviv. In an unorthodox (if one may use the term in this context) step, they decided to settle in the north of Tel Aviv, in a secular neighborhood, confident that they could become part of the social tissue of this neighborhood, while both retaining their beliefs and ways of life; indeed, they hoped to live among and learn from other groups in Israeli society. When her husband was appointed judge in a rabbinical court and her children were old enough, she hoped to pursue an academic degree in psychology. However, her husband, with her father's support, vetoed her wish to study, so instead she studied fashion design in the (secular) Shenkar School of Engineering and Design in Tel Aviv. Of this she wryly says, "…my father convinced my husband that it was just a school for seamstresses."

Adina was struck by the polarization of Israeli society that followed the assassination of former Israeli Prime Minister Yitzhak Rabin in November 1995 (by a right-wing Orthodox Jew who opposed the signing of the Oslo Accords). She felt a personal responsibility to try to bring the animosity to an end. Adina's attempt to convene mixed groups of secular and religious citizens to try to listen to and understand each other led her to the realization that such initiatives—even if important culturally and helpful socially—would not bring about the needed sea change.

Adina's development as an educationalist and a social activist was a long and slow one, living as she did within the restrictions of her family background and famous father, and it was forged through enormous strength of character and great patience. When her three children were all married and settled, she finally hit upon the idea of a university offering professional skills to ultra-Orthodox women. Her father had once suggested that the community was in need of its own social workers; that was one of the seeds of her vision. "When I came to him with the idea of establishing a Haredi University, he was happy and blessed me. Apparently everything has its own time," she says. *HaAretz* commented, "Her whole life story seems to be arranged to culminate in poetic justice. She, who was not allowed to study, opened the gates of education to Haredi women and men." "I think Haredi society should be based on Torah learning," she says, "but at the same time everyone who wants to acquire a profession should be allowed to do so."

The latest development at Haredi College is a collaboration with the Ben Gurion University of the Negev to offer a course in clinical psychology for women identical to the course offered at the Be'er Sheva campus. The four-year course will be taught by Prof. David Leiser of Ben-Gurion University of the Negev, and will result in a certificate to practice clinical psychology. The students are to undergo therapy (with female therapists) as part of their studies—and her father has again given his blessing. "This is a new Haredi femininity," she says, "the recognition that a 40-year-old woman can still develop and realize one of her longings…I was searching for meaning…I looked for something to do that would remain after me, something to generate change." She has found it. ♦

DINA BUCHBINDER AURON

MEXICO

Nutrition/Wellness

Tolerance/Pluralism

Youth Development

Dina Buchbinder Auron has introduced an innovative, action-oriented education model called Deport-es para Compartir to a Mexican education system that has long struggled with passivity and rigidity. Deport-es para Compartir empowers teachers from a variety of school settings to foster social and environmental awareness while also teaching values, such as teamwork and fair play.

THE NEW IDEA

The Deport-es para Compartir (DpC) model's emphasis on active education deems it inherently different from most forms of formal education in Mexico. On the most basic level, DpC is built upon learning through physical activity, particularly interactive games and simulations rather than traditional sports (i.e. which often bare negative associations of competition and athletic ability). The use of play and physical movement not only encourages a more active lifestyle for Mexican children, but it also makes learning more fun and increases student retention. Moreover, using games as an educational tool enables the students themselves to discover the value of intangible principles like teamwork, fair play, gender equality, tolerance, and respect. DpC is designed to promote collective action as a means to solving local problems. Rather than merely reading about social and environmental problems in their textbooks, students are encouraged to create pragmatic solutions and implement them in their schools and homes.

The content covered by DpC revolves around three main topics: The United Nations Millennium Development Goals (MDGs), healthy lifestyles, and diversity. By structuring lessons around the MDGs, DpC allows children to discover how the problems that they see in their own communities, such as poverty, disease, and discrimination, are related to global problems that are similar in nature—a comparison that undoubtedly heightens their awareness of social and environmental actions. This interconnectivity applies equally to solutions as it does to problems; through DpC, students realize that the sum of local actions can have an impact that extends far beyond any individual community. Besides broadening student's horizons through the MDGs, DpC also exposes students to external contexts through games, activities, and an exchange of homemade "treasure boxes" between different Mexican communities. This exposure allows Mexican children to experience and appreciate diversity without ever leaving their local communities.

While elite private schools often possess the sole access to Mexico's innovative educational curricula, Dina is determined to cast a wider net and include all types of rural and urban school settings in DpC's network, including public and private schools, as well as indigenous shelters in the most marginalized communities. DpC has a particular focus on these indigenous communities in Mexico's poorest states, such as Oaxaca and Chiapas; Dina understands that if DpC achieves success there, it can achieve success anywhere. Not only is this the population most in need of educational resources, but it is also the most isolated from the outside world, and therefore, the most disenfranchised. By bringing DpC to these communities and linking them to other types of school settings where DpC operates, Dina and her team are empowering children, their families, and their teachers to understand that they are part of a larger ecosystem and to participate actively in solving local and global problems.

Dina wants all children in Latin America to enjoy learning and growing with Deport-es para Compartir, empowering them to change their world.

THE PROBLEM

Passivity and boredom have long plagued formal schooling in Mexico. Very few teachers actively encourage student participation, while even fewer focus on creative problem solving and teamwork. The poorest, most isolated communities—which generally are predominantly indigenous—often suffer the worst problems with educational quality. A high student-to-teacher ratio, multi-grade classrooms, and the use of Spanish rather than indigenous native languages all contribute to lower scholastic achievement levels among indigenous students. According to Mexican government statistics on basic education, school absentee rates, failure rates, and desertion rates are all twice as high for indigenous versus non-indigenous student populations. Nevertheless, the problem of rigid, passive education is endemic to many Mexican schools, not just indigenous communities. Government agencies and citizen organizations (COs) have unsuccessfully attempted to implement a variety of educational programs in public schools. Students often do not find the programs, which lack mechanisms to measure impact, engaging. To some extent, the rigid structure of the Mexican education system influences broader societal attitudes, with widespread paternalism and apathy in place of active civic participation.

DpC is improving the lives of children by using the power of games and physical activities to integrate universal values and generate an active awareness about their rights as well as global issues.

Many of Mexico's marginalized communities remain disconnected from the outside world, because of their physical isolation and dwindling populations. Without reliable phone and Internet connectivity, residents of rural communities are often unaware of the connections between problems, actions, and consequences on a local, national, and global level. Having seen little beyond the village or town where they have always lived, many Mexicans have a natural distrust of unfamiliar ideas and people—including Mexicans from other parts of the diverse country. As a result, Mexico has long struggled with the question of how best to handle diversity-related issues.

In addition to being an entrenched problem in Mexican education, inactivity is now rapidly becoming a problem in Mexican's daily lives. As in the U.S., lifestyles in Mexico have become increasingly sedentary as the economy has evolved. Combined with unhealthy diets, inactive lifestyles are contributing to a growing obesity epidemic in Mexico, where 52.2 million people—over half the population—are now overweight or obese. Since the topic of nutrition is generally not covered in schools, weight-control problems are becoming ever more noticeable in children. If children are not exposed to healthy eating habits and regular physical activity from an early age—either through their families or their schools—they risk forming life-long habits that increase their chances of obesity later in life.

THE STRATEGY

Dina's inspiration for Deport-es para Compartir comes from the United Nations Association in Canada's program, Sport-in-a-Box. Dina, however, has taken the basic concept of using active games to teach children about the MDGs to a heightened level in Mexico. Not only has she and her team worked unceasingly to adapt the concept to Mexico's social and cultural realities, which are very different from Canada's, but they have also integrated new elements like including parents participation, impact measurement and diversity-based pedagogy through the DpC lessons and the inter-school exchange of "treasure boxes." By dedicating much

more time and energy to training teachers as multiplicative change agents, DpC—in its first two years in operation—also managed to scale over 10 times as quickly as the Canadian program.

Dina identifies the communities where DpC will be implemented by collaborating with two large federal agencies: The Secretaría de Desarrollo Social (SEDESOL—Ministry of Social Development) and the Comisión Nacional para el Desarrollo de Pueblos Indígenas (CDI—National Commission for the Development of Indigenous Communities). Both SEDESOL and CDI were so impressed with early pilot results from DpC that they have partnered with Dina over the last couple of years. By leveraging SEDESOL's and CDI's existing networks of program offices, the DpC team is able to penetrate isolated communities quickly and efficiently. Some of the regions where DpC works are so sparsely populated that indigenous children actually live and attend school in centralized shelters during the week, then return to their parents' villages on the weekends. These indigenous shelters are critical to DpC's strategy of reaching the poorest students and their families.

By the end of 2010, DpC's successful train-the-trainer model impacted 28,000 children in 16 Mexican states in just two years.

Rather than deliver the DpC lessons themselves, Dina and her team gather schoolteachers and indigenous shelter directors for intensive three-day trainings during which the adults experience the same games, activities, and group reflections that they will later lead in their classrooms. The teachers have learned a strikingly similar lesson about the effectiveness of experiential learning: By participating in the DpC sessions themselves, the teachers grew sincerely invested in the program's value and have since become her champions and change agents, with a current ratio of 400 trained teachers to just 25 DpC staff. Each teacher or shelter director is assigned a DpC liaison to offer support throughout the semester-long program as they implement it in their respective schools and shelters. The liaisons are responsible for supporting the teachers and shelter directors via phone and e-mail communication, and every semester the DpC team physically visits about half of the participating schools and shelters throughout the country. The liaison system not only supports teacher's needs, it enables DpC to monitor program implementation and maintain quality control.

Each of the 8 DpC sessions focuses on one of the 8 MDGs: eradicating hunger and extreme poverty; achieving gender equality; reducing infant mortality; improving maternal health; fighting HIV/AIDS and other infectious diseases; achieving environmental sustainability; promoting economic development; and forming an international alliance to tackle global problems. Every session consists of a physical game or activity designed to teach students about that week's topic while bolstering values like fair play and respect, in addition to a closing group reflection asking students to synthesize what they have learned.

One of Dina's first priorities has been impact measurement, so she has collaborated with a statistician at the prestigious Colegio de Mexico Institute to design evaluations for participating students, parents, and teachers immediately before and after the program as well as six months later. The evaluations assess the children's understanding of global social and environmental problems; their perspectives on topics like teamwork, gender equality, and their ability to impact their communities; and, their level of physical activity. Since 2008, the evaluations have consistently revealed a significant impact in all these regards on the children who have participated in DpC, particularly immediately after the program, but also six months later.

> "In 2007, Dina co-founded 'Sharing the Joy of Sports.' Its work rests on acting, and sharing. Participants think about the relevance of sports and physical activity to their daily lives."
>
> —*International Youth Foundation*

While Dina and her team will continue to grow DpC's impact organically by training more teachers and involving children's parents, Dina's strategy for firmly establishing DpC nationwide in Mexico involves introducing the program into public school curricula through the Secretaría de Educación Pública (SEP—Department of Public Education). Having already formed alliances with SEDESOL and the CDI, Dina has a strong probability of securing the government support necessary to integrate DpC into the standard national curriculum. In terms of international expansion, Dina plans to leverage her affiliation with the Mexican branch of the World Federation of United Nations Associations, a network of COs in different countries dedicated to promoting United Nations programs, to lay the foundations for DpC chapters in other countries, beginning with Central and South America and the U.S. In addition, Dina is frequently speaking at international youth leadership conferences, where she has sparked much interest among other young leaders to replicate DpC in their home countries. While international chapters of DpC will be expected to raise their own local funds in the medium- to long-term, Dina knows that DpC's achievements align closely with the objectives of major international and multilateral organizations like USAID, the Global Children's Fund, the European Union, UNICEF, Ford Foundation, and the Inter-American Development Bank, all of which she views as potential providers of seed funding for international replication.

THE PERSON

Growing up in a Jewish family in Mexico, Dina was often labeled as "different" during childhood. It was only when she enrolled in the Colegio de la Ciudad de México, a high school with a large international student population, that she finally interacted with a diverse group of young people from different backgrounds. Her high school years represent one of the happiest periods of her life, providing her with a window into the value of diversity. Another element that greatly shaped Dina's childhood and adolescence

was sports. As a child, Dina often invented active games with her brother, and when she grew older she learned and played a wide variety of competitive sports. She continues to believe wholeheartedly in the positive influence that an active lifestyle has on the psychological and physical development of children, with whom she has always had a natural connection with, as a nanny, tutor, and camp counselor.

Despite being young, Dina has already had significant experience in developing civic participation and awareness. At university in Mexico City, she organized a highly successful electoral simulation to combat the apathy of her classmates and motivate them to participate in the electoral process. She also organized a forum to expose her classmates to various issues regarding immigration and human rights, particularly with respect to Mexico's most disadvantaged ethnic groups. In addition to being active on political and social issues, Dina contributed to the cultural life of her university through the coordination of artistic events and the creation of an indoor soccer team.

Upon graduating from the Instituto Tecnológico Autónomo de México (ITAM—Autonomous Technological Institute of Mexico) with a degree in International Relations, Dina participated in a global youth leadership conference in Japan. There she met Dara Parker, a young Canadian who worked for Sport-in-a-Box under the aegis of Canada's United Nations Association. Dina was fascinated by Dara's descriptions of Sport-in-a-Box and decided to bring the concept of active education built on the MDGs to Mexico. She adapted the model to the Mexican context and added innovative new elements like impact evaluation and a focus on involving diverse ethnic and socioeconomic groups. Dina identifies deeply with DpC because the program's principles and values—physical activity, civic participation, diversity, imagination, and the importance of childhood—are also her own. Her dream is for all children to learn how to carve out their own roles to create impact in the communities where they live and, by extension, within the larger global context. ◆

REGINA CABRAL

BRAZIL

Education Reform

Microenterprise

Youth Development

Regina Cabral is tranforming the education system in the state of Maranhão and beyond to ensure that all educational opportunities crafted for youth are closely integrated with their own development needs and that of their communities. Regina is infusing the public high school curriculum with professional and entrepreneurial education thus unleashing the true productive potential of each region where she works.

THE NEW IDEA

High school education in Brazil, for the most part, fails to prepare youth for university and the professional world. Regina is addressing this issue by transforming the way public education is delivered, starting in one of Brazil's most underserved states: Maranhão. The basis of her work entails the integration of three goals: The development of entrepreneurial abilities at a young age, the promotion of citizenship, and the enhancement of local development through teaching, research, practical experiences, and student-led community projects.

Before establishing her Centers of High School Education and Professionalization (CEMPs, by its Portuguese acronym) Regina undertook a study on the state of high school and professional education in Maranhão. The study was financed by UNICEF and gave her the opportunity to analyze hard data and most importantly, to learn from youth about their needs and desires relating to education. The CEMPs emerged from the realization that youth education needed to be closely linked to the working world and local development for it to become relevant and impactful.

The model is firmly based on the idea that, even in precarious situations, youth can develop the necessary critical thinking skills to become agents of change and create community-led solutions. The new school curriculum developed through CEMPs trains educators in new and improved teaching methods and allows students to gain both knowledge and skills through a combination of "traditional" classes and the development community projects supported by Formação, Regina's organization. These projects do not simply serve the purpose of enhancing young peoples own development, but are designed to also contribute to the economic development of the region. Regina has already created seven CEMPs and more than 1,000 youth have graduated from this new high school model. Her approach holds promise for the

country as a whole, as it is integrated within the public education system and enjoys great support from the citizen sector, the Ministry of Education, and UNESCO—an intricate part of her national spread strategy.

THE PROBLEM

Access to adequate secondary schooling is one of Brazil's biggest challenges in the field of education. Years after guranteeing universal primary education, federal, state, and municipal governments have yet to make progress on ensuring access to high school education in Brazil. According to the Institute of Applied Economic Research (IPEA) in 2007, while there were 136,903 municipal primary schools throughout the country, it only could account for a total of 17,874 secondary schools nationwide; rendering high school education out of reach for more than 1 million Brazilian youth. In addition, of those who graduate from elementary school, only 48 percent continue their studies and only 13 percent of the population pursues university degrees. This is alarming. as the Brazilian economy continues to grow, the demand for a highly educated work force also increases.

Regina believes young people in any situation can become agents of change, if they are offered the knowledge and skills of "traditional" courses and community development projects.

In addition to needing to create better conditions for youth to access secondary education, the prevalence of high school drop out rates throughout Brazil points to the fact that the content taught must also undergo profound transformations. The current high school curriculum does not give youth the full set of skills and abilities they want, or what they need to enter the job market, become critical thinkers, and active citizens. Education remains quite theoretical with very little space for creativity and experimentation. Acquiring experiential and experimental experiences in a diversity of subjects is instrumental to prepare youth to enter the professional world. Because of lack of appropriate training and continuing education opportunities, teachers are also ill-equipped to respond to these needs. Unfortunately, the lack of coordination and sometimes tension that exists between municipal, state, and federal jurisdictions also makes it difficult to incur changes that increase the quality and relevance of the education system.

Youth in Brazil are among the most vulnerable: Unemployment rates for this population are extremely high and few personal and professional development experiences are available. The situation is most pronounced in underserved areas of large urban centers as well as in the interior of the country, the Northeast most specifically. The prevalence of poverty in those regions and low economic development rates contribute to a culture of passiveness and apathy. With a high unemployment rate and the frustrations it entails, violence is becoming a common coping mechanism. These circumstances lead many youth to leave their hometowns in the pursuit of work opportunities. Many end up working under extremely poor conditions on farms and plantations in other states such as Mato Grosso, Sao Paulo, Pará, and the south of Maranhão.

THE STRATEGY

The idea of establishing Centers of High School and Professional Education (CEMPs) emerged in Regina's mind in 2003, as she was developing a thorough study of the education system in Maranhão. The research was underwritten by UNICEF, led by Formação, and most of its inputs came from the youth. Instead of crafting just any project relating to youth for UNICEF, Regina decided to map the needs and desires of youth within the realm of the regular education system. She examined high schools and professional education institutions throughout Maranhão and retrieved public information from the Secretariats of Education, corporate-sponsored schools (referred to as Sistema S in Brazil), and public and private schools. She also used studies on Brazilian legislation relating to high school education, professional education, and the potential economic development of Maranhão.

As part of her research, Regina facilitated a series of debates and ran various surveys with students, teachers, school principals, parents, and Secretaries of Education. The seminars she ran with youth were of particular importance to her approach because they allowed her to establish a strong dialogue about their current educational needs and deisres. Regina did this not only to gather the best data possible, but to empower the youth in leading the development of a new system of education for Maranhão.

> "The program supports the creation of innovative social, cultural and economic enterprises by youth from the 10 municipalities served by the cluster."
>
> —*W.K. Kellogg Foundation*

Regina used this analysis to create—with the youth's participation—a series of courses that would eventually be implemented in the CEMPs. In 2004, the first CEMP was established in the municipality of São Bento, Maranhão in partnership with the Municipal Secretariat of Education. In 2005 Regina opened another CEMP in a neighboring city, Palmeirãndia, and by 2007 seven new centers had been launched in Baixada, a rural region with the lowest human development index in Maranhão.

The CEMP framework is structured around three pillars: 1) a General Education program, which corresponds to the regular curriculum as established by the Ministry of Education 2) a Professional Education program established with the region's strategic development needs in mind: Each class was crafted to contribute to an enhanced quality of life and to the establishment of local ventures in the region and 3) an Incubator of Productive Projects: Be they social, economic, or cultural. By bringing these three critical elements together, Regina is adding applied research and entrepreneurial experiences to the high school curriculum in a way that had never before been done in Brazil. She is doing so in close collaboration with teachers and educators who receive continuous training and help adapt the curriculum.

Regina's organization has established 13 Information Technology Centers with 107 computers to administer courses.

Regina is thus giving youth the opportunity to take leadership roles in their own education, making it more relevant to them and their communities, and preparing students more appropriately to enter the job market as creative, critical thinkers. For example, CEMP youth act as tutors in adult literacy classes; they develop educational campaigns and seminars about local development, health, sanitation, and environmental issues; and they undertake research on the productive potential of their communities, among others. More than 1,000 youth have graduated from Formação's three-pillared education framework. Through the Incubator, Regina has organized market fairs to enable students to market their agricultural products, sweets, preserves, and crafts in cities throughout the region.

Regina has established strong partnerships with organizations such as the Kellogg Foundation, UNICEF, UNESCO, Caixa Econômica Federal, Fifa, and Instituto Oi Futuro. As a result, she has been able to open seven CEMPs, which, in the span of four years, have very concretely contributed to the local development of Maranhão. Formação has fomented the work of more than 90 student-led productive projects, including two agro-industrial projects, an industry not previously represented in the region. As a result of its strong focus on offering well-rounded learning experiences to its students, Regina's organization has also established 13 Information Technology Centers with 107 computers with Internet access where courses are administered. The youth have thus learned how to create animations, videos, and even websites. At the end of 2008, Formação and the Maranhão's Foundation for Research Support began a partnership to create a technology hub in Baixada, to enable youth to begin income-generating projects through projects related to information technologies. In addition, the organization, SERVLAGOS, is being created to help alumni of the program become technicians and enter the workforce.

Now that youth and educators are mobilized and collaborating, Regina is focusing her energies on two other important goals: The creation of the first local public university in Maranhão and the establishment of a community foundation. The first will allow Formação to extend its work in supporting the state's development potential, and the second will contribute to the creation of a permanent fund aimed at financing local development community projects. In parallel, Regina is building a spread strategy for the CEMPs to reach every region of Brazil through a partnership with the Ministry of Education and UNESCO.

THE PERSON

Regina was born and raised in the interior of the state of Maranhão. She learned from a young age to observe and identify the potential of people and places. Regina was always surrounded with great educators in her family, school, church, and community. Regina parents played a crucial role in her life. They acted as mentors and sacrified a lot to ensure that she would have access to the best education possible.

In 1985 Regina was invited to coordinate a youth and adult education project that included 100 classes from rural and urban areas of São Luis, Maranhão. She also led Brazil's Network of Literacy Support for a period of six years. It was during that time, at a young age, that Regina was able to truly get to know her country and its education systems various challenges.

Immediately thereafter, Regina was invited to become the Education Coordinator at the Education Secreatriat of São Luis and took on the role of Undersecretary of Education. After leaving these government posts, she was later invited to consult for the Ministry of Education where she stayed for three years. Although Regina is a great defender of public education, she realized that government bureaucracy was not compatible with her working style and her aspirations for large-scale change. She left the ministry to pursue bigger dreams.

Regina then established Formação, where she has been tackling the challenges of increasing the quality of education while making it locally relevant and intricately linked with Maranhão's development needs. Despite the precarious situation of her state, Regina has never stopped believing in and serving, its great potential. ◆

HEATHER CAMERON

GERMANY

Conflict Resolution

Gender Equality

By mobilizing a diverse group of actors from the national press to management consultants to university sports students, Heather Cameron is using boxing and self-defense training to help girls and young women develop the confidence, self-efficacy, and leadership skills to create strong inclusive communities.

THE NEW IDEA

Boxing is central to Heather's strategy to empower young women, especially those living in marginalized communities. Research has shown that sports in general, and boxing in particular, can play a key role in improving self-confidence and personal safety, aiding stress reduction, and contributing to the growth of an individual's self-discipline throughout puberty, as well as other times of personal development. These benefits are much needed, especially among some segments of Germany's immigrant communities, where girls and women's roles are limited; Heather uses sports as a vehicle to shift self-perceptions and challenge disempowering societal stereotypes. Among an important constituency of her target group, boxing is not perceived of as a sport or recreational activity, but as a self-defense tool, allowing socially conservative communities to approve of its introduction in an all-girl environment. Through partnerships with local organizations, girls participating in Boxgirls' programs also participate in other developmental programs addressing key life skills.

Heather aims to achieve three levels of transformation through Boxgirls International: 1) On a personal level, she knows that boxing will engage and empower girls in a physical activity in which they will excel, improving their health and building their confidence and aspirations 2) In combination with boxing, Heather aims for a broader transformation in which girls grow their leadership skills and are empowered to impact their communities; using skills-based curricula and outreach programs, ranging from personal safety presentations at schools for young girls and women to pursuing entrepreneurial activities through partner organizations 3) At the societal level, Heather hopes Boxgirls International programs and partnerships with citizen organizations (COs), governmental institutions, national Olympic programs, and so forth, will help to change the pervasive view of girls and sport by provoking discussion around the empowerment of girls.

THE PROBLEM

Strong girls make strong communities. Unfortunately, in many communities a girl's ambition and confidence are discouraged and many smart, confident girls turn into docile women. Heather locates Boxgirls' projects in challenged neighborhoods, i.e. economically less developed and often inhabited by migrant families facing social and economic hardships. Young girls living in such settings are often excluded from decision-making and have few opportunities to learn and experience leadership behavior. Instead, they are often taught that women's typical role in society is to please others and be subordinate.

Boxing strengthens girls' bodies and minds and helps them show the courage to take care of themselves.

Furthermore, during puberty disadvantaged young girls face many other identity issues, including changes in their body perception and self-image. The absence of positive role models and an overwhelming presence of "obedient" stereotypes hamper them from developing leadership skills and their potential to become effective changemakers. While middle- and upper-class girls have opportunities to develop into leaders (i.e. established programs seek them out), families of immigrant girls may see sport as a luxury. Due to cultural norms, many girls are discouraged from taking part in physical activities after puberty. Heather ensuring that the voices of young women from the marginalized parts of society are heard, and that they have the tools to help improve their living and working conditions.

German government programs have tried many approaches to integrating migrants, with various degrees of success. However, recent statistics on social mobility and access to further education show that Germany is still one of the worst countries in Europe concerning equal access to education and careers. German schools are also looking for new ways to increase school attendance, participation, and the performance of disadvantaged children. Thus, they are beginning to see sports as a solution to engage and shape young people. However, stereotypes around women and girls still create barriers against using sports.

THE STRATEGY

As a professor of educational science and sport for two and a half years, and a volunteer coach for over ten years, Heather is an expert on the positive effects that sports has on girls. Having experienced the power of women boxing during her studies in Canada, she realized that combat sport and particularly boxing, are strong tools to empower women. Boxing helps one understand the strengths, weaknesses and the physical, psychological, and spatial limitations of your body. As a contact sport, it also forces the boxer to confront their fears and redefine their self-image. Thus, of all sports, boxing is probably one of the most powerful to help achieve control over oneself and one's life.

Heather utilizes boxing to provide useful structured activities to teach girls self-efficacy, discipline, teamwork, and self-defense skills. Thus, her idea is not just to use girls' boxing to engage girls simply around sports, but to use boxing as a way to gain access to a specific group and help them understand their own strengths. Through boxing, girls are sensitized to gender issues and begin to question deeply rooted roles—discovering their potential and leadership skills. Thus, boxing becomes a force for change in communities, led by girls. For the first time in their lives, girls are encouraged to take on active roles in their communities and overcome their own, but also society's gender prejudices, at a critical stage of their physical and mental development.

Heather first founded a boxing club in her own neighborhood in Berlin, home to a high percentage of immigrant populations and among one of the most impoverished communities in Germany. Girls are recruited through an ambitious outreach process that includes a web and social media strategy, as well as active presswork with local and national papers. Once the girls are in the gym, Heather works with them to acquire sporting and other life skills through weekend seminars. With an all female training team, she ensures the gym environment feels safe and friendly for all the girls.

> "Cameron supports socially challenged girls to become the strong, independent, participating woman, that every girl has in herself and therefore creates a generation of changemakers."
>
> —*GlobalGiving*

This approach has already showed impressive results with the girls and has created new role models. Financed by the German Children and Youth Foundation, Heather's project was part of their "strengthening girls" program and had the best evaluation results among all the supported projects. Using this momentum and contacts from her university, Heather quickly spread internationally, starting Boxgirls International projects in Nairobi and Cape Town. There, in addition to their boxing training, girls have the chance to take part in conflict resolution and communications training, as well as activities with partners providing general health, HIV/AIDS, and domestic violence education.

Heather also works on an advocacy level, developing curricula in cooperation with leading sports education universities, advising the German Olympic Committee on sport and social inclusion, raising the profile of women boxing in the context of the London 2012 Olympics, and developing sector infrastructure with amateur boxing associations in Germany and abroad. Heather's efforts are helping to promote women in the boxing arena. London 2012 will be the first Olympics to include women boxers and there is already a significant change in the way national sport federations and ministries are beginning to support women's boxing.

Boxgirls International links innovative projects around the world using boxing as a catalyst for social change. The skills they learn in the ring, improve their strength and resilience, allow them to better negotiate the urban environment and bring them further in their schooling, family and career.

Heather is also spreading her program to schools, be it in Germany with Sicher im Kietz (German for Safe in the District) or programs run in Nairobi. The connection to personal safety is a key element of the program. She is also leveraging her impact through strong PR and media work and entering and winning several major awards (i.e. including the German StartSocial competition where Boxgirls was highlighted by German Chancellor Angela Merkel, and winning the Nike/Ashoka Changemakers competition). Heather and Boxgirls have built strong ties through domestic and international networks that have made her program expansion possible. She is also one of the founding members of the Women Win Foundation and a consultant to the International Paralympics Committee.

A key element of Boxgirls' growth and support has been to connect with leading corporate partners, particularly those focused on women's leadership. Rising leaders within corporations are invited for half-day and full-day workshops with Boxgirls and their students. These sessions are designed as broader corporate trainings for the women, where they both become inspired by the work with young girls, and participate in

many of the same physical and leadership training programs. Alumni of these trainings sessions become major supporters of Boxgirls' programs.

Heather's goal for expansion is focused on raising the profile of girls' boxing and developing a core training program, with modules that can be adapted and incorporated to suit the needs of the communities in which they are adopted. She plans to expand Boxgirls to several German cities, but anticipates that future expansion will partially rely on other gyms, girl's leadership programs, and other organizations adopting and developing Boxgirls as a core element of their programs.

THE PERSON

Heather discovered her passion for sport from an early age and for some time, she has been as active as an athlete. At the age of 12, she deepened her engagement by taking the responsibility to be an official coach for a baseball team. Heather's love for sports also comes from her family, where her mother was an ice hockey volunteer administrator and took turns running the local, regional, and provincial hockey associations.

At 16, Heather started a software business, and has had several jobs in the IT and change management sector. However, having faced sexism and discrimination in sports and at work, she was determined to find a way to change it, and was constantly looking for a way to do more for her community, especially to change perceptions and the role of girls. Parallel to an impressive academic career (Heather has a Ph.D. in Social and Political Thought and was German Professor of the Year, 2009), she has been developing skills in various areas key to her project: Fundraising, strategic planning, and international quality assessment. ♦

LÁZARO CUNHA

BRAZIL

Access to Learning/Education

Higher Education

**Intercultural Relations/
Race Relations**

By creating educational programs that recognize Afro-descendents' historical contributions to science, Lázaro Cunha is breaking the scientific and technological divide that has kept the majority of Brazil's black population marginalized. Lázaro is popularizing scientific knowledge in order to strengthen the black movement within the knowledge society, while also increasing the country's potential for technological development.

THE NEW IDEA

While the Afro-descendant black population has made some progress in the educational system in Brazil, they have not made the strides hoped, particularly into the important and promising field of science and technology. As an activist of the black movement, engineer, and member of the Steve Biko Foundation, Lázaro understands that because racial differences are due to systemic problems, injecting them into the area of science and technology creates still more complexity.

To effectively include blacks in this promising field, Lázaro constructed the Program for the Promotion of Science Oguntec for Afro-descendants. It includes a political education proposal for popularizing science that takes in consideration the low self-esteem and the low educational levels among this population. One of the central points of Oguntec is the educational methodology for the youth of the program and schools and communities of the neighborhood, in which the scientific content as well as its experimentation, has Afro references that disprove stereotypes about blacks capacity to work in these fields.

In addition to educational work, Lázaro is active in the field of state and national public policymaking in the areas of education, and science and technology. Through partnerships with State Secretaries of Bahia and with a proposal to take the methodology of Oguntec to all public schools, he is putting the popularization of science as well as attention to the question of race, on the agenda. Within the Black movement, his signatory idea is to impel this population to catch sight of future tendencies and to update their demands with proposals of science and technology.

THE PROBLEM

Slavery in Brazil was abolished only 120 years ago without the country establishing any structural and systemic changes in the life of the black population. This reality continues to exclude blacks from work that has become international in scope and increasingly values activities linked to science and technology. Nevertheless, rather than seeing this field as having the potential to transform the black population, the tendency is to keep them from having access to this type of knowledge, thereby restricting the possibilities of development, not only of the black population but the country as a whole.

The majority of the black population is poor, and public education, which could reverse this situation, is of a low quality. While the difference between the black and white populations in education in general is evident, it becomes an abyss in the area of technology. The size of this abyss can be seen everywhere from the lack of black teachers in the physical and biological sciences, to the low enrolment of blacks in higher education courses linked to technology.

Black students have to contend not only with a poor quality of education and a lack of contact with the field of science and technology, but also with the absence of emotional support to encourage them to believe they can compete in this area. Schools, with their didactic books and mostly white teachers, do not often make any reference to successful black scientists, doctors, or engineers. The pedagogy employed in Brazilian education is conservative, theoretical, and technical. It offers little autonomy for students to learn through curiosity or the pleasure of working with science.

Black families encourage their children to enter what are considered to be the easier higher education courses, since they may not conceive the idea that their child could be a doctor. Children and young people are therefore raised in an environment that does not support a belief in their potential to enter promising areas such as science and technology.

According to data of the National Institute of Educational Research and Studies (INEP), the highest participation of black graduates in these areas occurs in the chemistry course, where only 3.6 percent of graduates are black. The Getulio Vargas Foundation (FGV) also identified racial inequality in access to digital means of communication; the percentages of access according to race: 41.66 percent Asian; 15.14 percent White; 4.06 percent Mixed race (pardos- descendent of African and White); 3.97 percent Black and 3.72 percent Indigenous.

This explains why the system of quotas—a great victory for the black movement—in Brazilian public universities does not guarantee the entrance of this population into courses in the technology area. The movement is still far from creating black professionals with a strong political and historical awareness in the debate about the human genome, for example. The organizations which fight for the democratization of access to quality public education are still concerned with the rescue of African artistic and cultural traditions of the black population. The black movement seems unable to see the new challenges of the "society of knowledge" and the benefits generated by the insertion of the issue of race into the areas of science and technology.

Therefore, to deprive 46 percent of Afro-descended Brazilians the possibility of access to this knowledge undercuts development aspirations as well, since it will not end the socioeconomic gap between the ethnic groups. As the most promising area, as much in the perspective of professional career as in the potential for social transformations, the work to stimulate and prepare black children and youth to explore the area of science and technology is a challenging task with tremendous potential.

Through partnerships and with a proposal to take Oguntec's methodology to all public schools, Lázaro is increasing interest in science, while also bringing attention to racial issues.

THE STRATEGY

Lázaro was a member of a group of black youth which created the Steve Biko Institute in 1992. Their first initiative supported the enrolment of black youth in higher education in Brazil—a pre-university entrance exam course for blacks rapidly spread throughout the country. Over the years as an integrant of the group, director of the institute, professor of the pre-university course and an engineer, Lázaro realized that the scarcity of

blacks interested and effectively working in the area of science and technology is profound. It has systemic consequences and will not be resolved only with the reinforcement of study (i.e. with extra classes).

To insert the question of the popularization of science and at the same time, to put forward the issue of race in the field of the promotion of scientific knowledge, Lázaro considered the educational deficits and stereotypes that surround youth; the deficiency of the education system itself to offer experimental contact with science; and the necessity to strengthen the self-esteem of black youth and their families. To address these issues, he created the Program for the Promotion of Science Oguntec in 2003. This has three lines of work: Raising the level of education and self-esteem of black youth for their entrance into higher education in the areas of science and technology; popularization of science; and digital inclusion.

In order to raise the level of education for youth who wish to follow careers in the areas of science and technology, Lázaro utilizes a methodology created by the institute of popular pre-university courses and emphasizes the disciplines in the area of physical and biological sciences (100 percent of the first students were approved). This course includes the subject of Citizenship and Black Awareness (CCN) and is one of the principal strategies to reinforce self-esteem among black students. The CCN classes are offered to youth throughout the three years they participate in the program. In addition to the specific classes of CCN, the sciences pedagogy celebrates Brazilian black thinkers and scientists formative to the history of science. These are important references to break the stereotype that blacks have do not aptitude in these areas.

Digital inclusion is another element that promotes "technological literacy," which permits youth to achieve a condition of equality in the competition with other youth for places in university and the job market. The IT laboratory installed in the institute is also utilized as a channel for influencing other organizations to elaborate their own proposals of science and technology promotion based on contact with the political-pedagogic proposal of Oguntec.

The line of the popularization of science encompasses both the youth participants in Oguntec and more far-reaching initiatives. The program youth are offered an "Introduction to Science and Technology" with the objective of promoting a real-life scientific and technological experience. The method is participatory and focused on practical experience. The theoretical knowledge, for example, is put into practice in the "Science and Technology Seminars," broaching themes such as micro-electronics, nanotechnology, biotechnology, mechatronics, robotics, energy sources, and the worldwide contribution of the African diaspora to science. Parents are informed of the work developed by their children, and will support them in their choice of a career in science and technology. To bring the youth closer to professional practice, visits to scientific institutions and technology companies are also made.

Additionally, in the line of the popularization of science, Lázaro is very clear that it is necessary to expose other youth and children to the scientific and technological contributions of the African people. Oguntec therefore offers a series of initiatives with presentations, expositions, and workshops about scientific themes in communities and schools of peripheral neighborhoods of Salvador, bringing the low-income population closer to the world of science and technology. The project also promotes the exchange of Brazilian students with overseas universities.

To reach a wider public, Lázaro has participated in decision-making in the public sphere, influencing the Municipal and State Secretaries of Education, of Science and Technology and of Promotion of Equality to incorporate practices of the popularization of science with references to the contributions of the black population. Together with the Municipal Secretary of Education of Salvador, for example, a KIT for the Training of Teachers (law 10.639), with a chapter about science and technology, which makes references to black scientists of importance to Brazil and the world, has already been published and distributed. Lázaro is also in discussion with the Secretary of Science and Technology in Bahia to create QuilomboTecs; a replication of the initiative of Oguntec in Salvador's public schools.

> "Oguntec, focused on the area of science and technology, prepares high school students from public school for college entrance exams and draws attention to the need for affirmative policies."
>
> —JLC News

The educating of Afro-descendents in the areas of science and technology also has great potential to transform the scene of this sector in Brazil. By participating in delicate debates, such as those concerning genetic ethnic differences, black professionals have a great chance to oppose the prejudicial positions that are consolidated in this area. Through his participation in events in the scientific area, Lázaro has already been able to include in the discussion the popularization of science and the question of race at both the state and national level. In addition, he made use of his master's degree on the Physics Faculty of the Federal University of Bahia, to systematize the impact of Oguntec in the scientific field.

Lázaro is now working to have his methodology disseminated nationally through the insertion of QuilomboTecs in public schools. A further front of expansion is to insert the black movement in the debate about science and technology, which takes place in Brazil and the world. In Lázaro's vision, the proposal of promoting access of blacks to the knowledge of science and technology enters in all of the affirmative policies necessary to reverse the situation of racial inequality in Brazil and, for this reason, must have the total support of the movement and the government.

The Steve Biko Institute has also begun to plan with the community the creation of an institution of higher education with focus on technology, regulated by the state and aimed at the black population. In this perspective, the expansion and strengthening of Oguntec becomes even more fundamental to the formation of teams of future professionals and professors of science not only for the education system but also for the future university.

THE PERSON

From his youth, Lázaro lived with leaders of the Black movement in Salvador, which included his brother, father, and mother. This put him in direct contact with the principal struggles of the movement and offered him a clear view of social inequalities in Brazil, increasing his perception of racism as an organizing element of poverty in society.

At the same time, Lázaro was always fascinated by mechanics. His father was a typewriter mechanic and this stirred an enormous interest in Lázaro about the world of science and technology. In adolescence, Lázaro took a vocational high school course at the Federal Technical School of Bahia, where he founded the first organization of black students in the school. Here, he utilized the knowledge acquired from living within the black movement to generate reflections about the exclusion of black youth from educational environments and acted to reverse the situation.

With this political and historical vision, Lázaro graduated with a degree in mechanical engineering from the Federal University of Bahia, overcoming every type of prejudice. His institutional experiences of a technical and scientific education confirmed his desire to work in science and technology. On the other hand, Lázaro understood the lack of the educational sectors preparedness to confront the challenges of inclusion and the education of a generation of students in technology. In addition to institutional racism, the antiquated state of the infrastructure, the lack of enthusiasm of the teaching staff, and the technical line of the course were disappointing to him after having experienced rich technological innovation and academic production.

Lázaro's interest in changing the educational model which he had experienced led him to develop a pedagogic proposal that reduced the damage caused to the self-esteem of the black population by the traditional Eurocentric and racist vision of education. In 1992, he participated in the creation of the Steve Biko Institute to bring the black youth of Salvador an education that integrally took into account their reality and their yearnings, guaranteeing their entrance to higher education.

In Lázaro's life trajectory, working directly in the area of education and the black movement, he recognized that his contribution in relation to the public policies of university quotas and of incentive to the preparatory pre-university exam courses for black students would not be enough to change the problem of the technological abyss between whites and blacks. With this in mind, Lázaro created the Program for the Promotion of Science Oguntec in 2003.

To date, 800 youth have passed through the institute. With Oguntec, Lázaro is achieving his principal objective of fostering a taste for science in young Afro-descendents and widening the horizons of this population. His intentions are to introduce black youths to the most recent areas of knowledge, generating greater opportunities for personal and professional development, and to produce more efficient and democratic forms of transmission of scientific knowledge. ♦

© Emile Benjamin

JOHN DANNER

UNITED STATES

Access to Learning/Education

Education Reform

By reconfiguring the school day and increasing the independency and efficacy of elementary-level charter schools, John Danner is allowing schools to deliver quality education to low-income students, while scaling with greater ease and resources.

THE NEW IDEA

John wants to close, at scale, the so-called achievement gap: The performance gap between students from low-income and middle/high-income families. He saw that by adjusting the traditional school day and staffing structure, he could achieve an overall higher-performing and scalable school network, characterized by teacher specialization, optimized student learning, and increased parent involvement.

The approach he and his team are introducing cuts by 20 percent the certified teachers needed for quality learning, freeing up $500,000 per school of 450 students and making it cash-flow positive on government funds alone from day one. This works due to a re-envisioning of the elementary-level school day, including the addition of a "learning lab:" A 100-minute session facilitated by non-certified, hourly staff (e.g. City Year volunteers). Facilitators earn less than teachers, and the "savings" is routed to optimize student achievement by focusing on developing teachers and school administrators, and stress-testing the industry's promising but nascent technology tools.

John and his team have begun their work in San Jose, with two schools fully operating and an ambitious expansion plan. While he is growing his school network, he also believes that independent replication of aspects of the model by other schools will open new possibilities for innovation and greater efficacy in the charter movement as a whole, particularly as it seeks to serve low-income students.

THE PROBLEM

The "achievement gap"—the gap in learning between students in low-incomes families and neighborhoods, and students in middle and high-income neighborhoods—is real and alarming, despite enormous investments of time, energy, and public and private funds. The charter school movement, now in its second decade (i.e. first state charter laws came out in 1991), has generated good ideas and models to address the gap, and the movement remains the most

promising vehicle for testing and spreading ideas and practices that work. But charters are not matched to the large scale of the problem.

And actually, a small slice of the charter pie is aimed at low-income students – less than 10 percent of charter schools are really focused here. That means fewer than 100,000 low-income students out of the 1 million total students currently enrolled in charter elementary and secondary schools. For those networks that do serve low-income neighborhoods, they are stymied. Even KIPP, the largest charter network serving low-income students, has 84 schools—a huge achievement, but it doesn't map to the scale and enormity of the challenge: Millions of children from low-income families, many also belonging to minority households and using English as a second language, get a subpar education that does not set them up to succeed in middle and high school, and adulthood beyond.

Limiting factors to growth run the gamut from having the right teachers and leadership, to getting real estate and leasing arrangements, to summoning the political will at a community or school board level. Charter school leaders spend their time battling the school board, worrying about the security of their classroom space and whether they can get their leases renewed, and managing a team of teachers who work 12-hour days, get paid very little, and—in elementary school—scramble to stay on top of the five or six subjects per school day. The best talent burns itself out in a couple of years, creating a talent problem that proves crippling.

Typically, charters cover their costs from two sources: The per child allocation from public funding, and some infusion of philanthropic support (between $200,000 and $1M on, say, a $4M budget). The lack of fiscal independence contributes to significant problems: The charter schools can not lease or build their facility, and visionary leaders spend time raising money from increasingly weary donors and worrying that donor fatigue and shifting public will close them up at the school board level. There are also scarce funds to invest in teachers and their development, with its obvious link to student achievement and longer-term sustainability.

In addition to the question of scale, there's the concern about quality. Teachers struggle to manage large classrooms while giving individual students what they need to develop optimally along their unique learning curve. This is especially pronounced in schools serving low-income students, as the spectrum of ability is large and often compounded by differing levels of English language proficiency. Technology-enabled learning tools offer teachers a way to deliver "mass individualized" learning. "Smart" software programs will recognize from a logon ID who a child is, what her instruction level is, how she learns, and so on. These technologies hold the promise of aiding schools and teachers enormously by allowing individualized learning in ways that challenge everybody, both the high-performers and those in need of remedial help. But the development of these technologies isn't moving quickly enough—in fact, it's quite nascent. As the industry evolves in the next 5 to 10 years to the standards of the gaming world, educators need to jump in and test and assess what's working and what's not, helping what will be a valuable and low-cost tool to evolve more rapidly and wisely.

THE STRATEGY

John reconfigures the elementary school day and instruction so that it works more effectively for overall learning, as evidenced by the high student achievement scores of the first two Rocketship schools. The mechanism that allows this to work is what John calls the hybrid model, which reduces by 20 percent the number of certified teachers required per K-5 school of 450 students by blending instruction from certified, higher-paid teachers and non-certified, lower-paid facilitators. The $500,000 per year that is "saved" is routed to a few important functions that ensure stability (i.e. real estate and leasing arrangements), optimize learning, and allow independence and growth of the network.

> "Rocketship has pioneered the transformative model, that combines outstanding classroom teaching to extend students' critical thinking skills, with individualized instruction and technology."
>
> —*Huffington Post*

The Rocketship approach melds broader platform learning, which allows teachers to specialize, with opportunities for individualized learning. Per day, students get 100 minutes of math/science, 200 minutes of literacy/social studies, and 100 minutes of "learning lab," which consists of independent reading, individualized technology-enabled learning, and various other enrichment programs, including music, and physical education (partnering with Ashoka Fellow Jill Vialet's Playworks for PE). The math/science module is taught by a certified instructor at the whole class level; the second module is taught by a certified instructor with a focus on smaller group learning within the context of the whole class; and the third module is tailored to the individual student and is guided by a non-certified instructor. Each student has an individualized learning plan, with progress assessed every eight weeks to adjust the plan. The bottom 25 percent of learners/performers get two hours of mandatory, small-group after-school tutoring.

Teachers, for their part, experience Rocketship as being radically different from the traditional elementary school both in terms of what they do day to day, and how they perceive career possibilities longer-term. The approach requires them to go deep, and deliver high-quality learning for the students in their care. They work with one grade level, and specialize in literacy/social studies or math/science—essentially a secondary school staffing model applied to elementary school. In terms of career path, a few things are important. First, they have someone looking after their development: This is the "academic dean," a role created with money freed up through the hybrid model. Teachers who join Rocketship are introduced to a career path from day one that includes moving into mentoring and administrator roles within the school, or taking on expansion and recruitment duties as the network expands. This allows promising, high-energy new teachers—more than half of Rocketship's staff are Teach for America alumni—to see where they are going, and feel nurtured to get there. The specialized focus cuts back on class prep time and allows teachers to become good at what they teach, and feel on the ball and successful, rather than completely swamped and ineffective.

In the Rocketship model, school leadership is managed by a triumvirate: The principal (ultimately in charge), the academic dean, and the operations manager. Most school districts roll all responsibilities into a single job, but specialized roles allow for greater efficacy, John and his team believe. Principals, responsible for the culture of the school, are identified 18 months in advance of a new school's opening, allowing time for training and teacher recruitment.

Moving out from students, teachers, and administrators, there's another role that's important to the short- and long-term success of the approach. The parents. John and his co-founder Preston Smith see parents as another key group to engage and mobilize—for the sake of currently enrolled students and for the expansion of the network, and its political independency. Teachers visit the homes of all students during the first semester, and hold monthly community meetings, with parent attendance of 70 percent. (John notes that there is some self-selection at play here—the parents who choose to enter their children into Rocketship following the lottery already agree with the Rocketship philosophy.) John sees enormous potential to harness parents and their will and enthusiasm to create political freedom for action—in other words, to favor locally elected leaders who support pro-charter policy.

Aside from arranging people in roles that work for them, Rocketship is positioning itself to contribute significantly to the development of improved technology tools that allow further individualization of learning. While the hybrid model isn't dependent on the technology, it has technology "in its DNA," as John says, and is attracting attention from the Gates Foundation and others to play a leading R&D role in stress- and performance-testing new tools, helping along technologies for elementary-level kids so that the tools get "smart" fast and with real-time feedback loops from the classroom. Harnessing technology for learning cuts costs, and segments learners in ways that push everybody at a pace that matches each child's capabilities.

In its first three years, Rocketship has demonstrated remarkable success as measured by student achievement scores, moving 91 percent of its students from the bottom two quintiles to the top three in the last year. The two schools to date, each with 450 students, serve a student body of which 73 percent are English language learners and 78 percent qualify for free or reduced lunches. It is the highest performing elementary serving low-income students in Santa Clara County, and the third highest in the state of California. As compared to elementary schools in Santa Clara County, Rocketship ranks (in API scores) 5 of 45, behind four schools serving student bodies of which 10 percent qualify for free and reduced lunches.

With direction from a great Board, which includes Senior Ashoka Fellow Don Shalvey, John and his team will create 10 additional schools in San Jose, then move their model nationally. In the next 30 years, the teams aim to introduce Rocketship schools in low-income neighborhoods of the 50 largest U.S. cities, reaching 20 percent of low-income, elementary school students—approximately 1 million students.

THE PERSON

John grew up in San Jose, California, the eldest of three children. His sister was born with severe brain damage and needed considerable care, and his brother was ten years younger. John says he felt like an only child. His mother started what became a robust organization to aid people with mental disabilities.

John got a computer when he was 12, when the first Apple II desktop came out. From about that age, he wanted to start a technology company. Following high school at a Jesuit-run, all-boys school in San Jose, John headed down the road to Stanford, and studied electrical engineering because it was a way to continue working with computers. He was a software engineer after college, and he loved it. Everything was changing and evolving rapidly in the technology world.

Five yeas into his life as a programmer, John still wanted to start a company. It was the mid 1990s and things were beginning to really bubble with the Internet. The possibilities for changing the world seemed endless. In 1994, he quit his job, and set about writing up ideas into business plans until one stuck. He, along with many others at the time, saw huge potential in commercializing the Internet, and after several iterations, he arrived at an idea: His company would write the code that places ads on Internet search engines and other sites. He walked into Yahoo's office when the company was 6 people, securing it as a first client. Making mistakes and learning along the way, he brought the business from just himself to 250 staff, and $40M (and slightly profitable) in four years before selling it. Two lessons stand out and apply to his work today: First, people are everything, survival and success depends on the team being outstanding; and second, different skills are needed when you start and when you build. In the start up phase, you throw yourself against the wall over and over until it breaks—these aren't the skills that allow you to build and sustain. John did learn to build, and he approaches Rocketship with that temperament, an ability to sustain short-term bumps and focus on the longer-term vision.

After John sold his company, the Jesuits called. They wanted money to build a middle school in a low-income neighborhood of San Jose. Instead of funding them, John offered to craft the plan, hire the teachers, and sort the budget. He became so inspired, seeing that a school could change an entire neighborhood, bringing it optimism about its future and its children. If you could do this at some scale, he thought, it would really matter.

Then John's wife, a lawyer, got a faculty post at Vanderbilt, and the family moved to Nashville for four years. John began a deliberate apprenticeship. He taught second grade for two years, learning what it takes to be effective in the classroom. Then he helped to start a KIPP school in one of the most challenging of Nashville's neighborhoods, an effort that exposed him to the importance of navigating politics and the constraints, many of them tied to financial dependence, that struggling charters face. He saw that despite its flaws, KIPP really got the middle school culture piece right—the teacher and principal recruitment and training. As with his company, he saw that if the people are right and see the right incentives and outcomes, you have the potential for a great school.

John is committed to seeing through Rocketship in the next 10 to 15 years. An idea that may emerge after is a global online education system, accessible to students throughout the world and tailored to their individual needs.

John lives in Silicon Valley with his wife and two children, ages five and seven. ♦

USHA TAMBA DHAR

CANADA

Access to Learning/Education

Equality/Rights

Usha Tamba Dhar is introducing new perspectives to the field of literacy education in Canada by providing local organizations with effective tools, trainings, and microfinancing to engage youth in their own literacy education. Tamba is addressing the shockingly high illiteracy rates in Canada, creating an easy to use, culturally appropriate, and spreadable set of methods to combat illiteracy. Tamba takes a unique approach to policy change in this area, by seeking recognition of literacy as a civil right.

THE NEW IDEA

Tamba is focusing on strengthening literacy in marginalized communities in Canada by implementing a strong community-based approach. Her approach is twofold: She builds her student's self-esteem and integrates community support to address low literacy rates in marginalized communities. The tools Tamba developed enable families and volunteers in the community to support youth to read and write. Her method gives mentors and parents techniques they can use even if they do not master English literacy skills—developing their own skills as they teach and become leaders and role models.

Tamba believes that an effective approach to literacy works equally well with 25-year-olds, street-involved youth, high school students with Down syndrome, and five-year-old refugees. Hence, she is reviving a traditional approach that has long been abandoned in Canadian schools and is based on four comprehensive steps. Tamba adapts her methodology to diverse groups and the materials she uses reflect their cultural and social realities, be they First Nations, street and homeless youth, immigrants and refugees, or youth with special needs (e.g. ADHD or learning disabilities).

To scale the impact of her literacy approach, Tamba provides microfunding to help community groups initiate or run literacy programs. Her grant program operates at a national scale. These partnerships also involve sharing her effective and inclusive manuals, as well as capacity-building trainings about literacy. To date, 150 organizations are using Tamba's materials and methodology or have received microfunding to increase literacy across Canada.

THE PROBLEM

According to *Statistics Canada*, 42 percent of Canadians are semi-illiterate. For the past 15 years there has been scarcely any improvement in Canada's 42 percent literacy rate (*The National*, 05/24/06). *The Toronto Dominion Report – Literacy Matters*, stated in 2007, "Four in 10 high school youth have insufficient reading skills. Two in 10 university graduates, five in 10 adults, and six in 10 immigrants also have insufficient literacy skills... While both levels of government are engaged in literacy programs, there is little evidence that it is working. Canada is losing billions because of illiteracy."

Illiteracy is a dynamic and severe social problem, particularly with Canada's diverse population. Marginalized groups such as immigrant communities need materials and methods of learning relevant to their experience to engage effectively with educational material. The school and social systems have failed to adapt to the reality of a multi-cultural Canada. Non-English native speakers who are not taught English literacy skills effectively in school often end up isolated in their classrooms.

By addressing marginalization, diversity, and illiteracy in a cohesive and systemic manner, literacy among Canadians can dramatically increase and Canadian society as a whole will benefit from a greater number of individuals being educated, employed, leaders, and entrepreneurs.

THE STRATEGY

In 1992 Tamba created Sage Youth to provide literacy support to marginalized communities in Ottawa. Through its programs, Sage Youth students move toward becoming "children in-opportunity." Since 1992, 8,000 youth have been supported through this program: 45 percent are homeless children and youth; 55 percent are new Canadians and 35 percent have special needs.

Through Sage Youth, Tamba is building self-esteem alongside literacy. She involves youth in mentoring programs about job preparedness and skills development, and encourages them to become active leaders and changemakers. Through this type of programming, Sage Youth students begin to see themselves as potential heroes and community builders.

Tamba's four step approach has proven to be highly effective. It increases 1) verbal skills 2) phonetic skills 3) comprehension skills 4) writing skills. Her materials are inclusive to all the populations they serve in a way that is culturally relevant, sensitive, empowering, and respectful. The combination of these four approaches is core to Tamba's methodology.

Sage Youth mobilizes 100 volunteers per year who become empowered to affect significant change in the lives of participants, to help them develop life skills, and to guide them in realizing their dreams. Tamba's training practices effectively engage community members with educational backgrounds ranging from a 5th grade education to a Ph.D. Her programs have expert staff members on site to assist with fine-tuning literacy and life-skills support to the needs of the individual student.

Tamba creates a space and programs that give their students confidence and a sense of joy and hope, while being able to measure their literacy developments qualitatively and quantitatively. It uses

a rigorous structure to evaluate social impact in its target areas. Through the use of a standardized measurement tool Sage Youth has demonstrated that its methodologies yield improvements three to four times greater than control groups for ESL students and double the rate of control groups for special education students. In addition, Tamba's organization monitors the number of successful community partnerships maintained in the areas of program delivery, volunteer recruitment, and program support. Sage Youth also diligently tracks student registration and attendance, and uses qualitative as well as quantitative methods to measure the impact of its leadership and employability programs. Finally, Tamba and her team assess the success of its volunteer engagement program by measuring volunteer registration, training, screening, and attendance records, as well as through occasional surveys. She continually uses these evaluative tools to improve her teaching and expansion strategies.

> "ELF provides literacy materials, training and micro-funding to over 160 community organizations across Canada as well as programs in orphanages in Ghana, Lesotho and Thailand."
>
> —*Community Foundation of Ottawa*

Conscious of the magnitude and hidden nature of Canada's illiteracy problems, Tamba decided it was time for her to disseminate her methodology more broadly. In 2002, she created the Excellence in Literacy Foundation (ELF), a sister organization in charge of spreading and replicating the approach through partner organizations. Workbooks co-authored by Tamba are used in over 150 communities across Canada and in orphanages in Ghana, Lesotho, and Thailand. Tamba has provided microfunding ($500 to $2,000) to nearly 100 organizations, and has offered trainings, workbooks, and evaluation materials to approximately 150 organizations across Canada and the world. ELF targets similar populations: Low-income, First Nations, new Canadians, homeless, and special needs communities. To date, 16,000 youth have participated in ELF activities, and Tamba's goal is to reach out to 3,000 youth yearly.

ELF measures success by evaluating 1) the number of programs introduced and served 2) the number children and youth served 3) the percentage of children served in each of the targeted high-risk communities 4) partnerships with dynamic, effective, ethical programs 5) the relevancy of materials, based on updates to student workbooks and partner training materials.

In addition, Tamba fosters large-scale change by partnering with schools to adopt her methodology, training tools and teaching materials. Tamba has currently worked with 27 in-school or school-supported programs. After various attempts of entrenching literacy into educational curricula through policy change, Tamba is taking an alternate approach by challenging Canada to recognize literacy as a civil right. The aim is to push the government to increase the human and financial resources necessary to address literacy in Canada. She believes that literacy is a birthright of Canada's children, and children all over the world. Tamba pursues public policy changes to ensure that all communities in Canada can receive adequate literacy development, thereby drastically augmenting literacy rates, and fostering a more representative and diverse body of leaders.

THE PERSON

Tamba chose to work around the social issue of illiteracy because she believes knowledge is freedom. Her father, who was very much involved in the Gandhian movement for independence in India, had a huge influence on her perceptions of what freedom means and its true reality. Her grandfather once told her father, "While you are all traipsing after this Gandhi fellow, remember that freedom is not a license. True freedom comes from a powerful mind. No one can take that from you." Tamba grew up in a family culture of community service. She was raised with a sense of civic responsibility to create opportunities for others. This is the work she has always envisioned for herself.

One of Tamba's first volunteer jobs was working at a day camp for children with developmental challenges. One of her kids was Carlos, a five-year-old boy with Down syndrome. His family was told that he should have been institutionalized at birth, that he would never speak, read, or be able to live a full life. One day driving back from a field trip on a school bus, Carlos fell asleep on her lap. He was curled up in a little ball. Very suddenly, he awoke, sat up, smiled at Tamba and spoke his first word "Tamba." The bus driver pulled over and everyone gave him a standing ovation. Years later, one of the directors at the camp informed Tamba that Carlos was in high school, mainstreaming in many courses, had a very pretty girlfriend, and was working on the weekends. At that moment, Tamba was hooked on what has now become her life's work.

Tamba's students at Sage Youth have also been a continuing source of inspiration, always giving her more reasons to continue to work on eradicating illiteracy in Canada and to help programs all over the world fight illiteracy in their nations. One of her first students at Sage Youth was an eight-year-old refugee from Somalia. When she was five, her father and grandfather had been killed in front of her. She had witnessed her mother and sister being gang-raped and her infant brother killed. Before the end of every Sage Youth session, she set aside her work to help a younger child learn the alphabet. She was then, and remains to this day, Sage Youth's youngest volunteer. Tamba later learned that she was a straight-A student, captain of her high school basketball team, and was moving forward with plans to become a pediatrician. These are the stories that encourage Tamba to continue to commit 100 percent to her vision of a completely literate Canada. ◆

SANDRINE FAUST

CANADA

Access to Learning/Education

Capacity Building

Education Reform

Sandrine Faust, who comes from a family of educators, is democratizing education and changing power dynamics between students, teachers, and parents through platforms that enable peer-to-peer tutoring among these groups. Sandrine's interactive website and phone help-lines allow for constant access to a wealth of resources and learning tools that help 1,000 children per night with their homework and turn them into peer educators. This engaging, inclusive, and thoughtful platform targets kids who are at-risk of dropping out.

THE NEW IDEA

Sandrine has created a powerful solution that helps kids stay in school and increases their confidence levels by providing children, parents, and teachers with the pedagogical support they need. As a teacher and the daughter of educators, Sandrine knew that to democratize education in Canada she would have to address three closely linked issues: The lack of incentive and support structures for children and youth to understand the value of education; many parents lack of confidence or preparedness to help their children with their homework; and low morale among teachers.

> "Thanks to [Sandrine] and her team, many children draw from the courage to pursue their studies,"
>
> —L'Universite de Quebec,
> Sandrine Faust, Person of the Year

Sandrine therefore set out to create an online platform that gives children 24-hour access to educators—including 50 teachers, their peers, and parents—who make themselves available to answer homework questions. Entering her website is, in essence, the equivalent of dialing 911 to get "emergency" support for homework. The teachers engaged in this initiative are active school teachers—this ensures their full awareness of the curriculum and also allows them to anticipate the types of difficulties faced by students. Moreover, because all questions can be answered by anyone in the online fora, Sandrine's platform also turns students into peer educators. This reversal of roles not only boosts their confidence and teaches them new skills, it also helps to test and master their knowledge, while increasing the pool of "service providers." All questions answered by students are reviewed and approved or edited by trained teachers. Parents also participate both by answering children's questions and receiving advice from the vibrant network of parents that participate on the platform.

Because many low-income students do not have access to a computer or the Internet at home, Sandrine installed interactive terminals in afterschool programs, libraries, and low-income housing to render universal access to her services. By creating and promoting a free, accessible, anonymous, and interactive system to assist students with their studies, Sandrine is preventing many students from dropping out of school. Her goal is to reach all students who need assistance, beginning with the province of Quebec. Sandrine's initiative is already being replicated in Ontario.

THE PROBLEM

It is now a broadly accepted fact that education can dramatically increase one's lot in life. Without a high school diploma, today's Canadian youth are not eligible to undertake postsecondary education, thus greatly restricting their earning potential. Yet according to the Ministry of Education, in 2008 almost 30 percent of Quebecois youth below the age of 20 failed to obtain their high school diplomas. The majority of these students (i.e. approximately 40 percent) report that they are simply not interested in pursuing an education. About 30 percent drop out due in large part to poor self-esteem and the difficulty of keeping up with the curriculum and/or adapting to the school system. The remaining 30 percent leave school for other reasons, such as health problems or anti-social behavior. Lacking proper support either at school or at home, students lose confidence and motivation. Although children and youth are told that education is important, because most do not have access to homework support resources, many become discouraged and conclude it may not be as valuable as adults make it seem. They therefore opt to get a job as early as possible, without fully understanding the long-term sacrifices their decisions entail. Ontario's students are slightly better off, but the fact that 21 percent of the youth do not graduate from high school remains alarming.

The factors connected with students dropping out of school are many and complex in nature. Not to be overlooked are the socioeconomic status, the family dynamic, the parents level of education, and health issues. Many families are ill equipped to help their children as they may not have the knowledge, language skills, or required time to do so. This issue is particularly acute in low-income or immigrant communities where families cannot afford the long-term tutoring many times needed in high school. In addition, teachers are often left to deal with these systemic issues on their own in the context of their classrooms. This has a significant impact on teacher's morale and ability to teach effectively. They rarely have the opportunity to work one-on-one with children and are barely ever thanked for the important work they do. Moreover, many teachers and school administrators have failed to embrace the digital revolution in their classrooms. This means teaching styles often do not correspond with what children need or want nowadays, thus causing an even greater disconnect between students and teachers.

Student drop out rates affect society as a whole. As a result of under-exploring and under-developing the individual talents of each student, the contribution each could potentially make to society becomes significantly limited. In addition, approximately 30 percent of high school dropouts fail to find employment, and

when they do, they receive on average $3,000 less per month than a high school graduate. As a result of poor education, many end up relying on social assistance from the government, costing Canadians around $4,320 per person per year and thus failing to offer them long-term solutions to increase their quality of life.

Allô Prof offers telephone service, cyberclass, forums, and a virtual library among its many resources.

THE STRATEGY

When Sandrine joined a new television program called Allô Prof created in 1996, the program was meant to help students do their homework by calling teachers who would answer their questions. In 1999, the program was reaching out to a small number of viewers and only 50 calls were answered every evening. As a result, Tele-Quebec, the network host, decided to discontinue the program. At that point, Sandrine, who began her involvement with the show shortly before it was taken off the air, saw an opportunity to develop a province-wide initiative to support students all across Quebec through the use of new technologies. She took leadership of the organization and radically shifted its mission and mandate with the clear goal of democratizing access to education and reducing high school drop out rates. Sandrine is on her way to giving all students in Quebec free, easy, and rapid access to homework and school-related support. She gained the support of parent and teacher's associations as well as school boards who put pressure on the Ministry of Education of Quebec to allocate a portion of its budget to her program.

The first thing Sandrine did in 1999 was to develop cyber-classrooms using screen-sharing technology. Allô Prof now handles around 1,000 calls (75 percent through web conferences and 25 percent over the phone) each night from youth all over the province. From a pool of 50 paid teachers, 20 are available every night to answer students' questions. During a typical call, which usually lasts between 4 and 30 minutes, students are referred to a teacher with a specific subject expertise. All teachers are well equipped to handle students' questions since they work in schools during the day and at the call center at night. Although the cyber-classes have allowed Sandrine to make the whole process more efficient, she decided to keep the original phone help-line to ensure that students, who have limited access to the Internet, are shyer, or need more hands-on support can readily obtain the help they need.

In 2001 Sandrine continued innovating by developing online forums, which have been critical to democratizing the roles students and teachers play in the field of education. There are currently six forums active 24-hours a day, and each supervised by one teacher. Anyone may post a question on the forums, and everyone is invited to answer. This sometimes means younger students find themselves tutoring older students. While Allô Prof teachers review every single post, the forums allow students to give back to their peers by supporting them. In addition, the exercise of explaining a concept to a fellow student deepens their understanding of that same concept and as a result, increases their confidence. The forums now have 45,000 participants. Sandrine has thus successfully multiplied the number of people involved in supporting others while also creating a vibrant community of peer educators and challenging the role of teachers as the sole or primary knowledge-holders. This success motivated Sandrine to launch a volunteer mentoring program in 2009, engaging high school students to help those in elementary school under the supervision of a teacher. Volunteers receive school credits for each call successfully answered.

In 2008 Sandrine created a library of online videos, mathematical games, and other resources to answer recurring questions about specific concepts students struggle with. In that first year, 75,000 downloads of these videos were registered. She created this online library of resources after noticing that many of the phone calls or cyber-class requests they received came from the students not experiencing the most difficulties. The library therefore allows the more pro-active students to find answers on their own, while Allô Prof phone lines and cyber-classes free up teachers' time to respond to the student's questions most in need of help. The virtual library is also used in class by teachers to explain specific concepts and to encourage autonomous learning.

A large number of teachers in Quebec are using Allô Prof materials not only because they are of high quality, but also because the technological element keeps their students engaged. They often use Allô Prof mathematical video games—which help students learn their multiplication tables, for example—as rewards. Allô Prof has a critical affect on teachers as well. Those who are employed by Allô Prof find a renewed commitment and love for their work because they notice outcomes immediately, and being thanked at the end of each phone call is critical. The entire classroom also benefits when students attend class better prepared to absorb new material as a result of getting the support they needed while doing their homework the previous night.

The program primarily targets youth when they are at home. However, the recent adoption of this program by the Ministry of Education of Quebec as the national service for homework support has enabled Sandrine to bring Allô Prof into municipal libraries, after school programs, and low-income housing units. To maximize her impact, she has focused the organization's expansion to low-income areas where the high school drop out rates are particularly high. The lack of technology in some of these new spaces inspired her to commission the creation of beautiful Allô Prof booths, thus giving students access to its services regardless of the "digital divide."

Over the next five years Sandrine expects to grow the number of calls answered from 270,000 per year to 1 million. By then, she aims to be working in all regions of Quebec, giving special attention to regions impacted by socioeconomic difficulties. By establishing local partnerships, working with key stakeholders, and raising the program's profile in each region, Sandrine intends to better tailor the program to suit local needs. Furthermore, Allô Prof will become a stronger ally for parents who struggle to balance the demands of their professional and family lives. The province of Quebec has set itself the goal of seeing 80 percent of its youth over 20 graduate from high school by 2020. Sandrine is determined to turn Allô Prof into one of the main strategies to achieve this goal and began replicating her program in francophone Ontario through a sister organization, SOS Devoir. Sandrine intends to systematize this approach to facilitate the replication of her model by partnering with other organizations across Canada.

THE PERSON

With her father the director of a school board, Sandrine grew up knowing and appreciating the value of education. She pursued a B.A. in business, quickly followed by a second B.A. in education for people with learning difficulties. Sandrine soon realized that if teachers truly focused on student's needs, they could contribute to significant changes in student performance and confidence.

When Sandrine started working at Allô Prof as a young tutor to a group of students in grade six, she was overwhelmed by their level of disengagement and the difficulty she had convincing them of the value of continuing their education. Yet she received instant gratitude from many students after giving them the support they needed to keep trying. At the time Allô Prof offered little more than a telephone service for children transitioning between primary school and high school. When the TV show ended and the future of the program was jeopardized, Sandrine felt it was an opportunity to harness the power of the advent of the Internet to foster social change. She took the leadership and redesigned the mandates and programs. Sandrine has since been motivated by the goal of offering every youth the opportunities they need to develop their full potential. She refuses to accept common comments affirming that low-income youth are "destined" to have fewer opportunities. Sandrine's nickname, "The Tornado", highlights the energy she puts into making change happen and into engaging a wide variety of actors in her campaign for education—the media, government, teachers, parents, and many more. Sandrine is expanding her programs beyond Quebec and envisions international reach. ♦

MIKE FEERICK

IRELAND

Access to Learning/Education

Mike Feerick is improving access to opportunity through ALISON, a new approach to skills training that offers increased employment competitiveness for users around the world, for free. The program, akin to an accessible online community college, is designed around a system of alternative certification and immediate competence testing. Mike is expanding offerings to mobile platforms, secondary school curriculum, and beyond.

THE NEW IDEA

Top quality, peer-reviewed online education and skills training can be provided for free. Mike's ALISON program offers free resources to "up-skilling" workers in everything from English to IT competency online. His work breaks down the barriers of expensive curriculum and limited access to educational resources, and offers verified, quality controlled tools with teacher groups, forums, and testing functions—built on a sustainable, self-funding business model.

Mike's work with ALISON focuses on competence rather than credential. It offers "generic" versions of well-known certificate programs such as the European Computer Driving License. Quality reputation is bolstered through "flash tests," quick 30-question overviews of course material which students, teachers, and potential employers can use to gauge current mastery and gain alternative certification—similar to the typing tests of a past era.

Community college is an underfunded and underdeveloped educational resource—Mike is offering the first freely accessible online community college, rather than an online university. There are many resources that offer free trials to computer literacy and other training programs, but Mike's alternative credential model is unique in that it offers a completely free full set of tutorials and fully-fleshed curricula created partially through open source methods, peer-reviewed to offer a markedly high level of quality.

THE PROBLEM

Online training is prohibitively expensive—there are a few growing online university initiatives that offer college-level curricula, yet they lack assessment tools. There is little on offer in terms of more basic training coursework free of charge, and thus little recourse for people hoping to advance themselves in their chosen field, but without the economic means to pay for expensive trainings. "Free" trainings available online almost entirely consist of samples of courses offered to entice individuals to buy the full course. Continuing education around the increasingly important skill of computer literacy, and gaining the credentials that can decide the difference between a job offer and a rejection letter, are outside the reach of many people who need them most. For example, CISCO certification, the "gold standard" for computer network programming, charges a rate of US$3,000, and the European Computer Driving License certification, a basic requirement for any IT job in Europe (and in many other areas) costs roughly US$750. Cost of certification tends to make up two-thirds of the total cost for these education programs. These high costs make training difficult or impossible for prospective workers in the developing world, the unemployed with little disposable income, and small business owners who cannot afford to train their workers to be competitive.

Education is a US$1.4T industry worldwide; however, the industry suffers from significant reinvention of the wheel and duplication of efforts. For-profit universities, which can comprise a US$6B market, prey on students looking to advance, but end up buried in debt for a non-accredited certificate. Whereas in community college, 50 percent of students fail out, and many take six years or more to complete a two-year associates degree.

> "ALISON now has over half-a-million registered learners in 200 countries worldwide providing over 150 courses at Certificate & Diploma level."
>
> —*Galway Advertiser*

While there are few systems of measurement and accountability for e-learning and online education, open source options—whether software or courses or otherwise—can lack quality control among the multiple providers. Employers depend on well-known, but expensive, certification schemes such as the European Computer Driving License because their quality is vetted. Online courses and free options for courses with few systems for quality control do not offer the same immediate name recognition or credibility. Also, a certification offers a record of demonstrated past competence in a particular skill—whether English or computers or otherwise—but offers little method for employers to check prospective employees' current competence. The gap in e-learning and online education opens a huge opportunity for new innovations that provide low-cost, accessible, quality training.

THE STRATEGY

Mike is aggregating high-quality, peer-reviewed content to make workplace skills training—and beyond—freely available to everyone. He is creating a new knowledge business to offer low-barrier access to an individualized skills education, and tearing down the boundaries erected by underfunded and low quality community colleges. Founded in April 2007, ALISON recently registered its 400,000 learner. Mike's larger vision is to become the world's largest learning site, with the deliverable of providing quality interactive multimedia education to anyone in any certifiable subject.

In 2010 ALISON published over 100 new courses, including the very successful Diploma courses, and monthly learner traffic rose to new highs in nearly every country worldwide.

Mike has structured ALISON to be an arbiter of quality for skills training courses. To combat the prohibitive cost of many training/credential programs, Mike and ALISON are creating free, open source versions of respected programs, adapting them to stay within relevant copyright laws. For example, ALISON's IT literacy offerings (the most popular ALISON course), ABC-IT, is adapted from the European Computer Driving License, and the English language program (the second most popular ALISON course) is drawn from the British Council curriculum. Many of the other courses are designed by the ALISON team or outside experts. Mike stresses that his work is by no means "the YouTube of e-learning," a free-for-all of self-created options with no vetting. Quality control, which is often difficult to ensure with online options, is secured through his use of adapted curriculum, a team of educators, and a strong international volunteer base. For example, Mike recently bought an interactive high school curriculum from the Australian government, and is working to make it available as a next step.

To supplement his adapted curriculum and other offerings, Mike has created an "alternative" certification function as well as competence tests for employer use. Users who have successfully completed a course can download a certificate, and Mike is working to integrate his programs into the accepted and recognized set of options—for example, the Board of Education in South Africa has accredited his ABC-IT as a recognized computer literacy training certification nationwide. To add validity to his training offers and create accountability, Mike provides services to employers, who can immediately test the skill level of potential

hires through "flash tests," which, similar to traditional secretarial typing tests, allow immediate measure of skill level at job interviews through a quick test of 30 random questions. Rather than relying on a TOEFL certificate earned many years previous, an employer can ask a candidate to take a quick aptitude test to check true competence and current understanding.

Mike has built these options to be especially useful for smaller businesses, believing that traditional training approaches impact businesses negatively in terms of time spent away from core activities. His online learning provides flexibility to small- and medium-sized enterprises, as it affords participants the ability to learn at their own pace, at any time and from any place including the home. Currently, he is designing an HTML-based mobile platform to make his offerings available to those without Internet or computer access. Mike's vision is the "creation of a turnkey universal curriculum," and an approach to education that overturns traditional "Victorian" models that do not individualize learning.

Mike has grown his model through partnerships with organizations and integrating it with institutions. Ireland's National Health and Safety Executive has contracted Mike and ALISON to develop courses focused on health standards, and they have also been contracted by WHO to produce IT literacy courses in French, and the Indonesian government for REDD forestry courses. The largest user of ALISON programs is the U.S. Department of Labor, which offers free ALISON e-learning programs through their unemployment website for prospective job-searchers seeking to increase their skills. Mike and ALISON have designed courses to test comprehension and offer certification in entrepreneurship texts such as *Stone Soup*. He is working to integrate the program into existing education programs, and gain widespread accreditation for his alternative certifications, much like in South Africa. Recently the Ugandan government donated money simply to provide ALISON with the means to publicize their programs across the country. He is growing his community of learners through these types of partnerships, word of mouth, teacher outreach, and is expanding his offerings through an extensive global volunteer network of translators and educators—including 300 volunteers in Egypt and 30 in Afghanistan. Mike's funding model is build almost entirely around online ad revenue, but also includes content development (i.e. government contracts) and a nominal charge for printing certifications.

THE PERSON

Born in the rural West of Ireland, Mike has had the challenges of accessing education imprinted on him from an early age. The first of his family to attend college, and engaged in entrepreneurial ventures since childhood, Mike was accepted to Harvard Business School at age 23. The school suggested he spend a year gaining experience before enrolling as he was much younger than the rest of the students. Faced with a year of waiting, Mike wrote a letter to a well-known businessman in Ireland, and talked his way into an extended apprenticeship. Mike offered him a deal—he would shadow him and learn the tricks of business success, in order to one day move back to the West of Ireland and contribute to building the community there.

An entrepreneur within both the social and business sectors and an accomplished musician, Mike moved from the U.S. to work in the London music industry, working on new Internet paradigms on traditional music. Later, he created and sold a successful telecom business called Yac. Mike's insights with ALISON draws from his extensive experience working in e-learning, primarily through a company he founded called Advance Learning, which offered per diem online curriculum. On a gamble, he took the US$1M worth of Advance Learning content and made it free online. He notes, "The day I learned about the Internet was the day I knew what would allow me to move back to the West of Ireland."

With his e-learning programs thriving, Mike fulfilled his promise, moving back to the small town of Loughrea, outside of Galway, where he and his wife still play traditional Irish music in pubs on Saturday evenings. Deeply tied to his Irish roots and local community, Mike, a "rebellious optimist" has created programs that work with the substantial Irish Diaspora. He founded an organization, Irish Charitable Trust, dedicated to the large numbers of Irish immigrants who move to England seeking opportunity but fall into alcoholism and destitution. Mike's own uncle was the driving inspiration behind the outreach efforts.

In a similar vein, as a hobby on the side Mike is crafting an additional initiative that has systems-change potential. Using his expertise with online communities and funded by his home community, he has created a program that reassembles scattered Irish communities around the world. He realized that it was possible to trace those immigrants who left Ireland by pinpointing their arrival points. Beginning with 30 parishes in Galway, Mike is reaching out to communities to find who left, connecting and reaching out to the far-flung descendants. Seeking to "reawaken family links" and transform "one-off roots trips" back to Ireland into ongoing relationships, returning descendants visit ancestral towns with someone local to meet them and are united in online communities. The program is tracing lineage forwards rather than backwards, and spurring the globalization of Ireland in a new and intimate way. Mike has found the levers he needs to move seamlessly through the business and social sector worlds, yet is deeply informed by his ties to home. ♦

CASEY FENTON

GLOBAL

Intercultural Relations/ Race Relations

Casey Fenton is cultivating trust and appreciation of difference through a global travel community that facilitates one-on-one interactions with strangers, orchestrated at mass scale.

THE NEW IDEA

Casey is reshaping the experience of travel and using it to essentially reset society's default to trust, appreciation of difference, and inclusivity. Through CouchSurfing, travelers and hosts of all sorts and backgrounds find each other and arrange free home stays, averaging five nights. The matching is orchestrated via the Internet, and the community is reinforced off-line by lively weekly meet-ups of hosts and travelers in many major cities across the world. Open to anyone who can access the website, the community is anchored by guiding principles and various measures, such as rating features that ensure that as the community grows, it adds intelligence, self-regulates wisely, and supports personal safety for traveler and host. While the average participant age is 28, members hail from every age group, participating as single travelers, pairs, and even as families. If a participant cannot travel for whatever reason—financial hardship, disability, and so on—the experience comes to them through the active role of hosting a traveler in their home. Begun in 2004, CouchSurfing engages over 2 million participants from nearly every country, democratizes travel and encourages CouchSurfing-enabled experiences to foster empathy and advance global citizenship.

THE PROBLEM

While our world is becoming ever more global, our growing interconnectedness does not necessarily foster tolerance or translate into increased trust among people. The events of 9/11 moved many Americans in the opposite direction, causing many to react with fear and encounter strangers—particularly strangers from different cultural backgrounds—with unease. Watch your bag. Suspect your fellow passenger. Be on alert. Add to this elevated mistrust-of-other the trend toward customization in many areas of life. Many tools, online and off-line, allow users to assert preferences—useful in many respects, but there's a danger that people will tune out difference altogether and further insulate themselves from viewpoints and people they do not like, or in many cases, simply do not have occasion to understand.

Travel can offer a profound experience of seeing and being inside another life, another place, another way of living. Direct contact, face-to-face conversation, and the experience of hosting or being hosted can result in more tolerance and acceptance than any media campaign could ever hope to effect. Yet the experience of travel has become so contrived and boxed in as to lose its transformative potential. Even those who can afford to travel are often limited by the ways and means of traditional tourism. Tourists drive to the next state or fly thousands of miles to visit exotic cultures only to stay in sterile hotel rooms and visit postcard-approved monuments. While most travelers want to have meaningful interactions with the people of the places they visit, the industry is set up to substantially shield the traveler from the experience and appreciation of difference.

Numerous cultural exchange programs have managed to break down the barriers, but these services tend to be expensive, focus on students, and facilitate singular experiences for a set period of time. Such efforts have important social impact, but most are exclusive to an elite group of people who can afford to participate. Even where institutions provide the experience to a disadvantaged population, they are limited by the time and money required to identify participants and homestay hosts and to facilitate the program. Importantly, the parameters of these programs, rather than the individual participants, drive the experience.

In the current digital age, the obvious next step in the evolution of exchange programs and fee-based hospitality services has been the migration to a vastly more scalable online infrastructure. A few of these services have made the transition and grown their membership to a degree, but their fundamentally closed nature has not changed and continues to limit their reach. Others have created a hospitality infrastructure but have lost the values-driven element to traditional exchange programs.

THE STRATEGY

CouchSurfing is fostering appreciation of difference by providing a forum where travelers can find hosts. It nurtures a diverse and trusting community within that forum, and creates opportunities for inspiring experiences among members of the community. The organization lives the values it promotes by operating with a new virtualized workplace model which has doubled output by relying on paid staff (whose hours are trackable).

The core of the CouchSurfing model is the online forum that encourages people to become "surfers" and "hosts" and allows surfers and hosts to find each other. By removing the participant selection component of exchange and homestay programs, CouchSurfing makes the opportunity to host a traveler or stay with a host accessible to everyone. To maximize opportunities to interact with someone different than oneself, CouchSurfing deliberately makes this forum a neutral space where persons of all nationalities, races, religions, ages, classes, viewpoints, and any other category can participate. All users of the forum have individual profiles where they can share information about themselves and any accommodation arrangements they may have available. In its initial years, CouchSurfing largely attracted young,

intrepid adventure travelers, but as the model has proven itself, the community is growing increasingly diverse. CouchSurfing's first strategic priority is to bring more and different types of persons into the forum. As such, Casey and his team are innovating ways to highlight more remote community members and their locales, to reach people who do not have Internet access, to build multilingual capacity, and to ease skeptics into the community through subsidiary shared-interest groups.

Casey did not set out to build just a forum, however. He recognized that achieving diverse and inspiring experiences would require nurturing a community conducive to that effect. As such, Casey has designed CouchSurfing as a community, rather than a service. It is against CouchSurfing's terms of use to charge for hosting services. This ground rule contributes to fostering the CouchSurfing community's most important value, trust. Staying at a stranger's home, or inviting a stranger into one's home, requires a significant degree of trust. Because the CouchSurfing community depends on trust to survive, it vigilantly protects this value within the community. It self-polices through a vouching system and through evaluations that hosts and surfers leave on each other's profiles after their CouchSurfing experiences. The CouchSurfing team has also implemented other measures to enhance trust and security, including a verification option for community members, safety guidelines for surfing and hosting, and other security measures in the event of criminal activity.

> "When Casey Fenton and his crew wanted to create a real-life community from a virtual one, they founded CouchSurfing, devoted to creating connections by offering free places to stay."
>
> —*Bottsnall*

CouchSurfing is continuously developing new ways to encourage people into more and deeper interactions and experiences, and monitoring closely what is happening and what is working. Those who are interested in the CouchSurfing mission but not yet willing or able to surf or host overnight can start by offering to merely meet up for a conversation. Those who do not know of or care about the CouchSurfing mission and are merely looking for free accommodation are also welcome to join the community. In either case, CouchSurfing creates a fun environment that encourages people to explore within the community. The team has created a particular volunteer role, Ambassadors, for veteran couchsurfers who viscerally understand the CouchSurfing mission and serve as promoters of that mission wherever they are in the world. Among other things, Ambassadors organize local gatherings of couchsurfers, providing an opportunity for hosts and travelers to socialize as a group, and thus making possible interactions beyond that between one host and one traveler. Casey is tracking the types of experiences people are having in order to develop CouchSurfing into a learning institution in empathy-building and intercultural understanding.

Furthermore, CouchSurfing is planning new initiatives that build off of the host and surf platform. CouchSurfing Cares will use the platform to connect persons who are displaced from their homes by natural disasters with hosts who can take them in for an extended stay. CouchSurfing University will connect young people who want to experiment with different career tracks with hosts who they can shadow temporarily in different professions.

Casey launched and helps run CouchSurfing through an innovative, resourceful, and mission-aligned "collective" model, through which he attracts highly skilled staff. In its first few years, from 2006 to 2010, CouchSurfing did not have a permanent location or paid staff. They set up temporary collectives in different cities around the world for a few months at a time. These collectives were live-work environments, where volunteers were drawn by the opportunity to travel to a new place and have all their basic needs met in return for their time and skills. Once open to anyone who wanted to contribute, as the organization has grown, CouchSurfing has developed a highly competitive recruitment process and is establishing several permanent collectives in different parts of the world. Using its new virtual workplace model, the team continues to innovate tools to make CouchSurfing experiences as positive and high-impact as possible.

THE PERSON

Due to his family's financial situation, Casey did not get to travel much growing up, and when he left home for college on the other side of the country, he was filled with a sense of adventure and passion for life. Restless in his hometown (i.e. he grew up in small-town New Hampshire), he finished high school in three years so that he could get out on his own. While college was inspiring, he left to start an Internet company and see how people lived in other parts of the world. As he traveled, he sought opportunities to interact with different people, places, and perspectives, but he found that the travel infrastructure disallowed meaningful connections and authentic interactions.

On a trip to Iceland, he tried something different: He sent an email to 1,500 university students in Reykjavik introducing himself and sharing his interest in staying with a local for a week. Several students responded, inviting Casey into their home. He found in the experience a new and transformative way to connect with people living in a place very different from his home.

Wanting to positively shape the world, Casey then worked for legislators and candidates for political office in Alaska. But a core insight had evolved from his Iceland experience and he began to feel more powerfully drawn to creating a community designed to foster appreciation of difference, a quality he felt was especially needed at this moment. Casey pulled together a team of co-founders, and after experimenting with a closed network, they opened it up to the world, inviting everyone to be a CouchSurfer. ♦

HANNE FINSTAD

NORWAY

Education Reform

Despite considerable economic resources, Norway ranks below France and Germany in science education. As one of the first masters students to work in gene technology in Norway, Hanne Finstad realized that you learn science by doing. Every scientist—like every social entrepreneur—had a moment that sparked his or her passion. Through Forskerfabrikken (Scientist Factory) Hanne is creating opportunities for as many kids to have as many moments of inspiration in science. Beginning in Norway, lagging behind Western Europe and Scandinavian neighbors of Sweden and Denmark, Hanne is building a civil society movement to change the way science is taught and perceived.

THE NEW IDEA

Hanne is creating a new generation of scientists, a culture of critical thinking, and broadening intellectual curiosity through a multi-pronged strategy to integrate in-depth, experiential science into classrooms. Hanne is operating on the realization that students must actively participate in science to understand it. Hanne's company, Forskerfabrikken, offers inexpensive two-hour science courses after school to "train young brains," enrich and speed learning, and position science as something fun and interesting. A corps of specialized teachers is drawn from scientific researchers and engineers to inspire, teach, and engage students around experiential learning.

Hanne is integrating this experiential approach into curriculum, offering modules for teacher lessons, textbooks, and extensive teacher training, which has raised test scores as well as offer consulting for schools to determine how to improve their equipment and build centers for science. Her work is building a new social landscape for science, based on an understanding of how people learn, and transforming science education into something compelling and accessible to all.

THE PROBLEM

Ineffective teaching does not create a citizenry of practical, curious scientists. Schools in Norway teach almost entirely theoretical science. Courses in science, from primary school to high school, revolve around reading about scientific ideas and then writing about them. This rote memorization is an ineffective method for learning about the abstract ideas that underlie all scientific study—

"conceptual ideas are tough for young brains" without seeing them in action. Also, Norway does not have a culture of school extracurriculars—after school activities are not provided by school systems, are expensive, and are rarely academic in nature. There is little to supplement an education outside of the school walls. Norway is somewhat notoriously behind even other Scandinavian countries in terms of science education, and the long-term impact is clear in terms of performance and interest. Chemistry has the lowest recruitment of any college subject in Norway.

While there are many teachers who are gifted at teaching, many lack the practical knowledge and experience. Teachers in Norway are not required to specialize in the subjects they teach for any age range of students. Below college level, teachers are not required to have taken any courses beyond the level they teach. For example, 70 percent of tenth grade science teachers in Norway have not studied science past the tenth grade themselves. Moreover, teaching method textbooks rarely enter classrooms and science training for teachers has remained the same for roughly 30 years. Recently, Norway teacher colleges have added a fifth year of specialized training for teachers—this is an ample opportunity to reform education pedagogy in the sciences.

> "Hanne is creating a new generation of scientists, a culture of critical thinking, and broadening intellectual curiosity through a strategy to integrate in-depth, experiential science into classrooms."
>
> —*Partnership for Change*

Even passionate science teachers struggle with dated equipment, texts, and lack of institutional commitment. Schools have extremely poor facilities for science and are not built to accommodate an experiment-based style of science education. Science books in Norway tend to cover developments and discovery up to roughly 1970, and talk in broad strokes for younger students rather than delving into details—neglecting the cutting edge science that is most relevant and compelling to young minds. For example, children can understand atoms at a young age, yet they are taught a simplified course work covering substances—a lost opportunity.

THE STRATEGY

Hanne, a cancer researcher and biochemist, created Forskerfabrikken to fill the gap in Norwegian science education and provide the experiment-based education that makes science come alive. She has crafted a strategy that targets young people after school hours, in schools, and the larger education system to change the culture of science; intervening with children, young people, the academic system and the media to create new ways of thinking of human potential and dramatically expand passion

in science. Her courses, designed to last between two to three hours and offered after school hours, are made up of 70 percent practical activities, with 30 percent focused on theory students see in action around the themes of chemistry, biology, and physics. Co-designed and taught by practicing scientists (Ph.D. students and experts) in working science labs at universities (or approximations in other spaces) the courses teach specific concepts such as atoms and gases through engaging story-based courses on "alien slime" or DNA sleuthing. Students wear lab coats, learn the scientific method, and practice the technical skills of science including safety and measurement. They are also provided with experiments and supplies to do their own projects at home. Hanne hopes to make it as natural for children to do science after school as sports.

Hanne realized that many of her scientific colleagues pointed to a time in their youth—roughly at age 8 or 10—when their interest in science was sparked. With Forskerfabrikken, she seeks to replicate those experiences to "open up minds to the invisible world." Initially begun with a focus on that age group, Hanne has since expanded her offerings to include longer courses for high school age kids, shorter courses for children in the first through fourth grades (ages 6 to 8), and weekend activities for families, with everything from "bug clubs" to magnetism to ice cream making. Her primary one-off courses are offered on a paid basis to students after school. She has recently been expanding her work to be available to children of all socioeconomic backgrounds, incorporating courses in the "leisure time clubs" available to low-income students, the "open school" which provides afterschool care for students with working parents, and providing general discounts. She is also partnering with schools to provide courses to immigrant children from conservative religious backgrounds who may not be allowed out for traditional activities. Beginning with 441 students in her courses in 2008, she has doubled the number each year and is on track for 1,600 students in 2010.

Hanne is building from her free-standing extracurricular courses to overhaul science education within the system. A for-profit company, she is focusing heavily on teacher training to provide the skills, specialized learning, and tools and ideas to offer vastly more students an active, experiment-based science education. Several thousand teachers have gone through her program—roughly 3,000 teachers in Oslo and Bergen, with collaborations with teacher's unions. Hanne's efforts have helped to overhaul new science training for teachers—colleges now require an additional year of specialized study, from four years to five. Hanne's teacher courses, her primary revenue source for Forskerfabrikken, strengthen the knowledge foundation, update teachers on the most up to date science, and guide them through the experiments that illustrate the concepts they teach. The results are promising: Teachers who underwent Hanne's training in 2006 achieved higher results in Oslo testing. Another study followed students for three years, from second grade through fifth grade, using Hanne's experiments and curricula. Out of 100 schools, the class was mediocre at best, ranking 50th out of 100 before the first year taught by Hanne's methods. By the third year, the class ranked in the top 10 percentile (9th out of 100) in science—one of the best schools in all of Oslo. Currently, she is engaged in a two-year contract which has trained 30 percent of all teachers in Oslo, with plans for the entire school system.

Since 2002, several thousand children have attended Forskerfabrikken. Today, it offers summer school and continuing education courses for teachers. By arousing children's interest in science and technology, Forskerfabrikken hopes to boost recruitment for research and technology in Norway.

Hanne is working to overhaul science education infrastructure and alter society's perception of science as removed from cultural life, emphasizing the contribution of science in all areas of society. Coupled with her teacher trainings and course offerings, she works with schools to conduct an "inventory" of their facilities and equipment, and makes recommendations for what they need to change/purchase to have a fully developed science department. Hanne has overhauled 85 schools through this process. Several municipalities have requested a full package, including courses for the first through seventh grades, planned experiments, teacher training, and facility inventory. Hanne is also working to get science accepted as part of the government investment in cultural activities. To further integrate her work into existing curriculum and teaching, Hanne has authored a science textbook for eighth to tenth grades, which integrates the experiments and active learning that is the basis of Forskerfabrikken. The text has 25 percent

market share in Norway. Hanne's board is exploring expansion in Denmark and Sweden through a franchise model.

Hanne has been working with a professor specializing in how brains learn to help hone her techniques. In all elements of her strategy she has emphasized the importance of specificity. Hanne feels that children's brain development and interest is enriched by learning science in an in-depth way at an early age—for example, learning atoms rather than simple substances (solid, liquid, and gas) kick-starts understanding. Currently, curriculum is slow moving; children do not learn about anything on a microscopic level until roughly age 15. She is adamant that "You can teach eight-year-olds biochemistry." Hanne has structured her extracurricular courses and teacher training to incorporate more specific and cutting edge science to children at an early age.

THE PERSON

Hanne's father, a geologist, helped spark her love for science when he gave her a telescope as a child. Together they explored the natural world on hiking expeditions and trips to his science lab. An athlete, Hanne was initially drawn to studying nutrition but then moved to biochemistry. During her studies, she supported herself by teaching science to teenagers. After earning her Ph.D., Hanne became a cancer researcher. At 22 she was an outlier in the scientific field in Norway—one of the first students in the country to focus on gene technology. She became obsessed by the question, "Why doesn't everyone love science as much as I do?" The answer became clearer once she began to see the dismal and dry curricula on offer. Hanne was struck by the gap between what was in the lab and what was communicated in coursework or the media.

Leaving the lab behind, Hanne began to work as a science writer and journalist, creating her own small company as a free-lancer. She drew from a history of small entrepreneurial ventures, such as a woodcutting business as a teen. Writing for a women's magazine, she was one of the only contributors with a scientific background, taking articles from such publications as *The Lancet* and explaining findings and implications in an easily digestible way. She honed her skills to engage people with science, and found communicating about science as exciting as the science. As an author, she interviewed scientists about why they loved their work, and what inspired them in the scientific field. Hanne began writing a column about fun science activities for a children's magazine. She was inspired by the dynamic science museums in New York and San Francisco, but felt they offered a static learning experience. Hanne began brewing the idea of a fluid and continuous science education that would become Forskerfabrikken. ♦

MERCHE GARCÍA VILLATORO

SPAIN

Citizen/Community Participation

Education Reform

Youth Development

Merche García Villatoro is bringing together key educational institutions to provide a holistic experience for children and youth beyond teaching formal skills, to include values such as empathy, democratic participation, and service. In doing this, Merche assists educational institutions, parents, and communities to understand that education goes far beyond the eight hours a day a child spends at school and involves them as key participants.

THE NEW IDEA

Merche is creating alliances with education-related entities—such as local governments, schools and high schools, parent organizations, and citizen organizations (COs)—to create comprehensive education models that include leisure time as a key component to children and youth education. Through a consensus building process that includes assessing needs and available programs, training volunteers and leaders, and creating a center for leisure time activities, she brings these components together to provide youth with a comprehensive education. Merche helps organizations put key competences, such as empathy, leadership, and citizen participation at the core of each activity. Additionally, Merche involves children and youth in planning and carrying out activities, thereby powerfully increasing the transmission of these competences.

In Spain (excluding the region of Catalonia) since there are very few entities using youth's leisure time as a values-building platform, Merche also uses these alliances to build locally managed youth centers—Esplais—which provide space and activities to train young people about the values needed to be successful in today's world. She has found, during her 24 years of experience working with youth, that leisure time is an ideal environment to develop children's and youth's sense of responsibility, citizenship, identity, integration, and other key concepts that cannot be fully transmitted in a formal school setting. Additionally, to allow access to as many children as possible, Merche applies a scaled pricing scheme to cover the costs for children from underprivileged backgrounds.

One of the differentiating factors in Merche's model is that all activities are aimed toward solving a social problem of the municipality where the center is located. Thus, each activity the participants propose or plan must include a way to improve the world around them. In doing this, young people acquire a deep sense of citizenship and empathy.

THE PROBLEM

With an average school drop out rate of 30 percent and a quickly increasing percentage of jobless youth (43.8 percent), there is a justified concern for the future of youth in Spain. To add to this concern, coinciding with most Western European countries, there has been a drop in young citizen participation, shown both in low rates of youth voter participation (i.e. lower than 40 percent for ages 18 to 25) as well as few youth-led COs. Many studies show that such high rates of school failure and the lack of interest in citizen participation are not only related, but point to a need to train children in value-based competences—not only skills—from a young age. In fact, the European Union recently established eight competences to be acquired through practice as a framework to rewrite national school curricula. These go beyond math and communication to include interpersonal, intercultural, social and civic competences, as well as critical learning and entrepreneurship. However, a static formal education system is unable to teach these competences, alleging that there is not enough time or qualified professionals to both instill competences and meet national curricular requirements in skills-based learning. Schools, and the time students spend in them, are proving to be insufficient to educate children in all the skills and competences necessary to be successful.

Merche is teaching young children valuable skills, such as empathy, to prepare them with a more holistic experience of learning beyond formal education.

Spain's transition from dictatorship to democracy was also a transition from an imposed set of religious values across society to avoiding imposing any particular system of belief. Thus, educators in public schools are generally uncomfortable correcting behavioral problems and are unsure how to instill good citizenship. Recently, the government created a compulsory school subject titled "Education for Citizenship" which attempted to cover this need, but has instead set the stage for a political battle between the governing and opposition party.

Another barrier to providing a comprehensive educational experience for children and youth is a general lack of coordination and networking among the key stakeholders involved in education. Ever changing curricular requirements from the central government have made teachers and school administrators resistant to external influences. Moreover, local governments are generally unfamiliar with their role to provide a fuller education in their local school systems. New laws and regulations at regional, national, and European levels are opening paths for collaboration but there are few taking up the task of coordinating such different groups toward a common goal.

> "Merche understands education as a common project in which each actor has a role to play and just needs the opportunity and the right tools to perform."
>
> —*Europa Press*

Although there are initiatives aimed to reach kids during leisure time, there are few examples that act as essential complements to formal education. On one hand, many leisure time initiatives are services designed to keep children entertained while their parents are unable to care for them. These are often expensive or when publicly funded, focused on providing a space for sports or other fun activities without much coordination with schools. The organizations that do offer fun value-based activities (e.g. Boy Scouts) tend to serve kids from fairly economically privileged families, which excludes a large amount of the population which have higher rates of school failure. Existing programs aimed to help children improve grades or find a job usually target youth older than 13, which is late to begin instilling values and competences in children.

THE STRATEGY

Merche is developing her model at a local level in different key municipalities in Spain, with the aim of enabling local values-based educational environments for kids to grow up in. To be successful, the model must be fully owned and managed by local stakeholders. She often refers to the saying: "It takes the whole village to educate a child," and, therefore has developed a very thorough and flexible process to involve key players in creating strong local alliances. To work in a given community she requires full commitment from the mayor, school and high school principals, representatives from parent organizations, and later, local COs.

The process of involving local entities to create and manage a coordinated Esplai consists of a series of steps that slowly convince each group to work together. As representatives from each group (i.e. a mayor, the local youth representative, a principal and a few key people in youth work) becomes a team and acquires a common vision, Merche helps them establish a base of values and, with this common thread in place, structures a series of activities and programs for youth based on these values. Finally, the group decides what kind of center is necessary to both coordinate these activities as well as offer a physical space for their youth. Additionally, Merche gives specific roles to each entity in the group, including participating from the beginning in financing the center they build. Generally, schools recruit students and faculty to plan and participate in activities, high schools recruit volunteers to assist in running the activities, local governments provide the space and one-third of the funding, and COs and parent organizations create a citizen-base to support the activities and spread the word.

After having interviewed close to 60 expert youth workers around the country in depth, identifying needs and key people, Merche is now working in three strategic regions—one has already established a center and is building teams in another seven. The process of involving representatives from local entities includes a series of steps beginning with a visit to a municipality where Esplai is already working. Generally, Merche demonstrates La Florida, the municipality where her center reaches over 900 children per year. She then offers local training courses for youth workers and volunteers and organizes a series of meetings to establish a plan and create a common project that includes what is already available and what needs to be done. Normally, after 9 months, the local alliance will have created a long-term plan and a temporary center to cover additional needs, co-funded by families, businesses, and local and regional governments.

In Merche's organization, older children often assist younger children, and the younger children have the opportunity to lead the older in a planned activity.

The methodology Merche uses throughout the activities is essential to create a learning environment in the communities where she works. The model consists of placing 10 key values or competences, as the common thread which underlies every activity. These include encouraging social inclusion and avoiding marginalization, entrepreneurial and leadership attitudes, space for democratic participation, local identity, caring for the environment, healthy habits, integrating people with disabilities, reconciling work and school with family time, preventing school failure and accessing the right to educational leisure time. Additionally, every 3 months there is a theme placed around activities, such as "gender equality" or "caring for the environment." To decide which activities to include and plan, youth workers propose ideas to the participants and volunteers who then choose either to do one of the activities or propose their own activities. Once the participants have decided what they would like to do for the trimester, the youth workers and volunteers help them prepare the activities by walking them through a pre-established planning tool, which includes general goals, specific goals, a budget, and so on. The participants are aware of the 10 key values and must include them in the activity planning, or change the activity. Throughout the process, children and youth learn to plan their own projects, and also deepen their understanding of the key competences while threading them through their projects. During and after the project, volunteers evaluate the progress and results with the participants in order to improve or change the course of the activity if it is not accomplishing what was originally proposed.

For example, a group of teenagers in the Canary Islands—while learning about the importance of recycling—planned a series of recycling parties to raise awareness and set an example of recycling. Their process included engaging their peers at local schools and high schools to present the project, involving faculty to help them understand what happens when one recycles, working with the local government to secure permits for events, and using their activity as a starting point for a recycling campaign. The result was a series of large events at a nearby beach with numerous stakeholders. The events not only raised recycling awareness, but perhaps more important, was the impact they had on the participants; recognized for their hard work and feeling valued for doing something useful for society.

Generally these centers divide children and youth into three groups: Ages 3 to 10, 11 to 14, and 15 to 17. Although some activities are limited to certain age groups, most of the activities mix different ages: The older help the younger or the younger lead the older in a planned activity. There are also activities that involve adults and the elderly; a central component of Esplai is to provide participants with a sense of belonging to a diverse community.

Merche's unique methodology not only leverages the participants' learning experience but also serves the community as a whole. Merche often says that a youth center, and any activity it does, must "face the neighborhood," meaning that everything must be structured to help others in the community. This is the key to the success of participants' growth, but also to citizen support of the center. As youth, often considered the problem, become the solution to different issues in the community, they gain neighbors trust and trust in Merche's work. In addition, Merche's methodology constantly involves parents and other family members in the activities, an essential aspect to consolidate the education processes inside homes as well.

After having worked in the region of Catalonia for many years, Merche has established a coalition reaching over 100 centers that operate under similar principles and serve 60 percent of youth. She has refined a working model to spread the essence of her work to the rest of Spain. Already Merche has created alliances in three regions around Spain (i.e. close to Toledo, Sevilla, and the Canary Islands), and one is managing its own center. Her goal is to have examples in 10 autonomous communities in the next five years and to build a network of Esplais that work regionally and nationally. Once this network is functioning, Merche believes that they will be able to slowly transform policies and mindsets to understand education as a process that includes leisure time as an essential learning space, as well as involve the whole community.

THE PERSON

Merche has been a key figure in youth and child development work in Spain for 24 years. She created her own leisure time education center, La Florida Esplai, in a suburb of Barcelona. Merche was one of the most active founders of Esplai Federation, which has held over 100 youth related entities in the region of Catalonia alone, and is the driving force behind its growth and spread. A key part of her work with the federation has consisted in finding the levers that have made some centers successful.

While working with youth and children, Merche spent a good amount of time spreading key programs to other centers belonging to the Federation in Catalonia, and working with partners in Spain. During these processes, Merche found that there seemed to be no specific initiative that leveraged leisure time to empower youth with empathy and citizenship. Surprised that no one seemed to have even attempted to take on this challenge, in 2007 Merche began meeting with experts in youth work throughout the 17 Spanish autonomous communities. After talking to nearly 60 experts and people working in the field, she concluded that no organizations were focusing specifically on preventing school and civic failure in children from a young age. Soon after, she put a plan together and began building a team to launch pilot models that applied the key principles she had discovered were successful in positively influencing and enabling youth.

In addition to her work on the ground, Merche has been involved in influencing regional and national policies and other key stakeholders concerning non-formal education. In addition to a brief stint establishing a youth policy with the government of her home city, she has presided over a series of regional and national boards and federations concerning youth and children. Merche's passion is to see a complete transformation in the national conception of education to include many more people and leisure time as essential pieces of a child's educational experience. ♦

LILY LAPENNA

UNITED KINGDOM

Access to Learning/Education

Non-formal Education

Youth Devleopment

Lily Lapenna created the first independent peer led youth banking program approved by the national banking regulatory body (Financial Services Authority—FSA) in England. In doing so, Lily is developing the next generation of financially literate and entrepreneurial citizens. In less than three years MyBnk has reached 20,000 young people across 57 partnering organizations.

THE NEW IDEA

Lily is fostering and educating a generation of young people who will become the enterprising and financially empowered citizens of the future. By working with young people, as young as nine-years-old, she is fundamentally changing the way they relate to finance, financial services, enterprise, and ultimately their attitudes toward achieving a fulfilled life.

At the core of Lily's approach is the insight that finance can be used not simply to encourage savings and thrift but also as an effective springboard for young people to launch new ventures. A related insight is that by giving young people the real experience of taking on the roles of various actors in the banking system, they sharpen their entrepreneurial skills and understand the entire ecosystem of creating and sustaining ventures.

The centerpiece of MyBnk's unique dual approach is the MyBnk-in-a-Box program. As a youth-focused and youth-led microfinance scheme, it emulates a real world lender-borrower scenario. Lily recognized that the principles behind microfinance have great power to shape a young person's future relationship with money and enterprise from the very earliest stages. By working with young people to create deep-seated habits, Lily will change their attitudes toward money in a powerful and holistic way, which will ultimately carry on into their adult lives. Through the banking scheme young people create and manage their own savings and take out small, interest-free loans to start their own ventures. They also assess the loan applications and manage the bank's finances, learning through experience about concepts such as interest, risk, ethical banking, and responsible lending.

By coupling microfinance inspired financial literacy with entrepreneurship Lily provides a unique learning experience that goes beyond learning about money, but also equips individuals to thrive in a fast-changing and dynamic workplace by learning financial concepts and tools to achieve their goals and unlock their entrepreneurial potential.

THE PROBLEM

In the United Kingdom the average personal debt of an adult is over £30,000 (US$46,500). Moreover, 91 percent of adults have never received any financial education. Against a social landscape where finance plays an increasingly important role, these statistics indicate a breakdown in the relationship between people and money, and young people are the most vulnerable, as many start their adult lives in debt.

Governments, citizen organizations (COs), and commercial banks are aware of the problem and have begun to take action to address it, albeit with notable shortcomings. The U.K. government has recently made an effort to build finance into school curriculum, but its delivery is static and abstract, as opposed to experiential and practical, and teachers do not feel confident or supported to teach it. Furthermore, pedagogical content is often supported by commercial banks, which arguably pursue a commercial agenda such as setting up teen bank accounts, thereby compromising the impartiality of the learning experience. Finally, current government policy overlooks the most vulnerable young people who are unable to attend school or trainings and are thus unable to access government programs that teach finance.

Solutions provided by COs, which rely on teacher buy-in and delivery, run into some of those same issues. Other approaches to financial literacy cater to teachers as opposed to young people and fail to maximize the learning experience for young people, as MyBnk has been able to achieve.

MyBnk teaches enthusiastic students at Rydens School.

THE STRATEGY

Lily describes MyBnk as born from a young person who wanted to take the reins of her future and enable other young people to do the same. Therefore, she began by listening to young people and understanding what aspects of money mattered to them and why. By taking the core principles of microfinance learned in Bangladesh, Lily's unique solution places her program at the intersection of microfinance and enterprise for young people. The program incrementally engages them, initially through a banking scheme, making them learn about money, then by linking savings to loans and teaching general concepts associated with money management, and finally by incentivizing them to start their own ventures. MyBnk engages young people in a unique process of self-discovery, ultimately unleashing their entrepreneurial potential.

Since its founding in 2007, MyBnk's youth advisory panel remains at the center of the program's decision-making process. MyBnk has grown into an organization of seven full-time staff, two consultants and five interns. It has ten branches across London and is working with 45 partner schools and other youth support organizations such as housing associations and the Scouts. Over

LEADING SOCIAL ENTREPRENEURS

20,000 young people from the ages of 9 to 25 have been exposed to one of the MyBnk projects, of which 10,000 have been directly involved with the microfinance scheme MyBnk-in-a-Box.

MyBnk aims to transform the way society relates to and uses financial services. To achieve this, Lily's approach focuses on intervening at an early age and reaching the largest possible number of young people. MyBnk's unique model is designed to deliver bottom-up, independent and holistic financial and enterprise education to children and young people from all walks of life within schools, youth organizations, and anywhere young people congregate.

This is the first ever FSA approved independent online and in-school banking scheme. Run throughout the year, the bank embeds finance and enterprise learning, with structured incentivized Savings and Loans Challenges.

At the heart of the model is the first ever, independent Financial Services Authority approved youth led banking scheme, designed to emulate a real bank that offers both savings and loans to its young customers. A group of young people is chosen to be the bank managers, their responsibility is to look after the savings, provide advice, authorize loans, and encourage the customers who take out loans to create their own enterprises. The bank is typically open during breaks and after school hours. As they are exposed to the basic concepts of personal finance i.e. the credit scoring system, interest rates, bank fees, and loan repayments, they develop an overall financial awareness that gives them the confidence to use finance in their favor. In addition to the MyBnk-in-a-Box scheme, the program is supported by a wide range of workshops and activities that are focused on enterprise and financial education, and which range from yearlong programs to shorter-term activities. Feedback from participants shows that the success of these activities is due to the fact that they are fun, accessible, stimulating, and adaptable. MyBnk also invites young people to question what banks do with their money and to consider ethical policies when shopping for a bank that suits their needs.

MyBnk programs are offered as an independent activity outside rigid lesson structures, during lunch breaks or after school hours, making them more appealing for participants. In order to de-couple financial education from a purely academic setting and reach the broadest possible cross-section of young people, MyBnk specifically reaches out to a variety of youth organizations other than schools. In doing so, MyBnk is capable of reaching the most vulnerable young people, For example, the Money Works program is designed to empower young people who are not in employment, education or training, and others provide teacher resource packages for structured learning programs around enterprise. This ensures that MyBnk is able to reach all young people, irrespective of background and ability.

Additionally, entrepreneurship education is weaved into everything MyBnk does. Lily understands that one of the many ramifications of a more financially literate person is increased confidence and enterprising ability. For this reason, MyBnk encourages young people to use their loans to set up their own ventures and think about how these may also have a positive impact on society. This is achieved through MyBnk's Ideas Generator Workshops and Business Battles initiatives, where young people work together to develop and pitch creative enterprise ideas. Through these mechanisms MyBnk uses microfinance as a tool to unlock potential and foster entrepreneurship. Furthermore, participatory education methods, such as enabling young people to run the bank, also incentivize entrepreneurship. Examples of the success of this approach include a car-washing service for teachers set up by a 14-year-old student who quickly repaid the loan and made a profit, and a school which after engaging with the program set up a record of 15 new businesses, including Fully Loaded which produced and delivered sandwiches to the school's teachers.

To further support its financial literacy work, and because it cares about innovation, MyBnk is developing a new product, Enterprise-in-a-Box, which enforces the delivery of their mission. This will provide young people with all the tools needed to create a social enterprise, giving them an extra boost to break the initial lack of ideas or the panic some face. MyBnk has also recently brought its central project online with the creation of the first online banking system for young people.

> "Empowering young people to build the knowledge, skills and confidence to manage their money effectively and make enterprising choices throughout their lives—these are the key drivers for MyBnk."
>
> —*Volans*

Key to Lily's success and penetration in the market has been the strong brand and reputation built around MyBnk, as well as a model that engages students and provides ongoing support to the teachers and adults involved, making it attractive for schools.

Part of Lily's spread strategy depends on working with local authorities to identify organizations that deal with vulnerable young people outside the education system. Local authorities also provide the funding to deliver the MyBnk program through their youth organizations, housing associations, and so on. Lily will expand the program by identifying more partner organizations in London and the South East region of England.

Lily has put considerable thought into a potential national franchising model, having mobilized MBAs to put together feasibility studies and to study other success stories such as that of Ashoka Fellow Jeroo Billimoria. She realizes that for the program to go national she will need to complete a stronger impact assessment piece and is already engaging with partners to identify the optimum framework to build her evidence base. One idea is to conduct a longitudinal study and analyze two control groups of young people at transitional moments of their lives. MyBnk is interested in understanding how their programs influence young people's choices throughout critical moments of their lives.

MyBnk is currently set up as a social enterprise with a diverse funding base that ranges from sales of services and programs to organizations working with young people, private donations, grants, corporate partnerships, and sponsorships. Lily has built MyBnk to be sustainable and remain relevant due to creative delivery programs, as well as how it raises funds. Lily's team is working toward a model that will increase the proportion of MyBnk's generated income to move away from traditional fundraising for core costs. On the other hand, Lily is very clear about offering the services to a wide range of young people and foresees that grant funding will still be needed for the maintenance of these specific programs.

THE PERSON

Lily comes from an Italian family but was raised in the U.K., where she moved with her family after her father was assigned to work in London. Despite the move, trips to Italy were very frequent and during these Lily spent a great deal of time with her family, particularly her grandfather, a respected and active member of the community in Abruzzo as well as Lily's great inspiration. From early on, Lily's grandfather instilled in her the values of altruism and doing good for others.

Lily remembers never being particularly academic and while she was in school she discovered a passion for theater, which she also describes as her coping strategy. During school she was always involved in setting up drama clubs, performing plays, and even managed to convince a traditional French Lycée to formalize its school theater company—a small revolution at the time.

Upon finishing school, Lily realized that she was not ready to throw herself into an acting career just yet. Instead, she felt compelled to spend time in Africa as a volunteer. After raising part of the funds for the trip, she spent nine months in Zimbabwe, where she received training in non-formal education and began to work at the local primary school. She describes this year as the most fulfilling year of her life, feeling for the first time a sense of real purpose. She stayed an extra year by which time it was clear to Lily that she wanted to spend her life serving others. Her newfound passion led her to Bangladesh, where she worked in the field with women and experienced yet a second insight. Lily witnessed how small loans were unleashing the potential of people by giving way to entrepreneurial ideas and ultimately acting as a powerful educational tool. The women were learning business skills, negotiation skills, finance and economy without even knowing it.

After spending time in Bangladesh and engaging in other humanitarian work, Lily returned to London with a number of ideas brewing. Her return to the U.K. also exposed her to new reality in Britain; one where she became aware of the serious social issues affecting young people like herself. As Lily's ideas matured, she realized that she wanted to marry some of the learning from Bangladesh with an issue that was very close to home: The lack of financial education for young people. Her idea was to use financial services as a practical learning tool to encourage young people to manage their finances and help the wider community. Lily plans to spread the program by identifying more partner organizations in London and England's South East region. When asked about the future, Lily sees herself fully engaged with MyBnk's growth and beams with excitement at both the possibilities and challenges ahead. ◆

© Darnel Lindor

CHANTAL MAINGUENÉ

FRANCE

Child Care

Citizen/Community Participation

Responding to the lack of adequate, affordable childcare solutions after school hours, Chantal Mainguené has created the first integrated, scalable afterschool program in France. By mobilizing latent resources in the community, Chantal is demonstrating how it is possible to offer a high-quality solution to low-income families, single parents, and parents who work outside of school hours.

THE NEW IDEA

Seeing single parents struggle to juggle their jobs, children's schedules, and bills, Chantal, a single parent herself, had a creative idea: Harnessing unused spaces at the bottom of housing projects, employing some of the 6,000 unemployed artists in Paris, and charging parents proportionally to their income, she created inimitable spaces in which children of diverse socioeconomic backgrounds could develop their creativity, empathy, and abilities through artistic activities. By tapping into the resources of her community, she developed Môm'artre, a unique comprehensive afterschool program.

Through Môm'artre, Chantal places a specific focus on supporting single mothers in keeping their job(s) or finding employment. Relieving these mothers from the constant stress of providing fulfilling environments for their children, Môm'artre also offers mothers space to work on their own situation and strengthen their ties within their community. Through toolkits, self-help groups, literacy classes, and targeted workshops, Chantal empowers them to manage the complexity of their lives and succeed as working mothers.

Chantal is now demonstrating the portability of her model through a franchise network and is stepping into every space where the right community resources are available. Already looking beyond 27 preselected locations in Paris, she is investigating densely populated suburban areas such as Saint-Ouen and Montreuil as well as exploring large cities across France.

THE PROBLEM

Elementary school classes in France finish at 4:30 pm and schools close at 6 pm at the latest. During this hour and a half after classes end and before children can return home, they are looked after, however, only routine activities are organized to pass the time. In addition, schools are closed on Wednesdays. In most cases, French school hours are a challenge to parents' working schedules.

Those who can afford it hire specialized afterschool care or babysitters, who ensure the logistics of bringing children to their various extracurricular activities such as sports, music, or arts. These activities take place outside the French school system, as the Ministry of Education is very resistant to mixing formal education with any optional activities and considers school grounds to be a sacred space for school learning. Even attempts from the Ministries of Sports and Youth to open schools at night and on weekends have repeatedly failed. Municipalities have also fallen short in creating acceptable afterschool alternatives, as the hours after 6 pm are overtime and caregiver unions lobby to protect the interests of their members; most being mothers themselves and wanting to take care of their own children.

Low-income families and single parents cannot afford extra childcare expenses, and their children walk home alone after 6 pm. They end up on the streets or home alone, which may contribute to poor school performance or delinquency. This problem is particularly acute in the case of singe parents (80 percent being mothers), which represent 35 percent of families in the Paris area and nearly 20 percent in the rest of France. Without a reliable childcare option, many fail to find or keep their jobs: Only 34 percent of single parents are unemployed. With on average lower levels of education and income, single parents are also less likely to send their children to extracurricular activities, which remain a privilege of the wealthy.

There are several employment programs and services designed for single parents, but they fail to reach their intended audience. Without adequate childcare options, which give priority to employed parents, single parents often skip the program's workshops and counseling sessions, which can endanger their access to benefits. This lose-lose situation often leaves single parents with low self-esteem, depressed, and isolated.

There are, however, many untapped resources in the community to support single parents and the multitude of challenges they face. For example, the bottom spaces of buildings are designated by law to be devoted to social projects. Another untapped resource is unemployed people. All across France, thousands of unemployed artists currently live on social aid and would love to share their skills and passion with children. In addition, many retirees would enjoy giving their time to volunteer, but lack the proper infrastructure and legal certificates to do so. Until now, there was no catalyst to creatively combine these resources into an adequate afterschool mechanism.

THE STRATEGY

Chantal designed Môm'artre to be the afterschool program of every child's dreams. At 4:30 pm, directly after school, volunteers go to four neighborhood elementary schools to pick up participating children and bring them to a space located within a few minutes distance. There, they first eat a healthy afternoon snack, before doing their homework with the help of volunteer retirees or with specific support if the teacher has recommended

it. As soon as they are finished with homework, children join arts workshops under the supervision of artists in residence and visiting artists. Here, they participate in creative group-projects that they present to their parents and community at the end of each trimester. After parents leave work, they can either take the children home or stay and work with their children on the projects. On weekends, activities are open to parents and children alike. The results are outstanding; teachers and parents agree that all 150 children registered at a Môm'artre center have developed outstanding creative and social skills, and demonstrate stronger empathy.

Môm'artre centers are rooted in their neighborhoods. During the day and late at night, they become community centers that host activities for the community and space for artists. As a result, centers become local pillars, attracting the volunteers and resources they need from the community.

> "The association offers day care for children six to eleven, adapted to the financial resources of families. The association has made artistic and cultural awakening the heart of its project."
>
> —Atelier-idf

Chantal has designed the service to be particularly accessible to low-income families and single parents, but to also be open to reflect true social diversity. For prices ranging from 10 cents to 7 EUR an hour, families are selected on criteria combining status, income, employment and working hours, transportation time, and number of children. In doing so, Chantal's centers represent the socioeconomic reality of the surrounding neighborhoods. Single mothers are given specialized support. Not only do their children benefit from the afterschool program (i.e. 35 percent of registered children are from single parent families), but toolkits are distributed to single mothers, and they are invited to join weekly self-help groups, in addition to having access to all the activities offered at the center. Chantal is progressively integrating partnerships with citizen organizations in order to provide employment workshops at Môm'artre centers, while children are engaged in other activities. Through this specialized support, she is creating a hub to empower single mothers.

Until 2008 Chantal juggled another job to raise her family. However, she is now devoted full-time to work on her project and developing a franchise of Môm'artre centers. Chantal has taken the lessons learned from her first center in the north of Paris and formalized a franchise model when opening her second center in the east of Paris, and a third opened at the end of 2010; three other projects are in preparation. She has identified 27 locations in Paris where her model could be readily implemented and is negotiating a framework agreement with those municipalities. She is also conducting feasibility studies in three suburbs. To make this possible, she has formed partnerships and obtained recognition from key local institutions. Chantal is working with the largest real estate developers to obtain adequate spaces in housing projects and exploring other ideas such as retirement homes and other vacant buildings. Chantal is combining funding from municipalities and private foundations and has become a reference model for the sustainability of other social enterprises in the region. Chantal is now lobbying to extend childcare allowances to the age of ten, as it currently ends at age five.

THE PERSON

During her childhood in Brittany, Chantal saw her father convert from market gardener to a humanist entrepreneur, heading a construction material company of over 100 people. She grew up convinced that anything is possible through hard work. Like her three brothers and sisters, Chantal moved to Paris, pursued management studies and married young. She embarked on a promising marketing career at a large insurance company, where she was in charge of launching new products. Soon after having two children, her husband abandoned her to move abroad, leaving her alone with their three-year-old and three-month-old daughters.

Chantal had to adjust and learn to juggle a managerial position with very young children in elementary school, with no adequate childcare program. She hired au pairs and tried to find childcare solutions in partnership with her neighbors, but soon realized that they were not sustainable solutions. Chantal grew tired and decided to take a sabbatical. For nine months she lived in Chile with her children and helped a friend set up her company. When Chantal returned to France, the idea of Môm'artre was born. After trying to resume her marketing career, she eventually realized that she was too obsessed with her idea, and with the support of her second husband, launched the first center in 2001. But with four children at home, Chantal took another job with Ashoka Fellow Danielle Desguées' organization, where she helped would-be entrepreneurs launch their ventures during the day. She worked on Môm'artre at night and on weekends, with the help of her new friend and Môm'artre director.

In 2008 Chantal continued to be impassioned about expanding Môm'artre. She decided to focus full-time on creating a franchise model, which she successfully accomplished with the launch of a second center in 2009. Recognized for her unique idea and entrepreneurial determination, the Municipality of Paris identified Môm'artre as the Parisian childcare solution at the European Childcare Symposium 2009, where Madrid was the first city to express interest in bringing Môm'artre to Spain. ♦

© Stefan Pucher

HEIDRUN MAYER

GERMANY

Early Childhood Development

Substance Abuse

Violence and Abuse

Heidrun Mayer's PAPILIO program teaches kindergarten children how to recognize and express emotions using a series of simple toys and lessons, greatly enhancing their resiliency, improving the pre-school environment and preparing them to become active learners and successful students. This emotional literacy program is spreading quickly through a social franchise model which trains educators and is transforming early childhood education practices throughout Germany.

THE NEW IDEA

Heidrun is changing the face of early childhood development in the education system through her newly developed, comprehensive approach to teach empathetic ethics and emotional literacy in German kindergartens. The program grew out of initial research from an international study on resilience factors for drug addiction and violence conducted at the Beta Institut, an Institute for Research and Development. Heidrun, who worked at the institute, recognized the broader potential of the research. Drawing from it, she developed the PAPILIO program to focus on building resilience factors in young children. She skillfully brought together a broad coalition, including scientists, 100 kindergarten teachers, over 700 children, 1,200 parents, as well as the world-famous puppetry of Augsburger Puppenkiste (i.e. Germany's most famous puppet theater), to develop the 2005 pilot program.

Papilio encourages socio-emotional competencies and reduces behavioral problems.

One of the central elements of the PAPILIO program is the use of storytelling to reach young children. Four puppets representing the emotions of anger, sadness, fear, and happiness are introduced to the children without any judgment that one is better than the others. To teach emotional literacy, Heidrun's model incorporates these figures, as well as other pedagogical tools in the form of a children's game, into the daily routine of the kindergarten classroom. The children learn to communicate their feelings, to overcome irritations about the behavior of other children and grown ups, and to empathize with others. These simple instruments have measurable long-term impact, such as reducing aggressive and violent behavior, improving the working environment of kindergarten teachers, as well as facilitating children's transition from kindergarten to school.

Today there are 137 PAPILIO trainers who have trained over 3,200 kindergarten teachers, reaching 58,000 children across Germany. To date, the Augsburger Puppenkiste has performed the PAPILIO story *Paula and the Trunk Pixies* in 122 cities, reaching nearly 30,000 children.

THE PROBLEM

Increasingly research on resilience in adolescents and adults is traced back to early childhood experiences. One key finding in studies of resilience is that children need to learn to speak about their own feelings and to communicate them to others in order to be able to empathize with their peers, which in turn is one of the key indicators for resilience against violence and even addiction. Some of the most important and formative times for young children are those years before entering school, from ages three to six. Heidrun recognizes this and works to incorporate all the important influencers on child development, including parents, families, other children, and teachers; who all have a critical role in helping children learn emotional literacy.

There are nearly 2.7 million children currently enrolled in kindergarten in Germany, which covers the ages from three to six. During these early years, children may deal with their emotions through defiance and anger, often resorting to aggressive and even violent behavior against others or themselves. Teachers and parents often feel overwhelmed by the aggression of young children, and may label this behavior as an illness, as seen by the increasing diagnosis of ADS/ADD and treating it with tranquilizers.

Nearly 200,000 teachers take care of these children in Germany. Although teachers must complete an apprenticeship of five years, the German education system lacks any unified training or certification standard or even continuing education requirements for kindergarten teachers and kindergartens. (In Germany's federal structure there is no single ministry of education or similar entity with responsibilities for national policy and standards.) In the current economic environment, kindergarten teachers are faced with worsening job conditions, characterized by declining teacher/student ratios and little support for continuing education and training. In a profession that is poorly paid, these conditions add to teachers' stress, and create a challenging environment for learning and education.

Papilio includes three intervention components: child intervention, kindergarten teacher intervention, and parent intervention.

THE STRATEGY

When Heidrun started to work with the independent research institute that was affiliated with the Betapharm pharmaceutical company, she discovered very interesting research for developing emotional literacy in kindergarteners on her desk. However, these ideas proved not to be practical enough to be implemented in kindergartens, nor were they fully informed by the latest research in the field. Through Heidrun's ability to translate the experience of the worlds of academic research and the practical worlds of kindergartens and children and parents, she took the seeds of the idea from the research and developed a comprehensive school-based program, PAPILIO (www.papilio.de).

The core elements of the program are stories and games that are implemented into the daily life of kindergartens. Each of these elements addresses different levels of human emotion, communication, and interaction. The story *Paula und die Kistenkobolde (Paula and the Trunk Pixies)* relays a narrative in which Paula is a little girl who plays with four puppets. The puppets represent the four most important emotions: Happiness, sadness, fear, and anger. Through the puppets, the children have the means to talk about how they feel—which becomes a regular part of their everyday preschool experience. Teachers and parents are taught the story and its uses so that it can also be incorporated into the child's daily routine at home.

Another element of the model includes the "mine-yours yours-ours" game, which is used to develop social skills and empathy. In this game, children learn to understand the importance of every person in a group, what a group actually means, and how groups interact. The children receive fun rewards to break down the complexity. A second element is the "toys are on holidays" game, where children learn to play without toys, discuss other possibilities of interaction and learn to participate in decision-making.

Heidrun's program was initially tested and evaluated over a two-year period in a group of 700 children, with very positive results. Among the findings—it led to less violent behavior among already aggressive children. Parents, teachers, and children all reported that the program produced a more friendly and respectful atmosphere.

> "Papilio is a program for kindergarten, it reduced or prevented the behavior problems and promotes basic social-emotional competencies."
>
> —Kindergarten Education Online Manual

In implementing the roll-out of the program, Heidrun established a network of partners in various German states, as no one national organization or institution could assist in its expansion. She has relied on diverse funders, ranging from state level ministries, health insurance companies, foundations, and companies such as BMW and the Robert Bosch Foundation. These partners ensure that the trainings do not become too expensive for kindergarten teachers.

Kindergarten teachers have been extremely receptive to the program and are helping to spread the concept. After a year of regular trainings, meetings, and psychological supervision, teacher's receive a certificate, which allows them to work in any kindergarten of the PAPILIO network. Additionally, kindergartens using the methodology receive a certificate and become official partners. There is a strong quality management system and rigorous evaluation in place. For example, regular meetings between PAPILIO trainers and teachers assure the quality of instruction and build a community between kindergartens, residential communities, and local companies.

Heidrun is now at an inflection point. Having developed the program inside the research institute, she has negotiated to take the program into a separate organization, PAPILIO, e.V., which she has founded to take the program to the next level. She laid the legal foundation for a spin-off company, negotiated the

new entities retention of the intellectual property, and has begun to attract major funding from new donors. Heidrun is also working to diversify her social franchise model to generate several income streams.

Heidrun is additionally working on expanding her program to children under three-years-old as well as to elementary schools (i.e. children aged six to eight). She is also in talks with other programs doing follow-up programs starting from there.

THE PERSON

Heidrun comes from a caring family. When her father had an accident when she was a teenager, the entire family had to stick even closer together and allocate duties in a new way. Through this experience, Heidrun had to take on responsibilities at a young age. Visiting her mother at her job in a daycare unit, Heidrun observed her work with small children early on. Even though her godmother wanted her to work in the pharmaceutical industry, Heidrun opted for an apprenticeship as a kindergarten teacher. Realizing that this apprenticeship did not equip her with enough knowledge to work with children the way she wanted, she studied social work with a focus on preschool and kindergarten.

One of Heidrun's first and crucial challenges was her work as a social worker in the city of Augsburg in the 1990s. Augsburg built homes for asylum-seekers, but had no strategy or plan to integrate them into the community. She established meeting places for asylum-seekers and the community, founded a job center, and even new kindergartens.

Searching for a new challenge, Heidrun opted to work for an academy, training kindergarten teachers. Through this work her entire perspective of kindergarten work changed, as she saw teachers overwhelmed by their work, without the means to cope with increasingly diverse groups of children, and increasing behavioral problems.

As an expert of skill-enhancement for adults, the Betapharm Research Institute recruited her to set up programs for its employees. This is where she found the "fruit basket" of PAPILIO, a basket of good ideas for kindergarten teachers developed by the local Rotary community. These ideas, however, were not suitable for implementation and not up to date with the latest standards of pedagogic insights. This is when Heidrun started to work with scientists to set out the new PAPILIO concept, and in the end, has successfully implemented it in several regions throughout Germany. ◆

ADITYA NATRAJ

INDIA

Access to Learning/ Education

Education Reform

The 2009 Right to Education Act makes free elementary education the right of every child between the ages of 6 to 14 years in India. This is a historic milestone for the country and implementation of this Act on the ground is a focal point of concern. Aditya Natraj envisages a major shift in education leadership, where the government school principal is perceived as a lever to affect large-scale change in a failing system.

THE NEW IDEA

Aditya's idea focuses on a deficient government school education system where over a 110 million school-age children are illiterate. He is using the lens of education leadership to focus on the school principal and their role which has thus been seen as an administrator—revisited with the aim of changing attitudes and perspectives.

By 2014, Natraj wants to demonstrate 1,000 schools which work.

Aditya is introducing a philosophy by which the principal must return to the concept of teaching, must be a teacher to provide effective leadership to the teaching-learning process, and must bring empathy into his engagement with staff, students, and the larger community.

For sustained impact, Aditya is also looking at ways by which the existing education infrastructure must support the school principal.

The increased engagement as an educator rather than a cog in the administration wheel, is returning the sense of dignity and respect the school principal has lost over time. The career graph of the school principal is getting revamped.

Aditya's intervention works at the level of the larger ecosystem by engaging with the government administrative machinery at village, cluster, block, and district, as well as state and central levels. The aim is to nurture and create a buy-in of his idea by all stakeholders and so evolve a system-wide solution.

THE PROBLEM

The quality of education remains a persistent problem in India's 700,000 plus public schools. The Assessment Survey Evaluation Research from 2008 for rural India reports that only 56 percent of fifth graders can read a second grade textbook in their mother-tongue; teacher absenteeism and low levels of teaching activity are visible problems; the gender divide is apparent as the number of girls in schools remains lower than the number of boys; and a small village government school in India may have under 50 percent attendance and low attendance, with high drop out rates being familiar issues.

> "Kaivalya Education Foundation's goal:
> train and equip principals to run schools better.
> Aditya Natraj wants to fix India's
> primary education system—
> one principal at a time."
>
> —*Business Outlook India*

The management of education on the ground is a frustrating experience for school principals and teaching staff. Many of them manage their own private schools on the side, having given up on the government school system and the children it is supposed to serve. The connection between teacher and students has broken down and when the teacher is physically present with students, invariably the rod rules. The principal hardly, if ever, steps into the classroom.

In these schools, the senior-most teachers are eligible to be the school principal after two days of administrative training. No other certification or course of education is required or provided. Thus, the education system and leadership is ill-prepared to engage with the children, their parents, and significant decision-makers in the community or with the government. The quality of education is dependant on a fractured system, with no coherent dialogue between the key players and no motivation to provide leadership direction.

In terms of the larger picture, one of the big missing pieces in government efforts appears to be in models of effective implementation that take into account the capacities, skills, motivation, and attitudes of the staff. By the time initiatives flow top down through the state, district, block, and cluster to a village school, the charge of engagement is lost. Teachers and principals are passive recipients of a job list and there is no question of a reverse flow of information to feed the system.

THE STRATEGY

Aditya's strategy adopts a multiple point approach. At the grassroots level, he and his team ensure the attentive and active participation of school principals in government schools through close interaction and deep engagement with them.

After spending months visiting over 15 universities and government training institutions in the U.S., U.K. and the Netherlands, Aditya also studied systems in Sweden, Singapore, Korea, Japan, China, and France.

Principals have to do more than accept an idea; they have to undergo training which is as per the in-service three-year Principal Leadership Development Program (PLDP) Aditya has designed. As a part of this training they have to be open to changing the ways in which they perceive their roles, including stepping into the classroom and teaching students. Many such elements designed to induce behavioral change and build empathy into the leadership process are at the core of the leadership training.

Support for the principals during the PLDP is provided through another initiative, the Gandhi Fellowships, which takes the form of a two-year placement for socially aware graduates from India's top colleges, in schools that are a part of Aditya's initiative. Selected graduates are mentored and trained to work with principals to help them turn their schools around in a symbiotic relationship where both parties stand to gain.

Aditya has been able to demonstrate results in Gujarat and Rajasthan, working with 200 principals in rural and urban government school environments. He is launching his program in tribal areas in Maharashtra. Aditya's spread strategy involves working closely with government machinery to gain government support and readiness to accept his model and implement it through existing infrastructure. Ensuring a good relationship with the government is a critical factor to achieve leverage in a large and unwieldy public school system. Aditya is in various stages of agreement, negotiation, and discussion with the central and state governments, education departments, State Sarva Shiksha Abhiyan offices and the State Institute of Educational Management and Training.

Aditya has extensively networked through collaborations and partnerships with technical organizations in the field of academic and education leadership, i.e. the Ravi Mathai Centre for Educational Innovation at Indian Institute of Management Ahmedabad, Bodh Shiksha Samiti, and Mercer Human Resource Consulting.

THE PERSON

Aditya grew up seeing the impact of education as well as the lack of it at close quarters. After a master's degree in economics, he studied Chartered Accountancy and Business Management. His family roots go back to rural India and in his lifetime he has witnessed the effect of a differential education, as some members of his family, including cousins, were deprived of an education due to poverty. Seeing the difference between careers and futures ensured by education and those hampered by the lack of it has been critical to his perspective.

Aditya worked in the corporate sector for well over a decade with multinational clients in India and the U.K. but found his calling in the development sector in the field of education. He joined a premier education nonprofit in Gujarat, Pratham, where he worked as Program Director for five years.

Aditya's idea took shape due to the strong impression left on him by the integrity and dynamism of one local school principal in India. His vision was to take forward what he saw by building an enabling system that could become a model for education leadership across government schools in India. These are the schools that cater to the poor and the marginalized who do not have access to optional educational opportunities available to the more privileged. Aditya aims to demonstrate how the public education system can be made to work by turning it around, reviving the faith of people in it, and thus opening a door to quality education for children that can help them escape poverty. ◆

BASTU REGE

INDIA

Access to Learning/Education

Education Reform

Employment/Labor

Bastu Rege is working with the informal labor force in the stone quarries of Maharashtra, a population estimated to be 3.5 to 5 million "identity-less" migrants who have been denied fundamental rights for decades. Bastu has set up a system of schools for the children of these workers called "Pashan Shala" i.e. quarry schools designed to serve this hard-to-reach group. The education model has grown from 119 children in 1997 to 92 schools in 2010 across 13 districts of Maharashtra. Pashan Shala is officially recognized as an innovative educational program under the Sarva Shiksha Abhiyan initiative of the Government of India, and a replicable model for children in similar circumstances across the country.

THE NEW IDEA

Bastu's organization, Santulan, uses a broad schools intervention through the Pashan Shala system of non-formal education in stone quarries as an entry point to improve the living conditions of the workers in this sector. After creating a climate of trust and acceptance in an extremely difficult environment, Bastu has been able to mobilize the community and bring them together to demand their rights.

Bastu meets with the stone quarry workers whose children attend his Pashan Shala.

The children of stone quarry workers are mostly found breaking stones in the quarries alongside their parents, some starting as young as four-years-old. At the first layer of intervention, his aim is to take these children out of the stone quarry work and to empower, enable, and support them through easy access to education.

As a direct consequence, changes are taking place in the world of stone quarry workers. Bastu has created a strategic window through which he infuses the process of change at multiple points. These changes are the most basic amenities which have been denied to workers for decades, including ration cards, access to public food distribution systems, health care services, insurance protection, voting registration, labor identity, housing, and sanitation, clean water, educational support and the dignity of life.

The stone quarry sector falls under the minor mining category and quarry ownership is dominated by those with strong links to political muscle power. Corruption is rampant, records are absent, (even in relevant government departments) and the administration has traditionally not shown the will to affect any positive changes in this sector. At the macro level of law and policy, advocacy and judicial action have been critical components of Santulan's work, resulting in visible change. Bastu is currently engaging the government on the issue of changing the legal status of stone quarries.

> "Founded by Rege in 1997, Santulan is an NGO which works for children, adolescents, youths, women and workers in stone quarries."
>
> —*Times of India*

THE PROBLEM

According to Santulan, in Maharashtra (2009 to 10) there were around 17,720 stone quarries and an equal number of crushing machines with approximately 20 to 30 lacs (2 to 3 million) direct and indirect workers in the quarry, ground-breaking, and crushing sector. This does not include workers who are employed for stone breaking at the road side, on hills or skilled stone cutters. The labor force in these stone quarries is a faceless, floating population of migrant workers caught in a trap of poverty, working in a sector where even minimum wages are not guaranteed. Amenities at the stone quarries are negligible; shelter comprises tiny shacks half the height of an average human being, drinking water is unavailable, health care facilities do not exist, and since quarries are located in remote areas, all forms of abuse and exploitation go unseen and unreported.

Individuals have no proof of identity or address and remain uncovered by government policy and schemes that would otherwise benefit them. Without ration cards or birth and death certificates, some estimate that there are as many as 5 million workers in the state of Maharashtra alone. The women and children employed in this sector are among the most deprived, with children suffering the maximum injustices. According to the International Labor Organization, worldwide estimates for 2006 were 126 million children (i.e. 1 in 12) between the ages of 5 and 17 have worked in the worst forms of child labor, such as stone quarrying. According to Anti-Slavery International's ILAB report of 2003, approximately 1 million children work in India's stone quarries.

Legally, stone quarrying is recognized as a hazardous industry, but stone quarry work falls into the category of small-scale and labor intensive in the unorganized sector. As a result, legal provisions and government policies and administration systems to protect and provide for workers in this sector are inadequate.

Other states across India also have a strong stone quarry sector with a similar floating population of migrant labor. Statistics and documentation of basic numbers for this sector are unavailable because of its status as "minor." Official reports on stone quarries do not include children on the workforce, show visual evidence of them, or have the correct number of quarries on paper, since illegal quarrying is rampant. Children working in stone quarries are a common sight. They are not contracted in any formal way; they are just there to help their parents. As a result, they receive nothing in the way of wages, rights, protection, or government education schemes.

THE STRATEGY

Bastu's strategy with the Pashan Shala innovation at its core uses education for liberation and to facilitate the process of community change. It took ten years, 1997 to 2007, to design, refine, implement, and achieve government recognition for the Pashan Shala model, thus bringing in the resources available to government schemes e.g. Sarva Shiksha Abhiyan to this target population. The Pashan Shala design has three levels of schooling for three age groups; otherwise older children looking after younger siblings would never be available to attend school. Across districts these schools have a year-round documents-free admission based on the "Saptrangi" (Rainbow card) system, so that moving between quarries does not disrupt their schooling. A residential school system for older children has also been integrated into the Pashan Shala scheme, with teachers recruited and trained from the community.

Education is a strategic rallying point to bring together the worker community, train, and lead efforts at self-advocacy, unionizing and increasing the space and visibility of stone quarry workers' issues on policy, legal, and administration platforms. As a part of the process of organizing the stone quarry workers, Bastu's organization is causing critical shifts in the system that has for decades denied them basic rights and human dignity. Beginning by working with a handful of children in 1997, the decade saw struggles and successes on many fronts to benefit over a 100,000 stone quarry workers. Not only has he opted to organize the workers into lobbying groups, Bastu has even organized children and young people, bringing them together through democratic and non-violent protest marches and training them in advocacy tools, teaching them their rights, and bringing forth declarations to present to the government.

Successful interventions have resulted in many "firsts" for this segment, including processing ration cards for some families, government insurance coverage, health programs, electricity and water, educational scholarships, free legal aid, self-help groups, and the creation of a worker's union and housing cooperatives.

Santulan has since worked on varied developmental, legal, and advocacy policy issues. They have determinedly incorporated legal battles when necessary, such as a drinking water issue that was finally resolved over a four-year period; after rallies, legal notices, and public interest litigation in the Mumbai High Court. Bastu is currently engaged in talks with the government for the creation of a Stone Quarry Workers Board and a Stone Quarry Workers Protection Act. This is a first attempt in India to evolve legal infrastructure that focuses specifically on this sector.

Bastu interacts with the Pashan Shala children in the classroom.

THE PERSON

Bastu grew up in rural India in a family of poor farmers and has experienced poverty and deprivation. This strengthened his determination to commit his life to the social development sector despite opposition from his father. Determined to complete his schooling and graduate, Bastu worked to put himself through a master's degree in social work to increase his own capacity as a development professional (1995). Less than a decade later, in the middle of his interventions with stone quarry workers, he felt the need to bring a legal perspective to his work and attained a law degree (2004).

Bastu's employment prior to setting up Santulan was with citizen organizations working on integrated development and capacity-building projects.

In 1997 Bastu began his work in the stone quarries motivated by an accident he witnessed which caused the death of a child by a stone crusher. His empathetic response to the extreme hardships faced by the children, women, and men at the stone quarries gained him the acceptance and trust of the workers, who came together to support the processes he initiated.

In the course of this work, Bastu and his associates have been at the receiving end of threats to their lives and property, with their vehicles, office, and data being torched and destroyed by criminal elements with high stakes in the quarrying and mining sectors. However, it is the support of the worker community that ensures the continuing progress of Santulan's work. ♦

SHAI RESHEF

ISRAEL

Access to Learning/Education

Capacity Building

Education Reform

Shai Reshef is the founder and president of the University of the People, the world's first tuition-free global online academic institution dedicated to the democratization of higher education. The institution was specifically created to serve poor, remote and disadvantaged populations. Shai introduced many innovations in setting up the project—including the use of Internet technology, peer-to-peer teaching methods, and a diverse network of students and volunteer faculty—to transform higher education from the privilege of "an elite" to a right of the disadvantaged in all parts of the world.

THE NEW IDEA

The Internet's great potential lies in its connectivity, and its ability to shrink the world, and to deliver goods, services, and information globally and nearly instantaneously. With increasing scale and spread has come a decreasing cost for Internet and wireless technologies. Shai took note of the Internet's growing reach and its relative affordability. Then, using his own academic and professional experiences as grist, he strung together a series of known but—together—revolutionary ideas to create his most daring, large-scale, and above all, practical, innovation yet: The world's first free online university.

Shai's University of the People (UoPeople) draws on a number of recent trends in e-learning and e-commerce and links them in a way not previously considered. The university is built around three pillars: (1) access to education as a human right (2) the freedom of information (3) the natural willingness of people to help one another. The first pillar is made clear in the university's mission statement: "Our fundamental belief is that all people, worldwide, should have the opportunity to change their lives and contribute to their communities, as well as understanding that the path to societal and individual prosperity is through education." The second pillar is manifested within the university through the use of open source software and other non-copyright materials such as curricula and lectures, while the third pillar is seen in the university's extensive use of professionals as volunteer teachers, best-practice peer-learning procedures, and current social networking systems.

Although the key ideas are not original in themselves, the combination of tuition-free university, education online, and peer-to-peer engagement is original. It took both resourcefulness

and courage to create this platform for providing tuition free educational services to people who could probably not access it otherwise. Shai connects those with a surplus of time and expertise to those with a dearth of educational opportunity and access to universities, and he does so via a sophisticated yet simple-to-use platform and on a global scale. The Open University is probably the most familiar long-standing model of distance mass learning which popularized higher education, which comes to mind when discussing the popularization and mass-dissemination of academia and academic knowledge. Yet despite its success in the West, and after more than fifty years of existence, its disadvantages are obvious: Not enough such universities were established in the developing countries, where such models are needed the most; these universities offer limited online possibilities; and, of course, enrolment in academic studies with them requires tuition fees.

Just like Ashoka Fellow Monica Vasconez of Ecuador, who created a virtual high school—an important and practical idea that is quite likely to spread well across the Andean region and the Spanish-speaking world—Shai's tuition free virtual university, which is now run in English, could well become a global and multilingual solution for a growing and pressing international need.

Shai with a group of Haitian students that attend University of the People.

THE PROBLEM

While it is true that more people have access to higher education than ever before, the accessibility and quality of education is vastly unequal. Huge populations remain underserved. Millions of bright, motivated students in Africa, Asia, and Latin America must compete for an increasingly insufficient number of college openings. A lucky few garner scholarships to institutions abroad, primarily in Western Europe and North America. For the majority, however, opportunities remain scarce. The limiting factors include: Distance from established universities; their fixed absorptive capacities; the costs of tuition, accommodation, and books and other materials; and courses which are sometimes of an unsatisfactory quality. At the same time, in the developed world, there are many professionals who have time and expertise to share, but few reasonable platforms upon which to do so. Shai's project addresses all of these issues.

In addition to these limiting factors, there are several logistical factors which limit opportunity. When conducted in real time, students and teachers are forced into a uniform mode of learning; they must all be physically present in the same room, digesting curricula at the same pace. In some cases, this is not only impractical but it is unfair to those students who learn at a different pace or who prefer a different mode of teaching. Shai's idea is to replace synchronic with diachronic learning schedules.

According to the United Nations Educational, Scientific and Cultural Organization (UNESCO), "The field of higher education is undergoing rapid and profound transformation: Demand is surging, providers are increasingly diverse and students are more mobile than ever. But national funding falls short of needs and stark inequalities remain at a time when higher education has a crucial role to play in addressing key social and economic challenges." With the number of college-age and college-eager students rapidly outpacing both material and human resources, there is a critical need for both more and smarter resources. Shai focuses on the latter, i.e. changing the means of delivery rather than funneling more funds into an established model.

Moreover, the idea of "addressing key social and economic challenges" can be seen more broadly as the creation of human and social capital, as well as an important contribution to democracy, civic engagement, and governability—that is, the development of a population of productive and responsible citizens who are in a position to assess and transform the societies they live in. Failure to achieve higher education is likely to mean, for a citizen, worse prospects of employment, and lower status economically with regard to health, and in quality of life in general. For a society, it can mean the waste of much human capital and much-needed opportunities for positive social and political change.

THE STRATEGY

Shai's strategy for the UoPeople can be broken down into three parts: Business (growth, accreditation, and legitimacy); administration (applications, staffing, and enrollment); and pedagogy (teaching methods, instructors, and curricula).

His business plan has been forming throughout his academic and professional life, but in early 2009 he began seeking public exposure. After an article was published in January in the *New York Times* about Shai and the UoPeople, thousands of people contacted him to report their excitement and potential involvement. Shai himself has taken his idea and operationalized it, using his own personal resources in delving into the details of marketing, registration, technology, coursework, teaching, administration, and accreditation.

In terms of growth strategies and middle- and long-term plans, the university accepted and enrolled 180 students for the September 2009 semester—the first semester of the university. The University has started to accept 100 new students per semester. In the future, the University plans to grow to reach a projection rate of 30 percent per term for approximately four years. At 10,000 students,

UoPeople will be financially sustainable. After that, the University will continue to grow and the surplus that results will be allocated toward reducing the processing fees incurred by applicants and students (minimal application and exam processing fees, which vary on a scale depending on the student's place of residence and the University grant provided).

> "Reshef unveiled University of the People, a tuition-free, online academic institution that aims to revolutionize higher education by making college-level studies accessible to students worldwide."
>
> —*Yale Law School*

Ranging from recent high school graduates to retirees, the first class at UoPeople is comprised of students from 49 countries spread across Asia, North America, South America, the Middle East, the former Soviet Union, Africa, and Europe. Within the first week, there were 5,200 total online postings (i.e. the method in which students correspond with each other and with their professors), with each student posting approximately 30 times. After the first few weeks of classes, students were surveyed for overall satisfaction. Their marks for UoPeople were 4.2 out of 5. Since this first survey, UoPeople has consistently received a 4.5 out of 5 satisfaction rating when surveying students at the start of each term.

In terms of how to's, UoPeople is currently based in California, with numerous staff and volunteers working around the world. Shai envisions global offices in developing countries. UoPeople has some paid staff and a large volunteer base including dedicated professors, working as the heads of the computer science, business and general studies departments.

An example of the opportunities that the model holds is evident in UoPeople's ground-breaking work in Haiti. Cognizant of Haiti's critical need, following 2010's devastating earthquake, UoPeople, with the support of the Clinton Global Initiative, committed to providing 250 local Haitian students with the opportunity to pursue higher education, tuition-free, in Haiti.

In order to enable Haitian students, many of whom do not have Internet access, to be able to undertake their studies, UoPeople seeks to establish Student Computer Centers, open to students who may study there for the duration of their degree. The Student Computer Centers are equipped with computers and high speed Internet connection, electricity, generators, furniture and security. Support staff manages the operation of the Centers.

The first Student Computer Center opened on November 18, 2010 in Thomassin, Port-au-Prince. The inaugural class consisted of 16 students, men and women ranging in age from 20 to 29. The students have access to the online courses at UoPeople at the Center which is operated by a local organization, the Haitian

Connection Network. Since 2010, a further two centers have opened and over 50 students from Haiti are currently studying with UoPeople.

With a convenient virtual address at www.UoPeople.org, UoPeople is available anywhere that a computer and Internet connection can be found. The students and professors who comprise UoPeople represent a diverse group, coming from both developing and developed countries around the world. Students apply online with a simple form (including 6 essays), but must submit hard copies of their high school diploma or equivalent GED certificate to the admissions office. Acceptance to the university is not automatic, but depends on several factors, including completion of two orientation classes and passing marks on an attendant exam. However, anyone who meets UoPeople's minimal standards is generally accepted. UoPeople strives to maintain its mission to democratize higher education, with the only reason students are not accepted currently (if meeting minimal standards) is because of capacity.

Shai with a student in Haiti.

The pedagogical idea behind the university is that studying within peer-to-peer communities is more motivating than just reading alone or listening to online lectures. Preliminary results indicate that students become more interested in their topics of study. They also develop confidence in their communication skills, general abilities and knowledge of their courses. Shai was inspired by the "learning by teaching" or "peer-to-peer teaching" methodology, which was developed over the last two decades by the online universities. This approach helps students to analyze, discuss and learn on a level they can relate to and understand. One advantage of using peer-to-peer teaching is that it puts the subjects into a context that is realistic and accessible.

The curriculum itself is developed by respected scholars and is overseen by instructors, who manage day-to-day coursework and questions, and act as a final reviewers on all coursework and grading. A community of educators, comprised of active and retired professors, master's students and other professionals,

participate in and supervise the assessment process. They will also develop ongoing procedures for curriculum evaluation and development. Currently, for the needs of the students, two programs are offered: Business Administration and Computer Science.

Finally, understanding the crucial need for ascertaining the quality of the University, some of Shai's heaviest costs so far have been on the licensure and accreditation processes. Since 2009 his efforts gained recognition from established academic and international institutions: he was approached by the Information Society Project at Yale University and is now the Project's partner in its digital education research program; Shai was also elected among the 100 most creative people in business in 2009 by *Fast Company* magazine. Additionally, the United Nations Secretaria has endorsed his plan, inviting him to become a High Profile member of its Global Alliance for Information and Communication Technologies and Development (GAID). In 2010, he was granted membership to the Clinton Global Initiative and was named the Ultimate Game Changer in Education by the *Huffington Post*. Over 3 million people voted in the Game Changer competition which honored leaders and visionaries in 12 different fields of action.

THE PERSON

Three strands have been present throughout Shai's life, gradually but tightly entwining over the course of time. First, there is his entrepreneurial nature, his pursuit of new ideas and hidden opportunities, his business sense, market acumen and excellent marketing skills. Second, there is his political activism, his urge to change society, to challenge conventional wisdom, and maybe to run a campaign or two. Finally, there is his passion for education. Shai is someone who not only seeks out learning for himself, but attempts to expand the educational sphere to encompass as many eager students as possible. These three strands—entrepreneurial, political, and educational—have woven together over the years to bring Shai to where he is today: The founder and president of the first free online university, the University of the People.

Shai studied political science at Tel Aviv University in the late 1970s while working as a carpenter with his father and as a research assistant at the university. He began his Ph.D. studies in political sociology at the University of Michigan, Ann Arbor, with this question: How do you change cultural and social values via education? Shai's findings led him in a new and surprising direction: He concluded that a prerequisite of social change is political change, especially legislation concerning economic incentives, safety nets, and legal protections.

Realizing that policy and social change go hand in hand, Shai returned to Israel in 1985, feeling the need to contribute to his own country's development. He joined the Israeli Movement for Citizens' Rights, and became the coordinator of the various branches of the movement. In addition, Shai became its director for special actions, organizing demonstrations, rallies, etc. He was also instrumental in developing and running an election campaign that resulted in four seats on the Jerusalem city council—the first time it had achieved municipal representation.

In 1989, Shai became the CEO of Kidum, a for-profit test prep company. His innovative, provocative marketing and operational approach positioned the company as the leader in its field.

In 1996, the large American learning company, Silvan, became Shai's partner in Kidum, the first time an American company had invested in an Israeli education business. At the same time, Shai was busy orchestrating an alliance with the British universities of Liverpool and Leeds. to create the first online university outside the United States. Initially called KIT Learning, this online venture represented the first collaboration between a private company and a university in order to deliver their core educational business. So far, over 2,000 students from 100 countries are registered.

In 2005, Kaplan, owned by *Washington Post*, offered to buy Shai's share of Kidum. The buyout afforded him time and funds to regroup, and to scan the horizon for the next "big thing"— which didn't take long to materialize. Cramster, an online study community, combined many of the elements that had initially drawn Shai to online education. Its model, developed by two young innovators, weds a for-profit company to a peer-to-peer learning model, social networking and open source technology. It was while involved with Cramster that the various strands of Shai's professional life began to converge. If online education broke down geographical barriers to educational access, Cramster's peer learning approach and open source innovations could break down financial ones. In 2009 Shai announced his latest initiative—and the one he hopes will have the greatest impact.

When asked about potential competition in this emerging field of free online education, Shai is generous: He believes that the more, the better. His main motivation is to give people solutions, and so transform society, rather than make money or dominate the market. Being first, of course, does have its advantages, and Shai seems perfectly placed to offer his wisdom and experience to new contenders. He knows that a university's quality is a function of three related factors: The number of people enrolled, its methods, and its experience, and he is committed to optimizing all three. Shai has been equally committed to optimizing another three elements in his own life, combining entrepreneurship, education, and political activism into the yeast that is catalyzing a major shift in global learning. ♦

FRANÇOIS TADDÉI

FRANCE

Access to Learning/Education

Education Reform

Higher Education

François Taddéi is breaking away from the elitist, top-down, and conservative model of the French education system that fails to prepare students to innovate and meet the complex challenges of a changing world. François is reinventing high school and college science education and laying the ground for a renewed, democratized knowledge industry. His integrated model marries a variety of disciplines, taps into private investments, and attracts the most motivated students who acquire, invent, and apply knowledge directly to groundbreaking projects. This research-based architecture is inspiring institutions across the French system and influencing education internationally.

THE NEW IDEA

Through an interdisciplinary, research-based and experiential approach, François is creating a university architecture that dramatically develops the creativity and empathy of students, accelerates cutting-edge innovation, and attracts private investment to public universities. His Frontiers of Life science program is a testing ground for new interdisciplinary frameworks at the undergraduate, master, and Ph.D. levels that foster collaborative spaces in which professors and students can co-construct knowledge. These educational frameworks then become references for any field of education and research.

To democratize participation in knowledge and ensure that all children have access to the same opportunities, François has applied his idea to create a research-based, interdisciplinary science summer camp and lab placement program for high school students in disadvantaged neighborhoods. This transformative experience empowers teenagers to become champions of science in their communities and places them on a track to academic and personal success. François is progressively expanding his approach to even younger groups through collaborations with educational institutions and is working toward an integrated primary and secondary school interdisciplinary program.

Convinced by the global need for democratic, participatory, interdisciplinary, and innovative education models, François is simultaneously building a global online platform that will make his framework of learning and research accessible to all students around the world. For instance, he is working with Chinese universities and Colombian officials to accelerate the spread of his approach.

THE PROBLEM

Like in most countries, the higher education system in France is facing immense challenges. On average, 40 percent of students who enter higher education institutions leave without a diploma. This can partly be explained by a demographic challenge: The number of university students has risen dramatically from 60,000 in 1938 to 2 million today. During that time, the higher education model has not changed significantly. France relies on a two-tier educational model. One tier is comprised of selective, elite colleges, which train tomorrows managers, higher civil servants, and engineers. These host 3 percent of students using 30 percent of the education budget. The second tier consists of public universities, which train researchers, teachers, and employees in all other fields of work.

François created the Interdisciplinary Research Center in Paris, which offers 3 programs integrated in the Liliane Bettencourt curriculum: A new undergraduate program, a Master's degree (Interdisciplinary Approaches to Life Sciences), and a doctoral school (Frontiers of Life).

Under France's education system, 97 percent of students go to universities, where education is free but also very hands-off.

There is no initial selection allowed in universities and many of the students are poorly oriented. Indeed, students need to choose a specialization straight out of high school. No public university offers interdisciplinary curricula, which limits opportunities for students to switch studies. In science, for example, students must focus on mathematics, chemistry, physics, or biology; they cannot combine the different subjects even if they are interrelated. Furthermore, lecturers still rely on chalk-and-talk rather than participatory pedagogies. This limits students' ability to think critically and does not give them any space to innovate.

This narrow focus is coupled with a lack of money invested in research, which explains why very few science students pursue research in France and prefer instead to conduct research in other European countries or the U.S. A postgraduate student in France earns an average of 25,000 EUR (US$35,325) a year, versus 50,000 EUR (US$70,650) in Switzerland. The 2007 reform opened universities to private funding for the first time, aiming at incentivizing innovation and competitiveness and making them more appealing and competitive at national and international levels. However, most professors and students have resisted this cultural change, while university administrations are not equipped to attract private funding.

The French higher education system in fact reproduces socioeconomic inequalities. Parents who have attended elite colleges and pursued intellectual careers encourage their children to pursue an elite education: In 65 percent of cases, the parents of elite students are top managers and executive leaders. On the contrary, in low-income groups, only one in ten high school students go to university and among them, most choose short, professional degrees. While science education in elite colleges is growing by 1 percent per year, it is dropping in universities. Thus, there exists a large, untapped pool of students who have the potential to bring tremendous energy and innovative ideas into the research field.

Science and research have not only been proven to be one of the key elements for competitiveness in any given nation, but they are also great experimental grounds that allow students to develop their creative, systemic, and critical thinking capacities, as well as their ability to collaborate. With the proper scientific background, anyone is able to look at a problem, set hypotheses, and imagine solutions. Given the space to experiment and the confidence that they can engineer solutions, these young people all have the potential to bring about critical changes in our societies.

THE STRATEGY

In François' approach to education, learning begins by questioning what we know and consists of progressively pushing the boundaries of our individual and collective knowledge. All through university, students of François' Interdisciplinary

CRI's main role is to promote new pedagogies to help creative students take initiatives and develop their research projects, with the help of mentors, research institutions, private companies, and foundations, such as the Bettencourt Foundation, which has supported many student-created activities.

Research Center (IRC) successively look at questions from both narrow and distant perspectives, from angles of biology, physics, chemistry, mathematics, history, and economics. They are led through a process of defining their own questions, collaborating, and looking for existing knowledge to build upon. Teaching is restricted to general frameworks and basic content that the students enrich and expand on through experiences and research.

This type of learning approach is radically new in the French system. Starting with his own experience as a researcher in biology and university professor, seeing the impact of his own interdisciplinary model on students' motivation and research outcomes, François combined some of the best practices he has seen abroad (particularly in the U.S.) and invented new ones to create the first Interdisciplinary Master's degree in 2005 around the Frontiers of Life, attracting some of the most brilliant students from France and abroad. These master's students grew to become so creative and cultivated with such radical ideas that François rapidly saw that they would not be able to find a graduate program to pursue their research. Therefore, he created his own version of a Ph.D. program, convincing 80 research laboratories throughout the region to host the students for their doctorate, while IRC became a platform for exchanges and collaboration between the students. François also realized that his student's creative ability and motivation was dramatically reduced during their undergraduate studies, as they were forced to focus on specific disciplines and fit into a mold. He hence decided to create the first interdisciplinary, research-based undergraduate program, which inaugurated in September 2011.

François' revolutionary approach is shaking the entire French higher education system by creating a track for public universities to compete with elite colleges. In the context of national reform, François has been able to convince the Minister of Research to allow for interdisciplinary, inter-laboratory research in the 2007 Law on Higher Education. Since then, and thanks to the precedent set by IRC, no less than a dozen interdisciplinary Ph.D. programs have been created in France, as well as a few master's programs.

François' approach is indeed overturning the resistance of universities thanks to its economic model: It is particularly compelling to private investors, whom universities desperately need. Supported by the largest foundation in France (Bettencourt Foundation), which is interested in investing in the future of French education, François has also convinced private businesses that his approach to research will bring about groundbreaking innovations

that they will benefit from. He has managed to attract sizable investments from companies like AXA and Orange. This is unheard of, as private companies tend to give to elite colleges and very rarely to public universities.

But François does not only want universities to be innovative, he also wants them to be truly accessible to all, especially to talented, motivated students from disadvantaged backgrounds. Targeting motivated high school students who would never have given themselves permission to pursue scientific studies, François launched the Science Academy in 2006 with his master's students. This unique program offers participation in research projects in some of the top labs in France, under the mentorship of researchers and students. The program also offers year-long mentoring and internship opportunities, as well as summer events, where participants present the results of their research to other high school students, who are then inspired to join. Every year, over 200 students participate, many whom go on to create science clubs in their high schools and pursue successful higher studies.

> "[François] was arguing for learning from biology, bacteria, symbiosis, history etc., a multidisciplinary way of rethinking education in our ever changing and globalizing civilization."
>
> —*Flickr*

Convinced that opportunities and creativity depend on experiences in the earliest years, François is now exploring the idea of experimenting with a complete educational model, starting in kindergarten all the way through high school, to be coupled with an interdisciplinary research lab on education and childhood development. He is also working with the largest science museum in France, which welcomes 700,000 children every year, to develop an experiential, hands-on program based on the same principles.

François sees the opportunity for his model to have a global impact. To host all the students of the twenty-first century, governments around the world would need to build one university per day and train professors every minute. Instead, François is creating an online platform for learners to collaborate, share, and experiment with his interdisciplinary model, with the potential to create the largest hub for research and innovation. He has convinced a leading Chinese university of the unique opportunity to provide its students with cutting edge knowledge and the highest innovation ability: Hundreds of Chinese students are currently engaged in developing the platform. François is also developing partnerships with the Colombian Ministry of Education, and the Grameen University.

THE PERSON

Born and raised in a very engaged Corsican family, in which relatives were either doctors in economics, professors of physics, or political and union leaders, François was demonstrating on the barricades of May 1968 at the age of one with his mother. Soon after, his father became the youngest university dean in France and was thereafter elected to Parliament. François was educated in a very liberal manner and never received a strict order growing up: He learned to only act based on his understanding and rational thinking. A natural born researcher, he loved playing games and notably became a chess champion.

Even though he was often bored in school, François brilliantly passed the entrance exams into France's top elite engineering school, Polytechnique, where he had the chance to be exposed to many disciplines and travel the world. During his military service, he served more time in jail than on the field, as he would not obey the orders with which he disagreed. After his studies, François decided to step off the beaten path and refused the higher civil servants career toward which he had been pushed. Instead, he embarked onto the unlikely path of research, which had always fascinated him. He chose biology because the discipline gave him the most space to innovate and experiment. François focused specifically on evolution biology and genetics, applying an innovative cross-disciplinary approach.

François' groundbreaking findings brought him many awards, which he systematically spent to engage other researchers and students into interdisciplinary, intergenerational research groups at INSERM, Paris Descartes University and five other labs around the Paris area. When François won the Bettencourt-Schueller Foundation Award for his work on bacterial evolution in 2003, he invested the monetary prize in laying the groundwork for an Interdisciplinary Research Center. Intrigued, the foundation staff thought he would fail. But he proved them wrong and later convinced them to support his successive endeavors. François also uses his networking capacity to navigate the highest decision-making at the ministerial levels and has successfully lobbied for the legal inclusion of interdisciplinary education in university programs.

In 2005, struck by the riots in the French suburbs, François decided that university education should be accessible to all and used some of his funding to create another citizen organization with his students. He launched the Science Academy, opening up the research world to marginalized youth and helping them develop their creativity and ambition. Ever since, François has strived to integrate his method at all education levels and is creatively partnering with museums, educational, and research institutions, to spread his vision. ♦

SENIOR FELLOWS & MEMBERS

Senior Fellows and Members are elected into the fellowship later in
the entrepreneur's life cycle than the Fellows introduced earlier in this volume.
They receive no stipend but are welcomed into the fellowship and greatly enrich it.

AICHA ECH-CHANNA

MOROCCO

Adult Education

Citizen/Community Participation

Gender Equity

Aicha Ech-Channa is changing societal perceptions of unwed mothers in Morocco, from a socially taboo group to an included and recognized population. By pushing forward legal reforms and developing the first program in Morocco to serve unwed mothers, Aicha is a national figure and advocate for all people.

THE NEW IDEA

Over the last quarter century, Aicha has been a tireless advocate for the social inclusion and equal treatment of unwed mothers. A pioneer of the field, Aicha has built a nationally relevant support model for unwed mothers and institutionalized legal reforms to support their recognition in society.

Aicha's Association Solidarité Féminine (ASF) has offered thousands of unwed mothers a shelter where they and their children are supported unconditionally. Approximately 100 women per year also participate in a three-year program, where they are offered psychological counseling and medical treatment as well as vocational programs which teach them new skills to become better prepared to enter the job market, thereby, gaining autonomy and a steady source of income. ASF also provides day care centers, both while women are preparing for future employment and after they have achieved it.

Beyond directly serving unwed mothers, Aicha has developed a dual strategy to increase paternal recognition and support for children born out of wedlock. She advocates for legal reform that requires fathers to take paternity tests, while she also mediates between mothers and fathers about the importance of parenting roles.

THE PROBLEM

Traditionally, in Islamic societies like Morocco, unmarried mothers are not supposed to exist. To become pregnant out of wedlock is not only regarded as extremely disrespectful to the community, but traditionally, it is illegal. These women and their families are condemned by Moroccan society and most families simply reject their unmarried daughters, leaving them to care for themselves and their children. Without the support of family members it is difficult for unmarried mothers to find a safe place to leave their children so that they can find work.

There is also little support given to unmarried women within the Moroccan medical system. If a woman goes to a maternity unit and

does not have a husband, the medical staff is obliged to call the police. The mother must appear before a judge who then generally rules that she is a prostitute since there is no other way to publicly acknowledge and recognize her pregnancy. In the past, women were sentenced to six months in jail, but because of the growing prison population, most unwed mothers now are simply fined. However, the US$50 to $100 fine is an exorbitant sum for most unwed mothers, and ironically, many have to work as prostitutes to pay the fine. This puts them at-risk of contracting sexually transmitted diseases, including AIDS. In this environment, the experience of mothering a child out of wedlock can shatter a woman's self-esteem and self-worth. In the end, many mothers become convinced that their babies are "children of shame" and thus treat them as such.

Because unwed mothers are often stigmatized, it is difficult to gather statistics that precisely describe the scale and severity of their social exile in the Maghreb and larger Arab World. However, the few official statistics and field studies in Arab countries indicate that the number of unwed mothers is on the rise. For example, in Casablanca alone, two of every five births are considered illegitimate. There are no official statistics for home births, abortions, or cases of infanticide. In Tunisia, statistics show that about 1,200 births occur out of legal wedlock every year. Many of these births are born out of common law marriages. A common law or *orfi* marriage is a simple contract drawn between the two partners and two witnesses. Historically, Islam's nomadic roots made this type of marriage ordinary, since there were long periods without access to a licensed marriage official. Today, this type of marriage is frequently used by young people to circumvent the prohibition of premarital sex, since a proper marriage requires a great deal of money. Due to the motivations behind common law marriages, often the couple keeps it a secret. This inevitably becomes a problem if the woman becomes pregnant. The man may decide to leave her rather than risk losing his honor, while the woman is left alone to establish his paternity and receive support for her child.

> "Aicha Ech-Channa, a Muslim Moroccan woman, has earned wide respect for her advocacy of human and civil rights for single mothers and their children."
>
> —*MoroccoBoard*

Due to the taboo nature of unwed pregnancies, as many as 600 to 900 Moroccan women secretly undergo abortions every year, according to a survey carried out by the Moroccan Family Association. The underground "clinics" that serve these women are frequently ill-equipped and staffed by poorly-trained doctors and nurses. These clinics represent a serious danger to the health of both the mother and the child. Women unable to afford an abortion, or who decide that the procedure conflicts too strongly with their personal beliefs and traditions, become society's scapegoats and are socially isolated; one response is the abandonment of out of wedlock children. In Morocco alone, over 5,000 children are abandoned each year.

THE STRATEGY

Aicha launched the Association for Women's Solidarity in 1985 to provide unwed mothers with the necessary skills to care for themselves and their children. Initially, she ran the center out of a basement in Casablanca, which served as a welcoming shelter and a place to be cared for, away from social stigma.

As Aicha realized the spectrum of support required beyond shelter, she grew the program, beginning with a daycare. The daycare, at the time, was supported by another organization that required the mothers to work in order to receive access to services. Aicha realized that it was very difficult for women to find work, given their social situation, and she resolved to address this issue. She convinced the National Union of Moroccan Women to donate a space where unwed mothers could cook various snacks and then built an infrastructure to resell these snacks as an income-generation strategy. Aicha was always preoccupied with ensuring that the women did not begin to expect handouts from her organization. To do this, initially ASF finances 75 percent of the costs related to their children's needs (i.e. medicine and food), but mothers are expected to pay the remaining expenses to learn how to be independent.

Aicha's organization offers single mothers and their children shelter and safety, while also receiving vocational training toward paid employment and increased independence.

From its humble beginnings, the association offers unwed mothers a three-year program whereby they become more independent each year. The central component is a vocational program where more than 50 women a year receive training in cooking, baking, sewing, and accounting. Program participants split their days between training programs and paid employment in the association's income-generating programs, including its three daycare centers and capacity-building institutes, two restaurants, four *kiosks* (small shops) and a *hammam* (fitness center and spa). The association also operates a support center, which receives about 600 visits a year and provides medical care. Over the last five years, 433 women were part of the association's intensive

rehabilitation programs and 3,000 received help and referrals at the job listing center.

Through their employment experiences women are encouraged to start and manage their own businesses. For example, when Aicha learned that a participant had made enough income to rent out her own kiosk, she decided to launch a program to rent kiosks to program graduates. Many women eventually buy and run them themselves and the three-year program is now designed to help them reach this goal. In the first year or two of the program, the entrepreneurs are trained as sales women and receive micro-loans to buy basic cooking materials or merchandise. Once these loans are paid back and they have grown a client base, ASF gives them the opportunity to rent the kiosks.

All along, Aicha knew that changing public opinion was as important as offering unwed mothers new opportunities and a place in society. The intense social stigma around single motherhood since 1985 has been subdued to the extent that Princess Lalla Salma, wife of Morocco's King Mohammed VI, visited ASF to witness the opening of the hammam in 2004, representing the start of a discourse among the royal family as well as a demonstration of the program's successful expansion. Aicha's work has received further legitimacy as a result of an aggressive communications strategy, which includes a strong media presence in local and international press, as well as on public television. Among the influential media channels she has chosen to target is Al Jazeera, which recently produced and aired a 45-minute interview in Arabic throughout the Middle East. Although many religious leaders have condemned Aicha to death as a result of this interview and many others, she is adamant that public education and transforming societal perceptions about unwed mothers are necessary tactics.

With support programs up and running as models for the rest of Moroccan society, Aicha turned her attention to changing public policy. The work of Aicha and other leaders in her field has helped to shape the evolution of government policy toward unwed mothers, most notably with the 2004 Family Law. Referred to as the *Mudawana* (family law), it was enacted after an active and open debate which engaged religious and secular bodies across Moroccan society. This new code, while still incomplete in addressing all challenges, was a progressive step toward bridging differences between the values and social benefits of religion and tradition, and the reality of changing norms. Extramarital sex is no longer a crime and paternity tests have become accepted as an appropriate way to hold fathers accountable for their children. (Morocco is the first Arab country to impose DNA tests.) The law also gives women the right to marry without the assent of a male legal guardian (i.e. customarily a father or brother) and the right to initiate divorce. In addition, it has abolished "repudiation," the practice by which a man could annul his marriage by a simple declaration of his will to do so.

Since the passing of the Mudawana, Aicha and her staff have begun to help women identify the fathers of their children. She has developed a dual strategy of advocating for legal reform to require fathers to take paternity tests while also mediating personally between unwed mothers and the fathers—to convince the men of the importance of recognizing their child and providing some form of support for the mother. Between August 2005 and August 2006, the association persuaded 60 men to take DNA tests, while only two DNA paternity tests were imposed by judges in an application of the new Mudawana code.

Association Solidarité Féminine has been influential in increasing women's rights with regard to marriage, paternity tests, and divorce.

Aicha's vision is for ASF to be a model in the Arab World. She will continue to communicate the success of her programs to change mentalities, break taboos and inspire other Arab groups to tackle the issue of unwed mothers. Aicha also wants sexual education in formal education to become the norm, a practice she believes is correlated to the prominence of unwed mothers. She is also working to increase the financial sustainability of the model developed by ASF, which is 50 percent self-financed through its income-generation programs and has been independently replicated by numerous associations in Morocco.

THE PERSON

Throughout her childhood, Aicha learned the importance of social networks and solidarity. At the age of three, her father passed away, and a few months later she also lost her younger sister. Being raised by a single mother was not well-accepted in Moroccan society, but thanks to the help of some of her father's friends, she was able to study in a distinguished French primary school, which her mother would not have been able to afford. Aicha's family also received considerable support from social workers.

In 1953 King Mohammed V was exiled to France, and Pacha El Glaoui began governing the city of Marrakesh, where Aicha grew up. This was a pivotal event in her life as it led her stepfather (her mother had remarried) to decide, as decreed by the Pacha government, that it was not appropriate for girls to study. He also forced her to start wearing a white headscarf. Aicha's mother, in

disagreement, daringly sent her off on a bus, alone, to live with her aunt in Casablanca to pursue her high school studies. Aicha's mother eventually decided to take a second risky decision by divorcing her husband a few years later and moving to Casablanca to be reunited with her.

At 15, Aicha was determined to move out of her aunt's tiny apartment with her mother. She became the breadwinner of the household at the age of 16 when she took up a job as a prestigious doctor's social-medical assistant. Aicha's co-workers quickly noticed that she was very competent and particularly valued her ability to listen and to empathize with others. One of her social worker colleagues insisted that she take the exam to become a nurse, and ensured her that she would take care of the school fees if she passed. Eventually, Aicha and her colleague convinced her university to give her a job, in addition to her scholarship.

While completing her studies, Aicha began to work for the Ministry of Public Health, delivering hygienic education workshops. She worked in many orphanages and began to notice the issue of abandoned children. Aicha's boss at the Ministry of Public Health had also taught her considerably about the taboo topic of planned parenting. Aicha became involved with a youth group and resolved to make family planning education one of their main goals.

Encouraged by another colleague, Aicha later decided to become a social worker. During that time, she witnessed unwed mothers in need of government assistance get turned away on a daily basis. She heard stories from these women of sexual violence, extreme physical and emotional suffering, and utter despair. Aicha resolved to dedicate her life to changing the social situation of unwed Moroccan mothers, soon after, she founded ASF.

Over 25 years, Aicha has faced many tests and challenges, including a government official decrying she be stoned, and in 2000, the threat of assassination for encouraging "sinful" behavior. The same year, King Mohammed VI gave her a medal and financial support. Despite all of this, Aicha has drastically changed society's perception of unwed mothers and their children, drawing strength from the humanity of the women and children with whom she works.

Aicha founded and served as president of a women's solidarity organization and is currently a prominent member of the Moroccan League for Childhood Protection. Her achievements have garnered much attention in the local, national, and international media; Aicha is the recipient of many prestigious awards, including the Opus Prize (2009). ◆

HILDEGARD SCHOOß

GERMANY

Child Care

Housing

Hildegard Schooß recreates community-based forms of care, volunteering and entrepreneurship in uniquely designed multigenerational houses. With hundreds of such centers across Germany, her program is a powerful antidote to individualism, isolation and exclusion that often characterize urban life by providing mothers, children, and the elderly with a vital space for community members to incubate new programs, services and businesses to serve their needs.

THE NEW IDEA

Hildegard's multigenerational houses challenge the marginalization of excluded groups by reintroducing venues that foster neighborhood relations. By adapting the African proverb, "It takes a village to raise a child," to industrialized societies, caring for children, the elderly, the sick, and the handicapped are collective and mutual responsibilities. Having been described as "public living rooms," the centers allow the elderly, women, and children to claim a public space. The multigenerational houses are managed and operated by their members, provide peer-to-peer contact and exchange on a drop-in basis. Basic social and family services are also made available, in addition to support for entrepreneurial activities and trainings by providing workspace, consultancy, and skill-building activities.

Multigenerational houses impact communities on several levels. They influence the quality of parenting and child-raising, as well as the quality of family relations. They also revitalize neighborhoods, bring new family services and facilities to the communities, and provide a platform for grassroots players to be involved in local governance. The multigenerational housing movement, which has been led by Hildegard since the 1980s, has contributed to the transformation of social institutions and changes in legislation. It has created a paradigm shift in the field of social work and social welfare: Mothers and families are no longer seen as mere clients of professional programs, but as active participants in local planning and decision-making.

THE PROBLEM

One of the consequences of the growth of the welfare state in Germany has been the segregation of beneficiaries into specialized welfare structures, versus integrating them into community life. As integrating institutions, such as extended families, religious institutions, clubs and associations play less of a role in bringing communities together, often professional activities do, for those economically inactive.

Family and community structures in contemporary societies are disintegrating. The economic demands for increasingly mobile workforces challenge the ability for families to serve as the primary social support system for their members. Frequent changes of residency and long distances between family members destroy established intergenerational support structures within families, leaving mothers, children, and the elderly on their own. Additionally, traditional neighborly help and solidarity, formerly existing in village communities, has been lost through the trends of urbanization and individualization common of modern lifestyles. Mothers, children, and the elderly too often find themselves marginalized and isolated from public spheres, deprived of participation and decision-making in public life.

New ways of fostering intergenerational community are needed as the family unit is shrinking in Germany and various groups are becoming more isolated and excluded from public life. Children experience limited access to peer contacts and to public spaces, due to the increase of single child families and better access to technology (i.e. computers and video gaming). Young mothers can undergo a loss of self-confidence when raising children, a task which demands different daily rhythms and priorities than those constituted by public norms and the labor market. Elderly people, as they leave the work force and become less mobile, often feel needless, lonely, and disconnected with the world. These communities need a place where they can learn to establish confidence in social contacts and relationships and develop trust in building democracy from the bottom up. Intergenerational houses provide such a space.

> "Hildegard was able to extend over twenty years of business center services for various groups from birth until a very advanced age."
>
> —*Sit Materskych Center*

THE STRATEGY

Intergenerational houses grew from Hildegard's own experience as a young mother without a solid social network. Realizing that it does indeed take a village to raise a child, Hildegard opened the first multigenerational center in 1980. Soon after, with support from academic researchers, she wrote up the concept of the centers, initially coined "mother centers." In 1981 Hildegard co-founded two more mother centers in Munich and Darmstadt and the National Family Ministry began funding the first three centers.

Since 2003 Hildegard has worked with the Family Minister of Lower Saxony to further develop the concept of mother centers, expand the number of new centers, and develop evaluation tools. When the minister became Federal Family Minister in 2005, Hildegard helped to introduce a national initiative, which spread the concept of "multigenerational houses" all over Germany. Today, over 100,000 Germans are actively contributing their skills to the community in 500 centers throughout the country. Today, that first center, based in Salzgitter has grown to 100+ members with more than 600 visits per day. It was recognized by the world exhibition (EXPO) in the year 2000 as an innovative concept for creating private-public space.

Hildegard's multigenerational houses are managed and operated by their members, provide peer-to-peer contact, and exchange on a drop-in basis.

Multigenerational houses differ from the traditional approach to social services in which an expert solves a problem for the client. The mother center philosophy turns this approach upside down: Everyone is good at something, so together the community has every skill it needs to thrive. Multigenerational houses are self-managed, community-driven organizations that facilitate service exchange based on reciprocity. Individuals, particularly the isolated and excluded, encounter a level of support and engagement—through volunteering, trainings, and personal connections—that German social services have failed to provide. In multigenerational houses everyday life competencies are focused, consolidated, and channeled into community leadership, regarding, i.e. public childcare provisions, quality playgrounds, safer traffic conditions, or family friendly urban planning, and housing. They offer a platform for the issues of parenting and for community interest to be linked to national campaigns and policies, to achieve a family and child-friendly society and environment.

Multigenerational houses reintroduce village structures within a modern city as they reunite private life with community bonds, bringing citizens into open houses and under the same room. The core of every house is a daily drop-in coffee shop with childcare for mothers and support for the elderly. The center offers infrastructure for micro entrepreneurial activity, involves projects that help lower expenses for families, and supports families with their everyday chores, as well as in times of crises. They include services such as a second hand shop, hair cutting, lunch meals, a toy library, sewing classes, and repair services. There are also trainings to help expand skills to re-enter the labor market, such as language courses and computer and job retraining courses. Holistic health services are also part of the daily program. Within the setting of multigenerational houses a range of family services have been developed, i.e. pick-up and escort services for children and elderly, janitor and maintenance services, and meal and shopping services. Housing these services under one roof creates an animated meeting point in the neighborhood for all generations. It places child and eldercare services in the context of genuine neighborhood relationships and networks.

In its early years, a key strategy responsible for the concept's growth was to publicize the centers through the members themselves. A scientific research team facilitated a process whereby the women involved in the first three mother centers wrote down their personal stories, relating how the centers had helped them. The book was later translated into many languages. When other mothers read the accounts, they felt inspired and encouraged to replicate the idea of mother centers for themselves and their communities. The book conveyed two basic messages to grassroots women's groups across Germany and beyond: "This is it!" and "We can do that, too!" The mother center movement is an outstanding example of scaling up and the transfer of grassroots best practices, using a storytelling format and peer learning strategies.

Multigenerational houses have become hubs for broader community engagement. Centers and their members are involved in various consultations, round-tables and planning boards, with regional and local government and municipal departments. They are seen as an important linkage to the community and are invited to give their views on a wide-range of issues. The houses are central players in a partnership network with other stakeholders in society: Pediatricians, psychologists, and family counselors often cooperate with the houses and some professionals see the centers as an important support system to reintegrate clients into the community. Co-operations with local unemployment departments and various educational institutions are further partners.

Today there are over 850 multigenerational houses worldwide, across four continents and in over 20 countries. The houses have primarily been transferred and replicated by the migration and remigration movements, particularly throughout Central Europe. New houses are developed by refugees who return to their countries of origin and want to spread the valuable community. Furthermore, the Mother Center International Network (co-founded by Hildegard in 1993) facilitates the international transfer of the houses by providing start-up support, consultation, training, and peer exchanges between centers. A further driver behind the transfer and marketing of the concept were the series of trainings and partner dialogues produced between 1990 and 2001 by the Grassroots Women's International Academies.

The successful replication of multigenerational houses has solicited the attention of governments around the world. As such, the houses have become an integral part of federal programs, such as in Germany, and are being officially endorsed by governments, such as the Czech Republic. A trend toward public finance of the centers has emerged and now is the main source of funding for the centers. As multigenerational houses grew in number and size, municipalities saw the value of the services and the community to a well-functioning society, not to mention the cost savings benefits to government welfare funding. The concept of multigenerational houses as self-managed spaces to meet the needs of society—and of mothers and families as active participants in local planning— is increasingly taking hold as government partnerships expand and more centers spread internationally.

THE PERSON

Hildegard grew up in a large family as one of 11 children. Her father, an entrepreneur, gave her much room for proactive individual initiative. Struggling with the mainstream school system as a child, Hildegard looked for alternative ways to express her creativity. After deciding to end her higher education Hildegard applied at her father's butchery, which she took over at only 20. After getting married to a manager and moving away from home she found herself isolated and without any social contact.

In 1980 Hildegard became a young mother while living far away from her extended family, in a new city. She knew that she did not want to live the typical life of a mother in a German city, alone at home with their children and isolated from society. Hildegard dreamt of a private-public space where everyone could contribute his/her talents in the form of support similar to an old village community just within the city. Acting on her dream, Hildegard rented a room and opened up the first mother center in Germany which acted like a public living room space. It quickly became the place for people of all generations to go to find interaction and assistance.

Today Hildegard is perceived as "Mother" of the mother center movement. To solidify the movement, she founded an umbrella organization and a service agency to lobby and support the existing multigenerational houses.

Today Hildegard works with many organizations as a consultant, mentor, mastermind, and thought leader of the mother center concept. ◆

MARIE TRELLU KANE

FRANCE

Citizen/Community Participation

Over the last 15 years, Marie Trellu Kane has designed a model to make citizen engagement a normal step in young peoples' lives and has thus created the infrastructure to help them become social changemakers. As thousands of young people continue to dedicate periods of their lives full-time to social and environmental organizations, Marie now positions her association as a genuine experimental lab dedicated to invent new ways for youth to commit to society and to create the tools for a new generation of changemakers.

THE NEW IDEA

Through Unis-Cité, Marie is the first to encourage and facilitate citizen engagement for all those between 18 and 25-years-old. Convinced that each individual has a role to play in solving social and environmental issues, she has removed financial and cultural barriers by designing and implementing a highly-valued volunteer civic service across France. On a volunteer basis, her programs have allowed thousands of young people to fulfil six to nine month missions within a partner network of 600 social organizations, and thus develop young peoples' empathy, open-mindedness, and leadership skills. To date, 115,000 persons have directly benefited from the work of the volunteers, and the success of her initiative convinced the French government to create the first National Civic Service Agency to scale-up Marie's model and foster a citizenship spirit among new generations of young people. Set up in May 2010, this agency officially recognizes and finances social engagement. It works hand in hand with Unis-Cité to actively support and engage at least one youth in ten, in each age group, to become an ambassador of change.

While developing the civic service, Marie has contributed to changing the entire social infrastructure to ensure these new changemakers reinforce the social impact of existing organizations. Efficiency-oriented, Marie supports partner organizations, which welcome young people in defining needs and objectives, structuring volunteering missions and dealing with management, integration, and training of the teams. By doing so, she ensures that on the one hand, young people accomplish useful and fulfilling missions and on the other hand, welcoming organizations benefit from professional, creative, and intrapreneurial volunteers.

Marie has thus successfully created all the conditions to further youth citizenship and promote youth social entrepreneurship. Benefiting from a large database of committed youth, powerful support from public and private partners, and national recognition, she now aims at reaching a second tipping point where young people not only understand and participate in social issues but also create their own solutions by starting their own social ventures. Cross-fertilization with existing programs—e.g. Ashoka Youth Venture—is a key component of Marie's strategy to set up new programs. Marie also works in Africa where she has already brought her expertise to build civic service in Burkina Faso. Observing the lack of existing social organizations there, she will focus directly on social entrepreneurship and partner with local networks to accelerate the implementation of her initiative.

Unis-Cité engages young people in improving their community, through projects developed in partnership with local solidarity associations, homes for the elderly, municipal services, schools, and leading citizen groups.

THE PROBLEM

Over the past decades, levels of citizenship engagement, individual responsibility and political engagement in France have been decreasing among younger populations: Since 1980 the abstention rate has risen (i.e. it was 70 percent for the ages of 18 to 24 in 2002) and volunteering activities have decreased by 15 percent since the 1980s. These figures underlie the lack of social opportunities, as well as the financial difficulties for youth to engage themselves in society. Facing the non-recognition of citizen engagement by public institutions, universities and employers, only 15 percent of young people become engaged in a social or environmental cause, whereas 70 percent declare they would like to. In the background, this retreat in citizen commitment is correlated with deeper issues like youth unemployment or deterioration of social diversity due to the ending of military service.

At the same time, citizen activities such as volunteering are still sources of economic benefit and creativity for the citizen sector. Time spent volunteering in France equals 820,000 jobs, 13 billion working hours or 16B EUR a year (National Statistics Agency, 2004). Besides, this workforce is an incredible source of innovation and new action for citizen organizations (COs). However, it is a well-known challenge that the management of the volunteer workforce requires human resources that organizations usually do not have. Moreover, volunteers often commit themselves without necessarily having the needed competencies to do the work presented to them. Also, the gap between old-school social organizations and young people's spirits does not facilitate the matching between needs and available will.

Culturally, a few young people consider they are part of the solutions, but are not used to creating their own projects. In France, starting initiatives and taking risks are often not recognized and valued—surveys show that half of young people in France dream of becoming public officers in order to benefit from job security. In a world that is changing rapidly, with pressing social issues, there is an urgent need to develop a new generation of changemakers; citizens that can handle social and environmental issues and find creative ways to solve them. This will be achieved by returning a sense of citizen engagement to youth and developing their entrepreneurial spirit.

THE STRATEGY

Over the years, Marie has progressively abolished all barriers to youth citizen engagement. She uses three strategies to promote youth civic service throughout France. First, she has formulated a unique program and a legal framework to facilitate hands-on civic engagement experiences to youth; second, she supports COs to better manage volunteers and work efficiently with this new generation of changemakers; and third, she gathers players in the field of youth civic engagement to develop youth social entrepreneurship. Together, these three approaches have created the foundations for an enabling and supportive environment for youth civic engagement in France.

Marie has designed a smart program highly valuable for volunteers in terms of developing professional skills as well as personal qualities. Organized in teams of eight people, volunteers engage in four to five different missions at diverse organizations over the course of their service year, and have the opportunity to learn about a range of social issues (e.g. exclusion, discrimination, poverty, intergenerational solidarity, and the environment). By using various means of communication in universities, but also in local citizen and sport associations in underserved areas, Marie ensures that teams mix young people from diverse backgrounds (i.e. privileged and underprivileged, students, low-qualified workers, and minorities). Beyond their work in the field, volunteers dedicate one day a week to group sessions where they reinforce their knowledge on social stakes, share their experiences and work on their professional project (i.e. they set objectives, conduct individual follow-up and search for potential employees after their year of service). The results are outstanding: 94 percent of unemployed volunteers find a job at the end of their service year, or go back to their studies.

> "[Marie] has developed good practice in management, governance and transparency, and created an incubator and social philanthropic seed money "for social entrepreneurs."
>
> —*ESSEC Business School Alumni*

Besides creating opportunities for young volunteers, Marie has also constructed the financial and legal framework for the official recognition of volunteers by the government. This enables young people to commit themselves for almost a year as volunteers in COs, and be recognized for their work. During the first six years of Unis-Cité's existence, Marie successfully financed all of her programs relying on private funds, brightly engaging the staff of companies to coach young people, and offering volunteering days as counterparts. In 2000 Marie made a substantial step by obtaining the legal recognition of "volunteer" status. This status makes it possible for youth to receive a financial compensation paid in part by the government as well as access to benefits—mainly health insurance coverage and a contribution to a public retirement pension scheme. In 2010, the creation of the National Civic Service Agency reinforced the financial and legal framework for volunteers by simplifying the administrative procedures to become a volunteer and by giving volunteers the equivalent of university credits for their work. Moreover, the government has budgeted 500M EUR (US$710M) to encourage and fund a critical mass of young people engaged in citizen actions.

Unis-Cité organizes outings for isolated senior citizens in retirement homes with theatrical productions, exchanges between a retirement home and a day care, and mural painting workshops.

While better positioning young people in COs or social departments of local public institutions, Marie realized that the majority of these institutions were not structured to welcome and manage volunteers. To overcome that situation, she dedicates a part of her resources to support these organizations in defining interesting missions and sharing the management of the volunteer teams. Consequently, 77 percent of her partners think that the volunteers' work is useful and efficient. As the number of volunteers will soon be sufficiently increased by the work of the National Civic Service Agency, Marie recognizes the importance of strengthening the organization's ability to receive and support volunteers. She is also setting up a for-profit consultancy that will specialize in the management of volunteers, with all profits reinvested in the core not-for profit actions of Unis-Cité.

Finally, Marie has set up national projects on topics where partners can interact, learn, and develop and implement solutions together, assisted by young volunteers. The availability of the volunteer workforce constitutes a great opportunity to develop new solutions and put them into place. Mediaterre, which raises awareness on energy consumption among underserved families, is one the national initiatives led by Unis-Cité and sponsored by the national electricity company and other public actors. Volunteer teams from diverse backgrounds are the best positioned to facilitate the dialogue and therefore are more successful in changing behaviors.

Marie has always considered civil service as a necessary first step in developing youth citizen engagement. The results of her work demonstrate the emergence of a new generation of changemakers: 88 percent of Unis-Cité volunteers report that

they better understand society and the complexity of social issues; 83 percent feel they now have the tools to act for society; and 76 percent feel more daring to take initiatives. Based on these results, and benefiting from her leadership in the field, Marie wants to expand her solution to other countries as well as experiment around new ways of engaging youth beyond service projects. The next key step is to encourage social entrepreneurship and support young people in creating their own social ventures, capitalizing on existing organizations expertise like Ashoka Youth Venture or Antropia, the social venture incubator created by Marie. From an international perspective, Marie has already participated in the replication of her solution in Burkina Faso, where 900 young people have been engaged as civic service volunteers. She is now thinking of an Africa-wide development strategy, while working on unifying existing European civil service organizations to strengthen the movement and add the entrepreneurial component.

THE PERSON

At 22, Marie chose not to embrace the traditional career of a business school graduate, provoking the disappointment of her middle-class family who expected her to pursue a classic and lucrative career. After many experiences in the citizen sector such as tutoring children and launching a branch of Les Restos du Cœur, a national CO which provides deprived families with inexpensive food and conducts awareness-raising campaigns on hygiene, vaccination, and AIDS in Africa, she had a key encounter with Lisbeth Shepard who launched the idea of civic service in the U.S. Marie realized that one result of the French welfare system is that people get used to waiting for social solutions from public institutions when a social problem emerges. She thus designed a program to awaken youth and to mobilize them around social issues. In 1994 Marie launched Unis-Cité with two peers from school. In only one year she was managing a CO with six full-time employees and a budget of 1.2M Francs raised from large private companies.

Marie rejects the increasing trend in French society of fatalism, pessimism, and disillusion of young citizens toward political action and citizen commitment. In order to bring back trust in citizen action, Marie believes in the importance of building bridges with private and public actors to spread her model and convince political decision-makers to bid on the potential of youth. Moreover, she wants diversity to become a powerful leverage to both improve the well-being of society and foster youth commitment. Marie's strong belief in diversity partially stems from her personal experience: Her husband and the father of her two children is Senegalese, and she particularly understands the challenges faced by people with mixed origins. This is why she has given an essential dimension to diversity within Unis-Cité. Marie's exemplary work in that field led her to join the advisory committee of the National Agency for Social Cohesion and Equal Opportunities.

Beyond Unis-Cité, Marie has launched and/or participated in many initiatives to create a stronger citizen sector and promote social entrepreneurship. In 1999 she founded a consultancy firm to professionalize management and organization practices for COs and support big companies in their sponsorship strategy. A pioneer in the academic system, in 2004 Marie co-founded the first graduate program on social entrepreneurship in France, at ESSEC Business School. A few years later, she launched Antropia, the first incubator in France for social ventures. ♦

BERNARD AMADEI

UNITED STATES

Appropriate Technology

Poverty Alleviation

Bernard Amadei is transforming the field of engineering, particularly mechanical and civil engineering, by revamping the traditional training model and establishing professional standards to integrate the field more closely with global issues such as poverty alleviation, hunger, and disease.

THE NEW IDEA

By engaging students, professors, and professional engineers in an experiential framework, Bernard is trying to shift the field to focus on truly sustainable engineering. The core of Bernard's work is to offer rigorous, meaningful opportunities to integrate two things: Learning engineering skills in an applied context, and playing a life-changing role in substantive, sustainable engineering projects in the developing world. Through the engagement of professors and practitioners, sustainable engineering is spreading and changing the way that the engineering profession is both thinking of and educating itself across the country, causing it to become an even more powerful piece of the solution for some of the world's most pervasive problems, such as poverty, pollution, hunger, and disease.

Bernard is accomplishing this in several related ways. First, in 2002 he created a new strain of Engineers Without Borders (EWB), first by establishing EWB-USA, an organization that not only sent students overseas to do short-term projects in developing countries, but also sought to educate those students more broadly and rigorously about development, and to do "real" engineering—pairing students with professionals to create sustainable, lasting projects, and to train local engineers and students to ensure the long-term success of the project. (EWB projects are the culmination of course study and planning, rather than an internship-type of experience.)

EWB-USA integrates the participation of faculty on over 200 of its 385 chapters. These chapters multiply their impact by igniting the interest of professors to change the curricula to fully embrace the notion of practicing sustainable engineering in their respective universities. Currently, there are 12,000 members in these chapters (USA) of which 45 percent are professional engineers (55 percent students).

Subsequently, Bernard co-founded EBW International, a network of EWBs worldwide who share his vision of students, professionals,

and local engineers planning and executing applied engineering projects as a key part of sustainable community development and poverty reduction. These groups are neutral/non-political and affiliation requires a screening process for matching ethics. To date, there are 45 chapters globally affiliated with EWB International.

Third, Bernard created an Engineering for Developing Communities Program at the University of Colorado Boulder in 2004, which has been so successful that it was endowed by the Mortenson Center in Engineering for Developing Communities in 2009. He is working to make this the gold standard of teaching engineering students in a radically new way about their profession—enabling them to think and work "sustainably," with an eye toward the whole community they are serving and will spread the teachings through the center's model for training engineers.

THE PROBLEM

Mechanical and civil engineers, particularly in the U.S., are well trained in the directly relevant fields of science and mechanics. However, their understanding of how their work can make a deep and lasting difference in the developing world is often narrow, and their career options are often the same. As such, there is tremendous wasted human capital among the ranks of engineers, many of whom, given cultural and technological shifts in society, are hungry to use their skills and knowledge in solving humanity's problems.

A partial solution did exist in the original EWB, begun in France along the lines of Doctors Without Borders. However, while it sends students on short-term trips, Bernard found that it did not place its work within a broader context of thoughtful, sustainable development. It has short-term aid as its goal, rather than maximizing the tremendous opportunity for students to see and practice engineering in the greater context of human development, to work alongside professional engineers in a meaningful way, and to train-the-trainer locally, so as to enable both the long-term maintenance of the project and the fostering and/or strengthening of an indigenous engineering capacity.

EWB-USA pairs students with professionals to create sustainable, lasting projects, and trains local engineers and students to ensure the long-term success of the project.

THE STRATEGY

In 1997, when Bernard's landscaper mentioned the need for an irrigation system in his native village, he volunteered to help. Two years later, the landscaper took him up on his offer, and Bernard gladly accepted. With his 12 students they raised US$14K for themselves, 2 professors and essential equipment. The success of that trip in 2002, and the student's eagerness for more, made Bernard curious. He began to sense the historical moment in which he was teaching, when engineering students, as well as many young engineering professionals, were no longer satisfied to join the ranks of traditional engineering societies, or overly concerned with the bigger picture their work might fit. Bernard began to have an implicit vision to use the gifts and skills of engineering to make the world a better place, to understand the communities where engineers worked, so they could better serve them. This vision included high levels of local participation, in-depth study of the communities they would serve, as well as greater development of the cultural context. In addition to high-quality engineering projects that were culturally relevant, maintainable, and sound. Early on he knew this would require including professional engineers in the effort (both pre-trip and during).

> "The group is changing the way engineering is taught by demanding that practitioners address the long-neglected needs of the billions of people who live without clean water or decent sanitation."
>
> —*TIME Magazine*

Bernard began by looking for anyone already doing this in the U.S., but found no one. So he went overseas and found EWB, and met with them several times. However, as they didn't share his same emphasis on the inclusion of education about development, professional engineers running the trips themselves (i.e. rather than simply sending students to work with citizen organizations), extensively training locals, and committing to a community for at least five years (so relationships can be built and greater impact can be achieved), he decided to simply start his own version of EWB from scratch.

At the same time, at the beginning of some joint projects in the field, other like-minded EWB chapters began to band together, joining in Bernard's vision for a more comprehensive approach. He decided to formalize their partnership in an entity called EWB International (2002), which is more of a decentralized network than a centralized organization, with EWB-USA as its connection point.

From 2002 to 2004 EWB-USA was a low profile on-campus program, as Bernard worked to break barriers with the university.

However, given his essential nature of education, planning, and involvement of professional engineers, he believed that creating EWB through universities was the best way to establish and grow EWB-USA. Bernard had two jobs. Although quite stressful, in 2004 his work paid off when the university saw enough potential in the idea to provide an assistant for Bernard—then EWB-USA really picked up steam. They received several outside grants (e.g. from Boeing, saying they needed leaders not just engineers) and their growth ballooned even more—working in 48 countries in 7 years.

In 2005 Bernard stepped down from the full-time running of EWB-USA (i.e. in addition to his teaching load) to focus on two things. First, as EWB-USA was evolving, he became more convinced that the traditional way engineers are educated is too narrow, and he saw more cases where good engineering did not equal good development. So he determined to create a new curriculum for educating engineers interested in working in development, just as business and architecture schools were beginning to educate those who wanted to lead in the social sector and/or in developing economies. Bernard wanted engineering students to understand sustainable engineering in the context of sustainable development, so he created a program (now the Mortenson Center), which allows students to learn not only engineering technology, but also economics, public health, politics (e.g. governance and security), and social entrepreneurship, using Ashoka and Ashoka Fellows as case studies! Its innovative, integrated approach has attracted large numbers of students, including more women than usual. The center is also developing methods and doing the necessary R&D to support that. Furthermore, the center also serves all other EWB-USA members and is the core of his system change mechanism. This is what makes EWB more than the sum of thousands of projects. The center was established in April 2009 with a US$5M endowment from a construction company. Bernard works full-time at the center and has five full-time and five part-time faculty members involved in its operations.

Bernard is also focusing on projects and relationships that will be pilots for using engineering as a vehicle to create peace. For example, through EWB International, he is working to bring together EWB-Israel and EWB-Pakistan in a joint project as part of the "Abraham Path Initiative," and is also working to bring together the Turkish and Greek elements of EWB-Cypress in a joint project. And though it is not without its challenges, Bernard has been working in the past couple of years in Afghanistan, to enable engineering projects that will play a role in stabilizing the country. Similarly, he has organized a multi-faceted course that not only combines the study of development with actual projects (like the center), but also true cross-cultural experience throughout. As such, Bernard will teach "Engineering for the Developing World: Middle East Approach," in Haifa, Israel next summer for 15 engineering students from CU Boulder and 15 from Israeli universities. It will feature morning classes in development (e.g. anthropology, culture, and geopolitics) and afternoon joint projects in Bedouin and Druze communities.

Bernard's goal is to conduct such classes in different areas in the Middle East, and elsewhere in the world.

Bernard is a model to his students in the practical application of engineering knowledge for the public good—spending some of his time inventing or spreading mechanical engineering solutions. For example, when he received a grant from a private donor interested in Afghanistan (i.e. where Bernard had been working on and off for five years), he used it to pair up a Nepali inventor of a press to make fuel briquettes out of trash, an Afghan businessman, and a group called Afghans4Tomorrow, whom he had known since 2007. To date, the project has involved over 82 orphaned, disabled, and formerly trafficked youth, who study in the morning and make briquettes in the afternoon. He says the project needs just one more year to become sustainable. When Bernard saw that quality was an issue, he got some of his students at CU to invent ways to ensure quality control for the briquettes. They are also examining the economic aspects, studying how a family might create a viable business from briquettes.

Engineers Without Borders-USA has touched the lives of more than one million people. It expects to impact two million more in the next four years.

THE PERSON

Bernard is the grandson, son and brother of bricklayers, and while his family has run a respectable and sound business for generations, he is the first in his family to go beyond a high school degree and their French village. Bernard learned the spirit of community, helping others in need, and loyalty from both of his parents. After a time of hard work mastering his chosen profession (a Ph.D. in engineering from UC Berkeley and extensive coursework toward a Ph.D. in theology), he worked for six months at a consulting firm and then joined Colorado University. Why? He knew he was a free spirit, and feared becoming a "gerbil." Bernard wanted to choose his own projects to study and found the three summer months crucial for working on his innovative projects with corporations (i.e. mainly R&D on his specialty—geotechnical engineering).

Almost immediately, he started engaging students in his work outside the university.

In fact, it was so fast paced that Bernard burned out. In 2005, after years of intensive travel to establish both EWB-USA and International, in addition to his full-time teaching load, he began to suffer serious physical consequences. In retrospect, he sees it as one of the best things that ever happened to him, because it forced him to slow down, to assess what was the best use of his time and talents, and to reorganize his life accordingly. So Bernard stepped down from the full-time running of EWB-USA and focused on International, creating the center at CU, and his inventions. He credits his wife and his mentors, with which he says he has always been blessed, with helping him learn and grow from what could have been a disastrous experience.

Bernard also understood his motivations more clearly. He knew he could never give up his EWB work because it was the marriage of his gifts and a fulfilling application of them. But Bernard also saw that his life was increasingly guided by one vision—that while one person can make a big difference, one person galvanizing a group is exponentially as powerful. Bernard's honesty and humility about this brief interlude in his story is very inspiring, and has clearly brought him stability, focus, and wisdom he may have not been able to achieve without it.

Bernard also sees the goal of his work with EWB-USA and International, and other projects and inventions, to use engineering as "compassion in action" and "a vehicle for peace." This broader yet deeper vision of his work has grown in the past few years, as he travels the globe's hotspots, such as the Middle East.

Bernard is married with two children, a daughter studying biomedical engineering, and a son studying film. He works full-time at the Mortenson Center that he launched and is fully committed to scaling up the impact of the center and his idea. In his free time, Bernard is an active volunteer at a homeless shelter and a children's hospital in Boulder, and likes to exercise, read, and travel. He is also a trained pilot of single and multi-engine planes, and is currently learning instrument flying. ♦

© Claudio Tavares/ISA

CARLOS ALBERTO RICARDO

BRAZIL

Appropriate Technology

Poverty Alleviation

Carlos Alberto "Beto" Ricardo has been a staunch defender of environmental and indigenous rights for the past 35 years. Beto is spearheading a socio-environmental development approach in Brazil, which brings the traditional knowledge and wisdom of indigenous groups to the forefront and entrenches their rights through public policy changes and economic undertakings.

THE NEW IDEA

Founder of two of Brazil's most important social, environmental and human rights organizations, Beto has been a pioneer in advancing the links between human rights, environmental protection, and sustainable development for over 35 years. He has done this through creating innovative "socio-environmental" solutions that have given indigenous groups the legal rights to millions of acres of land and the tools to remain on those lands in sustainable manners.

In the early 1970s Beto co-founded Brazil's leading citizen organization (CO), the Ecumenical Center for Documentation and Information (CEDI). By 1992 he had already left an extraordinary footprint on Brazilian history, bringing indigenous rights onto the agenda as Brazil's 1988 Constitution was being drafted and culminating in winning the prestigious Goldman Environmental Prize. But Beto viewed this merely as the beginning of Brazil's transformation, and in 1994 he formed a second major CO the Socio-Environmental Institute (ISA), whose new idea was to integrate new solutions that were both social and environmental. The groundbreaking nature of ISA's work was symbolized by the creation and wide adoption of a new term in Portuguese—socioambiental or socio-environmental.

ISA has pioneered the concept of integrating environmental protection and sustainable development with indigenous groups. ISA's work has achieved significant impact by influencing public policies and spearheading new laws while effectively developing 70 million hectares through three separate projects, in three different parts of Brazil. ISA has introduced integrated programs from satellite mapping and monitoring against land invasions, to sustainable income-generation, to schools and clinics designed and operated locally, to extending formal citizenship and advocating for needed national policy changes. These initiatives have become models for indigenous socio-environmental development in Brazil and around Latin America.

THE PROBLEM

Brazil is home to one of the world's most culturally and historically diverse populations: There are 220 indigenous peoples, 5,000 quilombola communities (descendants of Africans), caiçaras, (i.e. descendants of intermarriage between Portuguese colonists, indigenous populations and African slaves); caboclos ribeirinhos, (i.e. persons of mixed Brazilian indigenous and European ancestry); peasants and traditional communities making up 8 million people and occupying more than one-third of Brazil's territory. Brazil's biodiversity is also second to none. Nevertheless, Brazilians usually fail to see this incredible socio-biodiversity as a core asset. In fact, the environment and the various peoples who act as its guardian are still viewed as obstacles and symbols of underdevelopment. They fail to realize however that indigenous peoples, who are among Brazil's most vulnerable and poorest, subsist thanks to the environment and also help preserve it. In addition, these "forgotten" people are also constantly threatened by socio-environmental conflicts: Land ownership battles, large hydroelectric projects, and wood contraband, among others. Although the Amazon usually comes to mind when describing such situations, these unfortunate scenarios are also realities for people living in lesser known regions of Brazil, including the Vale do Ribeira, located between the states of Sao Paulo and Paraná, home to the country's biggest Atlantic Forest (Mata Atlântica).

> "Beto Ricardo has been a pioneer in advancing the links between human rights and environmental protection for over 25 years."
>
> —*Goldman Environmental Prize*

Although Brazil's citizen sector achieved important victories in the late 1980s and 1990s, which brought the government to recognize and protect environmental and indigenous rights, the challenges remain great. The development model adopted in Brazil has been ecologically devastating and has concentrated resources in the hands of the richest few, leaving the majority more impoverished than ever. Due to the economic incentives inherent to this model, practically half of Brazil's vegetation has been devastated. In fact, none of Brazil's successive governments have taken into account the environmental dimension of economic growth.

By omitting to recognize the social and environmental dimensions of development, Brazilians have begun to believe economic growth must come at the expense of environmental sustainability. Experience has increasingly shown however, that this belief could not be further from the truth: "Development" can only be development if it is sustainable. A drastic revision of the paradigm of 'growth at all cost' is in order. Unfortunately, Brazilians, and the world, have yet to realize that misery, hunger, and injustice are direct derivatives of faulty development models. Brazil's socio-biodiversity is its most promising asset, and all sectors of society must collaborate in order to achieve socio-environmental sustainability.

Beto considers ISA's mapping technology with musician, Sting, and former senator and Minister of Environment, Marina Silva.

THE STRATEGY

Beto began his work in the early 1970s as one of the founding members of CEDI, the most important Brazilian CO of the past 40 years. It fought the 25-year military dictatorship with facts, studies, ideas, and new proposals in the 1970s with the protection of the church, and in the 1980s, by offering an incredibly wide variety of new ideas to a country emerging into democracy and thirsty for new solutions.

Beto led CEDI's environmental programs in the 1980s, and when Brazil was drafting a new Constitution in 1988, his field research provided new insights and argued persuasively in support of indigenous rights and the future of the Amazon. As a result of the national concern that was generated, indigenous people were given stronger guarantees in the Constitution. In 1989, Beto was instrumental in laying the groundwork for an alliance between Indians and rubbertappers, two groups who coexisted in Brazil's vast rainforest, but who had traditionally fought each other. Beto also co-founded the Committee for the Creation of the Yanomami Park (CCPY) because in the late 1980s over 45,000 gold miners had invaded the Yanomami. In 1991, in significant part due to the CCPY's efforts, President Collor issued a decree creating a continuous reserve of 94,000 square kilometers for the Yanomami people. This set a major new precedent and led to the formal creation of hundreds of indigenous reserves which now cover nearly one-third of Brazil.

By 1994, the founders of CEDI agreed it was time to divide into various focused COs and Beto founded ISA, but with a more field and program oriented approach, as opposed to CEDI's over-arching recommendations. Beto realized that it wasn't enough to win formal rights to the land. He and his former colleagues at CEDI put together a comprehensive, and eventually an online,

mapping system. Not only do these maps give information on topography and vegetation, they also show activity in a given area, such as invasions and planned dam sites. Thus, Beto saw, and showed Brazil, that indigenous groups had been living for hundreds of years in harmony with the environment and that it was outsiders moving into the Amazon who were destroying the Amazon through slash and burn agriculture and huge, single-crop farms.

In Rio Negro, for example, Beto has created an Indigenous Sustainable Development Program that operates on indigenous territories spanning 10.6 million hectares, and serves nearly 40,000 people. (These indigenous territories were legally recognized as such by the Brazilian government as a result of a campaign coordinated by ISA.) The program has enabled the creation of schools planned and run by indigenous people, supported income-generation projects and implemented the Department of Justice's Balcão da Cidadania Program to offer citizenship education and juridical services to indigenous populations. In Rio Negro, the Balcão da Cidadania has allowed 4,193 people, of 19 ethnicities, to receive national identity documents and has offered courses on indigenous rights to these communities.

In the Xingu region, ISA's partnerships with indigenous groups have: Increased opportunities for dialogue with the broader Brazilian population; allowed indigenous populations to become political leaders; trained people in traditional resource management approaches; and protected the indigenous territories' borders. For example, as part of its resource management initiatives, ISA has successfully helped indigenous farmers to eliminate middlemen thus increasing their sales of local organic produce by 80 percent. ISA has also led the way in reforestation efforts in the Xingu region.

ISA's mapping technology and expertise have brought about important policy changes. The institute participates in the Amazon's Geographic Information System and is responsible for generating data about Indigenous Lands and State Conservation Units in six Brazilian states. The Ministry of the Environment recently solicited ISA's services seeking a socio-economic and environmental diagnostic of a territory spanning 7.9 million hectares in Para as well as alternative policy proposals. As a result, ISA suggested that the Ministry of the Environment create a mosaic of Conservation Units, an innovative proposal that bridges the gap between various forms of settlements and environmental protection.

So ISA has pioneered an integrated and more holistic approach of environmental protection and sustainable development, learning from and working with indigenous groups rather than imposing outside solutions. ISA quickly overturned the conventional "wisdom" of many years with facts and successful projects. Beto's mapping showed that, contrary to government reports stipulating that there weren't any indigenous groups in the huge state of Acre, there are dozens of different indigenous groups and thousands of indigenous people, now represented as a separate department within the state government. The institute has also dispelled the view that there was basically one overall indigenous group by mapping 220 indigenous groups and 5,000 quilombola groups (African descendants) living in almost all Brazilian states.

Moreover, ISA's efforts have affected public policies and have had a critical influence on judicial rulings. For example, in 2003, ISA was the first organization to get the Brazilian judiciary to recognize the environmental and cultural destruction caused by the construction of a highway in the middle of indigenous reserves. The Panara people were offered 1.2 million reais (US$690,000) in reparations, as a result of the judiciary's historical ruling.

ISA now has nearly 150 staff working on those three major projects and a couple of smaller, satellite offices. It acts as a trusted partner with the many indigenous groups, and as a bridge to international groups, which provide the majority of the institute's US$1.3M budget. In order to ensure the institute's sustainability, Beto and his team are actively seeking greater contributions from individuals, corporations, foundations, and governmental bodies in Brazil.

Beto aims to gradually step away from the day to day responsibilities of ISA and is already spearheading three major new efforts bringing together all three sectors of society. The first consists of turning food products from the Amazon region into gastronomic products highly demanded by "haute cuisine" chefs. The second initiative, named Passagem da Cidadania (Citizenship Boulevard), is transforming the old, run down historical center of the city into a hotbed for culture. Beto is also co-founding Brazil's newest environmental organization, the Institute of Democracy and Sustainability (IDS), bringing together prominent political figures such as Maria Silva (i.e. a highly respected environmental leader who worked along side Chico Mendes, and ran in the 2010 presidential elections), and business leaders such as Guilherme Leal of Natura. The IDS aims to bring environmental issues to the forefront of the public discourse by finding sustainable solutions to Brazil's most pressing environmental problems, while aptly avoiding the traps of party politics.

THE PERSON

Beto was born in 1950 into a family of Italian immigrants, which had been persecuted and lost everything during the Second World War. His father started as an office boy in Unilever and, as a self-made man, became the first Brazilian president of this major industrial company. Beto studied at one of the most progressive, intellectually demanding Catholic private schools in Sao Paulo. In 1970, a priest who had lived for three years in the Amazon invited Beto to go with him. This first trip to the Amazon changed his life.

The military government's policy was that the Amazon needed to be populated and integrated, because it was an empty territory and could be lost to foreigners; but Beto saw a wide variety of people from different looking indigenous groups. He began writing down in his notebook the names and locations of different groups, how many lived where in that area. Over 15 years, this mapping exercise grew and became the foundation for the path breaking mapping project, which changed the entire focus of the 1988 Constitution debate about indigenous rights.

After becoming one of the founding members of CEDI, he continued his work on mapping and understanding the indigenous groups, but still taught as a secure professor at Unicamp University. He and others had long been talking with leading intellectuals like Fernando Henrique Cardoso about the need to create an enduring civil society in Brazil as a counterweight to the military government and a business class focused on growth and wealth. So he quit his university position and worked full-time with CEDI focusing not just on his environmental programs, but also on professionalizing CEDI and preparing it as a platform to create a civil society. Twenty years later, the founders agreed to split CEDI into various spinoff organizations becoming a platform for an entire civil sector.

Beto therefore set off to create the Socio-Environmental Institute. He brought together CEDI's Indigenous Peoples in Brazil Program, the CO called Indigenous Rights Nucleus, environmental leaders and leading-edge academics, thus exemplifying the inseparable nature of their work. Not only did ISA introduce the socio-environmental concept in Brazil it also became a leader on the topic and effectively created an alternative approach to sustainable development.

As Beto looks to the future, he is convinced that his integrated socio-environmental approach aimed at deep impact in specific geographical areas has proven far more successful than isolated efforts along issues such as education, health, and so on. He sees a new era beginning in Brazil in which real collaborations (not just photo-ops) among the social, business, and public sector are starting to work on integrated development projects. He sees this change as driven not only by the failure of isolated efforts and programs to have a major social impact, but also by the realization by all three sectors that the planet and Brazil are at-risk and that new and innovative approaches are urgently required. ◆

JORDAN KASSALOW

UNITED STATES

Disabilities

Jordan Kassalow is addressing the market-failure for affordable eye care in the developing world, and the resulting economic burden of vision disability by transforming the eyewear delivery system to ensure that every person has access to the glasses required to live a full, productive life.

THE NEW IDEA

An optometrist and public health entrepreneur, Jordan has spent much of his career showing the link between vision and economic productivity at the base of the pyramid. He introduced improved care for river blindness, and founded the Global Health Policy Council at the Council on Foreign Relations.

Through VisionSpring, the not-for-profit organization he co-founded as Scojo in 2003, Jordan is creating new markets and delivering affordable glasses and other vision services and products to the world's poor. He does this by arranging low-cost manufacture of sought-after goods; distributing these through direct sales and partner organizations; and signaling a new market opportunity to industry players that currently pursue a high-margin, low-volume approach to sales in emerging markets. Jordan and his team have supplied over 400,000 pairs of ready-made glasses, contributing health and increased wage-earning capabilities to this underserved group and surfacing a demonstration model for the industry. Now he and his colleagues are piloting a "full service" approach that builds out a diversified product range, and approaches profitability through the introduction of some higher-margin products (i.e. prescription glasses) that are still affordable to customers earning as little as $4/day. The global system he has engineered links production in East Asia with consumers and VisionSpring teams in Central America, India, Bangladesh, South Africa, and Indonesia.

THE PROBLEM

For sighted people, good vision is inextricably linked to overall health and to economic productivity. If you can not see well, you often can not work and earn a living. While simple, ready-made eyeglasses can correct most common vision problems, millions of people who need glasses are not getting them. This often means they can not work and lead fully productive lives: The global cost of vision loss was estimated at $3 trillion in 2010.

The problem is not a new one, nor is the product that represents a solution—eyeglasses were invented in the 1200s. The distribution system has been evolving for 800 years to the point of near market saturation in most developed economies. The challenge—and opportunity—is reaching everybody else. An estimated 410 million people are unable to perform basic tasks due to presbyopia (i.e. blurry up-close vision, resulting in middle age) because they don't have ready-made glasses, and another 158 million are visually impaired because they have blurry distance vision (myopia) and do not have glasses.

Various charity-based organizations gather eyeglasses that are discarded from customers in wealthier countries. Through the best of intentions, these approaches are limited in impact and do not represent a viable long-term solution. While a market-based approach makes sense as a longer-term solution, cost and distribution are the big barriers, so challenging that most mainstream eyewear manufacturers can't see past them to the market potential. Manufacturers who sell in developing countries—most of the big companies are based in the U.S. and Europe—pursue a model that is low-volume, high-margin—and high cost to the consumer. In cities across much of the developing world, you can buy a custom pair of glasses from an eye doctor or optical shop for $40 to $60. But if you're earning the equivalent of, say, $4/day, there's nothing available anywhere near your price point.

> "Scojo Foundation broadens the availability of reading glasses worldwide by training, and equipping women entrepreneurs to start businesses that sell reading glasses to those who require them."
>
> —Changing the Present

THE STRATEGY

For its first eight years, VisionSpring focused solely on distributing ready-made, non-prescription reading glasses. Reading glasses are inexpensive to produce, do not require a doctor to distribute, and have a direct impact on the work and productivity of tailors, artisans, mechanics, and other professions common in many parts of the world.

Jordan and his team are iteratively evolving distribution approaches, and molding distribution/sales to fit the local reality. Distribution therefore looks quite different in different parts of the world. There are three main approaches: Direct sales, sales through distribution partners, and an emerging "full service" model.

To reach customers in rural areas, VisionSpring manages 50 Vision Entrepreneurs, the on-the-ground sales team. Typically women, Vision Entrepreneurs generate awareness, conduct screenings, and sell low-cost reading glasses in their communities. Jordan and his team have developed "Business in a Bag," a kit containing everything needed to launch a one-person eye care business. While VisionSpring began with this sales model, Jordan's team is now focusing efforts on this channel mainly to innovate, but is not actively expanding it, due to the expense of working solely in rural regions, low margins from the core suite of ready-made reading glasses and sunglasses, and increased demand from customers and Vision Entrepreneurs for additional affordable vision products.

To achieve greater scale, VisionSpring partners with distribution partners—citizen organizations with complementary rural sales networks, such as microfinance institutions and community health worker organizations. This approach allows greater impact without committing additional human and financial capital. Partners are attracted to VisionSpring because they can easily incorporate eyeglass sales within their programs and they receive product and training support. VisionSpring provides them with the Business in a Bag program, performs initial due diligence, conducts a pilot program to train-the-trainers, and provides ongoing support as the partner continues to grow the program. In 2008 Jordan developed a partnership with BRAC, which accounts for 75 percent of VisionSpring's sales. A challenge of this approach is that the sales team is not dedicated and may have a number of other products in their bag, many of them less expensive, repeat-sales items, like sanitary napkins and condoms.

To address some of the challenges of the other models, Jordan and his team are piloting what they call the "full service" model in peri-urban areas of El Salvador, India, and Indonesia. The idea emerged from a Vision Entrepreneur in El Salvador who felt that she was disappointing as many people as she was helping, because some clients needed prescription glasses and she had only ready-made. The full service approach provides affordable, high-quality prescription glasses as well as ready-made reading glasses and engages an optometrist to host regular campaigns from an urban/peri-urban optical shop. VisionSpring compensates Vision Entrepreneurs for creating demand in rural areas and driving targeted potential customers to the optometrist. Jordan and his team plan to scale this approach either by building the Vision Entrepreneur network or through the partner channel once refined and proven successful. In El Salvador, the team has developed relationships with local lens manufacturers to make low-cost prescription lens, and are showing the viability of a high-volume, low-margin approach.

Jordan and his team are always improving the cost of goods. Currently, they source manufacturers in China through a full-time VisionSpring staff member, who is constantly scouting the best manufacturers, negotiating lower prices, and ironing out other supply chain problems, such as efficient, on-time, cross-border shipping. At present, Jordan and his team are working with three Chinese factories for the manufacture of ready-made reading glasses. They are also looking at possible partnerships with U.S.- or Europe-based companies. Last year, they were 90 percent through a negotiation with a U.S.-based manufacturer who was willing to make the glasses at 25 percent less cost than directly sourcing the manufacturers. The company was sold, and new leadership did not want to pursue working with VisionSpring at this time.

Jordan is beginning to showcase the learning's by convening large eyeglasses companies in North America and Europe in an effort to show the potential of setting the industry on a course of high-volume, low-margin, which shows huge social and profit returns.

VisionSpring has teams in the U.S., India, El Salvador, and Indonesia. Because much of its operational expenses are handled by local partners, it operates on a lean budget—in 2010, $1.6M. VisionSpring is a not-for-profit and all revenue is reinvested in the organization.

THE PERSON

Jordan grew up in New York City, the son of an optometrist who built a special and successful practice with the city's wealthy, connected clientele. Jordan devised several small businesses as a child, showing an early instinct for entrepreneurship. His interest in and exposure to the developing world emerged from his love of the world's mountains and of climbing.

Jordan trained as an optometrist, taking a partner role in the family business. But his interest in the developing world drew him to participate in eye camps in Central America, where he saw the real need for vision services, and grew frustrated by the band-aid approach to meeting that need. He also arranged an apprenticeship at Aarvind Eye Hospital in India during its early years.

Jordan studied public health, becoming an expert in Onchocerciasis (river blindness). He led the Onchocerciasis Division at Helen Keller International and over an 8-year period took the two-country program reaching 50,000 people to a 9-country effort reaching 1 million people.

Through these experiences with eye care in developing countries, he began to focus strongly on the link between health—specifically eye health—and economic stability, for individuals and families and also on a larger scale of nations. Learning of his interests, one of his patients pointed him to the Council on Foreign Relations, where Jordan became a Fellow (1999 to 2004) and established the Global Health Policy Council, which sought to reframe investment in health not as a humanitarian concern, but as a matter of national and economic security.

Jordan lives with his wife and three children in New York City. ◆

MARTA MAGLIO DE MARTÍN

ARGENTINA

Child Care

Early Childhood Development

Health Care Delivery

Marta Maglio de Martín has changed the consciousness and behaviors of thousands of Argentine citizens and health professionals about the importance of breastfeeding as a crucial avenue to ensure the physical and emotional health of parents and children alike. By focusing on the first months of parents' relationships with their infants, Marta is strengthening family bonds and creating an enabling environment for the development of empathetic skills.

THE NEW IDEA

When Marta gave birth to her third child in the United States she was surprised to see how much attention was given to breastfeeding. This was an issue that had never come up in her native Argentina, neither with her doctor nor with her peers. Upon Marta's return to Argentina in the early 1970s, she set out to disseminate knowledge about this issue throughout the country, while developing mechanisms to support families through their transitions as parents.

What began as an exercise with a few mothers in her living room quickly transformed into a nationwide effort to disseminate knowledge and best practices around breastfeeding. Marta's approach is particularly powerful because it does not simply focus on the health benefits of breastfeeding, but rather makes the link with a broader understanding of what a healthy family constitutes. She recognizes that breastfeeding and many other prenatal and parenting best practices are important ways to ensure strong bonds between a child and his/her parents. By focusing on breastfeeding as a way to ensure empathetic family relations, Marta has contributed to an important transformation in Argentine society.

Marta has since established breastfeeding as a common practice throughout Argentina. She has done so by formally and informally training health professionals, parents, and educators about its benefits; leading massive public education campaigns; and creating public policies that guaranteed the rights of women to breastfeed, among others. In the early 2000s, Marta created the first nationally recognized postsecondary education degree in the field: Breastfeeding and Parenting. She is now pursuing partnerships with universities throughout the country to adopt this curriculum. Marta is doing so to ensure the growth of this profession, through a holistic approach that furthers the emotional and physical health of children and parents alike.

THE PROBLEM

When Marta began her work more than 30 years ago, citizens and doctors were generally unaware of the advantages of breastfeeding. Although it might have been obvious for a doctor in the U.S. to mention the health benefits of breastfeeding to a new mother, this was not at all common practice in Argentina. At the time, physicians emphasized the importance of promoting a mother's independence and a child's autonomy through bottle-feeding or administering powdered milk. It did not occur to them that these practices might fail to boost babies' immune systems and prevent ear and respiratory infections, stomach viruses, diarrhea, asthma, and a host of other illnesses. It was also not widely known among doctors for example that breastfeeding could help mothers recuperate more quickly after giving birth, or that it could prevent ovarian and breast cancer, postpartum depression and type 2 diabetes. Connecting with a baby at an emotional level was also overlooked as an important element to create important family bonds.

> "Marta Maglio Martin is undoubtedly a power plant project, a generator of new roads, a pioneer in addressing issues of motherhood, breastfeeding, family ties and special abilities."
>
> —*Revista Nueva*

In addition, very little attention was paid to the common challenges that affected new mothers. Nearly no support was given to women who experienced gradual weight gains as a result of their pregnancies; mastitis was not widely spoken about; finding breastfeeding alternatives for adopted children was never even identified as a potential issue; and the effects of breastfeeding on a mother's timely return in the workplace were generally ignored. Although it is recommended for women—who make up 45 percent of the Argentine work force—to breastfeed for approximately six months after a child's birth, national legislation and business practices did not foster a favorable environment for this.

The inadequacies of the health and justice systems to respond to pregnant women's needs at the time were mainly due to the fact that knowledge about these issues was not disseminated amongst Argentina's physicians or the general population. An obvious consequence followed: The inexistence of prenatal training programs targeting health professionals and health institutions. Not only were there no formal postsecondary education programs dedicated to breastfeeding, prenatal care, and childcare education in Argentina, there are also were no existing informal programs addressing these topics, be it through support groups or seminars catering to families or physicians.

THE STRATEGY

Marta began her work in the 1970s as a result of a strong commitment to turning breastfeeding into a common practice throughout Argentina. Her vision was to transform behaviors and consciousness among Argentine society by getting doctors, hospitals and health centers involved with this mission, as part of a broader approach to giving mothers and families the support they needed to raise healthy, empathetic children.

In order to realize this vision, Marta employed a five-pillared strategy. She focused on developing formal and informal prenatal and parenting education curricula; disseminated information about the importance of breastfeeding and related it to the physical and empathetic health of families; created spaces where families could get the emotional support needed; established designated breastfeeding public spaces; and affected public policy.

Marta started this work from her living room with a handful of mothers and two physicians, and quickly understood the extent of the need for education about parenting. She began working through community centers, health clinics, and churches in a number of neighborhoods in and around Buenos Aires to get the word out. Within two years, she had trained and mobilized 20 volunteer mothers capable of leading community support groups around such issues as breastfeeding and prenatal care, with a clear emphasis on the health of families. These efforts led to the establishment of the Liga de la Leche (Milk League) whose main goal was to create similar support groups in every province of Argentina as a way to spread information and best practices.

Marta later founded FUNDALAM to extend the scope and reach of her initiative from an informal education model to one that focused increasingly on the formalization of educational curricula about breastfeeding, prenatal care, and parenting. Realizing that parents were more likely to listen to their doctors than their peers, Marta developed courses specifically for health professionals working in public hospitals, health clinics, and community centers. She understood that she needed them as allies if her approach to prenatal care and parenting were to gain broad acceptance in Argentine society. These trained professionals then became trainers themselves. FUNDALAM provided them with the systematized methodology and marketing materials to distribute to their clients.

Through FUNDALAM, Marta also began to systematically train volunteers to replicate the Liga de la Leche experience nationwide expanding on the topic of breastfeeding and taking into consideration other pregnancy-related issues such as the needs of children with special abilities or that of pregnant teenagers. She realized that parents in both situations needed particular attention and support. Not knowing how to deal with the fear and guilt, many parents reject and feel uncomfortable breastfeeding their own child. Marta recognized this challenge and developed workshops and support groups to cater to those two populations' needs, with the clear understanding that building strong bonds between parents and their children in such difficult situations would greatly contribute to the health of the families. This approach to childcare helped many parents transform their relationships with their children and ensured their independency and intellectual development. Marta has also introduced capacity-building courses for Doulas—mothers who provide emotional support to women throughout their

pregnancies—focusing equally on the mother's and the child's health. FUNDALAM is currently undergoing a certification process to turn this course into a professional specialization in postsecondary institutions.

Some of Marta's most important contributions have been in the realm of public policy change. Marta has led the establishment of the first laws in Argentina guaranteeing the right of women to breastfeed. She is also responsible for extending maternity leave to up to an eight-month period for mothers with children with special needs. In addition, she has been able to shift public opinion about the need to have designated areas for breastfeeding and has introduced such spaces in a number of public institutions and private companies—e.g. Citibank, Deloitte, Coca Cola, and Philips—throughout the country. She has thus been able to revert a trend which was common among women in the 1970s, whom, in order to be truly independent, thought they had to give up breastfeeding. As a result of these efforts, Argentine women who want to remain active workers are no longer faced with an "either or" situation when it comes to ensuring the health and development of their children. Marta has also opened such spaces in two women's jails in order to help mothers create strong bonds with their children despite the difficult situations they face in prison.

Through a partnership with the National University of San Martín, Marta established the first post-secondary degree in breastfeeding and parenting.

Having truly established breastfeeding as a recognized best practice throughout the country—by law and now by popular consensus—Marta is focusing on spreading prenatal care and parenting education as an esteemed profession. Her current goal is to ensure that the next generation of health professionals, upon graduating from university, is prepared to support men and women through their transitions to parenthood. In 2002 Marta established Argentina's first nationally recognized post-secondary degree in breastfeeding and parenting through a partnership with the National University of San Martín. Thus far, 122 students have graduated from this program and 100 percent have been able to find jobs in this newly created profession. They are working in public hospitals, private practices, and community centers. Marta's goal for the next five years is to spread this successful experience to Argentina's main post-secondary institutions.

Having created the field of breastfeeding studies, prenatal care and parenting in Argentina, Marta is recognized as a thought leader on these topics and is continuously advancing research in the area. She has disseminated her approach through numerous conferences such as the International Congress for Family in the Americas and the Meeting on Breastfeeding for Professionals. In addition, she established a magazine, *Mamando (Breastfeeding)*, which was massively distributed on the Internet and in paper format to doctors, parents, and educators throughout the country. Marta has also led a number of large public education and media campaigns. One of the most influential, "Amamantar: Dale Amor y Salud a tu Bebe" (Breastfeeding: Giving Love and Health to your Baby), was the result of a partnership with the municipal government of Buenos Aires. It disseminated information about the importance of breastfeeding through advertisements on television, radio, and the public transportation system.

As a result of her work Marta has fostered the emergence of a number of replicators in every region of Argentina. Her leadership has also brought about the first breastfeeding support groups in Uruguay. Between 2006 and 2008, Marta worked with more than 5,300 mothers, 3,000 health professionals, 60,000 children and 50 Doulas. In those two years alone, she established more than six breastfeeding and breastpumping spaces and has affected the lives of over 70,000 families throughout Argentina.

Marta has in large part been able to spread her work through strategic partnerships. For example, she stepped in as the Argentine partner in the global UNICEF and WHO sponsored program Mother- and Children-Friendly Hospitals, which sought to ensure that hospitals become breastfeeding-friendly environments. Argentina now has 26 participating hospitals and the number is growing. The program helped hospital staff understand the importance of breastfeeding for the mother and her child.

THE PERSON

Marta obtained a degree in psychology and various certificates in mental health and therapy oriented toward family health. She first learned about the importance of breastfeeding and family bonds while living in the U.S. and giving birth to her third child. Through this experience she realized the huge gap needed to be filled in Argentina where health professionals and citizens did not even recognize breastfeeding as a potentially beneficial activity.

Upon moving back to Buenos Aires in 1972, Marta decided to fill the country's information gap. She undertook a nationwide effort that established breastfeeding as a recognized best practice to ensure the health of children, mothers, and families. Marta founded Argentina's Breastfeeding League and later FUNDALAM to materialize this vision. She has also participated in numerous networks and associations such as the World Movement of Mothers, the Scientific Committee of the Observatory on Maternity and the Association of University Parenting Majors. She is the author and co-author of many publications on the topic of breastfeeding.

Marta is the mother of six children and lives in Buenos Aires. ♦

ASHWIN NAIK

INDIA

Healthcare Delivery

Poverty Alleviation

Rural Development

Dr. Ashwin Naik, the co-founder and CEO of Vaatsalya, aims to provide affordable and quality healthcare services to India's underserved, rural, and semi-urban populations. The success of his healthcare service company has demonstrated the viability and potential of small- and medium-sized private hospitals to efficiently serve impoverished citizens in India. Furthermore, Ashwin is working to make these hospitals magnets for the growth of the service economy, especially in sectors such as pharmacies, diagnostic labs, and medical-related training.

THE NEW IDEA

Ashwin founded India's first network of hospitals that primarily focus on Tier II (semi-urban) and Tier III (rural) towns. Ashwin's model provides quality service at affordable prices, which he has achieved by establishing hospitals that are small and easily manageable. Moreover, Vaatsalya hospitals generally adhere to a collection of strategies, including accessibility, quality, and efficiency (i.e. reduction of expenditures and administration of minimal procedures). He has also developed partnerships with local organizations and has worked to acquire insurance (as a cost-reduction strategy) for patients. Ashwin's hospitals cater to middle- and low-income families. The hospitals have been successful in reaching a wide-range of clients, as 45 percent of Vaatsalya's patients travel from surrounding villages.

Ashwin adamantly believes that a holistic approach involving the addition of services and the discovery of new opportunities is essential to the enhancement of healthcare. Vaatsalya is indeed a pioneer in Tier II and Tier III communities, which have the potential for tremendous growth over the next five years. Ashwin's model is currently flourishing as it seeks to serve low-income populations in four surrounding states (Andhra Pradesh, Maharashtra, Kerala, and Tamil Nadu).

Currently, Ashwin is trying to develop "doctors as entrepreneurs" who will not only deliver quality services, but will also replicate and expand Vaatsalya's model on a larger scale.

THE PROBLEM

India presently suffers from a severe supply-demand disparity: Urban areas contain 80 percent of the hospitals, but 70 percent of Indians live in villages and semi-urban communities. As a result, access to quality healthcare in rural and semi-urban communities is restricted to low-budget clinics, charitable institutions and government hospitals. Individual doctors almost always arbitrarily define prices.

Since the 1980s, sector reforms and a series of liberalization policies have created new profit-making opportunities for local and international corporations in India's healthcare market. A new pro-market regulatory environment has further attracted private investment to the hospital sector. While India's demand for hospital care has increased, public and private hospitals have failed to deliver on either quality of quantity. With such an untapped market and a favorable regulatory environment, corporations see a tremendous growth potential in Indian hospital care.

THE STRATEGY

Vaatsalya hospitals have two primary missions. On the one hand, the company hopes to reduce the supply-demand healthcare disparity that currently exists between India's rural and urban populations. At the same time, Vaatsalya aims to create a viable, socially responsible opportunity. With a professed focus on "friendliness in service, affordability in cost, cleanliness in settings, and efficiency in operations," Vaatsalya's hospitals provide both primary and secondary care in five specializations—pediatrics, gynecology, surgery, internal medicine and nephrolgy/dialysis.

Ashwin has strategically established hospitals in smaller towns (and close to public transport) in an effort to provide greater accessibility for a wider range of residents. Although he believes that effective healthcare does not necessarily need to be "hi-tech," he stresses that it must be "hi-touch" and focus on effective and timely diagnoses, treatments, and prevention strategies. For example, Vaatsalya does not invest in expensive equipment (e.g. the company performs X-Rays but not CT/MRIs). Vaatsalysa also hopes to offer attractive returns to blended investors.

> "Recognized and applauded for its unique model that has a significant social impact and is financially viable at the same time, Vaatsalya has grown manifolds since its inception."
>
> —*DARE*

Ashwin is looking for semi-urban establishment locations, which contain adequate infrastructure and public transportation, to simultaneously offer access to local inhabitants as well as rural residents. His current client composition underscores the need for such a strategy: Currently, 30 percent of Ashwin's patients come from within a 5 km radius, while 70 percent travel over 30 to 40 km to access Vaatsalya's services.

When Ashwin first began thinking about Vaatsalya Healthcare in 2004, he aspired to attract young doctors to India's rural communities. This strategy was essential to the success of his rather unique business model to establish accessible, affordable healthcare

for rural and semi-urban consumers. In fact, Vaatsalya exercises frugality in all but one area: Doctors' salaries. The company offers a starting salary of Rs 40,000 (US$675) per month, which compares favorably with the average Rs 25,000 to 30,000 (US$450 to US$562) per month in cities. They normally recruit recent specialty graduates (from ages 32 to 38) who would typically start working as junior doctors in city hospitals. Vaatsalya, however, offers them promoted starting positions as specialists.

Ashwin is currently developing partnerships with insurance companies and tertiary care hospitals to expand the breadth and depth of Vaatsalya's services (i.e. currently, more than 90 percent of India's healthcare expenses are not insured). For example, Vaatsalya has launched a vocational "health worker" program to train vulnerable female villagers. He is also creating health-insurance products for employees in micro-industries, which are presently being piloted among family-owned small businesses. In addition to the outreach programs, Vaatsalya is working to attract patients by leveraging television and radio advertisements as well as doctor-call-in programs.

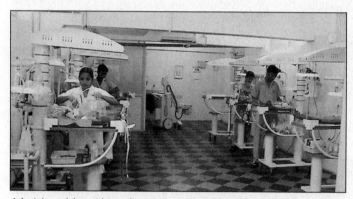

Ashwin's model provides quality service at affordable prices, which he has achieved by establishing hospitals that are small and easily manageable.

Vaatsalya operates as a low-cost model that promotes affordable and accessible healthcare services. The focus on efficiency, however, does not compromise quality. In some towns, Vaatsalya is highly regarded as possessing superior facilities (e.g. in Shimoga, Hassan, Gulbarga and Vizianagaram). Additional elements also make the model affordable, including a strategic focus on reducing the volume of in-house, administered tests. Vaatsalya, for example, outsources specialized diagnostic and radiology tests, such as thyroid testing and CT scans, which helps the company retain its focus on the five core specialist areas—pediatrics, gynecology, internal medicine, surgery and nephrology/dialysis. Vaatsalya charges Rs 100 to 300 (US$2.25 to $6.75) per bed per night and caters to basic needs defined by the five areas. Such a specialty enables Vaatsalya to address up to 70 percent of the local community's medical needs. Each hospital typically contains 70 beds and follows a "no-frills approach." For instance, Vaatsalya not only has a general ward that is much larger than most hospitals, but it also excludes air-conditioning, even in private rooms.

Ashwin is now exploring a local partnership route with revenue sharing arrangements, which will lower initial capital outlays (thereby lowering the pressure for immediate returns) and reduce real estate expenses. The company's strategically located hospitals in rural and semi-urban areas such as Hubli, Bijapur, Hassan, Vizianagaram, Narasanapetta and Shimoga further reduce both rental prices and wages for locally hired support staff. Collectively, these measures enable Vaatsalya to charge only Rs 6,000 (US$135) for a routine child delivery—as opposed to Rs. 12,000 to 50,000 (US$270 to $1,124) that urban hospitals typically demand. Ashwin has also established a three-tier pricing structure offering US$100 to US$300 for affluent populations and US$70 to $80 for low-income customers.

Ashwin intends to open hundreds of Vaatsalya hospitals across the country, which will have the potential to impact more than 700 million people. With US$5M venture capital from the Oasis Fund of Switzerland, Ashwin is preparing to serve an additional 1 million customers per year (against 175,000 per year now). He plans to use the money to establish 13 additional hospitals (for a total of 20 hospitals) in Karnataka, the company's home base, and elsewhere in southern India. With Oasis as a secured partner, Vaatsalya can also access the investor's extensive microfinance network to offer health insurance services.

Vaatsalya currently manages eight hospitals in Karnataka (i.e. with two more in the pipeline, one each in Karnataka and Andhra Pradesh) that are focused on primary and secondary care services. Vaatsalya plans to expand its network of hospitals to five states within the next three years. Aavishkaar, Seedfund, and Oasis Capital collectively fund Vaatsalya's operations. Once Ashwin has reached his initial goal of 20 hospitals, he intends to expand Vaatsalya to offer an additional 60 hospitals within five years, across five states.

THE PERSON

Ashwin has a medical degree from Karnatak Medical College, Hubli and a master's degree from the University of Houston, Texas. As a child, Ashwin witnessed the struggle his parents endured to access healthcare in one of India's many small towns. Such experiences have motivated and driven him to develop Vaatsalya and expand his model across India. Over the next five to ten years, Ashwin hopes to solidify the Vaatsalya model (i.e. leveraging a market-based approach to bring essential healthcare services to semi-urban and rural areas) and replicate it nationally.

Prior to starting Vaatsalya, Ashwin gained several years of experience in leading multidisciplinary teams in the U.S. and India. Before returning to India in 2002, Ashwin worked on the team that sequenced the human and mouse genomes at Celera Genomics, based in Rockville, Maryland. At Celera, he was instrumental in coordinating multidisciplinary teams to compile and analyze the human and mouse genomes, which resulted in the production of two publications in the leading international scientific journal, *SCIENCE*.

Ashwin has three patents with the United States Patent Office (with two patent applications on file). In addition, he contributed a chapter on the *Origin of Life*, which was published in the U.S. in 2004 and is based on his thesis work at University of Houston.

Ashwin has received widespread recognition for his work, such as the TED India Fellowship for 2009. ◆

LUH KETUT SURYANI

INDONESIA

Mental Health

Luh Ketut Suryani, one of Indonesia's 700 psychiatrists, is transforming the mental health field to address the country's growing number of mental health disorders. Using an approach that combines traditional healing methods with modern psychology, Suryani is providing a cost-effective treatment option available to all sectors of society.

THE NEW IDEA

Over the past two decades, Suryani has been spreading mental health care across Indonesia by not only making it more accessible to citizens, but also by redefining and expanding the definition of a "mental health care provider." Based on the simple premise that everyone can be a self-healer, Suryani has engaged a multitude of groups, including teachers, women, children, volunteers, senior citizens, and health workers, and has taught them how to cope with psychiatric issues. Perhaps most notably, she has successfully begun to partner traditional healers with modern psychiatrists to provide a holistic experience that includes community-based prevention, treatment, and rehabilitation.

> "Dr. Luh Ketut Suryani [is] a highly acclaimed western-trained psychiatrist and a leader in bridging indigenous Balinese knowledge and values with the western world."
>
> —*Voice of America*

Through Suryani's organizations, the Suryani Institute for Mental Health and the Committee Against Sex Abuse, she has developed and expanded a number of initiatives designed to treat patients. Using her innovative method, which she coined the "biopyschospirit-sociocultural" approach to psychiatry, Suryani's efforts combine meditation and spiritualism with modern psychological tools and practices. Local governments have adopted and replicated many of Suryani's methods.

THE PROBLEM

The number of reported psychiatric cases in Indonesia recently experienced a sharp increase. Many studies estimate that more than 1 million people between the ages of 15 to 34 commit suicide each year, which accounts for one suicide every 40 seconds. A 2007 study reported that the mental-disorder rate hovered around an alarming 11.6 percent nationally. Citizens suffering from mental health disorders often carry an enormous stigma and are subjected to discrimination and social exclusion. Due to the level of care required, many families physically restrain patients using chains, ropes, cages, or other confined spaces.

Psychiatric practice in Indonesia has traditionally centered on pharmaceutical treatments, rather than counseling and therapy. Many families, however, cannot afford even the limited and expensive drugs that are available. While traditional healers do present a potential solution, they are not yet a part of formal mental health services.

Despite the plethora of challenges surrounding mental health in Indonesia, primary health care providers still fail to prioritize the issue. Some doctors merely lack the skills and knowledge necessary to offer effective treatment. Patients, as a result, possess limited awareness about mental health disorders and perceive them as unpreventable and incurable.

THE STRATEGY

Suryani's strategy to expand mental health services across Indonesia relies on a multi-layered approach. On the one hand, her efforts aim to reintegrate traditional healers and partner them with the meager 700 psychiatrists working in Indonesia. On the other hand, citizens need to accept mental health as an integral part of local culture and care.

"Today's old age, for all its worries about degenerative disease and inadequate pensions, represents so complete a transformation that it may well be the greatest social revolution of the past century," says Professor Luh Ketut Suryani.

Suryani recently developed a referral system between traditional healers and modern psychiatrists, so that patients receive a holistic experience. Having been a traditional healer, Suryani understands the critical role that traditional healers play, as they are often the first level of support that patients seek. She deeply believes that traditional healers are an essential part of ensuring timely treatment and referrals; consequently, Suryani is currently working with religious leaders to engage and integrate more traditional healers.

To increase the demand for mental health services and ensure that disorders become less stigmatized, Suryani's focus includes services that are especially applicable to citizen's daily struggles. She targets groups that suffer from issues accompanying prenatal delivery and care, child abuse, aging, depression, as well as education. Suryani has extensively developed numerous initiatives to combat each.

In her efforts to aid the elderly and preserve their mental health, Suryani—since 1988—has been working to make senior citizens more socially active. Seniors form collaborative social groups, in which they manage activities, exchange information, and learn from each other. Suryani further links the groups with doctors and pharmacies to form partnerships that offer discounted services. More than 6,000 senior citizens have joined such groups across Bali.

At the same time, Suryani has developed a number of initiatives to treat children. As pedophilia became more common in the 1990s, for example, Suryani developed a spiritual hypnosis-assisted therapy to treat the post-traumatic stress disorders that ensued. In 2002, she established the Committee Against Sex Abuse, a citizen organization designed to provide children with treatment and rehabilitation as well as protection from sex offenders. The committee is comprised of police officers, volunteers, expatriates, and consulates. To provide preventative care, Suryani works with more than 5,000 elementary school teachers to offer child-development training.

In 2010, Suryani partnered with Indonesia's School for Health Science and began teaching students about her innovative hypno-birthing method—a prenatal care experience combining meditation and relaxation to expecting mothers in an effort to ensure that the fetus is surrounded by feelings of peace, love, and happiness. Numerous studies have shown that the birthing process forms the basis of a child's personality and ability to handle stress. Suryani and the School for Health Science are further partnering with Manuaba Hospital to apply the system in practice.

Through her organization, the Suryani Institute for Mental Health, Suryani has pioneered a community-based, affordable mental health treatment for the mentally ill, particularly for those who have been chained, confined, or jailed for multiple years. Her organization has not only provided more effective mental health services, but it has also served as an alternative to the inefficient and corrupt mental health system offered by the government. The program, furthermore, mobilizes families, communities, and local doctors; recovering more than 300 patients each year. Spiritualism, meditation, and acceptance are all among the practices espoused by the program.

In an effort to reduce the number of suicides and treat people suffering from depression, Suryani set up crisis centers in the districts of Karangasem and Buleleng. Leveraging support from the local governments along with her own resources, a center employs and trains a psychiatrist, field coordinator, staff members, and volunteers. They offer services via phone as well as in-person sessions, and always follow-up interventions by meeting with family and community members.

Suryani trains the elderly with meditation and relaxation to be in perfect harmony with mind, body, and spirit.

In cooperation with the Indonesian Psychiatric Association in Bali, Suryani also developed programs such as Understanding Yourself and the program for Balinese Women. Meditation sessions are organized for community members to foster discussion and share experiences. Such sessions enable people to confront, reframe, and cope with past traumas.

All of Suryani's initiatives have collectively formed a full model of mental health care for Bali. Some of her innovative methods have even inspired provincial and national governments to replicate her models. For example, Suryani's efforts have led to the government-led establishment of the Ministry of Health with Posyandu Lansia (Integrated Health Post for Senior Citizens) and Minister of Welfare with Karang Lansia (Integrated Community Leadership for Senior Citizens). Suryani is currently working with the provincial government to establish a senior center that can accommodate cross-generation communication and

understanding. She also partners with radio and television stations to more effectively market mental health treatment.

THE PERSON

Suryani was born in Singaraja, Bali in 1944 and raised in modest surroundings with six children. Her father was a nurse and an integral part of Indonesia's struggle against the Dutch. Suryani's mother was a successful business woman who supported the family's finances.

Motivated by a strong will to treat her young sick mother, Suryani learned meditation when she was only 14. While many of her family members initially doubted her abilities, they were surprisingly convinced to see her mother cured. Suryani then began treating sick people in her community through meditation.

After graduating from high school, Suryani studied medicine at Udayana University in Bali, where she specialized in psychiatry. In 1982, she received her degree as a psychiatrist—a profession she chose out of an innate curiosity to understand her upbringing and its effects on her current personality. In 1988 Suryani attained her Ph.D. from Airlangga University, Surabaya.

While working as the head psychiatrist at Udayana University in Bali, Suryani introduced a more efficient standard operational procedure to manage mentally ill patients. The procedure decreased the treatment from one month to six days in the residency hospital. While the procedure was initially accepted and did result in numerous adjustments, the hospital chief of staff eventually rejected it and discontinued its use.

Through her academic and clinical practices, Suryani has been resilient in her attempts to bridge indigenous spirituality with Western psychiatry and psychology. While many have criticized her findings, Suryani's approach is widely considered a breakthrough in the field of psychiatry. To further develop the field, Suryani retired from her position as the Head Psychiatrist at Udayana University and is now dedicating all her time to leading the Suryani Institute of Mental Health and the Committee Against Sexual Abuse. ♦

BARRY ZUCKERMAN

UNITED STATES

Health Care Delivery

Law and Legal Reform

Barry Zuckerman is broadening the notion of health delivery to low-income families to address social as well as biological determinants and focus resources on illness prevention.

THE NEW IDEA

Because of a family member's disability, Barry saw early on the struggles of parents and families trying to secure the right kind of care for their child, and experiencing great difficulty getting the various public systems to support their interests.

Through the lens of pediatrics, Barry has pioneered practical changes in the health clinic setting that fundamentally shift the tenor of care from reactive to preventative, especially for families living at or below the poverty line and experiencing such problems as inadequate housing, utilities shut-off in the wintertime, and food insecurity. Barry achieves this shift by showing the clear link between social determinants and illness in poor families; introducing non-traditional resources like lawyers and early education specialists into the clinic setting by creating new roles for them; and focusing everyone on fixing the root cause of illness at the same time they are addressing the presenting symptoms. Taken together, Barry's efforts help underserved families, save overall system costs, and achieve a profound mindset shift, orienting professionals accustomed to silos to a truly collaborative approach to illness prevention for low-income families.

Through medical-legal partnerships, Barry's current focus, he is pairing up front-line health providers and lawyers to deliver care to low-income families and, working together, to change the culture of health institutions. The partnership, now rooted in over 200 clinics, introduces legal staff – paid and volunteer – into the clinic setting by creating a funded role for them. Having piloted the effort at Boston Medical Center, Barry and his team are now advancing medical-legal partnerships as a national movement aimed at shifting care, professional training, and resource allocation to support illness prevention among low-income families.

THE PROBLEM

Many aspects of illness are not determined biologically, and cannot be corrected solely with a prescription. This is especially true for poor families, who contend with environmental factors relating to food and nutrition, housing, and so on that return them again and again to clinic settings and emergency rooms, contributing to poor health, worsening financial circumstances of already struggling families, and escalating health costs for the society.

Meanwhile, there are many existing social support services that can help if they are mobilized at the right moment – these include income supports for food insecure families, utility shut-off protection during the winter months, and mold removal from the homes of asthmatic children. But accessing these supports often requires some level of specialized help and information – it's a complex maze to sort out without guidance, especially if you're, for example, a single parent, working two minimum-wage jobs, and speaking English as a second language. For poor parents who need the most help, the resources are often absent to make these linkages work to prevent future illness.

There's also an issue of professional silos, and ingrained notions of what a doctor is and does, and what a clinic is responsible for in terms of health delivery. Doctors are trained to treat illness, prescribe drugs, and so on. And lawyers and early education specialists don't see their place in a clinic setting, or their role in health delivery. Lawyers can only respond in a reactive way – when the situation has reached a crisis point of job loss or eviction. The notion of preventative law as it relates to the health of poor families is not well established. The arrangement of professional inputs contributes to a system that is fragmented, reactive, and ineffective at supporting parents and families toward a path of health and wellness. It also contributes to high burn-out among doctors and lawyers, who grow frustrated at the limitations of their care.

THE STRATEGY

Barry's strategy operates on several levels and though organizations advanced since the early 1990s. Taken together, these efforts are changing the role and expectation of the health clinic in delivering a broad range of health solutions that prevent future illness.

To better serve poor families by augmenting the perspective and resources of medical staff, Barry brings nontraditional resources and insights into the clinical setting. Early on in his career as a pediatrician, he saw that sickness doesn't always have a biological cause, that many poor families face choices between heat in their house and food on the table – these choices greatly affect health outcomes but are often ignored in the clinic setting.

Beginning in 1993, he hired a lawyer for his clinic to help families unlock and access the host of legal remedies and resources that significantly impact health. The model that grew out of this experience is now advanced through the National Center for Medical-Legal Partnerships, which pairs up legal and medical professionals to ensure that care is delivered across the full range of health and social determinants. Barry kept the effort local in Boston until 2001, at which time inquiries from other institutions increased and the Center convened its first national conference to teach lawyers and health care providers how to adopt the model in their communities and institutional settings. In January 2009, Barry formed an organizational entity fully committed to national expansion and field reform. His team of three full-time staff is hosted by Boston University School of Medicine and Boston Medical Center.

The core components of a medical legal partnership include: provision of direct legal assistance to patient-clients at a healthcare institution; an established referral process and feedback referral loop between healthcare and legal providers; jointly created and led trainings for healthcare providers at a health institution; an on-site legal provider presence at the health institution at least part-time every week; active engagement by both clinical and administrative staff and leadership at a healthcare institution; jointly developed metrics and mandated data collection/sharing; joint medical and legal funding strategies to sustain MLP activity; and an aim toward jointly developed and led external systemic change efforts.

"Research has shown that the first five years of life are critical to a child's language development," says Zuckerman.

MLPs, which are now embedded in 200 hospital and clinic settings serving low-income patients, operate with little funding – most are funded by local contributions of $10,000 or $25,000 from community foundations and private investors. It is the responsibility of founding members – the medical and legal "champions" in a given clinic setting – to set in place the funding and build the chapter. Most of funding required pays the salary of a full-time attorney at a rate comparable to a legal aid salary. Barry and his national team handle dissemination of best practices among the network, match services to help legal and medical professionals interested in developing a partnership to find each other, and support implementation, knowledge sharing, and annual conferences.

Expanding the role of doctors (and lawyers) to include advocacy is another central thrust of Barry's work. To this end, the national center serves as a platform for advancing policy changes. In March 2010, medical-legal partnership teams representing 17 states met with nearly 70 members of Congress to share about medical-legal partnerships and their positive impact on vulnerable families across the country. The response was overwhelmingly positive. In the months after, the Center worked with policy consultants to prepare medical-legal teams—hosting webinars and trainings on how to prepare client stories and work effectively with legislators. In July 2010, the bipartisan Medical-Legal Partnership for Health Act was introduced, with the expectation for federally authorized funding of a nationwide demonstration project for MLP in 2011.

Central to spreading his core idea is Barry's focus on advancing and actively cultivating the right talent and professional orientation.

He does this on several levels: first, by engaging in his initiatives, doctors, lawyers, and other professionals learn by doing, and by realizing impact through a new model and approach. The second is actively working with professional programs to ensure that new graduates and trainees are exposed early in their training and careers to the model. The third is more selective: Barry cultivates entrepreneurs who will take the core idea and, through their own entrepreneurship and leadership, move it out significantly. For example, he worked with Ashoka Fellow Rebecca Onie for almost a decade to help her form and launch Project Health, now operating in six major U.S. cities. He also mentored Ashoka Fellow George Askew, whose Docs for Tots also embraces the core idea.

THE PERSON

Barry's early life exposed him to the struggles of his parents and grandparents as they tried to navigate the health and educational offerings available for one of their disabled family members. Barry's grandparents, émigrés from Russia, told him of the disrespect they felt at the hands of their doctors, who treated them poorly because they did not speak English well.

As a young man, Barry knew that he loved kids – he loved their joy and their autonomy, and thought he might be a teacher. Life decisions happen in a historical context, though, and to avoid fighting in Vietnam, he enrolled in medical school and set off on a pediatrics track.

> "Barry S. Zuckerman is the co-founder of Reach Out and Read, a national childhood literacy program in the United States, and the founder of the Medical-Legal Partnership model."
>
> —*Wikipedia*

As a practicing pediatrician, he grew frustrated and saddened by the limitations of care, especially when it came to providing care to poor families. Foregoing prestigious offers elsewhere, he came to Boston Medical Center in the early 1990s because he saw an opportunity to transform pediatric care as the chair of the pediatric department. As New England's largest safety-net hospital, 70 percent of the Center's patients live at or below the poverty line, it allowed Barry a laboratory to see problems, test solutions, incubate new ideas into organizations, and fundamentally change the institutions and professionals responsible for care delivery.

In 1989, he formed – with another pediatrician and several early education specialists – the national organization Reach Out and Read. Its aim is to help parents take their small children up a learning curve through early literacy. The effort relies on pediatricians to deliver books every six months, from the six-month check-up through to year 5. Doctors help parents see how to read aloud to their children and help them develop early language skills, as well as the social-emotional skills that are formative for the development of empathy. Reach Out and Read now reaches 3.9 million families, most of them low-income. Barry has started or advanced several other initiatives, including Healthy Steps, and Witness to Violence. He is now broadly scaling the approach he began developing in the early 1990s: medical-legal partnerships. ◆

PAUL TARYAM ILBOUDO

BURKINA FASO

Access to Learning/ Education

Adult Education

Education Reform

Thirty years ago Paul Taryam Ilboudo found a way to integrate trilingualism into teaching literacy. Instead of denying access to local languages in education, Paul engineered fast paced courses that use local languages as the building blocks for literacy. With increased student self-confidence and evident progress, this literacy could then become the grounds for students to learn new languages and subjects. By integrating local languages into education curriculums, Paul has empowered communities with the capacity to read and write, thus enabling them to excel in social, governmental, and educational systems.

THE NEW IDEA

Paul is revolutionizing existing education programs in Burkino Faso by demonstrating that illiterate African children can become literate through following a carefully crafted 48-day curriculum in their mother language. After completing the curriculum, previously illiterate students could solve math problems, read, and write. Before the civil war in the Central African Republic, Paul's approach also boosted child literacy rates to more than 80 percent in pilot project communities, however, much of his work was forced to stop due to rising local civil conflict.

> "[Paul] designed an intensive adult literacy training experiment and helped create the ALFAA method, which builds on literacy skills in African languages to promote the learning of French."
>
> —Wise-Qatar

With the return of relative political stability in the 1990s, Paul resumed crafting accelerated bilingual accelerated literacy programs for local farmers in Burkina Faso. In these programs, a person who had successfully completed the 48-day maternal language literacy program could then achieve basic literacy in French by following a successive, 150-day language training program. Using this process, Paul has introduced an adapted curriculum in schools that promotes balanced levels of high language proficiency in order to create a bridge to increase learning in other languages such as French or Arabic. Based on Paul's work, the Government of Burkina Faso recently signed a law requiring schools to adopt bilingualism.

Paul has since pioneered this work across Western and Central Africa as well as Madagascar in schools, farming communities, and citizen organizations (COs).

THE PROBLEM

During the French colonial period which lasted more than 60 years, French colonialists worked to delegitimize local languages in their efforts to reinforce French culture. In primary schools, teachers routinely told unrealistic stories about how their forefathers came from the French region then known as Gaul. Instead of using familiar local languages, schools taught in French, creating a challenging environment for students to succeed.

The former French colonies lacked teachers and adequate material to make literacy possible for an ever-growing young population. Using languages that the majority of the population did not understand as the medium of teaching had led to apathy among students, and limited curriculum development among their teachers. Students spent many years mastering the French language in order to begin learning other subjects. Most students could not receive help from their families because their parents did not speak French, and as a result students felt that dropping out of school was a better option.

THE STRATEGY

In the 1980s Paul's strategy was revolutionary: It identified what people were comfortable with, their local languages, and used this to help them become literate in French. Throughout his pilot projects and innovative curriculums, Paul has achieved wide reaching levels of literacy in the face of historic and emerging challenges.

Paul's solution is for each community to choose the language of primary instruction which is generally the one local language spoken by most of the people in a geographic area. In Ouagadougou, for example, where 80 percent of the people speak Moree, the population accepted Moree as the local language for the basis of primary level instruction. In Bobo Dioulaso, the majority speaks Dioula, and community members choose to use it as the primary level language of instruction. After years of patient work on bilingualism, Paul's effort to launch the first truly bilingual West African education system has been transformed into a legal mandate.

Paul sees his next challenge as creating a solution to support primary level Koranic Schools, which leave exiting students with narrow literacy in a language that is not spoken by other members of the local population, and without basic skills in math, science, or other subjects. Paul is beginning to advocate "trilingualism" as a response to this interest in learning Arabic. He proposes that students are trained first in their maternal language, French, and then are given an opportunity to transfer their literacy learning skills to Arabic.

THE PERSON

After completing high school, Paul became a primary school teacher but realized through his daily practice that the use of foreign language as a teaching tool was hindering children's development. He decided to change this by becoming a professional linguist and by using his expertise to lobby for a change in the role that maternal language plays in education. By 1979 he had completed master's degrees in linguistics and education science. In 1982 as a UNESCO consultant, he launched his first, highly controversial initiative that proved child literacy levels could rapidly and dramatically increase through a 48-day course of studies in a child's maternal language.

The success of that effort gave Paul the leverage he needed to launch national language programs aimed at raising adult literacy. He has received numerous citations and awards, and written several books and articles to guide teachers and students through the acquisition of maternal language literacy and bilingual literacy.

Paul is currently the representative for Swiss foundation Oeuvre Suisse d'Entraide Ouvrière and was the first volunteer representative for Ashoka in Burkino Faso. ♦

ORGANIZING THE MOVEMENT

Tipping the World:
The Power of Collaborative Entrepreneurship

PUBLISHED BY

McKinsey&Company
What Matters

By Bill Drayton — 8 April 2010

To QUESTION WHETHER SOCIAL ENTREPRENEURS can achieve large-scale change is to doubt the existence of Florence Nightingale, Maria Montessori, William Wilberforce, Fazle Abed, Jimmy Wales, or the 2,700 Ashoka Fellows!

After all, what defines the true social entrepreneur is that he or she simply cannot come to rest in life until his or her vision has become the new pattern societywide. Scholars and artists are satisfied when they express an idea. Professionals are when they serve a client well, and managers are when their organization succeeds. None of this much interests the entrepreneur. The life purpose of the true social entrepreneur is to change the world.

Ashoka creates detailed life histories of every serious candidate it considers for election into its world community of leading social entrepreneurs. We have learned to look for this central, gyroscope-like quality because it is so predictive of who will ultimately meet our standard for election, which is to create at least continental-scale pattern change in an important field such as the environment or human rights. This gyroscope kicks in as far back as childhood and continues to define the social entrepreneur's life decade after decade.

Once one understands this life-defining drive, a good many other characteristics of the true entrepreneur become obvious. They focus everyday on the "how to" questions. How are they going to get from here to their ultimate goal? How are they going to deal with this opportunity or that barrier? How are the pieces going to fit together? They are engineers, not poets.

For the same reason, they are attentive listeners and they are highly realistic. If something is not working, they want to know right away—and they will then proceed to change either the environment and/or their idea.

The entrepreneur's job is not to take an idea and then implement it. That is what franchisees do. The entrepreneur is building something that is entirely new—by constantly creating and testing and recreating and then testing and recreating again.

The true social entrepreneur also has an almost magical ability to move people, a power rooted in exceptional ethical fiber. He or she is always asking people to do things that are unreasonable—and people do them. The transaction starts with the other person knowing that he or she can trust the entrepreneur and then realizing that the entrepreneur and the idea are utterly fused—which is to say that they can trust the idea as well.

Finally, the entrepreneur has an inner confidence that most sense but do not understand. While others think entrepreneurs are taking risks, entrepreneurs don't see it that way because they have thought things through extremely well. They also believe in their ability continuously to adapt the idea as they drive toward a goal that they know is a huge win for everyone, and ultimately to reach that goal. They know, in other words, that they have the gift that brings the greatest happiness in the world, the gift of being able to give at the highest level.

Once one grasps who the true social entrepreneur is, one would have to be crazed to bet against him or her ultimately changing the world at large scale.1

Ashoka evaluates the impact of its Fellows five years after their election and start up. Several months ago, the Corporate Executive Board Company reported the results of a survey of Ashoka's impact, which they conducted in 12 languages across the globe last year. The results were completely consistent with the results over the prior eight years.

- Fifty-two percent of the Ashoka Fellows had changed national policy within five years of election. (The range over earlier years was 49 to 60 percent.)

PUBLISHED BY

McKinsey&Company
What Matters
By Bill Drayton — 8 April 2010

- Seventy-six percent had changed the pattern in their field nationally (on average 3.2 times) within the same five years.

These results are especially striking since five years is early in the lifecycle of the social entrepreneur.

However, these results only begin to tell the story of the social entrepreneur's impact.

Every social entrepreneur has a second dimension of impact that, especially at this moment in history, may well be more important than the impact he or she is having in pursuing his or her immediate social change objective.

Every social entrepreneur is a mass recruiter of local changemakers. Here is one of the few significant structural differences between the social and the business entrepreneur. The social entrepreneur has no interest in capturing a market and digging a moat. Instead, the goal is, indeed, to change the world.

The way social entrepreneurs do this almost always is to make their idea as understandable, attractive, safe, and as supported as necessary precisely so that local people in community after community after community will recognize that the idea would be hugely valuable to their community and also judge that they could make that idea fly. The moment one or several local people make that decision, stand up, and champion the idea, they have become local changemakers. They will disrupt local patterns; they will recruit others to be changemakers; and a few will later become large-scale social entrepreneurs in their own right.

The multiplication of such local changemakers is critical for several reasons. They will provide a large part of the long-term grassroots leadership for their newly adopted field. These engaged citizens are also key to deepening democracy because, as they master the issues and become a driving force within institutions, they and their colleagues will no longer be able to be ignored.

Most important, this multiplication of local changemakers is a central contribution to the most important historical transformation in the structure of society since the Agricultural Revolution. For millennia the social structure has been one where a very few people "managed" everyone else. This is a model that worked in a static period when those being managed essentially had repetitive tasks to do. However, we now live in a time where the rate and complexity of change are both escalating exponentially. This new environment requires a shift in the organization of both institutions and societies to one of flexible teams of teams that come together around whatever change opportunities exist and then reform around the next. In this world, everyone must be a changemaker. That is because you do not have a team unless everyone is a player—and, in a world defined by change, to play one must be ready to contribute to changemaking.

Social entrepreneurs are even more powerful when they collaborate with one another and/or with their business peers. Ashoka has always known that its ability to contribute comes largely through the mutual help and collaborations our community makes possible. A few examples will give you a feel:

- Even a few social entrepreneurs working together can be hugely effective. One Ashoka Fellow—Silvia Maria Carvalho, based in São Paulo—whose program transforms the perception of preschool from that of stigmatized warehousing to an important step in education, was able to turn trade union prejudice into support by working with an Ashoka colleague who employed large numbers of women to provide hot lunches in area factories by providing model facilities on site for their young children. An Indonesian Fellow named Iwan Nusyirwan spread a technique for growing mushrooms on wood chips floating in rice paddies, thus generating a new crop without requiring land, by sharing it with other Fellows looking for new job- and income-creating opportunities.

- Larger collaborations are even more valuable—be it Asian Fellows collaborating across the region to fight the cross-national trade in women and children or twelve Fellows working together to change prison policies across Latin America.

PUBLISHED BY

McKinsey&Company
What Matters
By Bill Drayton — 8 April 2010

- Functional collaborations add further leverage. As security conditions have worsened, especially in Latin America and Asia, Ashoka's mutual help Fellow security program has become more important, for example in connecting the dots to see danger on the horizon in Pakistan's tribal areas. Similarly, at least in Asia, the Fellows have learned how to help one another when disaster strikes locally. And more broadly, because the child of a social entrepreneur has a parent who is possessed by an idea and who may work in difficult areas, finding an engaged and supportive peer group can be hugely important for this Young Ashokan (and his or her parents), in order to help him or her gain a deeper understanding of the entrepreneurial parent and his or her work.

Community multiplies strength and impact.

Thus far we have seen that individual social entrepreneurs and, even more, groups of them that come together for mutual help and collaboration, produce extraordinary results.

Over the last half-dozen years we have been developing something with even more far-reaching impact—collaborative entrepreneurship. There has never been anything like it before.

Ashoka is always seeking out and helping to launch the best new ideas in the hands of the strongest entrepreneurs on every continent—without in any way predefining the idea fields. (If it sought to focus only on the areas it thought most important, it would always miss the newly ripe areas that the next wave of entrepreneurs are just beginning to develop.)

However, once there are several hundred leading social entrepreneurs in a field across the continents, one can be confident that a jump to the next paradigm in the field is near. Given how centrally important it is to each of these entrepreneurs to be able successfully to change the world, they make these life bets of where to commit very, very carefully.

The challenge, of course, is to detect what the next paradigm or "S-curve" is going to be. The Ashoka community has, over the last dozen years, learned how to study the questions these pioneer entrepreneurs ask and also the patterns among their answers in order to answer that critical question.

Once it is thus clear where the world must go, the community then determines what one or two things must happen if the world is to get there—and somewhere between a third and a half of the leading social entrepreneur Fellows then work together to tip the seven to ten countries that are critical ultimately to tipping the world.

For example, the 500 Ashoka Fellows whose primary focus is serving children and young people have figured out that the old paradigm that defines successful growing up as learning the world's existing knowledge and rules, while successful in a static world, is thoroughly inadequate in a world of escalating change. In this new world, all children and young people must first master a set of social skills that will enable them to be active contributors to change—empathy/teamwork/leadership/changemaking. The global team of leading social entrepreneurs must, therefore, ensure: (1) that every young child masters and practices empathy (see Ensuring Children Succeed in the Coming Everyone A Changemaker World [www.ashoka.org/printroom]), and (2) that all young people have the experience of seeing an opportunity to improve their schools or communities, building teams to do so, and later realizing that they have changed their world (see youthventure.org).

What distinguishes entrepreneurs from everyone else is that their job is to change the overall patterns and systems of society. Can there be anything more impactful than a global team of the world's best entrepreneurs who develop a strategy to tip the world toward a better future? ◆

---

[1] Any doubts about the impact of social entrepreneurs are partly the result of two misperceptions. First, whereas 30 years ago no one knew what the phrase "social entrepreneur" meant, now there are a vast number of people who call themselves social entrepreneurs who are really wonderfully good-hearted managers or professionals or, indeed, poets. They have little in common with true social entrepreneurs. Second is the notion held by many scholars, foundation executives, and others that social entrepreneurs should behave like and be measured by the same yardsticks as business. Social entrepreneurs are trying to change the world, not capture a market, therefore the standard measures of organizational size and growth are inappropriate.

ASHOKA LEADERS

ASHOKA CELEBRATES THE 30TH ANNIVERSARY OF OUR WORLD COUNCIL

We especially thank Marjorie C. Benton, who conceived the Council, and all the founder members for their vision and decades of leadership.

Marjorie C. Benton

Marjorie Benton has been a very wise counselor and active ally to Ashoka from the start. One of her greatest gifts was suggesting and helping to design the World Council, which is now reaching its thirtieth anniversary.

Marjorie, very much a fellow spirit, has founded and co-founded many socially important organizations including: the Chicago Foundation for Women; the Women's Issues Network; and The Peace Museum. Her leadership has left Chicago, America, and the world all better places. She has been board chair of Save the Children, and she served as a delegate to the United Nations special sessions on disarmament in the 1970s, and then as U.S. Ambassador to UNICEF.

Although her interests are universal, she has provided special leadership for women, children, and development.

WORLD COUNCIL CO-CREATORS

Fazle Abed

Fazle Abed is the founder and chairman of BRAC, the world's largest and one of its most excellent and entrepreneurial citizen groups. BRAC brings structural change to tens of thousands of villages on three continents through education, finance, and integrated development. Queen Elizabeth knighted him in 2010.

Robert Goheen

Robert Goheen was president of Princeton University and United States Ambassador to India. He long led the Carnegie program to strengthen teaching.

Peter D. Bell

Peter D. Bell served as president of CARE, one of the world's leading private relief and development organizations. He now is a senior research fellow at the Hauser Center for Nonprofit Organizations at Harvard University. He also co-chairs the Joint Learning Initiative on Children and HIV/AIDS.

Anupam Puri

Anupam ("Tino") Puri founded and managed McKinsey's practice in India. In 1996, he was elected a managing director, and from 1998 onwards, he oversaw all of McKinsey's Asian and Latin American practices. Tino was a founder board member of Ashoka.

Vera Cordeiro

One of the early Brazilian Ashoka Fellows, Vera Cordeiro founded Associacao Saùde Crianca which addresses the root causes that prevent poor families from providing adequate care to their children when discharged from hospital.

Sir Shridath Ramphal

Sir Shridath Ramphal is Co-Chair of the Commission on Global Governance and President of the World Conservation Union. He is Former Secretary General of the British Commonwealth, Chancellor of the University of West Indies and former Foreign Minister and Attorney General in Guyana.

Marian Wright Edelman

Marian Wright Edelman is a lifelong advocate for disadvantaged Americans and is the President of the Children's Defense Fund. Under her leadership, CDF has become the nation's strongest voice for children and families.

Muhammad Yunus

Nobel Prize recipient, Muhammad Yunus, provided the global leadership that made microcredit a universally accepted development tool. He went on to create a series of social businesses, including the largest telephone service in the region.

Ashoka Board

Richard Cavanaugh (On Leave)

Former President and CEO, The Conference Board
Former Executive Dean, The Kennedy School of Government
Harvard University

Bill Drayton

Chair and CEO, Ashoka: Innovators for the Public
Chair, Get America Working!
Former Assistant Administrator, U.S. E.P.A.

Mary Gordon

Ashoka Fellow
Founder & CEO, Roots of Empathy
Canada

Roger Harrison

Newspaper Executive and Chair, Leading Charities
Former Chair, Asylum Aid
Former Chair, Toynbee Hall
United Kingdom

Fred Hehuwat

Founder, Green Indonesia Foundation
Former Director, National Institute of Geology and Mining of the
Indonesian Academy of Sciences

William C. Kelly

Partner Emeritus, Latham and Watkins
President, Stewards of Affordable Housing for the Future (SAHF)

Gloria de Souza

First Ashoka Fellow, Elected 1981
Founder and Director, Parisar Asha Environmental Education Centre
India

Kyle Zimmer

Founder and President, First Book

North American Council

Marjorie C. Benton

Trustee, President's Commission on White House Fellowships
Former Chair, Save the Children
Former United States Representative to UNICEF

Richard Danzig

Former Secretary of the Navy

Lou Harris

Founder, Lou Harris and Associates

Peter Kellner

Founder and Managing Partner, Richmond Global
Co-Founder, Endeavor
Founder, Environmental Management and Law Association (Hungary)
Founder, Ural Petroleum Corporation

Eugene Ludwig

Chair & Chief Executive Officer of Promontory Financial Group
Former U.S. Comptroller of the Currency

Alice Tepper Marlin

Founder & President, Social Accountability International
Founder, Council on Economic Priorities

Theodore R. Marmor

Professor of Public Policy and Management and
Professor of Political Science, Yale School of Management

Senator Charles H. Percy

Former Chair, U.S. Senate Foreign Relations Committee
President, Charles Percy and Associates

Mark Talisman

President, Project Judaica Foundation

Richard Ullman

David K.E. Bruce Professor of International Affairs,
Woodrow Wilson School, Princeton University

Offices Worldwide

ASHOKA GLOBAL

1700 North Moore Street, Suite 2000
Arlington, VA 22209 1939, USA
T: 1 703 527 8300
F: 1 703 527 8383
http://www.ashoka.org

**ASHOKA ARGENTINA,
SOUTHERN CONE**

Juncal 840, 10°C
C1062ABF, Ciudad de Buenos Aires
ARGENTINA
T: 54 11 4393 8646
info@ashoka.org.ar
http://www.ashoka.org.ar

ASHOKA AUSTRIA

Herrengasse 1-3
A-1010 Wien/Vienna
AUSTRIA
T: +43 1 53706634
mringler@ashoka.org

ASHOKA BRAZIL & PARAGUAY

Rua Cubatão, 436, conj. 41
Paraíso
04013-001 São Paulo SP BRAZIL
T: 55 11 3085 9190
diretoria@ashoka.org.br
http://www.ashoka.org.br

**ASHOKA MCKINSEY CENTER FOR SOCIAL
ENTREPRENEURSHIP**

Brasil Rua Alexandre Dumas, 1711
Edificio Birman 12 12º andar
Chácara Santo Antonio
04717 004 São Paulo SP BRAZIL
T: 55 11 5189 1648
F: 55 11 5189 1462
carina@ashoka.org.br

ASHOKA CANADA

366 Adelaide Street West
Suite 606
Toronto, Ontario M5V 1R9
CANADA
T: 1 416 646 2333
F: 1 416 646 1875
canadainfo@ashoka.org
http://canada.ashoka.org

ASHOKA COLOMBIA

Calle 71, No. 5 23 Of. 501E
Bogotá, COLOMBIA
T: 57 1 545 1158, 57 1 211 9201
ashokacol@cable.net.co

**ASHOKA EGYPT,
MIDDLE EAST/NORTH AFRICA**

93 A, Abdel Aziz Al Saud, Manial
7th floor, Apt.# 1
Cairo, EGYPT
Postal code: 11451
T: (+2) 02 532 8586, (+2) 02 236 55336
F: (+2) 02 236 54404
ibibars@ashoka.org
http://www.ashoka arab.org

**ASHOKA FRANCE, BELGIUM &
SWITZERLAND (FRENCH-SPEAKING)**

Social Factory
3 Bd Saint Martin
75003 Paris, FRANCE
T: 33 (1) 80 05 96 55
amourot@ashoka.org
http://www.ashoka.asso.fr

**ASHOKA GERMANY & SWITZERLAND
(GERMAN-SPEAKING)**

Ashoka Deutschland gGmbH
Taunustor 2
60311 Frankfurt, GERMANY
T: 49 69 7162 5508
F: 49 69 7162 5700 (attention Ashoka)
info_de@ashoka.org
http://germany.ashoka.org

**ASHOKA GERMANY
YOUTH VENTURE**

Erkelenzdamm 59-61
Berlin D-10999
GERMANY
T: 49-30-7071-95444
halgandouzi@ashoka.org

ASHOKA INDIA

Ashoka Innovators for the Public
54, 1st Cross, Domlur Layout,
Bangalore 560071, INDIA
T: 91 80 41480496
sprakash@ashoka.org

**ASHOKA INDIA
CHANGEMAKERS.COM**

188/3/1A Prince Anwar Shah Road
Kolkata 700045, INDIA
T/F: 91 33 2483 8031
changemakers@vsnl.com
http://www.changemakers.com

**ASHOKA INDIA
LAW FOR ALL INITIATIVE**

188/3/1A Prince Anwar Shah Road
Kolkata 700045, INDIA
T/F: 91 33 2483 8031

ASHOKA INDONESIA

Jl. Durma II No.17
Turangga
Bandung 40264
INDONESIA
T/F: 62 22 7306914
ashokaindonesia@bdg.centrin.net.id

ASHOKA IRELAND & SCANDINAVIA

18 Eustace Street
Dublin 2, IRELAND
T: 353 1 881 4037
pohara@ashoka.org

ASHOKA ISRAEL

98 Ussishkin St. Tel Aviv
62031 ISRAEL
T: +972 524 508 408
ntsuk@ashoka.org
http://israel.ashoka.org

ASHOKA JAPAN

3-18-19 Toranomon, Suite 1602
Minato-ku, Tokyo
JAPAN 105-0001
T/F: 81-3-3434-0557
ashokajapan@ashoka.org

ASHOKA EAST AFRICA

Concert House | First Floor
Wood Gardens, off Wood Ave.
Kilimani Area, Nairobi, KENYA
PO BOX 101590–00101
T: +254 (0) 725 879 521
eastafrica@ashoka.org
Eastafrica.ashoka.org

**ASHOKA MEXICO,
CENTRAL AMERICA**

Ashoka: Emprendedores Sociales
Calle Tula Núm. 13
Col. Condesa
Delegación Cuauhtémoc
C.P. 06000, México, D.F, MEXICO
T: 52-55-5256-2820, 52-55-5256-2821
F: 52 55 2624 3210
ashokamexico@ashoka.org
http://mexico.ashoka.org

ASHOKA PAKISTAN

31B. Street 8, Sector F-11/1
Islamabad, PAKISTAN
T: 92 300 8297602
fashn2000@yahoo.com

**ASHOKA PERU,
ANDEAN REGION**

Prolongacion San Martín No. 12
(Edif. El Puente)
Depto. 602
Lima 4 (Barranco), PERU
T: 51-1-715-2233
Cel: 51-1-963-748-749
info@ashoka.org.pe
http://espanol.ashoka.org

ASHOKA PHILIPPINES

c/o Ateneo School of Government
4/F Ateneo Professional
    Schools Building
20 Rockwell Drive, Rockwell Center
Makati City 1200, PHILIPPINES
T: 632 899 4587
tlavina@ashoka.org

**ASHOKA POLAND,
CENTRAL EUROPE**

Chmielna 20/100
00 020 Warsaw, POLAND
T: +48 604 200 961
info_pl@ashoka.org
http://www.ashoka.pl

**ASHOKA MALI,
SAHEL/WEST AFRICA**

BP 105 A Kati Koko
Republique du MALI
T: 223 21 27 21 44
ctoure@ashoka.org
http://sahel.ashoka.org

**ASHOKA SOUTH AFRICA,
SOUTHERN AFRICA**

Ashoka Southern Africa
5th Floor, West Wing, Oak Place
352 Oak Avenue
Randburg, Johannesburg
SOUTH AFRICA
T: 27 11 3262736
F: 27113262704
ftoeffie@ashoka.org
http://southernafrica.ashoka.org

ASHOKA SPAIN, IBERIAN PENINSULA

c/o Joaquín Costa 15
Portal 3, Planta 3ª, 1 bis
28002 Madrid, SPAIN
T: 34 91 448 9255
F: 34-91-448-9962
coordinator@ashoka.org
http://www.ashoka.es

ASHOKA SRI LANKA

No 10 1/1, 08th Lane
Colombo 03, SRI LANKA
T: 947 736 494 96
ashokasl@sltnet.lk
http://srilanka.ashoka.org

ASHOKA THAILAND & BANGLADESH

101/8 Phahonyothin 32 Road
Senanikom, Chatuchak
Bangkok 10900, THAILAND
T: 66 2712 8610
thailand@ashoka.org
http://www.thailand.ashoka.org

ASHOKA TURKEY

Inonu Cad. Tarik Zafer Tunaya Sk.
Turkdogan İs Merkezi No: 8 kat 2/2
34427 Gumussuyu
Istanbul, TURKEY
F: 90 212 245 95 45
staluk@ashoka.org
http://www.ashoka.org/tr

ASHOKA UNITED KINGDOM

CAN Mezzanine
49-51 East Road
London N1 6AH
UNITED KINGDOM
T: +44 (0) 20 7250 8360
infoUK@ashoka.org
http://uk.ashoka.org

ASHOKA USA

1700 North Moore Street, Suite 2000
Arlington, VA 22209 1939
UNITED STATES
T: 1 703 527 8300
F: 1 703 527 8383
USProgram@ashoka.org
http://usa.ashoka.org

Volunteer Opportunities

As THE PROFILES IN THIS BOOK ILLUSTRATE, there is a wealth of experience and knowledge among the Ashoka Fellows. With a fellowship of more than 3,000 Ashoka Fellows around the world, Ashoka seeks to support and multiply the impacts of this community of most of the world's top social entrepreneurs in several ways. Ashoka provides professional services to support the Ashoka Fellows, promotes collaborations and mutual help within the global fellowship, and strives to build bridges between the Fellows and other key sectors of the world. Fellows, staff, and volunteers/friends work together to make all this possible.

Ashoka has always relied on the commitment of smart, able, caring volunteers. The Nominators, independent referees and panelists who scout and elect Ashoka Fellows, serve as volunteers. On-site supporters help out with myriad tasks for Fellows and in the Arlington Ashoka office and in offices around the world. Ashoka has also developed a virtual volunteer program, which allows interested supporters to offer support with research and networking for Fellows from all over the world.

> "Working with Ashoka's Fellowship Support Services has given me the opportunity to help Ashoka Fellows in a direct and personal way. Whether researching a request for information or helping Ashoka Fellows network, the goal is always the same—forging strong links throughout the Ashoka community—of which I am happy to be a small part."
>
> *Peggy Carr, Volunteer in the Ashoka Arlington office since 1987*

Ashoka welcomes and very much needs volunteers in a variety of capacities, depending on their location, interests and skills, and time constraints. A sampling of the broad areas where both virtual and on-site volunteers contribute include:

- Hosting Ashoka Fellows—hosts provide international Ashoka Fellows with accommodations for a few nights during their travels away from home, be it to the U.S., Brazil, or India.

- Translation—volunteers help fellows collaborate, translate Ashoka documents and newsletters for Ashoka Fellows and others in the community who do not speak English, and help, on occasion, with interpretation.

- Research projects—volunteers help with in-depth research projects to create information packages for Fellows in various thematic areas.

- Email bulletins, websites, and publications—volunteers assist with compiling, organizing, and formatting Ashoka's monthly bulletin of opportunities and news, which serves Fellows worldwide. Volunteers also are key to Ashoka's over 30 websites and its publications.

- Networking—volunteers help us by spreading key innovations, building understanding of social entrepreneurship and programs for the field, and through providing introductions within professional networks and organizations.

- Consulting to Fellow—this is a one-on-one relationship between a volunteer and an Ashoka Fellow, via email or in person, in which specific strategic and technical issues important to the Fellow's work are discussed and ideas and broad supports provided.

- Chapters—volunteers are central to building and leading chapters, e.g., in Washington, D.C., Boston, San Francisco, Johannesburg, and Bangalore. The chapters promote social entrepreneurship, import innovations, support Ashoka Fellows, and build smart bridges between their community and the global fellowship.

Please consider playing an important role in person and/or as a virtual volunteer for Ashoka in any of a myriad of possible ways! We also invite you to send us your ideas on other ways in which you could contribute. For more information about joining the Ashoka volunteer network, please visit our websiteatwwww.ashoka.org/volunteer or contact us in one of the following ways:

Fax: (703) 527-8383

Mail: Ashoka: Innovators for the Public
         Attention: Volunteer Coordinator
         1700 North Moore Street, Suite 2000
         Arlington, VA 22209
         USA

Email: volunteers@ashoka.org

Ensuring the Future: The Endowments

ASHOKA'S ENDOWMENTS provide an enduring base of support for innovation across the globe. Their growth also helps ensure Ashoka's long-term ability to serve a field that will be critically needed as long as society must adapt and change. Ashoka's endowments reached US$20 million in 2007 and have had positive investment results anually for over twenty years. Managed with a five-year perspective by three endowment trustees, the trustees invest with a long-team perspective and are committed to maintaining the real value of the funds before agreeing to disbursements. Given by both institutions and individuals, Ashoka endowments often create a permanent statement about or memorial to someone the donor especially loves or respects.

THE AMATERASU ENDOWMENT

For the support of women Fellows working outside the Americas in the areas of women's reproductive rights, women's empowerment, or sustainable community. Endowed by Katherine Victoria Randolph. Established in December 1999.

THE HENRY BEAL ENDOWMENT

In memory of Henry Beal, a founding friend of Ashoka and, before his death, one of its Endowment Trustees. He was one of America's most inspired and effective environmental managers and leaders. The endowment is focused on environment issues and AIDS. Established in 1992.

THE E. NOEL BERGERE ENDOWMENT

In memory of Noel Bergere who, though crippled by polio at three, became Master of the High Court. He was also a leader of the disabled and a patron of education in Australia. Focused on supporting a Fellow who is handicapped and/or whose work relates either to education or the law. Established in 1984.

THE JOAN BERGERE ENDOWMENT

Joan Bergere came to America as a young musician and later helped other young musicians get their first career opening at major New York City public concerts. She was a loving parent and also spiritually a citizen of the world with broad interests. Established in 1982.

THE BENJAMIN BLOOM ENDOWMENT

Ben Bloom was a successful lawyer and businessman who, as the son of immigrant parents, believed strongly in creating opportunities for others to succeed as he had succeeded. This endowment has been established to honor his principles to provide opportunities for those who are willing to work hard but need to be given a chance in life. Established in 1996. Unrestricted.

THE COLUMBIA ASHOKA FELLOWSHIPS I AND II

The Columbia Foundation created two endowments to enable Ashoka to elect more women as Fellows. Established in 1986.

THE C.M. CRESTA FUND

Established in 1986. Unrestricted

THE PADMA RAG DATTA ENDOWMENT

Dr. Padma Rag Datta dedicated his life's work to using science to improve human welfare and preserve the environment. His father, Parasuram Datta, founded a wildlife sanctuary in Assam and was a strong believer in social justice. The family wishes that their legacy be continued through this endowment so that Ashoka Fellows may find their own path to the simple and profound acts that make a difference. Established in 1996.

THE SARAH DUNBAR ENDOWMENT

Sarah Dunbar had an enduring concern for downtrodden people whose environment had been destroyed or reduced by modern times, especially by war and industry. Contributing to maintaining a people-friendly environment was another of her passions. Established in 2000.

ENDOWMENT FUND B

Established in 1999. Unrestricted.

THE MICHAEL FEIN HONORARY ENDOWMENT

This endowment is in memory of Michael Fein and his tremendous ability to touch so many lives. He was very passionate about the social enterprises that Ashoka fulfilled. Established in 2001.

THE MAURICE FITZGERALD ASHOKA FELLOWSHIP

Maurice Fitzgerald taught in the Philippines after the Spanish American War. He loved his teaching and the people of the Philippines. For a teaching and education fellowship. Established in 1986.

THE JOHN AND ELEANOR FORREST ASHOKA FELLOWSHIP

Established in 1986. Unrestricted.

THE FORT HILL ENDOWMENT FUND

Established in 1993. Unrestricted.

THE FOX PEACE ENDOWMENT

The Fox Peace Endowment is inspired by the Peace Testimony articulated by George Fox in 1651 and by the commitment of Tom Fox who was killed in Iraq in 2006 while serving as a witness for peace. Its purpose is to identify and launch social entrepreneurs and their projects dedicated to the development of structure, conditions, and communities that nurture peace.

THE BENJAMIN FRANKLIN ASHOKA FELLOWSHIP

Focused on education and matters related to science. Established in 1984.

THE BUCKMINSTER FULLER ASHOKA FELLOWSHIP

For Fellows working to alleviate hunger in South Asia. Established in 1983.

THE GENERAL ENDOWMENT FUND FOR ASHOKA

The General Endowment for Ashoka was established in 1998 from numerous individual contributions earmarked for endowment purposes. Unrestricted.

THE SANJOY GHOSE ENDOWMENT

This endowment is a tribute to the work and sacrifice that Ashoka Fellow Sanjoy Ghose made in building a culture of volunteerism and a sense of citizen responsibility among the youth in India's northeastern state of Assam. It is a legacy of the work he began to reorient the area's youth away from violence and anarchy towards constructive and active social involvement in the face of ethnic strife, insurgent movements, and state repression. Sanjoy was abducted on July 4, 1997. The United Liberation Front of Assam (ULFA) claimed responsibility for this event. Unrestricted. Established in 1998.

THE JAMES P. GRANT ASHOKA ENDOWMENT

Named for the late Executive Director of the United Nations Children's Fund (UNICEF) and created by his friends, colleagues, and family to "continue his life's work and world vision." The endowment's purposes include supporting innovative leadership that contributes to social development among children and the disadvantaged, developing new methods and low-cost technologies to further social development, and encouraging dialogue leading to policies that improve the lives of children and all humankind. Established in 1998.

THE ALBERT O. HIRSCHMAN FELLOWSHIP

Given to honor Professor Hirschman's long leadership in the field of practical, grassroots development. Established in 1986. Unrestricted.

THE JIMMY HOPKINS FELLOWSHIP

Jimmy Hopkins was a Judge of the New York State Supreme Court, Appellate Division. He was known as a very kind man who was a master of the law. Many of his decisions and interpretations are the basis of important legal precedent. For a Fellow in the legal or judicial arena. Established in 1997.

THE HARRIS AND ELIZA KEMPNER FUND
ASHOKA FELLOWSHIP

For support of Fellows working in Mexico. Established in 1989.

THE W. ARTHUR LEWIS ASHOKA FELLOWSHIP

Given to honor Professor Lewis's remarkably broad contributions to our understanding of development and of key areas of the world. Established in 1986. Unrestricted.

THE MACK LIPKIN SR. MEMORIAL ENDOWMENT

In memory of Dr. Mack Lipkin, a much loved friend and doctor who was also a leader of the medical profession and a founding friend to Ashoka. Dedicated to innovations in the effectiveness and humane quality of health care. Established in 1991.

THE JAN SCHMIDT MARMOR ENDOWMENT

Jan Marmor was a wise counselor to her family, friends, and patients. She was a fine poet and artist. She was a close friend to Ashoka from its launch. With commitment and love she built a family that believed that "no good idea should go unexpressed—or unheard." Established 2003.

THE FRANCISCO "CHICO" MENDES ENDOWMENT

In memory of Chico Mendes, a friend and early Ashoka Fellow. Chico created an approach to grassroots organizing in the Amazon basin that Gandhi would have recognized but that was adapted to his own, very different, environment. Chico, like Gandhi, was killed pursuing peaceful change. The preferred uses of the funds are grassroots work and environmental issues, though the endowment carries no restrictions. Established in 1988.

THE HELEN MERESMAN FELLOWSHIP

In memory of Helen Meresman, the personification of breaking boundaries with determination, grace, and charm. The Helen Meresman Fellowship was established by Roger Barnett in 1997. Unrestricted.

THE JAWAHARLAL NEHRU ENDOWMENT

Jawaharlal Nehru was far more than a great national leader: He helped build a global community; he was a democrat; he was a historian; and he used his reflective power to hold himself to a high ethical standard. Unrestricted. Established in 2003.

THE JACOB H. OXMAN MEMORIAL FUND

In memory of Dr. Jacob H. Oxman, a devoted husband and father, and a kind, caring, generous, and principled man. This endowment is used to support an Ashoka Fellow. Any additional funds can be used either to support another Fellow or to cover operating costs. Established in 1986. Unrestricted.

DIANE PIERCE PHILLIPS ASHOKA FELLOWSHIP ENDOWMENT

Diane Pierce Phillips led an exemplary life of spiritual integrity and servant leadership as a U.S. Peace Corps Volunteer, wife and mother, registered nurse, hospice volunteer, minister of the United Church of Christ (Congregational), and spiritual director. Established in 2003. Unrestricted.

THE DANIEL SAKS ASHOKA FELLOWSHIP

In memory of Dan Saks who, had he lived longer, would have changed U.S. employment policies even more profoundly than he already had. Dan was also one of Ashoka's earliest creators, beginning in 1963. Focused on creating work opportunities for the poor or otherwise disadvantaged. Established in 1986.

THE MORTON SAND MEMORIAL ENDOWMENT

Mort Sand, long a highly successful business entrepreneur, turned his energy and creativity to solving society's ills over his last decades. He helped build Ashoka's Entrepreneur-to-Entrepreneur program, opened business opportunities for Brazil's street girls through three Fellows there, and pushed for and was key to the launch of the Ashoka U.S.A./Canada program. The Mort Sand Endowment will be used in the U.S.A./Canada. Although it is unrestricted, the Endowment will give priority to enabling disadvantaged young people through opportunities in business. Established in 2002.

THE FATHER EUGENE WATRIN ENDOWMENT

In memory of Father Watrin, a remarkable educational founder and builder for over 50 years in Nepal and Ashoka's volunteer Representative there for our first 15 years. His special commitment to the Ashoka vision and to all in its community, which he did so much to build, exemplifies why he had such a powerful impact on all around him. His greatest legacy is the model of how to live life well through service that is both highly important and performed with the modesty of true caring, love, and faith. For the support of Fellows working in Nepal. Established in 2004.